File No. A 16-3
Serial: 01568
15 November 1944

INVASION OF SOUTHERN FRANCE

REPORT

OF

NAVAL COMMANDER, WESTERN TASK FORCE

Vice Admiral H. K. Hewitt, U. S. Navy

Published by Books Express Publishing
Copyright © Books Express, 2011
ISBN 978-1-78039-559-3

Books Express publications are available from all good retail and online booksellers. For publishing proposals and direct ordering please contact us at: info@books-express.com

UNITED STATES EIGHTH FLEET

File No.
A16-3

Serial: 01668   29 November 1944

CONFIDENTIAL

From: Commander U.S. EIGHTH Fleet
              (Naval Commander Western Task Force).
To   :   Commander in Chief, U.S. Fleet.
Via :   (1) Commander in Chief, Mediterranean.
            (2) Supreme Allied Commander, Mediterranean.

Subject: Invasion of Southern France.

References: (a) Articles 712 and 874(6), U.S. Navy Regulations.
            (b) COMINCH and CNO letter FF1/A12-1/A16-3,
                Serial 7152 of 29 October 1943.

Enclosure: (A) Invasion of Southern France, Report of Naval
                Commander Western Task Force, Commander
                EIGHTH Fleet, File No. A16-3, Serial 01568
                of 15 November 1944.

1.   In accordance with references (a) and (b), I submit herewith as enclosure (A) my report as Naval Commander Western Task Force for the invasion of Southern France.

                                    H. K. Hewitt
                                    H. K. HEWITT

Copies with Enclosure to:
  Distribution List

File No. A16-3
Serial: 01668

Subject: Invasion of Southern France.

DISTRIBUTION	No. Copies
COMINCH (For further distribution)	80
AGWAR	4
CG US Army Air Forces	2
CinCPac	6
CinCLant	2
ComServLant	2
ComDesLant	2
ComPhibTraLant	6
ComNavEu	1
ComNavForFrance	1
SACMed	4
DSACMed	2
Admiralty	7
CinCMed (For further distribution)	30
CG SOS NATOUSA	1
AFHQ (COT)	1
CG 6th Army Group	2
CG Seventh Army	2
CG VI Corps	2
CG 3rd Infantry Division (US)	1
CG 45th Infantry Division (US)	1
CG 36th Infantry Division (US)	1
CG MAAF	1
CG MATAF	1
CG MASAF	1
AOC MACAF	1
CG XII TAC	2
Navale France	2
ComAirLant	1
ComThirdFleet	2
ComFifthFleet	2
ComSeventhFleet	2
ComNorPac	2
ComThirdPhib	2
ComFifthPhib	2
ComSeventhPhib	2
ComEighthPhib	10
ComTwelfthPhib	2
COTC Pac	2
COTC Lant	2
ComPhibTraPac	2
ComBatPac	2
ComCruPac	2
ComDesPac	2
Army-Navy Staff College	5
Naval War College	5
USMC, Command and Staff School	3
Command and General Staff School, Leavenworth, Kansas	3
Army Air Forces Tactical Center, Orlando, Florida	2
Eighth Fleet	50

FOREWORD

The invasion of Southern France had a number of features which appear to justify a report which may serve for analysis and study with a view to further developing our proficiency in amphibious warfare. A long period of planning study was available, even though the final decision and the necessary forces were problematical until the final stages. This enabled planning procedures to be developed in detail and the lessons of previous large amphibious operations in this theater, in all of which this command participated, to be applied insofar as circumstances permitted. The number of units involved was so large that experience gained should be valid for the largest operations. Though, as expected, strong enemy coast defenses were encountered, the enemy lacked air strength and reserves for effective counter-attack. Therefore our operations were carried through without major changes forced by the enemy, and the efficacy of the plan for rapid build-up and maintenance of the Army was well tested. Lastly in the diversity of services and nationalities involved, there was presented an outstanding pattern of coordination and whole-hearted cooperation which is the keystone to success in amphibious operations.

INVASION OF SOUTHERN FRANCE

Table of Contents

Page

Part I PLANNING

Chapter 1 Appreciation

- Section 1.1 Introduction --------------------------------- 1
- Section 1.2 Background of Planning ----------------------- 3
- Section 1.3 The Objective -------------------------------- 5
- Section 1.4 The Naval Consideration of the Military Forces Available - 7
- Section 1.5 Survey of the Theater of Operations ---------- 10
- Section 1.6 Strategic Deception -------------------------- 11

Chapter 2 The Decision

- Section 2.1 Maintenance over the Beaches ---------------- 12
- Section 2.2 The Assault Area ---------------------------- 14
- Section 2.3 D-Day --------------------------------------- 16
- Section 2.4 The Assault Beaches ------------------------- 18
- Section 2.5 H-Hour -------------------------------------- 20
- Section 2.6 Summary ------------------------------------- 23

Chapter 3 Formulation of Planned Action

- Section 3.1 Analysis of the Decision -------------------- 24
- Section 3.2 Naval Planning Memoranda -------------------- 25
- Section 3.3 Preparing the Plan -------------------------- 28

Chapter 4 Assignment of Task Organizations

- Section 4.1 Attack Forces ------------------------------- 31
- Section 4.2 Gunfire Support ----------------------------- 32

Part II EXECUTION OF THE PLAN

Chapter 1 Campaign Narrative ----------------------------- 35
- D-Day -- 45
- Summary Statistics -- 133

Chapter 2 Intelligence

- Section 2.1 Surprise ------------------------------------ 134
- Section 2.2 Aerology ------------------------------------ 136
- Section 2.3 Enemy Coast Defenses ------------------------ 138
- Section 2.4 Underwater Obstructions and Mines ----------- 143
- Section 2.5 Enemy Air Forces ---------------------------- 146
- Section 2.6 Enemy Naval Forces -------------------------- 146
- Section 2.7 Beach Intelligence -------------------------- 147
- Section 2.8 Photographic Interpretation ----------------- 151
- Section 2.9 Rubber Topographic Models ------------------- 154
- Section 2.10 Panoramic Beach Sketches ------------------- 155
- Section 2.11 Combat Intelligence ------------------------ 158
- Section 2.12 Captured Equipment and Documents ----------- 162
- Section 2.13 Prisoner of War Interrogation -------------- 163
- Section 2.14 Press Relations ---------------------------- 164

- iii -

Table of Contents

Chapter 3 Operations

		Page
Section 3.1	Rehearsals	166
Section 3.2	Mounting, Sailing, and Staging of Assault Convoys	169
Section 3.3	Approach and Arrival of Assault Convoys	174
Section 3.4	Diversionary Operations	177
Section 3.5	SITKA Assault	181
Section 3.6	ALPHA Assault	184
Section 3.7	DELTA Assault	187
Section 3.8	CAMEL Assault	190
Section 3.9	Aircraft Carrier Operations	194
Section 3.10	Screening Operations	197
Section 3.11	PT Operations	204
Section 3.12	Minesweeping	207
Section 3.13	Navigation Units	216
Section 3.14	Reduction of Hyeres, Toulon and Marseille	218
Section 3.15	Seizure and Development of Port de Bouc	223
Section 3.16	Control of Post Assault Convoys	226
Section 3.17	Beaches and Ports	229
Section 3.18	Organization	231
Section 3.19	Postponement Directive	236
Section 3.20	Storm Plans	237
Section 3.21	Charts and Anchorages	239
Section 3.22	Reports	242

Chapter 4 Air

Section 4.1	Joint Air Plan	244
Section 4.2	Pre-D-day bombing	246
Section 4.3	Pre-H-hour D-Day bombing	252
Section 4.4	Post-H-hour bombing	257
Section 4.5	Fighter Direction Ships	260
Section 4.6	Air Support	264
Section 4.7	Fighter Cover	265
Section 4.8	Carrier Aircraft Operations	269
Section 4.9	Spotting Planes	271
Section 4.10	Air Raid Warnings	273
Section 4.11	Airborne Troop Movements	275
Section 4.12	Air/Sea Rescue Service	276
Section 4.13	Anti-Submarine Air Operations	277
Section 4.14	Aircraft for Mine Spotting	278
Section 4.15	Air Dispatch Letter Service	280
Section 4.16	Naval Air Liaison Officers	281

Chapter 5 Gunnery

Section 5.1	Bombardment	284
	Preparation	284
	Naval Gunfire during Assault	285
	Post Assault Naval Gunfire Support	285
Section 5.2	Ordnance Material	287
Section 5.3	Shore Fire Control Parties and Naval Gunfire Liaison Officers	288
Section 5.4	Anti-aircraft Gunnery and Aircraft Recognition	293
Section 5.5	Smoke Plan and Execution	296
Section 5.6	Ammunition and Smoke Supply and Expenditures	298

Table of Contents

Chapter 5 Gunnery (Continued)

		Page
Section 5.7	Chemical Defense	301
Section 5.8	Naval Combat Demolition Units	302
Section 5.9	Apex Boats and Reddy Fox (Demolition Outfit Mark 119)	306
Section 5.10	Woofus Craft - LCT(R), LCM(R), LCS(S)	309
Section 5.11	Mine and Bomb Disposal	311
Section 5.12	Light Indicator Net Plan	312

Chapter 6 Material and Logistics

Section 6.1	Planning, Preparation and Training Period	313
Section 6.2	Repair Facilities and Dry Docks	315
Section 6.3	Petroleum Installations and Supply of Petroleum Products and Coal	317
Section 6.4	Water Installations and Supply	320
Section 6.5	Provisions, Clothing and Small Stores, Ships Store Stock and General Stores	321
Section 6.6	Barrage Balloons	323
Section 6.7	Assault Maintenance and Build-up Period	324
Section 6.8	Losses and Damage	327
Section 6.9	Salvage and Fire Fighting	328
Section 6.10	Eighth Fleet Ships and Craft	331
	(a) General Remarks	331
	(b) Research and Development	332
	(c) Recommendations	333
Section 6.11	Beach Control Group and Beach Battalions	334
Section 6.12	Loading and Unloading of Ships and Craft	336
Section 6.13	Evacuation of Prisoners of War	339
Section 6.14	Opening of Ports	340

Chapter 7 Communications

Section 7.1	General	342
Section 7.2	Planning	344
Section 7.3	Cover Plan	346
Section 7.4	Flagships	347
Section 7.5	Deficiencies	349
Section 7.6	Call Signs	351
Section 7.7	Authentication	352
Section 7.8	Cryptographic Aids	353
Section 7.9	Voice Codes	355
Section 7.10	Special Codes	355
Section 7.11	Radio Channels	356
Section 7.12	Visual	358
Section 7.13	Radar and IFF	360
Section 7.14	Countermeasures	361
Section 7.15	Radio Installations and Equipment	362
Section 7.16	Conclusion	363

Chapter 8 Medical Department Operations

Section 8.1	General	364
Section 8.2	Force and Area Evacuation Officers	365
Section 8.3	Medical Sections of Beach Battalions	365
Section 8.4	Ambulance Boats	366

Table of Contents

Page

Chapter 8 Medical Department Operations (Continued)

    Section 8.5   Evacuation Ships - 367
    Section 8.6   Hospital Facilities in the Rear Echelon - - - - - - - - - - 369
    Section 8.7   U.S. Navy Casualties - 370
    Section 8.8   Casualty Reports - 370

Part III CONCLUSIONS AND RECOMMENDATIONS

Chapter 1 Conclusions

    Section 1.1   Planning - 371
    Section 1.2   Intelligence - 372
    Section 1.3   Operations - 374
    Section 1.4   Air - 377
    Section 1.5   Gunnery - 379
    Section 1.6   Material and Logistics - 379
    Section 1.7   Communications - 380
    Section 1.8   Medical Department Operations - - - - - - - - - - - - - - 381

Chapter 2 Recommendations

    Section 2.1   Planning - 382
    Section 2.2   Intelligence - 382
    Section 2.3   Operations - 383
    Section 2.4   Air - 385
    Section 2.5   Gunnery - 385
    Section 2.6   Material and Logistics - 386
    Section 2.7   Communications - 387
    Section 2.8   Medical Department Operations - - - - - - - - - - - - - - 387

INVASION OF SOUTHERN FRANCE

Index of Diagrams

Title	Diagram Number
Plan of Assault	I
Assault Convoy Routes	II
Follow-up Convoy Routes	III
Convoy Positions, 1200, D-4	IV
Convoy Positions, 1200, D-3	V
Convoy Positions, 1200, D-2	VI
Convoy Positions, 1200, D-1	VII
Convoy Positions, 2000, D-1	VIII
Convoy Positions, 1200, D-day	IX
Postponement Convoy Movements	X
Tracks of Diversion Forces	XI
Aircraft Lanes	XII
Night Retirement Areas for Gunfire Support Ships	XIII
Tactical Air Command Cover Plan	XIV
Minesweeping, South coast of France, Eastern Section	XV
Minesweeping, South coast of France, Western Section	XVI
Interdiction Targets, Pre-D-Day Bombing	XVII
Alpha-Sitka Areas, Naval Bombardment and Aerial Bombing	XVIII
Delta Area, Naval Bombardment and Aerial Bombing	XIX
Camel Area, Naval Bombardment and Aerial Bombing	XX
Toulon-Giens Peninsula Area, Naval Bombardment and Aerial Bombing	XXI
Marseille-Ciotat Area, Naval Bombardment and Aerial Bombing	XXII
Right Flank (Nice-Menton) Area, Naval Bombardment	XXIII
Ammunition Expenditures by Caliber	XXIV

Index to Figures

		Page
Figure 1	Army Units of the Western Task Force	8
Figure 2	Ships and Craft of the Western Task Force	30
Figure 3	The Sitka Assault	180
Figure 4	Assault Area Screen (15 Aug. - 25 Sept.)	198
Figure 5	Assault Area Screen (19 Aug. - 25 Sept.)	199
Figure 6	Marseille-Toulon Screen (Established 11 Sept.)	200
Figure 7	Toulon-Beachhead Screen (Established 11 Sept.)	201
Figure 8	Mines Swept, Golfe de Frejus	208
Figure 9	German Plan for Mining Toulon Harbor	210
Figure 10	Mines Swept, Marseille	212
Figure 11	Command Relationships	232
Figure 12	Joint Operations Room, USS Catoctin	263
Figure 13	Air Grid Map	267
Figure 14	Aircraft Carrier Force	268
Figure 15	Solid Concrete Tetrahedron	303
Figure 16	Daily Traffic Analysis	356

INVASION OF SOUTHERN FRANCE

PART I

PLANNING

Chapter 1

APPRECIATION

Section 1.1

INTRODUCTION

Part I of this report is concerned with the overall planning for the invasion of Southern France. The initiation of the planning activity of the Western Task Force was prompted by the preliminary directive to the Naval Commander for the invasion of Southern France, issued in Algiers by Commander-in-Chief, Mediterranean on 28 December 1943. That directive appointed Commander US Eighth Fleet as Naval Commander Western Naval Task Force (NCWTF), directing that the administrative title, Commander Naval Forces Northwest African Waters (ComNavNAW) be retained during the preparatory stages.

The planning group of ComNavNAW staff immediately began preparing plans for the invasion, based on the experience gained in the invasions of North Africa, Sicily, and Italy. At the time of the preliminary directive, there was no definite indication of which army units or which air units would participate. The identity of the naval forces to be available could be only approximated. Neither had it been decided where, on the coast of Southern France, the invasion would take place. Concurrently with this planning, on the echelon of the Mediterranean theater, army planners of the various sections of the Allied Force Headquarters, air planners of the Mediterranean Allied Air Forces, and naval planners of the staff of Commander-in-Chief, Mediterranean, also began planning for the invasion of Southern France. These plans were mainly concerned with training, mounting, and availability of troop units. Furthermore, during this period planning for other operations in the Mediterranean was being carried on and some operations were executed.

Planning sections of the commanders of the army, navy, and air forces concerned were, however, established in the Ecole Normale, Bouzareah, just outside Algiers, for the purpose of formulating the necessary detailed assault plans in as close cooperation as possible. This was in accordance with the requirements found most suitable for planning prior to the invasions of Sicily and Salerno. Headquarters of the Seventh Army, at the beginning of the planning period were at Palermo, Sicily. In May, Major General, now Lieutenant General A. M. Patch, US Army, who became Commanding General Seventh Army, and the principal members of his staff, arrived from the United States and established headquarters in Algiers with the sections involved in planning at Bouzareah. The rear echelon of the Seventh Army remained at Mostaganem, near Oran.

On 8 July 1944, the planning headquarters for the operation moved to Naples because AFHQ had moved there and it had been decided to train troops and mount the assault in the Naples area. There, the planning group continued to work in close collaboration with the staff of Lieutenant General Patch, who had been appointed Commander of the army forces, and with the staff of Brigadier General G. P. Saville, who had been designated Air Commander for the invasion. Both had been appointed coordinate commanders with Commander US Eighth Fleet prior to the move to Naples, but now for the first time it was possible to accomplish the planning of all three forces in one place with the respective commanders present.

In Naples, also, planning headquarters for the next lower echelons, the US VI Corps Commander, task force commanders, and division commanders were established in one building. General de Lattre de Tassigny, Commanding General of the Frency Army B (II French Corps), and his staff also established his headquarters in Naples for the final period of planning. In addition, headquarters Seventh Army had a French military mission and Commander Eighth Fleet had French liaison officers attached prior and after the move to Naples.

In accordance with the Naval Commander's responsibility, because he exercises military command over the assault forces until the army is firmly established on shore, the planning was in constant review from the viewpoint of a successful invasion rather than purely naval, army, or air interest.

The following discussion covers the development of planning from the time of the preliminary directive until the invasion on 15 August 1944.

Section 1.2

BACKGROUND OF PLANNING

The general situation in the Mediterranean theater, at the beginning of 1944, was that the allied armies in Italy were engaged in a difficult and bitter winter campaign, and the allied navies were in almost complete control of the seas. The landings at Anzio in late January met with such difficulty that it was uncertain what allied forces would be available to launch the invasion of Southern France when and if ordered.

Throughout the period from the beginning of 1944 until the execution of the invasion, intelligence reports indicated the gradual but definite decline in enemy naval strength. The disposition of the enemy army divisions along the coast of Southern France was reduced somewhat to meet the threat of invasion in Northern France. During this period, the German Nineteenth Army in Southern France showed a decrease from about 13 divisions and additional defensive zone units including two mobile divisions, or about one division for every 30 miles of coastline, to nine divisions when the assault was launched. The greatest single threat, of course, because of its high mobility, was the German Air Force.

On 15 April, the naval intelligence estimate concluded, "The enemy is now incapable of mounting an attack by surface ships against an allied task force in the Western Mediterranean. By far the greatest threat to an allied task force is from the air, from enemy controlled bombs and missiles."

The naval forces available for the Western Task Force in early 1944 were busily engaged in maintaining the Fifth Army on the Anzio beachhead. At that time, the number of craft in the western Mediterranean for an amphibious invasion of Southern France was considered inadequate for the scale of assault envisaged, and, due to operational losses in maintaining the beaches at Anzio, no definite estimate could be made of the numbers which might be available when the time came to mount the assault. The number of combat loaders in the theater was not considered to be sufficient to carry the number of troops and equipment proposed. The invasion of Northern France had a recognized priority on ships and craft of this nature. The Northern France (after the cross-channel invasion) and Indian theaters were possible sources for more ships and craft.

The number of gunfire support ships available in the theater was considered of secondary importance at this time, for it was felt that any necessities for gunfire support which might arise would be satisfactorily met from other theaters. The major problem in connection with making plans, therefore, was getting a definite allocation of ships and craft to be made available for the invasion of Southern France. As the months passed and preparations mounted for the invasion of Northern France, it became increasingly apparent that an allocation of ships and craft would not be made definite until the last stages of planning.

It must be appreciated that until the allocation of ships and craft was definite, the army was delayed in making a decision on how to execute the scheme of maneuver. Furthermore, it was impossible to complete the navy planning until the army planning was reasonably complete.

However, the navy planners considered everything possible prior to receiving a definite army plan. As early as 19 February, bids for transportation of naval base personnel in assault and follow-up ships and craft were issued. Construction work was commenced in Corsica to insure adequate supplies of petroleum products and establishment of PT bases and staging ports. The Invasion Training

Center was established at Salerno. Also, requests for the manufacture of naval bombardment ammunition in the United States were initiated.

The invasion of Southern France was an integral part of the overall allied strategy in Western Europe and was to be executed in conjunction with the invasion of Northern France, although subsequent thereto, and furthermore, from a strategic view point, the invasion of Southern France was based on the following assumptions made by Allied Force Headquarters on 22 December 1943:

(1) On the mainland of Italy, the allies were confronting the Pisa-Rimini line and as a result were not in possession of the port of Leghorn, and therefore, without detracting from the proposed invasion of Southern France, pressure was being maintained in Italy;

(2) Other forces in the Mediterranean were not engaged in offensive operations elsewhere;

(3) Internal security in North Africa was not a limiting factor in assessing available US and French divisions.

It will be noted that at this time, the invasion of Southern France was given a secondary priority to the allied advance in Italy. This priority was not changed until July, and consequently assignment of ships and craft and army forces continued to be the subject of overriding priority of the allied advance on the Italian front. Such a condition made it impossible to arrive at definite plans for the operation in Southern France.

The assumptions upon which the naval plans were based are identified in the Operation Plan, Annex A to this report. These were based on an estimate of the enemy defensive strength opposing the invasion. It was found, however, that in the short period from the invasion of Northern France to the time of the invasion of Southern France, enemy defensive strength decreased materially, due principally to thinning out of personnel by withdrawal of field divisions to the North; decline of air strength by withdrawals and damage; deterioration of logistics and lines of communication in France by air bombing and activity of French Forces of the Interior; and naval losses (especially U-boats) caused by accurate bombing of Southern French ports.

Section 1.3

THE OBJECTIVE

The preliminary directive received from Commander-in-Chief, Mediterranean, on 28 December 1943, embodied the following mission:

Task

    To establish the army firmly ashore;

    To continue to maintain and support the army over beaches until all need for maintenance over beaches had ceased.

Purpose

    To support the invasion of Northern France.

As a basis for planning, the preliminary directive gave the following points:

(1) Preparation for the invasion of Northern France was in progress and it was expected to take place during the first suitable day in May 1944;

(2) Decision had been made that a beachhead would be established on the south coast of France in conjunction with the invasion of Northern France for the purpose of supporting it;

(3) Composition of the army forces for the invasion of Southern France had not been decided but would probably consist of ten divisions, three or four US divisions, and the balance French divisions.

Ramifications of the strategic situation in the Mediterranean during the following months caused considerable uncertainty as to the decision to be finally made. There was the possibility under consideration by the Supreme Allied Commander, at various times, that other targets for invasion, for example, a landing in Greece or the Adriatic, might give greater support to the invasion of Northern France. In considering the implications of alternative operations, the Mediterranean Joint Planning Staff of Allied Force Headquarters on 15 June set as the basis of their assumptions the following:

(1) The overriding necessity is, at the earliest possible moment, to apply to the enemy all our force in the manner best calculated to assist in the invasion of Northern France;

(2) Destruction, in Italy, of the German armed force south of the Pisa-Rimini line must be completed, and there should be no withdrawal of any allied forces that are necessary for this purpose from the battle;

(3) A three division amphibious assault should be the basis for consideration;

(4) The forces in the Mediterranean should be prepared to launch an invasion by 25 July provided always that this would not limit the completion of the army operation south of the Pisa-Rimini line.

While these considerations were carried on by the AFHQ level, and the level directly above the Western Task Force, the planners of the Western Task Force were involved to the extent that they had to be prepared for any change of decision as to where the invasion was to be launched.

The mission stated in the preliminary directive of the Commander-in-Chief, Mediterranean, definitely indicated what was to be done by the Western Task Force, that is, to establish the army ashore and maintain it until a maintenance over the beaches was no longer necessary. Discretion was limited to the decision as to what sector or sectors in a general area would be utilized for the assault.

An exhaustive study of the possibilities of beaches in various sectors of the southern French coast was made jointly with the army. From the naval point of view, the aim was to pass upon the acceptability of assault beaches on the basis of (1) the ability of the naval forces under command of NCWTF to overcome enemy resistance in order to land the assault divisions and firmly establish them ashore, and (2) the ability of naval forces to effect the build-up and maintain the army over the same beaches or nearby beaches until ports were open. The second basis immediately gave rise to a subsidiary objective of the Western Task Force. It would be the responsibility of the naval forces to open and rehabilitate enough ports so that the necessity of maintaining the army forces over beaches no longer existed. In the proposed area of Southern France, Marseille and Toulon were the two major ports. Marseille alone probably could support maintenance shipping, but Toulon alone probably could not. An attack from the east of these ports, therefore, required considerations of capturing and re-opening Toulon and Marseille in succession. From the west, Marseille would remain the final goal for re-opening, but Toulon would have to be neutralized by capture.

The supposed objective of the enemy force was defensive in nature. His purpose was to prevent the assault and failing that, to delay the advance of the armies as long as possible, falling back to prepared positions where a decisive land campaign could be waged favorably to the enemy (as in the Rhone gap). Because of the weakness of enemy surface strength in the Mediterranean, the biggest problem confronting the naval forces was, consequently, not the approach, but rather the establishment of the beachhead, and the subsequent rapid build-up and maintenance of the army.

Section 1.4

THE NAVAL CONSIDERATION OF THE MILITARY FORCES AVAILABLE

The question of the identity of the military forces to be made available for the operation was of great concern to the naval planners inasmuch as three major problems depended on the final assignments. In the first place, it was desired that the assault divisions each be thoroughly trained in amphibious assault with the naval attack forces until the army and navy elements were firmly welded into a finished amphibious attack unit. Secondly, the broad problem of mounting and transporting the assault and follow-up forces required considerable planning, assignment of ships, and construction in the many mounting ports. This problem was jointly considered by the Movements and Transportation Section of AFHQ, Service of Supply, North African Theater of Operations (SOS NATOUSA), the G-4 section of the Seventh Army, and the Eighth Fleet planning and logistics sections. Lastly, after having the assault divisions assigned, it was necessary for these commands to work out their tactical assault plans with respect to definite assault beaches.

During the early period of planning, an assault with 2 or possibly 3 US infantry divisions having previous amphibious combat experience, plus 1 French armored command, was contemplated. The follow-up would include 5 French infantry divisions and 2 complete armored divisions. Because of the necessity of using army divisions with amphibious combat experience and because the units having the necessary qualifications were found only in the US Fifth Army, it was necessary to remove them from the Italian front. This withdrawal from the Allied Armies in Italy (AAI) raised the problem of where the divisions should be moved for training, refitting, and mounting. Originally, it was proposed to train the two US infantry divisions, the 3rd and the 45th, in the Salerno area, beginning as soon as the Pisa-Rimini line was established. In order to meet the original invasion date, May 1944, promulgated in the preliminary directive issued by Commander-in-Chief, Mediterranean, on 28 December, it was imperative that these two infantry divisions be withdrawn from combat sometime in April. At the same time, the 85th US Infantry Division was training in North Africa in the Oran area.

French divisions at this time had not yet been nominated, but they also would have to be withdrawn from the front, trained, refitted, and mounted. It was considered that training in the Salerno area might congest the port of Naples. Therefore, Sicily and the "heel" ports were considered as suitable places for refitting some of the French divisions.

Because of the distance the 85th Division would have to travel from Oran to the assault area, it was determined that that movement should be a ship to shore assault from combat loaded personnel and cargo ships. The 3rd and 45th Divisions would then make the assault on a shore to shore basis in craft, probably staging in Ajaccio.

Army operations in Italy, south of the Pisa-Rimini line, were not stabilized in time to meet the requirements for an operation in May. Consequently, craft and ships assigned for the invasion of Southern France were withdrawn for the invasion of Northern France. By the middle of June, the 3rd and 45th Divisions were released from the Italian front and, instead of the 85th Division, the 36th US Infantry Division was withdrawn from the Italian front for participation in the invasion of Southern France.

During this period of uncertainty as to which divisions would be assigned for the invasion of Southern France, naval planning was continued as far as possible. Corsica was being developed as an advanced supply depot. Petroleum storage, water storage, gasoline storage, and facilities for staging landing craft were in-

ARMY UNITS OF THE WESTERN TASK FORCE

The Seventh Army, Lieut. General A. M. Patch, USA

    Assault Forces (D-day and D plus 1)

        VI Corps (US), Major General L. K. Truscott, USA

            3rd Infantry Division (US), Major General J. W. O'Daniel, USA
            36th Infantry Division (US), Major General J. E. Dahlquist, USA
            45th Infantry Division (US), Major General W. W. Eagles, USA
            Armored Combat Command Sudre (1st French Armored Division)

        First Airborne Task Force, Brigadier General R. T. Frederick, USA

            2nd Independent Parachute Brigade (Br.)
            517th Parachute RCT (US)
            509th Parachute Battalion (US)
            1st Bn. 551st Parachute Regiment (US)
            550th Infantry Battalion (Glider) (US)
            Supporting Troops

        1st Special Service Force

        French Groupe de Commandos

    Follow-up Forces (Until D plus 20)

        French Army B (II French Corps), General d'Armee de Lattre de Tassigny, French Army

            1st (Fr.) Infantry Division (DMI)
            3rd Algerian Infantry Division (DIA)
            9th Colonial Infantry Division (DIC)
            1st (Fr.) Armored Division (DB) (less Combat Command Sudre)

    Build-up Forces (Until D plus 40)

        I French Corps, General de Corps Henri Martin, French Army

            2nd (Fr.) Moroccan Infantry Division (DIM)
            4th (Fr.) Mountain Division (DMM)
            5th (Fr.) Armored Division (DB)

Figure 1

creased throughout the island. In order to effect the build-up of the air force in Southern France, the Calvi-Ile Rousse area in northwest Corsica was selected as the logical base for loading air forces from Corsica to Southern France. This selection was made as a result of studies conducted by the representatives of the Naval Commander.

Whatever divisions were to be employed, it was known that they would be located in Italy. It was estimated that the assault would be mounted probably from the Naples area and routed through the Straits of Bonifacio, to the area in Southern France finally selected. This required the immediate sweeping of the Straits of Bonifacio and the restoration of aids to navigation. The follow-up would come from Oran, the "heel" ports and Naples.

The army force to be made available was considered sufficient, and had adequate combat training to indicate that they could make the invasion a success. However, since there was no decision as to when these troops would be made available and the Corps Commander and the Division Commanders were still engaged in combat, it was very difficult for the army to make any detailed tactical plan.

Airborne forces had been offered. Because of their dependence on weather conditions, their value was viewed with considerable doubt. Air support was considered adequate. It was not probable that air support would be increased by additional forces.

Resistance forces in the interior of France had been supplied and directed both from Great Britain and from the Mediterranean theater. Because of the prior commitments for the invasion of Northern France, the direction for these now came entirely from the United Kingdom. This created a more unified effort of all resistance groups. The problem of supply was met jointly by both theaters.

Section 1.5

SURVEY OF THEATER OF OPERATIONS

The study of characteristics of the theater was made by G-2 sections of the army and the naval intelligence section. At one time, the Sete-Agde area was carefully considered in order to execute an assault which would cut France in two by a thrust to the west with the Carcassonne Gap, Toulouse, and finally Bordeaux as the objectives. However, maintenance in this area was estimated to be most difficult because of the poor beach gradients, many lagoons, lakes, and canalized roads. For the thrust north along the Rhone Valley, it was determined more suitable to capture Marseille and Toulon from east of the Rhone delta, inasmuch as a landing in the Sete-Agde area would be separated from those two ports by the difficult terrain of the delta which could be flooded. It was concluded that the area close to the two major ports in Southern France, Toulon and Marseille, was most feasible for maintenance. It was early apparent from both army and navy view points that the most suitable area for the invasion was east of Toulon.

Section 1.6

STRATEGIC DECEPTION

As soon as the invasion of Northern France was launched, the allied forces in the Mediterranean gained a psychological initiative over the German defenders. From the concentrations that were apparent in the allied ports of the western Mediterranean, the Germans early knew that an invasion was in preparation. It was believed that they had concluded that we would invade Southern France, but it was further believed that they did not know when or exactly where. It was deemed wise to augment the strategic initiative by certain strategic deceptions.

The 91st Division at Oran, after having completed its amphibious training and having been ordered to the Italian front, was transferred from 16 to 19 June in a method carefully planned to simulate preparations for an invasion. In other words, for the mere transfer of the 91st Division from Oran to Italy, the troops were combat loaded on assault personnel and cargo ships. A complete psychological preparation was executed to simulate the launching of an operation. There is reason to suppose that German intelligence so interpreted the move.

Another aid to deception was the preparation for mounting follow-up divisions for the invasion in the "heel" ports of Italy. This move pointed toward a Balkan invasion. At the same time, the bombing of Southern France carried out by the Mediterranean Allied Strategic Air Forces (see Section 4.2, Part II, Pre-D-Day Bombing) was so coordinated with the entire bombing of Western Europe, over all of France, Northern Italy, and the Balkans, that no direct indication could be drawn from the bombing in any particular area.

During this period, also, the Carrier Task Force was ordered to the eastern Mediterranean. The move of AFHQ and the associated commands to Naples in early July, and the presence of the gunfire support forces at Malta and Taranto prior to the invasion, were all consistent with an intention to invade east of the Italian peninsula.

The strategic deception achieved for this invasion was due to the joint efforts of many sections under AFHQ, the Office of Strategic Services (OSS), and the US Eighth Fleet.

Chapter 2

THE DECISION

Section 2.1

MAINTENANCE OVER BEACHES

Reaching a naval decision involved approval of the beaches selected by the army for the assault based on the feasibility not only of landing but of subsequent maintenance over the beaches. The beaches should permit the troops landed to take their proper part in the military scheme of maneuver, and, equally important, should permit the maneuver to be sustained by continuing naval action.

It was considered that the beaches selected should be feasible both from the point of view of the hydrographic and immediate terrain features, and also from the point of view of the local military opposition to be overcome. When the hydrographic and immediate terrain features presented no choice, the natural and man-made military obstacles determined the choice to be made.

The following factors were stipulated and satisfied as considerations for adequacy of maintenance beaches:

(1) The length of beach suitable for landing;

(2) The number of landing points available to larger types of landing craft;

(3) The number of pontoon causeways which could be sited on the beach under consideration.

Assuming the beaches were adequate, the navy insisted that in order to maintain the army, the following considerations be met:

(1) Adequate unloading personnel provided in ships (The navy's experience indicated that 120 men were required in each combat-loaded transport and merchant ship);

(2) Adequate labor troops provided the Beach Group (The navy's experience indicated that 200 men per battalion combat team landed was the minimum required);

(3) All army echelons to have an understanding of the organization and operation of supply over beaches;

(4) The Beach Group Commanders to be familiar with the unloading plans;

(5) Adequate motor transportation provided with relief drivers to permit 24 hour operation between the beaches and the dumps, and control of this transport placed under the Beach Group Commander;

(6) The existing road nets to permit the moving of adequate tonnages from the dumps to the combat areas without interference from troop or weapon movements using the same roads;

(7) The Beach Group troops to be kept working at the beaches, that is, they were not to be withdrawn inland to reenforce combat elements.

The naval opinion was that at least 30 days of beach maintenance would be required before the ports of Southern France could be captured and rendered usable to insure the supply of the US Seventh Army and French Army B ashore. Due to the fact that, beginning in October, the weather of Southern France would hinder beach maintenance to a considerable extent, the navy advised that the latest date for execution of the assault should be 1 September.

Section 2.2

THE ASSAULT AREA

On 15 June, after a careful study, this command recommended dismissing from consideration the Sete-Agde area for the following reasons:

(1) The target offered no lee for off-lying shipping nor any port which could accommodate deep draft vessels, and all ships would have to be unloaded, therefore, by craft, boats, and DUKWs;

(2) The port of Sete is small, shallow, and very easily blocked, its capacity would be insufficient to support the forces landed, and hence beach maintenance for an extended period would be imposed upon us;

(3) Pontoons could not be maintained upon these beaches, inferior because of their poor gradients, during heavy weather, and destruction of the pontoons would seriously affect the supply of the army;

(4) Beach exits are very poor, requiring extensive construction, and owing to the large areas of lakes, lagoons, marshes, rivers, and ditches, the road communications would be canalized, restricting maneuvering of troops and the routing of supply lines;

(5) One division, which would have been the 3rd Division, according to an army outline plan, would have to land on the beaches north of Port Vendres, about 25 miles distant from the two division landing and hence the landings would not be in mutual support;

(6) Beach obstacles on the Sete beaches were more highly developed than in any other area along the south coast of France;

(7) This area was beyond the range of fighter air cover from Corsica;

(8) An assault in this area did not offer good terrain to the army leading to the early capture of Marseille and Toulon.

During the same period, the army developed outline plans for the assault in two other areas, the Rade d'Hyeres and the Frejus-Cavalaire area (see diagram I). The Army and Navy Task Force Commanders held that the Rade d'Hyeres area was not as favorable as the Cavalaire-Frejus area for the following principal reasons:

(1) Before the beaches could be approached, extensive minesweeping would be required and there were insufficient hours of darkness to achieve this for the areas required by the assault shipping;

(2) Any assault in this area would be completely flanked by gun positions on the islands of Porquerolles, Port Cros, Levant, and the surrounding mainland;

(3) The assault beaches and the shipping nearby would be within range of the many coastal defense guns in the Toulon-St. Mandrier area;

(4) The restricted waters would deny gunfire support ships freedom of movement, and the resulting concentration of ships would provide a good bombing target for enemy air forces.

The Cavalaire-Frejus area had been selected by this command as early as 2 March as the most suitable for an assault on Southern France. The reasons for the navy's recommendation of the Cavalaire-Frejus area were:

(1) Least distance from supporting airfields in Corsica;

(2) Favorable seaward approach with narrow coastal zone of waters suitable for enemy mining;

(3) Least density of enemy coast defense batteries, (within comparable distance of the objective) capable of ranging on approach, transport areas, and landing beaches;

(4) Good to moderate beaches with some well-suited for maintenance;

(5) Three small ports with limited facilities available, but with considerable anchorage;

(6) Bridgehead in this sector would provide suitable base for attack on Toulon and Marseille from landward;

(7) Apparent enemy estimate, as indicated by our evaluation of his defense activity, that the landing, which he expected, would take place on other sectors of the coast;

(8) The lines of transportation and supply could easily be severed by air force bombing, thus isolating the bridgehead and preventing the enemy from building up the forces opposing the assault on the coast;

(9) The area offered suitable sites for the employment of paratroops dropped on critical centers of road nets to block enemy troop movements;

(10) This area offered excellent sites for rapid construction of airfields and early establishment of fighters and bombers in Southern France to support the advance of the allied armies.

Section 2.3

D-DAY

Early in the planning period this command had set forth the view that D-day should not be later than 1 September. This was based on the considerations of beach maintenance and weather. It was believed that the Western Task Force should plan for a period of at least 30 days' beach maintenance before ports could be opened sufficiently to close the beaches. The fall storms along the coast of Southern France, locally known as "mistrals," could be expected frequently after 1 October, making beach maintenance no longer feasible. (It is interesting to note that 41 days were required before port operations permitted all beaches to be closed on 25 September.)

Early in June, it became evident that in order to assist the invasion of Northern France, a decision to launch the invasion of Southern France would have to be made soon. On 11 June, it was reported that the volume of supplies which had been collected for the invasion stood at 90%, and this figure was being progressively reduced by the existing priority of the Italian campaign.

On 12 June, the Supreme Headquarters Allied Expeditionary Forces planners in United Kingdom indicated that an invasion of Southern France no later than 15 August was desirable from the standpoint of giving optimum assistance to the invasion in Northern France.

On 14 June, the Mediterranean Allied Air Forces and the US Navy pointed out that a definite decision regarding the invasion was necessary at an early date. Until then, the allied armies in Italy continued to have priority on the use of craft. Training schedules were tight, because of the short time left until the latest acceptable D-day. This priority was, therefore, of great concern to the Commander Eighth Fleet for at any time during training or overhaul craft could be requested and taken for supplying the Italian front. At this time, the air forces planned to execute their build-up into Southern France from the Calvi-Ile Rousse area. Because the air forces required approximately 35 days to complete their transfer from the mainland to Corsica for this invasion, they were extremely interested in getting a definite decision.

On 14 June, G-4 of the US Army at AFHQ, notified SOS, NATOUSA (Service of Supply, North African Theater of Operations, US Army) that priority of supply would be given to the preparation of the invasion divisions and overriding priority to US divisions in order of their withdrawal from the Italian front. On the 16th of June, the Seventh Army troop list was reported complete, although the order of withdrawal of units from the Fifth Army in Italy was not. On 21 June, the Executive Planning Section of AFHQ, which included army, navy, and air planning representatives, was given the target date of 15 August.

In previous analysis, it had been determined that 38 days would be required to withdraw a division from the front, train, refit, and mount. Thus, the time element became increasingly important.

On the 24th of June, the US 36th Division was nominated to replace the 85th Division. It was determined that the 36th Division would require a longer period of training than the 85th Division, but it was estimated that the target date could be met. The assault divisions were now the US 3rd, 36th, and 45th Infantry Divisions. These three divisions constituted the US VI Corps, which was to make the assault.

The rapid changing of the forces allocated to the follow-up further complicated final assignment of forces. On the 26th of June, the French 4th Zouaves, formerly on the invasion troop list, were assigned to garrison duty at Elba. This move, however, released the 9th French DIC for the invasion. On the 28th of June, the 4th Zouaves were redesignated on the invasion troop list. At this time, Commander-in-Chief Mediterranean, stated it was important to replace the 9th DIC from Elba within the next eight days. These examples are selected to show the situation confronting army planners as they made final plans for the invasion based on the target date of 15 August.

On 2 July, the Supreme Allied Command decision was promulgated to authorities concerned and provided that:

(a) At the earliest possible date, the invasion of Southern France would be launched;

(b) Every effort would be exerted to meet the target date of 15 August;

(c) The operation would be prepared on the basis of about a three division assault, an airborne lift of a strength later to be decided, and a build-up to at least 10 infantry and armored divisions as quickly as resources made available for this operation would allow;

(d) SCAEF (Supreme Commander, Allied Expeditionary Forces, Commanding General of the invasion of Northern France) would release to Supreme Allied Commander, Mediterranean, as early as practicable, the additional resources required for the invasion of Southern France.

Section 2.4

THE ASSAULT BEACHES

On 8 July, in accordance with the AFHQ directive, all planning headquarters were moved to Naples; and, thereafter, working on the basis of a D-day no later than 15 August, the joint decision as to beaches to be assaulted was reached by the VI Corps and the Eighth Fleet planners.

The Commanding General of the US VI Corps was given command of the assault of the three US Infantry Divisions. Command of all landings on the flanks was retained by the Commanding General, Seventh Army. At this stage the latest army plan was to make a two division shore-to-shore assault, using craft, and, one division ship-to-shore, using combat loaders. This was based on the original consideration of mounting the 85th Division in Oran. Because of the long voyage, combat loaders were to be used for the entire division.

However, when the 36th Division was substituted for the 85th, which permitted mounting the 36th Division in the Naples-Salerno area, it was jointly agreed that one RCT of each division should be a ship-to-shore assault from combat loaders and two RCT of each division would be a shore-to-shore assault using craft staging in Corsica.

Two RCT in each division were to be loaded in 6-davit and 2-davit LSTs for the assault. One RCT in each division loaded in combat loaders, LCI(L)s, and LCTs, were to be landed as reserve waves.

While the selection of beaches to be assaulted was made by the echelon of the US Eighth Fleet and the Seventh Army, the assignment of beaches to divisions and RCTs was left to the echelon of the US VI Corps and the echelon of the divisions and attack forces, the forces which were to make the assault. Certain principles of coordination, however, were set forth.

Foremost was the necessity for a vigorous assault which would definitely secure the "Blue Line" (see diagram I) by D plus 1. It was considered that the beachhead must be of that area including high ground inland from the beaches in order to deny the enemy favorable artillery positions from which beaches could be shelled and to meet a concerted counter-attack which could develop at that time.

The beaches selected, therefore, should have adequate exits. Beaches 259 and 261 were each considered adequate for the landing of one division. Beaches 263A, B, and C were backed by steep hills and had only a single, narrow coastal road as an exit following the coast. Particular care was considered necessary on this beach to insure that supplies and personnel were not allowed to block the exits.

The beaches in the Camel area gave the greatest concern. Camel Red, beach 264A, was defended by the highest scale of underwater obstacles and beach obstructions in this area. Camel Yellow, beach 265, was a well-protected harbor well situated for a small boat landing. Photographs of the surrounding area showed it to be defended by small guns, pill boxes, machine gun emplacements, etc., far out of proportion to its value as a beach. Camel Green and Camel Blue, beaches 264B and 265A, permitted only a narrow assault. Both were fringed by hills with a narrow, winding road as the exit. It was considered essential that Camel Red be secured as early as possible for it was the only beach in the Camel area with considerable possibilities for maintenance and rapid build-up and to exploit the establishment of air forces in the Argens Valley.

The Frejus area was considered the critical area. Movement of troops inland toward Le Muy was expected to face a high density of field guns in a German training area about 5 miles northwest of St. Aygulf Pt. The dropping area in vicinity of Le Muy of the 1st Airborne Task Force to be occupied prior to H-hour by airborne troops was further insurance that the "Blue Line" would be properly secured on D plus 1.

Because the Golfe de St. Tropez might be heavily mined and the Delta assault beaches might not support the maintenance required, a plan was worked out whereby maintenance for the 45th Division could be executed over the north half of Alpha Yellow, beach 261. An administrative division line was thus set up so that the road from the Pampelonne Bay area to La Foux and Grimaud could be included in the 45th Division area.

Section 2.5

H-HOUR

The H-hour of 0800 was a compromise between two requirements. Primarily, it was necessary to have it late enough to permit adequate bombing and shore bombardment in sufficient daylight immediately before landing to destroy or neutralize the defenses. Secondarily, it was desirable to have H-hour as early as possible to permit unloading during daylight for a sufficient period to insure the establishment of a firm beachhead and build-up of forces more rapidly than the enemy could reenforce the defenders.

The experiences at Salerno and Anzio made it clear to the naval planners that it would be absolutely necessary for the assault of three divisions to be so overwhelming that a deep, firm beachhead would be established by the end of D plus 1. The area enclosed by the "Blue Line" (see diagram I) was set as the goal. Having secured this area it was considered that any organized counter-attack could not be launched before D plus 1; and furthermore, the possibility that the counter-attack could push our forces into the sea would then be considerably reduced.

The navy planners vigorously supported plans for a quick powerful army thrust inland in order to secure such a beachhead. This movement was necessary to make room on D-day for the personnel of three assault divisions, the French Combat Command Sudre, and the equipment with which the troops would fight. This necessary extension of the beachhead was enhanced:

(1) By the excellent, offensive spirit of the assault forces;

(2) By giving as much time as possible during daylight for efficient unloading.

It may be noted that at the end of D plus 1 the Seventh Army had secured the "Blue Line" and in many places advanced beyond it.

No reliance was placed on the efficiency of unloading after dusk when air and submarine attacks were considered likely. From the consideration of unloading alone, it was evident that the time of H-hour should be as early as possible.

Opposed to this requirement for unloading was the necessity of insuring that the initial landings would be successful. This required adequate time to neutralize the coast defenses. The coast defenses of the assault area for this consideration came into three categories:

(1) Coastal defense guns;

(2) Mines;

(3) Underwater obstacles and beach defenses.

To neutralize the coastal defense guns would require the most powerful, concentrated bombardment ever employed in the Mediterranean theater. There was one saving feature; the coastal defenses were not deep. Most gun positions could be reached by gunfire from seaward. Furthermore, assault troops could capture the coastal defense guns without penetrating very far inland. However, any period of time devoted to neutralization had to be kept to a minimum in order to give the maximum time for landing assault troops and equipment beginning as soon after the enemy had been alerted as possible, which in turn would give the enemy the shortest possible time to group his reserves for a concerted counterattack. This consideration dictated as short a period of pre-H-hour bombing and bombardment as possible commensurate with the scale of air effort and naval bombardment required and the light conditions during neutralization. Bombing and bombardment to be effective needed adequate daylight for spotting. As a matter of fact, some of the French bombardment vessels had no radar and therefore required light to be able to fix their positions with sufficient accuracy to fire indirect fire.

One further consideration in determining the period for bombardment was the probable absence of enemy naval forces. In every other invasion in the Mediterranean, a cover or support force was required nearby to defend the assault against possible surface attacks. Because of this situation and the heavy scale of coastal defense guns and reenforced strongpoints, it was early apparent that all heavy ships would be needed and could be employed in the bombardment. It was necessary, therefore, to have sufficient daylight time before H-hour, not only to execute the air bombing and naval bombardment with spotting, but also to permit the heavy concentration of gunfire ships to take up the most effective firing positions. This meant, in some cases, as a preliminary action, the neutralization of certain long range enemy batteries which threatened the approach.

It was also necessary in the compromise determining H-hour to consider the ammunition supply for bombardment. It was desirable to conserve the supply of ammunition for the probable continued use of the bombardment ships in supporting the Seventh Army's drive on Toulon and Marseille.

For this reason, prolonged naval gunfire was considered undesirable. By careful timing of air strikes against the gun positions, it was considered that neutralization could be accomplished by the combined and carefully integrated employment of air and naval bombardment, air bombing replacing a considerable portion of the naval gunfire for this period.

It was necessary to augment the fighter bombers with medium bombers and heavy bombers. The medium and heavy bombers had the problem of rendezvousing after mass take-offs in darkness. The mass take-offs in darkness could be executed, although it was the first time in the history of the 15th Air Force this had been done. For a concerted strike, rendezvous had to be at or later than first light and over some friendly land mark which could be identified. The northern parts of Corsica and the islands between Corsica and the Italian mainland were selected. This meant, however, that the earliest the medium and heavy bombers could bomb would be about 0700. In order to execute all the attacks, with careful adherence to scheduling, bombing could be completed by 0730. The fighter bombers made their attacks beginning at 0610, the earliest time of satisfactory light conditions.

It was considered that one-half hour was the maximum that could be allotted to naval gunfire alone based on the considerations of conserving ammunition. Furthermore, it was necessary to have bombing completed prior to the time the Naval Combat Demolition Units began their work of breaching the underwater obstacles. H-hour was thus determined to be 0800.

It remained to ascertain that there would be adequate time for minesweeping prior to positioning of gunfire ships. It was necessary to have an adequate period of darkness prior to first light to complete minesweeping of the assault areas. Naturally, the approach would have to be as late in the night as possible. It was known, however, that because of the sharp slope of the continental shelf, the minesweeping of the final channels would be of short duration and could be covered by pre-H-hour bombing and counter-battery naval gunfire. The period between the beginning of the minesweeping for the assault and the final minesweeping under neutralizing bombing and gunfire was thus adequate with H-hour at 0800.

The detailed considerations of bombing, naval gunfire, mining, Naval Combat Demolition Units and unloading plans are discussed in Part II, the Execution of the Plan.

While the gunfire support ships had a bare minimum of time for accurate, observed fire, the careful integration of the air bombing and the limited naval bombardment prior to 0800 produced a completely satisfactory neutralization of the assault area, conserved the limited supply of ammunition, and finally permitted such efficient unloading on D-day that the extension of the beachhead proceeded so rapidly that the Germans never had the opportunity for an organized counter-attack.

Section 2.6

SUMMARY

The Alpha, Delta, and Camel Attack Forces were simultaneously to place ashore the 3rd, 45th, and 36th US Infantry Divisions. The most difficult area for assault, the Frejus area, was to be given the added support of the 1st Airborne Task Force dropping in the Le Muy area.

The assault at 0800 on 15 August was to be preceded by the neutralizing effort of 1300 aircraft under the XII Tactical Air Command and 53 gunfire support ships. Commando landings were to be made prior to H-hour on the flanks on Ile de Levant and Ile de Port Cros to silence the gun batteries which were reported thereon and which commanded the approaches to Cavalaire and Pampelonne Bays; and at Cap Negre and south of Cannes at Theoule sur Mer, to establish road blocks on the flanks of the attacking troops. The Sitka Force was to execute the landings on the left flank, and the Special Operations Group was to land the troops on the right flanks during their diversion operations.

The French Armored Combat Command Sudre was to follow the assault troops on D-day over Camel beaches and push up the Argens Valley.

The immediate follow-up beginning on D plus one of the French Army B (the II French Corps) was to be made over Alpha or Delta beaches through the left flank for the drive on Toulon and Marseille, supported by the gunfire support ships reorganized within Task Force 86. The 1st Airborne Task Force was to hold the right flank.

For the build-up and the proposed thrust north up the Rhone Valley the I French Corps was to be landed in the captured and re-opened ports of Toulon and Marseille, or over beaches if necessary.

Chapter 3

FORMULATION OF PLANNED ACTION

Section 3.1

ANALYSIS OF THE DECISION

Obviously, no analysis of the decision as such could be made until the decision as to the selection of the beaches was complete, and since the VI Corps plan of the assault did not appear until 30 July, this command could not complete its plan until a few days prior, when an advance copy of the army assault plan was received. However, much of the planning had been done before this time.

The simple feature, timing; of (1) the approach, (2) neutralization of the islands, (3) troop landings, and (4) gunfire and air support, was early considered by this command far more important to the success of an amphibious invasion than any additional fairweather forces such as paratroops or airborne forces. Even though the decisions, first, that an invasion of Southern France would be executed, and secondly, that the Cavalaire-Frejus area would be selected for the assault were late in appearing, army and navy Task Force Commanders as early as March indicated their preference for the area. Consequently, the major part of the planning was along the single progressive line pointing toward that final area. Beaches had been thoroughly studied. The navy was prepared to accept or reject the beaches selected by the Corps for the assault in a minimum of time.

In April, it was recognized that the major naval problems of this operation would be:

(1) That the army would be landed at H-hour with such overwhelming, coordinated air and naval gunfire support that the situation would be most favorable for the army to exploit the beachhead;

(2) That the army would require continued support by gunfire in its coastal advance westwards towards Toulon and Marseille. Consequently representations to the proper naval authorities were made in an effort to concentrate adequate naval ships in support of the invasion;

(3) That the logistic support of the army by prolonged beach maintenance would be an essential feature of this operation, and the navy, therefore, made extensive plans to employ adequate facilities to fully cope with the problem;

(4) That the land campaign up the Rhone Valley would require a large build-up of reenforcements and increased logistics supply through full exploitation of the two naval ports to be captured, and therefore at this stage, naval planning gave careful consideration to marine salvage and reconstruction of ports.

In February, the training center was moved to Salerno in order to facilitate training of any elements which would be withdrawn from the Italian front for the invasion. The training center was well established so that by the time the divisions were withdrawn from the Italian front, the divisions and the amphibious groups which became the attack forces were readily molded into efficient units. During the period before the divisions were available for training, every effort was made to solve by experimental methods the problem of breaching underwater obstacles and beach defenses by actual rehearsal of the units that could be made available.

Section 3.2

NAVAL PLANNING MEMORANDA

In order to reach an early solution of the many complementary problems that present themselves in the execution of an amphibious invasion, the method of promulgating Naval Planning Memoranda was followed, commencing early in February.

NAVAL PLANNING MEMORANDA

No.	Section preparing memorandum	Section collaborating on the preparation
1 Security and Top Secret Procedure.	Intelligence	Communications
2 Code Words.	Intelligence	
3 Division of Responsibility for Planning and Preparation of Orders for Invasion of Southern France	Planning	Material and Logistics, Communications
4 Division of Responsibility between Army and Navy in Ports.	Planning	Material and Logistics, Intelligence, Communications, Deputy Chief of Staff
5 Responsibilities of the Beach Group	Planning	Material and Logistics, Communications, Gunnery
6,7,8,9 Description of U.S. and British Landing Craft and Transports	Material and Logistics	
10 Special Instructions for Merchant Ships	Planning	Material and Logistics, Communications, Gunnery
11 Naval Intelligence Outline Plan	Intelligence	
12 Beach Reports	Intelligence	
13 Beach Defenses (Enemy)	Intelligence	
14 Port Reports	Intelligence	
15 Astronomical Tables and Meteorological Information.	Intelligence	
16 Captured Equipment and Documents Directive	Intelligence	Material and Logistics, Flag Secretary, Gunnery, Communications
17 Press Relations and Photographers	Intelligence	
18 Censorship Directive	Intelligence	Communications

- 25 -

NAVAL PLANNING MEMORANDA (Continued)

No.	Section preparing memorandum	Section collaborating on the preparation
19 Combat Intelligence in Amphibious Operations	Intelligence	
20 Evacuation of Casualties	Medical	Planning, Material and Logistics
21 Prevention of Looting by Naval Personnel	Planning	Supply
22 Port Organization	Planning	Communications, Deputy Chief of Staff, Material and Logistics
23 Aircraft Spotting of Naval Gunfire	Air	Gunnery, Communications
24 Methods of Indicating Positions	Air	Operations, Intelligence, Planning, Communications
25 Control of Anti-Aircraft Fire	Gunnery	Air, Planning
26 Mine Sweeping	Minesweeping	Planning, Gunnery
27 Control of Craft and Boats	Planning	Communications, Material and Logistics
28 Convoys	Planning	Air, Deputy Chief of Staff
29 Countermeasures for Beach and Underwater Obstructions	Gunnery	Planning, Material and Logistics
30 Employment of Smoke	Gunnery	Planning, Material and Logistics
31 Employment of Rockets	Gunnery	Planning, Deputy Chief of Staff, Material and Logistics
32 Ammunition Reserves	Gunnery	Planning, Material and Logistics
33 Fuel and Water Arrangements	Material and Logistics	Planning
34 Salvage	Material and Logistics	Planning, Communications, Gunnery, Deputy Chief of Staff
35 Naval Orders and Instructions	Planning	Communications
36 Preparation of Communication Plans	Communications	
37 Schedule of Rehearsals and Mountings	Planning	Operations, Communications, Deputy Chief of Staff, Material and Logistics

NAVAL PLANNING MEMORANDA (Continued)

No.	Section Preparing Memorandum	Section collaborating on the preparation
38 Task Organization	Planning	Communications, Deputy Chief of Staff, Material and Logistics
39 Chemical Warfare, Poison Gas	Gunnery	
40 Prisoners of War	Material and Logistics	Planning
41 Barrage Balloons	Material and Logistics	Planning
42 Extra Light Indicator Nets	Gunnery	
Distribution	Flag Secretary	Deputy Chief of Staff

The Naval Planning Memoranda were given as wide a distribution as was deemed commensurate with security restrictions to all branches of the allied military services. New sections were issued and previous sections corrected weekly, and in this manner all elements of the Western Task Force were kept currently informed on the progress of planning for the invasion of Southern France. Even portions of the forces participating in the invasion of Northern France received all planning memoranda and current corrections.

It is believed that for a force of this size attempting to plan under the uncertain situation as it existed prior to 2 July, the distribution of planning memoranda is a most efficient method of preparation. No single document, and no one effort of planning after the invasion was finally decided upon, could have physically promulgated the necessary doctrine nor adequately treated the problem.

The formalized procedure of issuing planning memoranda and periodically correcting them for an operation of this scope is highly recommended.

Section 3.3

PREPARING THE PLAN

Daily conferences were held for the planners of the many services involved, in which joint navy and army outline plans were considered and discussed.

The number of personnel involved in planning was kept to a minimum. Code names were promulgated in order that all references to any geographical place or any operation would be given added security.

In solving the many complementary problems, tasks were assigned to various sections of the staff, and annexes for the Operation Plan were prepared by these sections. Roughly, the annexes were prepared by the sections covering the same topics in the Naval Planning Memoranda. The War Plans Officer, N-31, had the task of correlating and integrating the many parts into the final Operation Plan (see Annex A).

The annexes were correlated by the Planning Section and prepared in accordance with the following assignments:

Annex	Section assigned to prepare annex
A. Information Annex	Intelligence
B. Fire Support Plan	Gunnery, Planning
C. Communication Plan	Communications
D. Medical Plan	Medical
E. Logistic Plan	Supply, Material & Logistics
F. Air Plan	Air, Planning
G. Departure and Rendezvous Plan	Planning
H. Convoy Plan	Planning
I. Approach Plan	Planning
J. Minesweeping Plan	Minesweeping
K. Salvage Plan	Material & Logistics
L. Special Operations Group Directive	Special Operations, Planning
M. Screening Group Directive	Planning
N. Directive to USN Liaison, Beach Control Group	Planning, Deputy Chief of Staff
O. Directive to USN Liaison, French Ports	Planning, Deputy Chief of Staff
P. Intelligence Annex	Intelligence
Q. Instructions to Merchant Vessels	Planning, Deputy Chief of Staff
R. Air Beacon Directive	Planning, Air
S. Postponement Directive	Planning
Distribution	Flag Secretary

One feature of Annex B, Fire Support Plan, may be noted. This annex included the three major bombing plans of the XII Tactical Air Command, (1) the Pre-D-Day Bombing Plan, (2) the Pre-H-Hour Bombing Plan, and (3) the Post-H-Hour Bombing Plan. (See Sections 4.2, 4.3, and 4.4, Part II, for discussions of these phases of the operation.) This departure from the usual preparation of the gunnery annex was carried out to give emphasis to the bombing schedule where it was needed. It was expected that the fire support groups would become more familiar with and therefore would integrate their gunfire more completely with the bombing schedules, if the bombing schedules appeared in the Fire Support Plan.

It is believed that this method of focussing attention on the bombing schedules in the gunnery annex was sound. For tight time schedules of neutralizing effort, it is recommended that all neutralizing effort, air bombing, naval bombardment, and rockets be considered in a single annex.

Assignment of tasks, because of the lateness with which the final decision as to where the landings were to take place, was not as satisfactorily executed as would have been desired. The attack force commanders and the gunfire support commanders were kept notified of the changing situation as far as possible in Naval Planning Memoranda, briefings, and special letters. Laboring under the handicap of not having a definite Corps assault plan upon which to base their considerations, various commanders simultaneously carried out as much of their planning as was possible. Groups 1 and 2 of the Eighth Amphibious Force became Task Forces 84 and 85, respectively. Group 3 was organized under command of one of the attack force commanders upon his arrival from the invasion of Northern France and became Task Force 87.

When the VI Corps commander was given command of the assault of the three infantry divisions, the problem was posed as to the advisability of having an intermediate naval commander between the Naval Commander Western Task Force and the attack force commanders. This was considered unnecessary. Consequently, the Commanding General of the Seventh Army and the Commanding General of the VI Corps for the assault were dealt with simultaneously on the echelon of Naval Commander Western Task Force. This created no problem, however, in the actual assault and the simplification in the naval command was considered warranted.

No attempt has been made to reproduce the formulation of the planned action. Part II of this report covers the problems which were considered with the critical analysis of their success or failure.

SHIPS AND CRAFT
OF THE
WESTERN TASK FORCE

| Column 1
Listed in Operation Plan 4-44 | Column 2
Planned to be in assault area on D-day | Column 3
Actually in assault area on D-day | Column 4
Remarks |
|---|---|---|---|
| 5 BB (3 US, 1 Fr, 1 Br) | Same as column 1 | Same as column 1 | General notes: The designation "craft" used in this tabulation includes only non-ship-borne craft. Ship-borne craft are considered in Chapter 6, Part II. Column 3 has been included in this tabulation to indicate changes not foreseen in the Operation Plan. Increased numbers were usually due to more ships or craft being in operational condition than were anticipated in planning. Decreases on the other hand were usually due to break downs. |
| 3 CA (US) | Same as column 1 | Same as column 1 | |
| 18 CL (5 US, 7 Br, 6 Fr) | 14 CL (3 US, 6 Br, 5 Fr) | Same as column 2 | |
| 4 AACL (Br) | Same as column 1 | Same as column 1 | |
| 9 CVE (2 US, 7 Br) | Same as column 1 | Same as column 1 | |
| 3 DL (Fr) | Same as column 1 | Same as column 1 | |
| 83 DD (47US,27Br,5Fr,4Gr) | 77 DD (47US, 26Br, 4Gr) | Same as column 2 | |
| 13 DE (8 US, 5 Fr) | 7 DE (US) | Same as column 2 | |
| 2 KT (Br) | 0 KT | Same as column 2 | |
| 6 Sloop (Fr) | 0 Sloop | Same as column 2 | |
| 2 PG (Br) | Same as column 1 | Same as column 1 | |
| 25 PC (US) | Same as column 1 | Same as column 1 | |
| 31 SC (29 US, 2 Fr) | 29 SC (US) | Same as column 2 | |
| 25 AM (US) | 13 AM (US) | Same as column 2 | |
| 22 MS (Br) | Same as column 1 | Same as column 1 | 1 MS in reserve not listed in Op-Plan. |
| 39 YMS (32 US, 6 Br, 1 Fr) | 32 YMS (26 US, 6 Br) | Same as column 2 | |
| 28 ML (Br) | Same as column 1 | 27 ML | |
| 6 DanLayers (Br) | Same as column 1 | Same as column 1 | 2 DanLayers in reserve not listed in Op-Plan. |
| 3 ACM (2 US, 1 Br) | Same as column 1 | Same as column 1 | |
| 3 FDS (Br) | Same as column 1 | Same as column 1 | |
| 1 LSF (FDT) (Br) | Same as column 1 | Same as column 1 | |
| 2 AGC (US) | Same as column 1 | Same as column 1 | |
| 1 AVP (US) | Same as column 1 | Same as column 1 | |
| 9 AP (US) | Same as column 1 | Same as column 1 | |
| 7 APA (US) | Same as column 1 | Same as column 1 | |
| 5 APD (US) | Same as column 1 | Same as column 1 | |
| 7 AKA (US) | Same as column 1 | Same as column 1 | |
| 10 LSI (Br) | Same as column 1 | Same as column 1 | |
| 1 LSP (Br) | Same as column 1 | Same as column 1 | |
| 0 MT | 63 MT | Same as column 2 | Listed in Convoy Plan, Annex H to Op-Plan. |
| 1 AKS (US) | 0 AKS | Same as column 2 | |
| 1 AF (Br) | 0 AF | Same as column 2 | |
| 3 AE (2 US, 1 Fr) | 0 AE | Same as column 2 | |
| 5 ASIS (4 Br, 1 Fr) | 0 ASIS | Same as column 2 | |
| 1 AD (US) | 0 AD | Same as column 2 | |
| 2 AR (US) | 0 AR | Same as column 2 | |
| 1 ARL (US) | Same as column 1 | Same as column 1 | |
| 4 ARS (3 US, 1 Br) | 0 ARS | Same as column 2 | Listed in Salvage Plan, Annex K to Op-Plan. |
| 2 LSD (Br) | Same as column 1 | Same as column 1 | |
| 2 LSG (Br) | Same as column 1 | Same as column 1 | |
| 2 AC (Br) | 0 AC | Same as column 2 | |
| 11 AO (4 US, 7 Fr) | 3 AO (Fr) | Same as column 2 | |
| 5 YO (4 Br, 1 Bel) | 0 YO | Same as column 2 | |
| 4 YOG (Br) | 3 YOG | 0 YOG | |
| 5 YW (1 US, 3 Br, 1 It) | 0 YW | Same as column 2 | |
| 4 ATR (1 US, 3 Br) | Same as column 1 | 3 ATR (1 US, 2 Br) | |
| 7 ATA (3 US, 4 Br) | Same as column 1 | Same as column 1 | |
| 5 ATF (US) | Same as column 1 | Same as column 1 | |
| 6 YTL (US) | 4 YTL | Same as column 2 | |
| 2 YTB (US) | Same as column 1 | Same as column 1 | |
| 4 BAR (Br) | Same as column 1 | Same as column 1 | |
| 2 AN (US) | 1 AN | Same as column 2 | |
| 2 YF (US) | 0 YF | Same as column 2 | |
| 6 MFV (Br) | Same as column 1 | Same as column 1 | |
| 79 LST (73 US, 3 Br, 3 Gr) | Same as column 1 | 81 LST (75US,3Br,3Gr) | |
| 115 LCI (97 US, 18 Br) | Same as column 1 | 124 LCI (97US, 27Br) | |
| 124 LCT (64 US, 60 Br) | Same as column 1 | 142 LCT(77US,65Br) | |
| 30 LCT(R) (Br) | Same as column 1 | Same as column 1 | 14 LCT(R) manned by US personnel |
| 6 LCF (Br) | Same as column 1 | Same as column 1 | |
| 5 LCG (Br) | Same as column 1 | Same as column 1 | |
| 1 LCS (Br) | Same as column 1 | Same as column 1 | |
| 2 FT (Br) | Same as column 1 | Same as column 1 | |
| 42 PT (US) | Same as column 1 | Same as column 1 | |
| 17 ASRC (16 US, 1 Br) | Same as column 1 | Same as column 1 | |

Figure 2

Chapter 4

ASSIGNMENT OF TASK ORGANIZATIONS

Section 4.1

ATTACK FORCES

The task organization is shown in the Operation Plan, Annex A. It will be noted that each attack force commander had under his command for the assault, gunfire support ships, escort sweeper ships, and a certain number of salvage vessels. Subsequent to the assault, each of these three groups was reassigned to one commander for the entire invasion front. Task Force 80 contains several groups which might have been assigned to attack forces, for example the Special Operations Group, Screening Group, and possibly the Anti-Submarine and Convoy Control Group. However, it was considered that with one tactical commander co-ordinating the efforts of the entire operation, these task groups should be made part of a control force. They could then be assigned by simplest administrative procedure to any part of the entire operation.

The assignment of craft and ships to the attack forces was dependent on the final decision of the Corps and the Army as to the tactical plan of assault. Each division was to land with two RCT in assault and one RCT in the reserve. Consequently, each attack force had combat loaders and craft of about equal number. For the Sitka Force, Task Force 86, which was directed to secure the left flank by a pre-H-hour assault on the Isle de Levant and on the mainland at Cap Negre, LSIs and APDs were assigned.

Section 4.2

GUNFIRE SUPPORT

The gunfire support analysis for this invasion was developed in three steps:

(1) Selection of the areas of gunfire support responsibility for the:

    (a) Camel Attack Force,
    (b) Delta Attack Force,
    (c) Alpha Attack Force,
    (d) Sitka Attack Force (see diagram I);

(2) Analysis of the targets capable of opposing the assault;

(3) Assignment of ships with gunfire support groups.

The selection of areas of gunfire responsibility was made in the following manner. Any gun or defensive position that could oppose the attack of any force was considered the responsibility of the ships of the gunfire support assigned to that force. It was found that frequently one major caliber defending gun could range on two and sometimes more areas. From a study of the terrain surrounding the gun, it was assigned as a responsibility to the force on which it could most effectively fire. Thus, the areas were delineated on considerations of:

(1) Geographical features of the assault areas;
(2) The direction in which guns, which could fire on more than one area, could fire most effectively. These areas are delineated in diagram I.

The analysis of targets capable of opposing the assault was done in two steps:

(1) Major defense guns of 75mm or more;
(2) Minor defense (smaller) guns, strongpoints, casemates, radar, observation points, etc.

The major problem was to meet the German strategic coastal defense concept, that is, the building of many more gun emplacements than they occupied. Our photo interpreters listed three types of emplacements:

    (1) Occupied,
    (2) Unoccupied,
    (3) Dummy.

Obviously, these emplacements could not be treated as equally effective nor on the other hand could any one, even a supposed dummy, be ignored.

A second consideration was that certain guns were in such a position that their effectiveness was certainly not as great as other guns. Guns of reduced effectiveness due to location fell into two groups:

(1) Guns of which the effectiveness of their fire control could be reduced by smoke, such as the guns in the sheltered base of the Gulf of St. Tropez;

- 32 -

(2) Guns of which the effectiveness of their fire power would be reduced by firing at extreme ranges, of which were the guns on the flanks.

A consideration of these guns indicated some which could not be satisfactorily neutralized by naval bombardment. These were accorded high priority as pre-H-hour air bombing targets.

Assignment of ships to each fire support area was based on the relative defensive strength in major caliber guns, 75mm and above, of each area. It was considered that the fire support ships should be distributed in proportion to the major defensive gun strength of each area subject to the following provisions. The fire support strength of each attack force must in addition to being able to neutralize the major guns:

(1) Be able to neutralize minor defenses;
(2) Have a reasonable percentage of unassigned batteries for counter battery fire and for special missions.

It was determined that the number of gunfire ships available was not nearly large enough to meet the standards set forth in General Order 1-43, Standard Operating Procedure of Amphibious Force, Atlantic Fleet. However, it was considered that for a simultaneous three division assault, the entire offensive strength would be mutually supporting. Furthermore, the actual sea room was so small that the number of gunfire ships that could be employed simultaneously was limited.

The absolute necessity was therefore apparent of making the most advantageous use of the limited air power available for this invasion. Consequently, the integration of gunfire support and air bombing was planned to a finer degree than was ever before attempted in this theater.

The areas of responsibility are set forth in the information paragraph of the Operation Plan, Annex A. The actual positions of the gunfire support ships were assigned by mutual agreement of the gunfire support commanders in order to give the most effective fire support to each attack force.

In order to determine how many and what kind of ships should be assigned as gunfire support to the attack forces, the relative weight of the various targets was set up in this manner. A major gun position that was occupied and easily capable of hitting at least one attack area was considered an effective gun. It was considered to have full effect or a relative effect of unity (1.0). Unoccupied gun positions within range of the attack area were considered potentially almost as dangerous, but when considered as a group, a lower strength factor, 0.8, was arbitrarily assigned. In a similar way, guns which were possibly dummies were further reduced to 0.6. Coast defense guns firing at extreme ranges or guns the effectiveness of which could be reduced by smoke were also assigned a reduced ratio, i.e., 0.6 or 0.8 of the above pertinent ratio, respectively. The numbers of major defensive gun positions were tabulated with their relative effective strength determined by the ratios assigned to the reported condition of the emplacement.

Obviously, for any particular gun positions, this method of analysis was not necessarily accurate. However, for an area, the total overall effective strength in gun positions reduced as it was to a ratio could be very accurately shown as a comparison with any other area. Thus, by reducing the effective defensive strength to a ratio, there was a basis on which the gunfire support forces could be apportioned, and from a consideration of the characteristics of the batteries, the desirable positions of the individual ships were immediately indicated.

The strength of each gunfire support force in total batteries and weight of projectiles was therefore based on the relative potential defensive strength of the respective areas of responsibility. At first, it was considered appropriate to divide the gunfire support ships on the basis of nationality in order to put ships which had been trained under similar procedures in the same group. However, in order accurately to meet the ratio of potential defensive strength, it was more advantageous to distribute the ships on the basis of numbers of batteries, fire control installations, size of shell, etc. This assignment of mixed nationalities was very successful, and resulted in a highly satisfactory and well-executed, cooperative enterprise.

In order to adequately meet the defensive concept of building dummies and real guns, and occupying some and not others, this method of gunfire support assignment was found valid. While the values of the weights assigned to the various conditions of gun emplacements did not meet an adequate test in this invasion, this method of apportioning gunfire support ships based on a similar mathematical study is recommended for use in amphibious invasions.

INVASION OF SOUTHERN FRANCE

PART II

EXECUTION OF THE PLAN

Chapter 1

CAMPAIGN NARRATIVE

9 August 1944 to 25 September 1944

- - - - - - - - - - - - - - - 9 August 1944 - - - - - - - - - - - - - - - - - -

WEATHER

Partly cloudy skies with gentle winds and good visibility prevailed over all the western Mediterranean during the morning. Cloudiness increased rapidly during the afternoon in the Southern France-Corsican area so that by sunset skies were broken to overcast. Simultaneously winds increased to fresh southerly in Corsica and Sardinia. Conditions remained excellent over Italy.

ENEMY FORCES

Navy: It was estimated that the enemy naval forces which could be brought to bear against an invasion of Southern France consisted of the following types of vessels: Destroyers (DD), Torpedo Boats (TB), Escort Vessels (EV), Heavily Armed Vessels (HAV), German Schnellboote and Italian Motoscafi Anti-Sommergibili (MAS), Auxiliaries, and Submarines (SS). DD's correspond to our destroyers, TB's to our destroyer escorts, and EV's to our corvettes and PC's. HAV are fast converted merchant vessels used for escort duties. MAS correspond to our PT boats, and Auxiliaries are converted trawlers and yachts used for anti-submarine and escort duties.

Estimate of Enemy Naval Strength and Disposition was as follows:

	DD	TB	EV	HAV	MAS	SS	Auxiliaries
Toulon					1	3	2
Marseille			4	5	1		6
Port de Bouc					1		
La Ciotat							1
Nice					3		
Villefranche					4		
Cannes		1	1		2		
Genoa	1	2	1		2		3
Spezia		2		1	4		1
Port Lerici					2		
Unlocated			1		10		12
Totals	1	5	7	6	30	3	25

There was no submarine activity reported at sea in the Western Mediterranean. Photo reconnaissance showed the arrival in Genoa of one supply type and two 200-foot submarines which had been fitting out at

- 35 -

Spezia. One supply type and one 200-foot submarine still remained at the fitting-out basin at Spezia. All were believed to be human torpedo carriers and constituted a potential threat to the Western Task Force (WTF). Additional threats to the invasion of Southern France were the Italian destroyers Premuda, ex Dubrovnik, and Squadrista fitting out and nearly completed at Genoa. The probability of enemy employment of human torpedoes and explosive boats and perhaps a few midget submarines was emphasized.

Army: In southeastern France, from the Mediterranean Spanish border to the Italian border, the Germans were maintaining the Nineteenth Army. It was composed of the 242nd Infantry Division, the 189th Infantry Division, the 198th Infantry Division, the 244th Infantry Division, the 11th Panzer Division, the 338th Infantry Division, the 716th Infantry Division, the 148th Reserve Infantry Division, and the 157th Reserve Infantry Division. The Toulon-Agay area was being defended by the 242nd Infantry Division, which was a three regiment division made up mostly of young Nazis. The division was well up to strength. Coast defense divisions were re-enforced with Coast Defense Artillery, Marine Infantry, and other similar coast defense units. The other divisions were not at full strength, and some had non-German elements. The German occupation forces were being harassed by French maquis and the French Forces of the Interior (FFI) in many isolated localities.

Air : Enemy air strength in France and Italy was estimated to be as follows:

	S. France	N. France	Italy
Long Range Bombers	175	170	
Ground Attack		20	45
S/E Fighters	25	425	100
T/E Fighters	10	400	
Reconnaissance	30	70	45
Total	240	1085	190

It was estimated that the following reinforcements to Southern France could be made available:

Long Range Bombers	50 from North France
Ground Attack	20 from North France
S/E Fighters	60, of which 30 each from Italy and Southwest Germany.

The serviceability of the Long Range Bombers was estimated to be in the neighborhood of 50%, and that of the other types was estimated to be about 60 to 65%.

OWN FORCES

Navy: Most of the naval forces allocated for the operation were at their mounting ports, as follows:

- Naples: Combat loaders, landing craft, merchant vessels, and Sitka fire support ships.
- Taranto: Merchant vessels, personnel ships and Delta fire support ships.
- Oran: Merchant vessels and personnel ships.
- Palermo: Camel fire support ships.
- Malta: Carrier force and Alpha fire support ships.

Many of the ships allotted by Commander-in-Chief, Mediterranean (CinCMed) for the operation had not yet reported to Commander Eighth Fleet, because CinCMed's Op-Plan of 29 July 1944 directed that such ships which had not been operating under the orders of Commander Eighth Fleet previously were to consider themselves as being under his orders from the time of their arrival at the base ports from which they would sail for the operation, or from 24 hours before their time of sailing from that port, whichever was the later.

Army: The embarkation of the 3rd Infantry Division, the 45th Infantry Division, and the 36th Infantry Division (the U.S. assault divisions) began at Naples.

Air : As the first assault convoys, naval forces and support troops began to move out of Naples, Taranto and Oran enroute for the Corsican assembly area, fighter cover was provided by P-47s and P-39s of the 62nd Fighter Wing of Mediterranean Allied Coastal Air Force (MACAF). During the night, cover was furnished by Mosquitoes and Beaufighters and for the seaborne forces moving southwest from Taranto, Wellingtons supplied anti-submarine patrol.

Aircraft under the operational control of the XII Tactical Air Command (XII TAC) carried out fighter bombing missions from their bases in Corsica. These included six groups of P-47s, three wings of RAF Spitfires, one Squadron of A-20s, one Squadron of Beaufighters, two Squadrons of tactical reconnaissance Spitfires and one of P-51s and one squadron of photographic reconnaissance aircraft. Two groups of P-38s were furnished by the 15th Air Force. B-25s were based in Corsica and B-26s in Sardinia. The missions of these aircraft as part of general pre-D-day bombing were attacks against coastal defense guns, beach defenses, lines of transportation and supply, and radar installations.

IMPORTANT ORDERS RECEIVED:

None.

IMPORTANT ORDERS ISSUED

Commander Eighth Fleet placed Op-Plan 4-44 into effect at 0930B by dispatch, and at 1750B by further dispatch promulgated D-day as 15 August and H-hour as 0800B.

OPERATIONS

At 1000 LCT assault convoy of 145 LCT and 72 other ships divided into sections SS-1, SS-1A and SS-1B under tactical command of CTF 84 in USS Duane departed Naples for Ajaccio via route one (see diagram II), speed 5.5 knots.

OWN AND ENEMY NAVAL LOSSES

None.

---------------- 10 August 1944 ----------------------

WEATHER

Widespread thunderstorms with general low ceilings and poor visibility occurred in the Ligurian Sea with numerous rain showers in Corsica. Elsewhere in the Mediterranean it was cloudy with upper clouds. Winds were generally gentle with slight seas.

ENEMY FORCES

Navy: No comment.

Army: No comment.

Air : Evidence was received of a withdrawal of bomber units from Southern France and enemy strength in that area was re-estimated to be:

Long Range Bombers	130
Ground Attack	nil
S/E Fighters	20
T/E Fighters	10
Reconnaissance	25

OWN FORCES

Navy: LCT convoy was underway for its staging port Ajaccio. Other forces continued to assemble at their mounting ports except for convoys AM-1 and TM-1 which departed Oran and Taranto, respectively.

Army: The 3rd Division Infantrie Algerienne (3rd DIA) and the II French Corps completed loading vehicles and stores on motor transport (M/T) ships in Taranto area. The embarkation of personnel of the U.S. 3rd Infantry Division, the 45th Infantry Division, the 36th Infantry Division, the Seventh Army, the VI Corps, the Air Force, the 1st Special Service Force (1st SSF) in Naples; personnel of the French 1st Division Marocaine Infantrie (1st DMI), 3rd DIA, II French Corps in the Taranto area; and of personnel of the French 2nd Combat Command (2nd CC) in Oran was completed.

Air : Fighter bombers, P-47s, attacked Gun Positions in Cap Esterel, Cap Benat, Ile du Levant, Cap Camarat areas encountering no opposition. Weather conditions precluded complete execution of the pre-D-day bombing plan.

IMPORTANT ORDERS RECEIVED

None.

IMPORTANT ORDERS ISSUED

None.

OPERATIONS

At 1630 merchant vessel convoy TM-1, composed of 40 M/T ships and 12 escorts, departed Taranto for the assault area via route 2 (see diagram II), speed 7.5 knots.

At 1800 merchant vessel convoy AM-1, composed of 15 M/T, 9 other ships and 6 escorts, departed Oran for the assault area via route 3 (see diagram II), speed 7.5 knots.

HMS Ulster Queen was assigned duty as standby Fighter Direction Ship replacing HMS Stuart Prince in position shown for Stuart Prince in diagram I. The latter was re-assigned as Air Beacon Ship in Troop Carrier Aircraft lane, with subsequent duty as Fighter Director ship southwest of the convoy lanes (see diagram XII).

OWN AND ENEMY NAVAL LOSSES

None.

- - - - - - - - - - - - - - - 11 August 1944 -

WEATHER

Thunderstorms were general over the Tyrrhenian Sea and Italy with ceilings variable from near zero to 5,000 feet. In the remainder of the western Mediterranean and Southern France the weather was fair with moderate winds and slight seas.

ENEMY FORCES

Navy: Photo reconnaissance showed at Sete an Italian 210 foot EV which had arrived from Oneglia and a former French Elan class EV, previously noted at Porto Maurizio. Photo reconnaissance of Toulon showed the damaged battleship Strasbourg near the harbor entrance, indicating possible use as blockship, also 2 U-boats at the seaplane base apparently in active status.

Army: No comment.

Air : A JU-88 long range reconnaissance plane was reported over Oran engaged in observing invasion shipping. This was pursued by P-39s and chased into Spain, some damage being inflicted.

OWN FORCES

Navy: LCT convoy and 2 merchant vessel convoys were underway, 4 more convoys sailed, and the remainder of the assault convoys were nearly ready to proceed.

Army: No comment.

Air : The 87th Fighter Wing successfully attacked gun positions in Toulon and Savona areas. Forty-one missions of 410 sorties were sent with success against radar installations at Antibes, Cap Benat, Agay, Marseille and Cap Camarat. Medium bombers, 144 B-25s, hit gun positions at St. Tropez, and east of St. Raphael, with no enemy air activity nor any losses. In Sardinia area, anti-submarine operations were initiated following a report by fighters of two submarines 50 to 55 miles southeast of Toulon. Our own submarines were clear of the area and therefore "Total Bombing Restriction" was cancelled and four Wellingtons sent out to hunt for the U-boats.

IMPORTANT ORDERS RECEIVED

None.

IMPORTANT ORDERS ISSUED

CTF 86 requested CinCMed to hold F S Jeanne D'Arc in reserve at Naples.

OPERATIONS

At 1200 Sitka assault convoy SY-1, composed of 5 LSI, 5 APD and 1 DD, departed Naples for Propriano via route 1 (see diagrams II and IV), speed 14 knots.

At 2000 convoy special No. 2, composed of 1 AP, 1 LSI, 2 LST and 2 DD, departed Oran for the assault area via route 3 (see diagram II), speed 12 knots.

Delta gunfire support group composed of 2 BB, 3 CL and 8 DD departed Taranto for the assault area via route 2 (see diagram II), to be joined by 3 French DL off Bizerte.

OWN AND ENEMY NAVAL LOSSES

None.

--------------- 12 August 1944 -----------------------

WEATHER

Skies were clear to partly cloudy throughout the entire western Mediterranean with excellent visibility, gentle land and sea breezes, and slight seas.

ENEMY FORCES

Navy: On basis of photo reconnaissance enemy strength in invasion area was estimated as 1 DD, 5 TB, 8 EV, 6 HAV, 30 MAS, 3 SS, 25 auxiliaries.

Army: No comment.

Air : Enemy reconnaissance activity was intensified in the Corsica area, and he was able during the night to report concentrations of shipping at Ajaccio.

OWN FORCES

Navy: Five of the assault convoys were at sea, one was staging at Ajaccio, and four sailed. Other convoys completed preparations for sailing the following day.

Army: No comment.

Air : The Strategic Air Force proceeded with its part of the execution of of the XII TAC cover plan, directing missions against the three areas other than the assault area. Of these three, 139 B-17s and 94 B-24s were despatched against the Genoa-Savona coast. 257 B-24s hit Sete with good results. Gun positions at Marseille were attacked by 138 B-24s escorted by 48 P-51s.

87th Fighter Wing flew 386 fighter bomber sorties with good to excellent results which resulted in the destruction of bridges at Arles, Tarascon, and Avignon, contributing to the accomplishment of one of the primary missions of pre-D-day strategical bombing, the interdiction of the assault area to enemy replacement troops. Medium bombers, B-25s and B-26s, attacked gun positions in the assault area, mainly at Ile de Porquerolles, Cap Negre, and Cap Cavalaire.

IMPORTANT ORDERS RECEIVED

CinCMed directed NCWTF hospital ships not to broadcast their positions prior to noon of D-day and not to burn lights prior to H-hour.

IMPORTANT ORDERS ISSUED

Commander Eighth Fleet requested Senior Officer Inshore Squadron (SOIS) to establish a motor torpedo boat (PT) patrol off Genoa on the night of 12 August and subsequent nights to protect the right flank of the assault forces.

OPERATIONS

At 1230 LCI assault convoy of 115 LCI and 30 other vessels divided into sections SF-2, SF-2A and SF-2B and departed Naples for Ajaccio via route 1 (see diagrams II and V), speed 11 knots.

At 1530 LST assault convoy of 69 LST and 63 other vessels divided into sections SM-1, SM-1A and SM-1B under tactical command of CTF 85 in Biscayne and departed Naples for the assault area via route 1 (see diagram II), speed 8 knots.

At 2000 Sitka gunfire support group composed of 1 CA, 1 CL and 3 DD under tactical command of CTF 86 in Augusta departed Naples for the assault area via route 1 to point NH then along route 10 (see diagram II).

Aircraft carrier force composed of 4 AACL, 9 CVE and 13 DD under tactical command of CTF 88 in Royalist departed Malta for the carrier assault operating area via the standard westbound Mediterranean Secret Convoy Instructions route to the Tunisian war channel then along route 2 (see diagram II). The aircraft Carrier Force consisted of seven carriers of the Royal Navy and two of the United States Navy. Aboard each were 24 aircraft: Seafires, Hellcats and Wildcats in the Royal Navy carriers, and Hellcats in the United States Navy carriers. Fighter, fighter bomber, tactical reconnaissance, spotting, photographic, and rocket projectile aircraft were included. The latter type was in only the U.S.S. Tulagi and U.S.S. Kasaan Bay.

Thirty-six additional spare aircraft were based at Malta, and Casabianda in Corsica, as well as 5 Avengers for ferry operations and anti-submarine operations. Five night Hellcats were based at Solenzara, Corsica, for night carrier cover.

HMS Ulster Queen, standby Fighter Director Ship, sailed with convoy SF-2B.

The air sea rescue service ranging from Leghorn to Toulon reported the rescue of 3 airmen.

A channel 2000 yards wide through the Straits of Bonifacio was swept with Oropesa minesweeping gear, with negative results.

OWN AND ENEMY NAVAL LOSSES

None.

--------------- 13 August 1944 ---------------------

WEATHER

Fine conditions continued over the western Mediterranean with clear skies, excellent visibility, gentle winds and smooth seas.

ENEMY FORCES

Navy: Photo reconnaissance showed the Pomone class TB Bombarde at Cannes with 2 EV. The 2 EV were seen to have departed from Sete. An HAV arrived at Toulon, probably from Marseille.

Army: There were indications that the German Nineteenth Army expected an allied invasion in the Genoa area.

Air : Reconnaissance activity was continued and further reports of shipping in the Ajaccio area were made.

OWN FORCES

Navy: All remaining assault convoys sailed from their mounting ports. All convoys at sea were properly located and on schedule. (See diagram VI).

Army: No comment.

Air : Over 100 P-47s hit the airdromes of the southern Rhone Valley namely Salon de Provence, Istres, La Jasse, La Chanoines and Chateau Blanc near Avignon, destroying installations and many enemy aircraft. 626 heavy bombers were escorted by 33 P-38s and 208 P-51s which joined in the attack on gun positions, bridges and communications. Fighters and fighter bombers of XII TAC flew 416 sorties. MATAF informed XII TAC the Troop Carrier Command was authorized to drop window from 0315 to 0502 D-day.

IMPORTANT ORDERS RECEIVED

None.

IMPORTANT ORDERS ISSUED

CTF 86 directed USS Omaha to sail independently to arrive Ajaccio prior noon on D-day.

OPERATIONS

At 0530 personnel ship convoy TF-1 composed of 11 personnel ships and 7 escorts departed Taranto for the assault area via route 2 (see diagrams II and VI), speed 12 knots.

At 0930 Camel gunfire support group composed of 1 BB, 1 CA, 5 CL and 11 DD departed Palermo for the assault area via route 6 (see diagram II).

About 1400 the combat loader convoy, composed of 25 combat loaders, 1 BB and 16 other ships, under tactical command of CTF 87 in Bayfield departed Naples for the assault area via route 1 (see diagram II), speed 12 knots. NCWTF was in USS Catoctin with SF-1B.

At 1600 HMS Ramillies departed Algiers for the assault area via route 3 to position AF then 10 miles to the west of route 3, escorted by 4 DD detailed by CinCMed.

Merchant vessel convoy SM-2 composed of 48 M/T and 10 other vessels departed Naples for the assault area via route 1 (see diagram II), speed 9 knots.

From 1900 to 2030 convoy SS-1, SS-1A, SS-1B departed Ajaccio for the assault area. Three stragglers were sailed to join with SS-1B.

At 2000 Alpha gunfire support group composed of 1 CA, 5 CL and 6 DD departed Malta for the assault area via route 2 (see diagram II).

OWN AND ENEMY NAVAL LOSSES

None.

- - - - - - - - - - - - - - - 14 August 1944 -

WEATHER

Low clouds and indifferent visibility in the early morning formed over the coast of Southern France, dissipating by 1000. Throughout the remainder of the area visibility was average with clear skies; winds were generally calm with smooth seas.

ENEMY FORCES

Navy: Photo reconnaissance indicated the TB Bombarde and 2 EV had arrived at Toulon from Cannes, and that one HAV had departed from Toulon. At Genoa 2 TB, 1 auxiliary EV, and 3 MAS boats were in port, and 2 EV had departed, one arriving in Oneglia and the other at Porto Maurizio.

Army: The 338th Infantry Division sent one of its regiments northward, and the 11th Panzer Division planned to move tomorrow (D-day) to assist the German forces in Northern France. Enemy air reconnaissance sighted our convoys off Corsica and reported our approach to Southern France. The troops defending the Toulon-Ciotat area were alerted due to the approach of convoys at 2100.

Air : During the night the enemy was again able to view the invasion shipping in the Ajaccio area.

OWN FORCES

Navy: All assault convoys were enroute the assault area, and the Sitka assault convoy arrived there.

Army: No comment.

Air : The concentration of the many convoys in the waters of western Corsica and their outward swing to southern France necessitated fighter cover in greater numbers. Mediterranean Allied Coastal Air Force (MACAF) supplemented by 87th Fighter Wing flew over 200 sorties for this purpose. Medium bombers of Mediterranean Allied Tactical Air Force (MATAF) continued to strike gun positions, 62 B-26s and 144 B-25s hitting the assault coast from Rade D'Agay south to the Giens Peninsula. Light bombers, 36 A-20s, ranged inland striking fuel dumps and motor transport (M/T). Fighter bombers concentrated on radars with 107 sorties of their total 414 directed against Wurzburg, Freya and coast watcher stations at Nice, Cannes, Cap Benat and Cap Camarat. With no enemy air opposition, many buildings were destroyed or badly damaged. An allied fighter pilot and a German pilot of reconnaissance aircraft who had crashed between France and Corsica were brought in by an air sea rescue launch.

IMPORTANT ORDERS RECEIVED

From 0730 to 1800 CinCMed in HMS Kimberly watched the progress of the assault convoys through the Straits of Bonifacio. About 1430 he reported to NCWTF that all convoys were proceeding according to schedule, directed him to carry out the assault operation as promulgated, and advised that Supreme Allied Commander, Mediterranean (SACMed) concurred and had authorized heavy bombers to carry out pre-H-hour bombing of beaches using pathfinder procedure if necessary.

IMPORTANT ORDERS ISSUED

None.

OPERATIONS

About 0800 convoy SY-1 plus 11 PT and 4 ASRC departed Propriano to rendezvous with Sitka gunfire support group at point NH at noon. At 1400 another section of the Sitka force consisting of 5 MS, 4 ML, 1 Dan Layer and 1 AN departed Propriano for the Sitka assault area. Both groups arrived in the assault area about 2200 and assumed assigned stations by 2300. (See diagrams II, VII and VIII).

LCI convoy SF-2, SF-2A, SF-2B departed Ajaccio for assault area about 1700 (see diagram VIII).

Convoy Special No. 1 consisting of 3 tankers escorted by 2 PC departed Palermo for Ajaccio on a shuttle run.

At 1600 convoy SF-1 joined Camel gunfire support group at point AL, and at 1800 convoy SF-1A made rendezvous with Delta gunfire support group at 41° 55' N., 08° 26' E.

HMS Wheatland made rendezvous with TF 88 at point AH about noon to replace HMS Tumult, which was then ordered by CTF 88 to Ajaccio for temporary duty with CinCMed.

The first section of the eastern diversion unit consisting of HMS Aphis, HMS Scarab, 3 ML and HMS Stuart Prince departed Ajaccio at 0830 and the second section of 12 PT departed Bastia at 1800 to rendezvous at point D (see diagram XI) at 2130, when diversion measures were commenced. At 2230 HMS Stuart Prince detached from the eastern diversion unit to take station as radar beacon ship (see diagram XII).

The first section of the western diversion group composed of 1 DD and 4 ML departed Ajaccio at 1130, and the second section of 8 PT and 11 ASRC departed Calvi at 1400 to rendezvous at point K (see diagram XI) at 2005, when diversion measures were started, aircraft starting at 2030.

Window was dropped over each diversion unit until 0400 15 August.

Escorts furnished by CTG 84.7 relieved CinCMed's 4 DD of escort of Ramillies at 1800, position 40° 30' N, 07° 37' E. USS Cincinnati departed Gibraltar at 1800 for Oran.

Mindiv 21 took over the minesweeping of the Straits of Bonifacio from 13th M/S Flotilla.

OWN AND ENEMY NAVAL LOSSES

    None.

---------------- 15 August 1944 ----------------------
(D-day)

WEATHER

Low clouds formed over the Southern France coast after midnight, with local banks of thick fog in the eastern part of the Gulf of Lions. Lower clouds thinned by midmorning and dissipated by noon. In the remainder of the western Mediterranean, skies were clear throughout period with visibility of ten miles. Winds were light variable with calm seas.

ENEMY FORCES

    Navy: The arrival of the invasion forces found an EV of 210 feet, Camoscio, accompanying an auxiliary vessel, Escaburt, southwest of Port Cros. These were engaged and sunk by USS Somers at 0500. Off Alpha Yellow beach were five small units believed to be harbor patrol craft based at St. Tropez. These were encountered and sunk by minesweepers of the Alpha Attack Force at about 0500. Reports from photo reconnaissance indicated arrival 4 MAS at Imperia. The estimate of enemy naval strength significant to the operation was: 1 DD, 5 TB, 7 EV, 6 HAV, 30 MAS, 3 SS, and 24 auxiliaries.

    Army: Enemy resistance to our ground forces in the assault area was of limited character, consisting in the main of small arms and mortar fire. Contact was made with elements of the 242nd Infantry Division. An unsuccessful counter-attack was made against the French Groupe de Commandos in the Cap Negre area. No large vehicle movement toward the assault area was observed. No unexpected major units were identified.

    Preliminary interrogation of prisoners indicated that landings in the area of assault had not been expected until ships were seen in large numbers off the coast. Some prisoners stated that coast-watcher reports could not be transmitted to headquarters because of the disruption of communications by bombing and bombardment.

Air : Further withdrawals were made of the enemy bomber force from Southern France area. The remaining force was estimated to be as follows:

JU 88 (Torpedo bombers and flare droppers)	70
DO 217 (Radio-controlled glider bomb carriers)	20
S/E Fighters	20
T/E Fighters	25
Reconnaissance	20

In view of these reductions, it was estimated that the maximum effort that the enemy air anti-shipping forces could put forth would be 30 sorties per 24 hour period by torpedo bombers and 10 sorties per 24 hours by radio-controlled bomb aircraft.

During daylight hours, 18 ME 109s were engaged by our fighters and a total of 3 were destroyed. At 2043, a maximum of four DO 217s approached the Camel area first at about 15,000 feet, then dropped to about 8,000 feet. Bombs landed near the USS Bayfield and one glider bomb was released and effectively hit and destroyed LST 282 which was located about 600 yards off the beach at St. Raphael. The control plane operated over the land and was thus able to keep the LST between it and our jamming ships. This made it necessary for the jammers to attempt taking over control of a glider bomb approaching head on which is the most difficult angle for control. Although 22 jamming ships were on the glider bomb, control was impossible due to this new technique of coming in over the land. This was the first time this technique had been observed.

OWN FORCES

Navy: All convoys arrived in the assault area in accordance with the plan. WTF in the assault area on D-day comprised 880 ships and craft and 1370 ship-borne landing craft. This Allied naval force included 515 US, 283 British, 12 French, and 7 Greek ships and craft and 63 merchant vessels of various nationalities. Late in the afternoon, FS Lorraine and USS Nevada escorted by 2 DD departed for Propriano to remain there on call.

Army: The three U.S. infantry assault divisions (the 3rd, 36th, and 45th) were landed in force. The 3rd Infantry Division was landed on beaches in Cavalaire Bay and Pampelonne Bay and moved rapidly inland, leading elements reaching Grimaud, 6 miles west of St. Tropez. The 45th Division was landed on beaches in Bougnon Bay. Leading elements reached Plan de Tour, 4 miles northwest of St. Maxime. The 36th Division was landed over beaches east of Frejus and fanned out rapidly to the North, East, and West, reaching the high ground overlooking Theoule sur Mer from the South, and the ridge overlooking Frejus from the Northeast. The 1st SSF was landed on Ile de Levant and Ile de Port Cros. The French Groupe de Commandos was landed near Cap Negre and occupied high ground inland, repulsing an enemy counter-attack during the day.

The French Naval Assault Group was landed south of Theoule sur Mer and made contact with 36th Division. The 1st ABTF was dropped at first light and established themselves in the Le Muy area. (See diagram I). The VI Corps reported capture of 2,041 prisoners.

Air : At 0155, Airborne Diversion unit of five C-47s took off from Ajaccio, flew to the assault area and returned dropping window at regular intervals. At dropping zone near La Ciotat and Cassis, 300 dummies were expelled. Small arms fire was encountered over the coast but enemy action was ineffective.

Fighter aircraft of XII TAC began reporting to the Fighter Direction Ship for air defense of the assault area at 0550. The first patrol consisted of 12 P-38s and 8 Spitfires followed at 0615 by 16 P-47s. Thenceforth, patrols reported continuously and the schedule proposed in the Air Defense Plan was strictly maintained. Hellcats and Wildcats of TF 88 reported at assigned times later in the day. P-47s and P-38s carried bombs and attacked previously assigned targets as fighter bombers before reporting for fighter patrol duty. For day fighter cover over the beaches over 500 sorties were flown.

Beginning at 0644, medium and heavy bombers on their missions to bomb beaches and beach obstacles, reported by radio to the USS Catoctin. Warnings were sent by TBS from the Catoctin to the Task Force Commander of each beach area, of the number and type of approaching friendly bombers and the estimated time of their arrival over the target.

Alpha Beaches were bombed by 83 B-17s and 138 B-26s with excellent results. Weather prevented the complete execution of the plan in Delta area and the Southern section of Camel Area. The northern part of Camel was bombed by 162 B-25s with good coverage. Later in the day, 1215, Beach 264 A (Camel Red) was hit with 187 tons from 93 B-24s.

Supplementing the attacks by medium and heavy bombers, fighter bombers of XII TAC reported in the assault area beginning at 0550. Their attacks were directed against coastal batteries, and they hit gun emplacements which could be used against the landing beaches. Later in the day, highway bridges, motor transports, railroad tracks, beaches, and personnel movements were the object of their attacks in support of the landing effort. The rocket projectile aircraft of the US CVEs of TF 88, USS Tulagi and USS Kasaan Bay, were particularly effective in their destruction of motor transport. Approximately 750 fighter bombers sorties were flown by XII TAC and an additional 150 contributed by Aircraft Carrier Force.

Tactical Reconnaissance planes from 111th and 225th Squadrons were constantly in the assault and forward areas. Radio reports from them of action and disposition of enemy ground forces were received by USS Catoctin in addition to the routine reports made by the pilots upon return to their bases. Forty-five sorties by P-51s and Spitfires were flown from 0615 to 2015. Spotting aircraft reported to Gunfire Support Commander in Camel area as lifting of ground haze made spotting missions possible.

The Provisional Troop Carrier Airborne Division took off from their bases in the Rome area in the early morning, flying a course to the northeast of the convoy lane and guided to their landfall by their beacon ships.

Landfall was reached by the first Pathfinder planes at approximately 0315 followed an hour later by 396 troop carrier A/C which after dropping their troops in the vicinity of Le Muy returned to their bases. At about 1015, 71 aircraft towing gliders flew over the drop zones, cut loose their gliders and returned to base. This operation had been postponed two hours.

At dusk, about 2100, night fighter cover was provided as Beaufighters based at Corsica under MACAF reported to FDT 13 for night fighter patrol assignment in the assault area. The entire proposed schedule of 20 sorties was not accomplished, but since no hostile contacts were established during darkness, the proposed effort was not needed.

IMPORTANT ORDERS RECEIVED

None.

IMPORTANT ORDERS ISSUED

CTF 85, on the basis of the reports of amphibious scouts that the approaches to Delta beaches had no underwater obstacles, at 0543 cancelled use of drones in the Delta area.

At 1415, CTF 87 ordered the Red beach assault, scheduled for 1400 and delayed to 1430 by the Beach Assault Commander, canceled because of enemy shelling of the approaches, concentrations of mines, and the failure of the drones to function properly. He further directed that the forces scheduled for this assault land over Camel Green beach commencing at 1515, Z-hour (see diagram I), for which landing an alternate plan had been prepared.

At 0945, NCWTF by despatch indicated the intention to sail landing craft convoys from the assault area at 1800 to 2000 daily.

As the speed of unloading combat loaders permitted, NCWTF ordered their departure on D-Day. Six, scheduled to leave on D plus 1, were assigned to SRF-1 bound for Naples. Three, of which one was scheduled to leave on D plus 1 and two on D plus 2, were assigned escorts and organized as an unscheduled convoy ARF-2A bound for Oran.

OPERATIONS

Diversions:

The eastern diversion unit executed its operation as planned (see diagram XI). A force of 70 French assault troops landed at 0010 at Pointe Des Deux Freres south of Theoule sur Mer from 4 PT, while the rest of the unit carried out assigned screen and decoy functions. Shore targets were engaged from 0420 to 0510 and return fire received without damage. The western diversion unit executed its operation as planned (see diagram XI), except that because of fog and radar failures, only 1 of 11 ASRC assigned entered La Ciotat Bay to carry out the simulated landings. No enemy forces were encountered and no return fire was received. At 0423, 300 dummy paratroops were dropped northwest of Toulon. Both diversion units were re-assembled at Baie de Briande by 1100.

Sitka Force:

At 0030, advance scout and preparatory units of the Sitka attack force landed on the Islands of Port Cros and Levant and on Cap Negre. At 0130, the main assault units landed special service troops on the islands and French commandos on the mainland, and the Sitka diversion group commenced its operations at a point 3.2 miles bearing thirty-six degrees from Cap Titan (east end of Levant). At 0430, the diversion group withdrew, the PTs being released to CTG 80.5 and the 4 ASRC's to CTG 80.4. At 0500, the main naval assault units withdrew. At 0700, F S Lorraine joined the Sitka gunfire support group after minesweepers had swept a channel to Levant and between Levant and Port Cros without encountering any mines. At 0742, the French Commandos reported being bombed by own planes. At 0825, they were established ashore, but having difficulty with a battery on Cap Negre. By 1000, they had beaten back a counter attack and were in control of high ground and the south lateral road.

At 0920, initial resistance on Port Cros and Levant was overcome. The coast defense battery reported at the eastern end of the island was found to be a clever dummy. At 1506, 1st SSF reported 240 POW taken. At 1603, fighting against isolated strong points continued on Port Cros and the Levant situation was not clear. At 2234, resistance on Levant ceased. Two 81 mm mortars, 2 light machine guns, and 50 POW were taken, but a pocket of the enemy still held out in the old fort on Port Cros, preventing off-loading of radar equipment and installation of GCI (fighter director) equipment. An enemy battery at Cap Benat shelled Port Cros during darkness. An armed air reconnaissance was set up between Porquerolles and the mainland to prevent evacuation of that island.

Alpha Force:

The Alpha assault began at 0300 when the PC reference vessels took station 10 miles off Red and Yellow beaches, followed by the stationing of 5-mile reference vessels. From 0440 to 0630, minesweepers swept the gunfire support and transport areas, and the boat lanes to 1,000 yards of the beaches. No mines were found. By 0500, the gunfire support, LST, LCT, and combat loader convoys had arrived. At 0620, an SC took station at each beach as 2-mile reference vessel. At 0640, the LCI convoy arrived and with the LCTs and LSTs moved to the inner transport areas. At 0745, combat loaders moved in.

From 0710 to 0745, shallow minesweepers cleared the boat lanes from 1,500 yards to within 100 yards of the beaches. Gunfire support ships fired on assigned targets from 0700 to 0750, except when fire was lifted as bombers entered the area. Between 0710 and 0730, drones were detonated. A runaway drone exploded near and severely damaged SC 1029. Fifteen out of eighteen drones functioned as designed. One reddy fox was damaged in transit and sank before it could be used. From 0750 to 0758, rockets and inshore fire were poured onto the beaches. At 0800, the first assault waves landed. The first 8 waves landed on schedule with only slight hindrance from mines, enemy fire, and underwater obstacles. The existence of many shallow water mines on the right flank of Red beach delayed the ninth wave. USS Catoctin shifted from Alpha to Delta area at 0925. At 1030, LSTs were directed to beach pontoons and LCT(R)'s to proceed to Camel area. CG 3rd Division went ashore about 1045. By 1400, all

Yellow beach landing craft were unloaded and combat loaders were 10% unloaded. At 1545, all unloading over the northern half of Red beach was halted until mines could be cleared. By 1700, rate of loading accelerated and additional landing points were in use. By 1800, Alpha Green beach was opened, but exits were found to be heavily mined.

Delta Force:

In the Delta area about 0000, 1 PC took station as 4-1/2 mile reference vessel and disembarked scouts. Starting at 0200, PCs took station at 10 minute intervals as reference vessels at 7-1/2, 10, and 15 mile points. At 0300, minesweeping of transport and gunfire support areas and boat lanes was started. At 0440, the LCT convoy reached the inner transport area, and shortly afterwards, the gunfire support group arrived. LST and combat loader convoys reached their transport area at 0500. At 0800, LCI convoy reached the inner transport area.

At 0543, CTF 85 cancelled use of drones, as scouts reported no underwater obstacles. From 0650 to 0758, gunfire support ships fired on assigned targets, except when fire was lifted to allow bombers to make their attacks. From 0755 to after H-hour, fire was shifted to the flanks. From 0630 to 0705, shallow minesweepers swept the boat lanes from 1-1/2 mile reference point to 500 yards from the shore. From 0745 to 0756, the Delta beaches were drenched by close inshore fire and rockets. The initial assault waves on all four beaches landed at 0802. By 0910, the first 7 waves had been landed, and by 1100, the CG 45th Division was disembarked. CG VI Corps moved ashore in the afternoon.

No underwater obstacles or mines were encountered. There was only a small amount of mortar fire on Red and Green beaches, causing no damage or casualties.

Unloading from LSTs was accomplished dry on Yellow and Blue beaches and over pontoons on Red and Green beaches. By 1700 St. Maxime was captured. By 2145 all personnel and vehicles had been unloaded from LCTs, LCIs and combat loaders and unloading of merchant ships was underway.

Camel Force:

The Camel assault began when, at 0100, 2 DD, 2 PC and 1 SC took station as reference vessels in the assault area. At 0330 minesweepers began sweeping to within 2000 yards of the beaches. About 0400 the LST and LCT convoys arrived, and at 0500 the combat loader convoy reached the outer transport area. At 0515 LSTs and LCTs assembled in Blue and Green beach lowering areas (see diagram I). By 0600 2 SC took station to mark the line of departure and the gunfire support ships proceeded to their assigned stations. At 0710 LCI convoy reached the outer transport area.

From 0650 to 0800 gunfire support ships fired on prearranged targets, except when fire was lifted for seheduled bombing. At 0700 shallow water minesweepers commenced sweeping from 3000 yards to within 500 yards of the beaches. From 0752 to 0756 the beaches were drenched with rockets and close inshore gunfire.

The first wave landed on Blue beach at 0800 and on Green beach at 0803. Because haze and dust reduced the visibility to 50 yards near the beaches, Green beach first wave slowed to avoid rocks flanking the beach. Later waves landed on schedule. No underwater mines or obstacles were encountered. All troops and vehicles were landed dry. Two LCVP were sunk near the beach by enemy machine gun fire. By 1100 scheduled unloading at Blue beach was completed and it was closed out. At Green beach there was light machine gun fire from the flanks and Ile d'Or, and after 0930 some light artillery fire on the beach and approaches which continued throughout the day. In the forenoon LCT 339 and LCT 625 received shell hits, and in the afternoon LCT 610 and LST 51 were also hit.

At 0740 CG 36th Division requested that the Red beach assault force composed of the 142nd RCT with attached artillery, tank, tank destroyer and engineer elements, be landed on Red beach (264A) at 1400. This assault and Z-hour had been anticipated in NCWTF and CTF 87 plans; and bombing schedules, pre-arranged gunfire and transfer of reloaded rocket craft after their use in the 0800 landings on other beaches, were ordered accordingly. At about 1000, CG 36th Division moved ashore.

At 1110 the minesweepers, engaged in sweeping Red beach approaches were heavily shelled and retired before completing their sweep. During period from about 1220 to 1300 heavy bombers attacked Red beach. At 1234 the SC reference vessel started to lead 8 shallow water minesweepers toward the beach. At 1700 yards offshore a severe barrage was met. At 1500 yards the SC returned to its post. The shallow water minesweepers continued in to 500 yards of the beach, and returned to the line of departure at 1300, still under fire.

The gunfire support group commenced shelling Red beach at 1310. At about the same time two demolition units with scout boats and 12 explosive drones were sent in, meeting with heavy enemy fire. Three drones exploded on Red beach, 2 hit without exploding, 1 was last seen circling off the beach, 1 exploded on the left flank of the beach, 2 were boarded to regain control, 1 was sunk by a DD with gunfire when it reversed course and threatened our own ships, and two were withheld because of the fear that they also might run wild. Shortly after 1400 the Beach Assault Commander reported the situation to CTF 87 and stated that the assault would be carried out at 1430.

At 1415 CTF 87 ordered that the alternate plan for landing this assault force over Green beach be placed in effect and set Z-hour as 1515 (see diagram I). On the basis of the new Z-hour all waves except DUKW wave 4 landed on schedule on Green beach, which was still being shelled by enemy light artillery. By 1500 transports had shifted to within 5 miles of the beaches.

The above decision was made without knowledge of CG 36th Division who could not be reached ashore in time, but at 1740 he sent the following message to CTF 87, "I appreciate your prompt action in changing plan when obstacles could not be breached. Expect to take Red beach tonight, no matter how late. Opposition irritating but not too tough so far".

To open Yellow beach (see diagram I), 2 demolition units proceeded to remove the net across the entrance. This was accomplished at 1915 and by 2015 the beach was open for some traffic.

At 1930 LCI(L) 951 struck a mine in the Yellow beach area and sustained underwater damage forward.

Miscellaneous Operations:

Carrier force operating in the vicinity of the assault area about 30 miles off shore gave support with spotting, strafing and bombing missions, and provided own air cover during the day. At the end of the day's operations the carrier force retired southward. The three flight-deck LSTs arrived in the assault area as scheduled, and started launching their planes by 0930.

About 0200 PT 209, Antwerp and Stuart Prince took station as beacon ships until dark at assigned positions as air beacon ships. (see Diagram XII). PT 209 then reported to CTG 80.5. Antwerp was released to CinCMed and took station as an air sea rescue ship at 43° 15' N., 08° E., operating under SOIS. At 1930 Stuart Prince commenced patrol from 42° 40' N., 07° 15' E. to 42° 25' N., 07° 40' E., acting as air sea rescue ship and fighter director ship and affording radar cover for convoys. 29th ML Flotilla took station near 43° 06' N., 06° 54' E. to carry out air sea rescue work daily from 0645 to 2045.

The Ulster Queen (in position shown for Stuart Prince in diagram I), three GCI LSTs, FDT 13, and Catoctin arrived on schedule and took station in the assault area as fighter director ships (see diagram I). The Catoctin was in charge of AA defense and air raid warnings from 1735 when she relieved FDT 13 of this duty.

On D-day all targets were successfully engaged except two batteries on the southern approaches to Golfe de la Napoule that could not be located. About 15,900 projectiles 5-inch and over were expended, about 1,250 being of major calibre. White phosphorous projectiles were used effectively.

In addition to the pre-H-hour convoys, convoys SM-2 and Special No. 2 arrived, and 4 convoys containing 95 ships departed. CTG 80.6 in USS Jouett was established in Baie de Briande as convoy control assisted by 2 other DD and some PCs. An assembly area was set up ten miles east of Cap Camarat for merchant vessels bound for Ajaccio or Naples and for all LSTs, and ten miles one hundred twenty degrees from Cap Camarat for merchant vessels bound for Oran and all other landing craft regardless of destination.

The screen consisted of PTs and DDs. The PT patrols were ordered by CTF 84 to patrol Rade de Bormes on the west flank. DDs not part of gunfire support groups and about 24 PC were released to CTG 80.6 for screen or escort duties by CTF 84, 85, and 87. USS F.C. Davis reported to CTF 80 as controlled bombing jamming ship. By 0600 an outer screen of 17 DD was set up under CTU 80.6.10 (see diagram I). Later the central sector of the outer screen was moved 4 miles shoreward and the screen was increased to 25 DD backed by PCs and the convoy control DDs.

Unloading figures from preliminary action reports of task forces concerned were:

	Personnel	Vehicles	Tons
Alpha beaches	12,800	1,324	18,500
Delta beaches	33,000	3,300	Not reported
Camel beaches	14,350*	2,113*	Not reported
Total	60,150	6,737	18,500
Total to Date	60,150	6,737	18,500

*Estimated

OWN AND ENEMY LOSSES

Our losses were:

Sunk or destroyed:

    US LST 282 and 2 US LCVP by glider bomb.

    2 US LCVP by gunfire.

Damaged:

    US LCT 452, 610, 1013; HM LCT 307, 339, 625 by shell fire.

    US LCT 790; US LCI(L) 588, 590, 592, 595, 951; 5 US LCVP; HM LCT 552; HM ML 559 by mines.

    US LCT 1144; US LCI(L) 589, 591, 949 by under water obstacles.

    US SC 1029 by runaway drone.

    US YMS 3 by fouling minesweeping gear in propeller.

    US LCI(L) 190 by unknown causes.

Enemy losses were:

Sunk:

    2 Corvettes and 5 patrol craft.

---------------- 16 August 1944 ------------------

WEATHER

Conditions remained generally good over the entire area with only partly cloudy skies, good visibility, light winds, and calm seas.

ENEMY FORCES

Navy: Photo reconnaissance showed that 2 HAV arrived at Port de Bouc from Marseille. At Toulon, the French BB, Strasbourg, and the CL, Gallissonniere, were believed intended for use by the Germans as coast defense batteries because of the position to which they were moved.

Army: Enemy resistance stiffened. A counter-attack on the right flank was repulsed. In the north, resistance was scattered and uncoordinated. Thirty vehicles were reported moving south and southwest from Alessandria and about 30 vehicles were moving south from Turin. Captured troops were of low quality with a large percentage of Poles and over-age Germans.

Air : A flight of five JU 88s escorted by four ME 109s approached St. Tropez at 2050 at 20,000 feet. Upon reaching the Delta area, the enemy aircraft spread out and dropped anti-personnel bombs along the beaches there, resulting in 14 deaths and 36 other casualties. A glider bomb was also reported to have landed at dusk near USS C. F. Hughes, stationed on the eastern sector of the screen.

The enemy fighter force was reinforced by aircraft from Italy and the total strength in the invasion area was estimated as follows:

JU 88 (Torpedo Bombers)	75
DO 217 (Radio Controlled Glider Bomb Carriers)	25
S/E Fighters	50
T/E Fighters	25
Reconnaissance	20

OWN FORCES

Navy: USS Omaha arrived in the assault area.

Army: Commanding General, Seventh Army, disembarked from USS Catoctin and assumed command of the army forces of the Western Task Force with headquarters at St. Tropez at 2359.

The VI Corps pushed toward Collobrieres and Carnoules, northwest in the Argens River valley, and east toward Cannes. Corps headquarters was established at St. Maxime.

The 1st Regiment of the 1st SSF remained on Port Cros where some resistance continued. 2nd and 3rd Regiments assembled near Sylvabelle, on the mainland.

Elements of the 1st ABTF occupied Draguignan and Les Arcs.

The 36th Division consolidated its position on the right flank near Theoule sur Mer and moved to the vicinity of Vidauban and Camp des Cais.

Elements of the 45th Division moved through Vidauban and reached Taradeau.

Advanced elements of the 3rd Division reached Carnoules and Flassans Sur Issole, and other elements reached the area 2 miles east of La Londe - Les Moures.

The French Combat Command 1 began to land at 1200 and to move to an assembly area in the vicinity of Gonfaron.

At 1800, the II French Corps began landing over beaches in the St. Tropez-Cavalaire area.

Air : Normal beach cover of 36 fighters reported in the assault area at approximately 0550. Throughout daylight hours, 28 to 36 continuously patrolled beachhead area, with last patrol returning to its Corsican base at 2100. A total of 367 fighter sorties were flown. Fighter bombers returned to patrol after execution of their bombing missions. Fighter bombers of the XII TAC in 611 sorties attacked gun positions in the Toulon-Hyeres and Cannes areas. Road bridges, railroad bridges, rail and motor transportation, and strong points were destroyed. There were 96 fighter bomber sorties and 32 fighter sorties flown by the aircraft Carrier Force against trucks and railroad rolling stock. Tactical reconnaissance planes penetrated further inland and in the almost complete absence of hostile fighter activity furnished valuable information regarding many targets of opportunity.

Fourteen sorties of spotting planes co-operated with gunfire support force in Camel area. Spotting missions were flown from TF 88 when requested by Sitka, Alpha, and Delta gunfire support commanders.

Highway and railroad bridges in the lower Rhone valley were the principal targets of both heavy and medium bombers, with 108 heavies and 129 mediums in action.

Night fighters from MACAF reported in the assault area for control by FDT 13 or assignment to GCI ships.

Forward Fighter Control Unit of XII TAC which was dropped with the 1st ABTF reported by radio to the flagship.

One hundred twelve C-47's flew supply paradrop missions to 1st ABTF.

IMPORTANT ORDERS RECEIVED

None.

IMPORTANT ORDERS ISSUED

NCWTF directed CTF 84, 85, and 87 to release all battleships and cruisers no longer required by them to CTF 86, who was to retire all vessels practicable, giving priority in retirement to British ships and in employment to French ships, except that F S Jeanne D'Arc was to be released at once to CinCMed. Battleships in reserve were to base at Algiers; cruisers at Palermo or Naples.

CTF 85 released all gunfire support ships of TF 85 and directed that they report to CTF 86.

CTG 80.10 was established in USS Barricade in charge of all minesweepers with the tasks, logistics, communications, and organization set forth in the minesweeping Annex "J" to Operation Plan 4-44. Task force commanders were directed to turn over their minesweepers to CTG 80.10 on completion of specified tasks already underway in their areas. Three AM and YMS due in the assault area 25 August were also ordered to be transferred by CTG 80.6 to CTG 80.10.

OPERATIONS

Convoy control handled 76 ingoing and 86 outgoing vessels. Among the arrivals were the first three hospital ships, and the first of the PTs on the blood bank shuttle from Corsica.

The destroyer screen was reduced to 18 ships. Two PC commenced an anti-submarine patrol in the Straits of Bonifacio.

Jamming ships were assigned to CTF 84 and CTF 87 for protection against radio-controlled bombs.

The second diversion operation commenced at 1630 when the eastern bombardment unit (HMS Aphis, HMS Scarab, and 4 ML) left Baie de Briande for the Toulon area. At 2000, the western bombardment unit (USS Endicott and 2 PT) and the Ciotat assault unit (2 PT and 13 ASRC) departed, overtaking and passing the eastern unit about 2300. The first formation of window-dropping planes arrived over the diversion units at 2030; weather prevented continuation of the window dropping operation by later flights as planned.

Shore batteries on Cap Benat were neutralized by gunfire from USS Livermore. Port Cros, still holding out, was shelled with 284 rounds from Sitka gunfire support ships and its strong point struck by 6 hits from 16 fighter bomber missions. Camel fire support group attacked various targets on the right flank successfully.

HMS Antwerp was directed by SOIS to a new station at 43° 12' N, 07° 36' E to continue her air-sea rescue duties. USS Catoctin moved into St. Tropez Bay.

In Camel area, Frejus and St. Raphael were captured. In Delta area, Blue beach was closed, Green Two beach and the port of St. Tropez were opened, and CTG 80.2, U.S. Naval Liaison Officer (NLO), Beach Control Group, Seventh Army, disembarked and set up his headquarters with the army west of St. Maxime in the Gulf of St. Tropez. In Alpha area, Red beach was cleared of land mines and exits were constructed. Full tonnage capacity of beaches could not be exploited with road matting and engineer equipment available.

Minesweeping for an approach and anchorage in Rade de Bormes was started. Sweeping in Port Cros area had to be delayed pending its capture. Sweeping off Cap Benat was halted because of enemy gunfire. In Alpha and Delta areas, sweeping was nearly finished. Extensive loss of sweep gear occurred in sweeping minefields containing obstructions in the Gulf of Frejus.

Unloading figures based on preliminary action reports of the task forces concerned were:

	Personnel	Vehicles	Tons
Alpha beaches	4,058	1,094	9,000
Delta beaches	6,356	789	570
Camel beaches	Not reported	Not reported	Not reported
Total	10,414	1,883	9,570
Total to Date	70,564	8,620	28,070

OWN AND ENEMY NAVAL LOSSES

Our losses were:

Sunk:

US PT 202, 218; US YMS 24; HM ML 563 by mines.

Damaged:

HMS Brave (minesweeper) and HM LCT 591 by collision.

Enemy losses were:

None.

---------------- 17 August 1944 -------------------

WEATHER

The sky was partly cloudy over Western Mediterranean throughout the day except for general cloudiness with scattered thunderstorms over the land mass of Southern France in the afternoon. Visibility averaged eight miles during daylight and four miles during darkness. Surface winds were gentle easterly with negligible swell.

ENEMY FORCES

Navy: The ex-Italian EV, Capriolo, and 1 Auxiliary, Kemid Allah, were sunk by USS Endicott, HMS Aphis, and HMS Scarab off Cap Croisette. F S Strasbourg and F S Gallissoniere in Toulon harbor were damaged by naval and air attacks. Estimated enemy strength in the invasion area was 1 DD, 5 TB, 6 EV, 6 HAV, 30 MAS, 3 SS, and 23 auxiliaries. From the beginning of the operation to date, no submarine activity had been reported in the Western Mediterranean. Four MAS were sunk by US destroyers of eastern destroyer screen.

Army: Enemy resistance was fairly light except in scattered areas. Elements of the 189th Reserve Division Battle Group were reported crossing the Rhone River from the west at Arles. Elements of the 148th Reserve Division appeared opposite the US 36th Division. To date 7,845 prisoners have been captured by the Seventh Army.

Air : Two ME 109s reconnaissance planes approached Alpha area at approximately 1900 but were driven off. One of them was destroyed by A/A gunfire. At 2138, a JU 88 came in low and fast and was shot down in flames by the USS Champlin. At 2040, a maximum of six JU 88s approached the assault area. Anti-personnel bombs were dropped in the vicinity of St. Raphael and St. Maxime, but no damage was reported.

During a dusk attack, a glider bomb again landed near USS C. F. Hughes on the eastern flank, causing no damage.

During the day, allied attacks on the enemy bomber forces at Valence and Avon in the Rhone Valley claimed to have reduced these forces to the extent of 18 destroyed and 16 damaged. This, combined with further withdrawals, reduced the estimated enemy air strength in Southern France to the following:

JU 88 (Torpedo Bombers)	50
DO 217 (Radio-controlled glider bomb carriers)	20
S/E Fighters	50
Reconnaissance	20

OWN FORCES

Navy: HMS Ramillies escorted by 2 DD departed for Propriano; USS Texas and USS Arkansas with 2 DD sailed for Palermo to be onward routed to Algiers and Oran respectively. HMS Sirius and F S Jeanne D'Arc, both at Naples, were released to CinCMed. HMS Delhi was released by CTF 88 to CTF 85. HMS Tumult reported to CTF 88 for duty.

Army: The French Army B relieved the 3rd Division for the attack on Toulon. The II French Corps continued to land over beaches in St. Tropez area and commenced to assemble in vicinity of Bormes and Cogolin.

The US 3rd Division moved to the vicinity of Brignoles and Sollies-Pont.

Elements of the 36th Division remained in the Theoule Sur Mer area and other elements assembled in the Draguignan area. The 45th Division advanced west to the vicinity of Salernes and Carces.

Task Force Butler, composed of 2nd Battalion of 143 Infantry, 117 Cavalry Reconnaissance Squadron, 59 Armored Field Artillery Battalion, 753 Tank Battalion (less 2 companies), 1 company 636 Tank Destroyer Battalion and service units, was organized for a quick thrust to the north. It reached the vicinity of Digne.

Air : Medium bombers continued with success their attacks on the railroad bridges at St. Julien, Sisteron and Montpellier. Fighter cover continued over the assault areas, protecting ships and unloading activity against attack. There were 257 fighter bomber sorties, but fighter sorties increased to 581 as enemy airdromes were attacked. Many enemy aircraft on the ground were destroyed or damaged. Enemy motor transport also suffered greatly from these attacks.

Carrier planes flew 92 sorties of fighters and fighter bombers against land objectives, and 36 sorties for gunfire spotting. Two Hellcats were damaged, and one Seafire destroyed by flak.

Tac/R was extremely active, flying 42 sorties, many of them deep into hostile territory.

At 0759, 8 Seafires on patrol were diverted to attack an enemy corvette southwest of Cap Sicie. The corvette opened fire and shot down one aircraft in flames.

IMPORTANT ORDERS RECEIVED

CinCMed closed out his advanced command post at Ajaccio, returned to Naples, and requested NCWTF to advise ships and commands to route traffic accordingly.

IMPORTANT ORDERS ISSUED

CTF 85 and CTF 87 directed gunfire support ships to report to CTF 86 who thereupon assumed control of all gunfire support tasks.

Upon request by SOIS for 3 PT equipped with radar to act as eyes for his MTBs patrolling off Genoa, NCWTF directed CTG 80.5 to assign the desired number.

OPERATIONS

One convoy arrived in the assault area and five departed.

These convoys were made up of LSTs of the Calvi shuttle arriving and departing, 16 LCT(R) and 3 fast transports leaving for Ajaccio, and 11 personnel ships for Oran.

At 0001, Beach Control Group Seventh Army took over coordination of unloading priorities and beach operations on shore.

Obstacles, mines, and road blocks were cleared from Camel Red beach which was opened at 1900. Alpha Yellow beach was closed. Unloading at some beaches was hampered by the dusk smoke screen, which persisted under good conditions.

Because unloading progressed so favorably in the Delta area, it was found unnecessary to use the northern half of beach 261 for maintenance of the 45th Division The boundary proposed in Operation Plan 4-44 for administration only between the 3rd and 45th Divisions (see diagram I) was therefore never put into effect.

Delta area defenses were increased by a jamming ship and an A/A cruiser. An A/A cruiser also reported to Camel area.

The second diversion operation was executed almost as planned. From 0315 to 0400, four simulated assault waves of ASRCs entered the Bay of Ciotat, carried out assigned tasks including firing rockets and filling the bay with smoke, and withdrew undamaged despite heavy but inaccurate enemy fire accompanied by star and searchlight illumination. Between 0310 and 0435, the eastern and western bombardment units fired at assigned targets.

During the retirement, an ASRC picked up two radar targets believed to be friendly until they opened fire and failed to reply to challenge. Evasive tactics were employed by all ASRC present until 0555, when HMS Aphis and HMS Scarab arrived and the fight moved out of their range to the west. Only one ASRC was damaged, sustaining minor shrapnel hits. HMS Aphis and HMS Scarab continued the action, and were joined by USS Endicott at 0609. USS Endicott sustained 1 40 mm hit and several shrapnel hits, which wounded 3 men. By 0730, both the Capriolo and Kemid Allah were sunk about 13 miles bearing 168° from Cape Croisette light, and 211 POW were taken.

Port Cros surrendered at 1300 after a final attack including 16 fighter bomber sorties, 12 rounds of major caliber fire from HMS Ramillies, and 63 rounds from USS Augusta.

Minesweepers in Rade de Bormes were protected by a cruiser and two destroyers against fire from shore batteries.

On the right flank, nine fire support calls for silencing batteries in the Gulf of Napoule were answered by destroyers. Batteries on Ile Ste. Marguerite and at Cannes were silenced by cruisers and destroyers. Some enemy mobile guns were still active.

Effective 2100, IAZ (Inner Artillery Zone) times were changed from 2130 to 0550 to 2100 to 0600. There were five red alerts, involving groups up to four enemy planes. Five out of six friendly night fighters were fired on by ships when they strayed into the IAZ.

Minesweeping of Rade de Bormes was continued under gunfire protection, and minesweeping of the entrance of Rade d'Hyeres commenced. In the Gulf of Frejus, 7 magnetic and 39 contact mines were cleared. Two ships were mined. Maintenance sweeping of Alpha and Delta areas was continued.

Unloading figures from preliminary action reports of the task force concerned, were:

	Personnel	Vehicles	Tons
Alpha beaches	3,670	1,659	5,380
Delta beaches	8,691	1,454	3,290
Camel beaches	3,650*	787*	9,400‡
Total	16,011	3,900	18,070
Total to Date	86,575	12,520	46,140

‡Total to date for Camel beach.   *Estimated.

OWN AND ENEMY NAVAL LOSSES

Our losses were:

Sunk:

None.

Damaged:

US LCC 98; HM BYMS 2022 by mines.

Enemy losses were:

Sunk:

2 Corvettes by gunfire with 211 prisoners captured.

Damaged:

None.

---------------- 18 August 1944 -----------------

WEATHER

Partly cloudy conditions of 17 August continued except that heavy afternoon thunderstorms occurred over Corsica making airfields unserviceable.

ENEMY FORCES

Navy: Photo reconnaissance of Toulon harbor showed F S Strasbourg to be damaged and guns put out by action, and F S Gallissoniere capsized by allied bombing of 17 August. Estimated enemy strength capable of operating in the invasion area was 1 DD, 5 TB, 6 EV, 6 HAV, 26 MAS or S-boats, 3 U-boats, and 23 auxiliaries. A U-boat was reported to have fired on a P-38 at 1600, and then to have submerged at 43° 01' N, 05° 52' E off Toulon. Four motor torpedo boats attempting to penetrate screen were sunk by destroyer gunfire. They had departed from Monaco area about 2100 17 August.

Army: Enemy resistance stiffened on the left flank while the enemy appeared to be withdrawing on the right. Artillery was negligible. The Headquarters of the German XLII Corps was captured at Draguignan. Elements of three new divisions, the 198th, the 244th, and the 338th, were identified in the left half of the front. The bulk of the 11th Panzer Division was reported southwest of Avignon.

Heavy vehicle movements were taking place toward the south and southwest from Turin and Alessandria, in northern Italy. Increased movement was noted toward the west from the training area of the 11th Panzer Division.

Enemy capabilities at this time were (1) to exert maximum delaying action, (2) to re-inforce his present troops in the area, (3) to harass the Seventh Army by limited counter-attacks, and (4) to delay our advance to the west and maintain a stubborn defense of Toulon and Marseille. The last was believed to be the capability most likely to be adopted.

Air : At dusk, approximately five JU 88s passed over Camel beach 264 at about 9000 feet. One of these came down to 6000 feet and dropped anti-personnel bombs in the Delta area. These straddled the USS Catoctin. Two bombs hit the ship resulting in 6 dead and 42 wounded. At approximately the same time, one JU 88 fired a torpedo at FDT 13 in the Delta area. It exploded about 250 yards short.

OWN FORCES

Navy: The Diversion Group was dissolved; HMS Aphis and HMS Scarab were released to CinCMed; the MLs and USS Endicott reported to CTG 80.6 the PTs and ASRCs to CTG 80.5. F S Lorraine returned to the assault area.

Army: The beachhead was extended rapidly to the west and northwest with reconnaissance elements on the Durance and Asse Rivers.

Task Force Butler reached Castellane and continued to move rapidly north toward Digne.

The 36th Division reached Grasse, La Bastide, and Chardon. The 45th Division by-passed Barjols and reached a point 4 miles west of the town. Elements of 3rd Division occupied Brignoles against stiff resistance, reached La Roquebrussance 5 miles southwest of Brignoles, and advanced to Sollies-Pont.

The II French Corps continued to land in the St. Tropez area.

Air : Fighter aircraft (P-47's, P-38's, Spitfires, and Hellcats) on patrol furnished beach and shipping cover throughout the day. A total of 225 sorties were flown. Crash strips were put into operation at Ramatuelle and St. Raphael. Night fighter cover was provided by Beaufighters which reported in the area at about 2100. No hostile contacts were reported. Fighter bombers continued sweeps against motor transport and highways, finding many favorable targets in the rapidly retreating enemy ground troops because of a complete lack of enemy fighter opposition.

Because of the rapidly changing Bomb Safety Line, the 87th F.W., Corsican Base Operations of XII TAC, advised that fighter bomber missions would be changed to armed reconnaissance and when practicable air briefed by Joint Operations Room aboard USS Catoctin.

Carrier based fighter-bombers flew 48 sorties, and fighters carried out gunfire spotting missions with 16 sorties. Targets on lines of transportation and supply were the primary objectives, and rockets from Hellcats proved most effective. One Seafire was damaged by flak.

Medium bombers concentrated on the Toulon area, as 91 B-26s of 42nd Bomb Wing hit the gun positions at St. Mandrier. Ninety B-25s of 57th Bomb Wing covered the same area hitting the gounded battleship F S Strasbourg. Bridges over the Rhone were targets of the Mitchells. Intense and accurate flak was reported over the Marseille-Toulon coastal defense.

IMPORTANT ORDERS RECEIVED

None.

IMPORTANT ORDERS ISSUED

CTF 86 reorganized gunfire support ships, assigning 2 BB, 2 CA, 6 CL, and 11 DD to the forward area and 3 BB, 1 CA, 4 CL and 1 DD to reserve status, and dividing all forces into left, center, right and battleship support groups, plus escorts as designated.

OPERATIONS

26 ships arrived in convoys and 25 departed.

To aid in handling convoys, assembly points for shipping were moved 5 miles shoreward, and the three convoy control destroyers took up fixed stations, USS Jouett at 3 miles 90°, USS Benson at 5 miles 70°, and USS Niblack at 5 miles 150° from Cap Camarat. At the same time, a small pool of escorts at Ajaccio was assigned by CTG 80.6 to CTG 80.9 for assignment to convoys sailing ahead of schedule or for A/S operations.

About 0005, enemy motor torpedo boats attacked the center of the destroyer screen. Four DD joined in sinking 4 of the raiders and captured 33 POW. The USS Frankford suffered casualties from two torpedoes that exploded near her.

During the raid of the 5 JU 88s (see enemy air above), objects were reported falling in the water in Alpha area. All areas were blanketed by smoke at the time of the raid. USS Plunkett shot down one of the attacking planes.

In the action to reduce Porquerolles, 286 rounds were fired, part by F S Gloire in the Hyeres area, part by USS Quincy on targets in the Giens peninsula, and the remainder by F S Lorraine and F S Emile Bertin on Porquerolles. A PT sent into Porquerolles under flag of truce with demand for surrender was forced to retire when shelled from Giens. Bombardment was then resumed.

Three cruisers supported the advance of the 3rd Division in the Bormes area.

Destroyers fired on two small batteries near Cannes which returned fire. No fire was drawn from enemy batteries by a CL and two DD that entered Golfe de la Napoule.

Night fighter director equipment was landed on Port Cros.

Maintenance minesweeping in Alpha and Delta areas was carried out. In the Gulf of Frejus, 12 moored magnetic, and 40 deep-layed moored contact mines were swept. Rade de Bormes was cleared. At the entrance to Rade d'Hyeres, 11 mines and 3 obstructors were swept.

M/S Flotilla 5 was ordered, upon relief by M/S Flotilla 19, to relieve MinDiv 21 of maintenance of the Straits of Bonifacio.

A mine search from a PBY revealed a four row field running south from Cap Benat.

Delta 262N and Delta Red Two beaches were placed in operation.

The ship to shore rate of unloading was held down by lack of transportation and labor ashore. Available French labor was hired.

Unloading figures based on preliminary action reports of task forces concerned, were:

	Personnel	Vehicles	Tons
Alpha beaches	2,071	270	5,753
Delta beaches	1,409	614	3,767
Camel beaches	Not reported	Not reported	Not reported
Total	3,480	884	9,520
Total to Date	90,055	13,404	55,660

OWN AND ENEMY NAVAL LOSSES

Our losses were:

None.

Enemy losses were:

Sunk:

4 motor torpedo boats by gunfire; 33 prisoners captured.

Damaged:

None.

---------------- 19 August 1944 ------------------

WEATHER

Mostly clear skies, good visibility and gentle winds prevailed in the assault area with scattered thunderstorms in the afternoon over land masses.

ENEMY FORCES

Navy: Four MAS were shown by photo reconnaissance to have departed from Imperia. Off Toulon, an enemy submarine fired on an aircraft rescue group, then submerged.

Army: Enemy resistance north towards Digne was negligible. The advance to the east was bitterly opposed. Enemy resistance appeared disorganized.

Considerable military movement was taking place south down the Rhone Valley and southwest towards Carpentras.

Air : At 2043, a single enemy aircraft approached the Camel area at 1500-2000 feet and dropped a string of seven or eight anti-personnel bombs in the vicinity of four SC of the inner screen. The bombs exploded 20 feet above the water. No damage or casualties were reported. USS Brooklyn tracked two groups of low flying planes at 2100 that searched the Camel fire support group area for about an hour. At no time did these planes come nearer than ten miles to friendly planes patrolling the vicinity.

OWN FORCES

Navy: USS Nevada escorted by 2 DD returned to the assault area.

Army: The II French Corps began the attack on Toulon, supported by aircraft of the XII TAC bombing strongpoints in Toulon harbor.

The US VI Corps made crossing of the Durance River in the vicinity of Pertuis. Reconnaissance elements advanced to points north of Sisteron.

The 1st ABTF was augmented by the 1st SSF for the advance to the east on the right flank.

Air : With the rapid advance of our forces inland and the decreased probability of large scale enemy attack against the beachheads, fighter cover was reduced and the patrols placed further inland for interception purposes.

Aircraft of TG 88.2 destroyed 5 enemy T/E Bombers and damaged 1.

As the use of fighter bomber and tactical reconnaissance missions had become almost exclusively a support function of Army ground forces rather than support for unloading at the beaches, offensive control of these operations was set up at HQ XII TAC ashore and the Joint Operations Room of the USS Catoctin was relieved of this duty. Control of defensive fighters was maintained by HMS FDT 13.

At 1614, additional fighter cover was assigned to the gunfire support task force engaged in bombarding the defenses of Toulon.

245 medium bombers were dispatched against rail and road bridges in the Rhone Valley. 35 B-25s and 36 B-26s hit the heavy gun positions on St. Mandrier Peninsula at Toulon.

Carrier fighter bombers executed 12 missions with 72 sorties. Eight locomotives and 25 cars were damaged; 118 vehicles were destroyed or severely damaged. Five enemy planes were knocked out. One Seafire was lost.

The 324th Wing (RAF) of Spitfires began operations at Ramatuelle airfield near Beach 261. Cub spotting planes, PBYs used for aerial mine spotting, and transport planes began operations from this temporary newly-constructed field.

IMPORTANT ORDERS RECEIVED

None.

IMPORTANT ORDERS ISSUED

The destroyer screen was reorganized, reducing the patrol areas to lines with stations at 2 mile intervals and setting up two wing patrols outside the main line of patrol. CTG 80.5 was ordered to operate a PT boat screen eastward of Cap Ampeglio against enemy light surface forces.

OPERATIONS

Convoys arriving consisted of 29 ships. Departing convoys consisted of 64 ships. Seven LST were frozen in the Calvi shuttle and authorized to sail independently in order to expedite the moving of army air force equipment.

Two DD and two PC were ordered to report to CTG 80.9 to augment the A/S patrol off Propriano.

On the right flank, USS Brooklyn with 2 DD successfully engaged gun emplacements in Golfe de la Napoule, to the north of Cannes, and near Vignelon. Three cruisers fired 216 rounds in the vicinity of Hyeres and Porquerolles, encountering heavy flak west of Hyeres. FS Lorraine, USS Nevada, and USS Augusta, screened by 4 DD laying smoke and covered by 12 to 18 fighters, bombarded the Toulon area, firing 87 rounds on St. Mandrier and 124 rounds in Toulon with a direct hit on the Strasbourg.

Two night retirement areas in the carrier operating area were set up for gunfire support ships between $06° 21'$ E and $06° 35'$ E, south of $42° 55'$ N.

An air-sea rescue team was disembarked from HMS Ulster Queen and set up at St. Tropez with 3 Walrus planes and 3 high speed launches.

Delta Blue 262N beach and Camel Red 2 beach, eastern half, opened. Camel Yellow beach closed. Unloading delays were caused at Camel Red beach by lack of trucks to remove cargo and lack of beach space clear of mines.

Enemy gunfire from Porquerolles again hampered minesweeping in Rade d'Hyeres. Maintenance sweeps of Alpha and Delta areas were continued. With the sweeping of 10 moored mines and 3 magnetic mines, clearance of the Gulf of Frejus was completed and all minesweepers assigned CTF 87 passed to CTG 80.10's control. A total of 75 contact and 12 magnetic mines were swept in this area.

Unloading figures ‡ were:

	Personnel	Vehicles	Tons
Alpha beaches	Not reported	Not reported	Not reported
Delta beaches	Not reported	Not reported	Not reported
Camel beaches	Not reported	Not reported	Not reported
Total	Not reported	Not reported	Not reported
Total to date	106,999	15,695	31,439

‡ The figures for unloading beginning this date and all reported subsequently reported by US Naval Liaison Officer, Beach Control Group.

OWN AND ENEMY NAVAL LOSSES

Our losses were:

Sunk:

None.

Damaged:

HM ML 562 by shell fire.

Enemy losses were:

None.

---------------- 20 August 1944 -----------------

WEATHER

Fair conditions continued over the western Mediterranean with good visibility throughout day. Winds were southerly over southern Tyrrhenian Sea and along North African coast but were gentle easterly in the assault area, increasing to moderate after sunset.

ENEMY FORCES

Navy: Estimated enemy strength and disposition at this date were as follows:

	DD	TB	EV	HAV	MAS	SS	AUX.
Toulon		1	1			1	
Marseille			3	4			6
Genoa	2	4	2	1			
Spezia							2
Savona					3		
Unlocated				1	23		15
Total	2	5	6	6	26	1	23

Noteworthy was the change from inactive to active status of 1 DD at Genoa. Six inactive submarines were also at Genoa, of which 5 still presented threat of activity in the near future. They included the remaining 2 at Spezia, which had moved to Genoa since August 9th.

A radio direction finder bearing was reported by Radio Naples of U-boat within 30 miles of 42° 40' N, and 06° 40' E.

Army: Enemy resistance continued light and scattered; at Aix and Durance enemy opposition was fairly stubborn. Enemy capabilities were (1) to withdraw north up the Rhone Valley, fighting strong delaying action; (2) to launch a local counter-attack; (3) to launch a strong counter-attack employing the bulk of the 11th Panzer Division. Our strong advances to the west beyond Aix had out-flanked Marseille. The only capability, therefore, left to the enemy, appeared to be to withdraw up the Rhone Valley.

Air : An unknown number of reconnaissance aircraft flew over the transport area under cover of darkness.

There were 3 red alerts but only one enemy aircraft entered the beach areas, dropping anti-personnel bombs in the Camel area without casualties.

OWN FORCES

Navy: One group of CVEs retired to Maddalena in accordance with a plan to alternate carrier groups in the operating area for logistic purposes.

Army: The French Army B encircled Toulon and began moving west toward Marseille. Le Beausset and Bandol, west of Toulon, were captured. French forces approached Hyeres.

US Forces captured Aix and moved northward. Strong reconnaissance elements north of Sisteron captured Gap. The First Air Borne Task Force advancing east occupied Callion and captured high ground northwest of Cannes.

Air : Normal Fighter cover was maintained.

Fighter bombers continued attacks on gun positions particularly at Toulon and at Nice. The installations at St. Mandrier were hit by 121 P-47s each carrying two 500 lb. bombs. Ninety B-26s hit the same area with 161 1000 lb. bombs. Enemy anti-aircraft fire was accurate and intense and 28 aircraft were hit by flak and 3 destroyed. Excellent bomb patterns were achieved with possible direct hits. Gunfire spotting planes aided US and French cruisers in bombardment of targets at Toulon.

Carrier fighter bombers carried out 9 missions with 56 sorties, resulting in 9 locomotives destroyed, 2 damaged, and 118 vehicles destroyed. A special attack on coastal shipping damaged 4 F-lighters and caused 6 of them to beach. Four Hellcats and one Seafire were lost; 3 Hellcats and 1 Seafire were damaged. Out of 40 sorties flown for gun spotting, one Hellcat was missing. Friendly night fighters were fired on by ships in the assault area.

Two Spitfires, last light patrol, were fired on by both shore and ships at dusk. One had to crash land and was destroyed. They were fired on as they were coming in to land at their field with wheels down.

MACAF reinforced night aircraft search along convoy routes and areas adjacent to assault area against possible submarine menace.

IMPORTANT ORDERS RECEIVED

None.

IMPORTANT ORDERS ISSUED

Fifteen DD were assigned to the screen, two of these to proceed daily to Ajaccio for fuel and supplies.

OPERATIONS

Convoys contained 59 arrivals and 58 departures.

The land attack on Toulon was supported by air and sea forces. About 1,500 rounds were fired with excellent results on numerous targets. Enemy guns, at least one of 340 mm, on St. Mandrier answered the attack, firing about 60 rounds slowly but accurately with a range of about 14 miles. FS Fantasque and FS George Leygues were hit by 155 mm shells, and USS Ericsson straddled.

HMS Ulster Queen took up a new station at 140° eight miles from Cap Lardier. The MLs that had been with HMS Stuart Prince departed to take up patrol duty at Ajaccio.

Maintenance minesweeping was continued off the beaches. Sweeping in Rade d'Hyeres was again curtailed by enemy gunfire.

The port of St. Raphael was opened.

The rapid advance of the Seventh Army made it unnecessary to carry out the plan for opening the Lavandou and Hyeres beaches.

The Seventh Army assumed responsibility for evacuation of casualties. Adequate hospital facilities were by this time established ashore. Air evacuation with a capacity of 40 patients a day was inaugurated. Evacuation of casualties to hospital ships was centralized and limited to Delta Green Two beach.

Shortages of personnel and vehicles prevented full capacity of beaches and craft from being exploited but the army reported that the military requirements were being met and that the rate of unloading was satisfactory.

Unloading figures were:

	Personnel	Vehicles	Tons
Alpha beaches	3,402	193	5,939
Delta beaches	3,749	911	4,273
Camel beaches	700	450	3,200
Total	7,851	1,554	13,412
Total to Date	114,850	17,247	44,851

OWN AND ENEMY NAVAL LOSSES

Our losses were:

None.

Enemy losses were:

None.

--------------- 21 August 1944 -----------------

WEATHER

Easterly winds in the assault area increased to fresh during the day producing choppy sea with swell and surf of 3 to 4 feet. Elsewhere, wind was moderate southerly. The sky was partly cloudy, and visibility was good in all areas throughout the period.

ENEMY FORCES

    Navy: 1 MAS was sunk, 1 forced to beach, and 1 damaged by USS C F Hughes, USS Champlin, and USS Boyle. Estimated enemy forces were 2 DD, 5 TB, 6 EV, 6 HAV, 23 MAS, 1 U-boat, and 23 auxiliaries.

    Army: The bulk of enemy forces defending Aix withdrew during the night. A prisoner stated that the 11th Panzer Division was acting as a rear guard and that they were to fall back to the Rhone River. About 1,000 rear echelon troops, consisting mainly of administrative personnel, were captured at Gap. Many truck convoys were observed in the northern Italy area.

    Air : No comment.

OWN FORCES

    Navy: Fourteen British LCT(R) were released to CinCMed.

    Army: French forces closed in on Toulon from the east. Hyeres was infiltrated. Le Coudon was captured. Task Force Butler occupied Gap and reached a point 15 miles north of Aspremont.

    The Seventh Army to date had captured 13,658 prisoners.

    Air : MACAF established a temporary air-sea rescue base at Port Cros.

    US LST 394, which had been a night fighter control station and day radar reporting station was released by the Air Defense Commander.

    225th (RAF) and 2/33 (French) Tactical Reconnaissance Squadrons now based at Ramatuelle, gave greater range to reconnaissance efforts inland.

    PBY 29, a mail and mine spotting plane, lost a propeller while taxiing in rough water in Bay of St. Tropez, killing the pilot and damaging the plane.

    Anti-submarine patrols were authorized to fly at a minimum height of 800 feet when 12 miles or more from the south coast of France. Within this limit minimum height was established at 4,000 feet.

    Carrier fighters, fighter bombers, and reconnaissance planes made 148 sorties, striking at communications and sinking 8 F-lighters, 1 steamer, and 1 minelayer in the Toulon area. One Wildcat, 2 Seafires, and 1 Hellcat were lost to enemy AA fire.

IMPORTANT ORDERS RECEIVED

    None.

IMPORTANT ORDERS ISSUED

    At the request of SOIS, the PTs operating eastward of Cap Ampeglio were ordered under his operational control in order to coordinate air and surface forces in that area.

OPERATIONS

    Convoys arriving consisted of 30 ships, and departing convoys consisted of 36 ships.

CTU 80.6.8 was established at Ajaccio, and CTU 80.6.9 at Naples, to act as CTG 80.6's representative with respect to convoy control of those ports and to assist with the logistic needs of escorts.

A DD was designated to patrol off the central sector of the destroyer screen and establish communications with aircraft in the vicinity in the event of a submarine contact.

At 0115 off Ile de Lerins, 3 DD caught 3 E-boats attempting to sneak through the screen, and eventually destroyed them, capturing two survivors. One E-boat was not destroyed until 0400, when it was located by combined DD and cruiser-plane search.

USS Brooklyn and 2 DD carried out 5 shelling missions in the Golfe de la Napoule and drew return fire.

Bombardment in the Toulon area was carried out along the same lines as the previous day with good results. Coastal guns were less active, and no ships were hit despite some near misses. Enemy positions in the Giens-Hyeres area were neutralized after 250 rounds were fired. USS Philadelphia lost an SOC plane in this area.

Porquerolles was bombarded and two boats were sunk in its harbor. USS Eberle removed 140 Armenian prisoners from Porquerolles and reported that a strong point containing 150 Germans still remained. Two PT were sent on patrol to prevent their escape.

Disappearing ASV contacts and one sound contact near the assault area produced no definite indication of a submarine.

A line of night retirement from 42° 50' N, 05° 10' E toward 41° 55' N, 06° 00' E was established for CVEs.

Delta Red and Green beaches closed. Unloading continued normally despite a 19-knot easterly wind and a 2-foot surf.

Unloading figures were:

	Personnel	Vehicles	Tons
Alpha beaches	1,286	400	4,068
Delta beaches	367	246	2,250
Camel beaches	2,197	884	2,757
Total	3,850	1,530	9,075
Total to Date	118,700	19,779	53,926

OWN AND ENEMY NAVAL LOSSES

Our losses were:

Sunk:

None.

Damaged:

USS Mackenzie (DD 614) by explosions during depth charge attack.

Enemy losses were:

Sunk:

3 E-boats by gunfire.

Damaged:

None.

Prisoners:

140 Armenians from Porquerolles and 2 survivors from captured E-boats.

---------------- 22 August 1944 -------------------

WEATHER

Wind in the assault area died down to gentle easterly near dawn but by noon had increased again to fresh generating 3 to 4 feet swells with slight seas. Winds were moderate southeast elsewhere. Skies were clear to partly cloudy with good visibility.

ENEMY FORCES

Navy: Photo reconnaissance showed that HAV and EV of 210 feet had departed from Genoa, 5 possible MAS boats had arrived Oneglia, 1 auxiliary was at Monaco, and the Pomone class TB, Bombarde, and the EV of 210 feet were not noted at Toulon. Neither the TB nor the EV of 210 feet were seen later, and it was assumed that they were scuttled in deep water. The three SS at Toulon were not seen and at least one was believed to have put to sea. At Marseille, naval vessels and auxiliaries were not seen and were assumed to have been scuttled. Known to have been scuttled were the HAV Cyrnos, the HAV Ampere, and a third HAV. Also believed sunk were 2 Elan class and 1 Arras class EVs and at least 6 auxiliaries. Other auxiliaries were assumed to have been scuttled when French ports fell.

Units estimated remaining were 2 DD, 4 TB, 2 EV, 1 HAV, 23 MAS, 1 U-boat and 3 or 4 auxiliaries.

Army: No comment.

Air : No comment.

OWN FORCES

Navy: HMS Black Prince (CL) was released by CTF 86 to CinCMed. All British LSIs were released to CinCMed, and all APDs were transferred to CTG 80.6.

Army: The French Army B passed La Vallette and moved into the outskirts of Toulon. The VI Corps moving north had reached the Grenoble area. The First Air Borne Task Force advanced east to Mendelian and on toward St. Vallier.

The Seventh Army command post closed at St. Tropez and re-opened at Brignoles.

Air : Responsibility for Air Raid Warnings was assumed by Sector Operations Room (SOR) of 64th Fighter Wing ashore near St. Tropez. The area of responsibility extended seaward 40 miles from the coast. Three nearby temporary airfields were available and ten radar stations of varied types were in operation along the coast of Southern France. 64th Fighter Wing controlled day and night fighter defense but could delegate control of certain patrols to GCI installations at both ship and shore stations. With this transfer of responsibility ashore and a definite termination of the assault phase, the All Clear (condition White) was made standard in the beachhead area, replacing Yellow Alert (enemy air attacks may be expected), which had been in force during the assault period.

At 0625, Spitfires on normal patrol were fired on by ships about 10 miles southeast of Frejus.

Four Night Fighters were continuously over the assault area from 2030 to dawn.

Carrier based fighter bombers executed 11 missions with 84 sorties, destroying 3 locomotives and 2 armored cars and strafing 50 trucks. Deteriorating weather curtailed other scheduled flights. CTF 88.2 provided spotting planes as requested by CTF 86.

IMPORTANT ORDERS RECEIVED

None.

IMPORTANT ORDERS ISSUED

All American liberty ships were directed until further notice to sail to Oran on completion of discharge in the assault area.

OPERATIONS

Sixty ships arrived in convoy and 21 departed.

One DD was established on each wing of the screen to maintain communications with night searching aircraft and destroyer hunting groups.

Naval bombardment covered the area from Giens to Marseille in the third day of the action to reduce Toulon. USS Augusta fired 54 rounds; FS Gloire answered urgent calls from the Army in the St. Marcel area; HMS Aurora fired 78 rounds at Cap Brun scoring two direct hits; and USS Philadelphia neutralized targets near Giens. Coastal defense guns replied vigorously, shells from St. Mandrier landing near the Augusta at a range of 16 miles. A white flag was seen at one battery on the Giens peninsula, but the battery on Cap de l'Esterel continued to be active.

Bombardment of Porquerolles was continued, and a white flag was raised twice. At 1130, CTG 86.3 in USS Omaha accepted the surrender of the enemy garrison except isolated stragglers. Later, USS Eberle destroyed boats, barracks, and ammunition dumps, and removed 58 prisoners. USS Hackberry landed 190 Senegalese troops and USS Tattnall removed 150 more POW.

In Golfe de la Napoule, cruisers and destroyers successfully engaged numerous targets with the aid of shore and plane spotters, including 170 mm batteries, armored vehicles, pillboxes, and railroad guns. One cruiser had a near miss and two destroyers suffered personnel casualties.

A four-foot surf impeded the progress of unloading.

Unloading figures were:

	Personnel	Vehicles	Tons
Alpha beaches	123	568	2,696
Delta beaches	7,364	1,604	4,229
Camel beaches	1,703	871	2,394
Total	9,190	3,043	9,319
Total to Date	127,890	22,822	63,245

OWN AND ENEMY NAVAL LOSSES

Our losses were:

None.

Enemy losses were:

None.

--------------------- 23 August 1944 --------------------

WEATHER

The entire day was fine in all areas with scattered clouds, good visibility, and gentle shifting winds. No sea or swell was experienced.

ENEMY FORCES

Navy: No comment.

Army: No comment.

Air : USS Doyle reported that a plane flew over at 0043 at 60 feet altitude. The plane was identified as a HE 111. It was suspected that it might be engaged in mine laying. By this time, the enemy air forces had completed their evacuation of Southern France. The few forces remaining in Central France were estimated to be as follows:

Long Range Bombers	0
Ground Attack	0
S/E Fighters	15
T/E Fighters	0
Tactical Reconnaissance	10

These were considered to be located in the Dijon area. The enemy air threat to the invasion of Southern France had become negligible and was limited to possible sneak raids by fighter bombers based in Northern Italy.

OWN FORCES

Navy: HMS Ajax, HMS Argonaut, and HMS Orion of TF 86, and seven DD of the British 18th Destroyer Flotilla were released to CinCMed.

Army: The French Army B cleaned out pockets of resistance around Toulon and Marseille. The French Division Blindee (Armored Division) relieved elements of the 3rd US Infantry Division to the north.

Air : The 322nd Fighter Wing (RAF) of Spitfires moved in to base at Frejus Airfield, near St. Raphael.

Carrier fighter bombers carried out 16 missions with 110 sorties. Three bridges and 20 trucks were demolished; 6 railway tracks were damaged.

Air coverage of convoys continued to be flown from Corsican bases.

IMPORTANT ORDERS RECEIVED

None.

IMPORTANT ORDERS ISSUED

Five APD were ordered to be released by CTF 86 to report to CTG 80.6 for escort duty. CTG 80.5 was directed to establish a boat pool at St. Maxime and to replace PTs being used as couriers with ASRCs.

Decision having been made not to use the Hyeres beaches and anchorages, the additional minesweeping which would have been required was cancelled as well as plans for laying light indicator nets to protect the anchorages.

OPERATIONS

Only one convoy of 8 ships arrived, while five departed, consisting of 57 ships. The blood bank shuttle from Corsica to the assault area was taken over from the PT boats by airplanes.

A nightly PT patrol close inshore off Nice and Villefranche between Cap d'Antibes and Cap Ferrat was established to assist in fighting the explosive boat menace and to ward off E-boat attacks.

Bombardment of the coastal rim of defense continued from Marseille to Giens. A total of 825 rounds was fired. Spotting planes from cruisers reported 6 hits and 4 near misses on St. Mandrier targets, the same on Fort des Six-Fours, 6 hits on Cap Sicie, and 5 near misses on the big battery on Cap Cepet. White flags were seen at the latter point and on Cap de l'Esterel. USS Tattnall landed 136 French troops on the Giens peninsula at the close of the bombardment with no resistance.

On the right flank, 9 gunfire missions were undertaken. Several gun emplacements were dislodged, pill boxes were destroyed, troop concentrations were disrupted, and an oil storage tank was sent up in flames. At noon, the French tricolor was sighted on a tower behind Cannes.

A mine spotting plane sighted 2 lines of 30 mines from Porquerolles to Ile de Bagau laid 300 yards apart.

Unloading figures were:

	Personnel	Vehicles	Tons
Alpha beaches	958	575	4,997
Delta beaches	986	1,904	6,131
Camel beaches	642	311	5,300
Total	2,586	2,790	16,428
Total to Date	130,476	25,612	79,673

OWN AND ENEMY NAVAL LOSSES

Our losses were:

None.

Enemy losses were:

None.

---------------- 24 August 1944 ------------------

WEATHER

Skies were partly cloudy in the morning; mostly clear in the afternoon. Wind was moderate shifting in all areas and sea and swell were negligible.

ENEMY FORCES

Navy: Patrols on the eastern flank noted activity off Cap d'Antibes during the night and by gunfire broke up a possible attempt to launch an explosive boat attack. Photo reconnaissance showed 2 possible minesweeper auxiliaries at San Remo, 2 at Monaco, and at Genoa 3 EV, 1 auxiliary, 1 HAV, and 1 TB.

Army: Pockets of resistance and the crews of some coast defense batteries continued to fight in Marseille and Toulon. Our reconnaissance elements met no opposition at Arles. No enemy resistance was offered to occupation of Martigues, Argonne, and Cavaillonne. Cannes, Antibes, and Grasse were entered against light opposition. Some enemy resistance was met northeast of Grenoble. Enemy vehicle movements northward through the Rhone Valley continued.

Air : No comment.

OWN FORCES

Navy: British 5th MS Flotilla, engaged in sweeping the Straits of Bonifacio, was released to CinCMed because of the decreased danger of enemy aircraft laying mines there. USS Pepperwood returned to Oran. All British LCI(H)s were released to CinCMed.

Army: No comment.

Air : A safety lane 10 miles wide relative to base point 43° 00' N and 06° 18' 30" E was established for night fighters and intruders to pass through the IAZ on the southern coast of France. North of the base point, the lane extended five miles on either side of north south line through base point for 15 miles. South of base point, the lane extended five miles to either side of line bearing $130^\circ T$ from base point for 25 miles. Aircraft using this lane were required to fly above 6,000 feet.

Sixteen P-47s of XII TAC attacked gun positions in the Toulon area.

Fighter aircraft of the 324th Wing (RAF) moved to Sisteron airfield over 60 miles inland, indicating the general flow of tactical aircraft away from the beachhead area

Normal fighter cover of 4 aircraft with 4 more on call was provided the beachheads throughout daylight hours with 8 aircraft airborne for first and last light patrols.

Carrier fighter bombers carried out 14 missions with 58 sorties against communications. Flak over Marseille was intense. Two Seafires were lost and five Hellcats were damaged.

IMPORTANT ORDERS RECEIVED

None.

IMPORTANT ORDERS ISSUED

NCWTF ordered immediate effort to clear Port de Bouc and Etang de Berre.

OPERATIONS

Only one convoy of 3 ships arrived in the assault area and two convoys of 27 ships departed.

Off Cap d'Antibes, PTs and DDs on patrol noted considerable activity of small craft, and heard one explosion 100 yards away. Their presence probably prevented the enemy from launching an explosive boat or human torpedo attack. The nightly PT patrol on the west flank in Rade d'Hyeres was discontinued due to the reduced threat of enemy surface forces from the westward.

The port of Toulon remained uncaptured. Coast defenses in the Toulon area were hit heavily, with four cruisers firing 516 rounds. At the end of the day, only 3 batteries remained active, one on Cap Sicie and two on St. Mandrier. Off Marseille, USS Nevada fired 200 rounds on Ile Pomegues, and silenced all return fire except flak. On the right flank, 394 rounds were fired, destroying one railroad gun, setting a ship afire in the harbor of Nice, and damaging a bridge across the Var River.

Carrying out a decision by NCWTF to open up Golfe de Fos and Etang de Berre, minesweepers began sweeping at dawn on a line 190° from Port de Bouc light, covered by fighter planes and 2 DD. At 1400, the minesweepers, despite shelling from shore batteries which the fire support ships were unable to locate, had progressed to latitude 43° 20' N and swept 38 mines, assisted by plane mine spotting. At 1700, PT 555 hit a mine near Cap Couronne buoy but remained afloat.

Unloading figures were:

	Personnel	Vehicles	Tons
Alpha beaches	302	143	4,820
Delta beaches	1,230	967	7,209
Camel beaches	561	157	6,626
Total	2,093	1,267	18,655
Total to Date	132,569	26,879	98,328

OWN AND ENEMY NAVAL LOSSES

Our losses were:

Sunk:

None.

Damaged:

    US PT 555 by mine.

Enemy losses were:

    None.

---------------- 25 August 1944 --------------------

WEATHER

Mostly clear skies prevailed in all areas with good visibility. Surface wind was fresh northeasterly in the assault area, seas slight swell 2 to 3 feet. In other areas, wind was moderate southerly with negligible sea and swell.

ENEMY FORCES

    Navy: No comment.

    Army; At scattered and isolated strongpoints strong resistance was maintained. A considerable number of troops, some ex-Marseille, were reported by the FFI to be in the Port de Bouc area.

    Air : No comment.

OWN FORCES

    Navy: HMS Sirius arrived in the assault area and reported to CTF 86 for duty. HMS Aurora was released by CTF 86 to CinCMed.

    Army: The French Army B captured Toulon and La Ciotat, and continued to clean up pockets of enemy resistance on Cap Sicie, St. Mandrier, and in the port area of Marseille.

        The US VI Corps advanced up the Rhone Valley.

        The 1st ABTF occupied Antibes and Cannes and met stiff resistance on the east bank of the Var River.

    Air : Normal reduced day fighter and night fighter patrols of assault area were continued by XII TAC and MACAF.

        St. Mandrier Peninsula off Toulon and Ratonneau Island near Marseille were heavily bombed.

        Medium bombers, fighter bombers, and fighters were now operating in upper Rhone Valley. Carrier based planes provided air spotting missions for gunfire support ships and conducted tactical reconnaissance in Nimes and Montpellier areas to the west of the River Rhone. Carrier based fighter bombers completed without loss seven missions of 40 sorties to the west of the River Rhone, attacking bridges, troop columns, and army vehicles.

IMPORTANT ORDERS RECEIVED

    None.

IMPORTANT ORDERS ISSUED

None.

OPERATIONS

Seven convoys arrived with 146 ships, and two convoys departed with 30 ships. The A/S patrol by 2 PC in the Straits of Bonifacio was discontinued.

PTs and DDs on the eastern screen thwarted an explosive boat attack from Baie des Anges, avoiding damage from numerous explosions without being able to hit or capture any of the raiders.

The bombardment of St. Mandrier was continued with added intensity for the sixth successive day. At three locations, batteries remained active until 1600. In the Marseille area, 354 rounds were fired. On the right flank between Nice and Cannes, a cruiser and 3 DD carried out 5 missions against troops, mortars, and a small coastal defense battery.

Minespotting planes located a string of 20 mines 10.5 miles long bearing $258°$ from the southern tip of Ile Pomegues. Minesweeping up to the entrance of the Golfe de Fos was finished with the cutting of 13 French and 16 German snag-line mines. Shallow minesweepers continued their clearance work as far as Port de Bouc channel entrance, and a mine disposal party was put ashore.

Unloading figures were:

	Personnel	Vehicles	Tons
Alpha beaches	6,198	1,066	3,106
Delta beaches	4,858	210	2,155
Camel beaches	135	1	4,656
Total	11,191	1,277	9,917
Total to Date	143,750	28,156	108,245

OWN AND ENEMY NAVAL LOSSES

Our losses were:

Sunk:

None.

Damaged:

US LCI(L) 585 by underwater obstacles.

Enemy losses were:

None.

------------------ 26 August 1944 ------------------

WEATHER

Clear skies, moderate land and sea breezes, generally smooth seas and good visibility prevailed throughout.

ENEMY FORCES

Navy: Photo reconnaissance showed that the DDs, Dardo, Premuda and 1 S-boat had arrived at La Spezia from Genoa.

An attack by an estimated 10 explosive controlled boats was made on the eastern flank. Eight explosive type boats were sunk by US PT 552 and USS Livermore. Others were reported to have destroyed themselves when discovered. Control boats were believed to have escaped.

Army: The heaviest motor movements to the north to date were observed in the Rhone Valley. The enemy still held out on St. Mandrier Peninsula.

Air : No comment.

OWN FORCES

Navy: NCWTF released to CinCMed the following British ships: HMS Colombo, HMS Vagrant (tug), 29th ML Flotilla composed of MLs 273, 336, 463, 471, 469, 458, and HMS Nasprite (tanker). CTF 86 transferred the USS Kearney to CTG 80.6. NCWTF released USS Arkansas, USS Nevada, and USS Texas from the invasion area.

Army: In the Toulon area, an SOC reported that a white flag was flying over the battery at Fort de Six-Fours at 1140. The sectors of Le Bosquet and le Mourillon in the Toulon area were captured by the French Army.

Air : Eighty-seven medium bombers, B-26s, scored several probable hits in good concentration on gun positions on Ratonneau Island in Bay of Marseille. XII TAC provided additional fighter cover in the Golfe de Fos area from first light to dusk, for which USS Augusta was designated fighter direction ship.

Planes of TF 88 flew 10 missions of 38 sorties against targets in the Rhone Valley. Sixty trucks, 4 railroad cars, and one bridge were destroyed. One Hellcat and one Seafire were lost, and 6 Hellcats damaged by flak.

IMPORTANT ORDERS RECEIVED

None.

IMPORTANT ORDERS ISSUED

NCWTF extended Alpha area westward to include Isle d'Hyeres except as required for gunfire support operations in Rade d'Hyeres.

NCWTF informed all holders of ANOR-1 that a new air raid warning would go into effect at 1200, 28 August. The area was divided into two sectors by the meridian of 5° 30' E. Two Sector Operations Rooms (SOR) of 64th Fighter Wing would notify the SOPA in each sector of all air raids.

NCWTF at 1555 directed CTF 86 to sweep channels into Port de Bouc and Marseille in order to accelerate the opening of these ports.

OPERATIONS

Two convoys, one consisting of 13 M/T, 24 LST, 2 DD, and one consisting of 45 LCI, 3 Transports, 4 DD, departed the assault area.

The assault area destroyer screen was reestablished forming a 'V' with following coordinates for Easy and William Line: (1) 43° 25' N 06° 54' 15" E, (2) 43° 07' N 06° 52' E, (3) 43° 02' N 06° 31' 15" E. Stations spacing was one mile. Item line and How line were established ten miles to seaward of Easy and William Line respectively. A destroyer assigned to each of these lines was within voice communication distance of the screen and served as a picket.

HMS Delhi anchored in the assault area at 1245 to augment anti-aircraft protection. At 0230 off Cap Antibes, the PT screen intercepted an explosive boat attack aimed for the assault area. As the attack moved west, the DD screen also engaged the boats. USS Livermore and US PT 552 each destroyed 4 explosive boats. The PTs attempted to destroy the control boat, but it was able to reach the harbor of Antibes.

USS Gleaves, USS Niblack, and USS Benson made a sweep to Spezia from 0800 to 2000 in an attempt to intercept two enemy destroyers. Three enemy destroyers were reported to have been attacked by a patrol plane at 0730.

HMS Ramillies and HMS Sirius fired 93 rounds from 1230 to 1330 at targets on the St. Mandrier Peninsula, Toulon. FS Lorraine, FS Montcalm, FS Duguay Trouin continued the bombardment from 1230 to 1630. The cruisers closed to within five miles of the fortress. Only one round of return fire was reported by our forces throughout this bombardment. All ships ceased fire at 1630. Explosions and fires were observed. USS Augusta and USS Philadelphia fired 63 rounds in support of minesweeping operations off Marseille at the batteries on the Frioul Islands and Cap Croisette.:e.

Two cruisers and 4 destroyers were stationed for gunfire support on the east flank. FS Emile Bertin, USS Champlin, USS Edison, and FS Terrible fired on six targets in the Nice area. Good results were reported by SFCP on all targets. USS Boyle made hits on six guns on Cap Ferrat. USS Tuscaloosa, USS Boyle, and USS Champlin proceeded to within 4,000 yards of Nice and drew no fire.

An advance party of 20 men was ordered by NCWTF to make a preliminary inspection of the harbor of Port de Bouc. The party arrived at 1530 and reported to CTF 86 who was in charge of operations for opening the port. Upon completion of the survey, the party reported that the entrance was partially blocked by two sunken ships. The opening still remained 120 feet wide and 30 feet deep. In the inner harbor, two liberty berths were available.

No mines were reported during the maintenance sweep of the assault area. A 2-1/2 mile approach channel from 42° 59' N, 04° 52' E to entrance of Golfe de Fos was swept and reported clear. A total of 47 moored mines were cut and detonated. At 0600, sweeping of the fire support area commenced. At the end of the day's sweeping, 25 mines were detonated and the southeast portion was reported clear. The minesweepers were hampered by shell fire, loss of gear, and the use of a smoke screen. In Golfe de Frejus, the dangerous area near Isle de Lion de Mer was reported clear. Four mines were detonated during the minesweeping operation.

At 1120, USS Madison rescued a bomber pilot in the water 10 miles south of Cap Croisette.

Unloading figures were:

	Personnel	Vehicles	Tons
Alpha beaches	782	744	2,173
Delta beaches	857	1,808	4,247
Camel beaches	1,927	1,026	3,942
Total	3,566	3,578	10,362
Total to Date	147,326	31,734	118,607

OWN AND ENEMY NAVAL LOSSES

Our losses were:

None.

Enemy losses were:

Destroyed:

8 explosive motor boats.

--------------- 27 August 1944 -------------------

WEATHER

Moderate easterly wind was reported in the Tyrrhenian Sea with slight seas and negligible swell. Elsewhere, wind was gently shifting with calm seas. A minimum of clouds with fair visibility prevailed in all areas.

ENEMY FORCES

Navy: A fishing vessel was captured by USS Ericsson with U-boat crew of 46 men and 4 officers aboard who reported that they had tried to escape in a submarine from Toulon, but had grounded on an island off Toulon, and had destroyed the U-boat. She had stood out from Toulon 2000, 17 August to patrol the Toulon-Hyeres area, and although Allied vessels were sighted, no opportunity was given to attack. She was surfaced recharging batteries on the night of August 19/20, when she ran aground on a submerged bank. The two submarine contacts of 18 August and the D/F bearing of 20 August probably applied to this U-boat.

A small boat with 13 men attempting to escape from St. Mandrier was captured by USS MacKenzie of the eastern flank patrol.

At 0230, the PT patrol off Cap Antibes captured a motor boat with three German officers and two men. The motor boat was enroute from Toulon to Genoa.

Photo reconnaissance showed Dardo, Premuda, and S-boat to have returned to Genoa. An EV of 210 feet had changed from inactive to active status since last full cover of August 21. Enemy estimated strength was 2 DD, 4 TB, 3 EV, 1 HAV, 23 MAS, no submarines, and 3 or 4 auxiliaries.

Army: Enemy forces gave some resistance north of Montelimar. The French forces made no contact northwest of Avignon. Enemy prepared to withdraw from Var River Area.

Air : No comment.

OWN FORCES

Navy: NCWTF released USS Omaha, USS Marblehead, and USS Cincinnati from WTF. NCWTF released HMS Suroit (tanker) and HMS Stuart Prince (Fighter Direction Ship) to CinCMed.

CTF 88, Rear Admiral Troubridge, RN, in HMS Royalist, departed with all British carriers, HMS Caledon, and escorts at last light. CTG 88.2, Rear Admiral Durgin, USN in USS Tulagi, remained in command of the US carriers.

At 0800, ComDesRon 10 in USS Ellyson, assumed command of CTU 80.6.10, assault area screen, relieving ComDesRon 18 in USS Frankford.

Army: 1st ABTF crossed the Var River. 335th Engineers, US Army, were ordered to Port du Bouc to open the port. I French Corps began landing over the beaches in St. Tropez area. The French Army B reported that all organized resistance had ceased in Toulon, except for the St. Mandrier Peninsula. It was stated that no future naval fire support was necessary.

The Seventh Army since August 15th had captured 40,211 prisoners.

Air : Air attacks on Ratonneau Island continued with 75 B-26s and 90 B-25s bombing gun installations. Excellent results were obtained. The 324th Wing of the RAF moved inland to Sisteron from Ramatuelle, resulting in a slight decrease in fighter cover over the assault areas.

Carrier planes flew 6 missions with 34 fighter bombers in the Montelimar-Livron area. Two locomotives were damaged and two convoys of army vehicles were attacked. One Hellcat was damaged by flak.

IMPORTANT ORDERS RECEIVED

None.

IMPORTANT ORDERS ISSUED

NCWTF ordered CTF 87 to sail HMS Bardolf, USS Edenshaw, HMS Mindful; CTF 85 to sail HMS Barmond, Barford, and an LCT towing pontoon causeways; CTF 84 to sail HMS Barholm, HMS Empire Spitfire, HMS Empire Anne, USS Tackle, US LCT 16, 6 pontoon causeways, ATR-1, all to report to CTF 86 for opening Port de Bouc.

NCWTF approved reduction of escorts for convoys to fifty percent of the number listed in Op-Plan 4-44 with a limit of two escorts for all convoys. Valuable ships and ships carrying a large number of troops were to be provided additional escorts.

TU 86.5.2, ComDesDiv 32, in USS Boyle with USS Champlin was constituted as destroyer bombarding unit for the right flank.

OPERATIONS

Two convoys, one consisting of 2 LST, 1 APD, and one consisting of 2 LST arrived in the assault area.

A continuous LCVP patrol was set up in the Camel area for protection of ships in the anchorage against one-man torpedo attacks. It was maintained two hundred yards from Isle de Lion de Mer to Isle d'Agay.

At 1200, USS Haines reported a possible sub contact at 40° 39.5' N, 13° 14.5' E. Hedgehog projectiles and depth charges were dropped with no visible results. The ship remained in the vicinity for three hours then rejoined the convoy.

In the morning, HMS Ramillies fired 34 rounds at targets on St. Mandrier, Toulon. Later in the day, two French cruisers concentrated on the battery on Cap Cepet, St. Mandrier, firing 71 rounds. There was no return fire throughout the bombardment.

USS Boyle and USS Champlin covered the advance on the east flank. Ships fired against tanks, coastal defense guns and infantry in the Nice-Cannes area.

USS Murphy operating as a part of the carrier screen picked up three German aviators in a rubber boat at 1016.

At Port de Bouc, the USNLO was established. At 1706, the inner harbor was reported clear for accepting a cargo vessel of 22 feet draft and a tanker of 26 feet draft. US LST 134 with four pontoon causeway platoons of the 1040th Construction Battalion arrived at 1700 for salvage and rehabilitation work. The advanced communication unit was ready to operate at 2030.

Golfe de Fos was reported clear to the four fathom line. A total of 55 mines were detonated. The channel into Port de Bouc was reported clear at 1324. One YMS was ordered as guide into the port for incoming and outgoing vessels. All but two sectors in the assault areas were reported safe. A total of 173 mines were swept.

Unloading figures were:

	Personnel	Vehicles	Tons
Alpha beaches	635	266	3,662
Delta beaches	2,332	1,085	8,167
Camel beaches	167	297	5,404
Total	3,134	1,648	17,233
Total to Date	150,460	33,382	135,840

OWN AND ENEMY NAVAL LOSSES

Our losses were:

None.

Enemy losses were:

Captured:

1 fishing vessel and 2 motor boats, with a total of 68 prisoners.

- - - - - - - - - - - - - - - 28 August 1944 - - - - - - - - - - - - - - - -

WEATHER

Good visibility, partly cloudy skies, gentle winds, and calm seas prevailed throughout the day in all areas.

ENEMY FORCES

    Navy: Photo reconnaissance of Genoa showed that 1 EV of 210 feet and 1 auxiliary had left Genoa arriving at San Remo. Two War Partenope class TB were also in Genoa as was 1 EV. Another EV showed signs of soon changing from inactive to active status. Five minesweeper type vessels were at Villefranche and one at Monaco.

    Army: Enemy forces finally surrendered in Toulon and Marseille. There were 1,800 to 2,000 prisoners including an Admiral taken on St. Mandrier Peninsula. Reports indicated approximately 20,000 prisoners captured in Toulon and Marseille area. Coastal defense guns in the Nice area were turned inland in order to assist in defense of the Var River line. Increased numbers of truck convoys were observed going northward around Valence.

    Air : No comment.

OWN FORCES

    Navy: CTF 86 transferred USS Mackenzie to CTG 80.6. NCWTF released HMS Terpischore and HMS Termagant to CinCMed. NCWTF released USS Quincy from WTF.

    Army: At Toulon, the French Army B reported that all resistance had ceased and the Germans remaining on St. Mandrier surrendered to the French at 1100. At Marseille, the German General agreed to surrender, terms to become effective at 1300.

    The VI Corps advanced on Lyons. French forces moved northward. The First Air Borne Task Force occupied Nice.

    Air : With the surrender of the garrisons at Marseille and Toulon and the reduction of the gun positions on St. Mandrier, air activity in the beachhead areas was reduced to a minimum. Only fighter patrols still functioned, being furnished by 251st Squadron RAF based at Cuers airfield, 18 miles north of Toulon.

    Aircraft of the two US Carriers, USS Tulagi and USS Kasaan Bay, were active west of the River Rhone.

    These carrier aircraft flew 3 fighter-bomber missions of 18 sorties. They destroyed 23 motor trucks and damaged 14. One Hellcat was damaged.

IMPORTANT ORDERS RECEIVED

    None.

IMPORTANT ORDERS ISSUED

    At 0000, due to the lack of any air threat, the new convoy routes numbers 5, 22, and 23 were put into effect by NCWTF for convoys between Oran and the assault area. It was felt that now the convoy lanes could be moved westward from along the Sardinian-Corsican coast line.

    At 1335, NCWTF directed CTF 87 to turn TF 87 over to his Chief of Staff, and return to Naples to assume the duties of ComNavNAW (Adm.), (Commander, Naval Forces, Northwest African Waters, Administrative).

OPERATIONS

One convoy consisting of 10 LST, 2 AO, 1 APD, 2 PC, and one consisting of 2 LST, arrived in the assault area. A convoy consisting of 10 M/T ships, 8 LST, 1 AO, departed from the assault area.

The convoy assembly areas located five miles from Cap Camarat were cancelled. Ships in convoys for Oran were directed to anchor in the Baie of Briande and for Naples in the Baie de Bon Porte.

At 0500, the PT patrol off Cap Ferrat had contact with an unidentified motor boat. The boat was pursued and driven ashore near Villefranche.

LST 134 reported that six prisoners were accepted from a French fighting vessel off Marseille. The prisoners were attempting to escape from the Frioul Islands, when they were picked up by the French vessel.

USS Champlin and USS Boyle fired 11 rounds at targets in the Nice area in support of the ground forces of the east flank. The SFCP reported that the targets were well covered.

The Germans on the Frioul Islands refused to surrender to the French Army. Instead they offered to surrender to the Allied Naval forces. Consequently, a German officer, 2nd in command of the islands, came alongside USS Madison in a small boat to surrender to the Americans. A force of 850 men were stationed on the island. CTF 86 directed USS Madison to accept the surrender in order that the swept channel to Marseille could be completed without any further delay. It was also decided that 90 marines from USS Augusta and USS Philadelphia would go ashore to insure the terms for surrender were carried out. Final details were not completed until the next day.

Two channels were swept into Marseille. The first channel was on a $251°$ bearing from Marseille to the entrance channel of Golfe de Fos. The second channel was on a course $007°$ from position $43° 03'$ N, $05° 16'$ E to one mile off the Isle of Maire then $337°$ to the above channel. Three mines were swept.

Port de Bouc inner harbor was swept and the area was declared safe. There were no mines found.

All LST other than those assigned to the Calvi shuttle were ordered in the future to be unloaded at Delta beaches. The unloading figures were:

	Personnel	Vehicles	Tons
Alpha beaches	0	29	4,004
Delta beaches	457	461	7,882
Camel beaches	18	15	5,881
Total	465	505	17,767
Total to Date	150,935	33,887	153,607

OWN AND ENEMY NAVAL LOSSES

Our losses were:

None.

Enemy losses were:

None.

------------------ 29 August 1944 -----------------------

WEATHER

Haze restricting visibility to four to five miles occurred at daybreak in the assault area. This haze thinned rapidly, increasing visibility to ten miles. The morning was clear; the afternoon partly cloudy. Surface winds were gentle in the morning and became fresh southwesterly in the afternoon but died away rapidly after sunset.

ENEMY FORCES

Navy: During the shelling of Villefranche, 3 minesweeper type vessels were destroyed and 2 others damaged. Photo reconnaissance at Genoa showed that 2 EV of 210 feet had left drydock and might possibly become active soon.

Army: Enemy resistance in the Montelimar area collapsed. Demolitions were heard in the Nice area as the 148th Reserve Infantry Division began to withdraw eastward. A prisoner stated that artillery personnel in the Nimes area had received orders to return to Germany by their own resources.

Air : No comment.

OWN FORCES

Navy: CTG 88.2, in USS Tulagi, with USS Kasaan Bay and DesDiv 34 departed the assault area at last light.

CTG 80.10 relieved CTF 86 of the duties involving the supervision of opening the ports on the southern coast of France.

NCWTF released the following ships to CinCMed: BYMS 2009, 2022, 2026, 2027, 2171, 2172; 24th ML Flotilla composed of ML 259, 299, 337, 451, 456, 461, 478, LCG 4, 8, 12, 14, 20; LCF 4, 8, 10, 14, 16, 17; HMS Whaddon, Belvoir, Crete, Ramillies, Dido.

CTF 86 released USS Kearney to CTG 80.6.

Army: Loriol was defended successfully against counterattacks by the enemy.

The First Air Borne Task Force continued its movement to the east from Nice.

Air : LST 32 with GCI installation, and HMS Ulster Queen, stand-by Fighter Direction ship, were released by the Air Defense Commander.

The carrier aircraft flew their last 2 fighter-bomber missions composed of 8 sorties. One motor truck and one locomotive were destroyed and several were damaged. A reconnaissance was made up the Rhone River to within 10 miles of Lyon. No enemy movements were reported. One Hellcat was damaged.

IMPORTANT ORDERS RECEIVED

None.

IMPORTANT ORDERS ISSUED

None.

OPERATIONS

One convoy consisting of 2 LST and one consisting of 7 LST and 1 DE arrived in the assault area. A convoy consisting of 13 M/T ships, 1 YF, 3 DD departed from the assault area for Oran.

A PT patrol composed of 4 PT was established nightly, until further ordered, from the mouth of the River Var to Cap Ferrat.

At 0800, a German truce mission from the Frioul Islands surrendered unconditionally to the Commanding Officer USS Philadelphia. The 90 Marines, previously assigned, were landed in Frioul harbor which is located between the Isles of Ratonneau and Pomegues. USS Augusta, USS Philadelphia, and USS Madison covered the operation.

FDT 13, a fighter direction ship, arrived off Port de Bouc to assist in control of aircraft operating in the Marseille area.

Port Cros channel was closed due to the presence of shallow mines in the area.

At 0715, sweeping of a channel into the harbor of Toulon began. At the close of the day's sweeping, 33 mines had been detonated. The outer bay, Grande Rade, was swept to the boom at the entrance to the inner harbor. At Marseille, a channel was swept to the eastward of the Frioul Islands to the Isle d'If. Rade Marseille was swept for magnetic and moored mines. Thirteen mines were detonated.

Unloading figures were:

	Personnel	Vehicles	Tons
Alpha beaches	489	48	1,844
Delta beaches	235	495	7,699
Camel beaches	886	336	5,087
Total	1,610	879	14,630
Total to Date	152,545	34,766	168,237

OWN AND ENEMY NAVAL LOSSES

Our losses were:

None.

Enemy losses were:

Destroyed:

3 minesweeper type craft by gunfire.

Damaged:

2 minesweeper type craft by gunfire.

------------- 30 August 1944 ----------------

WEATHER

 Morning winds were light with visibility near six miles. Wind increased slowly from the southwest during the afternoon to become fresh while visibility increased rapidly to above ten miles. Sea was choppy with negligible swell except for near three feet on Alpha beaches. Wind died away to light variable after sunset.

ENEMY FORCES

 Navy: No comment.

 Army: No comment.

 Air : No comment.

OWN FORCES

 Navy: NCWTF released to CinCMed the British 35th Trawler Group composed of HMS Ailsa Craig, Mewstone, Skokholm; HMS Ulster Queen; HMS Bruiser; HMS Thruster; HMS Sirius; HMS Dido; HMS LCT(R) 366, 368, 423, 425, 439, 447, 448, 450, 452, 464, 473, 481, 482, 483; HMS LCI 308, 292.

 NCWTF released USS Tuscaloosa from WTF.

 ComDesDiv 25 in USS Woolsey with USS Edison relieved ComDesDiv 32 in USS Boyle with USS Champlin as CTU 86.5.2.

 Army: The First Air Borne Task Force continued its movement to the east beyond Nice. The movements of Army forces to the north were now pertinent to the naval operations only in the fact that they had advanced more rapidly than had been expected.

 Air : With the departure of Squadron VOF-1 aboard USS Tulagi and Squadron VF-74 aboard USS Kasaan Bay, all US Navy fighter aircraft were withdrawn from the operation.

IMPORTANT ORDERS RECEIVED

 None.

IMPORTANT ORDERS ISSUED

 CTF 86, with the completion of the left flank fire support, reorganized his task force into three main groups. The groups were (1) the control force composed of USS Philadelphia, 1 CL and 3 DD; (2) the Left Flank composed of FS Lorraine, 2 CL, 2 French DD; (3) the Right Flank composed of 2 CL, 1 French DD, 3 US DD.

 The 1st Beach Battalion was detached from CTG 80.2 at 1730 and was directed to report to CTG 80.8 at Marseille.

OPERATIONS

 One convoy consisting of 10 Transports, 4 DE, 1 DD, 2 PC; a second consisting of 14 M/T ships, 4 DE; a third consisting of 2 LST; a fourth consisting of 6 Transports, 3 DD; and a fifth consisting of 22 LST, 19 M/T ships, 1 LCT, 2 APD, 2 PC, 1 DD arrived in the assault area. One return convoy consisting of 12 transports, 1 LSI, 3 DD, and another consisting of 10 M/T ships, 2 LCI, 4 LST, 2 DD departed from the assault area.

After minesweeping in fire support area south of Cap Croisette, channels were reported safe by CTG 80.10. A total of 35 moored mines were swept. The channel eastward of the Frioul Islands to the anchorage in Rade Marseille was completed. LCVP shallow sweepers commenced sweeping in Bassins Joliette and Avant Port Sud. Toulon Bay and the approach channel to the inner harbor were reported safe by CTG 80.10. A total of 65 moored mines was swept. At Port de Bouc, the ship canal to Martigues was swept to the railroad bridge. No mines were swept and further sweeping was obstructed by the bridge which blocked the canal.

Unloading figures were:

	Personnel	Vehicles	Tons
Alpha beaches	8,200	1,273	627
Delta beaches	10,610	768	5,197
Camel beaches	552	255	3,348
Total	19,362	2,296	9,172
Total to Date	171,907	37,062	177,409

OWN AND ENEMY NAVAL LOSSES

Our losses were:

None.

Enemy losses were:

None.

--------------- 31 August 1944 -----------------

WEATHER

The sky was partly cloudy to cloudy with upper clouds. Visibility was generally good. Surface wind was gentle shifting except briefly in forenoon when it became moderate northeasterly. Sea was slight with negligible swell throughout period.

ENEMY FORCES

Navy: Four MAS were attacked by allied coastal forces off Portofino; 1 was reported sunk, 1 damaged. Two MAS were attacked by patrol off Savona; 1 was probably sunk.

Enemy estimated strength was 2 DD, 4 TB, 3 EV, 1 HAV, 20 MAS, and 3 or 4 auxiliaries.

Army: The enemy was withdrawing hastily northward from Valence, and from the area of Southwestern France. Mines and demolitions covered the enemy withdrawal eastward from Nice. Captured documents indicated the LXXV Corps, consisting of the 157th Reserve Division, the 5th Mountain Division, and the 148th Reserve Division were opposing the Seventh Army push to the east into Northern Italy.

Air : No comment.

OWN FORCES

Navy: HMS LCT 307, 380, 420, 554, 578, 620, 556, 561, 615, 548, 339, 412, 421, 535; HMS LCI(L) 133, 247, 251, 278, 280, 294 were released to CinCMed. USS Augusta, and DesDiv 32 composed of USS Boyle, USS Champlin, USS Nields, USS Ordronaux, were released from Western Task Force.

Army: Montpellier and Sete were reported to be in the hands of the French Forces of the Interior (FFI).

CG 7th Army at 2120 considered that there was no further need for gunfire support except that being provided in the Nice-Cannes area.

Air : No comment.

IMPORTANT ORDERS RECEIVED

None.

IMPORTANT ORDERS ISSUED

The PT patrol between Cap Antibes and Cap Ferrat was cancelled. Two PT were directed to patrol nightly between Cap Ferrat and Cap Martin remaining inboard of a line two miles off each cape.

OPERATIONS

One convoy consisting of 8 LST, 2 DD, 1 PC; a second consisting of 2 LCT; and a third consisting of 2 LST, 1 DE arrived in the assault area. A return convoy consisting of 5 M/T ships, 1 DD, 1 DE; a second consisting of 15 LST, 6 LCT, 2 DE; and one of 4 transports, 2 DD departed.

USS Woolsey and USS Ludlow covered the army east flank. USS Woolsey bombarded machine gun and anti-tank guns south of Monaco. An unlocated 88 mm battery returned fire throughout the bombardment.

USS Eberle and PC 1174 were stationed two miles south of the entrance of the mine swept approaches to Marseille, to guide vessels into the harbor.

In Toulon, good progress in sweeping the inner harbor was reported. LCVP shallow water sweepers detonated seven moored mines. Mine spotters using PBYs sighted 30 mines laid in shallow water in Eguillette Roads, Toulon. At Marseille, minesweeping continued in the inner Bassins with no mines reported.

Unloading figures were:

	Personnel	Vehicles	Tons
Alpha beaches	1,187	521	2,656
Delta beaches	10,791	1,131	5,012
Camel beaches	1,021	677	6,154
Total	12,999	2,329	13,722
Total to Date	184,906	39,391	191,231

OWN AND ENEMY NAVAL LOSSES

   Our losses were:

   None.

   Enemy losses were:

   Sunk:

   1 MAS by gunfire.

--------------- 1 September 1944 -----------------

WEATHER

Skies were cloudy in the assault area with upper and intermediate clouds, visibility was good, and winds were light variable increasing to moderate easterly near midnight. Elsewhere in the western Mediterranean, there were clear skies, good visibility, and light variable wind. Seas were calm throughout period in all areas.

ENEMY FORCES

Navy: Photo reconnaissance showed 2 DD and 2 TB at Genoa. One EV had returned to drydock.

Army: The enemy continued his retreat northward in Lyons area.

Air : No comment.

OWN FORCES

Navy: At 2321, the US Naval Detachment at Marseille was established.

Army: The Seventh Army to date had captured 59,931 prisoners.

Air : The Commanding General, 64th Fighter Wing released FDT 13 from duty near Marseille. At this date, all air control ships had been released and full facilities had been set up ashore for both day and night fighter direction.

IMPORTANT ORDERS RECEIVED

CinCMed requested that NCWTF release 12 LCI(L) and 12 LCT in addition to three already released for urgent operations.

IMPORTANT ORDERS ISSUED

NCWTF stated by despatch to CG 7th Army the following (in paraphrased form): "At present, my plan is:

"(A) In order to make as many shore side berths as possible available to shipping in the shortest practicable time, to clear the approaches to and Marseille harbor;

"(B) Concurrently with (A) above, to divert such personnel and equipment under my command, which cannot be gainfully and efficiently used in

Marseille, to clear the approaches to and Toulon harbor; and, during the time Army Engineers are not available, to clear the shore side berths as practicable;

"(C) And using my resources to open the Arles canal, clear the approach to Port de Bouc and the harbor thereat.

" Experience in this theater has shown that beach maintenance after mid-September is inadequate, and that it is essential to have protected ports available to insure adequate facilities to supply advancing armies.

"In order to accomplish the above:

"(A) Seabee personnel have been placed at Toulon and Port de Bouc;

" (B) All personnel and salvage equipment under my command are being brought up;

"(C) Such personnel and salvage equipment that can be employed gainfully in Marseille have been allocated to that port;

"(D) That additional equipment that cannot be used in (C) above has been temporarily allocated to Port de Bouc and Toulon;

"(E) The work of the Seabees will continue in Toulon and will be augmented by Army Engineers when rehabilitation work of the Army in Marseille on shore exceeds that of the Salvage Forces of the Navy afloat when the said Army Engineers will be diverted to help in the shoreside work at Toulon;

"(F) When the work of the Army Engineers in the rehabilitation of Marseille on shore falls behind the Navy Salvage afloat, Seabees will be diverted to Marseille to assist in the shoreside reclamation in that port.

"Mine disposal and salvage units of the Seabees will be employed in the removal of wrecked bridges, mines, and obstacles from the Arles Canal, with the objective of making this canal available to the other services for the use of small craft."

NCWTF directed CTG 80.6 that all available LST except those frozen in Ajaccio, Calvi, and Oran movements were to be diverted to Naples for inclusion in Naples LST movements commencing with the convoy from Naples scheduled for 4 September, in order to increase rate of build-up of the Seventh Army.

OPERATIONS

A convoy consisting of 5 LST, 1 DE arrived in the assault area. A return convoy consisting of 9 LST, 2 DE departed from the assault area.

USS Woolsey and USS Edison fired 384 rounds at batteries, strong points, troop movements in the Cap Martin and Monaco area. Good results were reported on all targets. Return fire was directed against both ships and spotting planes.

The seaward entrance of the channel to Port de Bouc was closed temporarily. Consequently, all traffic for the port was routed through the approach channel to Marseille, thence to Port de Bouc along the channel connecting the two ports.

A French tanker, Dauphine, two tugs and two barges were removed from the channel into Port de Bouc. The channel was then clear of all obstructions.

At Marseille, four magnetic mines were detonated in Avant Port Sud and Bassin Joliette.

At Toulon, YMS 21 was sunk by a moored mine in Eguillette Roads, inner harbor. Three additional magnetic mines were swept in Eguillette Roads.

LCMs began a 24 hour ferry service across the Rhone River at Arles and Vallabregues for transporting troops and equipment of the French Army B, the Seventh Army, and FFI forces.

Unloading figures were:

	Personnel	Vehicles	Tons
Alpha beaches	707	412	3,518
Delta beaches	2,998	978	3,497
Camel beaches	548	195	5,840
Total	4,253	1,585	12,855
Total to Date	189,159	40,976	204,086

OWN AND ENEMY NAVAL LOSSES

Our losses were:

Sunk:

US YMS 21 by underwater explosion.

Damaged:

None.

Enemy losses were:

None.

--------------- 2 September 1944 -------------------

WEATHER

In the assault area, skies were cloudy to overcast with general showers and thundershowers during the afternoon. A cold front entered the Gulf of Lions at about 1800 moving easterly at near 25 knots. Ahead of the cold front, winds were fresh northeasterly. Skies cleared at frontal passage and wind shifted to northwest 20 to 25 knots. Five hours after frontal passage wind increased suddenly to 40 to 50 knots with gusts to 66 knots. Offshore seas rapidly became heavy with swell of ten feet developing. On the assault beaches the short fetch prevented any development of material swell and seas were only moderate.

In other areas, sky was clear with good visibility and gentle southerly wind. Sea and swell were negligible.

ENEMY FORCE

Navy: No comment.

Army: No comment.

Air : No comment.

OWN FORCES

Navy: NCWTF released the following British ships to CinCMed: HMS Lookout, Zetland, Calm, Hailstorm, Kintyre, Nebb, Sahra, Satsa, Antares, Arcturus, Aries, Brixham, Bude, Polruan, Rhyl, Rinaldo, Rosario, Rothesay, Skokholm, Stornoway, Waterwitch, LCT 615.

NCWTF released US DesDiv 31 consisting of the USS Parker, USS MacKenzie, USS McLanahan, and USS Kendrick from WTF.

Army: Since D-day the Seventh Army had captured 61,716 prisoners.

Air : With the transfer from the coastal airfields of the 111th Tactical Reconnaissance Squadron to Valence and the 225th Tactical Reconnaissance Squadron to Sisteron, only one spotting mission per day was available for the eastern flank operations.

IMPORTANT ORDERS RECEIVED

None.

IMPORTANT ORDERS ISSUED

None.

OPERATIONS

A convoy consisting of 10 M/T ships, 6 LST, 4 LCT, 3 APD departed the assault area.

In the Saint Andre, Tubie, and Monaco area, USS Woolsey and USS Edison fired at targets comprising guns, mortars, troops, and tanks. The area was reported well covered.

At Marseille, one British and one French submarine arrived. These submarines were intended to furnish power for the army engineers in the port. One British LCM was mined at 2300 off the entrance to Vieux Port.

NCWTF in USS Plunkett departed the assault area to make an inspection of Port de Bouc, Marseille, and Toulon.

Unloading figures were:

	Personnel	Vehicles	Tons
Alpha beaches	0	0	3,855
Delta beaches	1,392	558	5,501
Camel beaches	14	0	5,690
Port de Bouc	0	0	73
Total	1,406	558	15,119
Total to Date	190,565	41,534	219,205

OWN AND ENEMY NAVAL LOSSES

Our losses were:

Sunk:

One HM LCM(3) by mine.

Damaged:

HMS Empire Ann by underwater obstacle.

Enemy losses were:

None.

- - - - - - - - - - - - - - 3 September 1944 - - - - - - - - - - - - - - - -

WEATHER

The cold front which moved over assault area on 2 September passed beyond Italy by midafternoon producing brief thundershowers at passage, rapid clearing afterwards, and shifting wind from fresh southerly to fresh westerly in the Tyrrhenian Sea. In the assault area, sky was clear throughout the day with storm winds in the morning subsiding gradually to 20 knots by midnight. Seas in the Gulf of Lions, Ligurian Sea and Corsican-Sardinian area were heavy with swell of 16 feet. Visibility was extraordinarily good, exceeding one hundred miles. Along the North African coast, there were cloudy skies, good visibility and moderate westerly winds with negligible sea and swell.

ENEMY FORCES

Navy: Enemy strength and disposition estimate based on photo reconnaissance was as follows:

	DD	TB	EV	HAV	MAS	AUXILIARIES
Genoa	2	3	1			
Spezia	Cover not complete.					
Savona				1		
San Remo						1
Unlocated			2		20	
Total	2	3	3	1	20	1

An Orsa type TB was believed to be dismantling at Genoa. Six submarines remained at inactive berths at Genoa. Only one auxiliary, an EV of 230 feet, was seen since August 22, and it was believed that all others were scuttled or sunk by naval gunfire when the French ports were taken. The DD Squadrista was believed to be nearly ready.

Army: No comment.

Air : No comment.

OWN FORCES

Navy: NCWTF released the following British craft to CinCMed: LCT 496, 535, 561, 344, 396; ML 555, 556, 559, 560, 566, 567, 568.

Army: No comment.

Air : Coastal airfields at Frejus, St. Raphael, Le Luc, and Ramatuelle were abandoned leaving only the 251st Spitfire Wing at Cuers for day fighter protection. Night fighter cover was furnished by MACAF.

IMPORTANT ORDERS RECEIVED

None.

IMPORTANT ORDERS ISSUED

NCWTF directed CTF 84 to release ships and craft assigned to CTG 84.9 to CTF 80 in order to organize a new salvage group.

OPERATIONS

A convoy consisting of 8 LST, 4 M/T ships, 1 APD, 2 PC arrived.

The PT patrol between Cap Ferrat and Cap Martin was cancelled due to weather conditions.

USS Philadelphia, USS Ludlow, and USS Woolsey in support of the army right flank, fired 16 rounds at troop movements in the Monaco area. Good results were reported.

In Toulon, French Engineers detonated three mines of the controlled minefield at the harbor entrance. The remaining seventy-two mines believed left in the field were to be detonated as soon as possible. The harbor area west of 172° bearing from pier 6 was considered unsafe due to mines. In Eguillette Roads, Toulon, three additional mines were detonated. In Marseille, Avant Port Sud was reported reasonably safe.

Unloading was reduced because of heavy surf on the beaches. Camel Green beach, 264B was closed. All Navy beach battalions were to remain on the beaches while maintenance continued over beaches.

Unloading figures were:

	Personnel	Vehicles	Tons
Alpha beaches	0	0	674
Delta beaches	0	111	4,768
Camel beaches	1	0	3,723
Port de Bouc	0	0	1,031
Marseille	0	0	856
Total	1	111	11,052
Total to Date	190,566	41,645	230,257

OWN AND ENEMY NAVAL LOSSES

Our losses were:

Sunk:

One US LCVP and one HM LCM(3) by storm.

Damaged:

US SC 535, 693; three US LCVP, and four HM LCM(3) by storm.

Enemy losses were:

None.

--------------- 4 September 1944 ------------------

WEATHER

Clear skies, excellent visibility and gentle variable winds prevailed over all areas except the Tyrrhenian Sea where wind was fresh northwesterly with moderate sea in the morning diminishing to gentle westerly, with slight sea, by the end of the period.

ENEMY FORCES

Navy: Genoa was subjected to air raid, which destroyed 1 active War Partenope TB, 5 out of the six inactive submarines, sank 3 and damaged a 4th EV, and sank the DD, Squadrista, thereby removing the threat of adding a DD and at least 2 EV to the enemy fleet. The submarine threat in the Mediterranean was now considered negligible. Although the possibility still existed of midget subs, no use had been made to date and none was seen by photo reconnaissance.

Enemy estimated strength was 2 DD, 2 TB, 3 EV, 1 HAV, 20 MAS, and 1 auxiliary.

Army: No comment.

Air : No comment.

OWN FORCES

Navy: NCWTF released the following British ships and craft to CinCMed: HMS Foula, ML 121, 338, 462, 554, 557, 564, 565, 575.

Task Group 80.11, Salvage Group, was established. This group consisted of all salvage forces less those required at the assault beaches. The primary task of this group was the opening of the ports.

Army: The First Air Borne Task Force was still operating east of Nice, attempting to enter Monaco against determined resistance. Lyons was occupied by the French 1st Division Blindee and the FFI.

Air : No comment.

IMPORTANT ORDERS RECEIVED

None.

IMPORTANT ORDERS ISSUED

NCWTF directed CTG 80.6 to release all British destroyers and other British escort craft by 15 September.

NCWTF informed CinCMed of his intentions regarding minesweeping of approaches, channels, harbors, and anchorages of Southern France. The intentions were with US minesweeping forces to maintain swept channels in Alpha, Delta, Camel, and Sitka as long as required by the army; and in Toulon, Marseille, Port de Bouc, Nice, and, as a refuge anchorage, the Rade d'Hyeres. NCWTF further requested that all available French Minesweepers in North Africa be sailed to the Western Task Force for minesweeping in, according to priority, (1) Golfe de Juan, (2) Baie de Ciotat, (3) Golfe de la Napoule, and (4) Golfe de Giens.

OPERATIONS

Four convoys, one consisting of 23 M/T ships, 1 DD, 1 DE, 1 PC; one consisting of 11 M/T ships, 2 DE; one consisting of 7 transports, 3 DD; and, one consisting of 50 LCI, 1 AF, 1 DD, 2 PC, arrived in the assault area. Two convoys, one consisting of 7 transports, 2 DD; and, one consisting of 10 M/T ships, 3 DE, departed the assault area. Craft in convoys from Ajaccio to the assault area and Calvi were frozen in that assignment. Ships in convoys from Oran to the assault area were to continue that assignment but additions were to be made to replace those released and to increase the number in accordance with the plan. The convoys from Naples to the assault area were to be composed of all LST available, after the above scheduled movements were provided for.

USS Ludlow fired 366 rounds at troop and vehicle movements in the St. Agnes area.

USS Tackle was mined while shifting berth in Port de Bouc. All ship movements in this area were suspended until 0800B, 5 September. A thorough sweep was begun in the harbor.

At Marseille, 12 magnetic mines were detonated in Vieux Port. Two mines were sunk near the north end of the outer mole.

At Toulon, three mines were cut and sunk in Eguillette Roads. A two mile swept channel from the Camel beaches to 43° 39' N, 07° 16' E off Nice was completed and reported safe.

Unloading figures were:

	Personnel	Vehicles	Tons
Alpha beaches	5,156	806	604
Delta beaches	1,820	393	4,550
Camel beaches	1,276	518	2,457
Port de Bouc	0	0	289
Marseille	0	51	202
Toulon	5	5	30
Total	8,257	1,773	8,132
Total to Date	198,823	43,418	238,389

OWN AND ENEMY NAVAL LOSSES

Our losses were:

Sunk:

None.

- 98 -

Damaged:

    USS Tackle (ARS 37) by mine.

Enemy losses were:

Destroyed:

    1 TB, 5 inactive submarines, 3 EV, and 1 DD by bombing at Genoa.

Damaged:

    1 EV by bombing at Genoa.

---------------- 5 September 1944 ------------------

WEATHER

Gentle winds continued in all areas with negligible sea and swell and good visibility but sky was cloudy with high thin clouds.

ENEMY FORCES

    Navy: A human torpedo attack was launched from direction of Menton at the USS Ludlow and FS Malin. The destroyers frustrated the attack by opening fire and dropping depth charges. No vessels were damaged, and 3 human torpedoes were sunk; 3 survivors were recovered by USS Ludlow.

    Army: No comment.

    Air : No comment.

OWN FORCES

    Navy: NCWTF released HMS Lauderdale, Pindos, FS Le Terrible, Le Fantasque to CinCMed.

    CTU 80.6.4 was constituted. It was composed of USS Niblack, USS Gleaves, USS Benson, USS Eberle, PC 1168, 1173, 1174, 1597, and acted as local escort and provided offshore protection for the approaches to Toulon and Marseille. CTG 80.6 was relieved of the duty of assault escort and convoy shipping control by CDS 10, CTU 80.6.7 in the USS Jouett, at 1200. CTU 80.6.10, the assault area screen commander, was relieved. CTU 80.6.7 assumed the duties of the assault area screen.

    In order to speed up the phased troop lift, preparations were made to employ the LST to their maximum capacity. It was estimated that to accomplish this, the turn around time of LSTs could be cut to eight days from Naples, twelve days from Oran, three days from Ajaccio. Starting with SM-7, it was estimated that between 24 and 26 LST would be in the Naples ferry service. They were to remain on the Naples run, until the build-up from that port was completed. The Oran ferry would have about 25 to 27 LST in service, until about D plus 37. At that time, the 10 LST from the Calvi shuttle would join the Oran ferry. The remainder of the convoy program remained unchanged.

    Naval activities at Propriano closed.

Army: The 1st ABTF held a line Utele-Sospel-Monaco.

Air : 325th Fighter Control Squadron of MACAF relieved 64th Fighter Wing of XII TAC of responsibility of air raid warning and protection from air attack of harbors and shipping in Southern France in area east of 05° 30' E Longitude. The 64th Fighter Wing of XII TAC remained responsible for the area west of that meridian.

IMPORTANT ORDERS RECEIVED

None.

IMPORTANT ORDERS ISSUED

NCWTF approved use of only 2 escorts for escort of M/T ship and craft convoys.

OPERATIONS

Three convoys, one consisting of 10 LST, 2 DE; one consisting of 48 LCI, 2 DD, 2 Corvettes; and one consisting of 8 M/T ships, 9 LST, 1 DD, 1 DE departed from the assault area.

FS Montcalm fired 443 rounds on troop movements between Monte Carlo and Sospel. USS Ludlow fired against coastal batteries from Monte Carlo to Menton. FS Malin fired 103 rounds against concrete emplacements north of Sospel. Coastal batteries returned fire intermittently throughout the day.

At Toulon, the first Liberty ship was berthed and readied for unloading. The shore-side rehabilitation party reported that piers and docks had been cleared for berthing 8 Liberties.

The harbor of Port de Bouc was reopened at 0800, after a day's sweeping with no mines reported. The first Liberty ship was berthed alongside Quai de la Caronte. An additional berth was reported available.

A sand bar was formed off Delta Beach 262 caused by the storm. Blasting proved ineffective; LSTs were still able to use the beach, however.

Minesweepers in Toulon swept four mines in Eguillette Roads. French Engineers set off six mines of eighty-four believed present in the controlled minefield across the harbor entrance. In Vieux Port, Marseille, one magnetic mine was detonated by LCVP (M/S). In the harbor of Nice, two mines were exploded and one was rendered safe. The entire harbor was swept for magnetic and acoustic type mines. The controlled minefield which consisted of twelve mines across the harbor entrance was eliminated. Eleven were detonated and one was found to be a dud.

Unloading figures were:

	Personnel	Vehicles	Tons(Dry)
Alpha beaches	880	672	1,402
Delta beaches	9,694	412	2,661
Camel beaches	1,397	1,179	4,356
Port de Bouc	0	0	70
Marseille	0	160	615
Toulon	0	0	105
Total	11,971	2,423	9,209
Total to Date	210,794	45,841	247,598

OWN AND ENEMY NAVAL LOSSES

Our losses were:

None.

Enemy losses were:

Sunk:

3 human torpedoes.

Damaged:

None.

- - - - - - - - - - - - - - 6 September 1944 - - - - - - - - - - - - - - - -

WEATHER

Broken to overcast skies covered the western Mediterranean with continuous rain, low ceilings, poor visibility and fresh to strong northeasterly wind generating surf of 5 to 7 feet in the assault area. Winds in other areas were moderate southerly with slight seas and swell of three feet.

ENEMY FORCES

Navy: No comment.

Army: No comment.

Air : No comment.

OWN FORCES

Navy: No comment.

Army: No comment.

Air : MACAF provided Marauders (B-26s) to search for human torpedoes in Menton area.

IMPORTANT ORDERS RECEIVED

None.

IMPORTANT ORDERS ISSUED

NCWTF issued to all Task Force Commanders the plan for the closing of the Alpha beaches. It provided as follows:

(a) TF 87 was to be dissolved and CTF 87 with staff was to return to Naples in USS Bayfield;

(b) CTF 85 was to take command of Delta and Camel beaches. The task groups and units reorganized by CTF 87 as necessary were to remain in the area for the continuance of the beach maintenance;

(c) CTF 84 was to return to Bizerte in USS Duane;

(d) CTU 80.6.7 was to form a new screen to protect Delta and Camel beaches;

(e) CTG 80.10 was to reassign the minesweepers as necessary to maintain the assault areas.

OPERATIONS

A convoy consisting of 2 LST and 1 DE arrived in the assault area.

CTF 86 established a schedule for ready and standby cruisers and escort destroyers on the right flank.

Two SOC (cruiser planes) patrolled off Menton from 0530 to 1130 to report any attempted attacks by human torpedo on gunfire support ships.

The PT patrol for today between Cap Ferrat and Cap Martin was cancelled due to weather.

Sweeping in Toulon continued and an additional mine was swept in Eguillette Roads. The channel of Port Cros was declared safe. A total of five mines were sunk.

The entrance channel on a bearing $251°$ from Marseille was widened to three miles.

In Nice, the channel to the harbor entrance was declared safe. Sweeping continued in the harbor.

Alpha and Delta beaches were forced to suspend operations about 1800 due to storm conditions.

At Toulon, the first liberty ship began unloading, and a second berth was made available west of pier 5. Additional space was also available for unloading 3 LST and 5 LCT. At Marseille, the 1040th C.B. unit reported with 4 causeways to be used for off-loading. At Port de Bouc, directions were issued that no liberty ships with draft exceeding 22 feet should enter. The SS John Hopkins had grounded temporarily on a sand bar alongside Quai de la Leque in the inner harbor.

Unloading figures were:

	Personnel	Vehicles	Tons
Alpha beaches	126	160	2,911
Delta beaches	1,361	531	2,999
Camel beaches	214	273	3,623
Port de Bouc	0	0	697
Marseille	0	204	793
Toulon	0	0	900
Total	1,701	1,168	11,923
Total to Date	212,495	47,009	259,521

OWN AND ENEMY NAVAL LOSSES

Our losses were:

None.

Enemy losses were:

None.

--------------- 7 September 1944 -----------------

WEATHER

A weak cold front passed across the assault area during the day, entering western part of Gulf of Lions early in the period and moving easterly at about 15 knots. In advance of the front, there was light intermittent rain, fresh easterly wind and a surf of 5 to 7 feet. Wind shifted to moderate westerly at frontal passage and slowly freshened to 18 to 20 knots. Swell on assault beaches diminished to one foot at time of arrival of the front while moderate sea developed offshore with low swell from west. Over convoy routes, sky was overcast with good visibility, moderate southerly wind and slight seas.

ENEMY FORCES

Navy: USS Madison and USS Hilary P. Jones reported attacks by explosive boats, 2 of which were sunk. These were guided by a control boat which escaped. PTs on flank patrol claimed 4 and probably 5 explosive boats sunk.

Army: No comment.

Air : No comment.

OWN FORCES

Navy: NCWTF released HMS Aldenham, Aubretia, Columbine, and FS Quercy to CinCMed.

Army: 1st ABTF maintained contact in Nice area. Armies to north were operating in area of Lyon-Besancon.

Air : No comment.

IMPORTANT ORDERS RECEIVED

   None.

IMPORTANT ORDERS ISSUED

   None.

OPERATIONS

   The gunfire support destroyers were attacked five miles south of Cap Ampeglio by explosive boats from 2350 to 0110, 8 September. USS Madison and USS Hilary P. Jones each sighted and avoided one explosive boat.

   FS Emile Bertin fired 114 rounds at vehicle and troop concentrations west of Sospel. One direct hit was also obtained on a pillbox at Castillon. USS Ludlow fired 179 rounds at troop concentrations in the same area. Both ships used SFCP and excellent results were reported.

   Fourteen LCM from USS Arcturus and USS Procyon returned from Arles to Port de Bouc. These craft, which arrived at Arles, 1 September, were used to ferry troops of French Army B, US Seventh Army, and FFI across the Rhone River. Task was completed and craft returned to the assault area in HMS Highway.

   At Toulon, the controlled minefield was rendered safe. Six mines were detonated and 36 were found to be duds. The field consisted of 84 mines with two connected to each lead. At Marseille, minesweepers detonated three magnetic mines in Vieux Port and one in Bassins Avant Port Nord and Joliette. At Nice, three magnetic mines were swept in the inner harbor.

   Unloading figures were:

	Personnel	Vehicles	Tons
Alpha beaches	0	0	873
Delta beaches	197	62	1,484
Camel beaches	329	100	3,961
Port de Bouc	0	0	810
Marseille	0	99	761
Toulon	200	0	1,020
Total	726	261	8,909
Total to Date	213,221	47,270	268,430

OWN AND ENEMY NAVAL LOSSES

   Our losses were:

   None.

   Enemy losses were:

   Sunk:

      6, possibly 7, explosive boats.

---------------- 8 September 1944 -----------------

WEATHER

Cloudy skies with high cloud forms covered western Mediterranean clearing near the end of the period. Visibility was uniformly good. Surface winds were strong north-westerly and westerly in the assault area generating eight feet of swell offshore and choppy seas with two feet of swell in unloading areas. Winds in the Tyrrhenian Sea were fresh westerly with moderate seas and swell of four feet.

ENEMY FORCES

Navy: No comment.

Army: No comment.

Air : No comment.

OWN FORCES

Navy: No comment.

Army: No comment.

Air : With the practical elimination of the probability of large or even medium scale hostile air attack, MACAF reduced the daily fighter protection for the assault area from dawn to dusk to one section of 2 aircraft in continual state of readiness at a nearby airfield. A dusk patrol of two aircraft airborne was also maintained. Night fighter cover of one aircraft was provided from 2030 each night to the following dawn.

IMPORTANT ORDERS RECEIVED

None.

IMPORTANT ORDERS ISSUED

NCWTF ordered Alpha beaches closed on 9 September. He further put into effect the plan for redistribution of the Western Task Force such that a sufficient force was retained under CTF 85 for maintenance of Delta and Camel beaches and the remaining forces were directed to the ports opened in Southern France for maintenance and build-up of the US Seventh Army and the French Army B.

OPERATIONS

A nightly PT patrol was established within three miles from shore covering the area from Cap Martin to Bordighera to repel raids by small craft. The PT patrol from Cap Ferrat to Cap Martin was ordered to patrol until 0900 each day, principally screening against human torpedo attacks.

FS Duguay Trouin fired 457 rounds at batteries, troops, and pillboxes in the Sospel area. USS Hilary P. Jones fired 44 rounds against machine gun nest in the same area.

At Marseille, the final phase of minesweeping prior to opening Port Vieux was completed. Two mines were detonated in Bassin Marechal Petain.

At Toulon, two mines were destroyed in La Seyne area. Two additional liberty berths were made available; one west pier 5; one east pier 5.

Unloading figures were:

	Personnel	Vehicles	Tons
Alpha beaches	0	0	926
Delta beaches	0	22	3,618
Camel beaches	50	0	4,128
Port de Bouc	0	0	1,014
Marseille	0	142	788
Toulon	181	0	1,050
Total	231	164	11,524
Total to Date	213,452	47,434	279,954

OWN AND ENEMY NAVAL LOSSES

Our losses were:

None.

Enemy losses were:

None.

--------------- 9 September 1944 ----------------

WEATHER

Strong westerly winds continued throughout the day along south coast of France with rough sea and swell of six feet while wind was moderate along Riviera and remainder of western Mediterranean with slight seas and swell of four feet. Sky was partly cloudy and visibility was excellent in all areas.

ENEMY FORCES

Navy: Photo reconnaissance showed 2 DD, 2 TB, 2 EV at Genoa and 1 HAV and 2 auxiliaries at Spezia.

Army: No comment.

Air : No comment.

OWN FORCES

Navy: NCWTF released FS Barfleur to CinCMed.

Army: The Seventh Army to date had captured 68,584 prisoners.

Air : XII TAC established advance HQ at Amberieu, about 30 miles northeast of Lyon.

Terminal in assault area for naval air transportation and mail from Naples, and for mine spotting aircraft from Ajaccio was moved from Ramatuelle airfield near St. Tropez to Cuers airfield near Toulon.

IMPORTANT ORDERS RECEIVED

None.

IMPORTANT ORDERS ISSUED

None.

OPERATIONS

Six convoys, one consisting of 30 LCI, 3 DE; one consisting of 14 M/T ships, 25 LST, 2 DD, 1 DE; one consisting of 6 LST, 2 DE; one consisting of 6 Transports, 3 DD; one consisting of 6 Transports, 3 DD; and one consisting of 20 M/T ships, 22 LST, 1 DD, 2 DE, arrived in the assault area. Two convoys, one consisting of 30 LCI, 1 DE, 1 Corvette; and one consisting of 12 Transports, 6 DD, departed the assault area.

The destroyer screen in the assault area was reestablished as follows: "E" line was on bearing 000° for fifteen miles from point EW (43°09'N, 06°51'E). "W" line was on bearing 268° from EW. Patrol line "H" was cancelled. Patrol line "I" was moved near the coast east of "E" line as a picket patrol against human torpedoes and E-boats.

USS Hilary P. Jones, firing 724 rounds, aided in successfully breaking up a counter-attack by enemy troops and tanks in the Castillon area. Troops were dispersed and some tanks destroyed. The second counter-attack occurred in the Bellenda area with USS Hilary P. Jones firing 330 and USS Madison 64 rounds. SFCP reported that many troops were killed and the remaining dispersed. At various periods of the day, harassing fire was delivered against flak wagons, machine gun nests and mortars in the Castillon area where USS Hilary P. Jones fired 227 rounds; in the Bellenda area where USS Hilary P. Jones fired 109 rounds and USS Madison 64 rounds.

Covering minesweeping in the fire support area off Menton, FS Duguay Trouin fired 85 rounds at light batteries at Bordighera.

At Toulon, two mines were destroyed in the La Seyne area. At Marseille, four contact mines were cut in the vicinity of the north mole. Magnetic sweeping of Vieux Port continued with negative results. In Bassin Marechal Petain, shallow sweeping commenced and twelve contact mines were destroyed. The opening in the north block was reported to be 200 feet wide and at least 23 feet deep. Within the opening, a channel 120 feet wide and 26 feet deep was available. At Menton, the fire support channel was swept from one mile south of Menton and extended five miles eastward. At Nice, the inner harbor was reported safe. A remaining ground mine was fired at 1100.

NCWTF in USS Catoctin proceeded to Toulon. The ship was moored in the inner harbor.

Alpha beaches closed at 1200. The total unloading figures over the Alpha beaches were 81,573 personnel, 15,675 vehicles, and 67,353 tons of cargo.

Unloading figures were:

	Personnel	Vehicles	Tons(Dry)	Barrels(Wet)
Alpha beaches	0	0	250	0
Delta beaches	12,275	873	1,167	0
Camel beaches	0	0	2,964	0
Port de Bouc	0	0	1,324	5,000
Marseille	0	142	1,219	0
Toulon	134	19	1,150	0
Total	12,409	1,034	8,074	5,000
Total to Date	225,861	48,468	288,028	5,000

OWN AND ENEMY NAVAL LOSSES

Our losses were:

None.

Enemy losses were:

None.

---------------- 10 September 1944 -----------------

WEATHER

The entire day was fair being partly cloudy with gentle variable wind, good visibility, and negligible sea and surf throughout all areas.

ENEMY FORCES

Navy: Attacks by human torpedoes were reported on the eastern flank lasting from daylight to shortly after noon, resulting in no damage to US ships and the sinking of 10, possibly 11 human torpedoes. These enemy attacks were made from the beaches of St. Martin and Ventimiglia in two groups of six human torpedoes. Three survivors were captured by US ships, and 3 others captured ashore by the Army.

At 0230, the PT patrol encountered one control boat and two explosive boats off Ventimiglia. One drone boat exploded and the control boat was driven to the beach.

Army: No comment.

Air : No comment.

OWN FORCES

Navy: No comment.

Army: Elements of French Army B made contact with US Third Army, 45 miles northwest of Dijon. To date the Seventh Army had captured 69,562 prisoners.

Air : Amphibious Catalinas, PBY-5As of French Squadrons VFP-1 and VFP-2 based in Corsica, used Cuers as a forward base for daily mine spotting missions. The area they covered extended from Nice to Agde, including harbors and their adjacent waters to the 100 fathom line.

Wellingtons and Venturas of MACAF provided daily patrol search for human torpedoes near Ventimiglia and Menton.

IMPORTANT ORDERS RECEIVED

None.

IMPORTANT ORDERS ISSUED

None.

OPERATIONS

A convoy consisting of 11 M/T ships, 25 LST, 2 escorts, departed assault area. The scheduled turn-around time for LSTs in convoys from Oran to assault area was reduced to ten days.

At 0800, a patrol of 2 DD and 2 PC was established to cover the coastal routes from the assault area to Toulon and Marseille.

USS Madison, USS Woolsey, minesweepers, PTs, and SOC planes from 0718 to 1247 engaged human torpedoes in the vicinity of Cap Martin and Capo Morto'a, expending 478 rounds of three inch caliber ammunition and 2386 rounds of close range AA ammunition.

USS Madison, USS Woolsey, and USS Ludlow fired 819 rounds at troop concentrations in the Bellenda area and east to Capo Ampeglio.

CTF 84 in USS Duane departed assault area for Naples at 2400. The ships of TF 84 were reassigned to other forces.

At Marseille, the area off the north end of the mole was swept to a depth of 120 feet. Two contact mines were destroyed. LCVP shallow sweepers in Bassin Marechal Petain detonated four contact mines. The final check sweep was made in Avant Port Sud. In Bassin Joliette, one mine was blown. Vieux Port opened with space available for 21 LCT. At Toulon, one magnetic mine was detonated in the La Seyne area. At Rade d'Hyeres, the sweeping of the anchorage commenced. USS Seer was damaged in Grande Passe (Isles d'Hyeres) by a mine which exploded off the port bow. One dead and twenty-one injured were reported. The sweeping of QB 353 between Port Cros and Porquerolles was cancelled.

Off Menton, sweeping was interrupted by enemy shore batteries and human torpedo attacks. The minesweeping ships lost two sets of magnetic sweeping gear and three sets were damaged by the enemy batteries. Following the attacks minesweeping continued while DDs rendered support.

Unloading figures were:

	Personnel	Vehicles	Tons(Dry)	Barrels(Wet)
Delta beaches	7,271	2,336	3,704	0
Camel beaches	3,046	1,321	5,546	0
Port de Bouc	0	0	1,367	5,000
Marseille	750	60	987	0
Toulon	0	0	975	0
Total	11,067	3,717	12,579	5,000
Total to Date	236,928	52,185	300,607	10,000

OWN AND ENEMY NAVAL LOSSES

Our losses were:

Sunk:

None.

Damaged:

US LCC 98; HM BYMS 2022 by mines.

Enemy losses were:

Sunk:

2 Corvettes by gunfire with 211 prisoners captured.

Destroyed:

2 explosive boats.

Damaged:

None.

--------------- 11 September 1944 ----------------

WEATHER

Fine conditions existed throughout period in all parts of western Mediterranean. Skies were clear, visibility good, wind gentle shifting, and seas calm.

ENEMY FORCES

Navy: No comment.

Army: No comment.

Air : No comment.

OWN FORCES

Navy: No comment.

Army: First Air Borne Task Force operated in vicinity of Menton and Tete de la Lavina.

Air : Aircraft of USS Philadelphia and USS Brooklyn provided continuous A/S patrol for FS Lorraine during bombardment on eastern flank.

IMPORTANT ORDERS RECEIVED

None.

IMPORTANT ORDERS ISSUED

None.

OPERATIONS

A convoy consisting of 5 LST, 2 DE departed the assault area.

In support of the 1st ABTF, USS Madison firing 30 rounds and USS Ludlow 261 rounds broke up a counter-attack in the Bellenda area. USS Woolsey fired 419 rounds, USS Ludlow 407 rounds, FS Malin 34 rounds at batteries, troops, strong points, and the human torpedo launching base at Ventimiglia. FS Lorraine fired 58 rounds at fortifications near Castillon with four hits reported by air spot.

At Toulon, in the dangerous area in La Seyne Bay, two mines were sunk. A total of thirty-seven mines had been sunk in this area. One magnetic and sixteen moored mines were swept in the northern sector of the Rade Marseille. In Rade d'Hyeres, sweeping of the anchorage continued.

Unloading figures were:

	Personnel	Vehicles	Tons(Dry)	Barrels(Wet)
Delta beaches	6,645	0	3,980	0
Camel beaches	347	476	3,238	0
Port de Bouc	0	0	1,227	10,000
Marseille	454	263	3,269	0
Toulon	0	0	850	0
Total	7,446	739	12,564	10,000
Total to Date	244,374	52,924	313,171	20,000

OWN AND ENEMY NAVAL LOSSES

Our losses were:

None.

Enemy losses were:

None.

--------------- 12 September 1944 ----------------

WEATHER

Gentle easterly wind during the day became moderate easterly near midnight. Mostly clear skies, good visibility, and calm seas continued throughout the period.

ENEMY FORCES

Navy: No comment.

Army: No comment.

Air : No comment.

OWN FORCES

Navy: The 8th US Navy Beach Battalion reported for duty at Marseille for supervision of craft unloading at hards and landing points.

Army: The First Air Borne Task Force repelled an enemy counter-attack in the Menton area.

Air : No comment.

IMPORTANT ORDERS RECEIVED

None.

IMPORTANT ORDERS ISSUED

None.

OPERATIONS

A convoy consisting of 4 LST, 1 DE, arrived in the assault area.

USS Ludlow and USS Woolsey fired 258 rounds at troops and batteries in the Bellenda area. Good results were reported by the SFCP.

At Marseille, sweeping continued in the inner Bassins. Five magnetic mines were blown in Bassin Joliette and seven in the three northern basins. At Toulon, all areas accessible to sweepers were reported safe. In Rade d'Hyeres, sweeping continued and no mines were reported.

Unloading figures were:

	Personnel	Vehicles	Tons(Dry)	Barrels(Wet)
Delta beaches	0	1,011	1,916	0
Camel beaches	1,004	158	4,431	0
Port de Bouc	0	0	1,357	25,000
Marseille	360	362	3,267	0
Toulon	0	0	850	1,591
Total	1,364	1,531	11,821	26,591
Total to Date	245,738	54,455	324,992	46,591

OWN AND ENEMY NAVAL LOSSES

Our losses were:

None.

Enemy losses were:

None.

- - - - - - - - - - - - - 13 September 1944 - - - - - - - - - - - - - - - -

WEATHER

Broken to overcast skies with a few light rain showers occurred in the assault area with the sky clearing near the end of the period. Wind was moderate easterly with slight seas and swell of three feet. Along the North African coast, wind was gentle easterly with negligible sea and swell. Visibility was uniformly good in all areas. In the Tyrrhenian Sea, there were cloudy skies, moderate northeasterly winds, good visibility, and a moderate sea with swell of four feet.

ENEMY FORCES

Navy: No comment.

Army: Increased army truck traffic was observed in sector of San Remo.

Air : No comment.

OWN FORCES

Navy: No comment.

Army: The 1st SSF of the 1st ABTF moved east of Menton and established a road block on main road north.

Air : No comment.

IMPORTANT ORDERS RECEIVED

None.

IMPORTANT ORDERS ISSUED

None.

OPERATIONS

Two convoys, one consisting of 4 LST, 1 DE; and one consisting of 10 LST, 1 DD arrived in the assault area.

USS Woolsey and USS Ludlow fired 320 rounds on call fire using plane spot, at troops, vehicles, and mortars in Capo Mortolo area.

Toulon and Port de Bouc each reported that the first Liberty ship was unloaded.

Unloading figures were:

	Personnel	Vehicles	Tons(Dry)	Barrels(Wet)
Delta beaches	0	0	2,180	0
Camel beaches	1,952	148	3,649	0
Port de Bouc	0	0	1,042	40,000
Marseille	100	142	3,085	0
Toulon	0	0	675	0
Total	2,052	290	10,631	40,000
Total to Date	247,790	54,745	335,623	86,591

OWN AND ENEMY NAVAL LOSSES

Our losses were:

None.

Enemy losses were:

None.

--------------- 14 September 1944 --------------------

WEATHER

Cloudiness continued throughout the day in the western Mediterranean with gentle easterly winds, good visibility, and negligible sea and swell.

ENEMY FORCES

Navy: Enemy merchant vessel and small craft in harbor at Oneglia were damaged from shelling by USS Ludlow.

Army: No comment.

Air : No comment.

OWN FORCES

Navy: No comment.

Army: No comment.

Air : MACAF relieved XII TAC of responsibility of air raid warning and air cover of ports and shipping in all sectors of Southern France.

IMPORTANT ORDERS RECEIVED

None.

IMPORTANT ORDERS ISSUED

NCWTF directed that Delta beaches with Seventh Army concurrence should close when the vessels of the D plus 25 convoys had been completely discharged. CTF 85 was directed to turn over command of TF 85 to CTG 87.11, Commander Unloading Control, Camel beaches.

OPERATIONS

Five convoys, one consisting of 4 LST, 1 APD, 2 DE; one consisting of 21 M/T ships, 2 DD; one consisting of 3 LST, 3 M/T ships, 1 DD, 1 PC; one consisting of 40 LCI, 1 DD, 1 DE; and one consisting of 20 M/T ships, 2 DD, arrived in the assault area. Three convoys, one consisting of 18 M/T ships, 1 DD, 2 DE; one consisting of 5 LST, 1 DE; and one consisting of 5 M/T ships, 1 LST, 3 DD, departed the assault area. The build up of the Air Force, accomplished by the Calvi convoys, was complete. The nine LST on that shuttle were directed to intra-theater movements of the Bomber Wing commands.

USS Ludlow fired 238 rounds in the Bellenda area on a counter-attack against the 1st ABTF.

USS Edison from 0910 to 0945 obtained several hits on a three hundred foot enemy merchant vessel off Capo Cervo; USS Ludlow fired 153 rounds at Oneglia harbor and obtained twelve hits on two ships.

At Marseille, minesweeping continued in the four northern basins and in Bassin Avant Port Nord, one magnetic mine was detonated near the north end of the mole. Bassins Marechal Petain and Mirabeau were reported reasonably safe. Off Menton, the minesweepers cut thirteen deep laid mines in an area two miles due south of Capo Mortola. Floating mines were also sighted off Capo Cervo.

Unloading figures were:

	Personnel	Vehicles	Tons(Dry)	Barrels(Wet)
Delta beaches	3,300	547	2,996	0
Camel beaches	364	40	4,290	0
Port de Bouc	0	0	1,515	9,600
Marseille	46	97	2,942	0
Toulon	0	0	725	62,055
Total	3,710	684	12,468	71,655
Total to Date	251,500	55,429	348,091	158,246

OWN AND ENEMY NAVAL LOSSES

Our losses were:

None.

Enemy losses were:

Sunk:

None.

Damaged:

1 merchant vessel off Capo Cervo, 1 merchant vessel and small craft at Oneglia by gunfire.

---------------- 15 September 1944 ------------------

WEATHER

In the assault area, conditions were excellent throughout the day with clear skies, good visibility, gentle shifting winds and calm seas. Elsewhere in the western Mediterranean, the sky was partly cloudy, wind was moderate southeasterly, and the seas were slight.

ENEMY FORCES

Navy: An enemy Italian type EV was damaged by coastal forces off Genoa and probably sunk. Estimated enemy strength was 2 DD, 2 TB, 2 EV, 1 HAV, 20 MAS, and 2 auxiliaries.

Army: No comment.

Air : No comment.

OWN FORCES

Navy: NCWTF released HMS Bicester, Blackmore, Liddesdale, Oakley, Themistocles, LCT 9, 17, 154, 160, 164 to CinCMed.

At 0001B, 15 September, 6 US Army Group assumed command of all allied ground and service forces in Southern France except those units assigned or reserved for assignment to Service of Supplies, North African Theater of Operations, US Army (Continental Base Section) and units assigned to Allied Force Headquarters and Headquarters North African Theater of Operations, US Army. At the same time 6 US Army Group passed to operational control of Supreme Headquarters Allied Expeditionary Force.

Army: The 1st ABTF established defensive positions from Menton to Larche Pass.

Air : XII TAC passed to operational control of SHAEF.

IMPORTANT ORDERS RECEIVED

None.

IMPORTANT ORDERS ISSUED

None.

OPERATIONS

A convoy consisting of 15 M/T ships, 3 DD, arrived in the assault area.

A cruiser plane at daybreak located several craft at Imperia harbor. Two DD attempted to bombard the harbor but the accurate fire from an unlocated shore battery prevented the ships from closing to less than 20,000 yards.

USS Hilary P. Jones fired 124 rounds with plane spot at troops and vehicles in the Bellenda area. Good results were reported.

At Marseille Bassins Marechal Petain and Mirabeau opened at 1200. Two and one half Liberty berths alongside Mole H and nine holding berths in Avant Port Sud were available.

At Marseille, minesweeping continued in Avant Port Nord and Bassin Wilson where one mine was detonated. Three magnetic mines were blown in Bassin Pinede. At Menton, minesweepers south of Capo Mortola destroyed 19 additional contact mines in the fire support area.

Unloading figures were:

	Personnel	Vehicles	Tons(Dry)	Barrels(Wet)
Delta beaches	0	0	1,102	0
Camel beaches	1,867	840	3,001	0
Port de Bouc	0	0	1,126	10,000
Marseille	10,109	49	3,241	0
Toulon	0	0	470	762
Total	11,976	889	8,940	10,762
Total to Date	263,476	56,318	357,031	169,008

OWN AND ENEMY NAVAL LOSSES

Our losses were:

None.

Enemy losses were:

Sunk:

None.

Damaged:

1 EV (possibly sunk) by gunfire off Genoa.

--------------- 16 September 1944 ----------------

WEATHER

Skies continued mostly clear with good visibility, gentle winds, and calm seas in all areas.

ENEMY FORCES

Navy: The PT patrol off Ventimiglia at 0230 picked up a radar contact one half mile off Capo Mortola. Four explosive boats and one MAS boat were pursued by the PTs. Contact was lost off Cap Ferrat. No return fire was received and hits were obtained on the escaping craft.

Army: Enemy forces doggedly held mountain passes east of Menton. The tunnel at Mt. Cenis was destroyed by enemy demolition units.

Air : No comment.

OWN FORCES

    Navy: No comment.

    Army: No comment.

    Air : No comment.

IMPORTANT ORDERS RECEIVED

    None.

IMPORTANT ORDERS ISSUED

    None.

OPERATIONS

Two convoys, one consisting of 8 LST, 1 PC; and one consisting of 15 LST, 2 DE, arrived in the assault area. A convoy consisting of 37 LCI, 2 APD, 2 DE, departed the assault area.

USS Edison fired 310 rounds at enemy batteries and troops in the Magliocca area. USS Hilary P. Jones fired 137 rounds at a command post, bridge, and guns in the coastal area from Capo Mortola to Capo Biamonte. The above ships also fired 50 rounds in support of the minesweepers at batteries on Capo Ampeglio.

At Marseille, two additional berths, one liberty and one coaster, were available in Bassin President Wilson. The total berths available were 3-1/2 liberty and 1 coaster. In Rade d'Hyeres, minesweeping of the anchorage area was completed and it was declared safe to the six fathom curve. The eastern limit was QB 352, located one mile south of Cap Benat to the Isle de Port Cros, and the southern limit QB 353 located between Isle de Port Cros and Isle de Porquerolles, in Grande Passe. The eastern entrance was off Cap Benat and the western entrance through Petite Passe. Rade Porquerolles was reported safe to the three fathom curve.

The port of St. Tropez and all Delta beaches were closed. Total unloading figures to the closing date were personnel - 119,954, vehicles - 25,176, and tons - 121,692.

Unloading figures were:

	Personnel	Vehicles	Tons(Dry)	Barrels(Wet)
Delta beaches	0	0	41	0
Camel beaches	480	444	4,318	0
Port de Bouc	0	0	1,155	0
Marseille	7,350	32	3,184	0
Toulon	130	0	500	29
Total	7,960	476	9,198	29
Total to Date	271,436	56,794	366,229	169,037

OWN AND ENEMY NAVAL LOSSES

    Our losses were:

    None.

    Enemy losses were:

    None.

---------------- 17 September 1944 ----------------

WEATHER

    Broken to overcast cloudiness prevailed throughout the area west of Corsica with a brief shower in the middle of the morning in the assault area. Surface wind was moderate easterly with swell of two to four feet. In the Tyrrhenian Sea, the sky was cloudy with gentle easterly wind and smooth seas.

ENEMY FORCES

    Navy: Photo reconnaissance showed 3 or 4 possible explosive boats and 2 possible MAS at San Remo, 2 possible MAS at Porto Maurizio, 1 MAS, and 5 possible explosive boats at Oneglia, and one MAS seen at sea off Cap Verde, bound west.

    Army: No comment.

    Air : No comment.

OWN FORCES

    Navy: No comment.

    Army: No comment.

    Air : Navy Blimp ZP14 arrived at Cuers airfield from NAS, Port Lyautey, for experimental aerial mine spotting and auxiliary duties.

IMPORTANT ORDERS RECEIVED

    None.

IMPORTANT ORDERS ISSUED

    NCWTF directed that the PT base be transferred from St. Maxime to Golfe de Juan or Nice.

OPERATIONS

    A convoy consisting of 2 LST, 1 M/T ship, 1 PC, 1 YMS, arrived in the assault area. Three convoys, one consisting of 8 M/T ships, 1 DD; one consisting of 8 LST, 1 DD, 1 PC; and one consisting of 1 LSP, 1 DE, departed from the assault area.

    USS Edison fired 153 rounds at batteries and 33 rounds at trucks in the Magliocca area using SFCP. USS Hilary P. Jones fired 106 rounds at coastal guns in the vicinity of Capo Biamonte. An SOC plane on reconnaissance patrol as far east as Capo Delle Melle discovered numerous small craft in the harbors along the coast.

USS Hilary P. Jones, with a Cub spotting, fired 162 rounds at small craft in San Remo harbor. The heavy flak and 88mm fire precluded accurate spotting by the Cub. Several straddles were reported on two MAS boats and large explosions were observed on the quay.

Unloading figures were:

	Personnel	Vehicles	Tons(Dry)	Barrels(Wet)
Camel beaches	2,211	620	5,302	0
Port de Bouc	0	0	1,003	25,000
Marseille	169	130	3,339	0
Toulon	57	8	450	90
Total	2,437	758	10,094	25,090
Total to Date	273,873	57,552	376,223	194,127

OWN AND ENEMY NAVAL LOSSES

Our losses were:

None.

Enemy losses were:

None.

--------------- 18 September 1944 ----------------

WEATHER

In the assault area and the Corsican-Sardinian area, the sky was overcast throughout the period with light rain during the morning. Surface wind was fresh easterly with moderate seas and surf of four to five feet. In the Tyrrhenian Sea, fine conditions prevailed throughout area with gentle southerly wind, good visibility, negligible sea and swell.

ENEMY FORCES

Navy: The only change in the enemy situation was the indication as shown by photo reconnaissance that Savona was being abandoned by enemy naval forces. Piers were damaged by mines as were cranes and other installations. The enemy naval strength was estimated as 2 DD, 2 TB, 2 EV, 1 HAV, 20 MAS, and 2 auxiliaries. Enemy traffic was restricted to the Genoa-Spezia area with occasional small units venturing as far as Imperia.

Army: No comment.

Air : No comment.

OWN FORCES

Navy: No comment.

Army: No comment.

Air : No comment.

IMPORTANT ORDERS RECEIVED

None.

IMPORTANT ORDERS ISSUED

Ships and craft were directed to sail between ports and beaches in the assault area unescorted. Destroyers and patrol craft covered the routes.

OPERATIONS

The beachhead DD screen for St. Tropez-Frejus area was reestablished with two lines as follows: One line with origin off Cap Camarat extended to the vicinity off Cap Roux was called K Line; the other, L Line, was a picket line in a north-south direction to seaward off Golfe de la Napoule.

USS Hilary P. Jones carried out a bombardment of San Remo and Porto Maurizio harbors. At San Remo, from 0707 to 0940, 223 rounds were fired. Many small craft were damaged and sunk and the harbor was in flames at the termination of the bombardment. At Porto Maurizio, from 1700 to 1800, 250 rounds were fired. Three small craft were sunk and five were reported severely damaged. Ammunition dumps and fuel tanks were set on fire. USS Madison successfully attacked and destroyed a 3000 ton merchant vessel off Capo Cervo. USS Ludlow answered army calls and fired 50 rounds on a battery south of Magliocca. All ships and spotting planes were subjected to heavy return fire.

At Marseille, five additional alongside berths were available. They were; one on each side of the east end of mole H, one at the end, and one on the north side of Traverse de Madrague, one on the north side of Traverse de Janet, one on the north side of the Traverse de Pinede. A total of 11 liberty holding berths and 10 liberty and one coaster alongside berths were available.

At Toulon, two additional liberty berths were opened along the mole in Missiessey Bassin. A total of 6-1/2 liberty berths were now available.

At Marseille, minesweeping continued in Bassin National.

Unloading figures were:

	Personnel	Vehicles	Tons(Dry)	Barrels(Wet)
Camel beaches	4,308	863	4,232	0
Port de Bouc	0	0	845	45,000
Marseille	177	476	5,278	0
Toulon	0	0	605	5,039
Total	4,485	1,339	10,960	50,039
Total to Date	278,358	58,891	387,283	244,166

OWN AND ENEMY NAVAL LOSSES

Our losses were:

None.

Enemy losses were:

Sunk:

One 3,000 ton merchant ship off Capo Cervo, 3 small craft at Porto Maurizio, and some small craft possibly at San Remo by gunfire.

Damaged:

Some small craft at San Remo by gunfire.

--------------- 19 September 1944 ---------------

WEATHER

In the assault area, the day began partly cloudy with fresh easterly winds and moderate sea. By 1000, rain began which continued throughout the day with occasional thunderstorms. Surface wind gradually increased to gale force, the sea becoming rough with swell developing to ten feet from the east. In the Corsica-Sardinia area, during daylight broken cloudiness prevailed with a few light showers; surface wind was fresh southerly with moderate sea and swell of four feet. Heavy rain showers began about sunset lowering ceilings and visibility, while the wind freshened to 25 knots, the sea becoming rough with swell of six feet. In the Tyrrhenian Sea, partly cloudy skies, visibility 6 to 7 miles, moderate southerly winds and slight seas prevailed over the entire area during the day.

ENEMY FORCES

Navy: No comment.

Army: No comment.

Air : No comment.

OWN FORCES

Navy: No comment.

Army: No comment.

Air : Navy Blimp ZP14 began daily search for unknown minefields, and plotted accurate positions of mines in known fields from east of Giens Peninsula to west of Marseille.

IMPORTANT ORDERS RECEIVED

None.

IMPORTANT ORDERS ISSUED

None.

OPERATIONS

Six convoys, one consisting of 19 M/T ships, 2 corvettes; one consisting of 9 LCI, 1 PC, 1 corvette; one consisting of 6 transports, 3 DD; one consisting of 14 M/T ships, 28 LST, 2 DE, 1 corvette; one consisting of 6 LST, 1 APD; and one consisting of 12 transports, 4 DD, arrived in the assault area. A convoy consisting of 30 LST, 1 LCI, 1 corvette, departed from the assault area.

USS Ludlow fired 52 rounds at troops in the Bellenda area. The area was reported well covered. USS Madison made a sweep eastward to Capo Delle Melle but no enemy were observed.

At Marseille, the Swiss ship Generoso was sunk by a mine in Bassin de la Gare Maritime, while being moved to permit minesweeping operations. Minesweeping continued in Bassin National. At Toulon, one additional berth was available at pier 3 east. A total of 7-1/2 alongside berths were available.

Unloading figures were:

	Personnel	Vehicles	Tons(Dry)	Barrels(Wet)
Camel beaches	1,455	468	2,638	0
Port de Bouc	0	0	1,822	15,000
Marseille	10,256	474	7,518	0
Toulon	433	0	1,133	247
Total	12,144	942	13,111	15,247
Total to Date	290,502	59,833	400,394	259,413

OWN AND ENEMY NAVAL LOSSES

Our losses were:

None.

Enemy losses were:

None.

--------------- 20 September 1944 ---------------

WEATHER

In the assault area, gales from the northeast and steady rain lasted until 0600 after which time the wind shifted to northwest and west with velocities of 20 to 30 knots in the afternoon, then diminished to gentle breezes by sunset. The sea was rough. The swell, 10 feet at beginning of period, diminished rapidly after noon. Around Corsica and Sardinia, strong northerly winds at the beginning of the period backed to west in the late afternoon. The sky was overcast with low clouds and passing showers. The sea was rough with swell along the west coast of 12 feet. In the Tyrrhenian Sea, showers and thundershowers occurred throughout the day. Wind was southwesterly 20 to 30 knots. Sea was rough with a swell of 8 feet from the south.

ENEMY FORCES

Navy: No comment.

Army: No comment.

Air : No comment.

OWN FORCES

    Navy: No comment.

    Army: 1st ABTF was fighting in area of Ventimiglia.

    Air : No comment.

IMPORTANT ORDERS RECEIVED

    None.

IMPORTANT ORDERS ISSUED

    None.

OPERATIONS

    A convoy consisting of 1 LST, 3 M/T ships, 1 PC, arrived in the assault area. Two convoys, one consisting of 7 transports, 3 DD; and one consisting of 12 transports, 3 DD, departed from the assault area.

    USS Ludlow fired 72 rounds at railyards and vehicle concentrations in the Ventimiglia area. The SFCP reported that hits were made on both targets.

    At Marseille, Bassin National was opened making four additional alongside berths available. Two were located on the south side of Traverse de Pinede, one at the end of Mole D and one at the outer end of the north side of Mole C. The total alongside berths available were fifteen liberty and one coaster. At Toulon, two additional liberty berths were made available, which were located at Pier Three East and Pier One West. The total berths available were seven and one-half.

    At Marseille, minesweeping continued in Bassin de la Gare Maritime. No mines were reported. At Port St. Louis, minesweeping commenced in the inner harbor. One magnetic mine was detonated.

    Unloading figures were:

	Personnel	Vehicles	Tons(Dry)	Barrels(Wet)
Camel beaches	3,323	800	829	0
Port de Bouc	0	0	1,288	0
Marseille	8,377	2,165	11,240	0
Toulon	750	439	1,361	1,100
Total	12,450	3,404	14,718	1,100
Total to Date	302,952	63,237	415,112	260,513

OWN AND ENEMY NAVAL LOSSES

    Our losses were:

    None.

    Enemy losses were:

    None.

- - - - - - - - - - - - - 21 September 1944 - - - - - - - - - - - - - - - -

WEATHER

In the assault area, Corsica, and Sardinia, the entire period was fair with only partly cloudy skies, light variable winds, good visibility, and calm seas. The Tyrrhenian Sea in the morning was marked by a continuation of rain and thunderstorms with strong southwesterly winds, moderate seas, and moderate swell from the south. In the late afternoon, the wind shifted to the northwest and subsided to moderate while the sky cleared to partly cloudy and sea and swell diminished to four feet. Along the coast of North Africa, westerly winds of 25 to 30 knots, accompanied by light rain and rough seas, diminished in the afternoon to 12 to 16 knots while sea lessened to moderate.

ENEMY FORCES

Navy: No comment.

Army: No comment.

Air : No comment.

OWN FORCES

Navy: Acting upon the orders of NCWTF, CTF 85 released all the British LCI(L) and LCT of his command to CinCMed. All ships of US DesRon 18 were detached from Task Unit 80.6.7 to return to the United States.

Army: No comment.

Air : No comment.

IMPORTANT ORDERS RECEIVED

None.

IMPORTANT ORDERS ISSUED

None.

OPERATIONS

Eight merchant ships and 9 LCI departed from the area. ComDesDiv 21 in USS Kearny relieved ComDesDiv 36 in USS Baldwin as the Beachhead Screen Commander. Fifteen vessels were assigned screening duties covering the ports and the one remaining beach.

USS Ludlow fired 70 rounds at supply dumps northeast of Ventimiglia. The area was well covered.

The Golfe de Juan was swept for mines to the five fathom curve. The entire swept area was considered safe. Concrete tetrahedra with attached teller-mines prevented sweeping inside the five fathom curve. A sweeping operation to Cannes commenced. The French reported the removal of 22 mines from Cannes Harbor. Sweeping continued in the harbors of Marseille and Toulon.

Unloading figures were:

	Personnel	Vehicles	Tons(Dry)	Barrels(Wet)
Camel beaches	5,501	1,362	1,828	0
Port de Bouc	0	0	2,904	0
Marseille	1,982	485	8,640	0
Toulon	1,203	311	1,874	1,344
Total	8,686	2,158	15,246	1,344
Total to Date	311,638	65,395	430,358	261,857

OWN AND ENEMY NAVAL LOSSES

Our losses were:

None.

Enemy losses were:

None.

--------------- 22 September 1944 -----------------

WEATHER

Conditions were good in all areas throughout the day as seas were slight, skies partly cloudy, visibility good, and winds gentle.

ENEMY FORCES

Navy: Intelligence reports were received indicating a concentration of midget submarines, human torpedoes and explosive boats in Genoa-Spezia area and enemy intention to press attacks on our Southern France convoys with these weapons.

Army: No comment.

Air : No comment.

OWN FORCES

Navy: No comment.

Army: No comment.

Air : No comment.

IMPORTANT ORDERS RECEIVED

None.

IMPORTANT ORDERS ISSUED

NCWTF instructed CTU 80.6.7 to strengthen the escorts of all convoys while north of the Straits of Bonifacio.

OPERATIONS

A total of 19 Combat Loaders, 30 LST, 1 LCI and 12 merchant ships departed with escorts in regularly scheduled convoys for Oran and Naples. USS Edison and USS Woolsey fired a total of 254 rounds in the Magliocca sector against a railhead, trucks, storage dumps and batteries. The target areas were effectively covered causing several explosions.

During the minesweeping operations two magnetic mines were blown at Marseille, one moored mine was sunk at Toulon and one drifting contact mine was destroyed in the Port de Bouc area. A channel from the Golfe de Juan north of the Isle de Lerins to Cannes was swept.

NCWTF conducted an inspection of the port and naval activities at Marseille.

Marseille reported 12 holding and 17 alongside berths available.

Unloading figures were:

	Personnel	Vehicles	Tons(Dry)	Barrels(Wet)
Camel beaches	0	0	1,566	0
Port de Bouc	0	0	2,157	0
Marseille	1,500	475	11,111	10,000
Toulon	278	463	2,569	3,873
Total	1,778	938	17,403	13,873
Total to Date	313,416	66,333	447,761	275,730

OWN AND ENEMY NAVAL LOSSES

Our losses were:

Sunk:

None.

Damaged:

US ATR-1 by submerged wreck in Toulon.

Enemy losses were:

None.

---------------- 23 September 1944 -----------------

WEATHER

With the exception of the southern part of the Tyrrhenian Sea, where skies were overcast with few light rains and moderate shifting winds, conditions were generally fair, the wind gentle easterly and southerly, seas slight, visibility good, and skies partly cloudy.

ENEMY FORCES

Navy: No comment.

Army: No comment.

Air : No comment.

OWN FORCES

Navy: No comment.

Army: No comment.

Air : Navy Blimp ZP14 maintained visual and radar watch in the approaches to Toulon harbor against surprise assault by small craft and human torpedoes on Allied shipping from 2000 this date to 0900 September 24.

IMPORTANT ORDERS RECEIVED

None.

IMPORTANT ORDERS ISSUED

None.

OPERATIONS

A convoy consisting of 2 LST and an escort arrived. Thirty-two escorts under the control of CTU 80.6.7 were with assigned convoys.

Twelve ships were initially screening the ports and beach area. Because of an intelligence report of the possibility of an enemy attack on shipping in Marseille and Toulon harbors by midget submarines from Spezia, the offshore and harbor patrols were increased. Counter measures in both harbors were instituted.

USS Woolsey and USS Edison on the right flank fired 67 and 52 rounds respectively at a railyard, personnel, batteries and on an observation post, all in the Ventimiglia area. The return fire was accurate and reconnaissance by Cub airplane was unable to locate the source. Minesweeping in the harbor of Marseille continued.

Unloading figures were:

	Personnel	Vehicles	Tons(Dry)	Barrels(Wet)
Camel beaches	0	0	1,243	0
Port de Bouc	0	0	2,113	0
Marseille	235	340	9,594	0
Toulon	302	617	2,566	0
Total	537	957	15,516	0
Total to Date	313,953	67,290	-463,277	275,730

OWN AND ENEMY NAVAL LOSSES

Our losses were:

None.

Enemy losses were:

None.

---------------- 24 September 1944 - - - - - - - - - - - - - - - -

WEATHER

In the assault area, the day began clear with light easterly wind and calm seas. Wind shifted to westerly at 0900 and gradually increased to become fresh by midnight with seas becoming moderate and swell developing to four feet. Visibility was good throughout period. Throughout the rest of the Mediterranean, there were gentle winds, good visibility, partly cloudy skies, and slight seas.

ENEMY FORCES

Navy: No comment.

Army: No comment.

Air : No comment.

OWN FORCES

Navy: Task Group 80.10 was dissolved. All minesweeping units thereof were released to Commander 8th Amphibious Force for reassignment. The majority of these units were retained in the forward area operating under Commander Escort Sweeper Group.

The program for the turnover of PCs, SCs, and YMSs to the French was put in effect. Toulon was selected as a base for this purpose.

Army: No comment.

Air : Patrol of previous night by Navy Blimp ZP14 was repeated.

IMPORTANT ORDERS RECEIVED

None.

IMPORTANT ORDERS ISSUED

Control of the use of PBYs for mine spotting was transferred to Commander Escort Sweeper Group.

OPERATIONS

Fifty merchant ships from Oran and Naples and 4 fast transports from Naples arrived with their escorts. Eight merchant ships departed for Naples.

USS Edison with USS Madison providing a smoke screen, fired 51 rounds at enemy artillery in the Ventimiglia area and 44 rounds at troops in the Magliocca area. The targets were reported to be well covered.

Awaiting to unload at Toulon were 39 merchant ships in the Grande Rade and 12 in the inner harbor. At Marseille there were 19 merchant ships unloading offshore and 16 alongside.

Minesweeping continued at Marseille. Vieux Port was reported open for LSTs with a channel width of 130 feet and a depth of 12 feet.

Unloading figures were:

	Personnel	Vehicles	Tons(Dry)	Barrels(Wet)
Camel beaches	0	0	583	0
Port de Bouc	0	0	3,005	20,000
Marseille	8,391	173	9,647	0
Toulon	1,200	573	2,496	0
Total	9,591	746	15,731	20,000
Total to Date	323,544	68,036	479,008	295,730

OWN AND ENEMY NAVAL LOSSES

Our losses were:

None.

Enemy losses were:

None.

--------------- 25 September 1944 ------------------

WEATHER

The period in the assault area started with fresh westerly winds, moderate sea, swell of four feet, and clear skies with excellent visibility. Wind backed to northwesterly at 0300 and increased to gale force by midmorning. The sea became rough and swell developed to ten feet. In the rest of the Mediterranean, a cold front moving easterly at near 20 knots passed over Corsica and Sardinia at near 0100 with showers and thunderstorms along the front and fresh southerly winds to eastward of front and strong west and northwest winds to the westward, raising rough seas and swell to eight feet in the Tyrrhenian Sea. Along the North African coast, wind was moderate northerly with passing showers, moderate sea and swell of four feet.

ENEMY FORCES

Navy: Threat against Allied naval forces and shipping off the south coast of France was maintained by operation of explosive motor boats and human torpedoes brought overland to San Remo and other ports and beaches of the Ligurian coast.

Army: An estimated five divisions of General Kesselring's forces were disposed along the general line of the Italian-French frontier and the Ligurian coast area. German troops in this area were being replaced to some extent by Fascist Italian troops and German headquarters and administrative units were known to be moving eastward in possible preparation for the eventuality of having to abandon Northern Italy.

Air : At this time, only reconnaissance sorties were carried out. These averaged two per day, usually over the Ligurian area and sometimes further south.

OWN FORCES

Navy: Camel beaches, the last remaining in operation, were closed, whereupon Task Force 85 was dissolved.

Army: On the right flank, the 1st ABTF held a line roughly along the French-Italian border touching the coastline about 3-1/2 miles west of Ventimiglia and 1-1/2 miles east of Menton. The line was Balzi - Rossi - Cima - Pongoiria - St. Antonin Chlle. The US Seventh Army, the French Army B, and the XII TAC, under the 6th Army group, now fought on the southern sector of the Western Front in the area Epinal-Belfort, having liberated Southern France, Central France, and so isolated Southwestern France that the trapped German forces were rapidly surrendering.

Air : With the departure of NCWTF from Toulon, the Southern France terminus of Navy mail and transport service was shifted from Cuers to Marignane airfield, near Marseille.

IMPORTANT ORDERS RECEIVED

None.

IMPORTANT ORDERS ISSUED

NCWTF instructed CTG 80.8 to release all British LCT assigned him on 1 October and sail them to Maddalena for onward routing by CinCMed. NCWTF ordered the Blimp K-112 to report to CTG 80.8 for continuance of experimental minespotting flights and essential patrol operations.

NCWTF reported intentions as follows:

(1) Continue gunfire support of 1st ABTF on eastern flank with gunfire support forces under command of CTF 86;

(2) Prevent enemy small craft raids from enemy held Ligurian ports by PT patrols basing in Golfe de Juan and under command CTF 86;

(3) Protect shipping in approaches to Port de Bouc, Marseille, and Toulon by patrol, screening, and minesweeping units assigned to CTG 80.8;

(4) Continue operation of intra-theater convoys for Army maintenance and build-up through Southern France ports with assignment of amphibious ships and craft and escorts to be made by NCWTF, 25 US DD, 9 French DD, 6 French sloops, and 17 US PC being presently available for this purpose.

OPERATIONS

One convoy, consisting of 18 LST with 3 escorts arrived. Four fast troop transports with 4 APD escorts departed for Oran.

USS Madison fired 200 rounds at a supply train in the Ventimiglia area. Air spot reported hits on locomotive, cars and tracks. USS Madison fired 77 rounds destroying an observation post at Via Crengo.

At Marseille, there were 16 alongside berths and 23 offshore berths being used for unloading. At Port de Bouc, an additional liberty berth was ready, making a total of three at this port.

Additional alongside berths at Marseille above the 16 now available depended upon the progress of underwater salvage. All the basins had been swept and were considered safe. Special precautions were again instituted on the night of 24-25 September to guard against small craft raids. Four craft patrolled the harbor entrance and the anchorage and small anti-limpeteer depth charges were dropped at irregular intervals.

Maintenance sweeping continued in the swept channels and port areas. 6 AM, 6 YMS, and 3 SC (Shallow Sweepers) under CTF 86 were employed in the Golfe de la Napoule and were available for necessary sweeping in connection with gunfire support areas. The remainder of the minesweeping forces in the forward area, 18 AM, 29 YMS, and 8 MMS, were under the operational control of Commander Escort Sweeper Group, Eighth Amphibious Force, with the following assigned minesweeping tasks being undertaken in addition to maintenance sweeping: (a) Port St. Louis; (b) Golfe de Gien; and (c) Baie de Ciotat. Upon the completion of the above tasks, the minesweeping plan required that French manned ships would assume all further minesweeping off the south coast of France.

At 1758, NCWTF in USS Catoctin sailed from Toulon to arrive in Naples during forenoon of 27 September.

Unloading figures were:

	Personnel	Vehicles	Tons(Dry)	Barrels(Wet)
Camel beaches	0	0	175	0
Port de Bouc	0	0	1,561	30,000
Marseille	313	190	7,595	0
Toulon	212	193	1,898	0
Total	525	383	11,229	30,000
Total to Date	324,069	68,419	490,237	325,730

OWN AND ENEMY NAVAL LOSSES

Our losses were:

None.

Enemy losses were:

None.

Summary Statistics
Invasion of Southern France
9 August 1944 to 25 September 1944

Ships and craft in the assault: 2,250.

Our losses were:

    Sunk or destroyed:

        1 US LST, 1 HM ML, 2 US YMS, 2 US PT, 5 US LCVP, 2 HM LCM(3).

    Damaged:

        1 US DD, 3 US SC, 10 US LCI(L), 5 US LCT, 5 HM LCT, 1 US AM, 1 US ATR, 1 US ARS, 2 HM ML, 1 HM MS, 1 US YMS, 1 HM BYMS, 1 US LCC, 1 US PT, 8 US LCVP, 5 HM LCM(3).

Enemy losses were:

    Sunk or destroyed:

        1 DD, 1 TB, 13 EV, 5 MAS, 1 merchant ship, 5 inactive submarines, 3 minesweeper type craft, at least 5 small craft, 16 explosive motor boats, 13 human torpedoes.

    Damaged:

        2 EV, 2 merchant vessels, 2 minesweeper type craft, an unknown number of small craft.

    Captured:

        1 fishing vessel, 2 motor boats.

Movement into Southern France, 15 August to 25 September, 1944:

	Personnel	Vehicles	Tons(Dry)	Barrels(Wet)
Alpha beaches (Closed 9 September)	81,573	15,675	67,353	‡
Delta beaches (Closed 16 September)	119,954	25,176	121,692	‡
Camel beaches (Closed 25 September)	66,888	18,229	146,974	‡
Marseille	50,569	6,711	99,171	10,000
Toulon	5,085	2,628	24,252	76,130
Port de Bouc	0	0	30,795	239,600
Total to Date	324,069	68,419	490,237	325,730

‡ For the beaches, the quantity of supplies in barrels(wet) was included in the tonnage.

Chapter 2

INTELLIGENCE

Section 2.1

SURPRISE

The Germans were well aware of the preparations in the western Mediterranean for the launching of a large amphibious operation. Photo reconnaissance - among other intelligence sources - kept him informed of the general nature and strength of our naval and shipping concentrations. Comparison of German and allied held coasts left little doubt as to the general objective of our preparations. However, various allied deceptive measures, carefully planned to mislead the enemy, taking full advantage of his partial knowledge, and carried out continuously throughout the planning and preparatory period, appear to have been effective in concealing our intention as to the actual sector of the assault. On D minus 3, the German propaganda radio broadcast the report that we were invading in the Genoa area. This report was apparently a "feeler." Although our first slow convoys were sighted after their arrival off the west coast of Corsica, the pre-invasion air bombing plans and the diversionary operations masked the target sector until it was too late for effective re-enforcement or strengthening of defenses to be carried out. (See Section 4.2, Pre-D-day bombing and diagram XIV; also Section 3.4, Diversionary Operations, and diagram XI.) Prisoners captured on D-day in the vicinity of Pampelonne Bay stated that the invasion was not expected there until early morning when large numbers of ships were sighted off the coast. Captured signal personnel said that they were unable to transmit coast-watcher observations to higher headquarters because of damage to communications.

In evaluating the degree of surprise, it must be considered that the Germans had few disposable reserves in the interior. The 11th Panzer Division straddling the lower Rhone Valley, was commencing to move north. The difference of a few hours or even a day in learning the exact place and time of our attack was not significant to the enemy in determining the movement and disposition of his available forces since the chief reliance for defense was upon minefields, underwater obstructions, beach defenses, and coastal batteries located in accordance with previous estimates of the most likely place to be attacked. Therefore, strategic deception during the months before the invasion assumed an importance much greater than tactical surprise at the time of assault. If, on a balance of suitability of beaches with relation to the objective against enemy expectations as evidenced by relative expenditures for local defense preparations, the amphibious forces struck the coast in a most favorable sector, it may be properly considered that surprise was achieved regardless of enemy knowledge of our movements in the last hours before the blow. Definitely, in this sense, surprise was achieved in the invasion of Southern France. In addition, a considerable measure of tactical surprise was achieved as indicated by the alerting of garrisons in the Toulon-Ciotat area at 2100, 14 August while garrisons in the Cavalaire-Frejus area appear to have been alerted some time after midnight, and by erroneous reports in enemy communiques and radio news broadcasts on 15 and 16 August as to the place of landings.

Review of events preceding the invasion of Southern France once again affirms the principle that effective confusion of the enemy leading to advantageous situations at the time of assault is attained not by negative concealment of our preparations with a "Chinese-wall" attitude but rather by a positive program designed to present multiple threats.

It is considered of particular importance and it is recommended that carefully planned measures to deceive the enemy, in respects which will facilitate execution of our plans, be initiated from the earliest planning stages of our amphibious invasion. The cover plan should keep pace with both our own preparations and the enemy reaction to them. Actual and not merely paper activities should implement the cover plan and utmost care must be devoted to the security, coordination, and execution of such measures.

Section 2.2

AEROLOGY

Weather during the approach and the initial assault phase was uniformly favorable for surface craft and indifferent for aircraft as was indicated by the results of research into the characteristics of the theater made during the planning stage; and as was forecast with confidence on 12 August. During the month of September there were four days when the wind reached gale force; but, in each instance its direction was offshore as had likewise been indicated as highly probable in the preliminary survey, hence, though strong, it materially interfered with unloading on only one day, 3 September. The weather at any one time was found to vary markedly with locality as had been anticipated.

The aerological personnel was divided into two units on 3 July, 1944. Unit "Afirm" was established in the force flagship and Unit "Baker" at Patrol Base, Calvi.

Routine weather forecasts, addressed to Commanders of Task Forces and Task Groups, were placed on the Naples "Fox" broadcasts twice daily by Unit "B", beginning 1 August. Beginning at H-hour 15 August these forecasts originated with Unit "A" and were placed on the force "Fox" broadcast. Elements forecast in these messages were wind, sea, weather and smoke laying conditions. Aviation forecasts were supplied by Unit "A" to the Commanding General, XII Tactical Air Command during the period he was embarked on the flagship until his establishment ashore in the assault area on 19 August. Regular aviation forecasts and warnings were supplied the Advanced Blimp Squadron, Cuers, from 17 September to 25 September, inclusive.

An advance unit of three men was stationed in Port de Bouc on 6 September and regularly made skilled observations of weather in that area until their withdrawal on 23 September.

A continuous radio watch on two receivers was maintained in the force flagship throughout the operation by operators specially trained to receive weather broadcasts.

Decrypted enemy reports from Germany and occupied Europe were received from Air Ministry, London, broadcasts. They were of immense value in making weather map analysis; and the disappearance of such reports from Southern and Western France after 21 August, without the substitution of allied reports from these areas, was keenly felt.

Reception of synoptic weather reports from Spain and Portugal was very irregular because of frequent interference. Reports when received were often mutually inconsistent. Only one report of winds aloft in the Iberian peninsula was received during the entire operation.

All aerological equipment functioned satisfactorily with the exception of the radio-sonde receiver. Soundings obtained with the radio-sonde equipment were uniformly incorrect or non-evaluable primarily because of interference from shipboard transmitters principally the TBS equipment.

RECOMMENDATIONS

The recommendations contained in the report of the Sicilian invasion were affirmed as valid. Additionally it is recommended:

(1) That necessary measures be taken to insure complete, accurate surface and upper air reports from friendly and neutral countries in the vicinity of operations. Where the weather service of such countries is inadequate, or unreliable, that it be supplemented by reports from own personnel in allied countries, and reports from commercial interests in neutral countries;

(2) That a rear-echelon unit, such as Unit "B" be regularly organized to provide information to task force commanders during periods of radio silence in the attacking forces and to make all forecasts in the event of a casualty to the force commander's flagship of such severity as to prevent the functioning of the flagship unit after H-hour;

(3) That radio-sonde equipment be installed ashore as near as practicable to the vicinity of the assault beaches. This could well be a part of the equipment of the rear-echelon unit recommended in (2);

(4) That parachute type droppable automatic weather stations be stocked in Aerological Supply Pools.

Section 2.3

ENEMY COAST DEFENSES

The Germans occupied the south coast of France in November 1942. They did not find an undefended coast as the French had always maintained Toulon as a fortress area and naval base. In addition to numerous coast defense batteries commanding the approaches to Toulon and Marseille there had been developed by the French a number of railway spurs for employment of mobile heavy artillery of long range. These defenses were taken over by the Germans practically without damage, and as the Allied campaign in North Africa progressed, increased attention was given to building defenses for the entire coast. After the Italian surrender in September 1943, defense preparations were intensified.

For the extensive construction involved in developing a continuous coast defense line the enemy had available the experienced TODT organization and nearby cement factories but the supply of guns and personnel was not unlimited and time was pressing so priority areas were determined for the build-up. The first priority was the Sete-Agde area, between the Spanish boarder and the Rhone delta. Battery positions were casemated and elaborate beach defense positions were devised consisting of pill-boxes, barbed-wire, land obstacles (curved steel rails, tank traps, hedge-hogs, etc.). Underwater obstacles (concrete pyramids with attached mines) were installed first along this portion of the coast line. The second priority of defense construction was the Marseille-Toulon coastal area. This area protecting the two major ports already had the heaviest coast defense battery concentration of the entire coast line. The rugged coastal terrain and the small islands flanking the approaches were developed for defense by modernizing French fortifications and by constructing new positions. Underwater obstacles next appeared on the embayed beaches of La Ciotat, Sanary and Bandol. The third priority appeared to be the coast line from Giens Peninsula to Nice. Although there was extensive construction of casemates flanking beaches, underwater obstacles (principally concrete pyramids and jetted wooden rails) appeared late in this area, being observed first on Cannes and Nice beaches a few months before the invasion and then on Camel Red, Alpha Yellow and finally Alpha Red. Installations of concrete pyramids on Alpha Red beach commenced only in late July and was in progress just before D-Day.

The overall system of enemy coast defense appeared to have the following objectives:

(1) To protect the naval approach to coastal areas of landing beaches and ports by an outer perimeter of defense consisting of minefields, nets and booms, and long range coast defense batteries sited on headlands and islands covering the approaches;

(2) To prevent or impede landings with an elaborate system of beach defenses including shallow water mines, underwater obstacles, barbed wire and land mines on the beaches, casemate guns and pill-boxes, many of which were sited to enfilade landing beaches;

(3) To obstruct exits from beaches and prevent movement inland with anti-tank traps and walls, road blocks, land mines, strong points and mobile batteries.

The defenses of the general invasion area are considered in the following paragraphs under type headings. Underwater obstructions and mines are discussed in Section 2.4, Part II. For further description of defenses found in each assault sector see Sections 3.5 to 3.8 (inclusive) of Chapter 3, Part II.

COAST DEFENSE BATTERIES

Heavy and medium coast defense batteries were located on headlands and positions flanking entrances to gulfs and bays along the coast line of the assault area (Cavalaire Bay to Agay Road) to guard the seaward approaches to the landing beaches. This sector contained 29 batteries (total of 88 guns), and 34 casemates (75 mm to 88 mm guns) which covered the approaches to landing beaches. There were approximately 199 batteries (75 mm to 340 mm) along the coast line from Marseille to Nice, totalling about 647 guns. 107 casemates were identified in this area containing generally 75 mm or 88 mm guns. The heavily fortified St. Mandrier Peninsula at Toulon contained 15 batteries with 43 guns, 3 medium dual purpose batteries of 14 guns, and 6 light AA batteries of 13 guns. The above figures do not include unoccupied or dummy positions which during the planning period could not be left out of consideration.

In addition to the coast defense batteries enemy mobile batteries were located in an artillery training area about 7000 yards inland from Camel Red beach. Five batteries were active there on D-Day and 3 of them, totalling 8-88 mm guns participated in the defense of Camel Red beach; two having been put out of action by naval gunfire.

NETS AND BOOMS

The ports of Marseille and Toulon, the small harbors St. Raphael, St. Maxime and St. Tropez, and the small inlet of Agay were obstructed by nets and booms. These were not of much effect as defenses since frontal assaults were not made on the harbors, and they were cleared with little delay by tugs and combat demolition units after the places they protected were captured from landward.

LAND MINES

Beaches were mined, in patterns ranging from a single row of Tellermines to patterns of four rows, as on Camel Red Beach. On Camel Yellow Beach, the first LCI(L) to beach set off an explosion of a row of mines along the water's edge for more than 100 yards, apparently from sympathetic detonation. Anti-personnel mines were encountered inland on exits from several assault beaches but not in large quantity. Inland from Alpha Yellow Beach many "SCHU" anti-personnel mines caused a number of casualties, usually the loss of one leg below the knee but with few deaths. Open fields back of beaches contained large caliber shells fitted with detonators and snag lines of light wire which were easily seen in daylight and hence were not very effective. Wooden anti-glider stakes were usually planted in the same fields.

Few booby traps were encountered. In many of the mined areas danger signs (skull-and-cross-bones with inscriptions in German and French) remained to mark genuine as well as dummy fields, presumably because the enemy was rushed from those areas. Reports were received of some dummy minefields having been left by the Germans with danger signs in English.

In St. Raphael, iron stakes about 12 inches high were placed in the pavement of streets leading to the waterfront, connected with trip wires and reportedly having a TNT charge under every third one.

BARBED WIRE

Wire patterns ranging usually from one to three rows were found on all the landing beaches. It was not effective, the design and construction being of poor quality. Inland of the beaches, barbed wire was used with road blocks, surrounding batteries and strong points, and on walls and buildings near the landing beaches.

ANTI-TANK WALLS AND DITCHES

Anti-tank walls were encountered on Delta Red, Delta Green, Camel Red and Camel Yellow beaches. They were approximately 8-10 feet high, about 3 feet thick, of reenforced concrete. The pillar type wall on Camel Red backed the entire beach area and was a formidable barrier to exit from the beach. Delta Red and Green beaches were backed by continuous walls.

These obstructions were overcome by engineer units and exits quickly made. Aerial bombing, naval gunfire and rocket barrages had little effect beyond chipping the top of the wall in a few places. However, general neutralization of other defenses and the enemy lack of reserve personnel largely nullified the effect of anti-tank walls and ditches as serious obstructions.

CASEMATES AND PILLBOXES

Casemates, pill-boxes, and machine gun positions were effectively sited to enfilade the assault beaches, and most of them were well camouflaged. For seven months before the invasion NCWTF photo-interpreters watched the progress of construction shown in aerial photographs, locating many casemates by this method since they could not be detected in the latest photographs after camouflage was completed. In the St. Raphael, Nice and Cannes areas elaborate camouflage in the form of wooden structures of buildings around the installation made detection from photographs impossible except in the early stages of construction. The buildings around the casemates were painted to depict curtains in frame windows, flower boxes were installed, and in some cases appropriate signs reading "CAFE", "BAR", etc. were used to conceal the identity of the buildings.

Very few casemates or pillboxes covering the assault beaches were destroyed by bombing or bombardment. For most part their temporary neutralization in sufficient degree for assault troops to land and advance inland apparently resulted from destruction or damage to service installations, observation posts, and communications; casualties to personnel without available replacements and reserves; and lack of determination on the part of the defenders.

FORTIFIED BUILDINGS

The enemy had evacuated buildings facing the shoreline. Windows and doors were walled-in with cement and barbed wire placed around the walls. Anti-tank walls blocked narrow streets.

NEW TYPES OF DEFENSES

Miniature "Goliath" or "Doodle-bug" tanks were found in underground shelters facing the beaches with runways of logs leading out of the shelters. Four such tanks were found on Alpha Yellow beach and four on Camel Red. Although they were loaded with explosives and apparently ready for action, none were used against the landings.

The coast defenses of the coast of Southern France were under close study by the intelligence and planning staff of Commander Eighth Fleet from December 1943. Analysis was directed toward evaluation of the anti-amphibious-invasion strength of the defenses in terms of our means to overcome the defenses in particular sectors.

SOURCES OF INFORMATION

The sources of information for intelligence evaluation of enemy defenses were principally:

(1) Aerial photographs, both verticals and obliques;

(2) French naval personnel who were familiar with the area and supplied geographic data and information concerning French installations taken over by the Germans;

(3) Agents' reports through various channels which supplied much valuable information serving to supplement and assist in the interpretation of aerial photographs.

DISSEMINATION OF DEFENSE INFORMATION

Based upon evaluation of information obtained from the above sources the following reports and graphic presentations were distributed to all commands concerned:

(1) Naval Planning Memorandum Number 13 issued March 4, 1944, with successive supplements, disseminated to all planning echelons the state of information on enemy coast defenses;

(2) A graphic presentation in the form of two gridded charts including the coastal area from Marseille to Nice and having printed thereon pinpoint location of all known coast defense batteries, target number, six-figure grid location, and tabulated battery and gun data as of 20 July 1944, were distributed to all commands and ships concerned with naval gunfire;

(3) Panoramic Beach Sketches (see Section 2.10, Part II) included all defense information applicable to the areas covered by the sketches;

(4) Collation Maps (1:25,000 military maps overprinted with defense information as evaluated jointly by the army and navy planning staffs) were distributed as late as practicable before the operation to naval as well as military units;

(5) The Information Annex to NCWTF operation plan contained description and annotated aerial photographs of enemy defenses in the assault area.

CONCLUSIONS

It is of utmost importance to the logical development of amphibious assault plans that during the planning period every possible source of information concerning enemy defenses be exploited and that this information be under constant review in close conjunction with the planning staff in order that our capabilities be applied with maximum effect.

Well organized graphic presentations adapted to the requirements of assault forces, gunfire ships and air spotters, and receiving wide distribution to all personnel concerned, contribute materially to the efficiency and effectiveness of the forces engaged.

The German defense system of the south coast of France was thoroughly planned and formidable. That it appeared to be of limited effectiveness against our amphibious assault can be attributed to the following factors:

(1) The enemy during the previous six months had erroneously estimated that the most probable place of attack was in other sectors and the actual assault area had lower priority in defense preparations. Red Camel beach in the Gulf of Frejus was approaching the planned defense pattern and had the very troublesome shallow-water mines laid but even here work had not progressed very far on installation of the second and third rows of mined underwater concrete pyramids. On a considerable number of assault beaches no underwater obstacles had been installed although a great many were placed off beaches west of Marseille and throughout the coastal area large numbers were found ashore ready for installation;

(2) The thinning out of defense personnel caused by movement of reserves to the Northern France front caused a situation where numerous defenses were manned by low category troops and mobile reserves were badly placed to effectively meet our invasion;

(3) With the success of the Northern France invasion and the growth of FFI activity throughout France the general enemy situation deteriorated progressively as efforts were made to move administrative and non-essential supplies and personnel back to Germany in spite of destruction and damage to lines of transportation and supply and growing shortage of fuel;

(4) Lack of enemy air power imposed great difficulty on his movements and permitted effective application of our air forces in bombing, reconnaissance, air spotting, and direct attack on his ground forces;

(5) Our generally accurate knowledge of the enemy defense preparations throughout the planning period enabled plans to be formulated which made most effective use of our available forces to fully exploit factors of enemy weakness. Adequate well-coordinated offensive power was concentrated on the particular points which could threaten the success of those plans.

Section 2.4

UNDERWATER OBSTRUCTIONS AND MINES

An important part of the enemy defense plan for the southern coast of France was the laying of off-shore minefields, including shallow water mines off likely landing places, and the placement of underwater obstructions close inshore. However, the characteristics of the theater presented special problems, both for defender and attacker, of which account had to be taken in developing our intelligence estimate.

The factor of greatest influence with respect to underwater obstructions was the negligible tidal range. This required underwater obstructions to be placed almost entirely by boats or barges and limited the construction work which could feasibly be done at the site of the obstacle. It also prevented full view of the underwater obstruction layout by aerial photography or reconnaissance at low tide and required demolition plans to be based entirely on the destruction of submerged objects.

The beaches of the southern coast of France are in general of moderate to comparatively steep underwater gradients, with the more gentle gradients off beaches to the west of the Rhone Delta and steeper gradients found to the north-eastward of Rade d'Hyeres. This factor limited the width of the zone of effective underwater obstructions. On a number of beaches in the Cavalaire-Agay sector the beaches were fronted with sandbars on which obstacles could be effectively placed.

With respect to moored mines the zone of mineable water was much wider off the coast in the Gulf of Lyons. Along the coast from Ile de Levant north-eastward the 100 fathom is about 3 to 6 miles offshore narrowly limiting the area in which it was practicable for the enemy to lay minefields. Shallow water mines - or antiboat mines with snaglines - could be laid, of course, anywhere along the coast.

The first step taken was to study the types of obstructions encountered and noted on the channel coast of France in order to estimate characteristics of those most likely to be employed by the enemy on the Mediterranean coast to meet the special conditions there. In the absence of confirming information these were estimated to be concrete pyramids, which could be readily placed with crane barges, and floating rafts or booms with mines attached which could be moored in place with small craft. Jetted rails or mined stakes would also be a readily available form of obstruction in areas having a sandy bottom offshore and wooded areas near the beaches to provide timber. This estimate was confirmed by agents' reports of construction of concrete pyramids and then visually in June by excellent low oblique photographs of beaches in the Sete area which indicated methods of manufacture and technique of placement. During June and July, as good weather and clear water photographic sorties were frequently carried out, obtaining thorough vertical and close oblique coverage, an accurate picture of the enemy underwater obstruction program was developed.

In accordance with his erroneous estimate of our intentions the enemy devoted the most attention to landing areas west of Marseille. It may be that more gentle underwater gradients existing there, with better conditions for placing obstructions, was also a factor. However, in the Cavalaire-Agay sector considerable progress was also made by D-Day. Up to 25 July no underwater obstructions had been placed off beach 259 in Baie de Cavalaire although it had been noted that a supply of concrete pyramids was located conveniently near the beach. By 15 August a large number with attached mines had been placed in one random row 14 to 17 feet apart and following in general the contours of the sand bar in depths 5 to 7 feet deep so that the tips were a little above or below the surface.

Off Beach 261, Baie de Pampelonne, wooden piling or stakes ranging from 10 to 14 inches in diameter with the tops projecting a small variable distance above the surface, were being placed. On 25 July there was an inner row about 2,600 yards long and an outer row about 1,800 yards long. They were set in a wavy pattern with the rows 10-12 feet apart and the piling spaced about 14-15 feet apart apparently following the sandbar 40 to 110 yards offshore. Installation was in progress up to D-Day, having commenced sometime between 21 May and 28 May. It was estimated that these piling would be mined and be connected with tripwires since they would be comparatively ineffective otherwise. In the assault they were of little hindrance, large gaps being opened by our Apex boats, and it was reported that an LCM could push over these piling without difficulty or serious damage. It is doubtful if the piling were in fact mined and it is probable that the enemy's installation program in this respect was incomplete.

Off Beaches 264 and 264A one row of concrete pyramids had been completed by 25 July and a second row was in progress. They were laid in a random pattern 13 to 15 feet apart 30 to 165 yards offshore in 5 1/2 to 6 feet of water. Work here commenced sometime after 11 May. These obstructions were individually mined with Tellermines embedded in concrete blocks. (For details and sketch see Section 5.8, Part II).

On the Delta sector beaches no underwater obstacles had been noted and none were found in the assault. This was also true of Beaches 264B and 265 in the Camel sector.

A shallow water anti-boat mine with long green lines attached which were of low visibility in the water and were made buoyant by being threaded through corks at intervals was considered a dangerous threat. From the Gulf of Fos westward a large number were found to have been laid along possible landing beaches but enemy resources apparently did not permit more rapid laying and only first priority in the enemy estimate had been accomplished. It is probable that a D-Day six weeks later would have found many of these in the assault sector.

The general plan for enemy offshore minefields appeared to be directed toward denial of approach to the ports and blocking of passage between islands or between islands and mainland. (See diagrams XV and XVI for number and location of mines swept on and after D-Day.) Information regarding off-shore minefields was based largely on agents' reports and French sources. Submarines operating off the southern coast of France had reported contacts with minefields from time to time. All available information was correlated and during July special attempts were made to confirm or disprove presence of enemy minefields in suspected locations with submarines using detection apparatus. Although the presence and location of some fields west of Toulon was confirmed, the results of the reconnaissance in the assault area were disappointing. In the Gulf of Frejus, where earlier reports had placed a minefield, and which it was estimated would probably be mined, the submarine on 28 July was unable to detect any mines after thorough coverage. The possibility of mines in the Gulf of Frejus was not dismissed but the well-laid field of 90 moored and 15 magnetic mines with numerous sweeping obstructors which were swept after D-Day was an unexpected obstacle in the landings. At the mouth of the Gulf of St. Tropez submarine reconnaissance indicated one definite line of mines and another doubtful contact. As these were in accord with earlier information from ground sources the existence of minefields there was accepted. However, no mines were found when the area was thoroughly swept. There was also a small minefield in the Baie de Cavalaire and this was indicated both by ground reports and submarine reconnaissance. In general the enemy plan appeared to be to lay dense fields across entrances of gulfs and bays and larger fields out several miles to seaward with a coast-wise traffic lane inshore.

CONCLUSIONS

The efficacy of underwater obstructions as a beach defense depends strongly upon selection of types suitable to tide, depth and current conditions. Individual mining of obstacles greatly increases their defensive value.

Shallow water anti-boat moored and bottom mines are a serious obstacle to amphibious landings because of the time required to clear them.

Underwater obstructions effective against landing craft can be accurately evaluated by aerial photography.

Mine intelligence is of utmost importance in planning amphibious assaults and is the most difficult feature of the enemy defensive strength to evaluate because aerial photographs or reconnaissance will not give direct information but only inferences based on activities of mine layers, routes of coastal traffic, and apparent restrictions on movements of fishing vessels. Deductions may then be drawn from those inferences when studied in connection with an analysis of characteristics of theater as related to mining. The highly effective mine spotting from slow planes or blimps can be expected to be available only after the area is secured.

RECOMMENDATION

It is recommended that experiment and research be directed toward means by submarine detection or otherwise of locating minefields off hostile coasts, particularly shallow water mines close inshore.

Section 2.5

ENEMY AIR FORCES

The intelligence estimate respecting enemy air forces was directed toward analysis of enemy air capabilities in opposition to our invasion. It was estimated that in line with the enemy overall air situation and his requirements for defense in Northern France and Germany his action against invasion naval forces would be limited to controlled bomb or torpedo attacks against shipping and mine-laying carried out at night. The area of water suitable for night mine-laying was, however, small and danger from this source was considered to exist in the invasion sector only in Gulf of Frejus, Gulf of St. Tropez and Rade d'Hyeres.

The day to day estimate of enemy air forces is included in the Campaign Narrative, Chapter 1, Part II. After D+6 enemy air forces were no longer considered an appreciable threat to our naval units.

Section 2.6

ENEMY NAVAL FORCES

Enemy naval forces in the Western Mediterranean during the planning period for the invasion of Southern France were estimated to be incapable of presenting any serious threat to our naval task forces. The submarine threat was steadily declining and after the highly effective bombing of Toulon in early July was of minor nature. Frequent photographic reconnaissance of enemy ports and reports from agents in Southern France were the principal sources of information on enemy units prior to D-Day.

The probable employment of explosive boats and human torpedoes from Ligurian Sea bases had been noted in the Information Annex to the Operation Plan. Explosive boats were first employed by the enemy on the night of 26 August and from time to time thereafter but with no damage to our forces and a high percentage of casualties to the enemy. Human torpedoes were first encountered on 5 September but their operations were also ineffective in the presence of vigilant light screening forces. A combination airplane - PT screen proved to be particularly effective in detecting and frustrating this type of attack. A number of prisoners and specimens of both types of craft were recovered and detailed information concerning them has been separately reported.

For day to day estimate of enemy naval forces see Campaign Narrative, Chapter 1, Part II.

Section 2.7

BEACH INTELLIGENCE

The intelligence collected, evaluated, and disseminated to all naval forces concerned in the operation comprised three phases:

(1) The problem presented during the planning stage in the selection of suitable landing areas and in turn beaches;

(2) The solution or choice of beaches based upon the evaluation of all available information;

(3) The final presentation, graphically and by description, disseminated to all forces prior to embarkation for the assault area;

(4) An evaluation of the degree of accuracy of this intelligence as compared with the actual conditions encountered on the beaches.

THE PROBLEM

The mission of capturing the ports Toulon and Marseille at the earliest possible moment in order to maintain and support the Seventh Army's advance up the Rhone Valley necessitated that such landings be made on beaches the suitability of which would be based upon fulfilling the following prerequisites:

(1) Suitable for 3 divisional assault and close follow-up divisions;

(2) Landing beaches possess adequate exits with or without preparation connecting with inland lines of transportation and supply and suitable supply dump areas to support maintenance over the beaches until ports opened and beaches closed;

(3) Beaches within reasonable range of the objectives of Toulon and Marseille;

(4) Enemy defenses not prohibitive for reasonable chance of success of approach to and landing on beaches.

SOLUTION

In the course of selecting the landing beaches for the invasion, the coast line of Mediterranean France from the Spanish to the Italian borders was studied with a view to selecting an area of landing beaches most favorable both in location and suitability for landing to fulfill the tactical plan of the Seventh Army. The navy planning staff, in joint planning with army, and air staffs, began the study of the Mediterranean coast of France for the above purpose about 28 December, 1943. Thus, an exhaustive study and evaluation of all beaches was possible and in turn valuable in the final planning phase requiring the selection of the particular assault area.

The western coastline from the Spanish boarder to the mouth of the Rhone contained feasible landing beaches in the Sete-Agde area only. The suitability of these beaches was limited by offshore sand bars, swampy terrain, numerous streams and canals, and restricted canalized lines of transportation and supply plus the fact that the area was distant from the Rhone Valley.

The Golf de Fos area, heavily mined, although containing flat beaches, was undesirable because of swampy canal areas, and having no port of any size capable of supporting assault divisions and maintaining the Army in its advance inland.

The Marseille-Toulon beaches were suitable as landing points from a purely naval view point but underwater obstacles, coast, and beach defenses were the strongest on the coast. The Cannes-Nice area was also very strongly defended in terms of actual installations backed by very steeply rising terrain.

The Cavalaire Bay-Agay area appeared to be the most favorable, because the beaches were fair to moderate and capable of absorbing a 3 divisional assault and subsequent maintenance over the beaches until the ports of Toulon and Marseille were opened. The defenses were strong but considerably less so than the beaches between Marseille and Toulon.

Factors leading to selection were:

(1) Favorable seaward approach;

(2) Narrow coastal zone suitable for mining;

(3) Least density of enemy coast defense guns affecting approach, transport areas and landing beaches;

(4) Good to moderate beaches, some well suited to maintenance.

Disadvantages accepted were:

(1) Poor road net and difficult terrain inland from assault beaches (if high ground back of beaches should not be captured early, the army would be in a difficult position and the unloading and the maintenance over beaches would be jeopardized);

(2) Distance from objective (about 38 miles from Toulon) and resultant necessity for considerable advance overland in order to capture a port;

(3) Necessity for maintenance and build up over beaches for an extended period of time.

The evaluated information which led to the above choice of landing beaches was drawn from the following sources:

(1) French Admiralty and British Admiralty charts were studied for data regarding fathom lines, soundings, charted rocks, and as a basis for estimated charted underwater beach gradients for determining the suitability of craft for landing on the various beaches (the large scale French charts, brought up to date in 1940, were particularly valuable in this respect);

(2) Ground information was secured from civilian agents and military intelligence services, emigres and refugees from the target area, prisoners of war, and French naval and military personnel who were particularly familiar with the area;

(3) Special studies such as I.S.I.S. publications, US Army Engineering Studies of Terrain and Landing Beaches, O.N.I. publications, H.O. Mediterranean Pilot, were consulted and pertinent information coordinated into the beach intelligence produced for the operation;

(4) The most valuable source of information was the study and interpretation of aerial photographs, both high altitude verticals and low obliques (the

location of sand bars lying offshore of assault beaches were accurately plotted, and, when weather conditions produced suitable visibility and surface waves, the wave method of determination of depths over sand bars and underwater gradients was used. The high degree of accuracy attained in such hydrographic estimates is in large part due to the knowledge and experience gained in previous amphibious operations and the improvement in the wave method technique as developed and extensively used in this theater);

(5) Recent tourist snapshots and commercial photographs were studied for information as to land marks or details as to terrain, vegetation and visual aids for identification;

(6) Submarine reconnaissance was carried out but was not successful in detecting enemy minefields or the absence of mines;

(7) Particular attention was given to an exhaustive study of the suitability of beaches for maintenance pending the opening of the ports of Toulon and Marseille.

INTELLIGENCE PRESENTATIONS

Naval Planning Memorandum No. 12 "Beach Reports" was issued 19 February with supplements periodically thereafter. By this means detailed beach data for all beaches under consideration was made available to subordinate commands in advance of the issuance of operation plans as a guide to training and early planning.

Beach intelligence, graphic and descriptive, disseminated to all forces prior to embarkation for the assault area, consisted of the following:

(1) Information Annex to Op-Plan 4-44, contained full description of the hydrographic condition of all beaches (location, depth of water over sand bars, beach exits, navigational aids for identification, suitability for types of craft);

(2) Panoramic Beach Sketches (see Section 2.10, Part II).

Beach intelligence material was designed for the particular requirements of the following:

(1) Amphibious Scouts;

(2) Beach Battalions;

(3) Personnel of all landing craft;

(4) Army engineering units, shore regiments, and transportation units for planning of routing of vehicle traffic.

RESULTS

A mobile survey unit surveyed the various beaches after the assault for the purpose of comparing actual conditions with disseminated information in order that lessons might be drawn for future evaluation of beaches. A special report is in preparation covering this survey of beaches.

Soundings were made off the assault beaches by naval personnel after the assault waves had landed. It was found that the actual conditions encountered on the beaches reflected a very high degree of accuracy in the naval planning evaluations.

It was estimated that Red and Green beaches in Delta area would require pontoon causeways for LSTs because of a sand bar fronting these adjoining beaches. The actual conditions encountered on these beaches confirmed this estimate.

Yellow and Blue beaches in Delta area were estimated to be suitable for all craft including LSTs (without pontoon causeways). LSTs beached dry on these two beaches. In Camel and Alpha areas the suitability or lack of suitability for beaching various types of craft likewise agreed with pre-invasion estimates.

The close agreement between disseminated information and actual conditions encountered effectively contributed to the well ordered landings of the assault waves, the rapid advance of assault troops inland, the lack of congestion on the beaches, and the rapid unloading of a great quantity of vehicles over the beaches and movement inland.

The contribution of accurate beach intelligence to the carrying out of the assault was evidenced by the efficiency achieved by both naval personnel and army assault troops knowing clearly in advance what to expect on the beaches and, aided by this information, being thoroughly prepared to carry out their respective planned missions.

Section 2.8

PHOTOGRAPHIC INTERPRETATION

Eight officers composed the Photo Interpretation Unit during the planning and execution of the operation. It was considered that their services could best be utilized during the planning stage by assigning each officer a specialized task. The information obtained by these different officers was correlated by the Intelligence Officer and furnished to the planners and commands concerned in the form of Naval Planning Memoranda. These were kept up to date and supplements issued whenever sufficient changes warranted. A description of their duties, with the number of photo interpreters assigned to each, follows:

(1) Joint Army-Navy Photo Interpretation Unit. This unit was made up of two naval officers and four army officers. Its task was general Photo Interpretation of all pictures obtained of the areas concerned, and to furnish defense information reports for Collation Maps used by all forces during the operation.

(2) Coast Defense Batteries. One officer was assigned to work on coast defense batteries exclusively, to effect a coordination of all photo interpretation information on batteries with all other available information. A coastal defense battery map of the assault and adjoining area of the Southern Coast of France was prepared for the operation showing the location, coordinates, and a short description of every coastal defense and dual purpose battery capable of firing on the invasion forces. It was distributed to all forces concerned and was used as a guide to assigned targets and for counter battery fire.

(3) Minor beach defenses were assigned to another officer. These included all active and passive defenses, except coast defense batteries, which could affect landings on potential assault beaches. The duties of this officer were to coordinate all photo interpretation information on defenses with all other available information. The memoranda issued on minor defenses usually included a map (scale 1:25,000) with all photographic defense information overprinted in red and all other defense information in purple. They covered every beach along the coastline being considered by the planners. The defense information in its final form was presented graphically on Panoramic Beach Sketches and Collation Maps.

(4) One officer was assigned the task of obtaining information relating to suitability of beaches and approaches. This necessitated obtaining the best information possible on exits, gradients, presence of sandbars, presence of offshore rocks, nature of bottom and suitability of anchorage. This was largely obtained from aerial photographs and correlated with information from other sources. For the operation the final information was presented graphically on the Panoramic Beach Sketches and Collation Maps.

(5) One officer was assigned to making panoramic sketches of all beaches selected for assault landings. (See Section 2.10, Part II for discussion of Panoramic Beach Sketches.)

(6) One officer was assigned to collect and collate all information concerning ports and harbors. Overlay sketches were made from photographs to show available facilities, depths of basins, potential blockships, and conditions of quays, railroads, etc.

(7) The Senior Photo-Interpretor coordinated the photo-interpretation aspects of the activities outlined above. His duties in cooperation with the army officer in charge of the Joint Unit included liaison with the wing or squadron responsible for photo reconnaissance, determination of intervals at which sorties should be flown over given areas, and of the type of sortie to be flown, designating focal length of camera to be used and scale of pictures desired. He was assigned the task of procuring different types of pictures. In some cases, clear water pictures along the coast were desired while in other cases wave pictures for determining gradients were required. Color pictures were obtained in a few cases and comparison made with ordinary black and white. Several sorties of low obliques were obtained which proved especially valuable in preparation of beach sketches and confirmation of beach defenses. Near the end of the planning period the Task Force Commanders were furnished with complete and repetitive photographic cover of their respective areas.

ASSIGNMENT OF PERSONNEL DURING THE OPERATIONAL PHASE

It was necessary to maintain contact between the Joint Army-Navy Interpretation Unit, part of which remained on shore, and the flagships of the assault forces. This contact was the responsibility of the navy and such information as was obtained by interpretation of new sorties was sent by dispatch to the Task Force Commanders. Part of the unit went ashore on D-Day and started functioning on D plus 10, at which time the remainder joined. The entire unit proceeded with the Seventh Army, until D plus 38, when the naval unit returned to the flagship of NCWTF and continued interpretation of areas still of interest to the Navy.

The completeness of available facilities in the Photo Interpretation Room and the proximity of the photographic laboratory and map reproduction unit aboard the flagship USS CATOCTIN made possible the rapid production of collation maps covering areas currently under naval bombardment.

In addition to the above, navy photo interpreters were assigned to units of the Western Task Force as follows:

(1) The coastal battery specialist was aboard the flagship of the support force, his duties being to aid the gunnery and intelligence officers in identification of batteries for counter battery fire and to brief the ship's spotting planes.

(2) One officer was assigned each of the following CVEs of the Carrier Force, HMS HUNTER, HMS STALKER, HMS ATTACKER, for the purpose of briefing pilots on bombing and spotting missions and for interpretation of any photographs which the squadrons from the CVEs were able to take. USS KASAAN BAY and USS TULAGI had naval photo-interpretation officers regularly assigned. These officers worked in close liaison with the naval element of the Interpretation Unit during the last stages of planning.

(3) One photo-interpreter was part of the operation intelligence section in the flagship of NCWTF to correlate all photo interpretation information which came in during the operation and to answer questions regarding the material published prior to getting under way.

CONCLUSIONS

From the photo-interpretation experience on this operation during both planning and operation stages the following conclusions are drawn:

(1) In an operation involving Joint Army and Navy forces a Joint Photo Interpretation Section is highly desirable to ensure that Army and Navy aspects are given full consideration in photo-interpretation and the resulting intelligence meets the needs of all services concerned.

(2) The additional assignment of photo interpreters to specialized study of various types of enemy defences and aspects of beach study has the effect of getting better information with less effort than if every interpreter is charged with all types of work. The development thereby of "expert consultants" on the various aspects of enemy information raises the level of general interpretation and directs the efforts of photo interpreters most efficiently in obtaining information for the planning or operation in progress.

(3) Graphic presentation of information is more effective than written reports particularly for documents to be used by invasion forces.

Section 2.9

RUBBER TOPOGRAPHIC MODELS

Facilities available in the Amphibious Training Force, Atlantic Fleet, were utilized for the construction of sponge rubber topographic models covering the coastline area for the invasion. Topographic models had been found very useful in preparation for the invasion of Sicily but the plaster models available at that time were cumbersome and heavy, presenting many difficulties in security, transportation and ready use on board ship. It was expected that flexible sponge rubber models would obviate these difficulties and broaden the field of their usefulness. These expectations were met in a highly satisfactory manner.

The construction of the models was requested in March as soon as the most probable area was indicated in preliminary planning. This was with the expectation that D-Day would be in June. The following instructions accompanied the request:

(1) Scale to be 1:10,000 horizontal and vertical;

(2) Sections to be no larger than 3 x 5 feet;

(3) Division into sections to be in accordance with limits furnished which were intended to include a probable landing beach in the central part of the model so that flanking landmarks would appear on the same section;

(4) Surfaces to be marked with British military grid.

At a later date, when it was known that the operation would be delayed, further sections were requested to cover flanking areas and the Hyeres Islands.

The quantity ordered was estimated on a basis of one complete set for each major Task Force Commander and appropriate assault beach sections for each assault group. Distribution to army forces was on the basis of a complete set to Army Corps and Division Commanders with appropriate assault beach sections to regiments. Army commands considered them extremely useful for briefing and study by assault units.

The principal uses for the models were study by Navy, Army and Air Force planning staffs and briefing of personnel enroute to the assault area. The light flexible sections were particularly convenient for this purpose as they could be carried about the ship and displayed in crowded compartments.

The set on the flagship was laid out on deck forward of the flagbridge and one level below so that from the bridge an oblique view of the entire coastal assault area was presented.

Section 2.10

PANORAMIC BEACH SKETCHES

    The term "Panoramic Beach Sketches", as produced for this operation by the Intelligence Section of NCWTF, refers to a series of 12 documents covering the assault beaches. Each document measures approximately 22" by 26". On one side of the document, at the top, is the sketch of the beach area, (scale about 1/5,000), a combined oblique perspective sketch of the assault beach and inland terrain including information as listed below. Under this sketch are two shoreline silhouettes sketched at water level, with the particular designated assault beach marked: one at close approach, the other at distant approach. At the bottom of this side of the document is a sketch of an overall oblique view of the entire assault area, showing the assault beaches of all three attack forces.

    On the reverse side of the document is a collation map (scale 1/25,000) of the beach area covered in the particular sketch including surrounding area not included in the beach sketch itself. This collation map was included in the document in order to supply army assault personnel as well as naval forces, in one composite document, a map showing terrain and defenses of the general vicinity.

    Panoramic Beach Sketches, in the form developed by the Intelligence Section of NCWTF, were used with marked success by naval and army forces during previous amphibious operations in French Morocco, Sicily, Salerno and Anzio. In the course of these operations, much improvement in technique has been made with the result that the Panoramic Beach Sketches used by our forces in the invasion of Southern France represented the best effort to date both in plan, scope of information, and technique employed in their production. In early stages of joint planning the Seventh Army adopted the Panoramic Beach Sketch as produced by this command as a standard document for distribution down to and including platoon commanders of troops in assault. Navy distribution was on a basis to provide all commands and units concerned in the assault including all boat coxswains. This required 6,000 sets for the army and 2,000 sets for the navy but the manifold advantages of army and navy joint operations in assault areas being conducted with identical intelligence and operational maps acceptable to both and meeting the requirements of both has been amply demonstrated in past amphibious operations.

    The Panoramic Beach Sketches produced for this operation present in one graphic, panoramic form, as viewed from seaward, all evaluated and coordinated information pertinent to the assault. Among the various features included are:

Beach Sketch:

    (a) Hydrographic conditions on and offshore of the assault beaches (2 fathom curve, rocks, shoals, sandbars, with depths over same, beach gradients, rock, sand or weed bottom, etc.).

    (b) Characteristics of the beaches (dimensions, composition (sand or shingle), dune area if any, with height).

    (c) Inland terrain (contour features, tree, scrub or cultivated areas, canals, streams, stone walls, buildings, fences, heights of rising terrain, cliffs, etc.).

    (d) Lines of communications (condition, description of beach exits and whether or not preparation required, net work of roads and description of same, railways, standard or narrow gauge, tunnels, etc.).

(e) Distance between important geographical points.

(f) Geographical names of localities, towns, rivers, mountains, bays, gulfs.

(g) Conspicuous land marks.

(h) Enemy defenses (strong points, observation posts, machine gun positions, pill boxes, casemates, barbed wire, underwater obstacles, sea, beach and land mines, AA, DP, medium and heavy coastal batteries, anti-tank walls and ditches, road blocks, fortified buildings, etc.).

Close and distant approach water level shoreline silhouettes:

(i) Sketches of both distant and close approach offshore water level silhouettes of shoreline, with designated assault beach area marked with conspicuous landmarks to aid in identification of the assault beach.

Overall oblique view of assault area:

(j) Sketch of overall oblique view of entire assault area from height of about 1,000 feet affshore to orient each attack force with complete assault picture.

Collation map on reverse side of document:

(k) Special collation maps on reverse side of each sketch covering the beach and adjoining areas not included in the sketch itself. This collation map, showing defenses, hydrographic and topographic information, serves as a handy supplement to the sketch when assault troops advance beyond the area covered in the sketch itself, and supplies naval forces with necessary information in the event action, such as new landings, should be made in areas of coast not shown on the designated assault beaches covered in the sketches.

The Panoramic Beach Sketches served the following purposes in this operation:

(a) Used for study by army and naval planning staffs prior to embarkation.

(b) Used for study and for briefing of all army and naval personnel concerned with the assault phase of the operation.

(1) Army Personnel: for study, briefing and use during assault by Army Corps, Divisional, Regimental, Battalion Commands, and distributed down to assault platoon level. Six thousand copies of each sketch were furnished to Seventh Army for distribution to forces including, in addition to combat infantry, the following units: engineers, shore regiments, transportation and supply, artillery, and tank units, etc.

(2) Naval Personnel: task forces and group staffs, gunfire support force, shore fire control parties, boat group commanders and coxswains, amphibious scouts, beach battalions.

On the basis of reports from personnel who used the Panoramic Beach Sketches during the assault, these sketches were of great value and assistance in the carrying out of the assault. The graphic presentation of all assault intelligence, with the sketching of terrain encountered and its connection with the respective missions of personnel involved in the assault, all in one composite document, has demonstrated its value in the phases of planning, briefing and actual assault.

Section 2.11

COMBAT INTELLIGENCE

The <u>Intelligence Mission</u> for the invasion of Southern France was:

(1) The provision of adequate intelligence of the enemy and of the theater of operations, in order to contribute to freedom of action in the operations contemplated;

(2) The exploitation of long-range technical, and counter intelligence from prisoners of war, captured documents, and sources in captured territory, in order to obtain information useful for future planning.

As a basic directive for the provision of adequate intelligence of the enemy and of the theater of operations the following listed <u>essential elements of information</u>, applicable to this operation, were promulgated to all units to serve as a guide in the search for and reporting of information:

(1) Will the enemy attack with submarines? Destroyers? E-boats? Floating or laid mines? Toxic gas? If so, when? Where? In what force? From what direction?

(2) Will the enemy air forces attack our convoys or supporting forces? If so, when? Where? Type and number of planes?

(3) Do offshore minefields bar approach to the assault sector? If so are they in location and numbers previously reported? What types? Moored? Controlled? Influence? Anti-boat? In what depths of water? What is location of enemy swept channels and areas?

(4) Do underwater artificial obstructions prevent landing on designated beaches? Types? Numbers? Strength?

(5) Do underwater beach gradients encountered by our boats and craft vary markedly from those expected? If so, what is suitability for types of craft? Frontage and location for each?

(6) Do natural obstructions hazard approach of craft to designated beaches? Rocks? Shoals? Are they visible? What depth?

(7) What is scale of effort by enemy coast defense batteries? What areas offshore are taken under fire? What is location, number, and caliber of guns?

(8) What damage to enemy defenses and batteries by our supporting gunfire? By our aerial bombing?

(9) How effective are enemy beach defenses? Is the enemy using new types of weapons or obstructions? Flame throwers or burning liquid on water? Smoke? Toxic gas? Is ground contaminated with toxic agents?

(10) How effective are enemy inshore defenses? Is the enemy preventing attainment of our designated beachheads and phase lines on schedule? What is line of contact with the enemy?

(11) Will the enemy counter-attack our beachhead forces? If so, in what strength? From what direction? How effective?

(12) Do local inhabitants aid our forces? If so, how effective is their assistance?

Account was taken of the fact that a large part of the information required could be reported by the Task Force and Task Group commanders under whose command ships, craft and boats encounter and observe the objectives. To organize and correlate this flow of information instructions relating to submission of reports - combining operational and logistic requirements - were promulgated in the Intelligence Plan.

On 17 June Naval Planning Memorandum No. 19, "Combat Intelligence in Amphibious Operations," was issued as the directive for the organization within amphibious task forces of means to provide the commander with information concerning strength, disposition and movements of the enemy in the assault sector and conditions on and offshore significant to the progress of the amphibious assault. This organization was based on the plan submitted to COMINCH in COMNAVNAW letter File No. A8-2, Serial 0860 of 10 December 1943. The assignment and principal intelligence functions of the following personnel were described:

(1) Naval Amphibious Scouts.

Number and assignment to depend upon the requirements of the beach locating and marking plan but normally one qualified officer was to be assigned to each combat loaded transport or group of craft embarking a battalion landing team. The scouts and their boat crews were to be especially instructed and trained in methods of inshore reconnaissance, identification of points on the coast from seaward, clandestine lanlings, location and marking of beaches on a hostile coast, and hydrographic reconnaissance during the assault. Enroute to the assault area the amphibious scout officers would brief assault boat officers and crews in the hydrographic and defense details of the assault beaches. After H-hour, in addition to hydrographic reconnaissance, they would maintain intelligence liaison with the beach battalion assault elements and the Beach Group Commander and serve as boat courier if required for the transmission of intelligence. The prime aim of the above functions, of particular application to a combat loaded transport, is to send in to the assault boat officers and crews thoroughly briefed on the conditions they are to overcome, on beaches quickly and accurately located, and to inform the commanding officer of the transport as promptly as possible of the beach and hydrographic conditions and the degree of enemy resistance on or near the beach.

(2) Beach Battalion Intelligence Officers.

The scope in area of the intelligence tasks under direct cognizance of the Beach Battalion Commander was considered to be that of an army division in amphibious assault. These intelligence tasks and functions were:

(a) To maintain close liaison with the naval task group commanders intelligence officer and with the G-2 of the army division embarked commencing with the training phase prior to embarkation and continuing until the division has moved inland after the assault;

(b) To coordinate all hydrographic reconnaissance within the task force area;

(c) To prepare and maintain situation maps and charts for the Beach Battalion Information Center;

(d) To coordinate the activities of the naval combat intelligence officers assigned on temporary duty to the task group;

(e) To prepare the intelligence section of reports by the divisional beachmaster to the task group or task force commanders concerned;

(f) To perform naval security functions for the divisional beach area;

(g) To receive and render assistance to navy accredited press representatives and photographers who land in the divisional area;

(h) To carry out the duties of Chief Censor for private correspondence of personnel of the naval beach battalion.

The above delineation of intelligence responsibilities was considered helpful and contributed to smooth integration of naval activity on shore with the overall effort.

(3) Beach Battalion Assistant Intelligence Officers.

For administrative purposes this term was applied to the specially qualified combat intelligence officers assigned to each task force for the period of the amphibious operation. For this operation six such officers, three with German and three with French language qualifications, were assigned temporary additional duty from Naval Intelligence Unit, US Eighth Fleet. For several months before the operation they were trained in interrogation, examination of captured documents, counter-intelligence, and naval responsibilities in port security. For the operation they were formed into three teams and participated with the task forces to which assigned in final training and rehearsals, thus having an opportunity to establish liaison with intelligence officers of the army division and naval task force, to study details of the operation in their sector, and to be equipped with field equipment, transportation and portable voice radio for rapid communication on the Beach Battalion circuit. Largely because of the innovation of this assignment some difficulties were experienced in the matter of equipment because Task Force Commander's plans did not in all cases include provision for it. The orders of these officers provided that they remain under command of the senior naval authority ashore upon withdrawal of the naval assault forces and that they report to the naval port command upon the capture of the ports.

The combat intelligence teams described above landed on D-Day with the follow-up waves and carried out the functions of:

(a) Preliminary interrogation of naval prisoners of war;

(b) Interrogation of civilian inhabitants;

(c) Search for and seizure of enemy equipment and documents;

(d) Liaison with army counter-intelligence, document centers, and prisoner of war interrogation teams, together with interrogation of army prisoners as practicable who might have information of naval interest;

(e) Reconnaissance on shore as required, to obtain essential elements of information listed above.

All of the above functions were carried throughout the assault period with highly satisfactory results. Numerous intelligence reports of immediate operational value were made to the Task Force Commanders concerned. The second part of the Intelligence Mission - the exploitation of the situation to obtain long range technical and counter-intelligence information - was also carried out by these teams with equally satisfactory results.

In addition to the combat intelligence teams each Beach Battalion had assigned specially selected French naval officers and ratings familiar with the locality. These served to provide local information and as liaison and interpreters in dealing with the local population and with the French Army follow up divisions. They were extremely useful in all phases of the assault and follow up period.

Upon the capture of Toulon and Marseille the combat intelligence officers were assigned for temporary duty to Commander Advanced Bases and contributed materially to rapid opening of the ports by obtaining information from captured documents, interrogation of prisoners of war, and civilians and by maintaining close liaison with military intelligence agencies.

CONCLUSIONS

The combat intelligence organization was sound, proved practicable, and produced a flow of information which was of material assistance to the conduct of the operation. Combat intelligence officers of suitable qualifications, in addition to the staff intelligence sections of task force commanders, are required to meet the onshore intelligence requirements of an amphibious force commander and to exploit the intelligence sources of naval interest in the beachhead.

RECOMMENDATIONS

(1) That the training of Amphibious Scout-Transport Intelligence officers and selected boat crews now carried on at Ft. Pierce, Florida, be continued and that training be kept realistic by return to the school after each major amphibious operation of a number of Amphibious Scout Officers who participated in the operation.

(2) That for each theater of probable amphibious operations a pool of combat intelligence officers of appropriate language qualifications and with suitable training and experience be maintained for temporary duty assignments to amphibious task groups. They should receive amphibious training and plans for the assignment of combat intelligence teams should include definite arrangements for transportation and radio communications.

Section 2.12

CAPTURED EQUIPMENT AND DOCUMENTS

The Naval Planning Memorandum entitled "Captured Equipment and Documents Directive" was issued by this command on 8 April 1944 as a basis for appropriate orders to be incorporated in the detailed plans of Attack Force Commanders. Every practicable effort was to be made to search for and collect enemy documents from captured or stranded ships, headquarters and naval offices on shore, signal and communication installations, and living quarters. A detailed listing of the types of documents particularly desired was set forth and instructions given for their marking. Where applicable, information of immediate operational value was to be extracted and disseminated to all commanders concerned without delay. Disposition of documents was to be in accordance with theatre directive which provided for forwarding army documents to the nearest army command and naval documents to the Joint Royal Navy - US Navy document center where analysis and evaluation was carried out and microfilm copies sent to both Navy Department and Admiralty, as well as dissemination, as appropriate, to operating forces in the Mediterranean.

Captured equipment was to be immediately reported - or if small in bulk - forwarded to NCWTF for disposition in accordance with AFHQ directives. These provided for joint inspection by interested services in the theater and eventual disposition of intelligence items in accordance with agreed policies of the Admiralty and Navy Department.

In addition to captures by the operating forces reliance was placed upon combat intelligence officers assigned for each assault area and the captured ports, on temporary duty from Naval Intelligence Unit, US Eighth Fleet. These officers were trained and briefed before the invasion with respect to local organization of enemy forces, location of headquarters, signal stations, offices, and living quarters of key officers. In addition there was to operate in the area, as close behind our lines as circumstances permitted, an inter-service intelligence collecting team, equipped with a portable microfilm unit. This team was to ensure coordinated effort of all intelligence agencies in the exploitation of material and documents left by the enemy. Close liaison was maintained between Eighth Fleet combat intelligence officers and this team.

The organization and procedures for recovering and exploiting intelligence from captured enemy documents and equipment was productive of valuable results. On D-day German mine-field charts of the Ligurian Sea were recovered. A combat-intelligence officer located, through interrogation of prisoners of war, and recovered, valuable communication and cipher documents. The greatest aid to the operating forces, however, occurred upon capture of Toulon and Marseille when intelligence officers located German harbor-blocking, demolition and mining plans which greatly facilitated the task of harbor clearance. The considerable flow of all types of documents to the Joint Document Center indicated that nearly all forces had become "document conscious" and that a few well qualified and trained combat intelligence officers, operating with definite targets based on thorough advance study of the local enemy situation, can effectively exploit the intelligence abounding in enemy documents available immediately after his retreat but most often lost or dissipated if not located and seized without delay.

It is recommended that the intelligence plan for any large amphibious operation include provision for the assignment of an appropriate number of naval combat intelligence officers with enemy document experience and that they be landed with suitable equipment as soon as practicable when a beachhead is secured in order to exploit intelligence from captured enemy documents.

Section 2.13

PRISONER OF WAR INTERROGATION

Only preliminary interrogation and that necessary to obtain information required for current operations was planned to be carried out in the theater of operations. Two US Navy U-boat personnel interrogators were attached to CSDIC (Combined Services Detailed Interrogation Center) near Rome, Italy. A mobile detachment from this center moved into Southern France about D plus seven. The US Navy interrogators worked with this detachment since a considerable number of U-boat personnel were captured in Toulon as well as one complete crew attempting to escape to Genoa in a schooner. In addition, as the German coast defenses were under naval command, there was much of naval interest in the interrogation of the German naval personnel captured by the army. The general procedure in such cases was to examine records at prisoner-of-war stockades and conduct preliminary interrogation to ascertain extent of knowledge of the prisoner and his apparent degree of cooperation. Promising cases were then removed to the CSDIC, Italy, for complete interrogation and preparation of reports.

Prompt prisoner-of-war interrogation in the captured ports of Marseille and Toulon produced information of great value in rendering safe areas in which ground mines had been planted and in minesweeping and clearance in the harbors. During the period of human torpedo and explosive boat attacks on the right flank of the assault sector a number of survivors were picked up by our naval forces. Preliminary interrogation of some of these prisoners by Commanding Officer, USS Philadelphia, produced information of operational value which was disseminated by dispatch.

CONCLUSION

Plans for a large amphibious operation should include provisions for the assignment and functioning of naval prisoner-of-war interrogators and the prompt dissemination of operational intelligence obtained from preliminary interrogation.

Section 2.14

PRESS RELATIONS

Twenty-one accredited war correspondents were attached to the United States Naval forces during the invasion of Southern France. These correspondents represented American, Canadian, British, French and Russian Press Associations, metropolitan newspapers, magazines and the radio field.

In addition to this coverage, three US Navy Combat Photographic Units, numbers five, eight and ten, consisting of 12 men and 3 officers, covered the operation for both motion pictures and still photographs. Other photographic coverage was provided by US Navy photographers. These photographers numbering 12 men, working under the direction of the Fleet Photographic Officer, obtained pictures of operations afloat, on the beaches and of conditions in the captured ports.

US Army mobile radio units were attached to the Western Task Force for the operation. These units, equipped with wire recorders, operated in ships of the shore bombardment groups and in aircraft carriers.

Two Marine Corps Public Relations Officers, two Marine Corps Combat Correspondents, and a Marine Corps Combat Photographer were attached to the battleship division during the assault. During the follow-up phase of the invasion, they accompanied units of the shore bombardment force and later visited enemy installations ashore. One official US Navy Combat Artist made the assault with the landing craft, and a public relations officer on temporary duty from the Office of Public Relations also covered assault landing operations.

The above personnel, both civil and military, obtained material which greatly supplemented the news releases furnished at AFHQ on the basis of NCWTF combined situation-intelligence reports.

During the assault and the follow-up period, navy public relations officers were assigned as follows:

(1) Public Relations Officer, US Eighth Fleet, in the flagship, NCWTF. Most of the censorship for naval articles and stories cleared from the assault area was performed in the flagship;

(2) Flagship, CTF 84, USS Duane;

(3) Flagship, CTF 85, USS Biscayne;

(4) Flagship, CTG 88.2 USS Kasaan Bay;

(5) Advanced post of Allied Force Headquarters. This officer was naval censor for copy returned by air courier to headquarters at Rome without naval clearance in the assault area.

A Royal Navy censor was attached to Allied Force Headquarters press unit established on the beach of Southern France on D-Day. Censorship rules in this theater are identical for both United States and Royal Navies and this officer handled United States Navy copy as well as that of the Royal Navy.

The assignment of all correspondents and photographers was coordinated with the Public Relations Officer, AFHQ, and Public Relations Officer, CinCMed, in order to ensure that the activities of all task forces, types of ships and craft, and services participating were reported to the full extent of the available means.

During the invasion of Southern France, a press correspondent was authorized, for the first time during operations in the Mediterranean, to send news stories by radio direct from the flagship. For this operation, US Navy radio circuits were used to transmit a maximum of 300 words twice each day, so that both morning and afternoon newspapers in the United States could be furnished with the changing picture of the invasion. These stories by a navy accredited correspondent aboard the flagship were written for, and distributed to, under pooling arrangements, all news services and correspondents represented at Allied Force Headquarters in Rome.

RECOMMENDATION

It is desirable that additional officers, trained in censorship and public relations, be ordered to a theater for temporary additional duty for major operations. They should be ordered to report several weeks in advance, if practicable, so that they may be thoroughly briefed in the organization of forces, theater security problems, and procedures for censorship.

Chapter 3

OPERATIONS

Section 3.1

REHEARSALS

Training of the naval forces for the invasion of Southern France was influenced by:

(1) The time of assembly in the Mediterranean of ships and craft.

Late in June, 28 LST and 19 LCT arrived from the United States, and twelve PC and 12 YMS arrived the latter part of July. The third week in July, 6 XAP, 24 LCI and 24 LCT arrived from the United Kingdom. These were followed by 6 AM and 6 YMS which arrived too late to be scheduled in the assault and proceeded to the assault area performing escort duty.

(2) Support of theater operations.

The Elba Operation took place the latter part of June; 4 LST, 20 LCI, and 20 LCT were involved. Ships and craft were also committed to the support of the Italian campaign. All landing craft were not released from these operations until 24 July, while DDs, PCs, SCs, and YMSs were employed until 6 August.

The first of the army divisions became available for training on 24 June. At this time, all escort sweeper ships and landing craft of the US Eighth Fleet were organized under Group I, Commander Eighth Amphibious Force. These ships and craft were intensively trained and later became nuclei for the assault force. Commander, Group II, Eighth Amphibious Force, the amphibious training commander, was engaged primarily in training the transports. The revised "Standard Operating Procedure", issued by Commander Eighth Amphibious Force, proved most valuable in carrying out the training program.

The third amphibious group commander arrived from the United Kingdom on 28 June. Commander Eighth Amphibious Force on this day promulgated an operation order which formed three amphibious assault groups.

Forces continued to be allocated as they entered the Mediterranean. Transports were assigned to the individual task groups on 12 July, while the escort sweeper ships and landing craft were assigned 21 July. Thereafter, stabilization of ship and craft assignments was stressed to permit close coordination between army and navy personnel, and familiarization of methods and procedures used by the respective commanders. British landing craft, composed of 7 LST, 25 LCI(L) and 87 LCT, which participated in the operation, were not definitely assigned until the final rehearsals were completed.

Amphibious training for the three army infantry divisions which participated in the invasion of Southern France was carried out in the Naples area. The 45th and 36th Divisions were trained at Salerno; the 3rd Division was trained at Pozzuoli. The decision to employ battle-trained divisions which were at the time fighting in Italy, and the probability that the trend of events in Italy would not allow their withdrawal to North African ports in sufficient time for training, strongly outweighed all other reasons for the selection of the training areas. Of especial concern, was the possibility that congestion of shipping in the Salerno-Naples-Pozzuoli area might so reduce shipping facilities as to cause the influx of supplies to fall below an acceptable minimum.

All divisions, having been withdrawn in the latter part of June, were subsequently made available for training by 8 July. Commander Eighth Amphibious Force was made directly responsible for training of all naval units. Commanding General, VI Corps, was responsible for preparation of the training schedule and supervision of the training of the VI Corps units. Decision was made by Commanding General, VI Corps, that in each division two RCT were to be trained in "shore to shore" landings, and one RCT in "ship to shore" landings. The training was to be realistic, objective, and based on the assumption that the assault would be made in daylight.

The 45th Division was able to complete for each battalion (a) one day on amphibious technique with LCVP and LCI(L), (b) one day and two night landings, (c) two RCT in "shore to shore" landings and the third RCT in "ship to shore" landings. Each regiment conducted one LCT night landing. The training was conducted during the period from 24 June to 14 July.

The 36th Division commenced training 8 July. Day and night landings with LST, LCI and LCT for both RCT and battalions were carried out during the period 14 July to 18 July. With the final RCT landing from transports on 22 July, all training for the Division was completed.

The 3rd Division commenced training 6 July and completed 27 July. Each battalion practiced landings from LCVPs, LCI(L)s, LCIs and LSTs. They off-loaded from LCI(L)s during one forenoon. They executed one full scale night landing in which a token number of vehicles were off-loaded. On 17 July one RCT landed from combat loaders in a "ship to shore" exercise.

The 1st Special Service Force with 4 APD exercised off Agropoli for a commando landing. On 4 August, they were joined by 4 LSI, 1 APD and 9 PT. After completing preliminary exercises, a full scale rehearsal was held, 7 August, on the Island of Ponza.

Gunfire support ships were assigned to Commander Support Force, Eighth Fleet, for training. A three-day bombardment exercise was held, which began 10 July at Camerota range, for the purpose of establishing smooth coordination between gunfire support ships and shore fire control parties composed of both army and navy personnel. Battleships, cruisers and destroyers conducted communication tests with aircraft spotting planes to acquaint all units in the use of the Mediterranean Bombardment Code.

Two US CVE departed the United States, 30 June, and conducted training for flight operations, glide bombing attacks and anti-submarine operations, while enroute to Oran. Prior to their departure 17 July for Malta, they supplied aircraft for spotting missions for gunfire support ships training in the Oran area. At Malta, the Carrier Task Force was organized into two groups. Two of the seven British CVE joined the American carriers to form one group, and departed Malta on 26 July for Alexandria in order to train as a unit and also to effect a feint to the east as part of the cover plan for strategic deception. The remaining five British CVE plus escorts assembled at Malta, the last week in July, as the second group and conducted intensive training for their future operations.

Specialized units were constituted into groups for training. Naval Combat Demolition Units were formed as permanent units to encourage the development, to increase the mechanical efficiency of the gear, and to permit complete familiarization by the personnel who were to operate the units. A special exercise was held 25 July to develope Standard Operating Procedure for these units. A sufficient number of LCT were equipped and trained for the launching of "DD tanks". A combined army, navy and air demonstration was held, on 20 June, at Salerno, in an attempt to develop the best method of clearing beach obstacles. Shore Fire Control Parties, both army and navy, visited gunfire support ships, where essential communication and gunnery conferences were held.

The 3rd Division completed its official rehearsal with a full scale landing at Mandragone in the Gulf of Gaeta, Italy, on 31 July. A total of 146 ships and craft were employed.

The second official rehearsal incorporated the landings for the 45th and 36th Divisions. It was also conducted as a communication and fighter director test, and involved the employment of all types of ships and commands. The XII Tactical Air Command provided high fighter cover for the surface craft and assault forces. The Provisional Troop Carrier Air Division, later called the 1st Airborne Task Force, provided nine pathfinders and ten three-plane serials for simulated drops over a designated dropping zone 5 miles west of Albanella, guided to their destination by beacon control ships. The 36th Division landed over the beaches at Mandragone and the 45th Division over beaches at Salerno. The Mediterranean Allied Coastal Air Force provided anti-submarine protection for surface craft, commencing at daybreak. One Group of the Support Force augmented the escort of the assault convoys to Salerno, provided simulated fire support, and then proceeded to Camerota area. The Air Craft Carrier Force, operating 40 miles off Salerno, covered the assault area with fighter protection and launched tactical missions dropping live loads on selected targets. All fighter director ships were in the Salerno area directing planes for night interception, employing aircraft recognition, and shifting control to other standby fighter director ships.

Rehearsals were conducted so nearly like the assault landing that practically no change in organization, assignment or procedures was made. Communication difficulties were encountered and remedied. Due to the absence of time for landing and reloading vehicles and cargo prior to the actual operation, the landings were restricted mainly to off-loading personnel.

RECOMMENDATIONS

(1) The same organization and procedures to be used during the actual assault should be used both in the training period and the rehearsal.

(2) Sufficient time should be allowed between the rehearsal and the final sailing date for the actual operation to permit unloading of vehicles and cargo during the rehearsal.

Section 3.2

MOUNTING, STAGING, AND SAILING OF ASSAULT CONVOYS

Mounting ports for all assault divisions withdrawn from the Italian front for the amphibious assault against the south coast of France were located in Italy. The shipping situation and the limited time available to train, refit and mount these divisions did not permit further transfer. The French divisions employed for the follow-up phase were, with the exception of one division in Corsica, mounted from North Africa.

Naples was selected as the principal mounting port for the assault and follow up convoys. The size, facilities, and central location, plus the important consideration that the 3rd, 36th and 45th Divisions were to train nearby prompted the utilization of this port to the fullest extent. To cope with the loading problem, an organization under Commander Joint Loading Control was established, the duties of which were to coordinate with Flag Officer Western Italy, NOIC (Naval Officer in Charge) Naples, Port Commandant Naples, representatives of each Army division, and with the Peninsula Base Section on the loading of all ships and craft. The transportation division of the Peninsula Base Section set up a similar organization known as Embarkation Group. These two groups coordinated the solution of all loading problems between the Navy and Army. As a result of the experience gained in the Anzio operation loading of each type of ship and craft was done in one area in accordance with a loading bill drawn up for the entire Naples area. The combat loaders and liberty ships were loaded in Naples harbor, the LSTs in Nisida, the LCI(L)s in Pozzuoli, and the LCTs in Baia. As a direct follow up, the landing craft type commanders were assigned the task of insuring that their craft were ready for loading at the places and times designated. Anchorage plans were distributed to all ships and craft and they were to remain at the assigned anchorages prior to and after the loading. A mounting schedule was drawn up by Movements and Transportation Section of AFHQ for all assault ships and craft and loading was completed by 8 August.

Oran was the second principal mounting port. It was planned to sail most of the French armored forces from this port. The Combat Command Sudre of the 1st Division Blindee (Armored) sailed in Special No. 2 to land on D-Day, temporarily attached to the US VI Corps for the thrust up the Argens Valley. The 2nd Combat Command of the 1st Division Blindee sailed in the D-Day assault convoy, AM-1. Much of the army build-up was mounted in Oran.

Taranto and Brindisi were loading ports for personnel, equipment, and supplies of the 1st French Infantry Division and 3rd Algerian Infantry Division lifted in Assault Convoy TM-1 and TF-1. There were no build-up convoys loaded or sailed from these two ports. These ports were selected to alleviate the congestion in the Naples area and to support the strategic deception envisaged in the "Cover Plan."

Agropoli, a small port south of Naples, was the mounting port for troops of the 1st Special Service Forces and First Groupe Commandos d'Afrique.

Malta was selected as the terminal port for the aircraft carriers and the Alpha Gunfire Support Group. To contribute to strategic deception, permit freedom of movement when getting underway, and to effect an even distribution of the major war ships, Taranto, Palermo, and Naples were used as the terminal ports for the Delta, Camel and Sitka Gunfire Support Groups, respectively.

Calvi and Ile Rousse, small ports in Corsica, were loading ports for the Air Force Units. Since these ports were capable of handling only 10 LST, the port of Ajaccio was selected for mounting the French 9th Colonial Infantry Division. At Ajaccio, a new hard for LSTs was constructed of sufficient capacity to accommodate the movement of the 9th DIC and an adequate bivouac area was available within 5 miles of the loading berths.

Because of the distance involved, it was decided to stage the landing craft and troops at some convenient point along the assault route. Ajaccio and Propriano were selected as staging ports for the LCT, LCI(L) and the Sitka Convoys. These two harbors located on the west coast of Corsica were situated approximately half the distance between the convoys' sailing port, Naples, and the assault beaches. They provided ample, protected anchorages and logistic requirements for the landing craft and facilities for a staging area for the troops. A total of 104 anchorages were available along the northern and eastern shores of the Gulf of Ajaccio and 20 large ship berths in Propriano. The plan was to have the LCT berths distributed along the eastern shore and the LCI(L) berths along the northern shore. In Ajaccio the LCTs departed prior to the arrival of the LCI(L) thereby preventing any confusion during the staging period.

Composition of the assault convoys was determined by type and speed of ships and the ports from which they were to sail. The sections within each convoy were composed on the basis of the attack force to which they were assigned. The high speed APDs and LSIs allocated to the Sitka Attack Force were sailed as a fourteen-knot convoy from the Naples area. The Combat Loaders and LCI(L)s were sailed in two convoys of three sections each containing ships of the Alpha, Delta, and Camel Attack Forces, as fast (11 to 12 knot) convoys from Naples. The LSTs and LCTs were sailed in a similar manner as medium (8 to 10 knot) and slow (5.5 knot) convoys respectively. The APDs and LSIs of the Sitka Attack Force were sailed as a special (15 to 18 knot) convoy.

Gunfire Support Commanders were given no specific instructions as to speeds or routes to be followed. They were directed only to effect their rendezvous at prescribed times and places with their Attack Force Commanders.

The Aircraft Carrier Force also was given no specific instructions as to speeds or routes other than to be in the assigned area on D-Day at the proper time.

Convoy routes were the responsibility of the Commander United States Eighth Fleet, subject to the policies and approval of the Commander-in-Chief, Mediterranean. The selection of the convoy routes was intended to meet the following requirements:

(1) Assault convoys should approach the assault areas during darkness;

(2) Routes should be within reach of maximum air coverage throughout;

(3) Routes should avoid interference with other forces;

(4) Routes should be clear of mineable water except where unavoidable, and then be only through swept channels;

(5) Routes should be such that the movements of all forces would be in conformance with the Cover Plan.

Convoy route requirements were met as follows:

(1) Attack convoys should approach the assault area during darkness. H-hour was set at 0800; combat loaders, LSTs and LCTs were required to arrive in the initial transport areas by 0500 and the LCI(L) by H-hour.

To meet this schedule, and also make an approach during darkness, the LST convoy (SM-1, 1A, 1B) departed Naples, Italy, at 1530, 12 August (D-3), and proceeded directly to the assault area. The LCI(L) convoy (SF-2, 2A, 2B) departed Salerno, Italy at 1230, 12 August (D-3) and staged through Ajaccio, Corsica, on 14 August (D-1); then, departing at 1630, sailed directly to the assault area. The LCT convoy, (SS-1, 1A, 1B) sailed from Naples, Italy, at 1000 9 August (D-6) and arrived Ajaccio 12 August (D-3). It staged at Ajaccio, Corsica through 13 August (D-2), then departed for the assault area. The Combat Loaders convoy (SF-1, 1A, 1B) departed Naples at 1400, 13 August (D-2) and proceeded directly to the assault area. The time of sailing the Alpha, Delta and Camel Gunfire Support Group was left to the discretion of the Task Group Commanders, who decided for their own commands that the Alpha Gunfire Support Group should arrive in the Alpha Gunfire Support area at 0500 and the latter two groups should rendezvous with their respective combat loader convoys at a position approximately 10 miles south of position AL (see diagram II) at 1800 14 August, and at 1600 14 August, respectively.

The Sitka Attack Force was required to be in the Sitka Assault Area at about 2130 on 14 August (D-1). The APD and LSI convoy (SY-1) sailed from Naples at 1200 on 11 August (D-4) for Propriano. After staging there, the ships departed directly for the assault area at 0800, 14 August (D-1). The Sitka Gunfire Support Group departed Naples 2000, 12 August in time to rendezvous with its assault force in position NA 1200, 14 August (see diagram II).

(2) Routes should be within reach of maximum air coverage throughout. The assault convoy routes were laid down in such a manner as to enable the Mediterranean Allied Coastal Air Force to provide maximum air coverage outside forty miles of the assault area, at which point the responsibility for the protection of the convoys rested with the XII Tactical Air Command.

(3) Routes should be laid down so as to avoid interference with other forces.

    (a) Convoys from Oran and Taranto-Brindisi were sailed along the regularly assigned Mediterranean routes until they turned northward for the assault area at positions AG and TO (see diagram II). Estimated times of arrival off the Straits of Bonifacio for convoys from Naples were prescribed at sufficient intervals to permit uninterrupted passage of each convoy through the swept channel. Camel Gunfire Support Group was sailed along a westerly route from Palermo to position AH (see diagram II). All Gunfire Support Groups were sailed separately and did not rendezvous with the assault convoys until (D-1) day. This relieved the Gunfire Support Group Commanders of the hazard of collisions with small craft, reduced the traffic passing through the Straits of Bonifacio, allowed freedom of movement for a longer period of time and provided greater protection against possible enemy craft;

(b) Definite courses and speeds were laid down for all except gunfire support and carrier aircraft forces to take in the event of postponement (see diagram X);

(c) Chartlets ("Mickey Mouses") showing the estimated positions at 0800, 1200 and 2000 each day from D-4 through D day of each assault were issued (for examples see diagrams IV through IX);

(d) Diversionary forces were, in part, sailed north from Bastia along the east coast of Corsica, thereby keeping them clear from other movements. (See diagram XI.)

(4) Routes should be laid clear of mineable waters except when unavoidable, and then only through swept channels.

Care was used in routing the Oran and Taranto-Brindisi convoys northward along the West Coast of Sardinia and Corsica to insure that the routes would pass clear of the dangerous mineable waters off the shores of those islands.

A check sweep was made of the Straits of Bonifacio on 10 August by the British 5th M/S Flotilla. On 14 August, Mine Division 21 was ordered to make daily sweeps from 14-18 August and swept the channel prior to the passage of the combat loaders. These minesweepers were also stationed at Maddalena in the event that enemy minelaying aircraft were used. The convoys from Taranto-Brindisi were routed through the Malta and Tunisian War Channels (see diagram II).

(5) Routes should be such that the movements of all forces were in conformance with the Cover Plan.

The convoys from Oran and Taranto-Brindisi were headed as long as possible on courses east and west, respectively.

Although the LCT, LCI(L) and Sitka Convoys were sailed in advance along a direct route from Naples to Ajaccio, the staging at Ajaccio provided a break in the timing had the convoys been tracked by enemy air reconnaissance.

Convoy courses were maintained in a northerly direction toward Genoa until off the northwest tip of Corsica where the approach lanes commenced. The eastern diversion group supported this threat by proceeding on a direct course to Genoa until 2300 (see diagram XI) at which time all craft in the assault had turned into the approach lanes.

COMMENT

Localization of ships and craft by type for loading greatly simplified the problem of control. All ships and craft were without exception loaded in time to sortie. In the Naples area, 307 landing craft, 75 combat loaders and merchant ships with 165 escorts were loaded and sailed for the operation.

Sitka assault and LCT Convoys staged at designated ports. Although the LCI(L) convoy arrived at its proper staging port on schedule, a possible epidemic of malaria threatened some craft and troops were not allowed to disembark. In the case of the Sitka Assault Convoy, the 1st Special Service Force in part failed to conform to the approved loading plans; for after staging there were 325 troops and 36 rubber boats aboard the Osmond Ingram, and it had been planned to transport 250 troops and 26 rubber boats. The Ingram had berths available for only 145 troops. As a result, USS (APD) Osmond Ingram was overloaded, slowed down in the final debarkation, and the boats were slightly delayed in the assault.

There were no submarine or air attacks to test the adequacy of the escorts allotted to the convoys but it is considered that the screening force was adequate to meet any such threat within the enemy capabilities.

All convoys sailed as planned without incident and rendezvous were effected as scheduled. The weather was excellent during the entire period that the convoys were underway, so that navigation difficulties were neglible. Some of the LCTs did straggle due to break downs within the convoy sections enroute to Ajaccio, but since they were staged at Ajaccio, the convoy was able to reform before departing for the final assault.

RECOMMENDATIONS

That, for the loading of a large amphibious expedition:

(1) Separate loading areas be assigned for each type of craft;

(2) Standard loading plans be distributed to all concerned;

(3) A Joint Loading Control coordinate craft and troop movements.

Section 3.3

APPROACH AND ARRIVAL OF ASSAULT CONVOYS

The approach plan of the Western Task Force was designed to enable assault forces to make an entrance into the three approach corridors in an orderly, timely and well coordinated manner, and to have an adequate run on the approach course to deploy for the assault.

The location of the approach lanes allowed a minimum period of contact by enemy shore-based radar, permitted adequate sea room for maneuvering the large forces involved, and did not interfere with the operations of the Carrier Force, Alpha Gunfire Support Group, Sitka Attack Force and Diversion Groups present in the same general area. To make a minimum run from a landfall from which ships and craft could secure an accurate navigational fix prior to departure for the assault area, the entrance to the lane was established as close to the west coast of Corsica as the minefields along the island permitted. The width of the three corridors was determined by the necessity for providing ample maneuvering space for the assault forces and their gunfire support groups. The Troop Carrier Air Command, Fighter Command and Bomber Command lanes were laid north and south of the convoy lane. The Troop Carrier lane overlapped slightly the inner north corner of the convoy lane (see diagram XII). The aircraft carrier operating area bordered on the southern side of the convoy lane toward the assault area for a sufficient distance to provide, if necessary, fighter support in case of enemy air attack. The length of the approach lane from the entrance point to the outer anti-submarine patrol area was approximately eighty-two miles on an axis of $308°T$.

Individual approach corridors for the Task Force Commanders were ten miles wide. Camel Force was assigned the right (northeasterly) corridor; Delta Force, the center corridor; and Alpha Force, the left (southwesterly) corridor. The outer limits of the corridors were bounded on the southwest by point AL and the northeast by point AO (see diagram II). All convoys were sailed with an interval of approximately eleven miles between each Task Force Commander's section so that all ships and craft would reach the entrance to the corridors simultaneously.

Assault convoys were released to their respective Task Force Commanders at points AL, AM, and AN. The convoys were scheduled to reach these positions in the following order to prevent any interference with other forces at the turning points into the corridors: LCTs at H minus 21 hours; LSTs at H minus 15 hours; Combat Loaders at H minus 12 hours and LCI(L)s at H minus 9 hours.

After entering the approach corridors, the sequence of operations was:

(1) All convoys assumed their approach dispositions. The cruising dispositions of the convoys in most cases were based on the assault plan and required only minor changes in positions of ships and craft for the approach. Delta and Camel Gunfire Support Groups took station 2,000 yards astern of the Combat Loader sections. Alpha Gunfire Support Group because it approached from the south and did not cross any convoy lane, did not rendezvous with Alpha Combat Loader convoy but proceeded independently to avoid the unnecessary confusion of a rendezvous at dusk.

(2) Speeds and courses of convoys were altered to conform with the set time of arrival for each convoy in its transport area. The scheduled times of arrival in the respective transport areas were LCTs at 0450; Combat Loaders and LSTs at 0500; LCI(L)s at 0800. The Alpha Gunfire Support Group was to be on station at 0400 ahead of the other assault convoys. Delta and Camel Gunfire Support Groups were scheduled to be in position in their fire support areas to deliver shore bombardment commencing at 0650.

(3) Reference ships and craft detached without signal and proceeded to their assigned stations. No beacon submarines were utilized and the reference vessels were relied upon for properly positioning the assault convoys. PC, SC and smaller craft were used except for the two outer reference ships in the Camel assault, which were destroyers. Because it was planned to have the Camel convoys make an 11° turn to the left from the end of the corridor to the transport area, one destroyer was detached at point AN from the Combat Loader Convoy to assume position at the turn off point in the corridor. The second destroyer also acted as reference ship and marked the right side of the Camel transport area.

(4) Minesweepers were detached at 0300 to carry out their tasks; they provided additional escorts to convoys passed on their way into the assault area. These ships and craft performed the only passing required in the approach. This was accepted in order to have some of the minesweepers act as escorts prior to executing their minesweeping tasks.

(5) Gunfire Support Groups of Delta and Camel Attack Forces were detached from convoys to carry out the prescribed pre-H-hour shore bombardment. Delta Gunfire Support Group detached from the Combat Loader Convoy on arrival in the assault area and crossed inshore of the transport area while proceeding to assigned Fire Support Areas. Camel Gunfire Support Group detached from the Camel Combat Loader Convoy at 0230 without signal, deployed to the left and right in advance of the convoy, and proceeded to the flanks of the transport area. Departing at 0610, they assumed their positions in the Fire Support Areas.

(6) All escort DDs and DEs other than those attached to the bombardment forces were automatically released and reported to CTG 80.6 upon arrival of convoys in the transport areas.

Sitka Force followed an approach course well to the southwest of the other three attack forces and reached the assault position CB (see diagram II) approximately 10 miles southeast of Ile du Levant at 2156, 14 August (D minus 1).

COMMENT

Prior to arriving at the release points the Combat Loader, LST, and LCI(L) convoys with Delta and Camel Gunfire Support Groups were roughly in columns of convoy sections proceeding north along the west coast of Corsica. In this manner when each convoy was abreast the convoy corridor, each of its three sections simultaneously made a column movement to the left into its proper lane. The passage of this heavy concentration of ships and craft was completed to the assault area without interference except for one minor incident. The Alpha Combat Loader section passed through sections of the slower LCI(L) convoy at dusk on D minus 1. This interference was caused by the LCI(L) convoy having sailed from Ajaccio one hour ahead of schedule and the Combat Loader Convoy being one half hour behind schedule. It occurred prior to last light and before either convoy reached the release point to the approach corridor.

The slow speed of the LCT convoy was viewed with great concern during the planning period. Many factors were considered which determined the speed of this convoy. The convoy was composed of various types of LCTs of British and US design. In order to provide a safety factor for the slowest type in the convoy, the LCT(3), the speed was limited to the cruising speed for that type. The general condition of a certain number of the craft caused by the long operating period which they had previously completed in this theater, did not allow the convoy speed to be based on the designed speed of the LCT(3). The task of towing pre-assault craft (LCM(R) and LCC) was also undertaken by the LCTs. It was impracticable to tow these craft by LSTs or LCI(L)s. The LCI(L)s could have steamed at the slow speed needed for touring; but since these craft carried personnel, it was felt in addition to other considerations that this would not be a justifiable risk to the personnel. The LSTs or Combat Loaders could not lift these craft because all available deck space was allocated for lifting LCMs required during the initial assault. The combination of these factors limited the planned speed of the LCT convoy to 5.5 knots. In order to reach the assault area by 0500 the LCT convoy had to be in the approach lane from 1100, 14 August (D minus 1). Although the approach was planned to be conducted as much as possible during the period of darkness, there were no other faster craft in sufficient quantity in the theater which could carry out the duties performed by the LCTs.

The convoy lane served its intended purposes of keeping ships and craft of each Task Force Commander separate and facilitated the fighter-cover pattern for the approach. As the ships and craft proceeded along the lane, they became increasingly concentrated, thereby shortening the area to be covered, allowing for a greater strength of aircraft over all ships and craft, and finally providing the proper, timely concentration for the assault.

The approach was planned so that no convoy would, with the exception of some minesweeping units, have to pass another, but the convoys would join in the assault area. This proved to be most helpful and no collisions or loss of time due to excessive diversions to avoid other convoys occurred. The combination of the relatively slow speeds of the convoys and unpredictable currents resulted in some navigation error by the time the convoys reached the assault area. A westward set initially presented some difficulty for the reference ships and craft in keeping station, but they were all on station when the first convoy arrived. Although other minor difficulties were experienced, they in no way affected the arrival of the convoys. All ships and craft arrived and reached their assigned stations in the assault area at the proper time.

Section 3.4

DIVERSIONARY SURFACE OPERATIONS

THE PLAN

The chief purpose of the diversionary operations executed prior to D-day was to present multiple threats to the enemy in order that he would be less likely to anticipate when and where the actual assault was to take place. The over-all cover plan to accomplish this purpose was put into effect long before the invasion. A discussion of the strategic and tactical air cover plans appears in Part II, Section 4.2 of this report. The strategic deception achieved by disposition of forces throughout the Mediterranean area is considered in Part I, Section 1.6. This section is devoted solely to the diversionary surface operations conducted by the Special Operations Group (TG 80.4) from D minus one to D plus two day.

The mission of the first special operation was to threaten successively the Genoa area, the Nice-Cannes area, the Sete-Agde area, and finally the Marseille-Toulon area. To accomplish this task, two small diversionary units were formed. The Eastern Unit was to sail along the west coast of Corsica on a northerly course similar to that of the main attack forces behind it, as though bound for Genoa. Since the shift of the main forces to a northwesterly course along the approach corridor would presumably become known to the enemy, the Eastern Unit was to shift its threat from the Genoa area to the Nice-Cannes area and carry out a minor demonstration in the latter area (see diagram XI). Meanwhile, a Western Unit was to proceed from Corsica as if destined for the Sete-Agde area. When off the Marseille-Toulon area well out at sea, this unit was to turn and proceed directly into the Ciotat area in order to stage a mock landing there. A second simulated assault was to be launched in the same place on the following night. Further special operations could be arranged if required, but no more were specifically scheduled.

The Eastern Unit consisting of 2 gunboats, 1 fighter director ship, and 4 ML was to depart from Ajaccio the morning of D minus one with fighter cover to keep enemy reconnaissance planes away, to be joined at 2130 by 12 PT from Bastia. At this juncture, 3 PT were to detach to proceed for anti-E-boat screen duties off Nice and 4 PT were to head for the Gulf of Napoule to land a group of 70 French Commandos at Theoule sur Mer (Pointe des Deux Freres). The main group was to continue north until 2330, aided in its attempted simulation of a large force by radar jamming and by creating many artificial radar targets from planes and by reflector balloons, and then was to turn west. At 2230 the fighter director ship was to detach in order to take station as an air beacon ship. After landing the commandos at Pointe des Deux Freres in rubber boats, the 4 PT were to cross to the eastern flank of the group and take station as an anti-E-boat patrol. The MLs and remaining PTs were to deploy off Antibes, employing radar counter-measures to attract attention while the 2 gunboats bombarded targets between Antibes and the Var River for about an hour. The whole group was then to proceed to Baie de Briande in the Alpha area to rendezvous with the Western Unit, the PTs being released to Commander Screening Group (CTG 80.5).

The Western Unit was to be composed of 1 DD and 4 ML from Ajaccio, to be joined by 8 PT and 12 ASRC from Calvi at 2100 on D minus one, about 25 miles south of the Hyeres Islands. At this time reflector balloons were to be streamed and radar counter-measures were to be commenced by the Unit and by covering planes to simulate a convoy 12 miles long and 8 miles wide, a much larger force than the Sitka Attack Force which would then be moving up to its assault position. At 0100 the group was to turn toward Ciotat. The radar station at Cap Sicie was purposely to have been left unmolested by bombers so that it could track this movement.

On arrival off Baie de la Ciotat at 0300, the DD and MLs were to deploy as a gunfire support force would, while at 0330 the small craft were to simulate a landing in the bay. Dummy radio traffic imitating a flagship and ships of an amphibious attack force and a fighter director ship controlling night fighters was to be put on the air. The small craft were to enter in waves, lay a smoke screen, fire a beach barrage, employ high explosive and smoke rockets, place special delayed-action demolition charges close inshore, use sonic apparatus to reproduce boat noises, and broadcast radio traffic suggesting the presence of an assault force of LSTs and LCTs. At 0400, 300 dummy paratroops rigged with demolition charges were to be dropped northwest of Toulon. Meanwhile, the DD and MLs were to bombard coastal defenses, screened by 4 PT on each flank. Prior to withdrawal, radio traffic was to suggest that plans had been thwarted and the operation would be tried again later. Upon return to Baie de Briande, the Western Unit was to combine with the Eastern Unit plus 4 ASRC to be released by Commander Support Force (CTF 86), refuel, and carry out a repeat demonstration at Ciotat that night.

EXECUTION OF THE PLAN

In general, the diversion operations were carried out as planned. Due to mechanical failures, 1 ASRC and 1 ML were left behind on D minus one, and 2 ASRC, 1 ML and 1 PT failed to make the repeat demonstration. Two ML were diverted to other uses prior to the repeat performance. Failure of a tanker containing 100-octane gasoline to arrive on time caused the repeat operation to be postponed a day and kept 6 of the 8 available PT from refueling in time to participate. Bad weather limited the planes used in the repeat diversion to an initial flight.

Enemy reaction to these operations was most satisfactory. Most of the coastal battery fire against the Eastern Unit was directed at the decoy screen and passed well over it, and the rest fell short of or burst in the air over the gunboats. The effect of the gunboats' bombardment could not be determined, though numerous bursts and several flashes of fire were observed. Shelling by the Western Diversion Unit drew no return fire except some AA bursts directed in the area where the white phosphorous shells exploded. Owing to fog and radar failures, two of the four ML did not carry out their bombardment schedule and only one ASRC actually entered Baie de la Ciotat. Three ASRC were deceived as to the location of Ciotat by what appeared to be two large "burning areas" that may have been electric decoys turned on to confuse air and surface forces, as they were seen to blink out in unison and come on again ten minutes later.

The repeat diversion produced considerable enemy reaction. Much shore fire was expended against the imaginary gunfire support and transport areas, but no serious hits were sustained. Searchlights, star shells and tracer fire were tried, but the smoke screen laid by the ASRC in combination with high-speed maneuvers allowed them to evade the barrage that crisscrossed the bay. It was noted that when radar target rockets exploded, enemy searchlights were shifted to train skyward during the dropping period. The gunfire support ships aroused heavy enemy fire, star shells, tracers and searchlights. Most of the hostile fire was inaccurate, perhaps due to the radar counter-measures employed, and caused no damage. Results of fire directed against enemy targets were largely unobserved. During the retirement, two German escort ships, the Capriolo and Kemid Allah, were met, engaged, and sunk by USS (DD) Endicott and HMS Aphis, and HMS Scarab, two gunboats. Only minor damage was received, and 211 prisoners were captured.

Since no further special operations were required, Special Operations Group (TG 80.4) was dissolved on D plus three.

CONCLUSIONS

Although sufficient evidence is not yet available to determine to what extent the enemy was deceived by the diversionary surface operations, it is believed that considerable success was achieved. At 0030 an enemy plane flew low over the Western Unit, and at 0335 a craft resembling an R boat passed near it in the fog, but it is not known what reports were made by them. For the first two days of the assault, enemy announcements credited the Allies with landings on a front stretching from Cannes to west of Toulon, and on D-day it was even declared that Cannes had been captured and that Antibes and Nice had been shelled by four or five battleships. It was also stated in communiques and over the radio that thousands of paratroops were being dropped northwest of Toulon, though this announcement was later retracted. Another D-day claim was that the first waves of a landing attempt east of Marseille had been frustrated when the allied ships inadvertently ran into minefields, forcing them to retire. Prisoner interrogation suggests that a second attempted assault in the Ciotat area was expected, that mobile units were kept in that area and additional ones called for in anticipation of such a move, and that four or five minor combatant ships in that area were ordered to watch for the approach of an allied sea-borne force. On D plus two radio Berlin asserted that the assault force, which had again failed in its attempt to land east of Marseille, was 12 miles long, which is the exact convoy size which the radar counter-measure plan intended to convey.

The numerous technical problems involved in the planning and staging of the diversion operations and the performance of the equipment used are discussed in reports of a higher classification. It can be said here, however, that PT boats would have been more satisfactory than ASRC because of their more silent running, greater range and better offensive power.

The diversionary surface operations required considerable special equipment and were difficult to plan and execute. Their functions varied but the picture presented to the enemy had to be consistent, and the tactical diversions had to complement the strategic cover plan. If they are to be used in the future, experience in these diversions confirmed the value of air support, the need for considerable fire power, and the importance of communication deception and radar counter-measures.

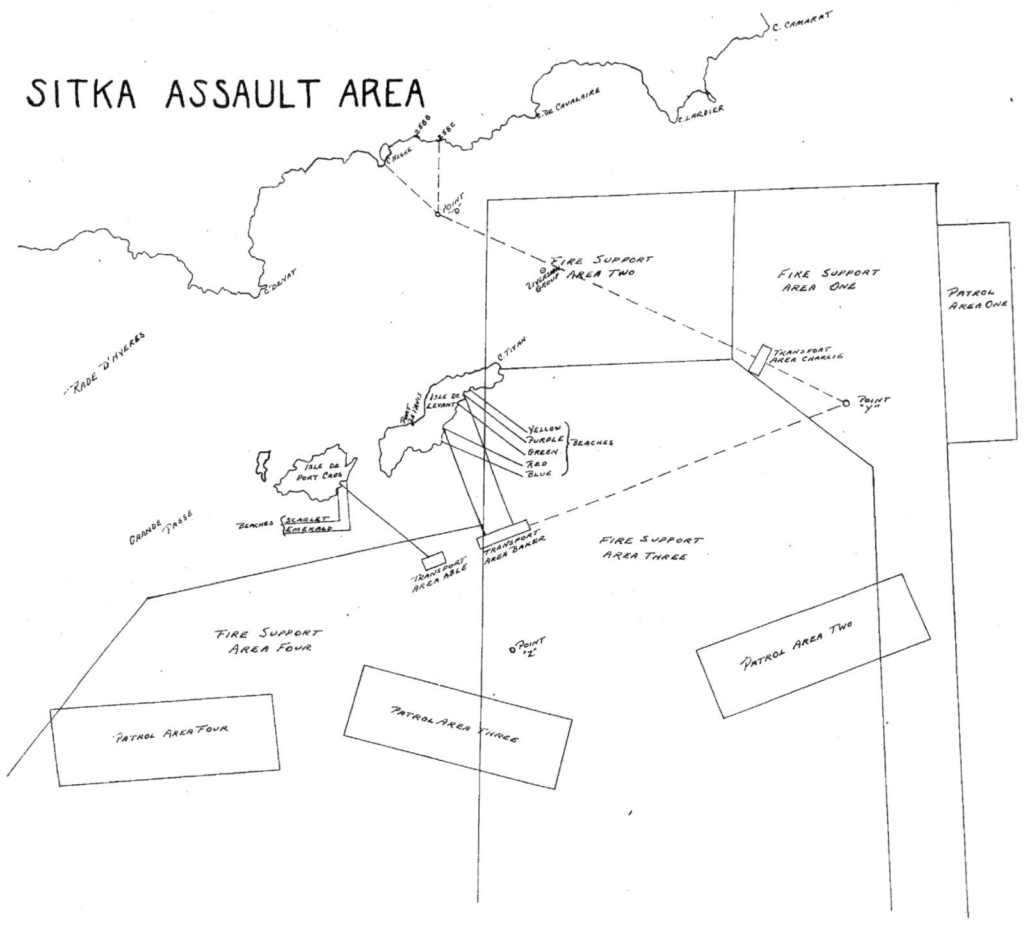

Figure 3

Section 3.5

SITKA ASSAULT

THE PLAN

The first task of the Support Force (TF 86) was to establish the Romeo Force, composed of French commandos, in the vicinity of Cap Negre and the Sitka Force, made up of 1st Special Service Force, on the islands of Levant and Port Cros (see diagram I). The objective of the Romeo Force was to destroy enemy defenses at Cap Negre, to block the nearby coastal highway, to seize the high ground two miles north of Cap Negre, and to protect the left flank of the main assault forces. Sitka Force was created in order to eliminate the threat to assault forces from enemy coastal defense batteries on Levant. The landings of these forces were to be made by stealth, without preliminary bombardment, about 6 1/2 hours before H-hour. No other method of achieving the desired end appeared feasible. The apparent battery of three 164 mm guns on the east end of Levant were so located that capture was the only sure way of removing them although they were considered critical targets in the pre-D-day bombing. An early seizure of control of the left flank area was necessary to prevent reinforcements from approaching from the west. The benefits to be derived from this pre-H-hour assault were believed to outweigh any disadvantages arising from a possible premature disclosure of allied invasion intentions, and it was expected that the diversionary operations conducted by the strategic air forces, the XII Tactical Air Command, and Special Operations Group (TG 80.4) would help to prevent this.

The Support Force was to arrive at Point Y at 2152 D minus one. (See accompanying figure). Within an hour, transports were to have taken station in areas A, B and C; cruisers, in areas 1 and 3; PT boat screen units, south of Toulon Bay, south and west of Porquerolles, and south of Grande Passe; and destroyers, in patrol areas 1, 2 and 3 until gunfire support should be required. By 0030 on D-day, advance units were to have landed for the purpose of identifying and marking the landing points and preparing the cliffs for scaling. Zero hour for the main landings was set at 0130.

Landings were to be effected by LCAs, LCP(R)s, LCRs, and kayaks with PT boats acting as control and close support vessels and LCMs to bring in supplies. About 1,400 men were to land on Levant to capture an estimated garrison of 400. On Port Cros almost 700 men were to attack a garrison believed to be around 200. Just east of Cap Negre 75 men were to go ashore, while on beach 258C, 750 men were to carry out the assault. All landings were to take place on rocky shores at the base of cliffs except the one on beach 258C, a small sandy beach with one exit to the main coastal road and believed to be without mines or obstacles but defended by three pillboxes. A battery of four medium guns was believed to be on Cap Negre, and probably some smaller guns. Port Cros was thought to be lightly defended by guns, and Levant likewise, except for the 164 mm battery on the eastern end.

At Z-hour, a diversion group consisting of 1 PT and 4 ASRC was to take station 3.2 miles 36 degrees from Cap Titan ready to cover the transports or the boat waves with a smoke screen if necessary and to attract attention by simulating an attack off Port de l'Avis if Sitka Force were attacked, or to the west if Romeo Force met opposition. In the event that the landing on the south shore of Levant should prove impracticable to carry out, an alternate plan for landing on a small sandy beach on the north shore was drawn up.

At 0500, ships of the Romeo Force were to withdraw to point Z, those of the Sitka Force to positions west of Z, and gunfire support ships to south of 43° 04' North preparatory to the arrival of Alpha Attack Force. At 0610 air bombardment of

Porquerolles, Cap Benat and the Giens peninsula was to commence. Bombing on Port Cros, Levant and Cap Negre was to be on call only. About 0630 FS Lorraine was to arrive from Alpha area for gunfire support duty. During the day minesweepers were to start sweeping fire support areas, an east-west channel north of the islands, and a channel into Port Cros through which US LST 32 could bring in GCI equipment. A net tender was to remove a net supposed to run between Port Cros and Cap Benat, preceded by minesweepers. At the close of the day the minesweepers and net tender were to base in Port de l'Avis, the gunfire support group was to go to its night retirement area, the PTs and ASRCs were already to have been released, and the transports were to have departed in the morning for Ajaccio for a lift of French troops.

EXECUTION OF THE PLAN

The Sitka assault was carried out almost as planned. The westerly set of the current gave trouble to transports, scouts and assault units, causing some delays. It probably was responsible for the main group of Romeo Force landing on beach 258B instead of 258C. Haze on the water made it difficult to see signals sent out by scouts and to identify the areas being approached from seaward. As a result, the scout signaling off beach 258C was not seen, and one LCA cut loose her rubber boats over a mile too far out.

No initial resistance was met on the islands, and only inaccurate machine gun and small arms fire on the mainland. The large coastal defense guns on Levant were found to be clever dummies. A pocket of resistance on the west end of that island was not overcome until 2330 D-day. Capture of Port Cros was not finally completed until 1300 on D plus two. Commandos on the mainland achieved their objective by 1000, after being bombed once by friendly planes and beating back one enemy counter-attack. Casualties everywhere were very light. No ships or craft were damaged or lost except one LCA that was hit by an 88 mm shell at Port Cros. No enemy naval or air engagements occurred except when the USS Somers, in patrol area three, opened fire on two enemy corvettes, Camoscio and Escaburt, at 0440 and finally sank both. It was not found necessary to execute any diversionary operations. No net was discovered between Port Cros and Cap Benat for the net tender to remove. The continued resistance on Port Cros prevented US LST 32 from off-loading GCI equipment as planned. All of the transports proceded to Ajaccio as scheduled except two that were retained to support the troops landed on the islands and to evacuate POW and casualties, and of these one finally got away at 1600.

CONCLUSIONS

The plan was sound and vigorously executed. Some degree of surprise was achieved, especially on the islands. It is probable that the deception achieved by the air and surface diversion groups helped considerably to offset the disclosure of allied intentions resulting from the Sitka attack.

It was well demonstrated, especially by the Romeo Force, that withholding fire as long as possible in darkness is the best protection for a small group of boats during an attack by stealth, and increases the chances of surprise and ultimate success. Flares, searchlights, star shells and gunfire in the area of the attacking force do not necessarily indicate detection by the enemy, and return fire merely provides a point of aim.

It was found that the British LCA was more maneuverable, less noisy and easier to handle than the US LCP(R) in landing on a rocky coast. Both types of craft executed their towing assignments well, and it proved feasible to tow three

LCR to a line with three lines per tow at 4 1/2 knots. PT boats were also used satisfactorily for towing LCR but should have been equipped with mufflers and were visible at twice the distance that the LCA was.

Owing to the excellence of weather and sea conditions, the suitability of the craft used was not fully tested. Had the weather not been good, it might have proved difficult or impossible to carry out the landings as planned, due to the rocky, unprotected nature of the points selected.

The number of men put ashore prior to Z-hour was so large that secrecy was jeopardized, but this was necessary for the purpose of affording security to the main assault in the event of discovery.

RECOMMENDATION

A boat similar to the British LCA is recommended for use in landings by stealth on rocky shores.

Section 3.6

ALPHA ASSAULT

THE PLAN

Alpha Attack Force was directed initially to establish the US 3rd Infantry Division (Reinforced) ashore on D-day in the Cavalaire-Pampelonne area. For the assault, about 1-1/2 miles on each of two sandy beaches about 2 miles long backed by a narrow belt of sand dunes were selected. Road and track exits were observed on both beaches, but some tracking through the dunes appeared necessary for wheeled vehicles. Sand bars created shoal water at varying distances and depths off both beaches. The beach in Baie de Cavalaire, Red beach, was 6 miles by land (13 miles by sea) from the beach in Baie de Pampelonne, Yellow beach (see diagram I).

Both beaches were mined, wired, and covered with pillbox and machine gun positions. The waters offshore were reported to be mined and any minesweepers in the area would be very vulnerable to shore fire. A row of concrete pyramids ran underwater in front of Red beach, and a double row of wooden pilings blocked the approach to Yellow beach. Both the pyramids and the pilings were believed to be mined to an unknown extent. The whole area was reported to be strongly fortified by coast defense guns, the most formidable of which were the 164 mm battery on the east end of Levant, 150 mm batteries on Cap Camarat and inland east of Red beach, and, a 220 mm battery overlooking one of the river valleys behind Yellow beach, but believed to be unoccupied.

In order to overcome these formidable defenses, every available weapon was to be utilized. The left flank was to be protected by commandos put ashore by the Sitka Force, during darkness, near Cap Negre, to block the approach from the west, and on Levant to capture the 164 mm battery. Commencing at 0550, fighter bombers were to attack designated points and any targets seen to be firing. From 0700 to 0730 medium and heavy bombers were to bomb the beaches and selected strong points. Gunfire support ships were to be ready to deliver counter-battery fire from about 0600. Cruisers and battleships were to fire on assigned targets from 0700 to 0750. Destroyers were to bombard beach areas from 0720 to 0750. Seaward areas to be used were to be swept from 0440 to 0650 by minesweepers covered by destroyers, and the inshore areas by shallow minesweepers between 0710 and 0745. The underwater obstacles and accompanying mines were to be cleared by the use of drones, reddy fox, bucket boats, explosive packs, and hand-placed charges. The boat waves were to be covered by close inshore fire directed onto the beaches from landing craft and rocket craft up to 0758 and by a protective smoke screen as required after H minus 15 minutes, and were to get through any uncleared obstacles by ramming or maneuvering.

Five miles offshore from each beach an inner transport area was laid out, and 5 miles to seaward an outer transport area was set (see diagram I). In each case the dimensions were 2 by 3 miles, with boat lanes 1000 yards wide. The dogleg 2 miles from Yellow beach was occasioned by the need to keep out of the Delta area. The bend in Red beach boat lane was planned in order to keep the outer transport area away from the Sitka area and from the coastal defense batteries believed to be on the eastern end of Levant. Upon receipt of word of the capture of these batteries by the Sitka Attack Force, all ships were to move to the inner transport area.

The plan of approach called for the stationing of a 10-mile reference vessel off each beach at 0300. The 5-mile and later the 2-mile reference vessels were to proceed in after the minesweepers. By 0500 the LST, LCT, combat loader and gunfire support convoys were to have reached the outer transport areas, followed by the LCI convoy at 0700. Alpha DDs and DEs, not part of the gunfire support group, were to be released to Commander Anti-Submarine and Convoy Control Group (CTG 80.6) upon arrival.

Two battalions of the 7th RCT and two of the 15th RCT were to land over Red and Yellow beaches, respectively, to be followed by the 30th RCT over Red beach and other troop units. The first two waves were to land in a "W" formation by five-boat divisions, so that a company with three rifle platoons would hit first at the center and on each flank while heavy weapons platoons would land on each side of the center, a minute later. Two LCT with DD tanks and tank destroyers embarked were to go in with the first wave. Within two hours the first nine waves were to land. Most of the LCT(R)s were to be sent to the Camel area for the afternoon assault. Nine sets of pontoons were to be sent over from the other areas to supplement the three initially in Alpha. A small beach in the eastern corner of Cavalaire Bay designated as Green beach would be opened if needed. Because of the danger of enemy reinforcements arriving from the west, the army forces landed were to strike north, overrun the St. Tropez peninsula, capture Cogolin, in conjunction with the 45th Division secure the roads around Grimaud, and push west to join the Romeo Force near Cap Negre as rapidly as possible.

For the assault phase there was an assault commander for each beach embarked in an LCI(L)(C). Under him were three sector commanders in LCCs, charged with control of all traffic, smoke laying, and close inshore fire in their sectors. The three sectors established were from the 2-mile reference point seaward, from that point shoreward on the left of the channel, and similarly on the right of the channel. When all the original assault troops were disembarked, a reorganization of forces was to be called into effect in order to take care of the maintenance and buildup phase. Ships and craft were to report for assignment of tasks under the new organization when finished with their assault tasks even though it had not yet been placed in effect. Existing forces, with addition of PTs to be furnished by CTG 80.5 for patrolling on the western flank, were to be reconstituted into a Screening and Smoke Group, Gunfire Support Group, Minesweeping Group, Salvage and Firefighting Unit, Area Unloading Control, Joint Loading Control, and Naval Beach Party.

EXECUTION OF THE PLAN

The Alpha attack was carried out almost as planned. No mines were found seaward of the underwater obstacles. Enemy gunfire was limited to mortar, machine gun and some 88 mm fire, causing little damage. As the batteries on Levant had not opened fire, ships started in from the outer transport area about 0700, even before word of capture was received. At times, smoke was so dense that active enemy targets could not be seen. Rocket fire proved effective, though the men in the first wave were endangered by the fact that some rockets from LCT(R) burst prematurely or fell short. All nine drones on Red beach detonated as planned, though they were concentrated too much on the left side of the beach because of reduced visibility. On Yellow beach, three out of nine failed to function properly. Of these three, one beached without exploding, one sank and then exploded without apparent cause on D plus two, and one reversed its course without being seen by the control boat and was detonated less than 50 yards from SC 1029, the 2-mile reference vessel, which was put out of action. It was not found necessary to employ any reddy fox, although one that had been damaged in transit sank before it could be used.

The first eight boat waves landed about on schedule. CG 3rd Division went ashore at 1045. On Red beach three LCVP and four LCI(L) were damaged by teller mines while beaching on the right end of the beach, requiring the landing area to be shifted to the left. Removal of land mines on this beach also occasioned some delay in unloading, as did a shortage of truck drivers and beach labor. Some speedup was effected by placing trucks in LCMs, loading bulk cargo in slings directly from ships into trucks, and sending the trucks from the LCMs to unload at the dump. On Yellow beach, all landing craft were unloaded by 1400, though fine sand and narrow exits resulted in considerable congestion. Green beach was surveyed and a seaward channel swept but could not be opened until land mines were cleared and exits created. Progress was such as to allow the plan for reorganization to be placed in effect at 1700.

CONCLUSIONS

In view of the obstacles to be overcome, Alpha attack was executed with a minimum of damage and delay. Enemy resistance was not nearly so great as had been expected, but in part, this can be accounted for by the overwhelming strength and precision of the assault that was launched. The severity of the aerial bombing prior to and on D-day, and the accuracy of the naval bombardment, proved to be the major factors contributing to the success of the attack. New weapons such as rockets and drones revealed weaknesses, but nonetheless, established their worth. Smoke was most effective protecting boat waves from enemy fire. Destroyers were employed to great advantage from 1200 to 1500 yards offshore to provide direct support for minesweepers and boat waves.

Careful planning, training, and organization also contributed greatly to the smoothness of Alpha attack. The value of objective and realistic training was thoroughly proved. The men who made the attack carried out their duties efficiently because during weeks of training they had practiced these same duties, using as nearly as possible the same terrain, objectives, procedures, equipment, craft, weapons, and organization as they were to use on D-day.

The division of each assault beach area into three sectors commanded by experienced officers worked out well, especially with respect to controlling smoke and keeping the task force commander fully informed. Use of a "W" formation for the first two landing waves, favored by the army, was very successful.

RECOMMENDATIONS

An organization of each beach assault area into separate sectors of command for the control of smoke, inshore gunfire, and traffic during the assault phase is recommended.

Section 3.7

DELTA ASSAULT

THE PLAN

  The Delta Attack Force had the initial task of establishing the US 45th Infantry Division (reinforced) ashore on D-day. Since it was not feasible to land on the beaches in the Gulf of St. Tropez owing to difficulties of preliminary mine clearance, and approach in the face of converging gunfire from three sides, four sandy beaches each about 400 yards long, located in Baïe de Bougnon between two headlands 3 1/2 miles apart, were selected. Red and Green beaches, adjacent to one another, had an anti-tank wall about 8 feet high extending along the back of the beaches for their entire length with only one exit. Sandbars prevented a dry landing on these two beaches, and rocks flanked their approaches. Yellow and Blue beaches were backed by a steep embankment cut through with only one exit on Yellow. The approach to these beaches was unobstructed except for some submerged rocks off Yellow. An excellent coastal road backed by hills lay just a few yards behind all four of the beaches. It was estimated that enemy demolition of this road would reduce maintenance capacity of the beaches. No artificial obstacles were believed to have been placed in the area to prevent an amphibious landing other than barbed wire and possibly land mines.

  Delta area was heavily fortified. From Cap St. Tropez to Pointe Alexandre there were five strong points covering the beaches, boat lanes and transport areas. Included among the defenses, there were estimated to be at least three 220 mm coastal defense guns at Pointe Alexandre, five recessed 220 mm guns near Cap St. Tropez (these proved to be 164 mm guns), and numerous smaller caliber guns and nests of machine guns. Many of these were lodged in pillboxes or casemates, connected by trenches or underground tunnels, and controlled from central observation posts. Two batteries of 155 mm guns positioned at the base of the Gulf of St. Tropez and a partially confirmed 105 mm howitzer in the Citadel of St. Tropez also constituted a major threat to the assault forces.

  The general plan of attack was to destroy or neutralize enemy defenses by air bombardment from H minus 130 to H minus 30 minutes, by gunfire from destroyers, cruisers and battleships from H minus 70 minutes to after H hour, and by close inshore fire from landing craft and rocket boats from H minus 15 to H minus 4 minutes. If necessary, the assault waves were to be hidden by smoke from enemy guns still in action. The seaward areas to be used were to be cleared by preliminary minesweeping, and by demolition units if required. The most difficult problem was the neutralization of coast defense guns. Shutting off the Gulf of St. Tropez guns by aerial smoke screen was considered, but rejected as too hazardous. The best position for shelling was in the right half of the gunfire support area, but little room existed there to maneuver the large ships needed for the heavy caliber gunfire required for neutralization.

  Following the arrival of reference vessels which were to take pre-arranged stations and disembark scouts, the LCT convoy was to arrive in the assault area by H minus 200 minutes, gunfire support ships by H minus 190 minutes, LST and combat loader convoys by H minus 180 minutes, and LCI convoy by H-hour. Landing craft and ships were to take positions in Transport Area One, with a small boat maneuvering area at the shore end (see diagram I), located 7 1/2 miles offshore. Combat loaders and cargo carriers were to stop in Transport Area Two, situated 10 miles from the beaches, or further out in a rendezvous and waiting area until called in. A single boat lane 1,000 yards wide was to serve both transport areas, splitting into four lanes 1 1/2 miles offshore. Most of the remainder of the rather confined area allotted to Delta Force would be left for gunfire support ships to occupy. A narrow strip of Camel area was to be shared with Camel gunfire support ships. Cruisers and destroyers were to move in from positions seaward of the transport areas to be at assigned stations on the flanks ready to fire by H minus 70 minutes. The battleships were at their assigned stations seaward of the transport areas on arrival. Seaward of the battleships, a rendezvous and waiting area was to be established. Each transport area and the waiting area were two miles square.

A major portion of the specialized landing craft for Red and Green beaches were to come from Transport Area One, and for Yellow and Blue beaches further out from Transport Area Two. Integration of the boat waves was to take place at a rendezvous point seven miles offshore. From there the waves were to be dispatched to the beach, under guidance of control vessels, about ten minutes apart. LCVPs of the first wave were to hit the beach line abreast about 50 yards apart. Two battalions of the 157th RCT were to land over Red and Green beaches and two battalions of the 180th RCT over Yellow and Blue beaches, to be followed by the 179th RCT and numerous other troop units.

A quick thrust inland was to be made after the landing, as the small Delta area needed a deep beachhead to prevent enemy gunfire from covering the unloading. At the same time, a push to the westward was to be launched in order to open up the small ports, excellent anchorage, and better beaches of the Gulf of St. Tropez, which was to be the primary area of maintenance. On the right flank, advancing troops were to join the forces from the Camel area in the Argens River valley. The northern half of Alpha Yellow beach, called Blue Two Beach, was to be cleared by the Alpha Force so that if at H plus four hours the Delta beaches were becoming too congested, a beach control group could be landed and part of the Delta unloading burden be shifted to this beach.

Upon order on D-day a reorganization plan was to be placed into effect. Only the groups and units necessary for maintenance and build-up of the beachheads were to be included. This involved disbanding all assault groups and creating an Area Unloading Control Group, a Joint Loading Control Group, and an Area Return Convoy Control Group. Of the previous organization, only the Naval Beach Party, the Escort and Screening Group, and the Minesweeping Group were to be retained. DDs and DEs which escorted the troop convoys were to have been turned over to Commander Anti-Submarine and Convoy Control Group (CTG 80.6) on arrival in the assault area. It was expected that the gunfire support ships might have been released prior to the reorganization, the destroyers to CTG 80.6 and the remainder to Commander Support Force (CTF 86); if not, the Gunfire Support Group was to retain its separate identity under the reorganization plan until released.

EXECUTION OF THE PLAN

All of the assault convoys arrived at their assigned stations on schedule. No mines were swept. No underwater obstacles were encountered. Aerial bombing before and on D-day and naval bombardment were so effective that by H hour all major guns had been damaged and most of the coastal defense crews had deserted their posts, been put out of action, or were unwilling to expose themselves in order to man their guns properly. No enemy shells landed in the transport areas. Only a few rounds of 75 mm and 20 mm fire and about 60 rounds of mortar fire were directed on the boat lanes, causing no damage.

LCM(R)s which were to come from HMS Eastway in the Camel area did not arrive in time to see action. Rocket fire from the boats that did participate was effective. More than 6,000 rockets were launched. Some of the rockets landed among the boat waves as a result of the rocket projectiles colliding in flight and the unforeseen number of shorts in the rocket patterns, but did no harm. Close inshore fire silenced casemated guns on each side of Blue beach.

The boat waves landed within a few minutes of scheduled times. Of the 12 amphibious tanks landed in the first wave, 5 were stopped on the beach by mines and steep sand, 2 were knocked out by road mines, and the remaining 5 were still operating at the end of the day. By 1100, the reserve regiment was on its way ashore, and CG 45th Division had disembarked. CG VI Corps moved ashore establishing headquarters in St. Maxime in the afternoon. The first pontoon causeway was sited at 1355 on Red beach, and by 1500 four had been put on Red and Green beaches. Unloading of LSTs over Yellow and Blue beaches was accomplished dry. During the afternoon minesweeping to the St. Tropez-St. Maxime line was completed.

By 1600, all scheduled assault and reserve troops had been landed. The reorganization plan was therefore ordered to be put into effect. The gunfire support ships had not yet been released, at this point, as previously anticipated, nor had it been necessary to unload over Blue Two beach in the Alpha Area. Otherwise, the assault was carried out as intended. During the day 11 combat loaders, transports and cargo ships, 30 LST, 41 LCT, and 36 LCI were unloaded over the four small Delta beaches, giving a total of 33,000 persons, 3,300 vehicles and an unreported number of tons unloaded. No navy ships and craft or personnel were either lost or injured, and there were only a few army casualties.

CONCLUSIONS

The fact that the Delta assault went off so smoothly was largely attributable to intensive training, careful planning, and the effectiveness of aerial and naval bombardment. Good weather and smooth seas were a contributing factor. Absence of mines and underwater obstructions helped to eliminate damage and loss. The success of pre-D-day pinpoint bombing was so considerable that the anticipated threat from coastal defenses never materialized and was easily disposed of on D-day by the closely coordinated naval and air attack.

It has been suggested that the danger of rockets falling into the initial waves could have been obviated by placing the rocket boats in front or on the flank of these waves. The first alternative would have lost too much of the last minute effect of the rockets, while the second proposal would have made the firing too inaccurate, even if the extremely confined space in Delta area had permitted this disposition. As the value of rocket fire has by now been thoroughly demonstrated, it is evident that the risk involved must be accepted. The danger can be minimized in the future by limiting the maximum distance permissible between rocket boats and the first wave and by improving performance of rockets and rocket launchers to reduce the number of wild shorts.

One of the most surprising features of the assault was the quantity of unloading accomplished over the small Delta beaches. Ideal weather conditions and lack of interference and obstructions help to explain this, but excellent training and organization, also, must be credited. The flow of traffic was aided by putting the reorganization plan into effect. The use of such a plan was an innovation that proved its worth.

RECOMMENDATIONS

In order to make a smooth and orderly transition from the assault to the maintenance and build-up phase of an amphibious invasion, a reorganization plan, to be placed in effect upon order from the task force commander, is recommended as a standard part of the operation plan.

Section 3.8

CAMEL ASSAULT

THE PLAN

The first task of Camel Attack Force was to establish the 36th US Infantry Division (reinforced) ashore in the St. Raphael-Antheor area on D-Day. The Special Operations Group was to assist by landing commandos on the right flank south of Golfe de la Napoule, during darkness, in order to block the main roads from Cannes to St. Raphael. The initial landing by Camel Force was to take place on Blue and Green beaches at H-hour (see diagram I). As Blue was a sandy beach only 80 yards long and unsuitable for vehicles, it was to be used only for landing personnel and light artillery, and was to be closed as soon as practicable. The beach and its approaches were believed to be without mines or obstructions and to be defended by a number of pillboxes and machine gun positions. A battery reported to be 149 mm, north of Cannes, threatened the right flank of this area.

Green beach was 840 yards long, but only 230 yards were workable. Wheeled vehicles would require matting to negotiate the beach, and it had only one prepared exit. The main coastal road and railway were less than 200 yards inland. The area was well defended by guns in casemates and pillboxes, by anti-tank guns, by machine guns, and in particular by a battery of 5 casemated 150 mm guns. The beach was believed to be covered with barbed wire but not to be mined. It was estimated to have very limited maintenance value.

Primary maintenance was to be over Red beach, located at the mouth of the Argens Valley in the Gulf of Frejus close to the main coastal road and railway, to the small port of St. Raphael, and to the town of Frejus and its airfield. About 850 of its 2730 yards were to be used for the landing. Wheeled vehicles would need mats. An anti-tank wall and ditch blocked all exit from the beach. The general area was very thickly studded with guns and the beach was covered by barbed wire and land mines. A row of concrete pyramids (in some places the rows were doubled or tripled, and reported to be mined) obstructed the seaward approach. Early reports indicated minefields in the Gulf of Frejus but submarine reconnaissance toward the end of July failed to find any trace of them. The assault on Red beach was to take place at Z-hour, which would be between 6 and 7 hours after H-hour. By H plus 2 hours CG 36th Division was to set Z-hour and would advise whether or not the assault on Red beach was to be shifted to Green or Yellow beach, for which alternate plans were prepared.

Yellow beach, located at the head of Rade d'Agay, was about 1/2 mile long with a very soft sand surface and exits to the coastal road and railway directly behind it. The inlet and beach were believed to be mined, and the entrance blocked by a net and boom. Gun positions of 88 mm, or smaller, strongly controlled the inlet and its approaches, threatening severe crossfire to forces attempting to enter. The beach was considered of limited value for maintenance. No landing would be made until the beach had been secured from landward and the inlet cleared of its obstructions and swept for mines.

Camel plan of attack was based on the estimate that Red and Yellow beaches and their offshore waters were too heavily defended and obstructed for assault, initially. Later in the day, more bombing planes and rocket boats could be made available, fewer coast guns would be active, gunfire ships would have more room to maneuver and could get in closer, and troops previously landed could eliminate the threat of heavy flanking fire.

Camel assault area was laid out with an outer transport area two miles square flanked by small craft reassembly areas about 12 miles offshore from Red beach (see diagram I). One destroyer was to act as reference vessel for this area and another to mark the approach to it. PCs were to take station to mark lowering areas for Green and Blue beaches, followed by minesweepers which were to clear the transport and gunfire support areas and the boat lanes. LCT and LST convoys were to reach the outer transport area at 0400; gunfire support and combat loader convoys, by 0430; the LCI convoy, at 0730. One combat command of the First French Armored Division was to arrive, about 1600, in Convoy Special No. 2.

One battalion of the 141st RCT was to land on Blue beach. The remaining two battalions, followed by the 143rd RCT, were to go ashore on Green beach; the 142nd RCT was scheduled for Red beach. Two LCT with DD tanks were to land on Green beach directly after the first wave. The touchdown of the first wave was to be preceded by naval and air bombardment, close inshore minesweeping and fire support, and rocket barrages. Gunfire support ships with air spot were to be ready to fire at 0610; those assigned beach neutralization were to take position by 0635. Both groups were to open on designated targets at 0650, lifting fire to the flanks and inland from 0755 to 0810, when pre-arranged shelling was to cease. Fighter bombers were to be in the area prepared to attack at 0550, and would bomb specified points from 0610 to 0730. Heavy bombers were to drop their loads from 0700 to 0730. Shallow water minesweepers starting at 0700 were to clear the boat lanes to within 500 yards of the shore. Rocket boats were scheduled to drench the beaches between 0752 and 0756. By 1100, all boat waves for Green and Blue beaches were to have landed. The pattern for Red beach assault was much the same as for Green beach, with the important addition of 12 Apex units to clear a path through the obstacles, and Naval Combat Demolition Units to complete the task of clearance. An evening bombardment of Frejus and/or St. Raphael was planned, to be executed if requested by the army.

On completion of the assault, Camel forces were to be regrouped to meet the problems of maintenance and build-up. Destroyers, not part of the gunfire support group, and PCs, on finishing their assigned tasks, were already to have been released to Commander Anti-Submarine and Convoy Control Group (CTG 80.6). The assault groups were to be disbanded. Forces remaining were to be organized in a Bombardment Group, Minesweeping Group, Escort and Screening Group, Salvage and Firefighting Group, Beach Group, Joint Loading Control, Unloading Control, Return Convoy Control, and Service Group.

EXECUTION OF THE PLAN

All convoys arrived in the assault area on time. The combat loader convoy was four miles out of position to the west but had gained its proper station by H-hour.

For the assault on Blue and Green beaches, the morning haze combined with clouds of dust raised by bombing made visibility difficult for gunfire support ships, spotting planes, and boat waves. Despite this, all major targets were demolished or neutralized by 0800, except one coastal battery east of Red beach which was destroyed later, and all boat waves landed substantially on time. No mines, underwater obstacles, or barbed wire were encountered. Enemy gunfire was sporadic and inaccurate. On Green beach there was some machine gun fire and, after 0930, some artillery fire. Only 13 fire support missions were requested during the day. Rocket fire was most effective, and no casualties resulted from rockets colliding in mid-air. All troops and vehicles landed dry, with few casualties and only light resistance. It was possible to close Blue beach by 1100. Landing conditions on Green beach were reported by the beachmaster to be excellent.

At 0740, CG 36th Division requested CTF 87 to carry out the landing planned for Red beach at 1400. The sequence of events leading to the decision of CTF 87 at 1415 to shift to the alternate plan and land the 142nd RCT over Green Beach is set forth in the Campaign Narrative for 15 August, Chapter I, Part II of this report. Among the factors of the situation at 1415 may be listed:

(1) Failure of the Apex boats to breach any part of the underwater obstructions known to exist off Red beach;

(2) Unexpected density of mines off the beach;

(3) Delay in approach of LCT(R)s and initial assault waves apparently because of enemy gunfire;

(4) Reported good progress of troops already ashore both in Camel and other sectors of the assault which might be expected to lead to the early capture of St. Raphael and Red Beach by land attack with considerably less loss than by amphibious assault under existing conditions;

(5) Known excellent landing conditions on Green Beach.

The landing over Green beach was carried out smoothly and efficiently on the basis of the Z-hour of 1515. From 1930 to 2000 a naval gunfire and army artillery barrage was fired on the Frejus-St. Raphael area prior to assault by land from the north and east. Clearance of numerous land mines on the beach and exit areas and the large and difficult minesweeping task delayed opening of Red beach until the evening of D plus two. In the meantime ships of Convoy Special No. 2 with the French Armored Combat Command unloaded over beaches in the Delta area.

At 1425, the army reported that only snipers and minor resistance remained in the vicinity of Rade d'Agay. By 1915, the net and boom across its mouth were cleared, and within an hour, Yellow beach was opened for limited traffic. No mines were swept in the Rade, but the first ship to touch the beach (LCI 951) set off a whole row of land mines along the water's edge. At 2015 the reorganization plan was placed in effect.

CONCLUSIONS

The success of Camel Force assaults on Blue and Green beaches resulted chiefly from the overwhelming pounding administered to the defenses of two beaches which the enemy apparently considered unlikely invasion landing points. This made possible an assault with few losses followed by a rapid advance overland to the only beach in the area fully suited for maintenance, and up the Argens Valley, to join the Airborne Force. As a consequence, the adverse effects on scheduled unloading of the failure to open Red beach from seaward on D-Day were held to a minimum. In view of the extensive clearance required, the progress of unloading had Red beach been assaulted from seaward at 1400 D-Day can only be conjectured but it is most probable that there would have been delay in any case. Scheduled unloading figures were attained by D plus six.

In connection with poor visibility at beaches resulting from haze and dust from bombing and gunfire, spotters placed in LCCs about 1,000 yards offshore proved most helpful.

White phosphorous shells were used successfully in a number of ways. In addition to their physical effect on enemy troops, they proved valuable for creating smoke screens, helping SFCPs to spot, and marking the location of an initial salvo. They were also employed for signalling when fire was lifted in a particular area to permit troops to move in at once, though this use was limited to situations where the signal could not be confused with their other uses.

The amount of unloading accomplished over Green beach was beyond all reasonable expectation for a space so small, and could not have been relied on in planning for the assault. The ideal weather conditions, lack of obstructions, neutralization of the opposition, and excellence of the beach, when taken with the speed and skill with which the landing craft were unloaded, helped to account for this unexpectedly favorable result. The efficient unloading on this beach reflects great credit on the shore party.

RECOMMENDATION

The positioning of a gunfire spotter in a small craft such as an LCC about 1,000 yards offshore is recommended for close gunfire support of the assault.

Section 3.9

AIRCRAFT CARRIER OPERATIONS

The aircraft carrier force (TF 88) was assigned the following tasks:

(1) To provide maximum practicable fighter protection and spotting aircraft to assigned attack sector;

(2) To provide close support missions;

(3) To provide own protection against enemy air and submarine forces.

The order for flights and assignment of sectors was issued by XII Tactical Air Command. In addition to the above assigned tasks, the carrier aircraft provided many strafing, photographic and reconnaissance missions.

Task Force 88 was organized in two groups as follows:

TG 88.1 (Rear Adm. Troubridge, RN)	TG 88.2 (Rear Adm. Durgin, USN)
HMS Royalist (AACL)(F)	USS Tulagi (CVE)(F)
HMS Delhi (AACL)	USS Kasaan Bay (CVE)
HMS Attacker (CVE)	HMS Stalker (CVE)
HMS Emperor (CVE)	HMS Hunter (CVE)
HMS Khedive (CVE)	HMS Caledon (AACL)
HMS Searcher (CVE)	HMS Columbo (AACL)
HMS Pursuer (CVE)	USS Jeffers (DD)
HMS Troubridge (DD)	USS Butler (DD)
HMS Tuscan (DD)	USS Shubrick (DD)
HMS Tyrian (DD)	USS Gherardi (DD)
HMS Teazer (DD)	USS Murphy (DD)
HMS Tumult (DD)	USS Herndon (DD)
HMS Tenacious (DD)	
HMS Navarinon (DD)	

Protection against air, surface and submarine attacks was provided by TF 88. Two anti-aircraft cruisers were assigned each group in addition to the destroyers. The carriers were never attacked by the enemy. On the nights of D day and D plus one, navigational flares were dropped in the vicinity of the carriers but there were no developments. Night fighter aircraft (Hellcats), based at Solenzara, Corsica, were on call to repel enemy air attacks against the convoy lanes or the carriers. On three occasions, night fighters landed on board and remained in readiness to repel night attack. The carriers did not have night fighter director equipment installed but could control the planes by the informative method. The Task Force was in the vicinity of the Fighter Director ship during darkness on D day and D plus one. For a more detailed discussion of operations of carrier aircraft see Carrier Aircraft Operations, Section 4.8, Part II.

Cruising dispositions were planned for any eventuality. The disposition of normal flight operations was generally used during the day. Carriers were stationed in a compact formation with DDs disposed to give maximum submarine protection and still permit them to readily assume close AA stations. The carriers turned into the wind together except when only one or two landings or takeoffs were involved. On these occasions, the carrier concerned would leave the formation escorted by a destroyer and maneuver as necessary to recover or launch the airplane. US CVEs had a two knot advantage over British CVEs. At times this factor made it difficult to keep the formation closed up at high speeds. The range of the Seafires employed by the British CVE was very short; they possessed about one third the endurance of the Hellcats. This caused more frequent turning into the wind during the day's flight operations than would normally be necessary for the CVEs carrying the longer ranged Hellcats.

Task Force 88 departed from Malta on D minus 3 and arrived in its primary operating area in time for the first scheduled flights on the morning of D day. An operating area well to the south of the assault and gunfire support area was designated for use of the aircraft carriers, (see figure Aircraft Carrier Force in Section 4.8, Part II). The carrier task groups operated separately but generally within visual signalling distance of each other. A fixed point, "Option", was chosen for each day's operations and the groups stayed within ten miles of that point each day. Decision as to the location of this point, each day, depended on the area of air support missions. For the first three days, the operating area was approximately 40 miles off the beaches. Three different point Options were chosen, each new point bringing the groups further west, until, on D plus 3, the third and final point Option chosen was twenty-five miles southwest of Marseille. The groups then operated from the vicinity of this point until their services were no longer required. Their missions on and after D plus 3 were mostly in the Rhone Valley and due to the short ranged Seafires it was mandatory that point Option was as close as possible to the hundred fathom curve.

Night retirement commenced immediately after completion of flight operations each day. Retirement was either toward a given position or along a prescribed course usually sixty or seventy miles distant from point Option. Carriers always arrived at the operating point for the day, before dawn.

The task groups took turns proceeding to Maddalena for logistics, rest and recreation. Both groups operated off the assault area from D day until D plus four, after which the following program was carried out:

	Departed Assault Area	Returned Assault area	Released from Assault Operations
TG 88.1	D plus 4	D plus 6	
TG 88.2	D plus 6	D plus 9	
TG 88.1	D plus 9‡		D plus 12
TG 88.2	D plus 11§		D plus 12§
TG 88.2	D plus 14		D plus 14

‡ Retired to Maddelena and released there on D plus 12.
§ Two British CVEs only.

Task Force 88 was dissolved on 29 August. US CVEs loaded spares and equipment at Ajaccio and proceeded to Oran to prepare for the return trip to the United States. British CVEs retired to Alexandria via Maddalena. The time on station of the CVEs carrying Hellcats that rendered support missions could have been increased had they been supplied with sufficient explosive rockets and 500 pound bombs.

The four British anti-aircraft cruisers and the screening destroyers had little or no problem due to complete lack of enemy opposition. Destroyers were assigned the additional duty of rescuing pilots who crashed in the vicinity, and, on several occasions, recovered aviation personnel.

Carriers rendered valuable support during the period of transition while landing fields were being prepared on captured territory near the beaches and while the air force was moving up planes and equipment from its bases in Corsica. The distance between land bases in Corsica and the assault area was not impossible for long range fighter planes to negotiate, but the floating fighter strips increased the effective radius of fighters and further insured a source of fighters for immediate coverage of the assault area. Carrier based planes were able to quickly penetrate distances up the Rhone Valley to a depth of 120 miles and caused much damage in the early days of the campaign when the Germans were rapidly withdrawing.

The following recommendations are made:

(1) Carriers comprising a Task Group should be homogeneous with the same speed characteristics;

(2) Four carriers of the CVE class is the maximum number to be operated in one task group for optimum efficiency;

(3) Adequate facilities and space should be provided on CVEs for the flag allowance when embarked.

Section 3.10

SCREENING OPERATIONS

The task of providing protection for ships participating in the operations off the Southern Coast of France required diverse screens. Task force commanders directly controlled certain screens off the beachheads, as did Commander Screening Group (CTG 80.5). The major task of screening offshore, however, was performed by Commander Anti-Submarine and Convoy Control Group, (CTG 80.6).

All available escort ships and craft were utilized for covering the assault convoys from the loading ports to the assault area. The escort DDs and DEs, with the exception of those attached to the bombardment group, were released upon arrival of the convoys in the transport area and reported to CTG 80.6 for duty.

Each task force commander was assigned an area of responsibility and controlled the operations of all screening ships and craft within that area. An inner screen composed of PC, SC, LCS, LCC, LCV(P) and LCM(S) was established, primarily to provide protection by the use of smoke for the anchorages, unloading areas and gunfire support ships if required. The shallow draft craft were stationed close inshore off the beaches and PCs and SCs were assigned patrol sectors around the transport areas. This group of larger craft, in addition, acted as an anti-submarine, anti-E-boat and anti-limpeteer screen. Minesweepers augmented this screen at dusk and dawn periods. Anti-aircraft cruisers and four ships equipped for jamming radio-controlled bombs were stationed in the areas for effective action against enemy aircraft and controlled missiles.

CTG 80.6 maintained two separate screens. Five DD constituted an inner screen as secondary defense against incoming E-boats and submarines, and for anti-aircraft defense of the convoy assembly area. The main destroyer screen, (Assault Area Screen - see figure No. 4) was initially organized into three sectors of responsibility covering the central, eastern, and western flanks of the assault area. Two DD pickets were stationed outside the sectors within voice communication distance. Complete cover of the entire assault area by this screen was lacking only at the southwest section in Alpha area. The existence of minefields in Rade d'Hyeres prevented use of destroyers there. CTF 84 established nightly PT patrol between Cap Benat and Ile du Levant to complete the screen.

The Assault Area Screen was established at 0600 15 August, and Screen Commander (CTU 80.6.10) was designated to be in direct control of its operation. A strong screen was considered necessary because of expected E-boat attacks and possibility of an "all out" submarine effort by the enemy with his last submarines at Toulon. The original screen, which was 50 miles in length, was composed of 26 DD.

No destroyers were permanently attached to the screen. CTG 80.6 rotated all destroyers into the screen so that ships would be relieved for logistic purposes, would alternate on assignments with the Gunfire Support Force (TF 86) operating on the flanks and would obtain escort duty; thereby affording an opportunity for all types of action.

The following modifications in composition and formation of the Assault Area Screen were made up to 25 September:

(1) At 2000, 15 August the central sector was moved four (4) miles shoreward (see figure 4) and reduced from 12 to 10 subdivisions.

(2) At 1600, 19 August the entire screen was drawn further shoreward, which lessened its length to 42 miles. The rectangular patrol areas were re-

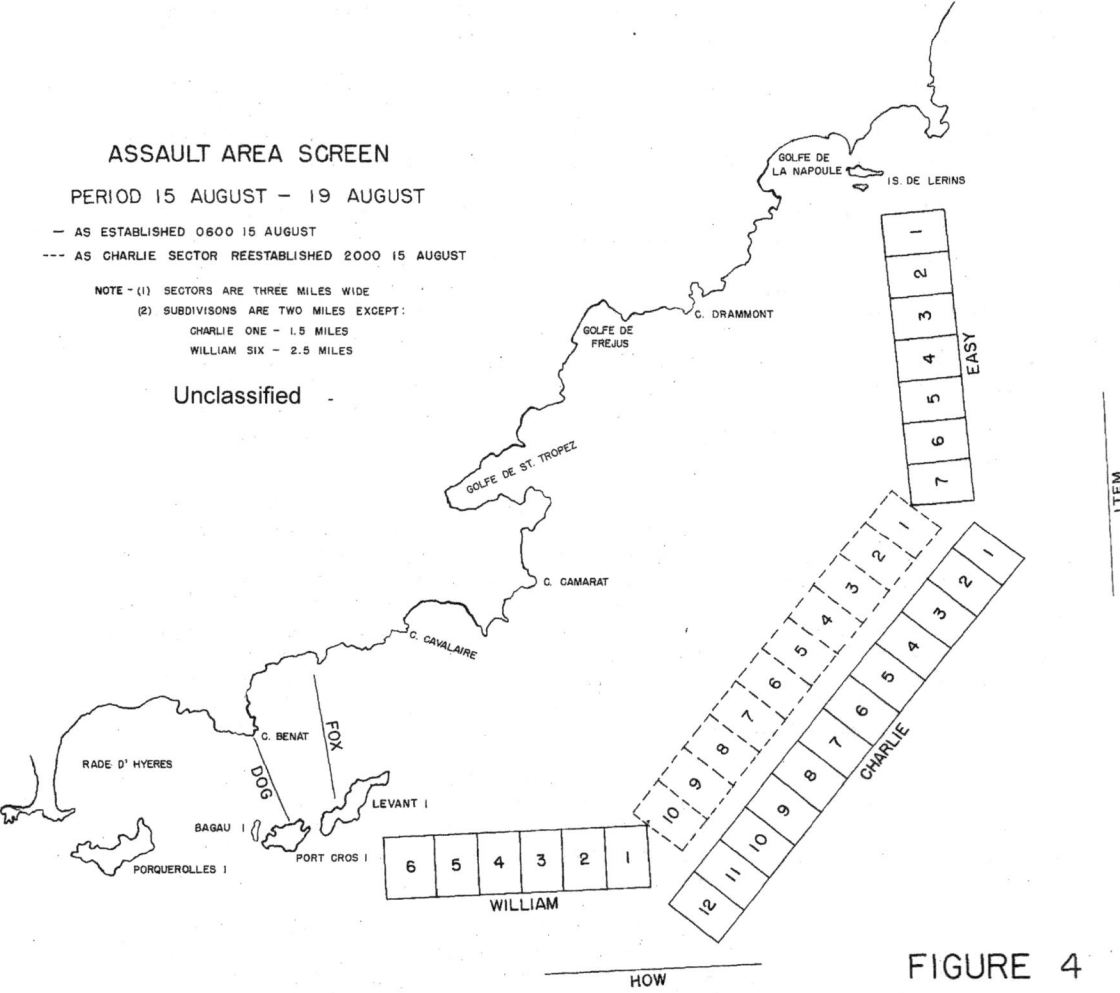

FIGURE 4

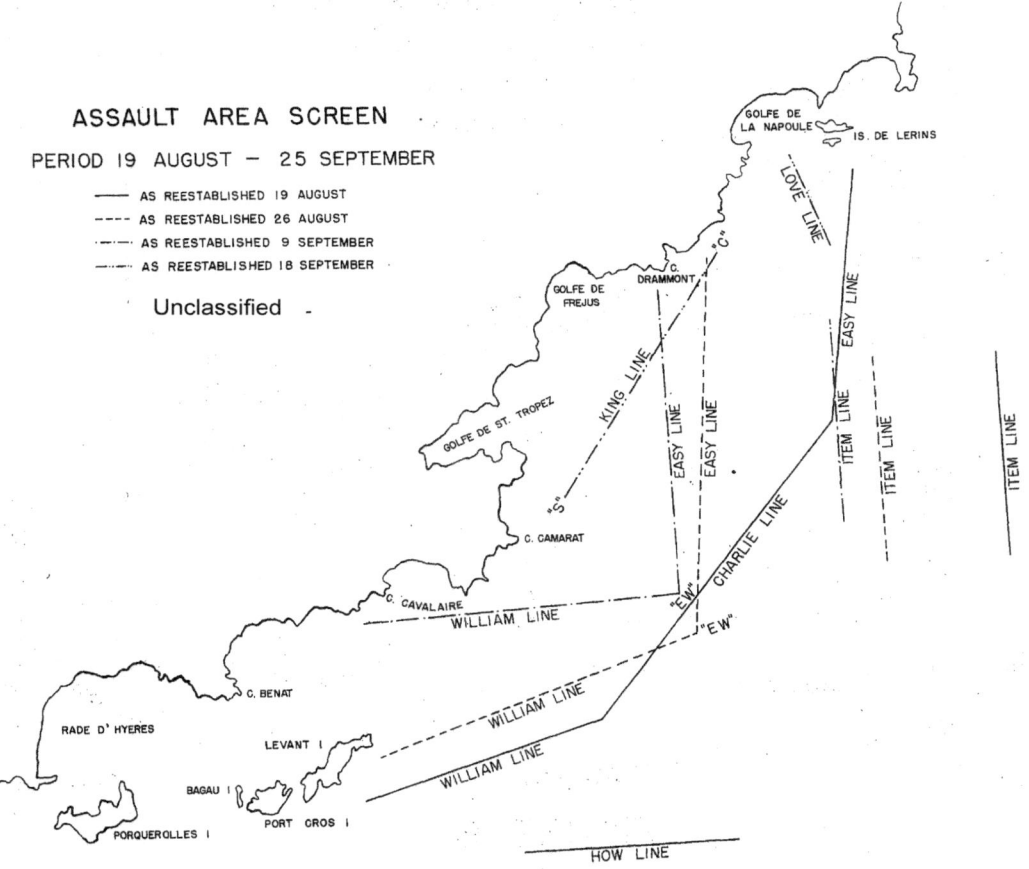

FIGURE 5

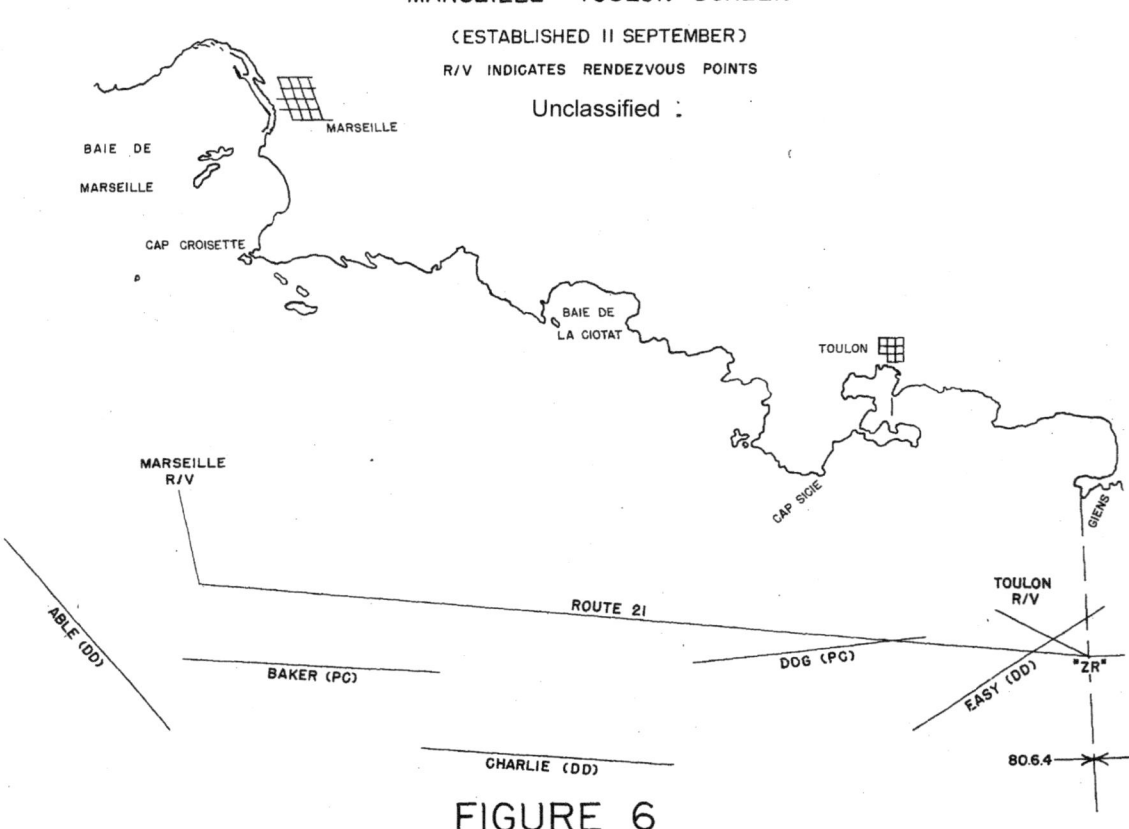

FIGURE 6

- 200 -

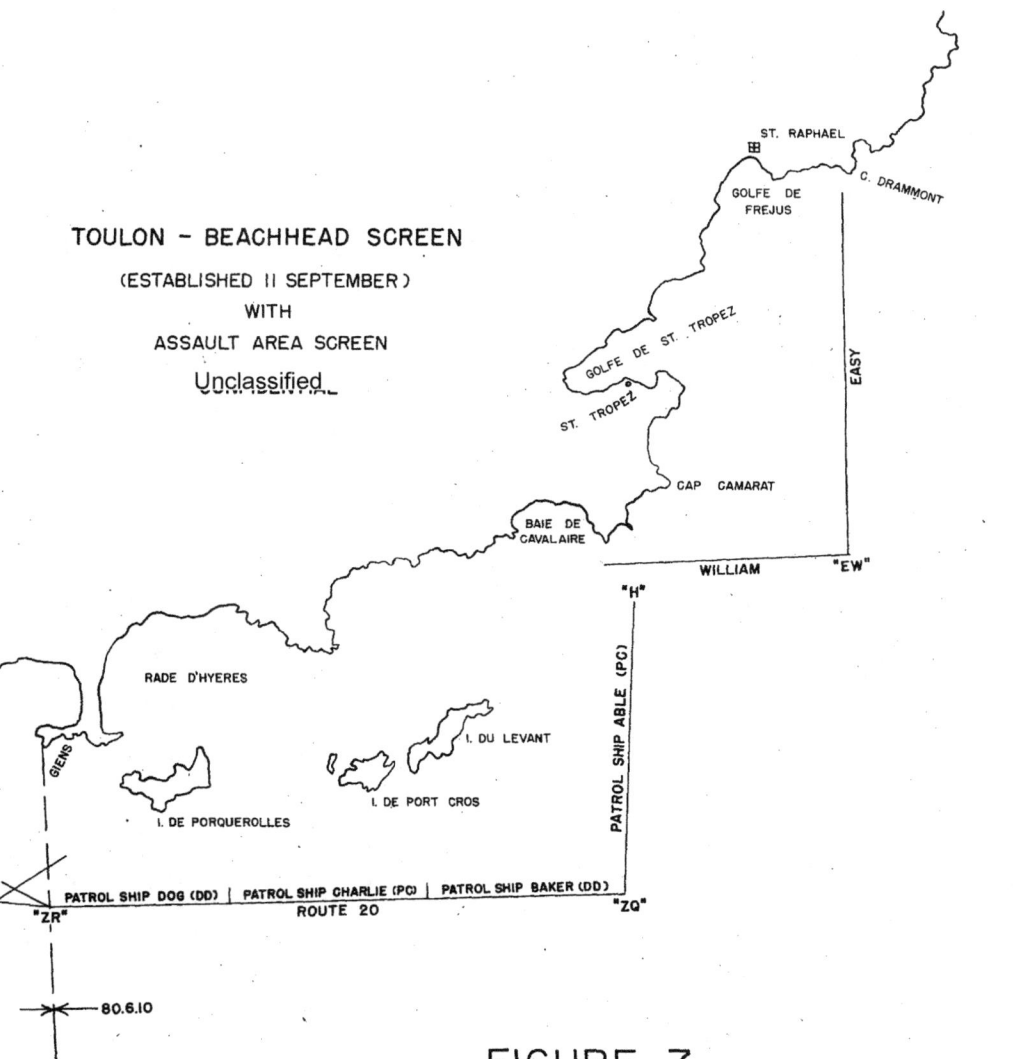

FIGURE 7

- 201 -

duced to patrol lines for each of the three sectors. The western picket was moved four miles to the north and the eastern picket four miles to the west. The number of ships employed varied from 13 to 15 DD (see figure 5).

(3) On 26 August the screen was reduced to two lines; the total length reduced to 34 miles. Pickets were readjusted accordingly (see figure 5).

(4) On 9 September the length of the patrol was shortened by reducing the angle between the lines. The western picket was eliminated.

(5) On 17 September the screen was reduced to one picket and one patrol line covered by 8 DD.

One DD on each flank of the assault area screen was assigned 22 August to effect necessary communications with night searching aircraft. A nucleus of a hunting group was organized in order to establish unity of control for action against enemy submarines and to insure early effective action on contacts obtained by aircraft at night.

CTF 84 maintained the nightly PT patrol on the western flank of the assault area on two patrol lines, Dog and Fox (see figure 4). No sightings or contacts were made, and it was discontinued on 23 August. Coincident with this, an inshore nightly patrol was established in the Golfe de la Napoule area on the right flank to screen against small craft raids (see "PT Operations," Section 3.11, Part II). This patrol was later increased to two sections with one in the van to engage the enemy when contacted, and the other to act as a supporting unit, if necessary. PTs also coordinated with picket DDs and DDs of the right flank gunfire support group.

Many ships were gradually diverted from the beaches to the ports of Marseille and Toulon for unloading. Ships were sailed intermittently and presented a constant demand for escorts. Protection had to be provided for the ships while in the ports. On 5 September, Commander Local Offshore and Harbor Defense (CTU 80.6.4) was established and set up a patrol composed of 4 DD and 4 PC off the approaches to the ports. It was decided on 11 September to maintain a continuous patrol controlled by CTU 80.6.10 and CTU 80.6.4 along the convoy route from the ports to the beaches (see figures 6 and 7). This permitted ships and craft to be sailed unescorted.

Special screens were organized to augment protection against specific types of attacks and to prevent attempted enemy operation in definite areas. An LCVP patrol was maintained approximately 200 yards from Ile du Lion de Mer to Ile d'Agay for the protection of ships in Camel area anchorage against human torpedo attacks. As a result of a reported submarine sighting, an anti-submarine patrol consisting of 2 PC was established off the Straits of Bonifacio. Both of these screens were discontinued, when the threat of attack became negligible.

COMMENT

The performance of the Assault Area Screen was flawless in all attacks which occurred. The screen destroyed or captured 5 MAS boats, taking 37 POW; 3 S boats, taking 2 POW; one fishing vessel, taking 50 POW who were an ex-German submarine crew, and 4 explosive boats all with no substantial damage sustained by the screening ships. These losses were in addition to the many enemy E-boats, human torpedoes, explosive boats and other craft destroyed by the PTs (see "PT Operations," Section 3.11, Part II) and by the Gunfire Support Ships operating off the right flank of the assault area (see "Campaign Narrative," Chapter 1, and "Bombardment," Section 5.1, both of Part II).

Numerous ASV contacts were obtained by aircraft prior to 22 August, but the information was not received by the screening ships within sufficient time to take effective action. The assignment of one destroyer on each flank of the screen for maintaining direct communications with the night searching craft was instituted to eliminate the difficulty. This duty in no way hampered the destroyers in carrying out their original task with the screen. It provided coordination of aircraft and DD effort against submarine contacts, particularly the threats during darkness.

The sector screen during this operation was considered to be much more satisfactory than the "endless chain" type of screen. It was composed of three individual screen sectors in which the two outer wings were controlled by sector commanders. The Screen Commander controlled the center sector and the entire unit. Conditions of the waters of the Mediterranean for echo ranging and underwater listening were considered poor. The sector type patrol under these conditions was considered more appropriate than the "endless chain" type. The ships were confined to definite patrol areas or lines thus enabling each ship to maintain a radar plot and the sector commander a master plot. This standard pattern on the radar scope was altered only by the approach of an enemy target on ship movements in the area. All plots or information received by individual ships were evaluated by the sector commander and relayed to the Screen Commander. Since the Screen Commander was informed daily of all ship movements with which the screen came in contact, identification of targets was simplified. Positions and names of screening ships were disseminated daily by dispatch to the task force commanders. This enabled them to determine the exact location of any attack.

Section 3.11

PT OPERATIONS

Three squadrons of 42 PT boats, assigned to Commander Boat Squadrons, US Eighth Fleet, participated in the assault. Of these, MTBron 15 was the only squadron which had previously taken part in a major assault. MTBron 22 and MTBron 29, which arrived in the Mediterranean by the second week in June, had participated in the Elba Island operation and patrolled from Bastia under the British SOIS (Senior Officer Inshore Squadron) against enemy coastal traffic in the Ligurian Sea. The activities of the 12 ASRC of ARBron 1, also assigned to Commander Boat Squadron, are discussed under Section 3.4, Part II, Diversionary Operations. On 31 July, all PT forces were withdrawn from active patrols in preparation for the assault on the south coast of France.

Commander Boat Squadrons Eighth Fleet commanded the Screening Group during the operation. For the assault, D minus 1/D day, the majority of the 42 PTs were assigned to other task forces and task groups as follows:

(a) Sixteen PT of MTBron 15 were allocated to Commander Sitka Attack Force. Eight PT divided into three screens were used to cover this force; 3 boats to the southward of Toulon Bay, 3 boats on a line southward and west of Porquerolles Island, and 2 boats to the southward of Grande Passe. Seven PT were used as control boats and inshore support for the assault landing craft. One PT with 4 aircraft rescue boats operated as diversion and screening unit for the commando landing on Cap Negre. A discussion of these appears under "The Sitka Assault" (see Section 3.5).

(b) Twenty PT were assigned to Commander Special Operations Group (CTG 80.4). The tasks assigned consisted of assisting in diversion operations staged on the eastern flank of the Nice area and on the western flank in the La Ciotat area. MTBron 22 participated in the former and 8 PT of MTBron 29 in the latter. The operations of these boats during this period are reported under "Diversionary Operations" (section 3.4).

(c) One PT was assigned to take station at position F (see diagram XII) as an Aircraft Beacon Ship from 0200, 15 August (D-day), until last light. This boat departed from Calvi in sufficient time to be on station and successfully completed its task.

On D-day, all PTs, with the exception of eight which remained with the Diversion Group until dissolved on 18 August, reported for duty to CTG 80.5 based in the Baie de Briande area.

Commander Task Group 80.5 was assigned the following tasks:

(1) To provide sufficient PTs to Commander Task Force 84 to maintain a nightly anti-E-Boat screen on the western flank of the assault area from D-day, until otherwise directed;

(2) To maintain a daily blood bank shuttle between Calvi and Delta Attack Force beaches composed of 2 PT, beginning on D plus one and extending to D plus ten, unless otherwise directed;

(3) To establish and maintain a PT boat pool in Alpha Attack Area from the morning of D-day for employment as directed by Naval Commander, Western Task Force;

(4) To maintain during darkness a continuous patrol in the Nice-Cannes area, beginning on D minus one.

PTs were made available to CTF 84 for nightly patrols in Rade d'Hyeres, between Cap Benat and Ile de Levant. The patrols were made in divisions of two boats each, the number of divisions ranging from one to three depending on the circumstances. These patrols never made any contacts and were cancelled on 23 August, owing to the reduced threat of enemy surface attack from the West.

The PT Blood Bank Shuttle commenced from Calvi on 16 August (D plus 1), and deliveries were made daily at the beaches in the Delta Attack Force Area. On 23 August, this service was taken over by airplanes which were then able to land on fields close to the assault area.

The boat pool was established on 15 August (D-Day) and operated from Baie de Briande until 23 August, when it was moved to St. Maxime. Assignment of PTs was made to the flagships of the task forces and task groups for smoke and close night screens, and, they were also used as courier boats, until relieved on D plus 10 day by the Air-Sea Rescue Boats (ASRC). From time to time PTs were assigned Commander Support Force, CTF 86, for a variety of duties in connection with supporting bombardment and accepting surrender of isolated defense units for the army movement to the west. Two outstanding incidents are described, briefly, below:

(a) On 22 August, PT 556 with a truce party from USS Omaha entered the harbor of Porquerolles. The party negotiated with the Commandant of the German Garrison and accepted the surrender of the island.

(b) On 24 August, PT 555 with a reconnaissance party composed of French and US Navy officers entered Port de Bouc to determine the status of the port. On their return trip from the port, the PT was mined off the entrance to Golfe de Fos.

The function of the eastern screen was performed on D minus 1/D-day by PTs assigned to the eastern diversion group. Thereafter, no screen was maintained until 23 August due to the presence of adequate destroyer screens. MTBron 22 was ordered on D-day to patrol eastward of Cap Ampeglio, and based at Bastia subsequent to D-day. Three PT from MTBron 29 on 17 August, were released from the assault area to act as radar lead boats in patrols off Genoa with British MTB, operating under SOIS Bastia. On 21 August, MTBron 22 was ordered under the operational control of SOIS Bastia to operate in coordination with air and surface forces in the north Ligurian Sea.

On 23 August, nightly patrols were established close inshore on the eastern flank off Nice and Villefranche between Cap Antibes and Cap Ferrat to guard against small craft raids including attacks by explosive boats and human torpedoes, which intelligence sources indicated could be expected operating from ports between the assault area and Genoa. PT patrols were organized in groups of two boats each; two groups operating on moonless nights and one on moonlit nights. Prior to establishing the patrols, daily contact was made with the DDs on the eastern flank before last light for the purpose of exchanging orders and plans for possible attacks and testing voice communications. During the period covered by the report, contacts were made on the following nights, and the results of the nights' engagements are given:

With Explosive Boats

    24/25 August - 3 explosions heard, which were believed to be 3 boats destroyed

    26/27 August - 4 boats destroyed

    27/28 August - results unknown

    7/8 September - 4 boats destroyed plus possibly one additional

    9/10 September - 2 boats destroyed

    15/16 September - contacts lost in attempt to overtake MAS control boat.

With Human Torpedoes

    10 September - 10 possibly 11 human torpedoes believed sunk

On 11 September, CTF 86 assumed operational control of all forces on the eastern flank, and two patrols of two PT were maintained nightly in the area.

COMMENT

Because of the nature of enemy craft, MAS-boats, explosive boats and human torpedoes, which PT patrols encountered, no torpedoes were fired by PTs while screening in the assault area. All enemy attacks were frustrated by use of close range gunfire of automatic weapons and depth charges. Enemy attacks by explosive boats and human torpedoes were launched from ports and beaches to the east of the assault area. Launching points were moved from the vicinity of Nice to San Remo as the 1st ABTF moved slowly eastward along the coast. The principal effort of both types appears to have been directed against destroyers and cruisers of the Support Force which were bombarding the coast, and against inshore elements of destroyer screens on the eastern flank of the assault area.

The initial attack by the "explosive boats" was detected close inshore. It is believed that the intention of the enemy was to penetrate the screen and attack shipping at the assault beaches. To counteract this, the PT patrols were operated off the suspected harbor bases and close aboard the intervening capes. Subsequently, the enemy moved well out to sea and was thereafter encountered from two to five miles offshore. Since, after the initial attack, it was learned that the explosive boats were guided by a control boat, the emphasis in repelling an attack was shifted to the control boat.

The first human torpedo attack occurred, 5 September, against the gunfire support ships operating off Menton. In order to break up attacks before they reached the gunfire support ships, SOC planes patrolled off the suspected launching area, from 0530 to 1100, and the PT patrol was extended over a longer period of time. The forward PT patrol operating from Cap Martin to Bordighera left station at day break; the patrol from Cap Ferrat to Cap Martin continued until 0900. The arrangement provided a strong defense against the human torpedo attack. Communications having been established, the SOC planes spotted the human torpedoes and the PTs destroyed them by gunfire. This method was found very efficient during the attack on 10 September, when 10 possibly 11 human torpedoes were sunk through the coordinated effort of SOC planes, destroyers, and PTs.

No PTs were sunk as a result of enemy action, but three were lost by mines; two in the Golfe de Frejus, and one off the approaches to the Golfe de Fos. Due to the increased effort by the enemy of anti-boat minelaying and the use of snag lines as a means for detonating them, the shallow draft of the PT is no longer a safety factor when operating in shallow waters.

Section 3.12

MINESWEEPING

PLANNING

The planning phase for minesweeping in the invasion of Southern France overlapped that for Anzio, especially in the procurement of minesweeping gear. In Salerno, the problem of supplying sweep gear had been serious, and until the establishment of the Spare Parts Distribution Center in Oran, and the fixing of Bureau Policy in January 1944, much confusion existed. From February 1944, the problem appeared solved and the minesweeping gear requirements for the operation were satisfactorily met.

The flow of sweep gear from Oran to Bizerte was adequate to maintain ample stocks in Bizerte in spite of heavy drains during and subsequent to Anzio.

A large part of the Bizerte stock (1500 tons) was moved to Ajaccio, Corsica, to be more convenient to the assault area; and prior to sailing, each sweeper was loaded with double her usual allowance of expendable items, such as otters, floats, cutters, chain slings sweep wire, etc.

It was also planned to carry additional sweep gear on the two ACMs which had been attached to the Eighth Fleet upon request.

Equipping 24 LCV(P)s with size 5 Oropesa gear and the training of the crews for these boats was undertaken because of the large amount of sweeping that had to be done close into shore.

Six SCs were converted to minesweepers and equipped with German SDG type gear. This gear can be towed by an SC up to 12 knots, and is not easily fouled even on sharp turns at high speeds. It doesn't, however, have the spread of the usual USN size 4 gear.

The first SC so equipped was successfully used at Anzio, and concurrently with the equipping of the 5 additional sweepers, the British equipped 18 MLs with the German gear. Fortunately, large stocks of this gear were found in the Italian ports.

Planning necessarily included attention to the procurement of specialized sweep gear to counter mines known to exist but not layed by the enemy in this theater.

The one main deficiency in the material planning was the lack of provisions for sufficient "Mother Ships" to supply fuel, water and provisions to the large number of small craft which made up the sweeper group. This was not an oversight in planning but more a deficiency in available craft of LST size and larger.

A carefully planned schedule for overhaul and progressive maintenance laid out by Commander Escort Sweeper Group, made it possible to have the entire US Navy sweeper force 100% operational on D-day.

Operational planning started with the preparation of Naval Planning Memorandum No. 26, in March 1944 by the Fleet Mine Officer, on the basis of experience gained in Sicily, Salerno and Anzio. In brief, the memorandum distinguished between the assault and the clearance sweeping carried out in previous operations and called attention to the fact that in the past, 5 YMSs had been able to sweep on the average about 1/2 square mile per hour and 5 AMs about double that rate. The use of heavily covered sweep formations in assault was stressed.

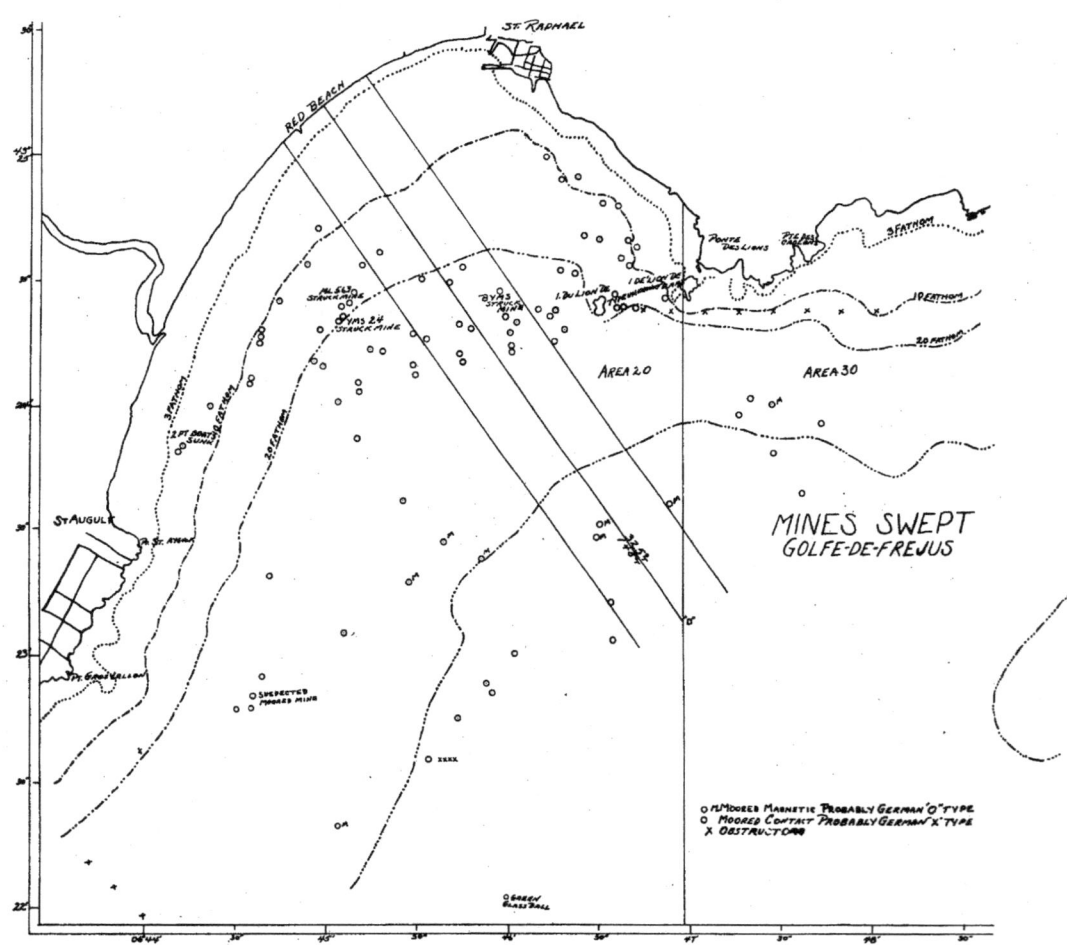

Figure 8

In April 1944, request had been made to Commander in Chief, US Fleet, for additional AMs and these were promised from the survivors of the Normandy invasion.

As the plans for the operation took more definite form, it was apparent that even with the help of all the British forces promised by Commander in Chief, Mediterranean, the minesweeping requirements would hardly be met. Therefore, on 21 June, 1944, Commander US Eighth Fleet requested 12 additional 180 foot AMs.

By July 1, it was clear that 9 220 foot AMs were to be expected from England, 6 180 foot AMs and 6 YMSs from the United States.

The total sweeper force to be available was 139 vessels of all types, 50 of which were British and 89 were US Navy.

The sweeping forces were distributed as follows:

United States		Great Britian	
AMs	25	Fleet Sweepers	17
YMSs	32	BYMs	6
SC (shallow sweepers)	6	M/S MLs	15
LCV(P)(sweepers)	24	Trawlers	4
ACM	2	Shore Ship	1
Total	89	Danlayers	7
		Total	50

Detailed planning for the minesweeping part of the operation, which occurred during the last four weeks prior to D-day, was done by the minesweeping officers of the various staffs. Only the Sitka force had no minesweeping officer.

The minesweeping plan for Naval Commander, Western Task Force, the first plan of this type put into effect in this theater, confined itself to setting up the framework for the post assault reorganization of the minesweeping forces, the methods of making reports, protection of the Straits of Bonifacio, and aerial minespotting.

For the assault phase, the sweepers force was to be divided so as to bring the sweeper units under the direct command of the several task force commanders. Following the sweeping of the assault area, that is on or about D plus 1, the minesweeping task group (CTG 80.10) was to be set up under the control force, and all minesweeping units were to report to him upon completing assault area sweeping. The minesweeping task group commander was then to plan and direct maintenance of the assault area and the sweeping in areas to the west in support of the army.

The general idea of the plans of the assault minesweeping may be had from diagram I and the following brief summary (for detailed discussion, the reports of the task force commanders should be consulted).

Sitka Planned to keep large ships in deep water and made the assault on Isles Port Cros and Levant without sweeping. With daylight the small channels into the Islands and the waters to the south and east of the Islands within the 100 fathom curve were to be swept.

Alpha This force, making assaults into Cavalaire Bay and Pampelonne Bay, planned two separate transport areas and assault channels. All the water in the area was to be used either as anchorage or fire support area so that the navigable water shallower than 100 fathoms was to be swept. The assault sweep and all clearance sweeping were planned for daylight.

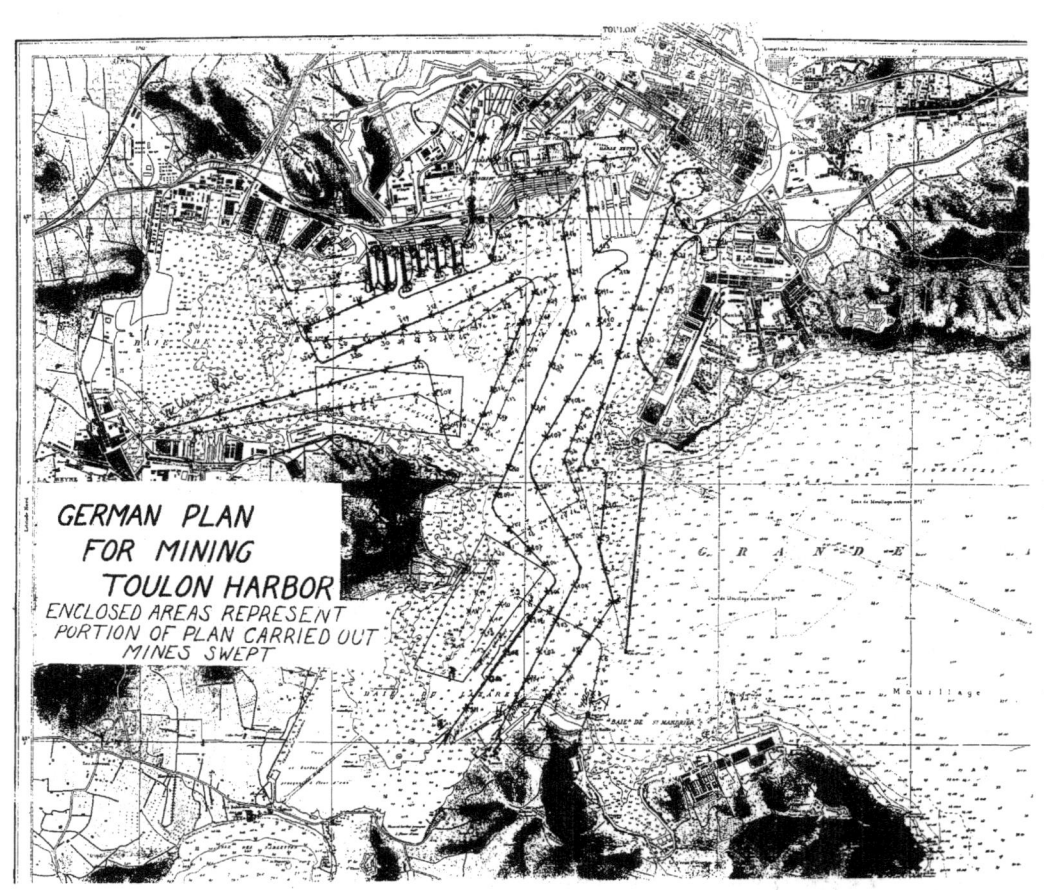

Figure 9

Delta   This force planned a single assault channel into the Bay of Bougnon. The assault sweep was to be made just prior to dawn and all clearance was to be made in daylight.

Camel   Four assault beaches were planned, two to be taken at H-hour and two later. Red Beach, just west of St. Raphael and the most important of the four, was to be assaulted at 1400 on D-day.

THE OPERATION (see diagrams XV and XVI)

The assault for Sitka, Alpha, and Delta proceeded entirely according to plan. No mines were swept by these forces.

The assault sweeping for Camel Green and Blue beaches was carried out according to plan. No mines were swept. Some delay was experienced with Yellow beach because of nets. As the sweeper formation proceeded into Frejus Gulf, at about 1400, it was heavily engaged by shore batteries and was turned back. The beach defenses were later neutralized from the rear and sweeping was resumed on D plus 1 day. Five vessels were mined in this vicinity during the next 24 hours by shallow layed contact mines.

An idea of the plan of the minefields in the Gulf of Frejus may be had from the chart.

The USS YMS 24 was mined while making a magnetic sweep behind the BYMs section which was sweeping for moored mines. ML 563 was mined rendering assistance. PT 218 was mined trying to cross the minefield. PT 202 was mined rendering assistance. BYMS 2022 was mined while sinking floaters.

Although the beach was opened at 1900 on D plus 2 day, it required four days intensive effort to completely clear the small gulf, of 90 shallow layed moored mines and 15 moored magnetic mines.

The only mines swept in the assault area were those found in Frejus Gulf, and these 105 mines caused a 48 hour delay in opening the beach even after all beach opposition had been silenced.

By D plus 4 all assault minesweeping had been completed and the sweeper forces had reported to CTG 80.10. The post assault phase, that of clearing the way into Marseille and Toulon was begun.

On D plus 4 the minespotting aircraft made its first sortie and located the minefield across the eastern entrance to the Rade d'Hyeres. Cruisers anchored very near the field were warned and the area was declared dangerous. This was the first aerial mine reconnaissance ever undertaken operationally.

By D plus 5, minesweeping operations had become stablized in the assault areas, that is, routine maintenance of anchorages and approach channels. It is worthy of comment, that the enemy attempted no aircraft minelaying operations.

From D-day on the enemy was very busy laying mines to the west of the assault area. The entrance to the Golfe de Fos was mined as was the St. Louis Canal, the Marseille Harbor, the Harbors of all the small coastal towns such as La Ciotat, Cannes, Nice, etc. An ambitious plan to mine Toulon Harbor was begun but was fortunately interrupted in the early stages. A chartlet of this plan which was captured after the fall of Toulon is shown.

In Marseille where the enemy had more time a plan similar to this was actually carried out.

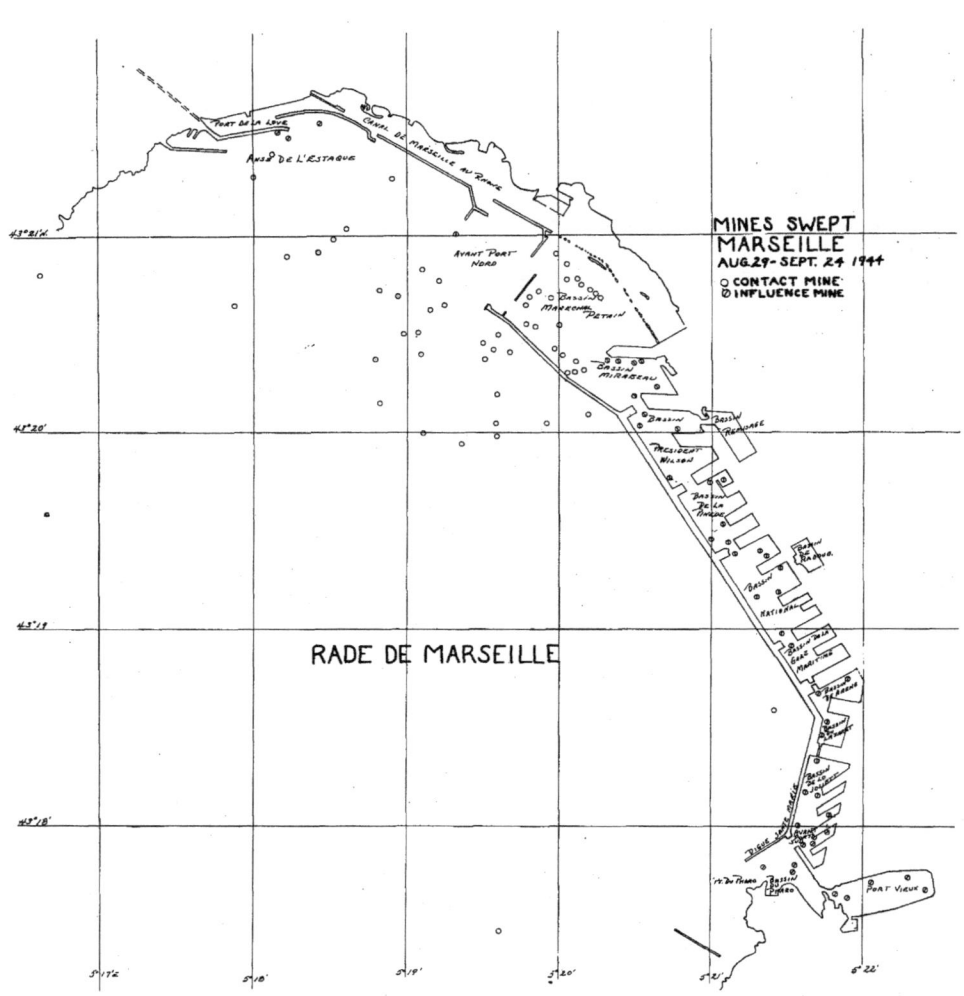

Figure 10

Warning of these fields was given by the local French authorities and by minespotting.

By D plus 12 the approach channel to Port de Bouc and the anchorage in the Golfe de Fos had been swept and declared safe. 102 mines were swept.

On D plus 16 Toulon Bay and approach channel were declared safe. A total of 74 mines were swept. At the same time the Marseille entrance channel and anchorage were reported swept.

By D plus 20 the coastal channel to Nice was declared safe. Sweeping of Toulon and Marseille Harbors was progressing slowly, one or more mines being swept each day.

D plus 26, Nice harbor was declared safe. USS Seer was mined in Rade d'Hyeres while sweeping.

Toulon Harbor was declared safe after sweeping in all areas not fouled by wrecked ships. 40 shallow layed contact mines were swept, largely by the LCV(P) sweepers.

A safe area in the Rade d'Hyeres was declared to serve as a refuge anchorage.

On D plus 40 CTG 80.10 was dissolved and responsibility for further sweeping in the forward area was turned over to CTG 80.8 who was directed to complete the minesweeping in coordination with the French.

SUMMARY

During the 40 days following the first assault, the entire south coast of France had been either swept free of mines or remaining minefields located and declared as dangerous areas. Six ports had been cleared.

No major loss was sustained due to the enemy mining effort and approximately five hundred and fifty mines were swept.

Moored Contact	463
Magnetic	70
Controlled	17
Total	550

The locations of the enemy minefields, the swept channels and anchorages are shown on the appended charts (diagrams XV and XVI).

Twenty four minespotting missions were flown and thirteen unknown enemy minefields located and reported. It is estimated that more than a thousand enemy mines were successfully by-passed in this way.

Fifteen casualties attributed to mines were sustained up to D plus 41. A list of the casualties follow:

	Ships	Location	Reason
(1)	YMS 24	Frejus Gulf	Minesweeping
(2)	ML 563	Frejus Gulf	Assisting YMS 24
(3)	BYMS 2022	Frejus Gulf	Sinking floaters
(4)	PT 218	Frejus Gulf	Trying to cross minefield
(5)	PT 202	Frejus Gulf	Assisting PT 218
(6)	ML 559	Rade d'Hyeres	Sweeping
(7)	PT 555	Port de Bouc	Trying to cross minefield
(8)	French launch	Port de Bouc	Assisting PT 555
(9)	French tug	Port de Bouc	Unknown
(10)	USS Tackle	Port de Bouc	Making fast to unknown buoy
(11)	1 LCM	Port de Bouc	Unknown
(12)	YMS 21	Toulon	Sinking floaters
(13)	USS Seer	Rade d'Hyeres	Sweeping
(14)	SS Morialta (Br. Coaster)	South of Marseille	Unknown
(15)	Swiss ship, Generoso	Marseille	Attempting to shift mooring

COMMENTS, ENEMY TACTICS AND INTELLIGENCE

In the operation relatively few new devices were used by the enemy as regards his mining practice. They are briefly:

(a) Laying of the small GZ type shallow contact mines near shore and close together (50-100 feet apart), apparently as a defense against landing craft. This type of field is extremely dangerous to all the standard types of mine sweepers and more sweepers were lost in this one operation than the total of others in this theater.

(b) Heavy mining of the waters of harbors, which were likely to fall into our hands, with contact mines and influence mines. This device more than any other slowed up the opening of Marseille and Toulon.

(c) Laying fields consisting of alternate snag line and shallow contact mines.

(d) Using long chain moorings and solid rubber rings fitted to the moorings wire to choke the mechanical cutters.

The delay experienced in opening the vital beach in Frejus Gulf indicates the possibilities of mining as a defense against an amphibious attack. It is probable that mining intelligence may become one of the most important factors in determining the time and place to make an assault against an enemy capable of exploiting coastal mining for defense.

Minespotting introduced a new factor in mine warfare and proved itself the most useful source of mine information inspite of its handicaps. Clear water, calm weather, and sunshine are required for minespotting; but the information is accurate and can be obtained from waters still under enemy control. It cannot be said, at this time, that water covered by minespotting planes with negative results is safe.

The expected mining by enemy aircraft after D-day, with new types of mines, did not materialize, presumably because of failing strength of the enemy air force.

PERFORMANCE OF SHIPS AND GEAR

The burden of the sweeping again fell to the YMSs and smaller craft (SC, ML, LCV(P) shallow water sweepers) although valuable maintenance work was accomplished by 180 feet and 220 feet AMs. Use of the AMs by the minesweeping group commander indicated a distinct hesitancy to put such large vessels in the danger consonant with clearing a new field. The wisdom of this decision is shown by the low casualty rate among the AMs without compromising the clearance of necessary areas. The restricted waters of French Riviera also hindered full employment of the AM type sweepers.

SC and ML shallow sweepers were invaluable for clearing a first passage through an enemy minefield and for sweeping in water shallower than 10 fathoms.

The LCV(P) shallow sweepers were necessary for clearing mines from the basins of Toulon and Marseille. Their maneuverability permitted sweeping around wrecks, buoys, and in the restricted waters of the basins. Their value in assault sweeping was not proved.

Performance of sweep gear was excellent in nearly every case. The supply of equipment was adequate in spite of the unexpected losses of magnetic tails due to gunfire and small craft.

Officers and men of the entire sweeper force performed their dangerous duties cheerfully and with despatch. On some newly arrived vessels there was a timidity on part of the officers to assume the risks necessary to the combat type minesweeping.

LESSONS LEARNED AND RECOMMENDATIONS

It is recognized that amphibious operations differ greatly, and what is urgently required by one operation is spare gear in another. Further, the minesweeping for this operation went in nearly every case, according to plan. Therefore the number of recommendations for future operations based on this experience is small. They are listed briefly as follows:

(a) The naval commander's staff and the staffs of each task force commander should have an experienced mine officer attached. The officer should be experienced in minesweeping and minelaying, and should have a knowledge of mine disposal procedure.

(b) The organization of the sweeper force under one command following the assault phase proved to be successful and is recommended.

(c) Minespotting from aircraft should be developed by technical research and its use extended.

(d) High speed sweepers of the SC type, which in this theater have been equipped with German sweep gear, need development.

(e) A more satisfactory shallow water sweep than the LCV(P), is required as these boats are not sufficiently seaworthy and cannot provide even limited quarters for officers and men.

(f) A very shallow draft sweeper of the skid type probably driven by an air screw is required for making a safe cut through fields of snag line and shallow layed moored mines.

Section 3.13

NAVIGATION UNITS

The landing plan was placed in effect as the assault convoys neared the end of the approach lanes. The timing of the landing schedule was exacting and called for close coordination of reference vessels, their relation to the incoming boat waves, the order of approach to the beaches, and methods of controlling the incoming waves. It is noteworthy that landing schedules were adhered to with remarkable accuracy throughout the assault.

The types of craft generally employed as reference vessels were SCs and PCs, because they had reasonably shallow draft and good navigational equipment including radar.

Reference vessels were detached from their respective convoys in time to be on assigned stations by approximately H-5 hours. The radical geographical contours of the assault coastline aided the reference vessels in making radar fixes; the vessels served as a check upon each other in their respective areas. The distance between the reference vessels employed in each assault area was generally the same. The seaward reference vessels were stationed 15 miles from the beaches in the vicinity of the transport area and the innermost reference vessels were about 1 1/2 miles from the beaches. PCs were the outer reference vessels, and SCs were the inner reference vessels. There were minor variations in all phases of the landing plan used in each assault area. With regard to reference vessels, Camel Attack Force used DDs for the 15 and 10 mile vessels. Delta Attack Force used a buoy to mark the 1 1/2 mile point. Alpha Attack Force was the only force which permitted minesweepers (AMs and YMSs) to proceed toward the beaches before the inner reference vessels were stationed, on the theory that the minesweepers were equipped as well as the reference vessels to navigate.

The reference vessels performed several functions in addition to marking the boat lanes. They served as Wave Control Stations, checking the waves to see that the schedule was being followed. The boat or craft waves were to be informed if the reference vessel was off station and were to be given the corrected onward course. Wave Control Officers were embarked on certain reference vessels to coordinate the movement of the waves. In the Camel Area a PC, acting as primary control vessel, led the first wave to the line of departure and relieved an SC stationed there. The SC relieved, then led the first wave into a point about 4,000 yards from the beach and remained there to guide the following waves. In each assault area alternate SCs and PCs were selected in the event of the loss or damage of any of the reference vessels. The USS SC 1029, reference vessel Able Yellow in the Alpha area, was severely damaged by the nearby explosion of a runaway drone, and a preassigned alternate reference vessel replaced it immediately. As an added aid to the landing craft the reference vessels had their smoke-pipes painted in accordance with the color chosen for the beach they were marking.

The order of approach and landing from the transport and lowering area was generally the same for all assault areas.

The initial wave was the largest wave. It was composed of the support craft and the first troop wave. The boat minesweepers led by an SC or an LCC in accordance with the respective assault plans proceeded first to conduct a sweep of the boat lanes to within 500 yards of the beaches. Where amphibious scouts were used, they preceded the initial wave and conducted a rapid hydrographic reconnaissance for natural and enemy placed obstacles. After H-hour some assisted the LCC in some of their control tasks and others were stationed on the windward flanks of the boat lanes near the beaches to smoke as ordered. The Apex units (these were employed in the Alpha area and at Camel Red Beach only), were directed by LCCs and positioned in the van of the support wave at firing time. Deployed behind them under the control of the LCCs and in the van of the first troop wave were the Woofus craft. The LCS(S) which fired rockets were stationed between the V formations of the LCVPs carrying troops and when ordered by the LCCs speeded ahead of LCVPs at firing time. On the flanks of the first wave were LCF and LCG to render close gunfire support as necessary. Also on the flanks were the LCTs carrying DD tanks. Each formation of LCVPs was led by an LCC which dispatched them to their assigned beaches. The LCT(R) followed behind the LCVPs keeping station on them and fired over them at the beach. LCCs which were not needed for immediate control at the beaches returned to the line of departure to assist in guiding later waves into the beaches. LCI and LCT were usually led in from the transport area by a designated craft of their own type. DUKWs were guided in by LCCs and in some cases by LCVPs and dispatched by these controlling craft when about 1,000 yards from the beach. All craft were cautioned not to pass the DUKWs too close aboard because of the danger of swamping them. In addition to LCCs, SCs also led in the later waves. These wave control vessels were at all times responsible for the formation, security and timing of the waves assigned them.

SCs and PCs once again proved their worth as reference and control vessels. LCCs were satisfactory but were not tested by conditions of heavy weather, and it is considered that there was too much equipment on this type of craft considering its small size. SCs with a draft of 6 1/2 feet would be more suitable. They are all weather boats, easily maneuvered, and can readily carry all the equipment necessary. Living conditions for extended service are also more suitable on SCs.

Section 3.14

THE REDUCTION OF HYERES, TOULON, AND MARSEILLE

CTF 86 with the gunfire support ships and minesweepers under his command was assigned the task of supporting the westward advance of the US Seventh Army and the French Army B for the capture of Toulon and Marseille. Gunfire support for the army's advance on the right flank was an additional assigned task. The naval gunfire support for the assault on D-Day was the heaviest concentration that has been provided for any operation undertaken thus far in the African and Mediterranean theater. Commander Support Force was able to draw upon these ships sufficiently to enable him to carry out all his assigned tasks on a long front and against formidable sea coast defenses.

Heaviest coastal gun concentrations were located in the vicinity of Toulon and Marseille and on Giens Peninsula near Hyeres.

The assault forces under CTF 86 were employed in carrying out and supporting Sitka assault (see Section 3.5, Part II). Sitka assault called for pre-H-hour landings on the Iles du Levant and Port Cros and in the vicinity of Cap Negre on the mainland. All these objectives were to the westward of the main assault beaches. The object of establishing forces at these positions was to protect the left flank of the main assault forces on land and sea from enemy troops and batteries.

Reduction of Hyeres included the reduction of the Iles du Levant, Port Cros and Porquerolles; Giens Peninsula, the area between the town of Hyeres and Cap Benat; and the clearance of the Rade d'Hyeres by minesweepers for gunfire support ships. This entire area was to the west of and adjoining the main assault area.

Sitka assault secured Ile du Levant on D-Day. The enemy garrison at Port Cros held out for one and one-half days beyond D-Day in an old heavily constructed fort. The Support Force was augmented by gunfire support ships released by the Attack Force Commanders of the three main assault sectors. Some ships were released on D-Day, and by D plus 2, all gunfire support ships were available and reported to Commander Support Force.

The left flank forces of the Support Force under CTF 86 for the support of the army's westward advance thus were increased to the following:

BB	CA	CL	DL	DD
USS Nevada	USS Augusta	USS Philadelphia	FS Fantasque	USS Plunkett
USS Texas*	USS Quincy	USS Omaha	FS Le Malin	USS Somers
USS Arkansas*		USS Marblehead*		USS Gleaves
HMS Ramillies		USS Cincinnati*		USS Eberle
FS Lorraine		HMS Aurora		USS Ericsson
		HMS Dido		USS Ludlow
		HMS Sirius		USS Kearny
		FS George Leygues		USS Madison
		FS Duguay Trouin		USS Rodman
		FS Montcalm		USS McCook
		FS Gloire		HMS Lookout
		FS Emile Bertin		

* Held in reserve.

Ile de Port Cros was the second Hyeres objective to fall. From D-Day until D plus 2, USS Augusta and USS Gleaves fired at the old fort, expending a total of 206 rounds of 8 inch and 1050 rounds of 5 inch projectiles respectively. In addition, 48 one thousand pound bombs were dropped on and near the fort. The fort was well softened up by the concentrated gunfire and bombing but the shelling did not completely knock this position out. CTF 86 ordered HMS Ramillies to fire 15 inch shells on this strongpoint. HMS Ramillies fired 12 rounds and shortly thereafter the fort surrendered, and Ile de Port Cros was in our hands.

CTF 86 on D plus three issued his post-assault plan to the gunfire support ships. It stated, "After the initial assault phase support the western advance of the army as directed by NCWTF. Valuable ships and limited gunfire available are to be employed only against targets of due importance. Sweep areas as necessary for the support of the western advance and the clearance of the Rade d'Hyeres." It was decided to advance the sweeping of the Rade d'Hyeres and to provide support for the minesweepers, and to commence immediately a naval effort to reduce Ile de Porquerolles and Presqu' Ile de Giens. The plan for the reduction of Ile de Porquerolles provided for a preliminary bombardment by USS Augusta and FS Emile Bertin followed by a demand for surrender to be delivered by a US PT boat bearing a white flag. A channel was to be swept the length of the Rade d'Hyeres from Cap Benat to Cap de l'Esterel on Giens Peninsula. Another area was to be swept in a north south direction between Ile de Port Cros and Ile de Porquerolles. Guns on Cap Benat and the Ile de Porquerolles were more of a nuisance than a hindrance to the minesweeping forces and gunfire support ships, but the batteries on Giens Peninsula, particularly those on Cap de l'Esterel, proved a positive menace and source of delay to all forces concerned. Enemy positions on Cap de l'Esterel had been subjected to repeated bombardments by the air force, especially before D-Day. The extreme range of the several batteries on Giens Peninusla was 22,000 yards. It was planned to use the lee of Giens as a shelter for gunfire support ships firing on the long range batteries on St. Mandrier Peninsula, but this was not possible until Giens Peninsula had been captured.

Minesweeping operations in the Rade d'Hyeres commenced on the morning of D plus 3 under enemy gunfire from Cap Benat. HMS Dido proceeded to neutralize the light batteries on Cap Benat. Bombardment of Ile de Porquerolles was carried out and USS PT 215 was dispatched with the truce party. During its approach to the island it was fired on by batteries from Giens Peninsula and forced to withdraw. USS Augusta thereupon reopened fire on these batteries. The softening up and gradual neutralization of Porquerolles and Giens continued. Minesweeping in Rade d'Hyeres was delayed by the fire of enemy batteries, especially by those on Cap de l'Esterel and those in the hills north of Rade d'Hyeres and by numerous underwater obstructions between Port Cros and Porquerolles. These were many underwater buoys attached to the anti-submarine and anti-torpedo net, sections of which had broken off and were in the Rade d'Hyeres. This minesweeping effort eventually had to be abandoned, but the main channel between Cap Benat and Cap de l'Esterel was swept after several delays and permitted access to gunfire support ships. The army was making rapid progress north of the Rade d'Hyeres and supported by the armor of the French 1st Armored Division did not feel the loss of the expected gunfire support, occasioned by minesweeping delays, too keenly.

The French Army B was steadily advancing westward along the coast at this time, occasionally leaving some forces to deal with pockets of resistance, as at Hyeres. The US Seventh Army was also rapidly pushing westward, but in general its elements were too far inland for continuous naval gunfire support. The Navy, besides aiding the mopping up of these rear areas had to maintain the pace of the army's advanced forces, which were reaching west of Toulon toward Marseille and Port de Bouc. Units of the French Army B were close to Toulon on D plus 4. During this approach to Toulon, army tank units were used with good effect against enemy batteries. Batteries at Ste. Marguerite, Pins des Galles, and Cap Brun which had been opposing the army's advance were knocked out by these units.

Toulon was surrounded with defense batteries with the heaviest concentration guarding the seaward approaches. Cap Sicie, to the west of and adjoining St. Mandrier Peninsula, had at least 13 guns capable of ranging 18,000 yards. Of all the guns located between Nice and Marseille 11% were located on the peninsula of St. Mandrier guarding Toulon Harbor and its approaches. St. Mandrier was the backbone of Toulon's defensive system with its 70 guns capable of firing on land and to seaward. Some 34 of these guns were able to fire at least 18,000 yards. Two batteries were twin mounted turrets of 340 mm taken from the old French battleship Provence and proved to be a serious obstacle to the gunfire support ships because our ships could not fire far enough to return the fire at the maximum range of these guns.

On D plus 4 a reconnaissance in force was planned by Commander Support Force to test the strength of the defenses around Toulon and particularly those on St. Mandrier. As Toulon Harbor and St. Mandrier were subjected to heavy aerial bombardment during the day, the naval shelling did not commence until 1600. For one hour USS Augusta, USS Nevada and FS Lorraine screened by USS Kearny, USS Ericsson USS Eberle and USS Gleaves conducted bombardment of St. Mandrier and Toulon Harbor using smoke cover and air spot. USS Nevada scored a direct hit on FS Strassbourg. Slight retaliatory fire was observed on this occasion.

Meanwhile Presqu' Ile de Giens and Ile de Porquerolles were kept under constant surveillance and bombardment and a rear guard action against the town of Hyeres was furnished gunfire support. Giens Peninsula offered good lee for ships bombarding St. Mandrier but it could not be taken advantage of until all of Giens and Ile de Porquerolles were neutralized. The situation on the morning of 21 August was that the French Army B was in the outskirts of Toulon and, to the northwest, was also approaching Marseille. The naval base and harbor of Toulon were in enemy hands as were Giens Peninsula, Ile de Porquerolles and the powerful St. Mandrier Peninsula. An effective fire support area in the Rade d'Hyeres had been swept on the previous day. USS Augusta, USS Philadelphia and HMS Black Prince demolished the Golf Hotel, an important enemy command and observation post near the town of Hyeres. All forces were readied for the reduction of Toulon and its immediate approaches by land and sea. Plans were being formulated for the reduction of the seaward defenses of Marseille.

On the afternoon of 21 August, USS Eberle noticed a small group of men on the southwest point of Ile de Porquerolles displaying a white flag. A boat was dispatched to the island and most of the Armenians who had fled from the German stronghold on the island surrendered. The German garrison was then shelled by USS Philadelphia, HMS Aurora and FS Lorraine. On the evening of 22 August, USS Hackberry supported by USS Omaha, landed Senegalese troops to garrison Porquerolles. Batteries on Cap de l'Esterel fired on USS Hackberry, but USS Omaha and USS Philadelphia silenced them. This left Giens Peninsula as the only enemy threat in this area. The guns of Giens had been firing at our ships at every opportunity, and despite the heavy return fire of our ships, a few batteries remained active. It was planned to use "heavy-fire-white-flag party" tactics on the morning of 23 August. However, before the bombardment began, planes reported white flags flying from various points on this peninsula. A party was sent ashore and found Giens Peninsula totally evacuated by the enemy. The entire area around the Rade d'Hyeres was now free of the enemy. A shelter in the lee of Giens was secured; all the available gunfire support ships and minesweepers employed on the left flank were free to concentrate on the approaches to Toulon and Marseille.

The westward advance of the army was so rapid that Toulon and Marseille were both under seige on 23 August (D plus 8). This called for a division of support forces with ships spread over a front of sixty miles on the left flank. In addition to the tasks of reducing the seaward defenses of Toulon and Marseille, CTF 86 was assigned the task of opening Port de Bouc (see Section 13.15, Part II). Minesweepers under Commander Support Force completed a swept channel in a north-south direction into the Golfe de Fos to Port de Bouc. This channel was out of range for fire support by light cruisers against batteries near Marseille so CTF 86 ordered an east-west channel swept in the Baie de Marseille. In addition to this, an area off Cap Croisette was to be swept for bombardment on the batteries on the Iles du Ratonneau and Pomegue. This last named channel was known as area Mars.

St. Mandrier had been previously subjected to aerial bombardments and with good results. Although aerial bombardment would have been useful at this time, the tactical situation was such that air support was needed to support the infantry advance in the north and destroy enemy truck convoys and troops which were fleeing northward. Strafing and air bombardment was vitally needed to render these mobile targets ineffective. A commando operation to destroy the 340 mm guns on St. Mandrier was considered in order to permit bombardment of the surrounding area at closer range, but it was not considered feasible due to the lack of air support which was being assigned the higher priority mission of tactical support of the infantry to the north. While naval gunfire support ships had been firing at St. Mandrier for six days, it was not until 25 August (D plus 10), that a determined effort with intense bombardment was made to force the surrender of the garrison there. In the absence of USS Augusta supporting the minesweepers south of Cap Croisette, Commanding Officer HMS Aurora acted as Deputy Support Force Commander for the bombardment of St. Mandrier. Together with HMS Ramillies, HMS Sirius, FS Lorraine, FS Montcalm, FS Fantasque, and USS Kendrick the heaviest naval bombardment of the campaign against St. Mandrier was carried out. On the following day the same ships with additional US destroyers again bombarded St. Mandrier from ranges as low as 10,000 yards. Army artillery fire was also employed with good effect. Very little return fire was experienced although several large shells, probably from the 340 mm guns, landed near FS Lorraine at a range of 30,000 yards. This bombardment was followed by a demand by the army for surrender. At this time cruisers were instructed to continue the bombardment that night. St. Mandrier was the last remaining center of resistance in the Toulon area. After some negotiations and without further activity the German Rear Admiral Heinrich Ruhfus, Commander of the Toulon area surrendered St. Mandrier and the remaining German forces on 28 August (D plus 13).

Since the active coastal and island defenses of the Marseille area were about one third of those encountered at Toulon corresponding time and effort were required by the gunfire support ships to reduce the Marseille area. The Iles du Ratonneau and Pomegues and Cap Croisette provided the key points of resistance to the minesweepers and gunfire support ships engaged in the task of opening Marseille. On 24 August, simultaneously with the arrival of the minesweepers, gunfire ships commenced the neutralization and reduction of the Marseille area. On D plus 11 and D plus 12, heavy aerial bombardments were effected on the Iles du Ratonneau and Pomegues. From D plus 9 through D plus 12, USS Augusta, USS Philadelphia and USS Quincy screened by US destroyers destroyed or effectively neutralized these same positions plus those on Cap Croisette. The army had quickly penetrated the defenses of Marseille and when the island strongholds were reduced the task was completed. Marseille surrendered on the same day as Toulon, D plus 13. The islands guarding the approaches to Marseille required more extended negotiations as they insisted that they would continue to resist if they could surrender only to the French. On 29 August, the Commanding Officer of USS Philadelphia with a detachment of marines from USS Philadelphia and USS Augusta landed on the Ile de Ratonneau and accepted the surrender of the forces on the island. This action was taken to avoid further delay in opening the way for the minesweepers to commence immediately their tasks of clearing the approaches and the harbor of Marseille.

Toulon was the most difficult objective of the gunfire support ships seeking to reduce the enemy defenses on the left flank. It was the hub of the German defensive system in this area. One of the more remarkable features of the defenses located here was the 340 mm guns on St. Mandrier Peninsula. They outranged all warships which were available to be brought against them. The positioning of the gunfire support ships was important. By taking positions in the lee of Giens and the Ile de Porquerolles ships were sheltered from German radar and visual observation. It was further contemplated and carried out that as soon as practicable long range ships were to take station to the south of Cap Sicie for the same reasons. In addition, the placing of ships to the east, southeast, and southwest of St. Mandrier permitted bringing that peninsula under a heavy crossfire so that guns in turrets and behind shields would be hit from the rear; at the same time naval gunfire ships were suitably dispersed.

Prisoners, fugitives from St. Mandrier batteries, taken from a small boat by USS Kendrick on 27 August stated that life on the fortress was possible by remaining in the tunnels but that naval gunfire had so reduced the gun positions and killed so many of the defenders that morale was very low. In addition it was reported that because the German headquarters had moved from La Vallette, east of Toulon, to St. Mandrier the food reserves were being rapidly exhausted.

Air spotting provided by carrier based fighter planes made the task easier and the gunfire more effective. In addition, spotting missions flown by army artillery observers in Cub and Sentinel airplanes together with Shore Fire Control Parties proved very helpful.

Teamwork between the minesweepers and the gunfire support ships was eminently satisfactory.

An interesting feature was the capture of some 1,200 prisoners by the support forces without the assistance of the ground forces.

While the naval gunfire support ships reduced many gun positions by their efforts alone, it is likewise true that of a substantial number of batteries destroyed, some were reduced by other means. This section deals with the role of naval gunfire support ships in the reduction of this area, but it is emphasized that the cumulative efforts and joint and carefully integrated action of the navy, airforce and army was necessary to achieve these results so effectively.

Section 3.15

THE SEIZURE AND DEVELOPMENT OF PORT DE BOUC

By D plus 8 (23 August), the army ground and air forces were moving swiftly up the Rhone Valley and the problem of keeping them properly supplied was a serious one. Demolitions effected and mines laid in the harbors of Marseille and Toulon, together with resistance of the German defenders, were delaying the opening of these ports. All the unloading was taking place over the beaches. Unloading was proceeding satisfactorily but it was realized that the expected forthcoming rough weather would render them untenable at times. It was highly desirable to obtain sheltered ports as quickly as possible for regular unloading in order to stabilize and shorten the lines of supply between the unloading points and our forces.

Coordinating with Commanding General, Seventh Army, on 23 August, NCWTF decided to open Golfe de Fos in order to provide entry into Port de Bouc and Etang de Berre. The low flat country north of Port de Bouc was ideal for establishing airfields to support our troops in event of heavy enemy resistance in the Rhone Valley. Port de Bouc was advantageously located to receive fuel and supplies necessary to operate these fields. Port de Bouc was situated adjacent to the mouth of the Rhone River about 20 miles west of Marseille. Reports indicated that the Germans had evacuated the town and that it was under French control. A small group of French Commandos and the FFI were patrolling the area. The port could be developed to accomodate about five or six liberty ships. A large tanker could be berthed at the petroleum basin. Considerable storage facilities for fuel were located at Port de Bouc. It was connected with Arles by a canal which could easily accomodate LCMs and which was blocked in several places by wrecked bridges and demolitions. A short channel, dredged to a depth of twenty five feet, connected Port de Bouc with the Etang de Berre. This canal was also obstructed by demolitions. It was planned that medium cargo ships would use the Etang de Berre as an anchorage if the opening of Marseille and Toulon were unduly delayed. Landing craft could be used to unload these ships and the nearby railroad and road nets leading up the Rhone Valley could be utilized after suitable repair.

Commander Support Force (CTF 86), was placed in charge of operations for opening the port. Minesweeping in the Golfe de Fos commenced at first light, on D plus 9, under the cover of fire support units and fighter planes. Shore batteries in the Cap Couronne area continually hampered the minesweeping, but the persistent efforts of the US cruisers and destroyers silenced them. On D plus 12 the minesweepers had completed their task of opening a channel to Port de Bouc and had swept a total of 173 mines.

PT 555 was mined at the eastward entrance to the Golfe de Fos on D plus 9, while returning from Port de Bouc with members of a French and American party that had been sent by CTF 86 to survey the situation. The PT evidently struck a snag line attached to a mine. The stern was blown off but the craft remained afloat. Five enlisted men were killed, and the remaining survivors were rescued.

From the number of mines laid in the Golfe de Fos it was evident that the Germans had prepared for an attack in this area. Intelligence reports derived from information freely given by the French population and a French Naval officer who had been parachuted into the area two weeks before D-Day indicated that the Germans garrisoned in the vicinity of Port de Bouc expected the invasion would strike the Rhone area, with the next best choice of invasion in the Marseille-Toulon area. Accordingly, thick minefields and heavy defenses were prepared in the area of the Golfe de Fos. The heavy aerial bombardment of the Southern Coast of France, prior to and on D-Day and the thrusts threatening their line of retreat, stunned the German forces left to defend this area, and a hurried evacuation was made. On D plus 1 the enemy hastily effected some demolitions damaging the quays and the shipyards in the port area.

On D plus 11 a US Naval reconnaissance party under the command of the senior staff planning officer 8th Fleet, acting under the orders of NCWTF, arrived at Port de Bouc to conduct a survey of the area.

The entrance to the port was partially blocked by 2 sunken French tugs leaving a channel 120 feet wide and 30 feet deep, sufficient clearance for a liberty ship. It was found that with the aid of salvage forces, berths could be made available for 5 liberty ships alongside the various quays and for one tanker at the Petroleum Basin. The enemy evacuated Port de Bouc so quickly that two barges loaded with contact and influence mines were found intact by the US Naval reconnaissance party. An abortive attempt had been made to detonate these mines; the US Naval mine disposal officer who accompanied the party rendered them harmless.

On D plus 12, the inner harbor was reported capable of berthing a cargo vessel of 22 feet draft and a tanker of 26 feet draft. US LST 134, with four pontoon causeway platoons of the 1040th CB, arrived for salvage and rehabilitation work. A company of 335th Engineers, US Army, also arrived to assist in opening the port. Twelve salvage vessels, US and British, arrived during D plus 12. An advanced comumnication unit was ready to operate that evening.

The principal salvage jobs necessary to clear the port for unloading ships were raising or moving a total of four medium sized ships sunk in some of the available berths, filling of craters exploded on the edge of one of the important quays, and removing or restoring five large cranes that were obstructing the Quai de Caronte, the largest quay in the port. Entrance to the Arles Canal had been blocked by one line of concrete pyramids, but the French had already partially cleared this entrance to a width of forty feet. The Arles Canal was reported to have a minimum depth of 1 1/2 meters (5 feet), a depth suitable for LCMs. Three bridges between Port de Bouc and Arles were twisted masses of steel blocking the canal but could be cleared. The RR bridge near Martigues had two spans destroyed, and these spans were blocking the entrance into the Etang de Berre.

Shallow minesweepers made a thorough sweep inside the Port, and, in three sweeps, no mines were found. On 5 September, while assisting USS Tackle to berth, a French tug grazed a nearby buoy; an explosion followed and the tug was sunk. USS Tackle was severely damaged. The exact cause of this explosion has not been determined. Although no booby traps were found in the port area, a mine may have been attached to this buoy. The port was closed for 48 hours and an additional sweep was made. No mines were discovered. Unloading cargo, discharging fuel and port clearance were therefore continued.

As a result of clearing the Golfe de Fos, 14 LCM from USS Arcturus and USS Procyon were able to proceed up the Rhone River to Arles on 1 September. For 24 hours a day until 7 September they ferried units of the French Army B, Seventh Army, and FFI across the Rhone both at Arles and at Vallabregues.

On 28 August (D plus 13), Marseille and Toulon surrendered and the priority need for Port de Bouc accordingly lessened as these two major ports were opened. Port de Bouc was then mainly used for petroleum discharge and storage. The bulk of the harbor clearance parties was released to hasten the opening of Marseille and Toulon. By 25 September (D plus 41), a total of three liberty berths and one tanker berth was cleared. This was sufficient for its role as an important auxiliary unloading port. The difficulties encountered in clearing the channel into the Etang de Berre combined with the early acquisition of Marseille and Toulon resulted in the decision not to use the Etang de Berre. By D plus 41 a total of 30,795 tons of cargo and 239,600 barrels of fuel had been discharged at Port de Bouc. The port served admirably as a staging point for small tankers that loaded and transferred fuel to the beaches and French ports.

The decision made to open Port de Bouc is considered sound and under the existing circumstances could have appreciably contributed to the success of the operations in the Rhone Valley. However, when Marseille and Toulon fell, surveys indicated that berths could be made available in these ports at a rate that exceeded previous estimates. Transportation facilities for moving supplies up the Rhone Valley were only sufficient to handle cargo discharging in Marseille, and the army was understandably reluctant to divert vehicles elsewhere. The momentum of our armies rapidly extended the lines of transportation and supply. Port de Bouc was relegated to a reduced but significant role. The unloading figures for Port de Bouc until D plus 41 indicate its substantial assistance. The cargo unloaded represented about 10% of that unloaded over all the beaches and about 25% of that unloaded through the ports. The fuel, discharged at Port de Bouc by D plus 41, was about 70% of the total fuel discharged in Southern France. This port continued to be an important unloading port for fuel.

Section 3.16

CONTROL OF POST ASSAULT CONVOYS

Primary control of post assault convoys was vested by NCWTF in Commander Anti-Submarine and Convoy Control Group (CTG 80.6), who was also directed to operate the main assault area screen and to assign jamming ships where needed, relief destroyers to the Support Force, and destroyers to diversionary or other special tasks. He was to base on Baie de Briande and Baie de Bon-Porte in the Alpha area (see diagram I). All traffic reaching or leaving the assault area was to funnel through his control. This involved directing arriving ships to the proper unloading place and assembling and sailing ships and escorts in return convoys. Close coordination with US Naval Liaison Officer, Beach Control Group (TG 80.2) and with the three assault force commands (CTF 84, 85 and 87) was necessary. A convoy schedule extending to D plus 70, and sailing routes, was established in NCWTF plan.

The three assault force commands had similar organizations. An Unloading Control Group received incoming ships, and a Return Convoy Control Group took care of sailing and escorting ships to TG 80.6. These were located offshore in LCI(L)(C). A Joint Loading Control Group dealt with the problems of the follow-up convoys in Naples and coordinated with the Army Embarkation Group and Base Section.

Task Group 80.2 acted as the shore link between the Army and the Navy. Its most important duty in connection with convoy control was to advise CTG 80.6 what ships were unloaded or moving out and where to direct ships of incoming convoys.

US Naval Detachment, Ajaccio, Calvi-Ile Rousse (TG 80.9) was assigned the task of loading and sailing convoys from Corsica.

Special instructions for merchant masters were contained in an annex to the operation plan and were distributed at briefing conferences prior to departure for the assault area.

By 0600 on D-Day, CTG 80.6 in USS Jouett, aided by two other destroyers and some PCs, was established off Baie de Briande. By 1000 he had established an assembly area 10 miles east of Cap Camarat for merchant vessels bound for Ajaccio or Naples and for all LST, and a second area 10 miles bearing 120 degrees from Cap Camarat for merchant vessels bound for Oran and for all landing craft. On D plus three, these areas were moved shoreward five miles, and the three control destroyers took fixed stations in order to be more easily located. Assembly areas were changed on D plus 13; ships bound for Oran were directed to assemble in Baie de Briande, while ships bound for Naples were to rendezvous in Baie de Bon-Porte. Use of Baie de Briande as a convoy control center was terminated on D plus 34, though the last beach was not closed until a week later.

To carry out numerous functions, CTG 80.6 was originally assigned 62 escort type ships. This total was supplemented on the arrival of convoys in the assault area during D-Day by escort ships not utilized by gunfire support groups. Destroyers, thereafter, were rotated between escort and gunfire support duty. The maximum number of ships under his control was 112 on D plus 8, of which 80 were allotted to escort duties. By D plus 12 the enemy threat had sufficiently decreased to permit reduction of convoy escorts to 50% of the scheduled number but not to fall below two per convoy. Requirements in the case of large troop carriers and valuable cargo ships remained unchanged. Subject to this exception, use of only two escorts for each convoy was approved on D plus 21. A week later LSTs were sailed with only one escort from Naples or Corsica to Southern France and on certain approved short routes. All British escorts were released by D plus 31. When the last beach was closed, 57 ships were available for escort duty.

On D plus six, CTG 80.6 found it expedient to establish Task Unit 80.6.8 at Ajaccio and Task Unit 80.6.9 at Naples to assist in convoy control and to handle the assignment and logistic needs of escorts at these ports. Stabilization of the convoy and escort situation permitted their dissolution on D plus 28 and D plus 32 respectively.

With the fall of Marseille and Toulon on D plus 13, planned coastwise routes from the beaches to these ports were placed in effect. The short route from Oran to Southern France was opened at the same time, since protection from the airfields of Corsica and Sardinia was considered no longer necessary. (See diagram III). The first liberty ship was berthed in Toulon on D plus 21. Task Unit 80.6.4, composed of 4 DD and 4 PC, was established at once to provide local escort and offshore protection in the Marseille-Toulon area. This task unit was dissolved on D plus 31, and a few days later unescorted sailing along the southern coast of France inside a DD-PC patrol was authorized (see figures 6 and 7). During the period from D plus 20 to D plus 30 Toulon roadstead was used for ships waiting to proceed to Marseille.

CTG 80.6 originally exercised direct control over convoys and their escorts and delegated control of the area screen to CTU 80.6.10. By D plus 31, it became feasible for CTG 80.6 to consolidate all his assault area tasks under a single command, CTU 80.6.7, and return to Oran for resumption of his administrative tasks. When the last beach closed on D plus 41, CTU 80.6.7 turned over to US Naval Liaison French Ports (CTG 80.8) his convoy control duties, retaining charge of escort and patrol assignments.

The planned convoy schedule was met and in some cases accelerated. Seven transports due to sail on D plus one and two on D plus two were able to depart on D-Day. LSTs assigned to the special priority air force lift from Calvi to Camel area did not leave on D-Day as scheduled, owing to the delay in opening Camel Red beach. They got away promptly the following morning, however, and ultimately completed their task ten days early. This was accomplished by freezing specified LSTs with assigned escorts in the shuttle and directing them to sail independently and to complete "turn-arounds" as fast as possible. LSTs of the Ajaccio shuttle, on which emphasis was also placed, finished their lift of ground forces two days ahead of the original schedule. In this instance also specific LSTs were frozen in the shuttle. APDs and LSIs running from Ajaccio to the assault area completed their task a day earlier than had been planned. All other convoys proceeded according to schedule, though fewer LCI lifts from Naples were required by the army than the plan specified. On D plus 21, the scheduled round trip time of LSTs was reduced three days on the Oran run, two on the Naples run, and one on the Ajaccio run. This was made possible by speedier handling of the ships at each end of their voyage and by opening of the short route from Oran to Southern France. Scheduled round trip time for Oran LSTs was reduced an additional two days on D plus 26.

The convoy control system was on the whole very successful. The chief source of difficulty was lack of adequate information. This produced mistakes such as loading or sailing ships for the wrong return ports and directing ships to the wrong beaches which occured in a very few cases. Another difficulty was the lack of coordination in requests for shipping by various army and air commands. This arose in connection with the LSTs, which were committed in specific groups to the task of building up specified forces in France, but were desired by the air force for lifts between Corsica and Sardinia and to Italy. Local naval commands were on a number of occasions faced with urgent demands for shipping made by high army or air commands. Sometimes these demands were acceded to, on the assumption that proper naval approval had been obtained. With communication facilities as crowded as they were, the mere task of establishing the propriety of a request required many valuable hours. The situation was eased when the Calvi shuttle LSTs completed their assignment and were made available for other air force lifts. The matter was clarified definitely on D plus 32, when SACMed ordered: "To avoid confusion and to insure that the desires of this headquarters are clearly presented to Commander Eighth Fleet, this headquarters is, effective this date, the only headquarters authorized to make requests on Commander Eighth Fleet for movement of landing craft and ships."

All convoys were planned to arrive in the assault area during daylight and to depart during darkness. On D-Day, NCWTF directed landing craft convoys to be sailed from Southern France between 1800 and 2000. The original plan for night sailings was not otherwise altered. Problems of night assembly were reduced by use of large luminous, numbered signboards on merchant vessels, as part of a system of identification by numbers in addition to names.

CTG 80.6 had a small staff without previous training in the specialized procedure in sailing convoys. Experience during the early part of this operation indicated the importance of thorough preparation and training for commands assuming convoy sailing functions.

The establishment of this command afloat rather than ashore proved very successful. It permitted active convoy control to be commenced early on D-Day. The ability to proceed quickly to any part of the invasion area and to move among the arriving and departing ships to anticipate difficulties and deliver instructions was also an advantage. Problems arising from being separated from unloading authorities ashore were largely met by the establishment of US Navy Liaison, Beach Control Group, (TG 80.2).

Section 3.17

BEACHES AND PORTS

BEACHES

See Section 6.11, Part II, for discussion of Beach Control Group and assignment of Beach Battalions.

Twenty-four pontoon causeways with crews were available. These were originally distributed on D-Day as follows:

Alpha Beaches	12
Delta Beaches	4
Camel Beaches	8

These were subsequently redistributed as more complete information on the beaches was obtained. Development of additional beaches suited for unloading LSTs without causeways eventually reduced the number required. In several instances causeways were moored to provide piers over which LCTs could be unloaded. Unloading was speeded up by mounting mobile land cranes on the causeway piers and handling supplies with cargo nets.

Although there proved to be an excess of pontoon causeways for use as originally intended at the beaches, this excess was rapidly absorbed by using them in captured ports for piers, ramps, and barges.

As port facilities were opened up at Port de Bouc, Toulon and Marseille, the assault beaches were progressively closed as follows:

Alpha beaches closed	D+25
Delta beaches closed	D+32
Camel beaches closed	D+41

The "Campaign Narrative" gives dates and details of beach operations throughout the assault and follow up period.

PORTS

In this operation the US Navy was committed to provide Port Parties for liaison and to supervise and coordinate command and other relations between the French Naval Commanders of captured ports and other allied commands; and to insure efficient operation of these ports. The operation of the ports was to be completely turned over to the French at the earliest practicable date, dependent on their ability to furnish competent personnel.

To accomplish the above CTG 80.8, US Naval Liaison, French Ports, set up headquarters upon landing between St. Tropez and St. Maxime. This was moved later to Marseille. It was contemplated originally that the Ports of Toulon and Marseille would be the only major ports involved. Before the fall of these ports, it was found expedient to open Port de Bouc, in order to provide adequate facilities for the support of our rapidly moving ground forces and to supply gasoline and stores for the air forces. Under CTG 80.8, there were eventually set up three Naval Detachments, each with a Commanding Officer, as follows:

CTU 80.8.1 - CO, NavDet Toulon
CTU 80.8.2 - CO, NavDet Marseille
CTU 80.8.3 - CO, NavDet Port de Bouc

Each naval detachment established quarters, supply, medical, and communication facilities, originally of a mobile nature and later more permanent in existing structures, rehabilitated as necessary. Each detachment had a Seabee Maintenance Unit detachment to perform utility and construction work.

A Port Director's office was established to supervise the routing and movement of ships and craft in each port. In each instance the French Navy set up paralleling opposite numbers, who eventually would take over all of the Port Director's functions.

Port salvage operations were accomplished by Navy Salvage Groups, and shoreside clearance was accomplished by Army Port Reconstruction Groups in Marseille and Port de Bouc assisted by Navy Seabees, and at Toulon by Seabees alone.

Specific features pertaining to salvage and shoreside clearance of Marseille, Toulon and Port de Bouc may be found in Sections 6.9 and 6.14, Part II of this report.

Functions of the US Naval Liaison Officer, French Ports, included the coordination of the turning over of ships and craft to the French, screening of requests by the French for materials, spare parts and the like from US Navy sources, and training of French personnel in the features of communications and port operations to meet the requirements of the army, for the support of which it was necessary to tax all facilities and equipment to the maximum.

As of D+41, the unloading facilities at the major ports were as follows:

Marseille

    16 Alongside liberty berths
    23 Holding berths
    45 LCT berths (bow on)

Toulon

    9 Alongside liberty berths
    31 LCT berths (bow on)

Port de Bouc

    3 Liberty berths
    1 Tanker berth

CONCLUSION

The organizational plans for port liaison were very effective, even though taxed by the introduction of an additional port.

The performance of liaison functions necessitates a supporting organization which tends to unduly expand if not carefully checked. The principal reason for the build up is the demands for services made by our own forces of the liaison organization, which can not be ignored, but which can be met only by expanding the organization from our own resources.

Section 3.18

ORGANIZATION

WESTERN TASK FORCE

The invasion of Southern France was executed by the Western Task Force under the overall command of the Supreme Allied Commander Mediterranean, General Sir Henry Maitland Wilson, GBE, KCB, DSO, ADC. Tactical command of the navy, army, and air forces of the American, French, British, and other allied nations, allocated for the operation, was jointly exercised by:

Naval Commander Western Task Force,

    Vice Admiral H. K. Hewitt, US Navy,

    Commander US Eighth Fleet;

Army Commander Western Task Force,

    Major General A. M. Patch, US Army,

    Commanding General Seventh Army;

Air Commander Western Task Force,

    Brigadier General G. P. Saville, US Army Air Corps,

    Commanding General XII Tactical Air Command.

Command of the army and navy forces of the Western Task Force after embarkation rested in the Naval Commander Western Task Force under the principle of unity of command, until Commanding General Seventh Army landed and assumed command of his forces on shore. This command was exercised as prescribed in "Joint Action of the Army and Navy (FTP 155, para 10)-Unity of Command." The Headquarters of Commanding General Seventh Army was established at St. Tropez and opened at 2359, 16 August. As the assault period of the invasion shifted into the build-up and maintenance period organization and command relationships changed to fit the situation. Figure 11 graphically indicates the principal command and coordination relationships of concern to NCWTF.

EIGHTH FLEET

The Eighth Fleet was organized on an administrative and a tactical basis. This organization was effective before and during the invasion. As ships and craft were withdrawn from the operation, they came under their Eighth Fleet administrative command. The administrative organization, promulgated in Operation Order 3-44, dated 8 July 1944, was as follows:

    (1) 80 Control Force

        80.1 Flagship

        80.2 Carrier Group

        80.4 Special Operations Group

        80.5 Boat Squadrons

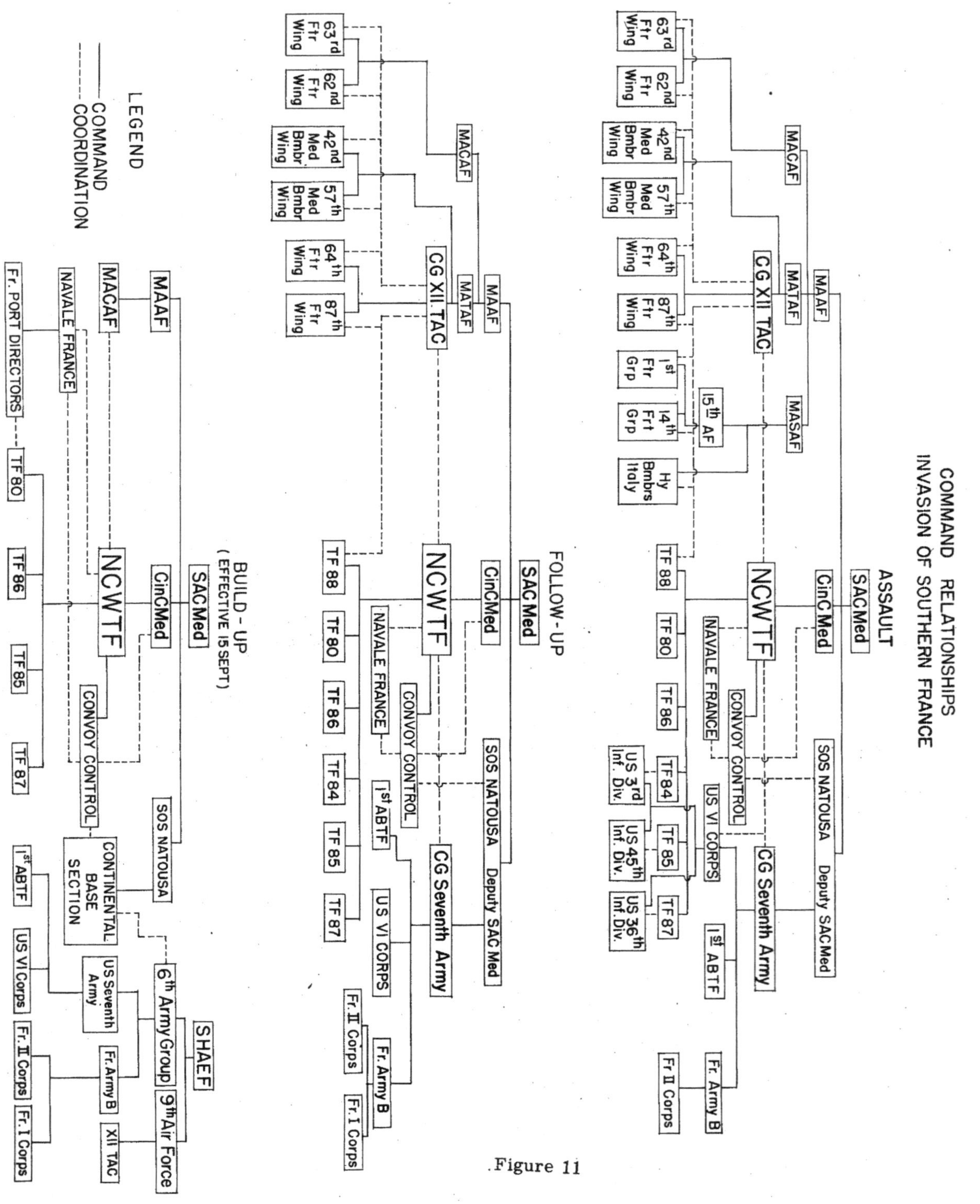

COMMAND RELATIONSHIPS
INVASION OF SOUTHERN FRANCE
ASSAULT
SACMed
CincMed
NCWTF
MAAF
MACAF
MATAF
MASAF
CG XII TAC
15th AF
63rd Ftr Wing
62nd Ftr Wing
42nd Med Bmbr Wing
57th Med Bmbr Wing
64th Ftr Wing
87th Ftr Wing
1st Ftr Grp
14th Frt Grp
Hy Bmbrs Italy
TF 88
TF 80
TF 86
TF 84
TF 85
TF 87
NAVALE FRANCE
CONVOY CONTROL
SOS NATOUSA
Deputy SACMed
US VI CORPS
US 3rd Inf. Div.
US 45th Inf. Div.
US 36th Inf. Div.
CG Seventh Army
1st ABTF
Fr. Army B
Fr II Corps
FOLLOW-UP
SAC Med
CincMed
NCWTF
MAAF
MACAF
MATAF
CG XII TAC
63rd Ftr Wing
62nd Ftr Wing
42nd Med Bmbr Wing
57th Med Bmbr Wing
64th Ftr Wing
87th Ftr Wing
TF 88
TF 80
TF 86
TF 84
TF 85
TF 87
NAVALE FRANCE
CONVOY CONTROL
SOS NATOUSA
Deputy SAC Med
1st ABTF
CG Seventh Army
US VI CORPS
Fr. Army B
Fr. II Corps
Fr. I Corps
BUILD - UP
(EFFECTIVE 15 SEPT)
SACMed
CincMed
NCWTF
MAAF
MACAF
NAVALE FRANCE
Fr. PORT DIRECTORS
TF 80
TF 86
TF 85
TF 87
CONVOY CONTROL
SOS NATOUSA
CONTINENTAL BASE SECTION
SHAEF
6th Army Group
9th Air Force
US Seventh Army
Fr. Army B
XII TAC
1st ABTF
US VI Corps
Fr. II Corps
Fr. I Corps
LEGEND
COMMAND
COORDINATION

Figure 11

                80.6 Destroyers

                80.7 Train

    (2) 81 Eighth Amphibious Force

    (3) 82 Moroccan Sea Frontier

    (4) 83 Naval Operating Base, Oran

    (5) 86 Support Force

    (6) 89 Miscellaneous

            89.1 Naval Advanced Bases

            89.2 Senior US Naval Liaison Officer, Italy

            89.3 Merchant Shipping Group

            89.4 Naval Detachment Naples

            89.5 Petroleum Division One

            89.6 Salvage Group

Since the administrative organization was devised to prepare for, maintain, support, and carry out offensive and defensive operations against enemy forces in the theater, only a minimum of change was required in preparing Operation Plan 4-44, dated 24 July 1944, which was the tactical plan for the invasion of Southern France (Annex A to this report).

Task Force 80, the Control Force, lost one task group and gained four new ones. Task Group 80.2, US Liaison, Beach Control Group, was created in order to take care of a special assignment peculiar to the invasion. The former Task Group 80.2, the Carrier Group, was set up as Task Force 88 in view of its increased importance. The Petroleum Group was brought under closer control by shifting its designation from Task Group 89.5 to Task Group 80.3. In order to take care of captured ports in France and important advanced ports in Corsica used for assault and follow-up convoys, Task Group 80.8, US Naval Liaison French Ports, and Task Group 80.9 US Naval Detachments, Ajaccio, Calvi-Ile Rousse, were established.

After the assault phase was over, two new task groups were formed under the Control Force. As soon as initial mine clearance in each of the four assault areas was completed, each task force relinquished control of its minesweepers, and they were placed under a single command, Task Group 80.10. This centralization of control was necessary in order to ensure proper division of forces for support of the eastward and westward movement of the army along the coast and at the same time for continued maintenance of assault areas. For the same reason it later became desirable to unify the salvage forces under Task Group 80.11, although in this case the assault force commanders were assigned a few salvage ships and craft to meet their local requirements.

Task Force 86, the Support Force, continued as such. CTF 86 commanded the Sitka Attack Force initially and, after the assault, all gunfire support ships.

For the invasion the ships and craft of the Eighth Amphibious Force, Task Force 81, were assigned to the three main assault forces, Task Forces 84, 85 and 87.

This constituted no great change, since Task Force 81 was organized to anticipate it. Eighth Amphibious Force Operation Plan D-44, dated 21 July 1944, contained three assault groups and divided transports and escort sweeper ships into groups of three, or into groups combinable into three. Training of all ships and craft was conducted in groups of three. Over-all control was retained by Commander Eighth Amphibious Force in order to provide proper allocation of forces for training, upkeep, and transportation needs. The unified control of all transports, escort sweeper ships, and landing ships and craft in one command achieved excellent results. A flexible command firmly directed was required in order to carry out a program of intensive training and material preparation for the invasion and at the same time to maintain Mediterranean commitments to other enterprises and to absorb large numbers of new ships and craft into the existing organization.

The training and material readiness program was carried out by establishing schools and bases at convenient locations. Preparation for the invasion was greatly assisted by distribution of naval planning memoranda and by development and practice of standard operating procedures. Training was rigorous and realistic, endeavor being made to approximate actual assault conditions in every possible way. Frequent inspections helped to maintain high standards on all ships and craft.

OPERATION PLANS

NCWTF operation plan for the invasion was made as complete as practicable, while preserving the initiative of the subordinate commands in working out details of assigned tasks. At the same time, adequate information and directives were included to facilitate the rapid preparation of attack plans. Sufficient detail was necessary in the NCWTF plans to ensure maximum coordination of all available effort and to reduce the amount of communication required to achieve it.

The plans were so complete that very few significant organizational changes were made during the operation. The large-scale reorganization of the attack forces for the new tasks arising at the close of the assault phase was accomplished according to plan, with little effort.

Distribution of NCWTF Operation Plan 4-44 was made to all commands and all ships and craft that were listed in the task organization, though ships to be retained in the rear area were provided only the annexes required for their individual needs. This wide distribution tended to endanger security and furnished many persons with information not pertinant to their assigned task, but is considered to have been justified. The risk of information leakage prior to departure for the operation was lessened by effecting complete distribution as late as practicable. In view of the enemy capabilities, likelihood of compromise by capture was reasonably slight. The difficulty of forseeing what information would be required and what could be dispensed with impelled wide distribution of the complete operation plan. A final briefing should be conducted to familiarize officers with the plan and to emphasize parts important in connection with their assigned tasks.

STAFF AND FLAGSHIP

During a large scale operation which may last a month or more, it is particularly important to have on board the flagship a balanced staff in sufficient numbers to carry out its functions efficiently and without physical exhaustion. Although over 200 more officers and men were crowded on board USS Catoctin for the invasion than normal berthing capacity provided for, at certain times more personnel could have been employed to advantage, if it had been practicable to accommodate them. In effecting the inevitable compromise that must be made between the physical limitations of the ship and the number of persons desired aboard, there should be eliminated from consideration all persons who cannot functionally justify their presence during the operation. In the present operation, the complex allied command made the problem an unusually difficult one.

On D-day, USS Catoctin had on board 1,214 persons, with normal berthing for 988. They were divided as follows:

Officers		Enlisted Men	
Ship's Company	49	Ship's Company	549
NCWTF Staff	80	NCWTF Staff	191
French Staff	3	Army	223
Seventh Army	10	British, French	21
VI Corps	30		984
XII Tactical Air Command	30		
2nd Air Combat Command	11		
Army Communications	5		
French Communications	1		
British Communications	3		
Army Liaison	1		
British Liaison	2		
War Correspondents	4		
SecNav	1		
	230		

As long as the Air Commander is aboard, or the ship is used for fighter direction, a complete air picture must be maintained, and no reduction of air personnel can be made. Under different conditions, fewer allied personnel might suffice.

In this operation the air commander was present in USS Catoctin, and the facilities of the ship were used for control of fighter bombers, for issuance of air raid warnings, and for secondary standby fighter direction. In accordance with the principle of unity of command it is believed sound to centralize tactical control as much as practicable.

Section 3.19

POSTPONEMENT DIRECTIVE

Because of the possibility of unexpected changes in weather along the southern coast of France a postponement plan was prepared. Because of the overwhelming force involved in the invasion of Southern France and the favorable naval and military situation it was agreed that the postponement would be executed only in event of adverse weather.

It was decided that the postponement, if ordered, should take place prior to 1200 August 14, D-1 for two reasons.

(1) At 1200, D-1 the slow assault convoys of LCTs, SS-1, SS-1A and SS-1B would have advanced one hour in the approach lanes. After that time it was felt that turning convoys of this nature about with the poor navigational equipment LCTs carry would be a greater risk than pushing them on in the face of the weather.

(2) Furthermore, the XII Tactical Air Command pre-D-day bombing plan was so designed to provide deception until H-16 hours. After that time bombing was to be concentrated on the assault area. To continue the deception, the postponement was requested by the XII Tactical Air Command to take place prior to the specific committment of the planes to the concentrated bombing effort.

The postponement was so designed that in general the convoys would counter-march and return to the 1200 D-1 positions on the day following. Small craft convoys were directed back into Corsican ports for protection. Convoys which would be in the swept channels of the Straits of Bonifacio at the time of postponement were in a position which prevented counter-marching. These convoys, therefore, were directed to complete their passage of the swept channel and then take such courses as to return to positions clear of the swept channel at corresponding times on the day following. The TM-1 convoy could not counter-march and retrace its course for 24 hours because on the second counter-march at midnight the convoy would have found itself in the narrow Tunisian War Channel. Therefore this convoy was directed to the west rather than to the east in its general counter-march. The tracks laid down for the convoys, especially the SM-1 convoys, the SF-1 convoys, and the AM-1 convoys, were designed to provide the greatest separation possible during hours of darkness and commensurate with the requirement to keep as close to shore-based air cover from Sardinia as was possible. (See Postponement Directive Chart; Diagram X).

The weather remained favorable, and therefore this plan was never executed. Consequently no conclusions may be drawn as to its effectiveness.

However, it is felt that one recommendation can be made in addition to the principles outlined above; that is, that when planning the postponement no convoy be expected to make a turn of greater than 45 degrees and special attention be given to keeping turns to the smallest practicable for craft convoys.

Section 3.20

STORM PLANS

THE PLANS

Each of the Attack Force commanders added a Storm Plan Annex to his Operational Plan. These three annexes were basically similar. Because of the fact that landing craft of all types are peculiarly vulnerable to storm damage by reason of their high freeboard and shallow draft, the great bulk of each plan dealt with specific types of landing craft and situations in which they may be found. The problems of landing craft beached, at anchor, or underway were treated separately. Special attention was devoted to DUKWs, which are very easy victims of rough seas, and to pontoon causeways, which are almost impossible to salvage after they have broached. The duties of the beachmaster, large ships, and the SOPA were set forth. Each plan called for issuance of a preliminary warning by radio or visual methods when the forecast indicated that certain conditions were likely to arise, and of a final warning when more severe conditions were predicted. Steps to be taken upon receipt of these two classes of storm warning were carefully elaborated. General instructions regarding storms were included, and the whole problem was made more vivid by citing instances of actual storms encountered at Anzio, Salerno, and Sicily and the ensuing damage.

EXECUTION OF THE PLAN

From 15 August to 25 September, unloading activities were curtailed and PT boat patrols cancelled, on a number of occasions, owing to strong winds and rough seas, but, only one storm of real intensity struck in the assault area.

For the night of 2/3 September the forecast predicted a 10 knot easterly wind with light showers after 0200 and the wind veering to northeast and increasing to 15 knots. By 2100, a strong northwest wind of 30 knots had developed. A violent mistral of 45 knots with gusts to 60 had arisen by 0200. The highest wind recorded was 58 knots with gusts to 66 knots. At noon the wind had reduced to 30 knots, and by nightfall was down to 15.

In spite of the suddenness and strength of this storm, the damage was insignificant. This resulted partly from the fact that the wind was offshore, so that its full effect was felt only by convoys at sea and by the ships in the Gulf of St. Tropez, and, partly from the alertness and good seamanship exhibited in carrying out the storm plans.

In the assault area, only one LCVP and one LCM were lost, and 25 ships and craft were damaged. At sea, two barges were lost and all convoys were delayed. All scheduled PT boat patrols, minesweeping, and air missions were cancelled.

CONCLUSIONS

The need for a storm plan in setting up the scheme for an amphibious invasion is clear. For the invasion of Southern France, where one of the largest landing craft forces ever assembled was to be sent into an area known for its severe autumnal mistrals, a storm plan was an absolute necessity. The provisions of the individual plans put forth by the Attack Force Commanders were based on long experience in this theater and are considered sound. The value of these plans was demonstrated during the storm of 2/3 September.

RECOMMENDATIONS

(1) Training of landing craft personnel should include thorough indoctrination in the art of handling landing craft in storms.

(2) A storm plan should be a standard part of any plan for amphibious operations.

Section 3.21

CHARTS AND ANCHORAGES

CHARTS

Apart from special charts presenting intelligence data, gridded charts and map charts for gunfire support ships, which were to receive a limited distribution in accordance with their purpose, every ship and command in the operation required navigational charts, which had to be of an appropriate scale. US Hydrographic Office (H.O.) Portfolio No. 29, which covers the southern coast of France, contained suitable large scale charts of the assault area with the exception of the Alpha, Delta and Sitka assault beach areas. Suitable British Admiralty (B.A.) charts were in existence, but, by the time the requirements were definitely known, late in July, it was too late to procure them in sufficient quantities for distribution to all US ships and craft requiring them. A new issue of large scale charts completely covering the assault area, had been announced in a Hydrographic Office serial of July, and, were promptly requested by Commander Eighth Fleet, but did not arrive until ten days after D-day. It was also discovered that many ships did not hold a complete H.O. Portfolio No. 29.

To meet the need for large scale charts it was found necessary to have numerous small map charts made by means of map reproduction facilities available on Commander Eighth Fleet's flagship and distributed among the ships and craft requiring them. These were supplemented by such B.A. charts and map charts, gridded or otherwise, which could be obtained from the limited supply in the theater. Although the gridded charts and map charts were planned for gunfire rather than navigation, they were found to be suitable for inshore work when used in conjunction with standard H.O. and B.A. charts and Notices to Mariners.

As suitable small and medium scale charts of the south coast of France were available, the only problem that arose was in connection with large scale charts. This was adequately solved prior to the departure of the invasion convoys and did not arise again until the capture of Port de Bouc, a move not contemplated in the original plan. At that time it was found necessary to reproduce 500 17" X 22" sections of large scale B.A. charts of the area using map reproduction facilities in the flagship.

The need for a complete set of up to date navigational charts of varying scales covering all areas subject to our amphibious invasions will always be a pressing one. This need was anticipated in the invasion of Southern France, though the problem proved to be more complicated than might have been expected and should have been considered at an earlier stage in planning.

The danger to security arising from procurement and distribution of charts of the assault area on such a large scale was partially met by obtaining charts of a much larger area than the assault area (thereby also providing for following the advance of the army in either direction), and by postponing and limiting distribution as much as possible. The map-charts, however, were prepared in two groups, the Sete-Agde area and the Marseille-Nice area. There was, unfortunately, a small gap at the mouth of the Rhone River, in the Port de Bouc area in which it was necessary to fire shore bombardment and for which there were no map-charts for gunfire.

Numerous illustrative chartlets and overlays were made for the invasion chiefly for insertion in operation plans. These proved most helpful, but their utility would have been increased if all of them had contained compass roses and notations as to their scale, and, in the case of overlays, the chart number of the original.

ANCHORAGES

Of the five major mounting ports, the problem of anchorages was critical only at Naples. From there the landing craft and combat loader convoys plus numerous other ships were to depart for the invasion. The staging ports of Ajaccio and Propriano presented difficulties because of the number of ships which were to stop there in comparison with the size of the harbors. The LCT and LCI convoys were to stage at Ajaccio, and the Sitka transport convoy at Propriano, while other ships were to be detached for or join from these ports. The smallness of the harbors at Ile Rousse, Calvi, and Ajaccio magnified the importance of the question of anchorages for follow-up and return convoys at these ports. In the assault area the Alpha, Delta, and Camel task force commanders and the main convoy control group had a considerable anchorage problem to secure maximum shelter and utility of position because the waters became deep very close inshore. As soon as the two major ports of Toulon and Marseille were opened and cleared of mines, an anchorage plan was needed to insure orderly handling of the large volume of traffic which was to arrive.

With the exception of the Camel area and the return convoy assembly area, anchorage charts were prepared for all the above-mentioned places. A chart was also prepared for the Rade d'Hyeres, though the plan to use this as an anchorage area was never put into effect.

The Naples anchorage problem presented the greatest complexity. Four main areas with 876 numbered berths were marked out: 222 berths at Salerno; 164 at Castellammare; 194 in the Bay of Naples; and 296 in the Baia-Pozzuoli-Nisida area. It was necessary for some of these places to be swept for mines in order to enlarge existing facilities. Signal stations had to be established at suitable points to insure rapid communication. Tugs, salvage craft and fire fighting craft had to be stationed so as to be equally available to the different areas. Provisions had to be made for additional anti-submarine screening, anti-limpeteer patrols and anti-aircraft defense. Coordination between the various commands ashore and afloat had to be arranged in order to avoid duplication of effort and confusion. Anchorage plans had to be laid out so as to provide maximum shelter and to simplify distribution of mail, personnel and supplies by small boats, loading, waiting for loading, and sortie; and, also, to accommodate the normal flow of shipping in each locality. At the same time, consideration had to be given to the minimum anchorage space and the proper depth of water suitable for each type of ship or craft. In the Baia-Pozzuoli-Nisida area, for example, 280 numbered berths for LCIs and LCTs with 250 yard circles in depths of from 1 to 40 fathoms and 16 numbered berths for LSTs with circles of 400 yards in depths of 5 to 35 fathoms were laid out. So many ships and craft were assembled in the Naples area that the controlling port authority had to rely largely on the anchorage plans for their location, though unfortunately these were not made and distributed prior to the time the invasion forces started building up there.

The anchorage plans proved invaluable in facilitating the rapid and orderly handling of large numbers of ships and craft, and for securing the maximum use of limited harbor areas, services, and defenses.

RECOMMENDATIONS

(a) It is recommended that the questions pertaining to charts and anchorages be dealt with as fully and as early as possible when planning for a large amphibious invasion, since many months are often required to secure charts that are not available, or, that have to be created, and the distribution of charts, also, consumes considerable time.

(b) Whenever practicable, chartlets and overlays specially prepared for use by invasion forces should contain compass roses, an indication of the scale used, and in the case of overlays, the chart number of the original. No overlay should be distributed unless its original has as wide distribution.

(c) It is essential to have available adequate chart reproduction facilities for an operation such as the invasion of Southern France.

Section 3.22

REPORTS

Instructions for making reports were contained in NCWTF Operation Plan 4-44 and in the supporting plans of subordinate task force commanders. In the case of the former, various annexes specified the special reports which were required. Reports as to matters of intelligence and operations, for example, were almost entirely covered in the Intelligence Plan.

Three types of reports were outlined in this annex:

(1) Reports of enemy contacts and of serious damage or loss to own or enemy major ships and craft were to be made immediately;

(2) A combined situation-intelligence report covering listed subjects and numbered serially was to be submitted daily as of 2400 by priority dispatch from commands directly under NCWTF;

(3) Important information of the enemy and special progress reports were to be forwarded as necessary.

These requirements did not suspend routine reports directed by current administrative instructions or Navy regulations.

The subordinate task force commanders dealt with the question of reports in a variety of ways. This was to be expected in view of the allied composition of the commands and the difference in the situation confronting each one. A greater degree of uniformity, however, would have been desirable, especially from the point of view of the higher echelon.

Certain problems with respect to the making of reports were common to all of the operation plans, and as to these some standardization is considered desirable. It is believed that the matter of reports can be appropriately dealt with in a report plan as a separate annex. Directives on the subject of reports should either be placed in this annex or incorporated in it by reference. Similarly, when a directive appears in this annex, cross-reference to it should be made in any other annex to which it pertains.

In connection with reports required at stated periods, it should be standard to prescribe the time the report is made or covers. All reports which the next higher echelon will use as a basis for submitting further reports should be scheduled to arrive at a suitable time. In the selection of a suitable time, the calendar day or week is of little importance compared with the convenience of the commanders who must approve or digest the reports and the desirability of transmitting reports in a period when the means of communications will be least burdened.

Conciseness in reports and the desirability of using other means of communication than radio should be stressed. The radio traffic burden may be further eased by limiting addressees to only those who need to know. Report directives should take into consideration radio circuits required for transmission to prescribed addressees, precedence required for the information contained, security classification necessary and the avoidance of duplication by requiring the same information from a number of sources when no confirmation is needed or requiring same unit to repeat information in separate reports in slightly different forms.

CONCLUSIONS

(1) Training and indoctrination should emphasize standardization in making reports;

(2) A report plan as an annex of the operation plan, containing clear and detailed instructions concerning all special and routine reports required in connection with the operation, is considered desirable for large amphibious operations.

Chapter 4

AIR

Section 4.1

JOINT AIR PLAN

In order to accomplish the mission of the early capture of Toulon and Marseille and the rapid exploitation of the Rhone Valley, the Mediterranean Allied Air Force (MAAF) was assigned the task of air support for the invasion of Southern France. MAAF issued a plan of air operations in which their headquarters exercised general control and coordination of the air operations and delegated the following responsibilities for the operation:

(1) Commanding General, Mediterranean Allied Tactical Air Force (MATAF) was responsible for:

    (a) The detailed planning of the air operation in conjunction with the army and naval forces employed in the operation;

    (b) The designation of suitable forces to maintain air cover over the assault area forces and for close air support of the operations;

    (c) The coordination of all bombing in the assault area;

    (d) The assignment of all medium bomber operations;

    (e) The conduct of intruder operations;

    (f) The protection of all convoys within 40 miles of the assault beaches until the Air Officer Commanding, Mediterranean Allied Coastal Air Force, (AOC, MACAF) took over the responsibility for the air defense of Southern France;

    (g) The conduct of Air Sea Rescue operations in the assault area by special agreement with AOC, MACAF who made suitable equipment and personnel available for these operations;

    (h) Organization and direction of Troop Carrier Operations, the routing of which was coordinated with AOC, MACAF and the naval commander.

(2) Commanding General, Mediterranean Allied Coastal Air Force (MACAF) was responsible for:

    (a) The defense of all convoys in the Western Mediterranean to a point 40 miles from the assault beaches, where the responsibility passed to MATAF;

    (b) In collaboration with the naval authorities and the CG MATAF, the conduct of special over-sea reconnaissance, anti-submarine and anti-shipping attacks in connection with this operation;

    (c) The conduct of all Air Sea Rescue operations outside of the area of the MATAF responsibility in coordination with the naval authorities.

(3) Commanding General, Mediterranean Allied Strategic Air Force (MASAF) was given the responsibility for the operation of strategic bombers. The requirements were determined by CG MATAF in collaboration with CG MASAF. CG MATAF was responsible for insuring that satisfactory arrangements were made for coordinating such attacks with other air action and the action of the naval and land forces engaged as follows:

(a) The Air Commander designated for the operation was the Commanding General, XII Tactical Air Command (XII TAC) under the direction of CG MATAF;

(b) The operations of carrier borne fighters were closely coordinated with those of the land based fighters by the CG XII TAC and the naval commander;

(c) Two long range fighter groups of the 15th Air Force were assigned to temporary operational control of the CG XII TAC.

In the working out of the detailed plans, such adjustments as necessary were made. These required close cooperation with the Navy when the embarkation ports, the courses of convoys, and the beaches on which the assaults were to be made were finally determined. Some of the adjustments were:

(1) Intruder operations made by MACAF Night Fighter aircraft when they were available;

(2) Spotting for naval gun fire by aircraft of XII TAC and carrier based aircraft and Army Artillery Cub planes;

(3) Aircraft lanes for special air operations were designated to keep aircraft away from combat and convoy shipping (see diagram XII).

The integration of the Air Plan with the Army plan and Naval plan is discussed in detail in the following Sections 4.2, 4.3 and 4.4. For a line sketch of Command Relationships see Section 3.20, Part II, Organization.

Section 4.2

PRE-D-DAY BOMBING

Pre-D-day bombing in support of the amphibious invasion of Southern France was carried out by (1) Mediterranean Allied Strategic Air Forces (MASAF), and (2) Mediterranean Allied Tactical Air Forces (MATAF), under the Mediterranean Allied Air Forces (MAAF).

STRATEGIC AIR FORCE BOMBING

The MASAF pre-D-day bombing of Southern France had as its objective the isolation of the assault area. In order to execute this, the strategic air force attempted to destroy all bridges over the Rhone River from its mouth to Avignon, over the Durance River from its juncture with the Rhone to Sisteron, over the Var River from its mouth to Annot, and the junction of all roads between the Durance and Var Rivers north of the invasion area at the foothills of the Alps. The plan further contemplated destruction of bridges, tunnels, and viaducts on all major roads, and the destruction of railway bridges, viaducts, tunnels, and marshalling yards in the proposed beachhead (see diagram XVII).

This plan was integrated with the strategic bombing of Western Europe from bases in England. Because it was integrated with the strategic bombing of Western Europe in such a way as to disguise the isolation of the assault area, it formed a part of the strategic air "cover plan." The "softening-up" process began on 29 April with the bombing of harbor installations in Toulon. From 19 May to 15 August, B-24s and B-17s dropped heavy bombs on specific targets in the invasion area in preparation for the landing operation.

This pre-D-day bombing program by the strategic air forces was carried on simultaneously with the strategic bombing of Western Europe, and it was believed that it was not immediately apparent to the enemy that the isolation of the assault area was being executed. Heavy bombers of the strategic air forces were bombing troop concentrations, marshalling yards, oil dumps, lines of transportation and supply in all of Southern and Central France. The immediate plan, however, the interdiction of the assault area, was gradually built up so that it reached its final crescendo on D-day. Until 0350, D-day, 5,408 sorties had been flown which dropped 6,704 tons of all types of bombs. Every bridge across the Rhone, Durance, and Var Rivers into the assault area was destroyed with the exception of one single track railroad bridge at Avignon. The heavy damage inflicted upon roads and railroads within the assault area contributed materially to the inability of the enemy to concentrate successfully his forces in this area subsequent to the landings.

TACTICAL AIR FORCE BOMBING

Planning for this phase of the pre-D-day bombing was by XII Tactical Air Command (XII TAC) planners in conjunction with navy planners, and the operation was under the command of Brigadier General Gordon P. Saville, USAAC, Commanding General of XII TAC. The XII TAC was assigned to provide tactical air support to the Western Task Force.

Pre-D-day bombing by the tactical air force was designed to (1) neutralize the main coastal defense batteries in the assault area which threatened the naval craft during the planned assault, (2) reduce effectiveness of coast defense troops by deterioration in morale resulting from these continued bombing attacks, (3) neutralize the main coastal radar stations in the assault area prior to the approach of the convoys, and (4) accomplish the foregoing without jeopardy to tactical or strategic surprise.

All aircraft that could be made available from the Mediterranean theater were assigned by MAAF to execute this pre-D-day bombing plan. Simultaneously, the MASAF strategic cover plan bombing of Southern France, and other bombing operations in support of the allied armies on the Italian front and in Yugoslavia were being executed by MAAF.

The pre-D-day bombing proposed by the XII TAC was at first objected to by the Commanding General of the Seventh Army and the Commanding General of the VI Corps on the ground that the bombing in the assault area might indicate the target area to the defending forces and thereby destroy the possibility of strategic and tactical surprise. The naval viewpoint was that with so many convoys approaching prior to the time of assault, and with even mediocre radar and coast watching, the attainment of tactical surprise was doubtful.

The ground forces were therefore urged to accept pre-D-day bombing of the assault target area. It was felt that the destruction of enemy defenses and radar installations would fully compensate for any effect upon the element of surprise. The army commands then concurred in plans for pre-D-day bombing with the provision that bombing should simultaneously and in roughly equal proportions be delivered at other plausible invasion areas on the south coast of France.

The invasion areas selected to effect this deception were (1) the Sete-Agde area, (2) the Toulon-Marseille area, (3) the assault area, from Cap Benat to the Vieilles d'Agay, and (4) the Genoa area (see diagram XIV).

The selection of targets was based on two factors. First, the bombing was to be directed against the heavy long range coastal defense batteries which could prevent the approach of gunfire support ships. These were termed "critical targets," and there were eight in the proposed assault area. See diagrams XVIII, XIX, XX. These eight batteries according to our intelligence were long range guns so located on the contours of the coast line that it would be extremely difficult for gunfire ships to approach if opposition by these guns was maintained by determined gun crews. Secondly, the bombing was desired to destroy or render ineffective the system of coast watcher radar stations. The selection of the coastal defense batteries as targets was by the naval planners while the selection of the radar installations to be bombed was made by the RCM (Radio Counter Measures) committee which functioned directly under the Commander-in-Chief, Mediterranean. (For a technical discussion of the RCM activities, see Part II, Section 7.14, RCM.)

Because there was the possibility of any one of the eight critical targets being destroyed by bombing or being obscured by weather, eight alternate targets of slightly less importance to the success of the approach were selected for bombing. Of course, there were many other targets which it would have been desirable to have bombed prior to D-day. However, the number of aircraft available and the necessity of maintaining deception in four separate areas required that the number of targets selected be kept to a minimum.

The planning of the pre-D-day bombing in the assault area will be considered in detail, for the other three areas were considered in an identical fashion to insure as complete deception as possible.

It was planned to have the pre-D-day bombing extend from D-10 until D-1. During the period D-10 to D-5, it was planned to drop fire bombs on the areas around the gun positions. Intelligence reports indicated that, at this time of year, forest fires could be expected to be particularly destructive. Beginning on D-5, demolition bombs were to be used.

For the assault area, the coastal defense batteries were selected as targets primarily because of their long range and commanding location. The objective was to destroy or damage these guns which might prevent the approach of the gunfire ships. This objective became especially important in the crowded Camel and Delta areas, in which the gunfire support ships had little maneuvering room (see diagram I).

For the Sete area, the Toulon-Marseille area, and the Genoa area, the process of selecting the potentially most dangerous targets was repeated. Beaches were selected to land a three division assault. Sea room to handle the same number of gunfire support ships, craft, and combat loaders, as was being employed in the actual assault, was determined. The restrictions to movement of the gunfire support ships due to mineable waters was also considered. Then the guns which could oppose the initial approach of the gunfire support ships were considered in order of potential fire power. (See Section 4.2, Part I, Gunfire Support, for the method of analysis of the potential strength of the gun positions.)

The detail of this consideration has been discussed because it was found that the pattern of bombing for an invasion of this sort was distinctive. Initially, for the three non-assault areas, the XII TAC planners selected the targets, and they were determined on the basis of air requirements. For example, guns on prominent land positions were selected for accurate bombing. Directions of the approach to give a clear bombing run were considered. Positions of AA defenses were naturally taken into account. It was found that the pattern of this type of bombing did not conform to the bombing in support of an amphibious assault. It was immediately agreed that for purposes of deception, the pattern in support of an assumed invasion would have to be accepted.

To aid the deception, the number of targets for bombing chosen in each non-assault area was the same as in the assault area, eight primary targets and eight secondary targets. Because of the distance to the Sete area, however, only eight primary targets were selected in that area, and for the same reason, the number of bombing missions was less.

The bombing of the radar installations was included in the pre-D-day bombing plan to destroy the radar capable of covering the approaches to the assault area and also to add deception by destruction in the three non-assault areas.

Scheduled in this pre-D-day bombing plan were 7 radar installations in the Sete area to be attacked on D-5 and D-3; 7 in the Marseille-Toulon area to be attacked on D-5, D-4, and D-1; 10 in the assault area to be bombed on D-5, D-3, D-1 (AM), and D-1 (PM); and 12 in the Genoa area to be bombed on D-4 and D-1.

The deception was to be carried out by bombing gun positions with equal weights in each of four areas from D-5 day until H-16 hours. For assigned targets in the assault area and in the Toulon-Marseille area see diagrams XVIII through XXII. It was considered that if the deception was maintained until H-16 hours, the defending forces would have no time to readjust forces to meet the assault. Therefore, after H-16 hours, which meant the afternoon of D-1 day, the assault area was to be bombed with all aircraft that could be made available for that purpose. During the bombing operations, counter-air force operations were to be carried out on D-6 and D-2 by MATAF.

The scale of effort was designed to effect some degree of neutralization of the batteries in the assault area. All forces were agreed that complete destruction of batteries was not to be expected. Any changes in the scale of effort in any locality or on any one day was to be compensated and to be reintegrated with the several requirements.

Photographic reconnaissance units were expected to select alternate targets when the main targets were seen to have been destroyed. This was done by MATAF units in Corsica.

Execution of the plan was controlled for the most part by MATAF. This was deemed necessary because the Commanding General of the XII TAC and his staff were embarked in USS Catoctin for the last two days of this plan and due to radio silence were not in a position to control it.

The fire bombs planned for D-10 to D-5 did not arrive in the theater until about D+8 and therefore were not used.

On D-5, the weather prevented heavy and medium bombers from executing the plan in the western part of Southern France. Fighter bombers, however, were able to get through in the Genoa area and in some portions of the assault area.

Of the eight designated primary targets in Genoa area, five were attacked, one of them twice, by approximately 30 P-47s with 15 tons of bombs with good results on D-5, and on D-4 a single attack was pressed home by six P-47s. On D-3, every one of the alternate targets was hit by 187 P-47s with 93 tons with excellent results. A general bombing of the Genoa-Savona area by heavy bombers also took place on this day with 122 B-17s and 80 B-24s dropping 543 tons of bombs.

The heavy bombers again made attacks on D-2 with B-17s and B-24s hitting six of the primary targets with 357 tons and two of the alternate targets with 161 tons.

On the morning of D-1, 205 B-24s returned to the attack with heavy concentration. Six of the primary gun installations were hit with 334 tons of bombs and two of the alternate targets with 122 tons. The scale of this effort was nearly commensurate with preparation for a full scale amphibious operation.

It may be noted that the greatest weight of bombs was dropped on the Genoa area on D minus 3. On that day, the German radio announced an Allied invasion in this area.

In the Sete area, sizeable raids were directed against the eight gun positions designated as primary targets on two separate days. The first raid on D-3 consisted of two missions. The first mission of 100 B-24s dropped 247 tons with fair to good results and the second of 134 B-24s dropped 333 tons with very good results. On D-2, seven of the same eight targets were again hit with varying bomb weights of 30 to 37 tons per target with excellent results. While this bombing was considered effective, it is questionable whether this scale of effort would have sufficiently indicated an amphibious invasion from the bombing effort alone. It will be noted that these efforts were scheduled for D-5 and D-3, but weather prevented the execution of the attacks until D-3 and D-2.

No attacks were made against Toulon-Marseille area on D-5 and D-4 because of bad weather.

On D-3, however, 120 B-24s dropped 252 tons of bombs on eight gun positions as substitute for failure of the missions of the two previous days. Medium bombers continued the attack on D-2 as seven of the eight primary targets and four alternate targets were attacked by 160 B-25s and 94 B-26s. On this day, 23 P-47s and 33 Spitfires also strafed gun positions which protected radar installations in the area.

On D-1, five of the primary targets and three of the alternates were objectives of a raid of 111 B-17s which dropped 306 tons.

The concentration of the bombing in this area extending from D-3 to D-1 is believed to have contributed to the desired deception, for prisoners reported the Toulon-La Ciotat area was alerted at 2100, D-1.

Coverage of the targets assigned in the assault area was practically complete with every primary target being attacked from four to eight separate times and seven of the eight alternate targets being hit at least once. Due to bad weather, no attacks were made on D-5. On D-4, the main assault began with the attacks that had been scheduled for D-5. All primary targets were hit with 593 tons of bombs dropped by 121 B-26s and 132 B-25s. Two of the alternate targets received 102 tons from 51 B-26s. Coverage of targets was good as was the concentration.

The alternate targets only were attacked on D-3 as four of the eight were hit with 333 tons from 138 B-25s and 24 B-26s.

On D-2 heavy bombers were used against two of the remaining alternate targets as 53 B-24s dropped 136 tons.

The primary targets of coastal defense gun installations were subjected to heavy bombing on D-1. Heavy bombers and medium bombers combined to give a thorough saturation. In one attack in the late afternoon, 90 B-24s dropped 223 tons and a half hour later, 105 B-24s dropped 261 tons. Twenty-seven B-17s added 87 tons more.

Medium bombers hit the same targets with 144 B-25s and 46 B-26s dropping 351 tons. Two of the alternate targets were hit by 91 B-26s with 94 tons.

This thorough concentration against gun installations was considered to have carried out the assigned plans satisfactorily. The greatest weight of bombs was dropped during the afternoon of D-1, after which adequate analysis of the raids would not give the defending troops time enough to meet our assault in the proper place.

The primary objective of neutralization of the critical batteries in the assault area was considered achieved to a most satisfactory degree. The secondary objective of not indicating our true assault area was also considered satisfactorily accomplished, for on D-3, the enemy guessed Genoa, and on D-1, he guessed the Toulon-Marseille area.

Of the 20 general radar locations of one or more installations scheduled for bombing, all but one were attacked with, however, only fair results. The situation on D-day was:

	Sete Area	Toulon-Marseille Area	Assault Area	Genoa Area
Stations attacked (D-5 to D-day)	5	5	6	4
Non-operational	0	1	2	0
Probably non-operational	0	1	0	0
Partially non-operational	1	1	2	1

Cap Sicie in the Toulon-Marseille area was purposely not attacked in order that aircraft and surface craft of the western diversion would be observed by radar in this area.

In analyzing the execution of this plan, it is apparent that the agency, set up to readjust the schedules for bombing gun positions when weather prevented the proposed scale of bombing on D-4 and D-5, did a creditable job. However, this organization was not thoroughly familiar with the disposition of the gunfire support ships during the approach. They were compelled to readjust the plan on the precepts stated in the plan. Consequently, the careful assignment in the plan of the alternate targets was excellent insurance.

CONCLUSION

Pre-D-day bombing in preparation for an amphibious invasion can be highly effective if the bombing plan is carefully integrated by navy-airforce planners. Selection of targets should be on the basis of attaining neutralization at the proper time of those enemy batteries critical to the success of the naval approach and amphibious assault. Deception as to the sector of assault can be made effective by bombing targets selected to picture impending amphibious assaults on other plausible areas if the selection takes full account of naval considerations and is carefully integrated with the overall cover plan.

Section 4.3

PRE-H-HOUR D-DAY BOMBING

The Pre-H-Hour D-Day bombing plan was executed under the command of the XII Tactical Air Command.

This plan was characterized by a high degree of coordination of all air commands and all gunfire support groups involved in the invasion of Southern France. The concentration of the destructive efforts of more than 1300 aircraft in an assault front about forty miles long in one hour and twenty minutes reflects the highest credit on the air forces supporting this operation. To accomplish this violent blow, timing to finer intervals than ever before had been attempted in this theater was used.

The purpose of the operation was to provide tactical air support for the invasion until H-Hour. It was designed to cause maximum damage to enemy coastal and beach defenses in the assault area with all forces available.

The following was the priority in the selection of targets:

(1) Counter-battery attacks coordinated with naval gunfire on enemy artillery that could be brought to bear on ships in the assault area;

(2) Enemy guns and other military installations which bore directly on the ability of our ground forces to advance inland from the beaches;

(3) Enemy light artillery and other military installations that were capable of delaying the planned D-Day advance in general;

(4) Destruction of any enemy airdromes in or within close fighter operating range of the assault area.

It will be noted that highest priority was assigned to attacks on coastal defense batteries which could oppose the approach of naval ships. The priority and the resulting preponderance of scale of effort directed against coastal defense batteries was primarily in tactical support of the navy. This was designed to give assurance that the naval gunfire support ships and minesweepers could get into position, in order that they, in turn, could support the approach of the landing craft and combat loaders. This priority was further subdivided into two phases. The first phase involved bombing attacks on long range coastal defense batteries which could hold the gunfire support ships outside their effective range. The second phase, during which it was expected the gunfire ships would assist in the neutralization of the shore batteries, included attacks on short range coastal defense guns which could oppose the landing of small craft at the assault beaches. Because of the short period between first light and the end of the bombing period, these phases overlapped.

The problem of timing involved a number of considerations which had to be carefully weighed and balanced. In the first place, it was agreed that the bombing should occur after first light on D-day. Furthermore, the bombing should cease prior to H-hour in order to provide a period for naval gunfire without dust to obscure observation. It was finally decided that all bombing should cease by 0730, on D-day, which would allow one-half hour for unhindered, accurate naval gunfire. It was the desire of XII TAC to accomplish as much destruction by bombing as was possible in the short period available. It was therefore planned that every aircraft available to the support of this invasion should make at least one attack during this period. This meant that naval gunfire was allotted a shorter period for support than normally would have been thought suitable. However, two considerations prompted the acceptance of this short pre-H-hour period for naval gunfire:

(1) The supply of ammunition in the Mediterranean theater for major caliber guns was limited;

(2) In order to support the advance of the armies to the west for the capture of Toulon and Marseille in an area well protected by many long range coastal defense guns, the expenditure of the supply of long range ammunition would have to be carefully controlled.

Aircraft for this pre-H-hour bombing flew from bases in Sardinia, Corsica, and Italy and from the nine escort carriers. This involved the problem of take-offs during darkness and rendezvous at first light.

In order to accomplish the neutralization of the coastal defense batteries during the approach of the ships in the assault area, selection of targets and timing of attacks was carried out in the same manner that would have been used if naval gunfire alone had been employed. Targets to be bombed were selected by Camel, Delta, Alpha, and Sitka gunfire support forces. Coordination was by XII TAC planners and naval planners of the US Eighth Fleet.

Attacks on the gun batteries were designed to achieve and maintain neutralization. The order in which this neutralization was effected was determined by the range and location of the gun batteries, based on intelligence reports. Guns which could reach the greatest distance to seaward were attacked first, and the attacks were designed to be continued until naval gunfire ships could move into position to continue neutralization with naval gunfire. That meant that some targets, so located that their guns could only reach naval ships when close inshore, were not attacked until later in the period of pre-H-hour bombing, and so timed as to effect neutralization just prior to the approach of the gunfire support ships which would continue the neutralization. For example, he long range guns reported to be on Cap Camarat were subjected to early neutr ization bombing attacks, whereas the guns located at the base of the Gulf of St. Tropez were assigned bombing attacks at a later time.

Considerations peculiar to the type of aircraft assigned for the bombing modified the timing. Whereas the fighter bombers could be assigned specific times at which to bomb their targets, the heavy and medium bombers could not be assigned so rigid a schedule. The decision as to whether fighter bombers, medium bombers, or heavy bombers were to attack any given gun position was made by the Air Commander on the basis of intelligence reports and aerial photographs of the target. Fighter bombers flying from carriers and bases nearby in Corsica were able to be over the targets considerably before the medium and heavy bombers which flew from a greater distance. Therefore, fighter bomber sorties were flown before the medium and heavy bombers could reach their targets.

The actual timing for the attacks was assumed to be practicable only after 0610 due to the conditions of light. Therefore, the entire scheduled pre-H-hour bombing had to take place between 0610 and 0730. For planning purposes, the smallest practicable interval was five minutes. Therefore, attacks were scheduled during each five minutes from 0610 to 0730. In order to maintain neutralization, it was desirable that these attacks be spread throughout the entire period of an hour and twenty minutes. In addition, it was considered that naval gunfire ships might be required to open counter battery fire prior to the scheduled time of 0730. In any event the gunfire ships were to be in position to fire at 0700. In order to give opportunity for some observation of naval gunfire, the interval between bombing attacks on each target had to allow sufficient time for dissipation of dust. It was determined, therefore, that no target would be attacked at shorter intervals than fifteen minutes.

On July 29th, NCWTF informed assault commanders, gunfire support group commanders, and other commanders concerned with the principal features of the pre-H-hour bombing plan and the timing of the attacks. On the basis of this schedule, the gunfire support groups were directed to establish their schedule of firing. This careful integration of bombing and bombardment was deemed necessary in view of the great number of coastal defense batteries and the short period of time available prior to H-hour to neutralize them.

It was planned to bomb each assault beach between 0700 and 0730 with anti-beach-obstacle bombs of weights ranging from 100 pounds to 260 pounds. Alternate targets were also assigned consisting of eight gun positions which could hinder the movement of troops inland from the beaches, and 16 strong points requested by the artillery sections of the Seventh Army and VI Corps. Furthermore, four flights were to bomb the batteries on Cap Negre as alternate assignments if the French Commandos failed to capture them.

In addition to execution of the bombing plan, the XII TAC provided fighter cover over the assault area, tactical air reconnaissance, and troop carrier aircraft cover.

This entire plan was to involve approximately twelve heavy bomber groups of the 15th Air Force, seven medium bomber groups assigned by MATAF, 408 fighter-bomber aircraft assigned by the XII TAC, 150 fighters of the XII TAC, 8 night fighters, 48 fighter-bombers and 16 fighters from TF 88. The total numbers of planes scheduled to bomb gun batteries were 464 fighter-bombers and 156 medium bombers. The numbers assigned to bomb the beaches were 304 medium bombers and 390 to 438 heavy bombers.

The execution of this plan exceeded expectations. The close interval schedule for planes flying from many distant locations was proved practicable.

In Phase I of the attack from 0550 to 0610, eight missions of four fighter-bombers each covered the assault area. They were assigned the mission of bombing gun flashes should they be observed. From Cap Roux in the northern part of Camel area, in a generally southwesterly direction through Rade d'Agay, St. Aygulf, St. Tropez, Pampelonne, Beach 259 (Alpha Red) to Cap Benat and Cap Esterel, five of these missions found guns firing and attacked. The other three missions bombed their alternate targets, which were enemy strongpoints in the same area designated by the army. After the attacks had been completed, 16 aircraft reported to the Fighter Direction Ship for defensive patrols over the assault area.

Phase II, the scheduled bombing of the coastal defense guns, was not completely carried out as low clouds covered many of the targets in the early morning. Of 29 gun position targets, 18 were reported definitely to have been hit at least once by waves of P-47s and P-38s. Three more were reported as probable hits on target, leaving eight untouched.

Of the eight targets not reported bombed prior to H-hour, only one was reported active after H-hour. The batteries over which the scattered low clouds were continuous enough to prevent all bombings were targets low on the scale of priority and had been assigned relatively few bombing missions.

Particularly successful attacks were carried to completion against installations near Cap Roux where 28 B-25s dropped 37 tons of bombs with excellent results, and gun positions near St. Tropez when P-38s dropped 25 tons with good concentration. Four 150 mm coastal defense guns near the Salins d'Hyeres were hit by 14 B-26s with excellent results. Three 220 mm coastal defense guns at Pte. Alexandre were attacked by 19 P-47s with 19 tons of demolition bombs.

Fair results were obtained on Cap Benat by 15 B-26s which dropped 20 tons, but another mission of 15 B-26s dropped only seven tons on Cap Esterel due to the covering haze.

The low clouds which prevented bombing of some of the targets requested by the navy shifted the weight of some of the bombing effort to the alternate targets, strong points, requested by the army. This shift in bombing effort to give tactical support to the army proved very advantageous in this instance.

Fortunately, the forces manning the coastal defense guns in the assault area were low category troops and furthermore did not expect the attack in this area until the morning of D-day. (See the report of enemy forces for D-day, August 15th, in the "Campaign Narrative," Part II, Chapter 1.)

As a result of bombing alternate targets, which were requested by the army because the coastal defense guns were either abandoned or weakly fought, this shift in tactical support more thoroughly paved the way for the quick movement of attacking troops inland from the beaches. Had the coast defense guns been vigorously employed, the joint control group in the flagship could have maintained the weight of the bombings on the gun batteries, as communications were excellent.

Rendezvous was a difficult problem. Most of the rendezvous points were over Corsica and in the period just prior to first light, there was some confusion. It was the first time that 15th Air Force heavy bombers had made mass take-offs in darkness. In general, the rendezvous were successful, but in a few isolated instances, aircraft were separated from their assigned flights, joined others, and returned to unassigned bases. A vertical search light beam, or "candle," was used as a beacon for the rendezvous of some units over Corsica, this proving quite effective. The pathfinder technique was used by some heavy bomber missions against the beaches.

Heavy bombers, principally, but also a few medium bombers were used for the attacks on the beaches and beach obstacles which constituted Phase III (see Diagrams XVIII, XIX, XX). This was executed with considerable success. For the attack on Beach 259 (Alpha Red), 180 B-26s were scheduled and 138 were dispatched. 135 B-26s dropped 186 tons of bombs. Coverage of the target was excellent with good concentration. Against Beach 261 (Alpha Yellow), 150 heavy bombers were scheduled, and 86 B-17s finally dispatched. They covered the entire beach area inland with 165 tons in heavy concentration. Attacks were made from 0700 to 0724 from altitudes of 12,500 to 16,000 feet.

Although 60 heavy bombers were scheduled for Beach 263A (Delta Red and Green), only 14 B-24s got through to drop 28 tons between 0705 and 0729. No results were observed due to the smoke and cloud cover which prevented maximum effort against the beach. The same situation occurred in general on Beaches 263B (Delta Yellow) and 263C (Delta Blue) but better results were obtained on the former. Over Beach 263B, 37 B-24s dropped 57 tons between 0705 and 0728 while only seven B-24s got through to drop on Beach 263C. In Camel area, only six B-24s hit Beach 264B, but over 100 B-25s covered Beach 265A in good concentration with 75 tons.

Communications between the incoming flights and the air section of the Joint Operations Room aboard the flagship were excellent and complete. The control of the flights was handled jointly by air, army, and navy officers conversant with air operations. Most of the flights, having been assigned a selected alternate, were prepared to bomb this alternate in case the primary target was obscured. However, the weather frequently obscured the alternates, as well, and the reassignment of targets of fighter-bombers was done by the joint control group in the flagship. The selection of second alternates, since the approach was progressing with meager opposition, was made from general alternates in the plan, which shifted about one fifth of the tactical support to the army.

CONCLUSION

It was brought out in this operation by the results of the execution of the scheduled bombing, how highly desirable it is to insure positive control of the tactical support resulting from the air effort, preferably by carefully pre-selecting alternate targets. In the selection of targets and alternates, the first objective should be support of the approach of gunfire ships. If communications then fail for some reason, execution of the air plan will neutralize the defensive strength of the enemy opposing the timely approach of the gunfire ships. By assignment of alternate targets, tactical support to the navy or the army can be controlled to the degree permitted by available communications. The experience with overcast and poor visibility suggests the desirability of alternate plans with the objective of achieving neutralization of long range coastal guns with heavy bombing by pathfinder technique while the gunfire support ships close the coast to bombard using radar control.

Section 4.4

POST-H-HOUR BOMBING

The post H-Hour bombing was intended:

(1) To destroy enemy coastal and beach defenses within the assault area;

(2) To isolate the battlefield area by destroying rail and road bridges across the Rhone, Isere and Durance Rivers, and blocking defiles and rail lines running through the Alps from the Isere southward;

(3) To attack troop movements within the area bounded by the Rhone and Isere Rivers and the western watershed of the Alps;

(4) To neutralize enemy airdromes operational in or within close fighter range of the assault area.

In an effort to achieve this purpose, attacks beginning on D-Day were planned against enemy military installations and gun positions, including coastal defense guns still in operation, road bridges, railroad bridges, and railroad tracks. By destroying the road and rail bridges it was hoped to hinder or prevent enemy replacements reaching their goal, and, by achieving rail cuts, it was hoped to disrupt enemy rail transportation to a considerable extent.

In addition to these measures, armed reconnaissance missions were planned against enemy troop and transport concentrations, and counter air force attacks directed against airdromes and aircraft capable of reaching the assault area. Close fighter bomber support of ground and naval forces was provided in operations westward from the assault area to Toulon and Marseille.

Since scheduling for post-H-Hour missions was so dependent on the tactical situation, planning was more general than for the pre-D-Day and pre-H-Hour bombing plans. After H-Hour the air support was expected to be shifted to the movement of troops inland with one exception, the support of the post-H-Hour assault on Camel Red beach. The planning for this assault was executed by representatives of the XII TAC and Camel Attack Force. For the movement of troops the primary coordination was between the XII TAC and the US VI Corps Artillery section and the US Seventh Army Artillery section. Coordination of the bombing and naval gunfire was by NCWTF.

Up to H-plus 6 1/2 hours, the maximum fighter bomber effort was directed against targets in the following priority:

(1) Counter battery attacks, coordinated with naval gunfire, on any enemy artillery that could be brought to bear on shipping of any type in the assault area;

(2) Enemy guns and other military installations which bore directly on the ability of our ground forces to advance inland from the beaches;

(3) Enemy light artillery and other military installations capable of delaying the planned D-Day advance in general.

After H plus 6 1/2, fighter bombers were used on armed reconnaissance missions against hostile troop and vehicle concentrations. Heavy and medium bombers were used in additional attacks against bridges spanning the Rhone and Durance Rivers.

The first heavy bomber effort, after H-Hour, was directed against Beach 264A, Camel Red beach near Frejus, from 1207 to 1217 D-Day. The plan called for 90 heavy bombers to attack this beach and the road from the beach to Frejus. Actually, 96 B-24s were dispatched and 93 hit this target with 187 tons of bombs from an altitude of 14,000 to 15,000 feet. This bombing attack was advance preparation for the assault on the beach which was scheduled for 1400 but cancelled by CTF 87 upon failure of drone boats to breach underwater obstacles. After the beach was captured from landward inspection indicated that the instantaneous fused bombs used had caused little damage to the defense installations. Photograph bomb plots also indicated that a large number of bombs exploded on the water offshore. Though the bombing undoubtedly neutralized defending personnel for its duration, the "softening" effect appears to have been much less than in the cases of bombing of beaches assaulted at 0800.

The heavy bomber effort directed toward the second objective, namely, the destruction of road bridges in the Rhone Valley, consisted of 27 B-17s and 115 B-24s which dropped 363 tons on three bridges just west of the Rhone River at Pont St. Espirit, Le Teil and Bourg St. Andeol, and one bridge east of the river just south of Valence. Traffic on the main north-south road in the Rhone Valley was greatly disrupted by this attack. As an escort to these missions against the River Rhone bridges on the afternoon of D-Day, 106 P-51s and 29 P-38s provided cover for the above B-17s and B-24s.

The plan provided a third objective, a group of bridges along the lower Rhone. 32 B-26s attacked the road bridge at Arles, and 36 B-26s struck the bridge at Aramon. Each of the bridges at Roquenaure and Tarascon were hit by 36 B-25s completing the day's effort by medium bombers to deny the use of the main roads of the Rhone Valley to enemy forces.

In addition to heavy bomber and medium bomber targets, the plan called for approximately 550 fighter bomber sorties against 98 selected targets including guns, strong points, road bridges, and rail cuts. About 750 fighter bomber sorties were carried out on D-Day and most of the targets were successfully attacked. Some which were missed on D-Day were hit on D plus 1.

Over 375 tons of demolition bombs were dropped as well as incendiaries. Rocket projectile aircraft were used for rail cuts, and against transport concentrations. About 150 tons were dropped on guns, and a similar amount on bridges which were the targets given the greatest attention.

One group of 56 P-38s attacked road bridges and gun positions in the battle area.

Guns on Cap Salins were attacked, and 23 tons of bombs were dropped on gun positions north of Frejus with good results. Marshalling yards at Cavaillon were strafed. During this attack, 24 of these P-38s encountered 17 ME-109s and were forced to jettison their bombs in order to press home their attack against the fighters. Three of the enemy were shot down without loss to our planes.

Smaller attacks were made against fighter control stations, headquarters, and radar stations which had been overlooked or insufficiently damaged in the pre-D-Day bombing.

The development of the beachhead and its rapid extension, necessitated modification of the original plan in so far as fighter attacks against assigned targets were concerned. It became necessary to substitute targets which were more favorable, and fighter bombers and armed reconnaissance missions ranged far beyond the enemy lines.

With this rapid advance of ground forces away from the beaches, the Bomb Safety Line soon passed beyond the area in which many of the planned targets lay. For this reason after D plus 1, the bulk of the fighter bomber effort was directed against targets of opportunity in the enemy rear, such as motor transport, railroads, barges, bridges, and troop concentrations.

At times it was necessary to brief fighter bombers while they were enroute from Corsica to the assault area in order to prevent possible attacks on positions which had already been taken by our forces or, to assign new targets which had been reported by tactical reconnaissance aircraft. (See Section 4.6, Part II, Air Support.)

On one occasion, a flight leader returning from a bombing mission, saw a target of over 20 boxcars and engines on a railroad near Pertuis. Being unable to take the target himself, the information was relayed through USS Catoctin to an armed reconnaissance mission known to be in the area and it successfully attacked the target. Again, a carrier based Tac/R mission sighted a large group of armored vehicles east of St. Maximin. This information was transmitted by the same method to a carrier-based Hellcat mission which entered the area a short time later. The target was successfully attacked by the Hellcats which destroyed over 65 armored vehicles and troop carriers (see Section 4.8, Part II, Carrier Aircraft Operations).

The reduction of the coastal batteries particularly at Toulon and Marseille was a major problem after D-Day, and a continued bombing effort was made against the heavy gun installations at St. Mandrier peninsula near Toulon. These attacks, beginning on D plus 1, were continued through D plus 5. During that period, 328 medium bomber sorties were flown against this target, dropping more than 600 tons of bombs, of which 150 tons were special armor piercing. The area was well covered and reports indicate that a generally good concentration on the target was obtained, with some direct hits.

Road and rail bridges crossing the Rhone, Isere and Durance rivers, were attacked by 255 heavy bombers dropping over 650 tons of bombs, on D-Day. From D-Day to D plus 5, these bridges were attacked by 664 additional medium bomber sorties, dropping over 1200 tons of bombs. Of this total 395 sorties were flown on D and D plus 1, dropping more than 750 tons of bombs.

Enemy airfields were attacked on D-Day by 68 medium bombers sorties dropping 62 tons of incendiary and fragmentation bombs. After D-Day, these fields were attacked by a total of 71 medium bomber sorties, dropping more than 90 tons of bombs.

CONCLUSION

The naval commander of an amphibious invasion is vitally concerned in the development of post-H-hour bombing plans with respect to:

(1) Coordination with available naval gunfire;

(2) Destruction or neutralization of enemy installations effecting execution of landings or maintenance operations;

(3) Routes followed by bombers and recognition procedures.

Section 4.5

FIGHTER DIRECTION SHIPS

Fighter direction was assigned as a task by the Air Commander Western Task Force to the Commanding General, 64th Fighter Wing who became Air Defense Commander. He carried out his preparations in conjunction with the Eighth Fleet Planning and Air Sections. Three ships for fighter direction were employed, each one of which could be assigned the mission of complete control of fighter aircraft in the assault area.

Fighter Direction Tender 13, in which the Air Defense Commander was embarked, was designated Fighter Direction Ship for the entire operation. It was a British manned, converted LST, equipped especially and solely for fighter direction duty and had performed this duty in the Normandy invasion. GCI radar provided information on movements of aircraft and Type 11 radar was used as a standby. The GCI presentation was remoted to two skiatrons in the operations room. Performance of radar was as satisfactory as the ship's geographical position permitted, but the IFF interrogator left much to be desired. The VHF Direction Finder was seldom of use in locating aircraft, at times having an error of as much as 40 degrees. Nine VHF receivers and transmitters (BC 639 and 640) provided communications with aircraft and other ships and were augmented by various HF and FM sets. In general the use of a horizontal filter table instead of a vertical board was satisfactory.

During the invasion, 64th Fighter Wing provided the majority of personnel which was supplemented by personnel of the Royal Air Force normally aboard. Officers and men from 64th Fighter Wing were not placed aboard FDT 13 in time to enable them to become thoroughly acquainted with the equipment and sufficiently briefed in their various jobs. The original position of the FDT 13 in the assault area was set forth in the Operations Plan, Annex A, and is indicated in diagram I. The Air Defense Commander was given full authority to alter this position within the anti-submarine screen of destroyers. The ever present problem during amphibious operations of land echoes on the face of the radar oscilloscope, was only partially solved by this comparatively limited freedom of movement.

HMS Ulster Queen, also British manned and equipped, was designated as first standby Fighter Direction Ship, with a combined British-American staff for air control. Its radar facilities were excellent and included a British 279 and 281 for air search, a GCI for air search and height finding, and a 277 microwave surface search and air height finding set. Identifications and tracks found by these sets were passed on to other ships in the control net, to aid in identification of aircraft in the area. The control room was well suited for the task assigned and was prepared to assume all fighter control duties. A vertical plot board was utilized with control officers and liaison personnel arranged before it with three remote radar scopes (PPI), a skiatron and intercept boards available. The GCI controller was in the ajacent compartment. Sufficient VHF, HF and FM radio channels were available for assuming all control duties. The position assigned to HMS Stuart Prince in diagram I was occupied initially by HMS Ulster Queen which replaced HMS Stuart Prince as standby Fighter Direction Ship.

The flagship of NCWTF, USS Catoctin, was assigned control of offensive fighter bombers and duty as second standby for direction of fighter defense, in case both FDT 13 and HMS Ulster Queen became inoperative. To carry out this dual role, a special Army Air Force unit, 2nd Air Combat Control Squadron (Amphibious), was provided. A few officers of the 64th Fighter Wing of the XII Tactical Air Command who were thoroughly familiar with operations in the area were placed aboard in key positions. The Air Commander and his staff were embarked in USS Catoctin. Radar equipment included one air search SK radar for detecting aircraft and two SG radars for surface or low-flying aircraft search. No height finding radar capable of control of night fighters was available. Eight VHF transmitters and receivers supplemented by HF and newly installed FM equipment provided excellent communications between aircraft, other ships and USS Catoctin.

All aircraft control was maintained in the Joint Operations Room (see figure 12) which had displays for both surface activity and air activity. This room was redesigned after arrival of the ship in the Mediterranean area to meet combined requirements of US Eighth Fleet and Army Air Forces. Navy operations utilized one-half of the compartment for displaying surface and ground activity, while Air Forces and their liaison personnel used the other half. An additional plot was maintained in Combat Information Center for the ship's information and for air raid warning while underway before and after the assault phase. As NCWTF was in USS Catoctin, no definite position in the assault area was assigned her, and she ranged along the coast from Sitka to Camel Areas, finally anchoring in the Gulf of St. Tropez. Her radar was also affected by the land mass but not to the extent of rendering it unserviceable.

Two specially equipped vessels, LST 32 and LST 394, were provided with GCI radars, and furnished information on aircraft movements during daylight hours and controlled night fighters during darkness. Their positions in the assault area are shown in diagram I. These LST-GCIs each used a separate VHF reporting channel, but enemy air activity did not prove sufficiently great to require such ample provision. Had hostile activity produced the expected amount of traffic, separate channels in all probability would have been necessary.

Fighter Direction Tender 13 controlled defensive fighter patrols (see Section 4.7) beginning at 0550 on D-Day and, with a few minor exceptions, maintained control until 1200 on D plus 7.

Radar information was received by FDT 13 and other fighter direction ships from sources afloat until such time as shore stations were placed in operation. The first shore installation was completely set up by D plus 2 and others followed rapidly. Seaborne sources from which information was derived were standby Fighter Direction ships, including the flagship, the two LSTs in which were mounted GCI radar, and battleships and cruisers of a Naval Radar Reporting Net. As planned, this net made available sixteen ships, only four being used at any one time. These four ships reported on a single radio channel using frequency modulated equipment UFS 50. Only hostile and unidentified tracks were passed, and since such traffic was light, the efficiency of the net was never seriously tested; but insofar as it was required, it functioned satisfactorily as an auxiliary source of radar information. The requirement that the four guard ships be designated, one from each support area, was particularly fortunate. These four ships, together with the three fighter direction ships, formed a very complete radio net which could give excellent emergency service during temporary failure of other nets. The new FM (UFS 50) communication channel was loud and clear most of the time, but of limited range. Where radar reception by a single ship is subject to interference from land echoes, a net of this type is very valuable. It is essential to hold a conference of the CIC officers of as many radar guard ships as practicable prior to an operation so that they may be briefed on a standard operating procedure.

CONCLUSIONS

Fighter direction ships or fighter control ships are indispensable in any amphibious assault in which a large number of aircraft play a prominent part. The basic requirements or specifications of a fighter direction ship for this use are:

(1) Adequate radars, including a height-finding type.

There are many types of radar with definitely proven characteristics and a combination of the best types now available should prove adequate. One suggested combination which is available immediately for ships of the US Navy is one SK for air search, one radar of a type similar to the AI-Mark 8 for search of the area directly overhead, one SM (or SP) for height finding and two SG for surface and low flying aircraft search. Land echoes will always be present when a ship is close inshore in an amphibious assault. Land echoes can be expected with available ship borne radar operating off hilly or mountainous coastlines. Until such time as an airborne search radar is developed to insure complete coverage of air invasion coastline regardless of elevations, radar blind spots must be covered by specially stationed fighter patrols, (see Fighter Cover, Section 4.7, Part II).

(2) Radio channels (VHF, HF, and FM) necessary to air control.

Such channels not absolutely essential should be eliminated. The radio equipment at present in USS Catoctin, which is normal AGC installation plus modifications of Joint Operations Room (see figure 12) made for this operation for use of 2nd Air Combat Control Squadron (Amphibious), has proved extremely well suited for control of offensive missions.

(3) Freedom of movement.

This must be permitted to insure geographical positions best suited to operational efficiency of equipment. If the overall naval situation is such that proper escort can be provided, it is recommended that such escort be given the fighter direction ship, thus affording freedom of movement outside the normal anti-submarine screen with protection against enemy air, surface and undersea attack.

(4) Protection.

Against minor surface or air attacks protection may be achieved by:

(a) Adequate armament including radar controlled guns;

(b) Assignment of escorts for this sole purpose as suggested in paragraph (3).

(5) Operations room.

A large well ventilated air-conditioned operations room with adequate lighting and emergency lighting and ventilating facilities to accomodate a large number of personnel is desirable (see figure 12).

(6) Personnel.

Thoroughly trained personnel entirely familiar with all installations and the plan of operations are necessary. Equipment is too often blamed for failure when the deficiency lies in the lack of trained personnel, thoroughly familiar with the equipment. Too much stress cannot be placed on the necessity for efficient radar scope readers, the heart of any fighter direction and air warning system.

RECOMMENDATION

It is recommended that when an amphibious flagship (AGC) with communications similar to the USS Catoctin is available, this ship be utilized for the control of offensive air action and that fighter defense be controlled by the **fighter direction ship.**

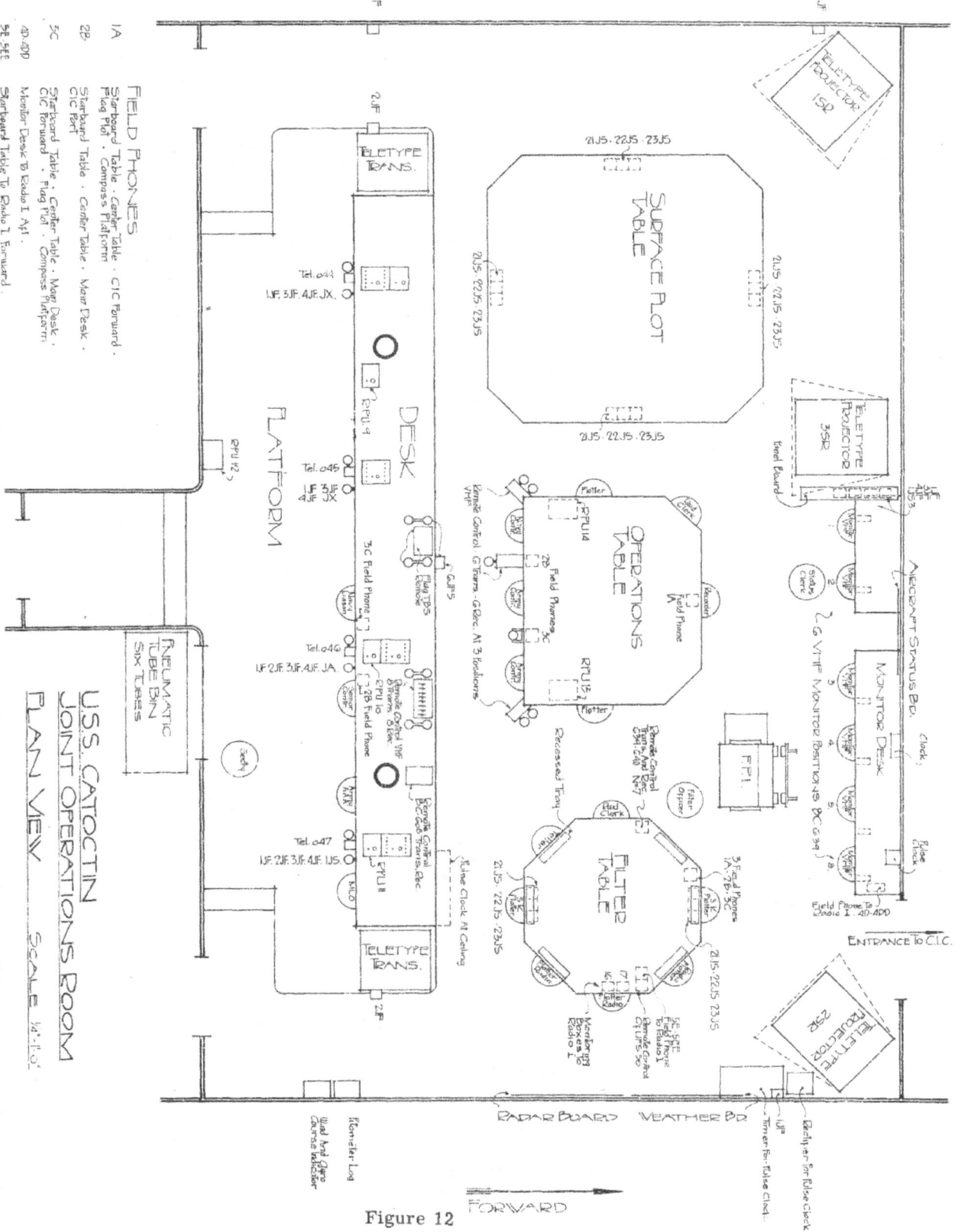

Figure 12

Section 4.6

AIR SUPPORT

Air support was furnished the operation by heavy, medium, and light bombers, and fighter bombers, and its complete integration with naval gunfire and ground force attack contributed greatly to the success of the landing and the rapid advance inland.

The three phases of pre-D-Day, pre-H-Hour, and post-H-Hour bombing demonstrated the splendid performance of all types of bombers in the initial stages of the assault. Fighter bombers were particularly useful in the subsequent development of the advance.

The use of fighter bomber and armed reconnaissance missions was determined by XII Tactical Air Command after consultation with Seventh Army and VI Corps in USS Catoctin. The controlling of these missions was by controllers in the Joint Operations Room and the centralization of all functions in USS Catoctin made immediate action possible.

The general plan of operation was that fighter bomber missions were determined by Headquarters, XII Tactical Air Command in USS Catoctin, scheduled by 87th Fighter Wing in Corsica, and flown by P-47s and P-38s based in Corsica and by carrier based Hellcats, Wildcats, and Seafires of Task Force 88. Each aircraft, before taking off, was briefed thoroughly and assigned a primary and an alternate target. As these aircraft entered the assault area, they reported by VHF radio to Joint Operations Room, USS Catoctin, and were given final instructions as to which target to strike. At times, an entirely new target was assigned because of an advance in the Bomb Safety Line which placed the primary target within a restricted area, or because of the discovery of a more important target of opportunity. Targets of opportunity such as enemy troop or vehicle concentrations were discovered by tactical reconnaissance planes (Tac/R) or by returning fighter bomber missions, when in and forward of the combat area. These targets were reported by radio to USS Catoctin where the Commanding General, XII Tactical Air Command decided whether the regular missions should be replaced with a new assignment of greater importance. In this way it was possible to take advantage of the extremely rapid movement of our ground forces, with a rapidly shifting Bomb Safety Line. Because of the rapidly changing situation, the 87th Fighter Wing, Corsican Base Operations of the XII TAC, advised that on D plus 3 all fighter bomber missions would be changed to armed reconnaissance missions, and when practicable, briefed over radio by J.O.R., USS Catoctin. Forward elements of army ground forces also notified J.O.R. of enemy strongpoints and made requests for air support. Many enemy dislocations were caused or accentuated by these extemporaneous missions. In several missions where identification of the target proved difficult, the fighter bomber was instructed to establish radio communication with the Tac/R plane making the report. Then, the Tac/R plane actually led the fighter bomber to the desired target.

During the first few days of the operation, aircraft assigned to regular defense patrols were used also for air support. These flights came into the area half an hour before their patrol time loaded with bombs, and were directed by the controllers either to their briefed targets or to a new assignment. However, due to the rapid advance of our ground forces, targets were beyond range of combined fighter bomber and fighter patrol missions.

During the four and one half days that USS Catoctin controlled this type of offensive action, several hundred fighter bomber missions of all types operated in the assault area. Targets destroyed consisted of motor transport, railroad installations and rolling stock, road and rail bridges, coastwise ships and craft, canal barges and particularly enemy concentrations of vehicles and troops. The procedure for these operations, considering the negligible air opposition to be expected and the rapidly changing ground situation, was highly successful in the efficient application of maximum available offensive effort.

Section 4.7

FIGHTER COVER

Fighter cover for the initial assault area was provided from first light to last light principally by aircraft of the XII Tactical Air Command from bases in Corsica. As airfields became available in Southern France either by capture or construction, fighter squadrons were based there. Fighter cover was augmented from D-Day to D plus 4 by aircraft of Aircraft Carrier Force (TF 88) which maintained station generally to the south and west of the assault area at distances of 20 to 60 miles. (See figure 14).

Four patrols were established providing low, medium and high cover, with total number of aircraft on patrol at one time varying from 28 to 32. In general, Spitfires were used as high cover, P-38s as medium cover, and P-47s and F6Fs as low cover. The exact positioning of patrols and assigned altitudes are illustrated in diagram XII. Until D+2, the majority of low cover patrols and many of the medium cover patrols were used on fighter bomber missions before being ordered on patrol as defensive fighters. Control of fighter cover was maintained by FDT 13 with HMS Ulster Queen as standby. USS Catoctin was second standby and performed only minor duties in this capacity. All fighter cover missions reported to FDT 13 when entering the assault area and patrols were assigned by use of a special Grid Map (Air) (see figure 13), which was given to each pilot and furnished as well to all Fighter Direction ships. Direction and positioning of fighters were by reference to this special Grid Map. Geographical locations and topographical features were also used as check points to effect the proper disposition of fighter cover.

The original patrols used for the first few days covered the beachhead areas closely, following the coast from Cap Roux (K4) to Cap Benat (F8) and Port Cros (G9). (See figure 13.)

Due to absence of enemy air activity, fighter cover flights were often able to remain in the area beyond their scheduled patrol time. Thus they were available to search for aircraft that had crashed or been forced down and when available fuel permitted they circled such aircraft until arrival of the Air/Sea Rescue Unit.

As ground forces advanced it became advisable to move the patrol lines inland. Using figure 13 for reference, these patrols were established as follows:

(1) High cover (22,000 feet) from H5 to C6 and return;

(2) Medium cover (9-12,000 feet) from J2 to C6 to E9 and return along the same route;

(3) Two low cover patrols (6,000 feet), the first from K3 to F5 and return, and the second from F5 to D9 and return.

Night fighters from Corsican bases were provided by MACAF with patrols of six aircraft at dusk and dawn and four aircraft during the remainder of the night. They reported to Fighter Direction Ship, FDT 13, upon reaching the assault area and were controlled by her, or assigned for control to the LST-GCIs, or HMS Ulster Queen. In later stages of the operation, night fighters were assigned for control to GCI installations ashore.

Fighter cover for convoy protection to a point 40 miles off the assault beaches was furnished by MACAF from Sardinian and Corsican Bases. From a continuous patrol of 12 aircraft over the convoy lane on D-1 the scale of effort was gradually reduced as enemy action permitted and fighter fields were established in Southern

France.

CONCLUSIONS

Fighter Cover must be assigned on standing patrols with two definite factors in mind:

(1) Direction from which and altitude at which enemy attack is most probable;

(2) To fill in blind spots of radar coverage which are almost certain to be present in an amphibious assault.

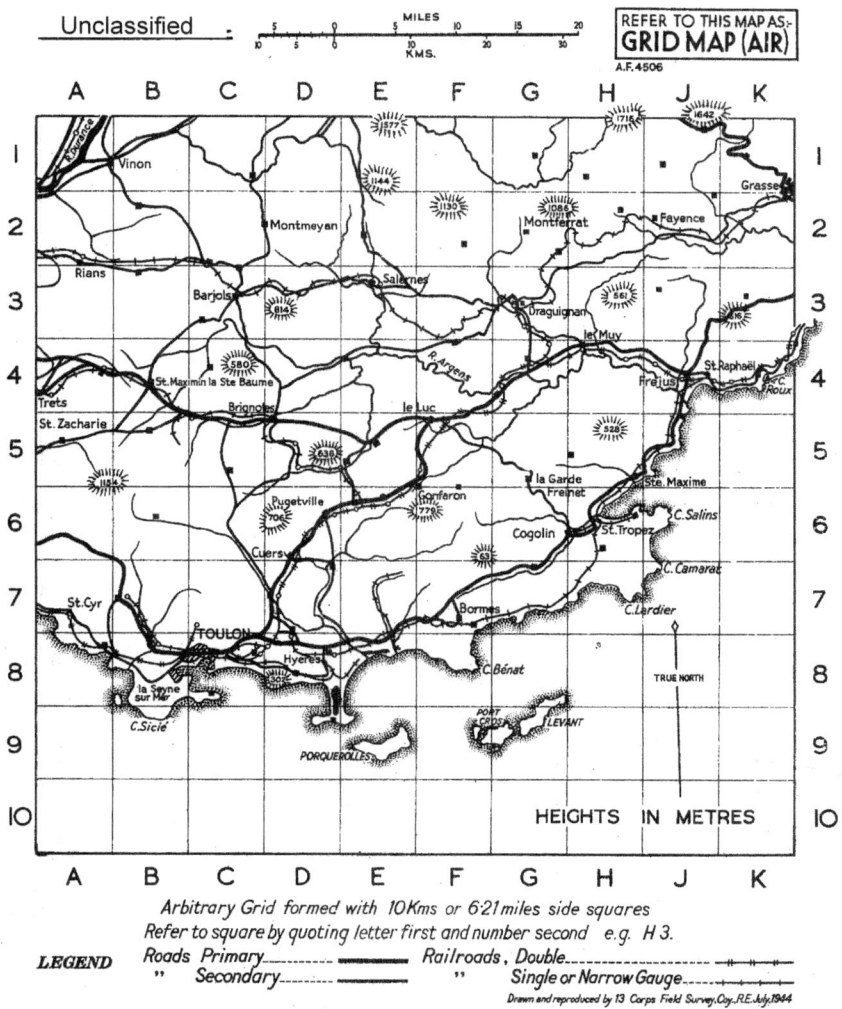

GRID MAP (AIR)

On the actual grid map, roads were indicated in red and the grid overlay indicated in blue. This afforded the chart greater readability than is possible in this black and white copy. Actual size was 9 X 11 in. Charts were issued to each pilot and each fighter direction ship. It is recommended that charts of this type be issued, not only to aircraft pilots and fighter direction ships, but whenever possible to each ship in the force as well. During air alert the position of the attacking aircraft can be more closely defined than is possible under the present system. Positions of friendly fighters can be indicated by the same method.

Figure 13

- 267 -

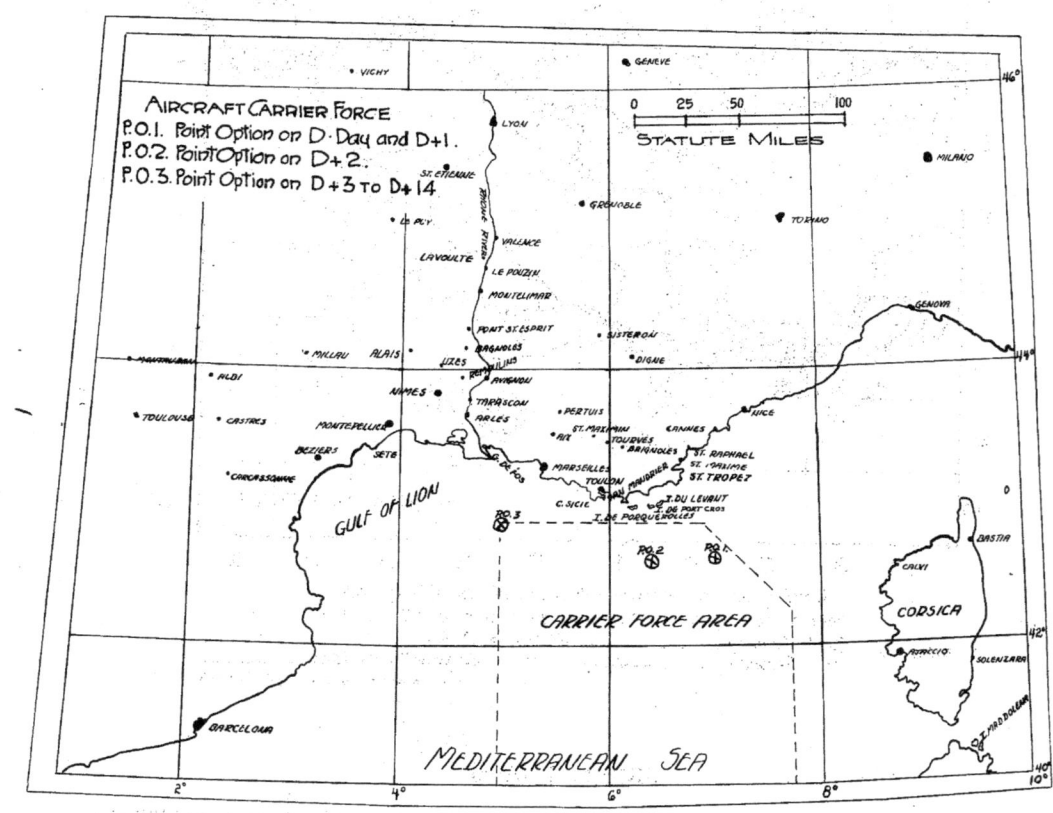

Figure 14

Section 4.8

CARRIER AIRCRAFT OPERATIONS

The Aircraft Carrier Force, Task Force 88, commanded by Rear Admiral T. H. Troubridge, DSO, Royal Navy, was comprised of seven Royal Navy and two US Navy CVEs with their attendant escorts. It operated in two loosely coordinated groups. In Task Group 88.1 commanded by Rear Admiral Troubridge, were five British carriers, two anti-aircraft cruisers, and seven destroyers. Task Group 88.2 under command of Rear Admiral C. T. Durgin, US Navy, was composed of two US carriers, two British carriers, two anti-aircraft cruisers, and six destroyers (see "Carrier Operations," Section 3.9, Part II).

Carrier aircraft aboard numbered approximately 24 per carrier. The Royal Navy Squadrons were composed for the operation as follows: In Task Group 88.1 - HMS Attacker and HMS Khedive carried Seafires of the 879 Squadron and 899 Squadron respectively. HMS Pursuer and HMS Searcher carried Wildcats of 881 Squadron and 898 Squadron respectively, and HMS Emperor flew Hellcats of the 800 Squadron. In Task Group 88.2, HMS Hunter and HMS Stalker carried Seafires of 807 Squadron and 809 Squadron respectively.

The US Navy squadrons were VOF-1 in the USS Tulagi and VF-74 in USS Kasaan Bay. All were Hellcats. In addition seven night fighters of VF(N)74 and five Avengers were based at Solenzara and Casabianda in Corsica for night carrier cover, anti-submarine, and ferry operations. Spares were based in Corsica and Malta.

The carrier force was (1) to provide its own fighter protection both day and night to guard against enemy air, surface and underwater attack, and (2) to furnish all remaining available aircraft to a pool available to the Air Commander for missions deemed most important from the overall viewpoint. Missions assigned to carrier aircraft included spotting for naval gunfire, fighter cover for the beaches, bombing and strafing, tactical and photographic reconnaissance, and armed reconnaissance.

It was thought initially that the weight of effort of carrier aircraft would be devoted to spotting of naval gunfire, but as the battle developed, fighter bomber and armed reconnaissance missions became an important part of the assistance that carrier aircraft rendered the entire operation. As a result of the rapid progress of the assault forces in establishing beachheads, spotting missions required of TF 88 were largely confined to the Marseille and Toulon areas. Spotting aircraft remained on call and were assigned missions at the request of CTF 86. Their activities are discussed in "Spotting Planes," Section 4.9, Part II.

The Aircraft Carrier Force operated within the area shown on figure 14 with the approximate position on D-Day as far eastward in the area as practicable. As the invasion progressed westward and northward up the Rhone Valley the carrier force shifted its position to the western edge of the area to give greater range to its fighter bombers and armed reconnaissance aircraft which executed their missions to the north of Lyon and to the west of Toulouse.

This movement of the force to a point relatively close inshore was made possible by the fact that there was negligible enemy air opposition. It became apparent that carrier aircraft were available for offensive missions in enemy territory to a depth somewhat beyond the range of fighters based in Corsica. The Anglo-American team of Seafires for short range missions and Hellcats and Wildcats for longer range sorties was particularly useful in destruction of enemy motor transport, troop concentrations, road bridges, rail nets and railroad equipment.

That this was effective beyond expectation is evidenced by the following message from the Air Commander to the Commander Aircraft Carrier Force:

"I would like to express my appreciation for the outstanding work they (carrier aircraft) have done and of their perfect cooperation. I consider the relationship and cooperation of this force to be model of perfection and a severe standard for future operations. Today I personally counted two hundred and two destroyed enemy vehicles from four miles west of Saint Maximin to two miles east of Le Luc. This is positive proof of an excellent job. I would be grateful if you would thank all concerned for an outstanding success and a definite contribution to the present rapid advance of the ground forces. Well done and thanks."

Fighter cover of the beachhead area and tactical reconnaissance missions were dispatched as directed by the Air Commander from the aircraft pool placed at his disposal (see "Fighter Cover," Section 4.7).

The general procedure for carrier aircraft on beachhead patrol or air support missions was as follows:

Upon taking off from the carriers the Fighter Direction Officer of the carrier force notified the air control ship in the assault area of the type of aircraft, call sign, attack order and mission and targets on which the aircraft just airborne had been briefed. As the mission reached the assault area, its leader called in to the fighter direction ship if on patrol missions, and to the amphibious flagship if on offensive missions, for confirmation of the targets on which they had been briefed aboard the carrier, or assignment of a new mission by the forward fighter control ship. While in the forward area they remained under the control of the forward control ship, and upon completion of the mission the aircraft reported their departure from the area to the forward control ship. This ship in turn notified the carrier flagship of the release of the mission and of the fact that it was on its return journey.

This system of control existed when the Air Commander was in USS Catoctin. When XII TAC headquarters was established ashore on D plus 4 the carrier flagship assumed control of the offensive missions. No defensive missions were furnished the assault area by carriers after that date.

The offensive direction of carrier based aircraft is of utmost value, and it should be carefully considered in any plan for an invasion in which the carrier forces are to be used close inshore.

The assignment of carrier aircraft to fighter bomber and armed reconnaissance missions in much greater number than was contemplated at the start of the operation presented difficulties particularly in the case of the US Navy carriers. The training of US pilots had directed emphasis toward fighter tactics, anti-submarine screening, gunfire spotting with little or no time devoted to tactical and armed reconnaissance and in the accurate reporting of enemy movements and concentrations.

CONCLUSION

The employment of carriers in inshore assault operations proved very successful. When the enemy air force is weak and dwindling, severe damage can be inflicted upon his ground forces even in the face of accurate intense flak such as was encountered in Southern France. Destruction of motor transport concentrations, either in transport pools or along the road is of great advantage, denying the use of the roads to the enemy during daylight hours.

Section 4.9

SPOTTING PLANES

The naval bombardment during the amphibious assault was observed by spotting aircraft as well as Shore Fire Control Parties and destroyers.

High performance spotting aircraft were furnished by 111th, 2/33, and 225 Tac/R (Tactical Reconnaissance) Squadrons of XII TAC and by TF 88, Aircraft Carrier Force, which supplied Hellcats and Seafires for this purpose. Initial missions called for simultaneous spotting for four gunfire support groups on four beaches and required a complex communications plan. Nine VHF and three HF channels were required to handle the traffic. Initially 111th Tac/R Squadron with naval pilots from cruisers and battleships flying P-51s was assigned to Camel Area, Task Group 88.2 to Delta Area and Task Group 88.1 to Alpha and Sitka areas. Task Force 88 used Hellcats and Seafires as spotting planes. The complete plan was included in detail in Appendix I to Annex F to Operation Plan No. 4-44.

Each spotting mission consisted of two fighters, one to spot and the other to "weave" astern. The spotter reported the fall of shot and the weaver reported presence of anti-aircraft fire and hostile aircraft. This second pilot was qualified to take over the spotting duty in case the spotter suffered casualty or communication failure.

All spotting was done in accordance with the Mediterranean Bombardment Code (MBC) which was proved extremely valuable in that it set forth a standard procedure for the varied air and naval forces that this operation required. The procedure outlined in this code is quite similar to that of the US Navy.

Unfortunately a ground haze over the assault areas handicapped observation by air spotters until nearly noon of D-Day although many valuable observations were reported prior to that time. After that time, spotting missions gave excellent assistance. With the advance of the ground forces toward Toulon and Marseille, Aircraft Carrier Force moved westward as well (see figure of Aircraft Carrier Force in Section 4.8, Part II) and assumed responsibility for all spotting missions in that area. Spotting planes were of great assistance to CTF 86 in the bombardment of gun installations at Toulon and Marseille. The pilots were thorough and aggressive in the face of intense flak. Spotting was at an average of 6,000 feet if target was clearly visible. Many pilots found it necessary at times to dive to within a few hundred feet of target to observe fire and to ascertain damage. One pilot was shot down while spotting for naval gunfire on enemy heavy gun installations at St. Mandrier, near Toulon. He parachuted from his plane, was captured and subsequently rescued as our forces captured Toulon. The reports by pilots of damage inflicted by gunfire were generally optimistic when compared with later examination of the targets.

In some instances spotting missions assigned for bombardment of a specific target, discovered that the target was unoccupied or had been eliminated. These aircraft were then assigned by the firing ship to tactical reconnaissance missions in an attempt to find a target of opportunity. It would seem more advantageous to leave this reconnaissance function to regular Tac/R missions and call only for the spotting planes when it was definitely determined that they would be of use.

In addition to land based P-51s and Spitfires, and carrier based Hellcats and Seafires, cruiser and battleship based SOCs were employed in the spotting of naval gunfire.

Experience in Sicily indicated that these types were vulnerable to enemy fighters, but they had proved to be of considerable value at Salerno. Since intelligence reports indicated that we should have almost complete control of the air, the decision to carry ship based planes into the assault area was made, with the provision that only those ships carrying aviation gasoline aft retained their aircraft while all others landed theirs. A certain reshuffling of pilots and planes between cruisers and battleships was necessary.

Under the condition of little enemy fighter opposition the SOC proved to be most valuable in spotting naval gunfire. When they stayed well away from flak areas they were unmolested and capable of carrying out many missions. One SOC was lost to flak when it ventured too near a heavy flak area. Some commanding officers reported that the launching and recovery of ship based aircraft was an embarrassment to fire support ships during the early stages of the assault for the aircraft required recovery at inconvenient times.

Field artillery Cub planes were also used to spot naval gunfire. The advantages of this type of air spot are that the planes are controlled by the army being supported and are operated from forward areas, which enables them to be assigned a mission, get into the air, adjust gunfire, and return to base in a matter of minutes. Initially the spots made by the Cub planes were sent to the Shore Fire Control Parties, where they were converted into naval spotting terminology and relayed to the fire support ship, but finally it became the practice for the Cub plane to communicate directly with the firing ship.

Section 4.10

AIR RAID WARNINGS

The task of initiating Air Raid Warnings during the Invasion of Southern France was initially assigned by NCWTF to an officer attached to his staff and embarked in the Fighter Direction Ship, HM FDT 13. Instructions were that a red alert was to be called when any unidentified aircraft were, or were believed to be, within 50 miles of the assault area.

During D-Day numerous red alerts were called, which interfered with the unloading of ships and the necessary rest of crews of all ships in the assault area.

In order to curtail the number of doubtful alerts and to achieve a balance between adequate warning of hostile attack and uninterrupted unloading of transports NCWTF decided that Air Raid Warnings would be called from USS Catoctin, effective 1735 D-Day. Alerts were called by direction of NCWTF from the Joint Operations Room of USS Catoctin until 1200 on D plus 7. At that time this responsibility was assumed by the Air Defense Commander ashore and warnings were issued by the Sector Operations Room of the 64th Fighter Wing which had been established near St. Tropez.

During the period that Air Raid Warning was the responsibility of NCWTF 25 Red Alerts were called of which 9 were definitely identified as hostile attacks. The total number of unidentified tracks that appeared on the Filter Table of the J.O.R., USS Catoctin, was 298. Reasons for inability to identify many of these as tracks of friendly aircraft were as follows:

(a) The IFF equipment aboard the HM FDT 13 was not satisfactory. It covered such a narrow sector that the signals were frequently missed. The equipment was also not functioning properly for over an hour on D-Day and several times thereafter;

(b) Planes (P-51s and P-38s) of two Fighter Groups assigned to XII TAC did not carry IFF and were frequently plotted as unidentified tracks;

(c) Friendly bombers occasionally approached the assault area from enemy territory, having completed their missions, without switching on their IFF;

(d) Incomplete information on the movements of all friendly aircraft;

(e) Carrier aircraft returning to base switched off their IFF in order to use the homing beacon;

(f) The air raid warning officer, not being aboard the fighter direction ship, could not immediately request that patrolling aircraft be ordered to investigate unidentified plots.

The IFF equipment aboard the flagship performed most satisfactorily. Many unidentified tracks reported by the fighter direction ship, radar guard ships, and shore based radar were identified as friendly by the flagship. However, due to the location close to mountainous country, all tracks reported by the other ships and shore based radars were not always picked up by the flagship radar.

While it is recognized that compromise and enemy use of IFF is a source of weakness, it is considered desirable in order to reduce the number of unnecessary alerts in amphibious operations:

    (a) That only the most satisfactory type of IFF equipment be installed in the fighter direction ship and all radar guard ships;

    (b) That there be more thorough briefing of all friendly aircraft on the rules governing the use of IFF during the operations;

    (c) That carrier-based aircraft switch on their IFF intermittently while homing;

    (d) That the fighter direction ship and the air raid warning ship, if other than the fighter direction ship, be fully informed of all movements of friendly aircraft as far in advance as possible.

It is recommended that whenever practicable the representative of the Naval Commander call the air raid warnings from aboard the Fighter Direction Ship until such time as shore facilities can be installed to assume this function. The Fighter Direction Ship is in the position to receive the most complete information on all air activity, friendly and hostile, both from radar sources and from fighters directed to intercept doubtful aircraft.

If it becomes necessary to place the responsibility for air raid warnings in a ship such as a flagship, close liaison and interchange of information between that ship and the fighter direction ship becomes most essential.

Section 4.11

AIRBORNE TROOP MOVEMENTS

The mission of the Provisional Troop Carrier Airborne Division (PTCAD) in the invasion of Southern France was to carry the parachute troops and tow the glider-borne elements of the 1st Airborne Task Force, Seventh Army, to the drop and landing zones in the Argens Valley between Le Muy and Carnoules. The mission of the 1st Airborne Task Force was to block the movement of enemy reserves into the assault area from the north and northwest. This was accomplished with great success. A decisive factor in the development of the allied plan in the initial stages proved to be the successful exploitation of the wedge driven in the enemy positions as a result of the landing of the airborne task force. Through this wedge light armored columns thrust northward, and subsequently the enemy forces were split into three separate groups.

During the planning stage the naval commander was concerned to make certain that a corridor was chosen through which the PTCAD aircraft could fly to the drop and landing zones without being fired on by allied ships or beach anti-aircraft. Through the closest coordination of the commanders of the several services a satisfactory corridor was selected (see diagram XII). No single instance was reported of allied ships or beach AA firing on Troop Carrier Aircraft.

In order to assist the PTCAD aircraft to reach the landfall at Le Trayas, the navy provided three beacon ships which were stationed prior to 0300 D-Day at positions in the center of the corridor at thirty-mile intervals from a point off the north tip of Corsica (see diagram XII). On each ship the PTCAD placed a team equipped with aeronautical navigational aids, Eureka beacons and Holophane lights. The PTCAD aircraft flew over the beacon ships on schedule and the navigational aids functioned perfectly; the Eureka beacon reception was from 25 to 30 miles and that of the Holophane lights was 1 to 10 miles. Several pilots reported that the beacon ships were somewhat off station but not enough to cause confusion. This cannot be considered as an adverse criticism as the practical impossibility of keeping exact station when beyond radar contact with land through many hours of darkness is obvious.

The magnitude of the PTCAD D-Day operation and its skillful execution is demonstrated by the following facts: aircraft made 807 sorties, 446 carrying paratroops and 361 towing gliders and lost only 3 aircraft and 9 gliders. It is even more remarkable when one considers that approximately one half of the 807 sorties were made in darkness and were further handicapped by a ground fog up to 500 feet at the drop zones. In spite of the dense fog a very high percentage of the paratroops were dropped either directly in the drop zones or in their close vicinity. There were no fatalities and no injuries to any PTCAD personnel in powered aircraft in the invasion. Only two aircraft incurred minor battle damage as a result of the operation. Attention is drawn to the fact that the above statistics apply only to the role of the PTCAD in the operation and do not deal with any operations of the 1st Airborne Task Force subsequent to arrivals over the drop and landing zones.

The night of 6/7 August an exercise, was carried out. PTCAD participated and the group leaders of the PTCAD aircraft flew on a course over the beacon ships under conditions similar to those to be met in the actual operation.

This exercise is considered to have been extremely valuable.

RECOMMENDATION

It is recommended that in joint operations involving air-borne troop landings in conjunction with amphibious assaults beacon ships be trained by rehearsal with the troop carrier command involved.

Section 4.12

AIR-SEA RESCUE SERVICE

The responsibility for the rescue of aircrewmen from the sea in this operation was delegated to the Mediterranean Allied Coastal Air Force (MACAF) and to the XII Tactical Air Command (XII TAC). During the approach phase MACAF's responsibility was for all the sea area from the Italian, Corsican and Sardinian Coasts to the French Coast. In the assault phase the XII TAC became responsible for the area within a 15 mile radius of the principal Fighter Direction Ship, FDT 13. When the XII TAC became established ashore on D plus 7 it assumed responsibility for an area extending between the flanks of the assault area and for forty miles to sea. During the last phase when XII TAC moved inland and was replaced by MACAF, responsibility for all rescues reverted to the latter.

HMS Antwerp as an air sea rescue ship, was located (see diagram XII) midway between the south coast of France and Corsica in the Tactical Aircraft lane and FDT 13 was stationed 10 to 15 miles offshore in the center of the assault area. Two high speed launches (HSL) were attached to the Fighter Direction Ship and two pinnaces to HMS Antwerp for air sea rescue work. In Corsica and Sardinia there were based 10 HSLs and 2 pinnaces together with 16 Warwick and 7 Catalina aircraft. Air patrols were flown along the aircraft lane from D minus 3 until D plus 9. During the two week period from 9 to 23 August, MACAF flew 274 sorties, and in cooperation with sea rescue craft, rescued 91 allied aircrewmen.

ANTI-SUBMARINE AIR OPERATIONS

In conjunction with the surface screen MACAF provided anti-submarine Air Search Patrols and convoy protection in all areas where an attack might be expected. Prior to and during the operation, day and night continuous patrols were flown on these missions. They were not discontinued until D plus 10, when it was considered that all submarine threat had disappeared. In the assault area two destroyers of the anti-submarine screen were designated daily to act in conjunction with aircraft. In case a contact was made, a coordinated hunt could then be quickly conducted with the destroyer going to the position of contact and directing the aircraft in the type of hunt the destroyer commander had determined upon. No actual contact with a submarine was made in this operation. However, a contact was reported and some difficulty was experienced in communications between the aircraft and the destroyer, indicating the necessity for adequate destroyer-plane exercises to test communications and work out procedures.

Section 4.14

AIRCRAFT FOR MINESPOTTING

An innovation in underwater mine detection was introduced in this operation. Catalina (PBY-5A) aircraft operated over and near the assault area on visual minespotting missions. Allied air superiority permitted these operations soon after the beachhead was established.

In early July, Catalinas of VFP-1, French Patrol Squadron, were offered to the Mediterranean Allied Coastal Air Force (MACAF) for Air/Sea Rescue and Minespotting during the invasion of Southern France. It was intended to base the required number of planes at an airfield in Corsica to be designated by MACAF.

At the outset, MACAF welcomed the offer and stated that they could use all the planes that could be provided. It was intended that 8 planes be based in Corsica in order to have 6 operational at all times. The 8 planes were flown from Agadir to Port Lyautey where they underwent a refresher course training in water landings and take-offs.

Shortly thereafter, MACAF advised that they had sufficient Air/Sea Rescue aircraft and that no VFP-1 planes would be required. Since, however, NCWTF was interested in minespotting, MACAF granted permission for 3 Catalinas to be forward based in Corsica in order that 2 planes would be operational to be called to the assault area as required.

During this time, MACAF had been requested to plan an Air Dispatch Letter Service (ADLS) of 2 flights daily between the assault area and Corsica. This request was not granted by MACAF because the operation was not considered feasible with planes available. MACAF then proposed that the service be performed by aircraft from VPF-1 and the following joint program was finally arranged:

(a) 5 Catalinas from VPF-1 to be based at Ajaccio;

(b) Minespotting missions to be flown upon request through MACAF representative aboard flagship to MACAF control in Corsica;

(c) ADLS flights to be flown under control of MACAF as long as they did not interfere with minespotting which was granted a higher priority.

The Catalinas reported for temporary duty to the Air Sector Commander, MACAF, Ajaccio, Corsica early in August in accordance with Commander Eighth Fleet's directive. They were under the operational control of CG 63rd Fighter Wing of MACAF located in Bastia, Corsica, and depended upon land lines for communications with the 63rd Fighter Wing.

During their first training flight a newly laid minefield was discovered in the waters between Corsica and Elba.

On D plus 1 a dispatch was sent requesting 2 minespotting flights on D plus 2. Owing to a delay in communications no missions were flown on D plus 2 and the initial flight was made on D plus 3. During the first 3 days of operations seven sorties were flown during which 9 minefields were discovered containing 229 mines. Some of these flights were made under intense AA fire and poor sea conditions. Through 24 September, when Commander Escort Sweeper Group assumed responsibility for requesting minespotting flights, the area from Nice to Agde including harbors and adjacent waters to the 100 fathom curve had been searched and over 600 mines had been discovered.

Minespotting aircraft were assigned by MACAF on the basis of the priority stated above. No provision was made for ship to aircraft or ship to base communication. This proved to be costly both in aircraft, personnel and equipment. Two minespotting aircraft were damaged in rough water landings costing the life of one pilot and the total loss of one aircraft. In another instance a PT boat was mined a half hour after a Catalina discovered the minefield but had no opportunity to report it. Lack of speedy communications with Ajaccio resulted in unnecessary flights when weather in the assault area prohibited effective missions.

During the minespotting and minesweeping operations, the efforts of the French PBY Minespotting squadrons VFP One and VFP Two were supplemented by two US Navy nonrigid air ships (blimps) operating out of Cuers airport near Toulon. The first blimp from ZP squadron 14 NAS, Port Lyautey reported to NCWTF on 17 September 1944. In addition to the development of known and the discovery of unknown minefields, it served as a valuable safeguard with the use of its MAD gear during night patrols against attacks upon our ships at anchor in Toulon Roads threatened by enemy small surface craft and submarines.

A thorough examination of the entire coastline of Southern France between the Spanish and Italian borders was made extending to seaward to the one hundred fathom curve. This was conducted by the PBY airplanes for the initial coverage with their higher speed, and by the blimps which examined reported areas more thoroughly and accurately. The following advantages accrued from the use of blimps:

(1) By use of the radar equipment, the position of individual mines could be accurately established and plotted

(2) The ability of the blimp to set a low ground speed enables it to examine carefully any suspected area. In cooperation with mine sweeping craft which the blimp coached either by means of a loud speaker or VHF radio, it was found possible to warn surface craft of mines which could not be seen from the surface. This accelerated the rate of sweeping and increased the degree of safety.

Under favorable conditions of air superiority, which is essential because of the extreme vulnerability of this type of aircraft to enemy fighters and to anti-aircraft fire, blimps can render valuable assistance to minespotting and sweeping operations.

Information gained from minespotting missions proved to be extremely useful and it is strongly recommended, conditions being favorable, that they be employed to the fullest extent in the discovery and survey of unknown minefields. When employed in connection with amphibious operations planning should include provision for adequate communications for control and reporting minefields, base facilities as near the area of operations as practicable, and close liaison with minesweeping commands.

Section 4.15

AIR DISPATCH LETTER SERVICE

The Mediterranean Allied Coastal Air Force (MACAF) in mid-July recommended that Catalinas (PBY-5As) of VFP-1 be made available continuously for two Air Dispatch Letter Service (ADLS) flights per day, commencing D-Day, from Ajaccio, Corsica, to the beachhead. This was not found feasible and a counter proposal was made as described in the preceeding Section 4.14, Aircraft for Minespotting, based on priority of missions.

The first ADLS flight was flown from Ajaccio landing early D-Day morning in the approaches to the Gulf of St. Tropez. Two flights daily were made through D plus 6 when owing to high seas one of the aircraft was damaged in landing resulting in the cancellation of one flight. On D plus 7 transport aircraft were operating from the Ramatuelle Airfield and the last ADLS flight by VFP-1 Catalinas was made that afternoon.

ADLS missions proved of great value. However, they must be carefully planned in every detail in order to provide an efficient service with minimum expenditure.

Section 4.16

NAVAL AIR LIAISON OFFICERS

The necessity of close liaison with the various air forces participating in this assault was foreseen from previous experience in combined amphibious operations in this theater. Moreover, Naval Air Liaison Officers were already maintained with those air commands under the Mediterranean Allied Air Forces (MAAF) with whose daily operations the Eighth Fleet was directly concerned.

During the planning of the invasion of Southern France, these officers were assigned to temporary duty with one or more of the following air commands:

(1) Mediterranean Allied Tactical Air Force (MATAF).

(2) Mediterranean Allied Coastal Air Force (MACAF).

(3) XII Tactical Air Command (XII TAC).

(4) CTG 88.2.

(5) Provisional Troop Carrier Air Division, USAAF.

(6) 2nd Air Combat Control Squadron (Amphibious), aboard USS Catoctin.

(7) 64th Fighter Wing (MATAF).

(8) French Naval Aviation, Navale France.

Some of these officers were temporarily attached directly to the commands concerned, others visited the various headquarters as planning required. It was the function of all of them to keep this command advised of the developments in the air plans for the operation, the organization and location of air units, air force decisions and policies in regard to specific questions.

After the plans had been approved, liaison officers were attached to those commands and units where their knowledge would be of most value during the operation, as follows:

(1) MATAF

(2) XII TAC (Adv)

(3) XII TAC (Ops) and 87th Fighter Wing

(4) 64th Fighter Wing

(5) 325th Fighter Control Sector (63rd Fighter Wing)

(6) CTG 88.2

(7) CTF 86

(8) French Naval Aviation, Navale France

(9) VF(N) 74

MATAF. It was the function of the Naval Air Liaison Officer (NALO), assigned to the CG MATAF, to interpret the naval plan and its subsequent execution, to maintain information of shipping movements and naval statistics and to keep NCWTF informed of the results of the bombing program as they affected the Western Task Force. This officer also accompanied the CG MATAF during the briefing of the various medium bomber and fighter wings under his command, being charged with the presentation of the naval plan to these wings.

XII TAC (Adv). The NALO assigned to CG XII TAC, the Air Commander for the operation, went ashore with XII TAC (Adv) on D plus 4. He had frequently visited this command on special missions during the planning stage, so that he was already familiar with this headquarters. His duties in the assault area were to keep the Air Commander and his staff advised of the naval requirements for air cover and naval gunfire spotting planes. He also assisted in **returning** escaped naval pilots, who had been shot down, to their own ships and stations. He kept NCWTF regularly informed, by daily report, of the status and location of airfields and air units, the results of missions flown and such other information as was specifically requested.

Liaison with XII TAC (Ops), 87th Fighter Wing, 64th Fighter Wing and 325th Fighter Control Sector was maintained by a team of one officer and three men (quartermasters) who were assigned successively to these headquarters as they were respectively concerned with the air defense of shipping in the assault area. Their duty was the maintenance of a convoy plot for the information of the Air Controllers at these control centers, in order that special cover could be assigned when desired. The officer of this team sent daily reports to NCWTF via the NALO at XII TAC on the number of sorties flown on air defense patrols and on any incidents encountered by these patrols.

The Naval Fighter Direction Officer who served with the 2nd Air Combat Control Squadron (Amphibious) aboard USS Catoctin was also assigned to 64th Fighter Wing in the assault area. He had made several previous visits to that command and XII TAC during the planning and assisted in the integration of Fighter Direction ships involved in the operation and in the coordination of shipborne and land based air control.

During the initial assault, two officers were assigned to temporary duty on the Fighter Direction ship, HM FDT 13, where they were charged with the responsibility of initiating air raid warnings to the fleet. They were in direct liaison with the Senior Fighter Director and the CG 64th Fighter Wing, the Air Defense Commander, aboard the same ship, until they were recalled to perform the same duties on USS Catoctin on D plus 1.

CTG 88.2. The officer assigned to the staff of CTG 88.2 for duty with the Carrier Force had formerly been assigned as liaison with MACAF and his experience with the air force organization in the theater was valuable in the coordination of the Carrier Force plans. During the operation he kept NCWTF informed of the progress of carrier operations. Together with the Naval Liaison Officer, Royal Navy, assigned by CTF 88 to XII TAC (Adv) both in USS Catoctin and later ashore, this officer assisted in the coordination of the missions furnished by CTF 88 both for air cover over the beaches and for close support of the assault area where these missions came under the direction of the XII TAC Fighter Directors.

CTF 86. The Naval Air Liaison Officer assigned to the Staff of CTF 86 in USS Augusta was to serve, if necessary, as standby in succession to the Staff Air Officer for NCWTF. He actually served as liaison officer to the Deputy Air Commander who was on board the same ship with his staff.

The officer appointed for liaison with French Naval Aviation went ashore with the commandant of that organization and was occupied in assisting to organize the program of minespotting by air from the French PBY-5As based at Ajaccio in Corsica.

VF(N) 74 was a unit of 7 Navy night fighters (F6Fs) under the control of and providing night fighter protection for the Carrier Force, from a base ashore at Solenzara in Corsica. The NALO assigned to this unit assisted in coordinating the operations of these planes with those of the other night fighters under MACAF.

CONCLUSION

In large combined operations the assignment of liaison officers as described above, especially when the commands involved are so varied and geographically dispersed, is highly desirable to provide the naval commander information of air plans and operations and to present the naval aspect to the air commanders.

Chapter 5

GUNNERY

Section 5.1

BOMBARDMENT

PREPARATION

During the winter months, when preliminary planning for the allied landing in Southern France had commenced, allied fire support ships in the Mediterranean supported the Fifth Army's left flank and the forces on the Anzio beachhead. The army became well acquainted with naval gunfire and appreciated its capabilities. Both British Forward Observer Bombardment officers, Naval Gunfire Liaison officers, and air spot were used, and the need for a common shore bombardment procedure and code became more apparent. Commander-in-Chief, Mediterranean and Commander US Eighth Fleet intensified efforts to obtain a common allied code. Representatives of the Royal, French and US Navies, of the US and Royal Air Force and US Army and Royal Artillery were assembled and preliminary work started on a shore bombardment procedure and code which would be used in future amphibious operations by the allied services in the Mediterranean. Many differences of opinion were eventually reconciled, and the Mediterranean Bombardment Code was published and promulgated.

Aerial observation has long been recognized as a most effective spotting and reconnaissance agent but SOC aircraft from US cruisers had suffered heavy losses in Sicily, while at Salerno, P-51 aircraft performed brilliantly as spotters with negligible losses. Due principally to the efforts of Commander Cruiser Division Eight, spotting by high performance aircraft was emphasized and naval aviators from US cruisers were trained and flew combat missions in P-40 and P-51 aircraft. As a result of a recommendation by Commander Eighth Fleet, army pilots, when observing naval gunfire, were directed by US Army Chief of Staff to use US naval spotting procedure. Thus, there developed in the theater an appreciation of the task of spotting naval gunfire; and army and naval aviators, flying high performance aircraft who could spot for fire support ships, became available.

When the French reserve ammunition problem began to be solved, and it appeared that reserve supplies would be available for practice bombardments and future operations, French ships were assembled at Oran and trained in communications and shore bombardment technique by Commander Cruiser Division Eight. Co-operation was eager and results excellent. It was not until the latter part of June, after the bombardment of Cherbourg, that Commander US Eighth Fleet learned the quantities of US 8" and 14" ammunition available for the operation in Southern France. British reserves were considered adequate, but French inadequate. Later, Commander Cruiser Division Eight visited ports in the United States and conferred with commanding officers of ships and flag officers tentatively assigned to Commander Eighth Fleet for the invasion of Southern France. The shore fire control problem was emphasized with particular attention to observation by high performance carrier based aircraft.

The Tarawa landing pointed out the need for close observation of gunfire immediately preceding and subsequent to the landing of the initial wave. At the bombardment range near Arzew, Algeria, it was determined that it was feasible to control and spot close supporting and covering fire from an LCC off-shore, and it was recognized that an army artillery officer, familiar with the army scheme of maneuver, should be the off-shore spotter.

Many enemy airfields were near the target assault area, and as the greatest threats to allied ships and shipping were the German Air Force and coast defense batteries, it was expected that great quantities of smoke might be used. The procurement of adequate smoke apparatus and materials was initiated early. Excellent cooperation was received from the Chemical Warfare Officer of Allied Force Headquarters and Seventh Army. The army supplied fog oil, smoke pots and floats, and FS smoke mixture.

Initial planning was handicapped by lack of definite information concerning availability of fire support ships and reserve ammunition. It was known that the extensive coast defense system of Southern France was formidable, particularly in the Toulon-Marseille area, and that continued fire support would be required by the army in its advance to the westward.

NAVAL GUNFIRE SUPPORT DURING ASSAULT

For the first time in a Mediterranean amphibious operation, large scale pre-assault naval and air bombardments were employed. Sixty allied ships, including battleships, heavy and light cruisers, destroyer leaders, and destroyers fired approximately 650 missions in support of Seventh Army from D-day to and including the 25th of September. The defenses of Southern France were strong, but were not manned with great determination by the enemy at all places. The construction and location of coast defense batteries and strong points were such that they would have offered serious opposition to the landing had heavy pre-assault bombardment and well coordinated close supporting fire not been carefully integrated and executed according to plan. All weapons - bombs, naval gunfire, explosive boats, rockets, and smoke - were combined into an overwhelming, concerted blow of only one hour and fifty minutes duration which dazed and weakened the enemy; and the army was placed ashore with extremely light losses.

Naval bombardments and aerial bombings carried out during the assault are shown graphically in diagrams XVIII to XX inclusive.

POST-ASSAULT NAVAL GUNFIRE SUPPORT

Post-assault gunfire support was provided for both east and west flanks, with the latter - the advance on Toulon and Marseille - marked by the greatest weight of naval gunfire ever employed in the Mediterranean against enemy positions.

The army's advance to the eastward was rapid, resulting in an extremely fluid situation. Requests for support were sporadic, and the naval ships supporting the right flank found themselves in a standby status much of the time. Because of the rapid advance, it was difficult for Shore Fire Control Parties to keep the ships informed of position of own troops. This often resulted, when requests for fire were received, in delays while the ship sought authentication of the request.

The capitulation of the peninsula of St. Mandrier climaxed an intensive, prolonged period of bombardment and bombing. Enemy personnel in the deep underground spaces were completely protected from bombs and projectiles, but surface communications were badly damaged, and numerous gun positions were put out of action during the siege. The ground in the vicinity of the two 340 mm twin mount turrets was ploughed by bombs and naval gunfire. One of the turrets was hit, probably by a bomb. This turret had previously been put out of action by sabotage or accident, and it is believed that it was not in commission on or after D-day. The muzzle of the left gun of the other turret was hit by a large fragment, which put that gun out of action. At the time of surrender, the right gun was still serviceable. A separate report on damage to the two 340 mm turrets has been forwarded to the Chief of Naval Operations and the Bureau of Ordnance. These guns were highly critical to our neutralizing efforts, because they could outrange all of our gunfire support ships.

Gunfire support on the right flank served to keep a constant pressure on the retreating enemy. Accurate fire from cruisers and destroyers prevented effective rear guard action. Working well behind the enemy lines with air spot, gunfire support ships dispersed troops, damaged strong points, and generally kept the fleeing enemy under harassing fire. Unusually profitable missions were fired by USS H. P. Jones against the harbor of San Remo on 17 and 18 September. Expending a total of 223 rounds of 5"/38 AAC, the following damage was inflicted:

Flak battery silenced - one gun destroyed;
Direct hit on tug;
4-5 small scows damaged and probably destroyed;
2 MAS boats destroyed;
2 ammunition dumps blown up;
Coastal freighter set on fire;
3 probable drones exploded;
3 ammunition barges exploded;
Fire and explosion on jetty.

The Commanding Officer of USS H. P. Jones attributes his success to the pilot of the spotting aircraft, a seaplane from USS Philadelphia.

All reported fire support missions and aerial bombardments in the Toulon-Giens area are shown in Diagram XXI; that of the Marseille-Ciotat area in diagram XXII. The naval bombardment on the right flank is shown in Diagram XXIII. Diagram XXIV tabulates the total expenditure of ammunition by calibers from D-day, up to and including 25 September, D + 41.

Section 5.2

ORDNANCE MATERIAL

The performance of ordnance material was excellent. A few minor casualties were reported. USS Endicott reported difficulty with breech blocks in three out of her four 5"/38 guns. The trouble developed after a diversionary bombardment. Apparently a high rate of fire was maintained. The guns became very hot and the breech blocks were closed with great difficulty during a surface action which later developed. Normally during a shore bombardment, slow, deliberate fire should be employed, but in an anti-aircraft or surface action, a high rate of fire is desired, and the 5"/38 caliber dual purpose guns are normally capable of delivering such fire.

The majority of allied fire support ships were equipped with modern fire control equipment and radar. A notable exception was the French **battleship** Lorraine which, with obsolete equipment, conducted accurate fire against St. Mandrier defenses. US 6"/53 caliber cruisers with modern fire control equipment and radar are capable of rendering highly effective supporting fire.

The performance of the high explosive and armor piercing, large caliber projectiles was excellent. No report of dud naval projectiles has been received.

The value of tracers in medium and large caliber projectiles is questioned. If the approximate location of a ship using tracer fire is disclosed, her bearing can be ascertained within reasonable limits. On dark nights sufficient illumination is supplied by tracers to disclose own forces between firing ship and target. With modern radar control, the tracer appears to be obsolete.

White phosphorus projectiles were effectively employed by US destroyers. As the supply was critical, each fire support destroyer was allowed only fifty. The WP projectile is very useful for night bombardment as it bursts on impact and gives a bright glow visible on clear nights for twenty thousand yards. In addition, it is an excellent anti-personnel weapon. It has been the experience of US destroyers in this theater that no arbitrary fuze spot is necessary. The shell will burst just short of the target if fuze is put in automatic with no correction. When smoke screens are laid, deflection spots are necessary to correct for the effect of the wind on the smoke. An excellent smoke screen was laid by USS Nields using WP projectiles on **Camel Red** beach during the approach of the assault and landing craft. It is recommended that more attention be given to the employment of white phosphorus projectiles and that a minimum of 100 projectiles be allowed each destroyer assigned fire support duties.

Beedex units were used for the first time in an operation in this theater. The Beedex is a radar beacon mounted in an LCC or other small craft or carried ashore by Shore Fire Control Parties, and is utilized by fire support ships to obtain accurate range and bearing in connection with fire support missions. Tests prior to the operation indicated accurate range and bearing data up to about 35,000 yards. The equipment was little used during the operation, so there is insufficient data to conclusively evaluate its performance in action. It is considered, however, that the potential possibilities of the Beedex merits further development, particularly for use in areas where gridded map-charts of the assault area are not available.

Section 5.3

SHORE FIRE CONTROL PARTIES AND NAVAL GUNFIRE LIAISON OFFICERS

US Shore Fire Control Parties were attached to the three US Infantry Divisions and the 1st Special Service Force to spot naval gunfire, British FOBs (Forward Observers Bombardment) to the French Infantry Divisions and Commandos, and both US personnel and British FOBs to the Provisional Airborne Division.

In the case of the three US Infantry Divisions, one Shore Fire Control Party was attached to each battalion, a total of nine being required per division. These Shore Fire Control Parties were of the standard organization used in this theater in past operations, as follows:

	Army Section	Navy Section
Army Artillery Officer (Forward Observer)	1	
Naval Gunfire Liaison Officer		1
Section Chief (Army Sergeant)	1	
Army Radio Operators (Voice)	2	2
Army Radio Operators (Key)	2	2

Both the army section and the navy section were provided with an SCR 609 (crystal controlled, two channel, battery powered, frequency modulated, lightweight radio set) and a jeep mounted SCR 284 (low powered 3800-5800 kcs. voice or c.w. radio.) The SCR 609 was hand carried during assault, and was the primary communications between naval vessels and the spotters. The jeep with SCR 284 was landed later with other army vehicles, and formed a standby communication channel.

In addition, a Naval Gunfire Liaison Officer and a naval section of a Shore Fire Control Party was attached to each US Infantry Division Artillery Headquarters. He was equipped with a jeep in which was mounted an SCR 608 (crystal controlled, ten channel, dynamotor powered, frequency modulated) and an SCR 193 (similar to the SCR 284 but somewhat higher powered and with a slightly wider frequency range.) These Division Naval Gunfire Liaison Officers by using their SCR 608 were able to monitor the spotting circuits of all Shore Fire Control Parties in the division and the common calling frequency. Unfortunately, the Naval Gunfire Liaison Officer attached to the 36th US Division (Right flank) was killed when US LST 282 was hit by a bomb when beaching. One of the battalion Naval Gunfire Liaison Officers was called back to Division Artillery Headquarters as a replacement, but lacking the SCR 608, his usefulness was somewhat impaired.

The three Shore Fire Control Parties with the Special Service Force consisted only of the army sections. Because of the nature of their assault on islands with no beaches, it was possible to equip them only with SCR 609. In review, it would have been wiser to have sent at least one Naval Gunfire Liaison Officer with the Commanding Officer, Special Service Force. As it was, there was no naval officer on the islands during the assault able to advise him of the capabilities of naval gunfire.

One US Shore Fire Control Party provided with special equipment for airborne operations and two British FOB parties were dropped with the Provisional Airborne Division. So far as is known, they had no requirements for naval support. They were able to establish communications with the Fire Support Group Commander.

Two British FOB parties landed with the French Commandos.

The French 1st DIM (Moroccan Infantry Division) had five British FOB parties; while the French 3rd DIA (Algerian Infantry Division) and the French 9th DIC (Colonial Infantry Division) each had two British FOB parties attached. There was a British Bombardment Liaison Officer at each of the French Division Headquarters, and one at the French II Corps Headquarters. Each of these FOB parties consists of a Royal Artilleryman and several Royal Navy wireless operators. They are equipped with a British#22 set (of approximately the same frequency range as the SCR 284 but somewhat lower powered) mounted in a White Scout Car. These FOB parties are permanent organizations, forming a part of the British Combined Operations Bombardment Group#2. As such, they have taken part in all amphibious operations conducted in the Mediterranean.

Because of the Army scheme of maneuver, the US Shore Fire Control Parties with the US Infantry Divisions landed in assault and provided the shore spotting agencies on D and D plus one. The French Divisions carried out the reduction of Toulon and Marseille. Consequently, the FOB parties provided the spotting agencies for naval gunfire on these two cities. Artillery officers embarked in LCSs and LCCs were stationed off each assault beach to adjust naval fire until the regular Shore Fire Control Parties arrived ashore and established communications. This spotter insured proper coordination of the close supporting beach preparation fire with the approach of the first assault wave to the beach.

As a result of experiences of the Anzio beachhead, it was considered most desirable to have a Senior Naval Gunfire Liaison Officer ashore with the Army Corps Headquarters. Accordingly, a Senior Naval Gunfire Liaison Party consisting of one Commander, USN, one Lieutenant Commander, RN, and one Major, US Army, and two Army radio operators, were landed on the morning of D plus one and were attached to US VI Corps Headquarters. The duties of this party included:

(a) Advising the Naval Task Force Commander and the Fire Support Group Commander of the tactical situation ashore;

(b) Coordinating the control of naval gunfire among the different types of spotting agencies, SFCP, naval aviation, land based high performance aircraft, and army air observation posts (Piper Cubs, etc.);

(c) Advising the Corps Commander and the Artillery Commander as to the proper employment of naval gunfire in support of the army ashore and in conjunction with field artillery support;

(d) Recommending to the Fire Support Group Commander as to the assignment of naval gunfire support.

Because of the rapid advance of the VI Corps inland, fighting had passed out of the range of naval gunfire, except on the right flank, before this party had begun to function. The Senior Naval Gunfire Liaison Party then transferred to the French Army B and coordinated all naval support incident to the reduction of Toulon and Marseille.

Because of the great overland distances involved between the various army command posts and the coast, the radio facilities provided this party proved inadequate. They were equipped with an SCR 608 and SCR 193, both mounted in a single jeep.

To insure positive radio contact at all times between the Senior Naval Gunfire Liaison Officer and the Fire Support Group Commander it is considered that an ideal set up would consist of an SCR #393 with two receivers (this is a medium powered transmitter with a wide frequency range) and an SCR 608 both mounted in a 2 1/2 ton truck. The truck should be enclosed by a canopy to permit work at night under blackout conditions. A minimum of two jeeps, each with an SCR 609 or SCR 610 would provide the necessary transportation between the various headquarters. Sufficient radio operators are needed to permit twenty-four hour watch standing for extended periods of time. In addition to the Senior Naval Gunfire Liaison Officer, the party should include an army artillery officer, and two junior naval officers for coding, decoding, and general liaison.

The Bombardment Calling Wave (BCW) was employed throughout the operation. In this system, there is a frequency that is common to all firing ships and all Shore Fire Control Parties. Furthermore, it is continuously guarded by the Fire Support Group Commander. Any Shore Fire Control Party that does not have a ship assigned, or is unable to contact an assigned ship, guards the BCW. If he requires naval support, he requests it from the Fire Support Group Commander, who assigns him a ship. The Shore Fire Control Party then shifts to his spotting frequency and establishes contact with the ship so assigned. Actually, two BCWs were employed, one a c.w. frequency and the other a common calling frequency for the frequency modulated SCR 608-609-610. During the assault there was such an organization for each infantry division and their Fire Support Group Commanders. During the follow-up phase, the support was divided into a right flank and left flank arrangement.

The principle of the Bombardment Calling Wave is an excellent one. However, this circuit must never be used for any administrative traffic. The Shore Fire Control Parties, with their comparatively weak radio sets, were sometimes unable to get their requirements for naval support through because a more powerful transmitter was engaged in sending a long dispatch.

The problem of providing a spotting agency to control naval gunfire during the "touchdown" of the troops, extending to the time when the regular Shore Fire Control Parties were landed and functioning was easily solved. This is an especially critical period, for the pre-H-Hour bombardment must be lifted inland and to the flanks as the first wave lands. Yet it is possible that some troublesome machine gun can pin the troops to the beach and no way may exist for naval support to neutralize it because as to doubt of location of own troops. Off each assault beach an army artillery officer was embarked in an LCC, PC or LCS that would be near the beach during the early phase of the landing. The spotter was furnished an SCR 609, and one or more destroyers assigned to support him. The spotter was either a member of a Shore Fire Control Party attached to a battalion landing in reserve, or was from the division artillery section. This system proved most effective.

The Combined Assault Code (CCBP 0130) was used by all Shore Fire Control Parties and Naval Gunfire Liaison Officers. In general, it was satisfactory. However, it consists only of three letter groups and garbles cannot be cleared. Consequently, one garble is quite likely to render an entire message unintelligible. Furthermore, it is a very slow and tedious process and when a message runs to one hundred or more groups well over an hour may be required to encode and check. For liaison officers who are required to send detailed situation reports, some sort of a mechanical coding machine would seem to be more appropriate.

The Mediterranean Bombardment Code, (MBC) was employed by all spotting agencies. The code was evolved by representatives of the allied services in the theater to fill a long-felt necessity -- a self-evident code which could be used by any combination of allied services. Essentially based on CSP 2156B, the code was in two parts. Part I, called "Naval Bombardment with Ground Observation" contained the procedure and code for use between Allied Ships and ground observers or links. Part II, "Naval Bombardment with Air Observation" consisted of the procedure and code for use between allied-ships and aircraft. The code was devised on the premise that the line of fire method of spotting was superior to the clock code for the various services involved, in that more practice is required by a spotter to become proficient in "clocking." It was felt that spotting agencies would have no trouble in visualizing the line of fire. Reports from fire support ships and spotting agencies indicate that the Mediterranean Bombardment Code was readily and effectively employed.

STANDARD FORM FOR REPORT OF SHORE BOMBARDMENT FIRE MISSIONS.

In order to facilitate the collection and analysis of shore bombardment data, it is proposed that a standard form for reporting pertinent data on each land target engaged be devised and issued to the fleet, just as is now done for anti-aircraft actions. Shore bombardment is receiving more and more attention as the war progresses, and when it is noted that the total of 556 bombardment missions reported by the fire support ships at Salerno was greatly exceeded by the ships supporting the Southern France landing, the need for a standard report form becomes evident, if a thorough bombardment study is to be made. Having felt this need as a result of Salerno, Commander Eighth Fleet included as an appendix to his gunfire support plan for the Southern France landing a form for the "Report of Fire Missions" which listed the following data for each land target engaged:

(1) Target numbers and map reference.

(2) Type target.

(3) Date - zone time of call for fire.

(4) Times of commencing and ceasing fire.

(5) Type of fire and method of observation.

(6) Initial navigational range.

(7) Initial spot.

(8) Number of rounds fired in ranging and in fire for effect.

(9) Total number of rounds fired and type of ammunition.

(10) Effect and remarks.

This form was incorporated into the action reports of many of the fire support ships, and it is believed that these data together with the ships' location during the shoot would comprise the basis of a form that could well be used throughout the navy in reporting shore bombardments.

ASSIGNMENT OF PRIORITY TO CALL FIRE TARGETS

In almost every landing operation there have been times in which various army units have found themselves in critical situations and have transmitted "Urgent" requests for assistance to fire support ships. Consequently in both CSP 2156(B) and the Mediterranean Bombardment Code provision was made to facilitate transmission of such requests. Likewise in almost every operation there have been occasions in which naval gunfire has been requested at such targets as general areas in which enemy activity has previously been observed, locations of suspected enemy batteries or troop concentrations, potential enemy OPs, and buildings which might contain enemy troops. Sometimes it is necessary for a fire support ship to move into unswept waters or within range of menacing coastal batteries to fire at these rather dubious targets and in many cases the risk to the ship is not justified. Therefore it is suggested that prior to landing, the Naval Gunfire Liaison Officers should be carefully briefed on the area in which they will operate with regard to the depths of the adjacent water, known or suspected enemy minefields, coast defense guns, and how close inshore the various types of fire support ships can be expected to maneuver without being seriously jeopardized. Further, it is possible that a complete system of classifying the importance of opportunity targets for use by the spotter or Naval Gunfire Liaison Officer in the call for fire message would be of value to commanding officers of fire support ships in deciding whether or not to risk their ships in particularly hazardous situations. Such a classification might use the terms "Urgent" or "Immediate" to indicate extremely vital targets at which fire is needed promptly, "Important" to indicate important targets against which immediate fire is not a necessity, "Routine" to denote targets which are not vital but are nevertheless appropriate targets for naval gunfire if it can be brought to bear without grave risk to the supporting ship, and "Possible" to indicate targets which are suspected targets or areas at which harassing fire would be appropriate provided there are not more important targets accessible and a fire support ship is known to be available for the mission.

Section 5.4

ANTI-AIRCRAFT GUNNERY AND AIRCRAFT RECOGNITION

RULES FOR ANTI-AIRCRAFT GUNFIRE

As in previous amphibious operations in the theater, special rules governed control of anti-aircraft gunfire in assault areas. These rules were based upon the current instructions for the Mediterranean station but modified somewhat as a result of experiences in the Northern France invasion.

The resultant rules were compromises between the desires of the air forces, army and navy. Experiences of missing targets due to dense, low clouds and overcast conditions in Normandy made the air force representatives keenly interested in as low a minimum altitude for flying as practicable. Furthermore, air intelligence indicated that in the invasion of Southern France we would have overwhelming air superiority; and, consequently, the air forces strongly recommended that there was no necessity of anti-aircraft gunfire in the assault area, that the air cover could defeat any air attack within enemy capabilities.

The naval viewpoint on the subject of minimum altitude was based on an analysis of weather conditions. Realizing the necessity of having a minimum altitude low enough to insure effectiveness of the bombing effort, the visibility conditions were thoroughly considered. A study of Naval Planning Memorandum No. 15, Astronomical Tables and Meteorological Information, showed that from thermodynamic considerations, morning visibility would be poor, less than two miles, in the assault area on 12% of the mornings, or one out of eight days. At Nice, visibilities of less than 2 miles were never observed in a period of nine years. Low overcast was to be expected only infrequently. Ceilings were expected to be generally above 5,000 feet. It was considered, therefore, that the problem of aircraft being required to fly low to find their target area was not as pressing as in Northern France where the condition of dense low clouds was prevalent.

A morning haze in the assault area was expected, but by 0800, H-hour, at this time of year, it would begin to lift. Thus, from a minimum visibility of two miles, or about 10,000 feet on 12% of the days, the visibility by the time the troops were ashore should be adequate and obviate the necessity of flying close to our naval forces.

The naval viewpoint also considered that prevention by our supporting aircraft of all enemy air attacks was most probably impracticable of achievement, even with overwhelming air superiority. It was also considered that unnecessarily severe restrictions on AA gunfire would have an adverse psychological effect on the ship's crews manning the guns and the commanding officers charged with the responsibility of defending their ships.

Therefore, from a gunnery standpoint, AA rules for the invasion of Southern France permitted more latitude to the gunners than the rules for the Normandy invasion did. For example, in Normandy, the ceiling below which it was permitted to fire at any aircraft not recognized as friendly was 1,000 feet, in Southern France it was 3,000 feet.

The rules for the operation are briefly summarized:

(a) On D-Day (from 0000 to 2130).

    A special belt was created, extending between two lines parallel to the coast, one 5,000 yards to seaward and the second 12,000 yards to seaward. Within this belt all allied aircraft were required to fly above 5,000 feet, and anti-aircraft guns were free to fire on any aircraft not recognized as friendly that flew below 3,000 feet. To shoreward of this belt allied aircraft were free to fly at any altitude. To seaward of this belt allied aircraft were to conform to the normal Mediterranean rules when in the vicinity of ships at sea. Ships and craft outside the special belt were not to fire at any aircraft unless it was recognized as hostile or committed a hostile act.

(b) On D + 1 and subsequent days (from 0550 to 2130).

    A special belt was created, extending between two lines parallel to the coast, one 12,000 yards to seaward and one 3,000 yards inland and extending along the coast between the points where the bombline cut the coast. Within this belt both anti-aircraft batteries aboard ship and anti-aircraft artillery ashore were free to fire at any aircraft not recognized as friendly that flew below 3,000 feet, and were prohibited from firing at aircraft flying above 3,000 feet unless recognized as hostile, or, observed to have committed a hostile act. Within this belt allied aircraft were to fly above 5,000 feet.

(c) At night (from 2130 to 0550).

    An area was created whose seaward limit was 12,000 yards from the coast, and whose landward limit was 12,000 yards inland from the coast, and extending 12,000 yards outward from any beach activity. This area became an Inner Artillery Zone within which the normal theater rules for an I.A.Z. governed.

(d) At all times, both day and night, minor warships, merchant ships, and craft were totally prohibited from engaging any aircraft within 12,000 yards of the assault coast unless directly attacked with torpedoes, bombs, or by fighter aircraft.

These rules were predicated upon an overwhelming allied air superiority, and upon the ability of the Air Force to keep enemy aircraft away from the assault area during daylight. There were no known incidents of allied aircraft being fired upon by allied ships or craft. During dusk, however, several such incidents did occur. This was at a time when the rules were about to change, and the only period of the day when enemy aircraft succeeded in penetrating into the assault area. As in the past, the principal offenders were over anxious gunners on smaller ships and craft. Visibility conditions were about as expected except that the morning haze was localized by the wind, which condition completely obscured some small portions of the ground from the pilots for short periods. The minimum altitude of 3,000 feet was never an obstacle to efficient air support.

It is believed that the anti-aircraft gunnery rules are still too complex. So many participating commands are interested in establishing the rules that the final wording is needlessly detailed. In the invasion of Southern France the different anti-aircraft defense areas were too small. Any radical change in rules between vague geographic areas or between different periods of the day lead to confusion. Aircraft and ships alike moved from an area with one set of rules to an area with another set without realizing it. In the final analysis early and continuous emphasis on aircraft recognition and an early appreciation by pilots that they ought to fly outside range of friendly ship-borne guns are the fundamentals of successful control of anti-aircraft gunfire.

ANTI-AIRCRAFT GUNNERY

There was insufficient anti-aircraft activity to provide a good analysis of the performance of anti-aircraft batteries. The German Air Force appeared only at dusk during the first few evenings of the assault and attacked with glider and anti-personnel bombs. The LST 282 was struck by a glider bomb on the evening of D-Day and anti-personnel bombs, dropped haphazardly through a smoke cover, resulted in casualties in the force flagship on the evening of D + 3.

Two enemy aircraft are known to have been destroyed by anti-aircraft guns. Using full radar control, USS Champlin shot down a JU-88 with the first salvo. USS Plunkett also scored a hit on a JU-88 which caused the aircraft to crash. There are no reports of the use of Mark 32 fuzed projectiles.

The education of 40 mm and 20 mm gunners is not yet completed. Automatic weapons still persist in opening fire at targets well beyond their effective range. Constant emphasis of this subject has somewhat improved the fire discipline of automatic weapons, but it still required constant vigilance on the part of experienced personnel to prevent those with little or no battle experience from firing at targets well beyond range of the weapons.

Many ships still fail to appreciate the accuracy of radar and continue to open fire using rangefinder ranges. Visual range finding during a twilight period is known to be unreliable. Use of radar must be stressed and anti-aircraft director personnel must be well drilled in its use. The dusk period, when last light patrols are still in the assault area, and night fighters are arriving, is the critical time for gunnery action.

The performance of ordnance anti-aircraft equipment was most gratifying. Casualties were almost non-existent.

AIRCRAFT RECOGNITION

There is still room for improvement in aircraft recognition. On one occasion, P-38s, the most distinctive American fighter, were fired upon by allied ships. It is axiomatic that efficient aircraft recognition will breed good fire discipline.

Section 5.5

SMOKE PLAN AND EXECUTION

As a result of experience in the Salerno and Anzio landings where the effective use of smoke contributed materially to the defense of the assault forces against enemy air attack, the value of adequate smoke cover was emphasized to those charged with the preparation of smoke plans for the operation against the southern coast of France. It was recognized that large transport areas must be covered quickly and detailed plans prepared by the Attack Force Commanders provide for such cover.

All available types of smoke producing apparatus were to be used. Worthy of special mention is the British LCM smoker. This craft mounts an aircraft engine and propeller which efficiently spreads a cloud of chlorosulfonic acid smoke emitted from a large tank carried in the well of the LCM. Seven of these craft were available with three specially fitted British LCTs for tenders. Light weight Besler smoke generators (Model 374) were available for mounting in LCVPs, LCCs, and other small craft. The heavy Besler generator, Model 317, was mounted in LSTs, SCs, and in new LCI(L)s. Two destroyers were equipped with Model 374 Besler generators.

During the planning stage it was emphasized that smoke must be emitted initially from all ships and craft equipped to make smoke, regardless of wind direction. This action is necessary to obtain a quick smoke cover of the transport area and in addition, produces a large screen which extends to leeward of the actual area to be covered. The result is that only the approximate location of shipping can be determined from the air. Trials with fog oil and chemical smoke in a force 1 breeze showed that both types had good persistency under usual Mediterranean aerological conditions and that chemical smoke tended to rise faster than smoke made by fog oil. Accordingly, plans were made to employ both chemical and fog oil smoke in order to produce an effective screen.

Each beach battalion was provided with eight Besler Model 317 smoke generators and fog oil for covering the beaches and to assist smoke apparatus afloat when the wind was off-shore. Each liberty ship in the first convoys carried 102 M-1 smoke pots and 102 M-4 smoke floats. Prior to departure from the assault area, each ship delivered 20 M-4 smoke floats to the Beachmaster. A reserve supply of chemical smoke was thus built up at each beach.

Detailed plans made by Attack Force Commanders provided for expeditious smoke cover of each transport area by employing in each area British LCM smokers, SCs, LCCs, and LCVPs equipped with Besler generators, augmented by LCVPs, LCSs, and other craft carrying smoke pots and floats. Plans provided for smoke patrols to windward with other smoke craft in the transport areas ready to smoke on sound signal. The British LCM smokers were controlled by radio, either from LCT tender or Attack Force flagships. In some cases, the control of smoke was difficult. Beach Battalion smoke did not function as well as anticipated. Control of smoke was difficult due, primarily, to inadequate lateral communications along the beach, and to the fact that beaches were heavily mined in many localities. Whistle signals for control of smoke should be paralleled by radio. This holds for LCVPs, LCCs, and other small craft as well as for the British LCM smoker whose airplane engine makes communication by radio imperative.

Minesweepers working in the Gulf of Frejus were handicapped by smoke laid at dawn. Land marks were obscured thus decreasing the accuracy of the narrow channel sweeps. Cases of smoke interference with unloading were reported. Such interference must be expected and accepted if the decision is made to cover transport and beach areas with smoke.

Due to the inactivity of the German Air Force, the use of smoke was generally limited to routine dawn and dusk coverages. Twenty minutes were normally required to produce an effective smoke cover of a transport area. A few daylight screens were initiated upon the receipt of red alerts, but these alerts were short lived.

During the siege of the defenses of Toulon, where enemy coastal batteries were a grave threat to fire support ships, screening destroyers provided effective smoke cover for battleships and cruisers engaged in bombardment missions.

Section 5.6

AMMUNITION AND SMOKE SUPPLY AND EXPENDITURES

The allocation of heavy cruisers and battleships as fire support ships for the operation required that there be assembled in the theater reserve stocks of 8", 12", and 14" ammunition. In previous Mediterranean operations, no US ship had mounted guns larger than 6". Consequently, there did exist considerable reserve stocks of US Navy ammunition, 6" and below, in the theater. The scale of the proposed operation required that these, also, be increased. During the early months of 1944, Commander in Chief, United States Fleet, was requested to provide reserve ammunition as follows: For BBs - 1 fill HC, 1/2 fill AP; for CAs - 2 fills HC, 1/2 fill AP; for CLs - 3 fills HC, 1/2 fill AP. The problem was further complicated by the scarcity of ammunition for the French OBB, cruisers, and destroyers that were to be assigned. A program was underway in the United States to manufacture and deliver to North Africa, powder and projectiles for the French ships, but the delivery dates promised were too close to the planned target date to permit any reliance being placed on availability. Only 191 rounds of HC and 1970 rounds of AP existed for the French OBB Lorraine. None was being manufactured in the United States. It was determined that US Army 155 mm HE projectiles could be fired from the French 155 mm naval gun. 152 mm ammunition was being manufactured in the United States, and 8000 rounds were on order. There were some reserves in the theater for British ships, and additional quantities were to be sent from the United Kingdom.

When it was determined that the operation against Southern France would be delayed until some time after the invasion of Northern France, reserves of US Navy ammunition, 8" and larger, were sent to the United Kingdom from the United States. Such ammunition as remained after the completion of the channel operation would become available for the operation against Southern France. Planning was accordingly handicapped by uncertainty as to the quantity of naval gunfire that could be spared for pre-H-hour bombardment and how much must be retained for the follow-up phases. Some uneasiness was experienced as intelligence continued to report increased strengthening of the coast defenses of Southern France. In June, the following major caliber ammunition reserves were allocated to the theater, in addition to whatever might have remained at the end of the Northern France operation:

```
 500  -  14" HC
 160  -  12" HC
 140  -  12" AP
1000  -   8" HC
1000  -   8" AP
```

USS Mount Baker arrived with ammunition direct from the United States in July, and USS Nitro arrived in early August with the remnants from the Northern France operation.

A summary of the reserve ammunition in the theater on D-day follows:

US Navy

```
14" AP -   373            6"/47 AP   -     5,130
14" HC -     0‡           6"/47 HC   -    23,500
12" AP -    82            5"/38 AAC  - 2,050,000
12" HC -   302            5"/38 Com  -     2,975
 8" AP - 4,032            5"/38 Ill. -     1,760
 8" HC - 3,300            5"/38 WP   -         0‡‡
```

- 298 -

‡ Earlier reserves of 14" HC required to replenish USS Texas and USS Nevada.

‡‡ All reserves of 5"/38 WP used to increase destroyer allowance to at least 50 rounds each.

Royal Navy

```
15"   HC  -    500
15"   APC -    460
 6"   HE  - 13,200
 5.25" HE - 34,000
```

French Navy

```
340 mm AP  - 1,970      152 mm HE  -     0
340 mm HE  -   191      138 mm HE  - 6,000
155 mm AP  - 1,500      138 mm AP  -   800
155 mm HE  - 1,500      130 mm HE  - 2,640
152 mm AP  - 2,626       90 mm     - 9,010
```

Shore stocks of US Navy ammunition were at Naval Operating Base, Oran; Advanced Amphibious Training Base, Bizerte; and Naval Operating Base, Palermo. Principal stocks of British ammunition were at Malta and Naples, while nearly all of the French ammunition had been moved to Ajaccio, Corsica, in July. It was not considered prudent to base either USS Nitro or USS Mount Baker in Corsican ports until it had been definitely determined that German air opposition would be negligible. Yet, it was imperative that the US and British reserve ammunition be closer to the assault area than any of the above mentioned ports. Commander in Chief, Mediterranean made available four A.S.I.S. (Ammunition Stores Issuing Ships) Empire Spinney, Empire Gat, Procris, and Fendris, to carry and issue US Navy ammunition from Corsican ports. (An A.S.I.S. is a small, coaster type ship of about 700 tons with about 9 knots speed, ideally suited for this purpose.) British Navy ammunition reserves were carried to Corsican ports in four additional A.S.I.S., Pacheco, Woodlark, Sutherland, and Brittany Coast. Such French naval ammunition reserves as were not already ashore in Ajaccio were in FS Barfleur, an armed merchant ship.

All reserves of US Navy ammunition, 8" and larger, were divided equally between USS Mount Baker and USS Nitro, the former initially based in Oran and the latter initially in Algiers. Reserves of 6" and smaller, depth charges, 40 mm and 20 mm were in the A.S.I.S., while a reserve of aviation bombs and machine gun ammunition was carried in two of the A.S.I.S. On D-day, Procris, Fendris, Pacheco, Sutherland, and Barfleur were in Propriano, while the remainder were in Maddalena.

Small stocks of 40 mm and 20 mm were ashore in Ajaccio, Calvi, and Ile Rousse for landing craft of all services.

Ammunition expenditure by calibers is shown in diagram XXIV. Because the movement of the army to the west was so rapid, with the consequent capture of the coastal defense batteries and field guns, the expenditure of ammunition was well within the limits of the available supply.

Because the need for fighter cover and spotting missions decreased, carrier based fighters were assigned armed reconnaissance and fighter-bomber tasks. The original plan did not visualize heavy bomb and rocket expenditures, but as carrier based aircraft cooperated with the XII Tactical Air Command in the pursuit of the enemy and destruction of his lines of transportation and supply, the initial supply of bombs and rockets proved inadequate. Additional reserves were obtained from British ships. Rockets were most effectively employed in attacking motor and rail transport.

The expenditures of ammunition for the US carriers were as follows:

USS Tulagi

```
     55 - 350 lb. depth bombs
     16 - 100 lb. G.P. bombs
     64 - 500 lb. G.P. bombs
     11 - 1000 lb. G.P. bombs
     17 - 500 lb. British bombs
     28 - 250 lb. British bombs
    200 - Rockets, Mark 7 with H.E. heads
    160 - Rockets, British, with H.E. heads
     16 - Rockets, British, with A.P. heads
193,000 - Rounds .50 caliber.
```

USS Kasaan Bay

```
      9 - 100 lb. G.P. bombs
     11 - 250 lb. G.P. bombs
     67 - 350 lb. G.P. bombs
     98 - 500 lb. G.P. bombs
     18 - 1000 lb. G.P. bombs
136,775 - Rounds .50 caliber.
```

Reserve smoke materials were more than adequate for the operation. First line reserves of all types of smoke materials (less acid smoke mixture) were carried in LST mother ships in the assault area. Reserves of chlorosulfonic acid smoke for the British LCM smokers were stored in three British LCT smoke tenders. Secondary reserves were located at Ajaccio, Naples, Palermo, Bizerte, and Oran.

The following smoke materials and equipment were available for the operation:

Type of Apparatus or Material	Quantity
LCM Smokers, British	7
Besler Smoke Generator Type 374	61
Todd Smoke Generator	9
Chlorosulfonic Acid for LCM Smokers	2,000 tons
FS Smoke Mixture	640 (55 gal. drums)
FM Smoke Mixture	500 (55 gal. drums)
Fog Oil	9,376 (55 gal. drums)
M-1 Smoke Pots	75,617
M-4 Floating Smoke Pots	20,179
Mk.3 Smoke Pots	6,578
Mk.2 Smoke Floats	3,428
Mk.3 No. 24 British Smoke Pots	20,000
Mk.6 British Smoke Floats	300

Because of slight enemy air activity and the early capture of the majority of coast defense batteries, smoke expenditures were light.

Section 5.7

CHEMICAL DEFENSE

Based upon the assumption that the enemy was capable of initiating chemical warfare, but most probably would not resort to it, the following precautionary protective measures were taken:

(a) For naval personnel landing on the beaches:

  (1) Each individual to carry a gas mask (army lightweight service mask M3-10A16 or British equivalent) with the following additional equipment in the gas mask carrier:

   (a) Individual protective cover (cellophane cape).
   (b) 2 pair eyeshields.
   (c) One tube BAL and one tube of S461 or S330 ointment.

  (2) A complete suit of protective clothing to be made available to each individual. This clothing not to be worn or carried, but to be landed as soon as practicable after the assault and kept readily available.

(b) For naval personnel embarked in craft that would beach:

  (1) Each individual to carry the gas mask and carrier containing the items listed above.

  (2) A complete protective clothing outfit for each crew member to be carried in each craft that would beach. This clothing not to be worn but kept readily available.

(c) For ships and craft that would not beach:

  (1) Gas masks and protective clothing to be distributed to accessible locations throughout the ship or craft.

Section 5.8

NAVAL COMBAT DEMOLITION UNITS

A total of 16 Naval Combat Demolition Units were available for the operation by June. Intelligence reports continued to indicate that beach and underwater obstacles were being strengthened in the target area, and, that by mid-August, they would probably be most formidable. Additional Naval Combat Demolition Units were requested and sent from the United Kingdom. As a result, a total of 41 Naval Combat Demolition Units were available for the assault.

It was known from photographic reconnaissance that underwater obstacles were in place, or were in the process of being placed before the beaches in Baie de Cavalaire, Baie de Pampelonne, and Golfe de Frejus. Those in Cavalaire and Frejus were known to be concrete tetrahedra, while many more were seen on dry land, apparently waiting to be laid. A heavy net was known to lie across the entrance to Rade d'Agay, and this would have to be removed before Yellow Camel beach could be used. Beaches in the Delta sector were apparently free of underwater obstacles.

In regard to underwater obstacles, great concern was felt in the planning stages, for there appeared to be no tried and tested method for breaching them. Few lessons could be learned from the invasion of Northern France because of the dissimilar conditions. The tidal range in the English channel was great and obstacles would be exposed at low water. In the Mediterranean, the tidal range was negligible, and the enemy's problem of placing formidable obstacles was simplified.

A beach obstacle board was appointed with members from both the US Eighth Fleet and Seventh Army. A beach, heavily defended by concrete tetrahedra, jetted rails, horned scullies, and Belgian element "C", was constructed in Salerno Bay for training and experiment. Explosive boats and other explosive means developed at Fort Pierce, Florida, were tried. None of these promised a complete solution. Even though a channel was created through the obstacles by explosive boats, "reddy fox", or other means, there still remained the problem of buoying the channel so that the assault boat could find it. Furthermore, to clear a sufficient beach frontage to handle the assault waves without undue bunching of the boats would require a great number of explosive boats.

The target date drew near without a solution having been reached. By elimination of various proposed methods, it became evident that:

(1) Explosive boats could be used, but they would clear only isolated channels, if any, and few of the assault boats would find the channels;

(2) Some assault boats could, from intelligence reports, pass between obstacles, and losses must be accepted in order to place large numbers of troops upon the beaches;

(3) Final reliance must be placed upon the Naval Combat Demolition Units to clear channels for the later waves and the larger landing craft by the use of hand-placed charges.

Each Combat Demolition Unit consisted of one officer and five navy enlisted men. Each unit was augmented by five US Army enlisted engineers.

Additional duties were assigned to certain of the Naval Combat Demolition Units to operate the rocket LCMs (Woofus) and the explosive boats.

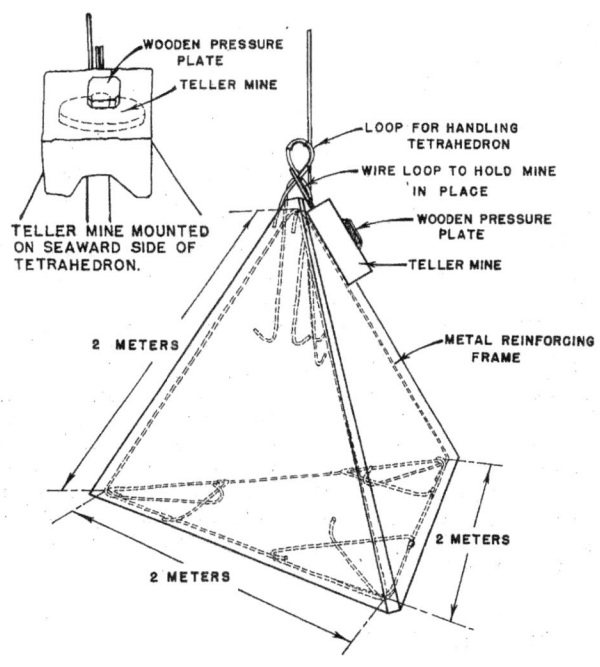

SOLID CONCRETE TETRAHEDRON (Underwater Obstacle) AND ATTACHED TELLER MINE.

FIGURE 15

Each unit landing on the beach had one LCVP with a crew of four experienced small boat men. In addition, the control boats for the explosive boats were loaded with hand-placed charges, and, after the completion of their primary duties, they became available to assist the Naval Combat Demolition Units on the beaches. Among the equipment carried in the Naval Combat Demolition Units' LCVPs were 2,000 pounds of tetratol prepared in 20 lb. packs, shallow water diving gear, two rubber boats, rations, and water. Lift of Naval Combat Demolition Units' boats to the assault area was made in LST davits and in LSDs. In accordance with the plan of attack, the first waves passed through the obstacles without attempting to find channels made by the explosive boats, and the Naval Combat Demolition Units landed at H + 10 to begin hand-clearance of the underwater obstacles.

A brief resume of clearance by beaches follows:

Baie de Cavalaire (Alpha Red)

LCVPs with Naval Combat Demolition Units landed on the beach at H + 10 minutes. In the meantime, the explosive boat control boats recovered other Naval Combat Demolition Unit personnel from the LCM(R)s, and with Reddy Foxes in tow, stood by on call to assist in the hand removal of obstacles. A total of 8 officers and 80 men (one-half US Army engineer personnel) were thus available. It was estimated that they could clear about 150 yards of obstacles per hour. The Reddy Fox was to be used for post assault clearance of obstacles if it was required. It was found that the obstacles extended for about 2,000 yards along the beach. The obstacles were concrete tetrahedra, as expected, and the majority of them were mined. A sketch of this obstacle is shown. They were in a single row, placed about 15 feet apart. They were about 6 1/2 feet on a side, about 5 1/2 feet high, reinforced with 1/2" steel rods. The depth of water was about five or six feet, so that the tops were just about at the surface. A tellermine, encased in concrete with a 4" X 4" wooden board covering the pressure plate, was found on almost every obstacle. To clear, two twenty pound packs of tetratol were placed on each obstacle, hung saddle fashion from the top. The Naval Combat Demolition Units cleared about 200 yards per hour, and by the evening of D-Day the beach was practically cleared.

Baie de Pampelonne (Alpha Yellow)

Eight officers and 80 men (one-half US Army engineers) were available to clear obstacles on this beach. It was estimated that they could clear about 150 yards of obstacles per hour. They also landed at H+10 minutes, and began clearance. The obstacles on this beach were wooden piling, apparently jetted in, 15 to 20 feet apart, and in two rows about 20 to 25 feet apart. The pilings were 12-14" in diameter, and many had been sawed off so that the tops were about 2' below the surface of the water. No mention is made in any reports of mines being found on these pilings, although it had been anticipated that they would be found. 3,400 yards of obstacles were removed D-Day, at a rate of about 350 yards per hour. The removal technique was the same as with the tetrahedra. It was noted that LCVPs, LCMs, and LCTs were able to push over these obstacles with little or no damage to the boats.

Cap Drammont (Camel Green)

Five Naval Combat Demolition Units followed the second wave in the assault. No obstacles were found.

Rade d'Agay (Camel Yellow)

Two Naval Combat Demolition Units had been held in reserve. At 1600 on D day, upon orders, they proceeded to Rade d'Agay to remove the net from across the entrance. From seven to forty pounds of tetratol were used on each float, thus permitting the net to sink. This operation was completed in approximately four hours.

Golfe de Frejus (Camel Red)

At 1200 D+1, Naval Combat Demolition Units were ordered to begin removal of underwater obstacles, working from the seaplane jetty at the southwest end of the beach towards the northeast. The obstacles were concrete tetrahedra about six feet high with three foot sides for a base, set in 7 to 9 feet of water. On the extreme northeast for about 400 yards they were placed in two rows and in some scattered sections in three rows. On the extreme southwest they were very thickly placed, some with bases touching, and averaging about four feet apart. On the southwest end of the beach no obstacles were found mined, but on the northeast half, all were mined. The mines were secured with wires to the seaward side, some in a one foot cubical container but the majority in a rectangular cement shell about one foot square by two feet long Each possessed a cylindrical wooden contact maker about four inches in diameter and four inches in height. Two twenty pound tetratol packs were place on each pyramid about two-thirds of the way from the top with primacord leads to a trunk line. They were fired electrically in segments of about 400 yards. About 16 hours were required in order to remove all obstacles from the beach.

Naval Combat Demolition Unit officers unanimously recommended that the size of the unit be increased to ten men. Prompt clearance of all underwater obstacles is imperative in order that the heavier landing craft may beach with army equipment. A need was felt for an amphibious vehicle that could be used for the transportation of explosives and equipment up and down the beach. Lateral communications on the beach between Naval Combat Demolition Units were found wanting, particularly when attempting to coordinate clearance detonations.

Section 5.9

APEX BOATS & REDDY FOX (DEMOLITION OUTFIT MARK 119)

Apex boats (remotely controlled LCVPs carrying 8,000 pounds of high explosive) performed with varying degrees of reliability, and results obtained varied, accordingly, from good to worse than none.

Tests conducted on the experimental beach in Salerno Bay had shown that the boat could and would clear the proposed area of all obstacles if properly placed and sunk. The chances seemed only fair that this could be done. With the best of visibility conditions it was difficult to guide the boat to the proper section of the beach and scuttle it before it had forced its way through the obstacles and driven onto the beach. With reduced visibility this would become almost impossible. Radar control tests from LCC indicated that the boat could be guided to the proper section of the beach with reasonable accuracy, but that the proper point for scuttling could not be determined with sufficient accuracy. Further attempts were made to devise a means of clearing a channel wider than that given by the detonation of one boat, both, by separately placing Apex boats at properly spaced intervals along the beach, and by using parasite boats. In the parasite method, either two or four LCVPs were guided by the Apex boat in the center, the Apex towing and the LCVP motors running at slightly slower speed and with rudders set in a direction to cause the LCVPs to turn away from the Apex in the center. This resulted in a V formation of three or five explosive loaded boats upon which a reasonable degree of control could be exercised. Primacord and electric detonation circuits were rigged from the Apex to the parasites. The method gave considerable promise, but the extensive rigging required in the assault area and the increased probability of malfunctioning due to additional complications caused it to be discarded.

Fifty-four Apex boats and twenty-seven control boats were available for the operation. Technical personnel were furnished by the Bureau of Ships to instruct crews and provide maintenance of technical equipment. Naval Combat Demolition Units were assigned to operate the Apex in combat. Apex boats and control boats were lifted to the assault area in LST davits and in LSDs.

A resume of performance follows:

Alpha Sector

Baie de Cavalaire (Alpha Red)

Nine Apex were detonated on the beach, three of them at H - 50 minutes, three at H - 45 minutes, and three at H - 40 minutes. The majority of the boats detonated on the center and left sections of the beach. Improvised mechanical stops had been devised for these Apex, consisting of two 2 1/2" X 10" planks bolted on each side of the boat. Special scuttling charges were fitted to these crutches to blow them off when the Apex scuttling charge was fired, allowing the boat to sink. Time for examination of results did not exist, for the Naval Combat Demolition Units landed at H + 10 minutes to complete the removal of the underwater obstacles. It does seem likely, however, that these Apexes were most effective in destroying mines on the obstacles within a large radius, and, also, in destroying a great number of shallow water and land mines. This is evidenced by the fact that not a single landing craft was damaged by mines on the left and center sections of the beach where the Apexes detonated. On the right hand part of the beach, where no Apex detonated, seven LCVPs were destroyed, three LCI(L)s and one LCT were damaged by mines while beaching.

Baie de Pampelonne (Alpha Yellow)

Nine Apexes were sent against the beaches in waves of three, prior to H-Hour. Six functioned as designed. One ran through the obstacles, broached on the beach, and did not detonate. The presence of 8,000 pounds of high explosive on the beach gave the assault commander considerable concern, but he reasoned that since concentrated bombing, naval gunfire, and detonation of the other Apexes in the immediate vicinity had not set it off, that it was probably safe. It was rendered safe by a Naval Combat Demolition Unit after the assault, and, later was towed to safe anchorage by the salvage unit. A second Apex sank in ten feet of water and did not detonate. On D + 2, as a shallow-water mine sweep was passing the general vicinity, the Apex detonated. At the time, an LCC was moored to an LST pontoon causeway about 75 yards away. This LCC was put out of action completely, the engine being torn loose from the bed plate and heavy structural damage incurred. The third Apex apparently made a 180° change of course during the approach and stood out to sea. It was not observed by the control boat because of the haze and dust from aerial bombing. The control boat thought it had beached, and gave the detonating signal. At the time, the Apex was about fifteen or twenty feet off the bow of USS SC 1029 which was acting as a reference vessel. The resultant detonation severely damaged the SC and critically wounded four men.

No opportunity existed to examine the effect of the Apex that functioned properly, as the Naval Combat Demolition Units began an immediate clearance of underwater obstacles with hand-placed charges.

Delta Sector

Baie de Bougnon (Delta Red, Green, Yellow, and Blue Beaches)

The task force commander cancelled the use of Apex boats on the basis of intelligence reports that no underwater obstacles existed. None were found.

Camel Sector

Golfe de Frejus (Camel Red)

Twelve Apex boats were to be used against this beach. It was, by far, the most formidable beach to be assaulted. A discussion of obstacles appears in Section 5.8, Part II, Naval Combat Demolition Units. The time for assault was set at H + 6 hours. Two Apexes in the first wave went out of control. One of these was boarded and defused after a ten minute effort to regain control. The second Apex was sunk by gunfire from USS Ordronaux when it headed for the assault waves, out of control.

In subsequent waves, two more went out of control. One of these was boarded and defused. The other one was last seen circling close to the beach.

Five Apexes hit the beach as directed. Of these, two did not detonate but were destroyed where they were found by hand-placed charges the next day after the beach had been taken by assault from the shoreward side.

Two Apexes were not launched.

An inspection of the beach on D + 1 by Naval Combat Demolition Units failed to disclose any gaps in the underwater obstacles or craters. The automatic buoy drop for marking channels had functioned in only one case.

Technical recommendations have been made to Bureau of Ships in separate correspondence. These boats should have distinctive markings so that other craft and ships can avoid them if they go out of control.

The Apex has two definite disadvantages:

(1) The Apex may run wild or detonate prematurely and destroy own craft and ships;

(2) It may not detonate after reaching the beach, thereby creating a hazard that may deny full use of the beach. Despite the somewhat limited success in this operation, the continued use of Apexes is recommended. In the meantime, vigorous steps must be taken to increase their reliability and positiveness of control.

It was not planned to use any Reddy Fox in the pre-H-Hour clearance of obstacles. However, several were to be taken in tow by landing craft which would lie to off the beaches. If Naval Combat Demolition Units required them for hand-placing to remove obstacles, they would be called in. Many of the Reddy Fox sank while in tow. None were used as planned because of the additional time required to place them, the possibility of creating an undesirable sand bar, and the danger of striking mines on underwater obstacles while moving them into position.

Section 5.10

ROCKET CRAFT - LCT(R), LCM(R), LCS(S)

LCT(R)s are British craft, one type mounting about 800 five inch rockets and another type mounting about 1,000. It is possible to carry one reload aboard, although approximately four to five hours should be allowed for refilling the launchers. LCT(R)s carry radar and are thus not dependent upon visibility conditions to position themselves for firing. The range of the rocket is fixed at 3,500 yards. Ninety seconds is required to launch the entire load. Either high explosive or FS rockets are available. Thirty of these craft were used in the operation, distributed as follows:

ALPHA

Red Beach 6; Yellow Beach 4.

DELTA

Red Beach 2; Green Beach 1; Yellow Beach 1; Blue Beach 2.

CAMEL

Red Beach 6; Green Beach 6; Blue Beach 2.

Fourteen of the craft were manned by US Navy personnel, and sixteen by British.

The reserve of rockets available permitted putting from 50% to 100% of a reload in each LCT(R). Inasmuch as the Camel Red Beach assault was scheduled for H + 6 hours the majority of the LCT(R)s from other beaches were to proceed to the Golfe de Frejus immediately after discharging their first load. They were to load en route and stand by for the assault on this beach. When the assault on Camel Red Beach was cancelled, there were seventeen LCT(R)s ready to launch their rockets when the assault waves started in.

The LCT(R)s fired at area targets, beginning at H - 10 minutes. It was necessary for them to fire over the first wave. In almost every case numerous shorts, caused by collision of the rockets, landed around the boats of the first wave. Some damage was caused, the full extent is not known but at least one LCM(R) was hit.

Targets assigned LCT(R)s should, if possible, be so situated that they will not be required to fire over the landing waves and accompanying craft. The destructive effect of rocket fire is so great that it should not be dispensed with on a defended beach.

Twenty one LCM(R)s (Woofus) were to be used. These were operated by Naval Combat Demolition Unit personnel. An LCM(R) carries 120 7.2" demolition rockets and has a range of about 300 yards. The range can be increased slightly by using a larger rocket motor, but the increased dispersion nullifies, to a great degree, the ability of the weapon to clear a path through barbed wire and land mines. The "Woofus" were distributed as follows:

ALPHA

Red Beach 7; Yellow Beach 7.

DELTA

Red Beach 2; Green Beach 1; Yellow Beach 2; Blue Beach 2. The LCM(R)s for the Delta Beaches Yellow and Blue arrived from the LSD too late to be used in the assault.

Performance was excellent. They deployed just ahead of the first wave and fired at H - 2 minutes.

The range of the "Woofus" should be increased by about 100 yards to protect personnel from fragments. This should not be done, however, at the expense of the small patterns that the weapon now possesses.

LCS(S)s fired at targets of opportunity, beginning at H - 5 minutes. They carried a reload of smoke rockets which were used with good results.

Section 5.11

MINE AND BOMB DISPOSAL

The seven bomb disposal units and five mine disposal units available for the operation were attached temporarily to Task Force Commanders as follows:

CTF 84	2 Bomb Disposal Units	1 Mine Disposal Unit
CTF 85	1 Bomb Disposal Unit	1 Mine Disposal Unit
CTF 86	1 Bomb Disposal Unit	1 Mine Disposal Unit
CTF 87	2 Bomb Disposal Units	1 Mine Disposal Unit
CTG 80.8	1 Bomb Disposal Unit	
Commander Escort Sweeper Group		1 Mine Disposal Unit

Each unit was equipped with transportation and a minimum of gear, and the mine disposal units carried no diving equipment during the assault phase. Upon completion of duty with the Task Force or Group Commander, each disposal unit reported to Mobile Explosives Investigation Unit which on D+26 had established headquarters at Marseille.

Few enemy bombs were dropped. Guided missile attacks were made against shipping, and only anti-personnel bombs were employed by the enemy air force in haphazard attacks at dusk. Bomb disposal personnel were not called upon to deal with any enemy bombs but were employed ashore in disposing of a few allied bombs and rockets, and enemy demolition charges and booby traps.

The Mine Disposal Units were extensively used in disposing of the many enemy mines encountered in the ports of Southern France. The enemy was particularly successful in placing mines where sweeping was most difficult and troublesome. The Mine Disposal Units rendered invaluable service in the opening of Port de Bouc, Marseille, Toulon, Cannes, and Nice.

The following ordnance was disposed of or rendered safe by disposal units:

- 14 bombs
- 151 sea mines
- 102 prepared and placed demolitions
- 169 projectiles and rockets
- 175 land mines
- 119 grenades
- 197 pieces miscellaneous enemy ammunition
- 1 German human torpedo
- 16 tons of stored enemy explosive

Thirty-two diving operations were completed.

COMMENTS

With the exception of the German human torpedo, there was little of ordnance intelligence interest recovered during the operation.

The immediate availability of bomb and mine disposal personnel during an amphibious operation is necessary in order to deal with fouled mines, unexploded bombs, and to assist naval personnel ashore in the removal of enemy demolition charges and booby traps in buildings and areas under naval control.

At least one vehicle per disposal unit should be supplied for the assault phase as transportation is often required for the safe removal of explosives.

Section 5.12

LIGHT INDICATOR NET PLAN

The plan anticipated that it would be necessary to use the Rade d'Hyeres as a sheltered anchorage for supply ships unloading over the beaches until such time as the ports of Marseille and Toulon were opened. To provide protection from submarine attack, preparations were made to enclose the Rade d'Hyeres, except at its eastern end, with a Light Indicator Net. The net was to be laid in the passes between Levant Island - Port Cros Island, Port Cros Island - Porquerolles Island, and Porquerolles Island - Cape Esterel. A total length of net of 6.6 miles was required (see diagram I).

The net was brailed and stopped to the contour of the bottom, and divided into three lengths, corresponding to the three passes in which the net was to be laid. The complete net was placed in two LCM(3)s at Oran. The LCM(3)s were lifted to Ajaccio in LSDs some time prior to the operation. It was intended to further lift the two LCM(3)s to the assault area in an LSD when they were required.

A heavy mine field was found to exist between Port Cros and Porquerolles which made the laying the net in this pass impracticable and unnecessary. Moreover, as a result of the early fall of Toulon and Marseille, it was decided not to use Rade d'Hyeres as a merchant ship anchorage. Consequently, the Light Indicator Net was never laid.

Chapter 6

MATERIAL AND LOGISTICS

Section 6.1

PLANNING, PREPARATION AND TRAINING PERIOD

Planning commenced on 28 December 1943 and the Logistics Annex to NCWTF's Operation Plan 4-44 was completed on 22 July 1944. Throughout this period it was necessary to maintain close liaison with commands of the Royal Navy and the French Navy to insure adequate logistic support for all allied navy ships and craft scheduled to be employed in the invasion of Southern France. The amphibious landing in the Anzio-Nettuno area north of Naples, Italy, on 22 January 1944; the subsequent long period of build-up and maintenance for the US Fifth Army; the frequent withdrawal and subsequent reassignment of ships and craft to the US Eighth Fleet; the late arrival of ships released from forces taking part in the invasion of Northern France; and the late date on which the final D-Day and scale of the assault was promulgated - all tended to increase the problems inherent in readying for action so large a force.

The following table supplements the foregoing remarks and is indicative of the constantly changing situation during the planning, preparation and training period:

	LST		LCI(L)		LCT	
	Withdrawals	Assignments	Withdrawals	Assignments	Withdrawals	Assignments
OCTOBER 1943	10	-	24	-	10	-
NOVEMBER	36	-	-	-	32	-
JANUARY 1944	20	10	-	-	4	1
FEBRUARY	2	-	-	-	1	-
APRIL	23	26	30	-	19	26
MAY	3	3	-	27	-	3
JUNE	-	9	-	13	-	9
JULY	-	43	-	24	-	21
TOTAL	94	91	54	64	66	60

It was necessary hurriedly to establish an amphibious training base at Salerno and to locate ashore at Salerno, Naples, Nisida and Pozzuoli the numerous activities required to support a large number of ships and craft and to prepare them for large scale operations. That this was accomplished under adverse conditions and that the results were generally excellent reflects great credit on all officer and enlisted personnel of the Amphibious Force, Eighth Fleet, which included ships of the Escort Sweeper Group.

The success of this and other amphibious landings in the Mediterranean has been due in large part to the outstanding support rendered by shore based activities and by repair ships based at friendly ports at some distance from the area of assault.

The logistic support planned for this operation was far more extensive than in previous operations in the Mediterranean due to:

(1) Greater distance from major repair yards;

(2) Anticipation of large scale enemy action from shore batteries and aircraft;

(3) Probability of extended period of unloading over assault beaches prior to capture of Toulon and Marseille;

(4) Expectation that such ports would be severely damaged and would require extensive harbor clearance.

Section 6.2

REPAIR FACILITIES AND DRY DOCKS

The assault and follow-up convoy schedules involved departures from widely separated Mediterranean ports and necessitated dispersion of repair facilities afloat and the creation of additional shore based repair units to augment those already established.

USS Vulcan (AR-5) was based at Mers el Kebir, Algeria, adjacent to dry-docking facilities at the Naval Operating Base, Oran, Algeria, and the Naval Supply Depot, Oran, Algeria.

USS Delta (AR-9) was based at Naples, Italy, adjacent to dry-docking facilities at that port.

USS Denebola (AD-12) staged at Cagliari, Sardinia. As enemy action decreased, USS Denebola shifted to Ajaccio, Corsica, on 14 August, to Gulf of St. Tropez, France, on 3 September, and to Toulon, France, on 16 September. On 23 September, USS Denebola proceeded to Naples to relieve USS Delta, the latter ship then being required at Palermo for post-operation overhaul of ships at that port.

USS Achelous (ARL-1) proceeded with the assault convoy to Ajaccio, staging there until 19 August when the risk involved warranted anchoring this ship in Canobies Bay, Gulf of St. Tropez. Upon closing of all beaches, USS Achelous was shifted to Toulon.

HM LSE-2 arrived at Ajaccio from the United Kingdom on 29 August and staged there as relief of USS Achelous until 2 September when this ship moved via Marseille to Toulon, arriving there 8 September. Later, when relieved there by USS Achelous, HM LSE-2 sailed to Marseille.

US LST-387, which had suffered major damage by enemy action prior to the invasion of Sicily, and had been fitted out as an immobile repair ship, was based at Bizerte, Tunisia.

Two British LCT(2) with British Landing Craft Repair Units embarked were assigned for repair of craft operating off the assault beaches.

Three US LST and four British LCI(L) were designated respectively as Mother Ships and Craft. Each LST and LCI(L) so designated carried a special repair party together with tools, equipment, and spare parts for the repair of craft operating off the assault beaches.

Repair facilities ashore were located at Gibraltar, Oran, Algiers, Bizerte, Palermo, Malta, Naples, and Taranto.

The principal PT Base was located at Maddalena although the engine overhaul base at Bizerte continued to function. Minor PT Bases close to the assault area were established at Bastia and Calvi, Corsica.

In addition to the above, the following repair facilities were specially provided:

    (1) Mobile Landing Craft Repair Unit No. 2 (British), consisting of 4 officers, 53 men, and 33 vehicles, arrived in the assault area on D+5, and was assigned to Marseille upon the occupation of that port.

(2) Amphibious Boat Pool Repair Unit No. 1 (Mobile), consisting of 3 officers, 39 men, and 18 vehicles, staged at Ajaccio and was later transferred, one section each, to Marseille and Toulon to assist in repairs to craft operating in those ports.

(3) British 258th LCI(L) Flotilla Maintenance Party and British 5th and 96th LCT Flotilla Maintenance Parties were staged at Ajaccio preparatory to joining up with LCI(L) Mother Craft and/or for augmenting repair parties in captured ports as required.

(4) US Amphibious Repair Unit No. 2, consisting of 2 officers and 22 men (in reality a modified E-8 functional component), was assigned to Calvi to provide repair facilities for LSTs shuttling from that port.

(5) US Amphibious Repair Units No. 3 at Palermo and Nos. 4 and 5 at Bizerte were organized and alerted but were not required in the forward area. Each of these units consisted of 3 officers and 37 men, with special tools, equipment and a reserve supply of spare parts.

In addition to graving docks and floating dry docks at principal repair yards in the Mediterranean, 100 ton, 250 ton, and 350 ton pontoon dry docks were located at Bizerte, Naples, Palermo, Maddalena, and Ajaccio. One 350 ton dock accompanied the USS Achelous to Gulf of St. Tropez and thence to Toulon, and one 350 ton dock accompanied HM LSE-2 to Toulon and thence to Marseille.

The arrival of these pontoon dry docks in the assault area greatly facilitated repairs to LCTs and LCM(3)s. A pontoon causeway was also used to advantage in repairing LCM(3)s. These craft were hoisted using the crane on USS Achelous and were then lowered on the causeway.

Two British LSDs (HMS Highway and HMS Eastway) took part in the operation, the former having been fitted with special blocks to provide dry-docking facilities for LCI(L), LCT, and LCM(3). However, other important duties assigned these ships precluded their use for dry-docking purposes except for a very short period of time. Their value in amphibious operations is discussed elsewhere in this chapter.

Section 6.3

PETROLEUM INSTALLATIONS AND SUPPLY OF PETROLEUM PRODUCTS AND COAL

Large stocks of coal and bulk and packaged petroleum products were maintained at Oran, Algiers, Bizerte, Palermo, Cagliari, Taranto, Malta, Augusta and Naples. Large reserve stocks were held at Casablanca and Gibraltar. However, in order to provide fueling facilities to permit expeditious fueling of small ships and craft staging in and shuttling from Corsican ports, Petroleum Division One was formed and assigned this responsibility.

French Navy installations at Ajaccio had a capacity of 135,000 barrels of black oil and 11,000 barrels of diesel oil. The following table indicates the additional tankage erected in Corsica, all figures in barrels:

	BLACK OIL	DIESEL OIL	100 OCTANE
AJACCIO	120,000	20,000	20,000
CALVI	-	10,000	10,000
ALCAJOLA	-	10,000	-
ILE ROUSSE	-	10,000	-

Extensive distributing lines were laid connecting tank farms with fueling connections on two piers in Ajaccio harbor and to LST hards in Calvi and Ile Rousse.

Additional storage was available in tankers and barges located in Propriano harbor south of Ajaccio and in Ajaccio harbor. The total floating storage was 60,500 barrels of black oil and 7,400 barrels of diesel oil.

Italian fuel installations at Maddalena were repaired by Engineers of the Royal Navy and these stocks were augmented by additional floating storage at that port.

Petroleum Division One personnel, equipment, tank farm materials and five 70 ton capacity wooden fueling barges were readied for transfer to the assault beaches immediately after the initial assault.

The following installations were erected on assault beaches by this unit:

ALPHA - One 2000 barrel tank for diesel oil.

DELTA - One 2000 barrel tank for 100 octane gasoline.

CAMEL - One 2000 barrel tank and one 5000 barrel tank for diesel oil.

Connections were made to fueling barges secured to piles off the beaches. Special mooring buoys were placed off St. Raphael for tankers discharging 100 octane gasoline at that port for use by the Army Air Force.

As beaches were closed, fueling installations were dismantled and moved overland to major captured ports for use there as required.

A shuttling schedule was prepared covering the movements of four black oil, four diesel oil and four 100 octane gasoline tankers and two colliers to insure adequate fuel in the three assault areas. Other tankers and colliers were held in reserve at Maddalena to replace possible losses.

In addition, four US Navy AO were available in case the situation required their services in the assault area, and they were staged as follows:

    Winooski (AO-38) - Palermo

    Chiwawa (AO-68) - Naples

    Chemung (AO-30) - Mers el Kebir

    Cowanesque (AO-79) - Mers el Kebir

Fortunately, it was not necessary to call these tankers forward. Shore stocks at Ajaccio were kept filled by tankers shuttling from Palermo and those at Naples by tankers shuttling from Augusta.

HMS Dewdale and HMS Ennerdale (LSG) which were converted from tankers each carried 7,000 barrels of diesel oil and 28,000 barrels of black oil which was available in the assault area until D+4 when these valuable ships were released. Six British MFV (French manned) accompanied the LCT assault convoys to serve as mobile service stations for small craft in the assault area. Each carried 1000 gallons of 80 octane gasoline and 1000 gallons of diesel oil plus small amounts of lubricating oils.

LST Mother Ships were fueled from tankers immediately after the assault to provide fuel for small craft operating off the assault beaches.

Large stocks of lubricating oils were available at all fueling ports, and each tanker carried maximum permissable deck load in drums as applicable to the type of ships or craft expected to fuel from such tankers.

All shore fueling installations and tankers were provided with adaptors to insure expeditious fueling of United States, British, French, Greek and other allied ships.

The division of responsibility for the rehabilitation of fuel installations at Toulon, Marseille, and Port de Bouc, was the result of careful study and mutual agreement of all services under the supervision of Petroleum Section, Allied Force Headquarters.

Anticipating large scale demolition, the major portion of two D-4 functional components (medium tank-farm units) was ordered for direct shipment from the United States to arrive in Toulon on D+20, the assumption being that tankage erected in Corsica and on the assault beaches could be dismantled and used in Marseille as necessary on or about D+45. However, the installations allocated for naval use in these ports had not been severely damaged, and immediate repairs and extensions of pipe lines to fueling berths were undertaken.

The following bulk storage was made available for naval use, quantities are in barrels:

Location	Plant	Black Oil	Diesel Oil	80 Octane	100 Octane
Marseille	(Shell (Jupiter)	140,000	70,000	-	-
	(SGHP (St. Joseph)	180,000	-	-	-
	(La Pinede Fueling Depot	18,000	12,000	10,000	10,000

Location	Plant	Black Oil	Diesel Oil	80 Octane	100 Octane
Toulon	(Parc du Lazaret	260,000	62,000	-	-
	(Parc de l'Eguillette	-	-	5,000	5,000

In addition to adequate fueling facilities for allied naval and merchant ships it was a responsibility of NCWTF to supply increasingly large quantities of black and diesel fuel oils for army and civilian requirements subsequent to D+30. Preparations were made to meet these requirements.

Section 6.4

WATER INSTALLATIONS AND SUPPLY

In anticipation of the usual critical water shortage in the western Mediterranean during the summer months and in order to provide an adequate supply of potable water for ships and craft staging in and shuttling from Corsican ports, Petroleum Division One erected tanks and installed distilling units as indicated in the following table:

Location	Storage in Barrels	Distilling Capacity in Gals./24 Hrs.
Ajaccio	13,000	25,000
Calvi	10,000	10,000
Ile Rousse	10,000	10,000

Distribution lines were run to all fueling berths.

Twenty-six LST were equipped as water carriers to supply potable water over the beaches immediately after the assault and during the maintenance period. The army requirement was 350,000 gallons of potable water from D to D+5 inclusive.

LSTs designated as Mother Ships were equipped with distilling plants. One water barge (YW) was assigned to each assault area and a fourth and larger water barge (YW) was placed on a shuttling schedule from Naples and Maddalena to the assault area. Unfortunately this ship, the British ship Myriel, arrived in the assault area with salt water ballast and the subsequent delay in reloading and returning to the assault area created a shortage which, while at no time critical, necessitated the transfer of small quantities of water from other sources. The need for a greater number of YWs had been forseen but they were not available in the Mediterranean theater, and it was recognized that strict rationing would be necessary on the part of all hands. Merchant ships carried surplus water but were often reluctant to discharge any appreciable quantity because of probable shortage at the next port of call. It is recommended that in the future the instructions to merchant ships specifically provide for the transfer of water in the assault area.

Ships of the French Navy presented a serious problem due to the small capacity of their distilling plants or the entire absence of such installations.

Upon entry into Marseille, Petroleum Division One ran water lines to fueling berths paralleling the fuel lines. Water tanks having a total capacity of 14,000 barrels are being rehabilitated at the Lazaret fuel depot in Toulon. Pending completion of these installations and due to the length of pipe lines it would be necessary to lay to the port area in Toulon, water barges were retained at these ports to supply the forces afloat.

Section 6.5

PROVISIONS, CLOTHING AND SMALL STORES, SHIPS' STORE STOCK AND GENERAL STORES

Fresh and refrigerated provisions were available to all ships and shore activities prior to the assault from AFs arriving from the United States.

US LST Mother Ships and British LCI(L) Mother Craft anchored off assault beaches and later berthed in Marseille and Toulon, were kept filled to capacity and provided reasonably adequate sources of provisions for small ships and craft.

Fortunately, conditions were such as to permit USS Tarazed (AF-13) and USS Saturn (AF-40) to provision ships and shore activities in the assault areas and in Marseille and Toulon commencing on 6 September and 22 September respectively.

Dry provisions were available at Oran, Bizerte, Palermo, Naples and in AFs.

Ample stocks of survivors clothing were located at Oran, Naples, Palermo and Ajaccio. Limited stocks were carried in APA, AKA, XAP, LSI and in LST and LCI(L) assigned duty as Mother Ships and Craft.

USS Pleiades (AK-46) staged at Palermo and was available in the assault area and in Marseille commencing on 5 September to supply forces afloat and shore activities with clothing and small stores, ships' store stock and general stores.

USS Capella (AK-13) arrived "castor loaded." Due to early withdrawal of large combatant ships USS Capella was released after only partially discharging at Oran.

Reserve stocks of minesweeping gear, fog oil, smoke pots and floats, ammunition and other consummable supplies were established at Ajaccio.

YF-445 and YF-447 arrived from the United States under tow on 1 August. Crews were provided and hurriedly trained. Three 20 mm machine guns, a portable distilling unit and four 625 cubic foot refrigerator boxes were installed on each ship. These ships arrived in the assault area on D+5 and D+10 respectively and were subsequently employed in the support of the forces afloat. A coaster, HMS Hebe II, had been designated for similar duty in order that each of the three assault areas would be benefited by such service. However, the refrigerating plant of this ship was inoperative and could not be repaired in the time available.

British LCI(L)s, designated as stores carriers, were employed shuttling from Naples to the assault areas to supply their LCI(L) Mother Craft. APA, AKA, XAP and LSI were directed to discharge provisions and stores in the assault area as time permitted. Due to the rapid unloading of combat personnel and cargo, only small quantities of provisions and stores were obtained in this manner.

Ample refrigerated storage was found immediately useable in Marseille and in Toulon. This storage proved of immediate value to supply the large number of small ships and craft basing on these ports.

Three British LCT(1) were loaded with chemical smoke acid and served as tenders to supply six British LCM(3) smoke producing craft, all being assigned equally to the three Attack Force Commanders.

Army personnel embarked in allied navy ships including LSTs were subsisted by such ships except that in some cases the number of troops embarked in LSTs required a modification in the navy ration and augmentation by the army.

The army provided rations for all army personnel embarked in LCI(L)s and LCTs. The navy provided hot soup and coffee when practicable.

Throughout the entire operation US Navy provisioning facilities were made available to allied ships and craft when necessary. This applied particularly to craft assigned unloading duties and to auxiliaries which remained off the assault beaches without relief until the closing of such beaches.

Combatant ships of the French Navy were rotated as necessary to enable them to provision in Oran or Algiers.

Frequent distribution of mail in the assault areas was effected by utilizing ships in follow-up convoys and by daily US Navy plane service. One British LCI(L) was assigned as mail carrier to serve British personnel attached to craft remaining in the assault areas.

Section 6.6

BARRAGE BALLOONS

With few exceptions all merchant ships, APA, AKA, XAP, LSI, LSP, AP, LST and auxiliaries entering the assault areas were equipped with barrage balloons.

Insofar as possible those flown from US Navy ships were helium filled, the balance were hydrogen filled.

Efficient maintenance and servicing units had been set up in Oran, Algiers, Naples and Taranto by the Royal Navy. Royal Air Force hydrogen plants were in operation.

In order to provide servicing and replacements in the assault area, two British Fleet Tenders (FT) and three British LCT(2) were assigned as Balloon Tenders. The former carried the administrative staff and some spare gear. The latter were manned with experienced personnel and fitted out with hydrogen generating units and spares. One LCT(2) was assigned to each attack force commander. Two LCVP from the LST Mother Ships reported to the balloon tender in each area for use in transferring balloons. Losses due to anti-aircraft fire or electrical storms were expeditiously replaced.

In order to insure immediate protection against enemy strafing attacks on assault beaches and over pontoon causeways, 90 LCT (US and British) were equipped with barrage balloons at Naples and Salerno prior to departure in the assault convoy.

Two enlisted men from three US Army Barrage Balloon Batteries were embarked in each LCT designated. One hand winch and one inflated VLA balloon was provided. Upon arrival on the assault beaches, barrage balloons were walked ashore by US Army personnel tending them.

Losses enroute to Ajaccio (reported as 20) were replaced at that port.

Barrage balloons were ordered flown at operational height or close hauled as directed by task force commanders.

In future operations it is recommended that pre-arranged signals by flag hoist be promulgated in the logistic annex, in the communication annex and in the instructions to merchant ships to insure prompt action in close-hauling balloons at sunset, in case of approaching storms or for other reasons.

Upon closing of the beaches, maintenance parties were established ashore in Marseille and Toulon to service ships arriving at those ports. Balloon tenders were then released.

Section 6.7

ASSAULT, MAINTENANCE AND BUILD-UP PERIOD

Almost without exception ships and craft were operational and sortied as directed in the assault convoys. Many of the United States and British craft had been operating continuously for 18 months and much credit is due the personnel directly connected with their short pre-invasion overhaul.

A total of 902 ships and craft and approximately 1200 ship-borne landing craft were assigned to the Western Task Force. In addition 103 merchant ships arrived in the initial convoys on D and D+1 days carrying 100 United States and 70 British LCM(3) for use in unloading ships anchored off the assault beaches.

From D-4 to D+15 approximately 825,000 barrels of black and diesel fuel oils and 131,000 barrels of potable water were discharged to ships and craft from Corsican ports. A total of 305 ships and craft were fueled and watered in thirty hours during the staging period at Propriano and Ajaccio enroute to the assault.

As a result of the swift advance of the US Seventh Army and the reduction in requirements for sustained naval gunfire support, demands for black and diesel fuel oils in the assault area and in Corsica were less than anticipated. Tanker shuttling schedules were therefore modified. With the exception of a delay in the arrival of the gasoline tanker Empire Lass in the Alpha area on D-Day and the necessity to transfer, during the assault phase a gasoline tanker from the Delta area, no serious difficulties were encountered.

It was not possible to brief commanding officers or masters of tankers prior to the operation, and in a few instances these officers had not received a copy of the Logistics Annex. Commanding officers of all auxiliaries should be briefed, and if practicable the vast amount of paper work covering plans and operation orders should be screened in order that only those pertinent to the auxiliaries concerned will be forwarded for study and execution.

All auxiliary ships anchored off the assault beaches together with LST Mother Ships, LCI(L) Mother Craft and craft assigned salvage and fire fighting duties were readily distinguishable by designating flags flown at the yardarm. In addition, tankers, colliers and water barges indicated by flag hoist the quantity of fuel oil, coal and water respectively remaining on hand for discharge.

Logistic support in the assault area for small ships and craft, particularly LCM(3)s assigned for unloading duties, has always presented numerous problems. Any attempt to standardize a plan for such support would be futile. The conditions anticipated must be used as a basis to determine the best means to provide support with the facilities available.

In this operation it was expected that unloading over the assault beaches would continue for several weeks, possibly for 90 days. Numerous PC, SC, YMS, YTL and PT together with 130 LCTs and approximately 200 LCM(3)s plus other small boats would require logistic support in varying degrees.

The Attack Force Commander in each of the three assault areas was assigned one US LST Mother Ship and one or two British LCI(L) Mother Craft. In addition to providing berthing, messing, repair, fuel and water facilities, these ships and craft carried maximum quantities of provisions, clothing and small stores, canteen stores, lubricating oil, smoke pots and other miscellaneous consumable supplies.

Each US LST Mother Ship was of the six davit type with 150 portable standee bunks installed in the after end of the tank deck and each carried six LCVPs for use in the area. Two 625 cubic foot refrigerators boxes and one portable Cleaverbrook distilling unit were installed on the main deck. LSTs assigned this duty were designated from those equipped with elevators to facilitate handling stores and repair materials and had not been previously equipped with Badger distilling plants.

The following is quoted from the Action Report of the Commanding Officer, US LST 74 which served as Mother Ship in the Alpha area and is representative of the valuable services rendered by ships assigned this duty:

"The following information covers, in part, the work performed by the US LST 74 in the period from D-Day to 1200, 8 September 1944:

Ships and craft watered and fueled	225
Water issued	552 tons
Fuel issued	945 tons
Fog oil issued	200 drums
Smoke pots and floats issued	1,752
Ships and craft repaired	109
Patients treated	76
Ships and craft provisioned	194
Provisions issued, dry	132 tons
Provisions issued, fresh	64 tons
Average daily berthing	256
Average daily rations	307
Total ships and craft alongside (LCVPs excluded)	416"

British LCI(L)s assigned as Mother Craft in support of personnel manning LCTs and LCM(3)s were admittedly less adequate than LSTs, but no more LSTs could be spared for this duty.

The Mother Ship idea is sound but in order to accomodate a large number of small boat crews it is considered that LSDs are more suitable than LSTs. The additional docking and repair facilities of LSDs are necessary with particular emphasis on their ability to lift 20 LCM(3)s in case of inclement weather and for underwater hull repairs. In the invasion of Southern France only two LSDs were made available, and these ships were required to transport warping barges, LCM(3)s, pontoon causeways and other small craft during the maintenance period and could not be made available for Mother Ship duty. In an operation of this size and under the conditions that were known to exist the availability of six LSDs would have been most desirable.

The increasing number of craft fitted for and assigned special duties in amphibious operations presents a complex problem in lifting them to the assault area. Under favorable conditions attack transports (APA) and cargo ships (AKA) can, and in this theater do, carry additional LCVPs at the rail supported by cargo booms.

Once the planning for an operation dictates the acceptable minimum number of LCC, Apex boats, LCVP shallow water minesweepers, LCM(3)(R) Woofus craft, LCM(3) Smokers and other special types to be lifted, it follows that LSDs in sufficient number should be assigned for this purpose. Subsequent to the assault, LSDs can assume their secondary but not less important function as Mother Ships.

Three LSDs had been requested from British sources but only two were made available subsequent to the invasion of Northern France. As a result it was necessary to load certain craft required in the Delta area in LSDs destined for the Alpha and Camel areas. Priority in loading for the assault was given to the LCM(3) Smokers, and the balance of lift available was in accordance with Attack Force Commanders requirements for LCM(3)(R)s (Woofus), LCVP shallow water minesweepers, and Apex boats.

Even in the Mediterranean where tidal conditions are ideal, it is not recommended that small boat crews and repair units be based ashore during periods immediately following an assault. Surf conditions and storms inevitably cause serious damage to beached craft, and it is not practicable to set up berthing and messing facilities for the large number of officers and men assigned to LCM(3)s arriving in the assault area in merchant ships. Later, if protected waters or small harbors are found suitable, an amphibious boat pool can be established and shore based facilities, if warranted, can be set up.

A temporary PT Base was established at St. Maxime, Gulf of St. Tropez, adjacent to the gasoline storage tank erected by Petroleum Division One.

Pontoon causeways augmented the damaged mole at this port and provided a reasonably safe harbor for PTs and air-sea-rescue craft.

One PT was designated as a tender, and adequate stores and spare parts were carried on board. The procurement of additional items was facilitated by using the PT making daily trips from the PT Base at Calvi, Corsica.

RECOMMENDATION

That LSDs and ARLs be allocated commensurate with the number of small ships and craft to be tended.

Section 6.8

LOSSES AND DAMAGE

A summary of losses and damage appears in tabular form in the daily reports in the "Campaign Narrative," Chapter 1, Part II. For a summary of the period, see page 133.

All US ships and craft damaged in this operation have been or are being repaired and will be fully operational within a short period with the following exceptions:

(1) USS Seer (AM-112) - temporary repairs to be completed at Palermo about 10 November, 1944. Ship to return to United States under own power for permanent repairs.

(2) PT-555 damaged by mine explosion has been stripped and sunk.

(3) LCC-25498 damaged by mine explosion was scheduled to be stripped and scrapped. This craft was identified as LCC 98, its short designation, in the "Campaign Narrative."

Information relative to status of repairs to damaged ships and craft of allied forces participating is not available.

Section 6.9

SALVAGE AND FIRE-FIGHTING

Fire-fighting schools were conducted at Palermo, Oran and Bizerte during the months preceeding this operation and were well attended by the operating forces.

Three officers experienced in fire-fighting who had been ordered to the Eighth Fleet by the Chief of the Bureau of Ships were assigned to act in an advisory capacity to task force and task group commanders.

Ships and craft designated for salvage and fire-fighting duties were divided into three groups and assigned to the three Attack Force Commanders. LCI(L)s and LCT(5)s assigned to these groups carried assault troops and vehicles respectively and immediately after the initial landing were available for salvage and fire-fighting duties.

The average group was constituted as follows:

Shallow Water Group	Deep Water Group
3 LCI(L)	2 ATF
1 LCT(5)	1 ATA
2 LCM(3)‡	2 ATR
1 Pontoon Warping Barge	1 British Boom Vessel (Similar to an AN)
2 YTL	1 YTB

‡ Note: These LCM(3)s were in addition to those carried by APA, XAP and AKA. One LCM(3) on each ship of these types was equipped for and assigned to assist in salvage work on the assault beaches.

Normal complements of these ships and craft were augmented by personnel qualified for salvage and fire-fighting work, and additional gear was provided to meet anticipated requirements based on past experiences in the Mediterranean.

The value of these specially fitted LCI(L)s and LCT(5)s in amphibious operations is such that they should not be required to participate in the initial assault, but rather, that they remain off the assault beaches to be available immediately for salvage and fire-fighting duties.

LCI(L)s were altered for salvage work by installation of heavy bitts, stern chocks and heavier stern anchor and anchor wire and were fitted out with necessary miscellaneous gear.

LCI(L)s designated for fire fighting were equipped with gasoline driven fire pumps and fitted out with required quantities of foam, hose and associated equipment.

LCT(5)s were equipped with sheer legs forward having a lifting capacity of thirty tons powered by a gasoline driven winch mounted on deck forward of the superstructure.

Task force commanders and others directly connected with the operations off the assault beaches were unanimous in their favorable comments on the success of the shallow water salvage and fire-fighting groups as organized.

Typical of the work performed, the following summarizes accomplishments in the Alpha area from D to D+10:

(1) Underwater repairs to 26 ships and craft;

(2) Retracted 37 craft stranded or broached on beaches;

(3) Cleared 76 fouled propellers;

(4) Assisted in extinguishing grass fires on shore;

(5) Assisted in salvage of army observation plane.

Services of a senior salvage officer and an experienced fire-fighting officer were available to each Attack Force Commander.

Ships and craft assigned were organized so that shallow water and deep water salvage and fire-fighting could be undertaken independently, and yet each was prepared to assist the other.

Salvage tugs (ARS) were stationed at Calvi and Ajaccio for the purpose of intercepting and relieving tugs towing damaged ships from the assault area.

Subsequent to the assault phase these salvage tugs together with other ships and craft in the salvage groups were despatched to Toulon, Marseille and Port de Bouc to assist in harbor clearance of these ports.

The harbor clearance work was undertaken by combined forces of the US and Royal Navies. Personnel were staged at Mediterranean ports and ordered forward as required. Advance parties were embarked in ships in the assault convoys to obtain data as to special equipment required to expedite harbor clearance.

The original plan was based on the clearance of Toulon and later of Marseille. The rapidity of entry into all ports in the assault area necessitated harbor clearance and rehabilitation to be undertaken simultaneously at Toulon, Marseille and Port de Bouc.

Harbor clearance units consisted of two US Navy groups, each of 10 officers and 100 enlisted men, and two Royal Navy groups of somewhat smaller complement.

British salvage ships were extremely useful because of their capacity to make heavy underwater lifts. These ships with the assistance of the four US LCT(5)s fitted for salvage were extensively employed in all ports.

In spite of the extensive damage by allied bombing and by enemy demolition the three ports were satisfactorily cleared to permit the closing of all beaches prior to 25 September.

RECOMMENDATIONS

It is recommended that the alterations to LCI(L)s and LCT(5)s for salvage and fire-fighting be standardized and that such craft be organized as shallow water salvage groups.

At least fifty percent of the complements of such craft should be composed of personnel trained in salvage and fire-fighting.

Each LCI(L) and LCT(5) assigned should be provided with a small shallow draft power boat to facilitate inspection of stranded ships and craft. (LCVPs are too large and draw too much water for this purpose).

LCT(5)s fitted for salvage should carry a small repair party with necessary equipment to accomplish minor repairs to damaged ship-borne landing craft and an adequate stock of spare propellers.

It is recognized that the recommendation to include LCT(5)s in a specially organized shallow water salvage group is based on results obtained in shore to shore operations. However, the results obtained on assault beaches are of such value as to warrant LCT(5)s being transported in LSDs to the assault area where distance or weather conditions prohibit such craft proceeding under their own power.

Section 6.10

EIGHTH FLEET SHIPS AND CRAFT

GENERAL

The performance and material reliability of all ships and craft were excellent. This is of particular importance with regard to ships of the amphibious force and is the anticipated reward for long periods of training and the standardization of proven methods.

USS Nevada and USS Texas each reported excessive temperatures below decks during prolonged periods at general quarters. USS Nevada also reported considerable difficulty experienced with interior communication equipment as a result of prolonged firing of the main battery.

Alteration requests from USS Catoctin have been submitted separately recommending an additional distilling plant and improved ventilation. Already favorable action has been taken on the former by the Chief of the Bureau of Ships.

USS Barricade and USS Planter (ACMs) were employed as flagships and tenders for minesweeping operations and were most satisfactory for this purpose.

LCP(R)s carried by APDs were in poor condition upon arrival in the Mediterranean and in some instances were not equipped with underwater exhaust. Even when so equipped, these craft are noisy compared with British LCA. In order to land troops from APDs, experiments were conducted with US Army M-2 assault boats and with US Army 10-man rubber boats. The latter proved more satisfactory and were used in the Sitka Assault, each LCP(R) towing nine rubber boats on three tow lines in tandem, at a speed of approximately 4.5 knots.

LCCs were available for the first time in the Mediterranean and were employed as control boats, messenger boats, smoke boats (fitted with small Besler generators), and to augment the E-boat screen. Opinion as to satisfactory performance and usefulness of these craft is as varied as the duties to which assigned. Three were carried by XAPs, the remainder being towed to the assault area.

It is considered that LCCs have a definite applicability to amphibious operations, their importance varying with conditions anticipated. They should be available to task force commanders for such use as they deem most appropriate in the execution of their detailed plans.

The following summarizes advantages and disadvantages reported and is submitted without further comment:

Advantages	Disadvantages
(1) Low silhouette.	(1) Range and efficiency of radar fall off rapidly in rough water.
(2) Maneuverability.	(2) Not a good boat in rough sea.
	(3) Heavy and awkward to hoist out from APA.
	(4) Displaces LCM(3) on APA.
	(5) Light construction results in damage when going alongside ships when used as messenger boats.

The US LCM(3), converted to LCM(3)(R) "Woofus" craft and the British LCM(3)s, used as smokers, were of necessity old boats and therefore difficult to maintain in operational condition.

RESEARCH AND DEVELOPMENT

As a result of research and experiments initiated during the preparation and training period, and in order to insure adequate facilities to conform to requirements developed during the planning, the following is a summary of the more important work accomplished:

(1) Twenty US LSTs were fitted to side-carry pontoon causeways. Necessary fittings were manufactured and issued to the British to fit out one British and three Greek LSTs to side-carry pontoon causeways.

(2) Three US LSTs were designated as Mother Ships, each fitted with portable distilling plant and two 625 cubic foot refrigerator boxes.

(3) Special ramps for GCI equipment were installed on the forecastle of three US LSTs by the Ship Repair Yard, Naval Operating Base, Palermo. These ramps can be disassembled and stowed on board when not required.

(4) A new LST flight deck was developed by the Ship Repair Yard at Naval Operating Base, Palermo. Three sets of standardized design were manufactured and installed on three US LSTs. When not required, the equipment can be disassembled and stowed on the tank deck.

(5) Six US LCI(L)s were specially fitted for salvage and fire fighting and three US LCI(L)s were fitted for salvage duties only.

(6) Eleven US LCI(L)s were equipped with additional communication facilities and were designated LCI(L)(C), Command Flagships.

(7) Bulwarks of fifty LCT(6)s were altered to provide portable sections to permit side-unloading.

(8) Four US LCT(5)s were fitted with sheer legs and specially outfitted for shallow water salvage work.

(9) Twenty-four US LCM(3)s were fitted with rocket racks and were designated LCM(3)(R) or "Woofus" craft.

(10) Several LCVP were fitted with minesweeping gear for shallow water minesweeping.

(11) As indicated elsewhere in this chapter, certain British craft were assigned special duties and each of these was altered and fitted as necessity dictated. The more important were three LCT(1) Smoke Tenders, six LCM(3) Smokers, three LCT(2) Balloon Tenders, two LCT(2) Repair Craft, and four LCI(L) Mother Craft.

(12) One British LST was converted for use as a Fighter Direction Tender in the United Kingdom and was designated as HM LSF 13.

(13) Additional anti-aircraft armament was installed on many of the ships assigned to the Eighth Fleet, the most important being that on destroyers and destroyer escorts with the concurrent removal of torpedo tubes and mounts.

(14) The large number of army ground force and army air corps staff personnel to be embarked in flagships and the resultant increased demand for communication facilities necessitated a considerable amount of work to be accomplished in USS Catoctin, USS Duane, and USS Biscayne.

RECOMMENDATIONS

(1) That the Research and Development Center, Amphibious Training Command, US Atlantic Fleet study the problem of landing troops from APDs. Boats with tows provided should be capable of embarking all troops in one wave. Speed is not important. Silence and reliability are mandatory.

(2) That electric air compressors be added to allowance lists of APA, XAP, and AKA for use in inflating tires of vehicles prior to unloading.

(3) That the adequacy of ventilation in the forward section of the well deck of LSDs be investigated. Reports indicate fumes accumulate in the space below the superstructure when landing craft engines are being warmed up.

(4) That a public address system be installed on LSTs with outlets on the main and tank decks.

(5) That propeller guards be installed on the smoke producing unit of LCM(3) Smokers. This was recommended but not accomplished prior to this operation with the result that one British naval officer was decapitated.

Section 6.11

BEACH CONTROL GROUP AND BEACH BATTALIONS

Three Beach Battalions (the 1st, 4th, and 8th BB) were employed in this operation. One was assigned to each divisional assault area. For the first time in this theater, a US Naval Liaison Officer (Beach Control Group) was designated to coordinate the activities of all Beach Battalions. Headquarters for this function were established west of St. Maxime with the Commanding Officer Beach Control Group (Army). The Naval Liaison Officer reported directly to NCWTF on strictly naval matters, and in turn controlled the employment and distribution of Beach Battalion Units to meet the requirements of support of the US Seventh Army over the beaches.

The organization proved to be most effective, but its success is entirely dependent on an adequate communication system. During the first few days, landline communications between the Beach Control Group and the three beach areas were not satisfactory, largely due to the time required to span the 60 miles or so of coastline that were involved. The latter was an army responsibility. It is believed that more study should be given to effective radio communication facilities for the Group and the Battalions to serve until landlines can be installed.

A supply officer and storekeepers should be assigned to the Naval Liaison Officer to facilitate problems of subsistence and supply to all naval units operating on or from the beaches.

During this operation, the Naval Liaison Officer was frequently called upon to provide services such as transportation and the like to naval officers visiting the beaches on duty.

Fortunately during this landing operation few underwater obstacles were encountered, and the beaches were well adapted to the beaching of landing craft. In a few instances pontoon causeways were required for the discharge of LSTs and LCTs. In general, within a few days after D-Day, sufficient beaches were located by survey to handle LSTs without the use of causeways. Except for brief periods of squalls, weather and surf conditions were excellent throughout the entire period and enemy action was negligible. Consequently, there was very little emergency salvage work required, and the control of boat traffic was relatively simple.

Beach operations were terminated on 25 September, at which date the ports of Marseille, Toulon, and Port de Bouc were capable of absorbing the tonnage previously handled over the beaches. The 1st Beach Battalion was sent to Marseille on 30 August to handle naval features of the operation of the landing craft hards in that port. Upon closing the Camel beaches, units of the 8th Beach Battalion relieved the 1st Beach Battalion at Marseille.

The Beach Battalions were well trained and equipped, and performed their functions most satisfactorily.

Although not included in the operation plan, it is considered that Pontoon Causeway Crews, on landing, should report to the Beach Control Group and in addition to the Beachmaster at the site of their operations. In fact, this was actually done, but was not clearly understood by all hands. Problems of supply and maintenance of these crews would be greatly simplified if the plan provided for this organization.

CONCLUSION

Two factors led to the success of beach operations:

(1) Provision of a responsible naval officer (Naval Liaison Officer) to coordinate the naval activities at and between all beaches.

(2) Beach Battalions trained and rehearsed with the Army Shore Parties with which they were to be associated in the actual operation. In this way, complete coordination of Army and Navy forces was assured.

Section 6.12

LOADING AND UNLOADING OF SHIPS AND CRAFT

With few exceptions all ships and craft in the assault convoys were loaded in the Naples-Salerno area. Merchant ships were loaded at Naples, Taranto and Oran.

Loading of ships and craft other than merchant ships in the Naples-Salerno area was coordinated by a Joint Loading Control Officer (US Navy) in close liaison with the Transportation Division of Peninsular Base Section (US Army). The US Navy loading control officer subsequently coordinated loading of ships and craft in Corsican ports in follow-up convoys.

LOADING SUMMARIES

	PERSONNEL	VEHICLES, TANKS, GUNS	MISCELLANEOUS
NAPLES (assault convoys)	98,455	16,077	-
NAPLES (follow-up convoys thru 18 September)	130,817	28,625	-
CORSICAN PORTS (follow-up convoys)	68,496	13,373	1,954 horses and mules 21 planes

In previous operations in the Mediterranean the coxswains of small craft and drivers of DUKWs experienced difficulty in locating merchant ships to which they were ordered to proceed for unloading. To overcome this difficulty preparations were made:

(1) To provide two transport area beacon buoys for use off the assault beaches in each of the three assault areas, and

(2) Assignment of numbers to each merchant ship prior to the assault, such numbers being painted on large sign boards secured to each side of each ship. These sign boards were illuminated at night by low visibility lights shielded to prevent their being visible to hostile aircraft. Experiments were conducted with luminous paint and with luminous tape. The latter proved more satisfactory and was used in the preparation of many of the numeral sign boards. Actually however, any good outside white paint on a black background proved satisfactory and in some cases, the numerals were painted directly on the side of the ship.

Unloading of ships and craft in the assault convoys was expeditiously accomplished. APAs, XAPs and AKAs were loaded with personnel and vehicles only and employed LCTs to augment their own shipborne landing craft.

APs and other large personnel ships transferred troops expeditiously in LCVPs, LCM(3)s and in many cases in LCI(L)s.

Pontoon causeways were shifted from one beach to another as circumstances required. Twenty-four complete pontoon causeways were available, the standard of one to every six LSTs having been increased to provide against anticipated losses from enemy action or weather, and for use in captured ports to increase the number of alongside unloading berths at damaged piers.

All US and British LCTs were retained in the assault area for unloading purposes. These and the army DUKWs were augmented by 218 LCMs, 170 of which were loaded on merchant ships, the balance arriving on two British LSGs and one British LSC. However, many of the British LCMs had been employed in several previous operations and most of those assigned to the LSGs and LSC were hoisted in and released when those ships departed from the assault area on D+4.

LCMs were used mainly for unloading of vehicles, particularly during the initial phases and are superior to LCTs for this purpose.

In general their crews and repair personnel, both US and British, established an enviable record in maintaining these craft in an operational status over a prolonged period. The performance of British and US LCTs was likewise excellent.

Information was not available from the US Seventh Army until a very late date as to the number of merchant ships scheduled to load at various Mediterranean ports, which of these ships would lift LCM(3)s, and to which assault area they would proceed for unloading. It was therefore necessary to establish an amphibious boat pool and on very short notice transfer LCMs to the loading ports finally designated. The most objectionable result of this delay in promulgating important data was in the lack of detailed orders and information which it was possible to disseminate to the LCM crews, to the Commanding Officers of LST Mother Ships and to Traffic Control Officers designated for each area. The assignment of craft remaining in the assault area for unloading purposes into small groups with the chain of command clearly defined should be included in the operation plan and should be covered in detail in the plans of individual attack force commanders.

Changing priorities of unloading merchant ships and the diversion of these ships from one beach to another during the period immediately following the assault further complicated the unloading plan.

The shortage of labor on the beaches, the serious shortage of vehicles to transfer stores from the beaches to the dumps, the necessity to ferry stevedores from one merchant ship to another and the failure of merchant ship crews to be alert in handling lines for craft alongside - all had a direct bearing on the rapidity of unloading.

Instructions to merchant ships required each ship to show by flag hoist the percentage of cargo in tons remaining to be unloaded. This was not adhered to in many instances.

Dunnage thrown overboard by ships anchored off assault beaches and wire rope and lines discarded by LSTs as they approached the beaches resulted in minor damage to and fouled propellers of numerous craft.

A shortage of cargo nets carried by merchant ships prevented carrying out on a large scale the system of leaving packaged stores in cargo nets in LCTs to be off-loaded in nets by cranes on the beaches or pontoon causeways. An examination of unloading statistics indicates an advantage in tons per craft per day for net unloading compared to bulk unloading.

Again, the shortage of vehicles was so acute and the distance from the beaches to the dumps so great as to warrant loading trucks in LCM(3)s for direct loading into trucks from merchant ships. This in effect turned the truck loaded LCM into a DUKW and could be feasible only in cases where the distance from shore to merchant ship was small in comparison with the distance from beach to shore dumps. Here again the cargo was left in slings and unloaded by crane at the dump.

In general, the facilities provided by the forces afloat for delivery of cargo to the beaches far exceeded the capacity of the army to unload and transfer cargo from the beaches to supply dumps.

In view of the above situation one assault force commander has recommended that the present division of responsibility between army and navy for maintenance of the army over beaches be changed and that the navy be responsible for all unloading and for delivery of supplies to the beachhead supply dumps, maintaining equipment and personnel necessary for that purpose afloat and ashore.

This command does not concur for the following reasons:

(1) It would be necessary for the Navy to maintain, equip and train a large organization comprising stevedore labor, unloading control organization, and truck drivers, equipped with trucks, beach and road improvement machinery, cargo handling equipment. This organization and equipment functioning during the period of beach maintenance would not have useful naval employment between amphibious operations.

(2) When beach maintenance ends under the present division of responsibility the navy has only the Beach Battalion to withdraw while the army engineer and labor elements are absorbed in army supply and transportation duties.

(3) While for planning purposes the highest practicable rate of unloading over the beaches must be anticipated, the actual military situation in the operation, losses, expenditures and enemy threat to merchant ships off the beaches are considerations in determining the priorities and the unloading rate to be achieved. The situation in Southern France was such that it was considered a sound military decision to pursue the defeated enemy and accept a long haul from beaches to dumps at the expense of the rate of unloading merchant ships anchored in an area of slight enemy air and naval action.

(4) Inefficiency in merchant ships when compared with the individual spirit, initiative and achievements of navy crews is a handicap in employment of merchant ships in amphibious operations which placing of navy stevedores on board would not be likely to cure. The primary purpose of their employment in large scale transportation to the assault area was satisfactorily accomplished. A ready spirit of helpfulness to boats alongside and eagerness to work in or out of hours to further the common goal is not at present notable in the concept of duty held by some of our merchant crews.

Thorough planning in close cooperation with the army command based upon the present division of responsibilities with the factors set forth in Section 2.1, Part I, receiving special consideration, remains, it is believed, the most satisfactory solution of the problem of maintenance of army forces over beaches.

A statistical summary of unloading data appears on page 133 of "Campaign Narrative," Chapter 1, Part II.

Section 6.13

EVACUATION OF PRISONERS OF WAR

A total of 38,833 prisoners of war were evacuated over assault beaches, the majority to Naples and Oran. Those seriously wounded were embarked in hospital ships, others in various types of personnel ships, merchant ships specially fitted to carry troops, LSTs and LCI(L)s.

In a few instances, due to changes in destinations of LSTs, prisoners of war were returned to Corsican ports. It was found imperative that notice of such changes or diversions be given to Beach Masters and Beach Group Control Officers in sufficient time to insure proper loading of ships and craft in returning convoys.

Guards were assigned by the US Army, the number being based on characteristics of individual ships and number of prisoners embarked.

Before evacuation, prisoners were searched, deloused, tagged and provided with life belts under army supervision. Rations were provided by the army for the return voyage. Guards embarked in US Navy ships were subsisted by the Navy.

Section 6.14

OPENING OF PORTS

The original plan contemplated opening of the ports of Toulon and Marseille in the order named. The shoreside clearance work was scheduled to be performed by US Army Engineer Port Clearance Units.

PORT DE BOUC

Due to the rapid advance of the Seventh Army, and the stubborn resistance to capitulation of the enemy forces defending Toulon and Marseille, it became apparent that some other port would have to be exploited in order to expedite delivery of supplies to the army, and gradually relieve unloading operations over the beaches before the onset of bad weather. Furthermore, the beaches were becoming more distant from the front daily, making the transportation and supply problem increasingly difficult.

In view of the above, NCWTF on D+10 issued orders to open Port de Bouc, to the west of Marseille, and near the mouth of the Rhone. Since army engineers and their equipment were tied up in the working of the beaches, and standing by to enter the major ports of Marseille and Toulon when they should fall, it was decided to assign four pontoon causeway platoons from the 1040th C. B. Detachment to perform the shore clearance work.

The work involved removal of five demolished bridges from the Arles Canal and clearing wreckage from demolished cranes on the docks in the port itself. Equipment available for this work consisted solely of standard causeway operating equipment - bulldozers, welding and cutting equipment. In addition, six pontoon causeway piers were installed to increase unloading facilities. Causeways had been moved from the beaches when no longer needed. Work was started on D + 13 and completed about D+25, at which time the C. B. Detachment was ordered to Toulon to assist in shore clearance at that port. By that time, a small army engineer unit was on the site to continue dock improvements.

As a result of the above, six liberty berths and one tanker berth were made available for use, and the Arles Canal was cleared permitting water transportation of supplies by LCM to Arles, about thirty miles inland.

Although army headquarters had no plans for its development and was unable to undertake the entire project due to limitations of personnel and equipment, Port de Bouc provided an excellent point to discharge gasoline and supplies for the support of the air forces.

TOULON

Upon the fall of Toulon and Marseille (practically simultaneously) on D+13, the army modified its plan of port clearance, to the extent that all their engineer forces would be employed at Marseille to the exclusion of Toulon. This decision was prompted by the fact that the reopening of rail outlets from Toulon would take considerable time, Marseille had a far greater number of prospective berths, and they considered the numbers of their personnel and equipment were sufficient to work only one port at a time.

As in the case of Port de Bouc, NCWTF considered the development of all practicable protected unloading berths to be of paramount interest from the navy's point of view. Surveys indicated that some berths could be provided at Toulon far in advance of any that might be expected at Marseille. Consequently, NCWTF, on D+15, directed that US Navy units in excess of those required at Marseille be employed in the port clearance of Toulon. (See "Campaign Narrative," 1 September, page 91.)

Five pontoon causeway platoons were transferred from the beaches for this project. These were later supplemented by the four platoons from Port de Bouc.

The port area of Toulon was badly damaged by intensive bombing by our forces and demolitions of the enemy. Practically all buildings were demolished, roads and streets blocked and torn up, and docks damaged and blocked. Scuttled ships blocked most of the berths.

With limited equipment and no land crane facilities, debris was cleared, roads opened, dock areas leveled, wrecks bridged to provide unloading berths, and ramps built up to the roofs of dock structures to provide access for trucks to otherwise useless unloading berths. In one instance, a demolished large swing bridge had to be cut up and removed from the channel leading to some inner basin berths. Local materials, such as lumber, spikes, welding and cutting gases, and the like were procured through local French naval and civilian agencies, since no provision for such a project had been made by the US Navy, for reasons mentioned above. The availability of many types of materials was quite remarkable, and made it possible to solve what would have been otherwise insurmountable problems. A great amount of ingenuity on the part of C. B. personnel overcame many obstacles, especially the lack of cranes for lifting heavy objects.

Prisoner labor was utilized extensively, and the French arsenal personnel followed up and improved the initial rough developments.

No attempt was made to perform any work that did not contribute to the earliest practicable availability of unloading berths.

Work was started on D+20 and by D+41, there were nine liberty berths and thirty-one bow on LCT unloading berths available.

On 25 September, the army was utilizing Toulon for offloading of personnel, civilian supplies, and motor transport. Relieving Marseille to this extent would appear to have fully justified the work performed. The unloading at Toulon through D+41 amounted to:

      5,085 personnel
      2,628 vehicles
      24,252 dry tons
      76,130 barrels (wet).

MARSEILLE

The navy undertook no shoreside clearance work at Marseille, other than to furnish eight bulldozers with operating crews from 1040th C. B. Detachment. These were used to assist the Army Port Reconstruction Engineers. On D+17, the army requested that all work be stopped at Toulon and Seabees with equipment be transferred to Marseille. When they were informed that these Seabee units were equipped for only a limited range of work, it was agreed that the bulldozers were all that could contribute to their efforts.

COMMENT

Throughout all port clearance operations, the very closest liaison and coordination was exercised between the ship salvage and shoreside clearance units. This insured the most expeditious development of unloading facilities to support the allied armies.

Chapter 7

COMMUNICATIONS

Section 7.1

GENERAL

    Communications during the invasion of Southern France were very satisfactory reflecting careful and thorough communication planning, and intelligent and conscientious execution of the Communication Plan. Not only were adequate communications for an amphibious force of large magnitude and diverse composition to be provided, but also additional problems were introduced by the following conditions:

    (1) The change in the composition of the forces available for the operation during the planning period;

    (2) The late arrival in the theater of many key units;

    (3) Participation by many units without previous amphibious experience;

    (4) The magnitude of the RCM installation necessary for planned operations;

    (5) The change from assault to post-assault task organizations particularly of gunfire support forces;

    (6) A considerably higher traffic load than in previous operations. (For the period D-Day to D+30 the average number of groups handled by the amphibious flagship of NCWTF was 79,932 groups daily. This did not include voice traffic).

    Factors which contributed to successful communications in this operation were:

    (1) Application of lessons learned in previous operations;

    (2) Adequate time for planning;

    (3) Close liaison with the communication staffs of the Army, Royal Navy, and Air Forces involved in the operation, and with AFHQ;

    (4) Simplification of the cryptographic systems employed;

    (5) Preparation of an operational call sign book;

    (6) Improvement of communication facilities in the amphibious flagships, particularly the flagship of NCWTF;

    (7) Use of high speed automatic circuits on the rear links from the force flagship to Naples, and use of a high speed teletype keyed circuit between NCWTF and assault force commanders;

    (8) Adequate exchange of communication liaison personnel, particularly with French ships.

    The supply and distribution of adequate cryptographic aids to units widely separated and arriving just prior to the operation posed a considerable problem. Temporary installation of RCM equipment also presented a major problem. This was true because knowledge of the approach disposition of the various task forces which was essential for a sound RCM plan was not available until a short time before the operation, at which time those vessels which required fittings to best accomplish the purpose were widely dispersed.

The high degree of cooperation between communication organizations of the Army, Royal Navy, French Navy, and Air Forces was gratifying. The Army and Air Forces were particularly helpful in supplying to naval forces certain radio material which contributed to the successful conclusion of the operation. During Mediterranean operations close liaison has been established between the communication organizations of CinCMed and Commander US Eighth Fleet, which greatly contributed to the solution of special problems incident to the operation.

Mobile truck-mounted communication units were successfully employed. Such units were established in Corsica prior to the operation to meet the communication requirements of advanced units established on that island. Mobile mounted units also proved extremely satisfactory in the captured ports. These latter units were initially landed over the assault beaches on D+5. Efficient communications were established in captured ports shortly after their fall.

NAN equipment was not used in this operation.

Section 7.2

PLANNING

Communication planning began in February 1944 when a small group of communication representatives from the staff of Commander US Eighth Fleet was established in Bouzareah with the planning section. Communication planning representatives of the Seventh Army and MAAF were also located at this headquarters. In July when the combined planning staffs moved to Naples, a communication planning office was maintained in the same building with the combined operation planning staffs of the various forces involved. Communication planning officers of the assault force commanders were also established in Naples at that time. It is considered that this close proximity of the planning sections contributed materially to the coordination of communication plans. In addition liaison officers, one each from the US Army, the Royal Navy, and the French Navy, were assigned to the staff of NCWTF for communication planning. They provided valuable assistance in the preparation of those parts of the communication plan in which these services were involved.

From the inception of communication planning primary consideration was given to the elimination of unsatisfactory features experienced in previous operations in this theater.

The frame work of the operational call sign book was completed and arrangements made for the book to be printed immediately after the units and task organizations were definite. Provision was made that adequate cryptographic publications would be available at the proper issuing offices for the large numbers of dispersed units requiring them for the operation. Attention was given to the simplification of the assault cryptographic systems for use by Allied Forces.

Frequencies in this theater are allocated by AFHQ to the major naval, ground, and air force commanders. These in turn allocate frequencies to subordinate commanders. The US Naval Forces thus receive their frequency allocations through CinCMed. There is usually an insufficient number of frequencies to meet the demands of the forces operating in this area for a large scale assault. Frequency allocation for the invasion of Southern France was difficult for the following reasons:

(1) Aircraft spotting was furnished the three major support forces by:

    (a) XII Tactical Air Command,

    (b) US carrier planes,

    (c) Royal Navy carrier planes,

    (d) US cruiser spotting planes,

    (e) US Army Artillery liaison planes.

Crystallization of the sets for the above planes was necessary to furnish the required flexibility.

(2) Expansion of the ship-shore fire control communication organization.

(3) The mixed composition of the major assault forces, each including combat loaders and landing craft.

In July, AFHQ established a joint RCM Board for the invasion of Southern France. US Navy communication planners participated in its activities.

Successful effort was made through planning to simplify the Communication Annex of the Operation Plan for the invasion of Southern France in comparison with those of previous operations. Appendices which had peculiar application to limited units were not generally distributed. The plan was formulated with the aim of relieving, insofar as practicable, Attack Force Commanders of the necessity of duplicating essential communication information in their individual plans. Periodically the assault force communication planning officers were given as much information on all pertinent communication matters as was available in advance of distribution of the plan.

Section 7.3

COVER PLAN

The impossibility of concealing the fact of an impending assault in the Western Mediterranean was accepted. Efforts were made to disguise traffic patterns to deny the enemy information of the predicted time of the assault. To accomplish this the following action was taken:

(1) The Senior Officer's Broadcast was inaugurated 1 August by CinCMed. Dummy traffic was transmitted on this circuit preceding the operation.

(2) Dummy traffic was placed on fixed circuits which carried the bulk of outgoing traffic from operational commands at Naples to maintain a normal traffic flow after the departure of NCWTF.

(3) Dummy traffic was also placed on the harbor circuit.

In addition to the above, Royal Navy traffic to the Eastern Mediterranean was maintained at a high level to preserve enemy interest in that locality (see Section 1.6, Part I, Strategic Deception). US participation in this was not possible because of lack of US activity in the Eastern Mediterranean.

Section 7.4

FLAGSHIPS

USS Catoctin, which served as the flagship of NCWTF proved to be very satisfactory from a communication standpoint. Prior to the departure of USS Catoctin from the US for this theater, a communication officer with previous amphibious training in this command was, at the request of Commander Eighth Fleet, ordered to the flagship to make a study and submit recommendations for the improvement of the communication facilities installed. This officer also carried out the same procedure in USCGC Duane (flagship of CTF 84). The information gained permitted the correction of certain deficiencies, resulting in improvement of communication facilities in these ships. Further communication tests were conducted in USS Catoctin during the training exercises at Arzew in June 1944 and in the rehearsal for the invasion of Southern France held in the Salerno-Capri area. Deficiencies noted were corrected, particular attention being given to elimination of interference within the ship. Both the ground and air force commands in USS Catoctin were assigned adequate facilities to meet their requirements. It is considered that the number of transmitters employed,

    4 low frequency

    26 high frequency

    15 very high frequency

was the maximum number practicable; 110 receivers were utilized. Additional equipment was neither necessary to the task, nor desirable in the interest of efficient communications.

Particularly useful were the high speed automatic installations which were used on the Rear Link to Naples and on the Force Fox circuit. USS Catoctin functioned as standby fighter director ship and controlled the offensive fighter bomber missions until control was established ashore. These functions were performed satisfactorily. However, in this operation the scale of enemy air opposition did not complicate their execution. The decision to utilize a fighter director ship separate from the flagship is considered sound.

USS Plunkett was designated standby flagship for NCWTF, and additional temporary equipment was installed in this ship to provide emergency communication facilities.

USS Augusta (flagship of CTF 86) also served as alternate command post afloat for Commanding General XII Tactical Air Command. Additional temporary radio equipment was installed in this ship to meet the requirements of the latter.

Flagships of the Assault Force Commanders for Alpha, Delta, and Camel areas were:

    Alpha - USCGC Duane

    Delta - USS Biscayne

    Camel - USS Bayfield

USCGC Duane reported this area in April 1944. Having been previously fitted as an amphibious force flagship, the communications equipment and facilities installed were considered satisfactory. Interference tests were conducted and minor alterations and additions in communication equipment were made. USS Biscayne, originally the AVP 11, was converted for use as an assault force flagship in this area, and has been used as such on previous amphibious operations. This ship from a communication standpoint was not considered satisfactory. Prior to the operation, a communication board was assigned to study and make recommendations to improve the communication facilities. Insofar as practicable, the recommendations of the board were carried out with resultant improvement. Permanent improvement in communication facilities is considered necessary if the ship is to be used as a flagship. Recommendations to accomplish this have been made the subject of a special report. The communication facilities in USS Bayfield (flagship of CTF 87) were considered satisfactory.

Nine US LCI(L)s were utilized as amphibious flagships on regimental combat team level within the assault forces. Additional radio equipment and personnel were provided. They were also fitted with CCMs prior to the operation, which greatly increased their efficiency.

Alternate flagships with adequate communication facilities to fulfill the function of the ships they would be required to replace were not available. The multiplicity of the radio circuits required in the flagship of NCWTF and the flagships of attack force commanders could be duplicated only by ships equipped with approximately the same radio and radar equipment. Such vessels suitably equipped have not been available in previous amphibious operations in which the Eighth Fleet has participated. The loss of USS Catoctin or any of the assault force commanders' flagships during the assault would have had serious effect on operational communications. Provision was made to meet such a contingency by installing additional radio facilities in the ships assigned as relief flagships, but it is considered that alternate flagships with comparable communication facilities are particularly needed in large amphibious operations, and should be provided.

A specially equipped amphibious flagship for the naval commander of an amphibious task force, and adequate flagships for the individual attack force commanders are a necessity. Not only during the assault, but particularly in the follow-up period did USS Catoctin prove her worth in handling communications. NCWTF remained in the assault area for a period of approximately five weeks. Communications of administrative character as well as those connected with the assault follow-up and the opening of captured ports were handled. The traffic load during this time was often comparable with that of the peak load during the assault. An improvised amphibious flagship would not satisfactorily have met this situation.

Section 7.5

DEFICIENCIES

During the invasion of Southern France as in previous amphibious operations of this command, deficiencies in communications were noted, the most noticeable being:

(1) Breaking of radio silence on TBS circuits prior to H-hour;

(2) Overloading and improper use of TBS circuits;

(3) Misuse of higher precedences;

(4) Overloading of Task Force Commanders circuit;

(5) Lack of security on voice circuits.

RADIO SILENCE

Although specific instructions had been issued cautioning against such unauthorized transmissions, radio silence was twice broken on the TBS for testing purposes on D-1 day. While there is no indication that these transmissions adversely affected tactical surprise, it is considered a dangerous practice which might well have given aid to the enemy.

TBS CIRCUIT

Lack of proper circuit discipline made it necessary for NCWTF on two occasions to direct discontinuance of this channel for other than operational traffic. The overloading of this circuit was caused by:

(1) Unnecessary transmissions and repetitions;

(2) Passing of lengthy despatches which should have been passed by other means.

To relieve the congestion on the TBS circuit consideration was given to establishing additional channels. While such an arrangement would reduce the load on the single TBS circuit, additional channels would introduce complications for those ships having but one TBS which were not considered acceptable.

MISUSE OF HIGHER PRECEDENCES

Placing of unwarranted precedence on despatches resulted in needless delays in clearing more important messages.

OVERLOADING OF TASK FORCE COMMANDERS CIRCUIT

On several occasions Task Force Commanders 84 and 86 reported backlogs of traffic which they were unable to clear on the Task Force Commanders circuit. To relieve this situation, alternate frequencies were established and traffic cleared. A heavy traffic load on the Task Force Commanders circuit was contemplated. An alternate VHF radio teletype circuit between NCWTF and CTFs 84, 85, 86 and 87 was provided. This circuit effectively removed a considerable load from the Primary Task Force Commanders circuit, and provided satisfactory communications, when the flagships were in close proximity with no intervening high ground.

LACK OF SECURITY ON VOICE CIRCUITS

The use of the telephone on shore as a rapid means of communication has resulted in the misuse of voice circuits on shipboard. Voice codes possess little security. The interception of voice transmissions provide valuable information to the enemy, therefore the voice transmissions should be confined to subjects where speed of transmission outweighs security.

Continued efforts have been made toward correcting these deficiencies with a resultant improvement in amphibious communications.

Section 7.6

CALL SIGNS

Call signs in combined operations invariably present a troublesome problem. Encipherment of normal call signs during a large amphibious operation in which forces of several nationalities participate is not acceptable because of considerations of speed, security, and efficiency. At the inception of planning for the invasion of Southern France work on a call sign book was started. Difficulty was encountered due to the continuous changes in the units allocated for the operation and the late receipt of the task organizations of Task Force Commanders. It was impossible to list all participating commands in the book when it went to press. To cover later additions, blocks of call signs were reserved as spares, and specific assignment of these was made and disseminated as information became available. A total of 1476 call signs was allocated. To provide limited security, four columns of call signs were prepared, each of which was made effective at a specified time during the operation.

Comments on the call sign book in action reports have been consistently favorable. "Number-letter-number" call signs were allocated to major army and air force commands and to all navy commands which it was known might take part in the operation, except landing ships and craft (for which a system of call signs using designating letter followed by hull numbers is effective). These call signs were specified for use on both W/T, Voice circuits and Visual.

Use of "number-letter-number" call signs on voice circuits has received both favorable and unfavorable comment. Where voice transmissions are logged it is much easier to log this type of call sign than a codeword call sign, but on the other hand, it is considered easier to memorize a codeword call sign. This is important on tactical voice circuits in connection with such duty as screening operations and submarine hunts, where speed is paramount.

For the above reasons the assignment of a codeword voice call sign in addition to the "number-letter-number" call sign would be desirable in destroyers, cruisers, aircraft carriers and battleships.

The NCWTF Operational Call Sign Book provided call signs for the principal army and air force commands for use on navy circuits only. Sufficient US Army and US Army Air Force call signs were extracted from the appropriate Army SOIs to provide the allied navies with the necessary call signs after these commands moved ashore. When this occurred some confusion resulted in that some navy-originated despatches continued to use the NCWTF operational call signs for army and air force traffic. Such a change of call sign system is not desirable, and in the future it is intended to arrange with the army and air force commands to continue the use of special operational call signs assigned to them as long as assault communications are in effect.

Section 7.7

AUTHENTICATION

From D-Day to D+5 edition 6 of CCBP 0122 (Challenge and Reply, first method) was authorized for all authentication except in communications with aircraft and airborne Shore Fire Control Parties. On D+6 this edition was superseded by the current area edition. Due to probability of compromise airborne Shore Fire Control Parties were provided special authenticators. The use of CCBP 0127 and 0128 was not considered during the planning stage as it appeared doubtful that these publications would be available in sufficient time to permit distribution.

It was reported that the assault edition of CCBP 0122 was compromised shortly before its supersession. This possible compromise apparently had no unfortunate consequences. However, it must be appreciated that the compromise of a widely held authenticator system might be extremely helpful to the enemy in deception. In the future therefore, it is intended to withhold the distribution of the basic authentication system from Class 1 holders afloat and from units operating on shore in the assault area. A special authenticator system can be constructed which will meet the requirements of these units. Although there was little need for an authentication system during the invasion of Southern France, it is considered sound policy to make provision for such a system in future amphibious operations.

Section 7.8

CRYPTOGRAPHIC AIDS

During the planning stage, action was taken to attain insofar as practicable, reduced but adequate cryptographic holdings to meet the necessary security requirements for units which would engage in the operation.

The Combined Coding Machine (CCM), with CCBP 0102 for class 5 and equivalent holders and CCBP 0131 for class 3 and equivalent holders, was prescribed as the common high-grade system for all services. The planned distribution of this system was realized with the exception of a few Royal Navy ships and two French destroyers. In a few cases, British commands afloat were handicapped by having only one machine aboard flagships. This situation can be rectified in the future with the increased availability of CCMs. Instruction in operation and maintenance of the CCM was furnished the Royal Navy by technicians from Commander US Eighth Fleet over a period of several months prior to the operation. Also US Navy communication liaison officers were placed aboard French ships for the operation. Both procedures proved helpful. The CCM meets the need for rapid secure communications within and between combined allied services for amphibious operations, which need had not previously been met. It was found possible just prior to the operation to provide CCMs to the 9 LCI(L)(C)s, which craft were used by the three major assault forces as amphibious flagships for the task group commanders on regimental level. Reports that this provision proved exceptionally useful have been received. To enhance the security of combined CCM channels it is recommended that they be provided with rotating indicators.

The Combined Assault Code provided a low-grade system for general distribution to all echelons having radio communications. It was also prescribed for use as a voice code. Three successive editions were used. Only the first-used edition of the Combined Assault Code was held by army and air force authorities. After D+5, therefore, it was necessary either for navy non-holders of the CCM to use CSP 1606 for traffic containing army or air force addressees or for a navy addressee to reencrypt for delivery. This unsatisfactory condition should be eliminated in future operations through joint agreement that all services hold the same low-grade system universally during the post-assault as well as during the assault period. At the same time provision must be made so that army and navy shore units operating where the danger of physical compromise is greatest hold only the effective edition during the assault phase. Garbles were encountered in the use of this three-letter code which were often difficult to clear. It is believed a four-letter code with a garble table would prove more satisfactory, and that increased efficiency in its use would result even though transmissions would be increased through addition of the extra letter to each code group.

CSP 1511/12 was prescribed for use within US Naval forces participating in the operation. It was not extensively used and opinion is divided as to its usefulness and necessity. Since instances may arise when secret information must be passed by units who do not hold CCMs, its continued retention for the above purpose is contemplated.

Since circumstances in the Mediterranean are such that ships holding class 2 or lower allowances normally never find it necessary to use world-wide cryptographic systems, steps were taken to reduce their holdings on 1 July. All world wide cryptographic publications were deleted from the list of required holdings for class 2 and below ships, and various other reductions were made in the holdings. As a result, minor war vessels, which comprise the major portion of the Eighth Fleet, were not required to bag and leave ashore any publications.

From experience gained during this and past operations it has been established that area publications to be used for an assault can be most satisfactorily issued in the area of operations. It is recommended that a policy of area distribution be adopted.

Section 7.9

VOICE CODES

A voice code, "NCWTF Voice Vocabulary," was prepared in booklet form and given wide distribution. Comment received from the task force commanders relative to the usefullness of the voice vocabulary varied. In addition to "NCWTF Voice Vocabulary," the Combined Assault Code was authorized for use as a voice code for transmissions requiring a higher degree of security.

A code such as "NCWTF Voice Vocabulary" can prove useful, but its limitations as to security must be understood. If properly used it can delay correct enemy interpretation of intercepted traffic in the early stages of an operation, when such delay is most important.

The advantages of speed gained from voice transmission are lost when encryption is necessary. Until efficient scrambling devices are perfected which will permit rapid voice transmission with the requisite security, it is considered loss of speed must be accepted and the most satisfactory voice code possible must be prescribed for use with emphasis placed on necessity for proper procedure, security, and circuit discipline whenever used.

Section 7.10

SPECIAL CODES

A special Mediterranean Bombardment Code was prepared by representatives of allied forces for use by Naval Gunfire Liaison Officers (NGLO) and Shore Fire Control Parties (SFCP). Based on CSP 2156B, this code contained two parts, one for use between ships and ground observers, and one for use between ships and aircraft. This code proved satisfactory in all respects.

The communication plan for this operation contained a compilation of code words of special interest and of special signals authorized for use during the operation. Circumstances necessitated little use of some of the code words, such as those assigned for RCM communications. It is considered, however, that the assembly of miscellaneous code words and signals in one place has merit. It obviates necessity for resort to several publications and pamphlets to obtain the required information.

DAILY TRAFFIC ANALYSIS - NCWTF FLAGSHIP (USS CATOCTIN) DURING THE INVASION OF SOUTHERN FRANCE

	DATE	TOTAL SENT	MSG'S REC'D	TOTAL SENT	GROUPS REC'D	SERVICES HANDLED
Aug.	15	472	783	35960	55709	114
	16	609	840	56081	60343	128
	17	592	900	46999	65485	125
	18	512	751	37354	56505	112
	19	598	620	46569	46009	187
	20	543	557	49285	43336	155
	21	533	637	51478	48678	204
	22	473	609	34891	42453	163
	23	716	662	56303	49161	295
	24	655	605	51046	36410	238
	25	695	701	48480	46484	245
	26	704	696	51092	47868	273
	27	665	769	49307	51621	267
	28	625	718	42874	45753	277
	29	642	718	42345	45287	287
	30	670	708	44066	53909	246
	31	566	668	39899	43525	201
Sept.	1	603	759	35749	42657	308
	2	572	767	35237	55996	250
	3	568	546	34556	40924	262
	4	596	659	44579	36597	279
	5	593	651	37887	43476	265
	6	545	567	45564	32721	233
	7	603	600	40359	36554	265
	8	651	653	44592	41896	263
	9	672	666	44158	40245	241
	10	591	691	39196	49369	290
	11	503	611	32961	39643	305
	12	545	744	38173	54269	229
	13	548	697	37671	49180	320
	14	620	748	40601	49199	315
	15	648	750	53823	47299	369
	16	434	707	32202	44651	260
	17	516	617	36600	38272	289
	18	552	658	31772	38966	365
	19	554	627	42023	40524	292
	20	560	661	37600	39123	300
	21	568	600	38169	40522	268
	22	470	639	38210	39107	264
	23	506	549	44837	35800	167
	24	472	509	41452	35064	194
	25	163	473	14335	31079	97
Totals		23923	28091	1736211	1881680	10217

GRAND TOTAL 3,617,891

Figure 16

Section 7.11

RADIO CHANNELS

The frequencies allocated and the radio channels provided proved to be adequate. Considering the number of units employed, the circuits in general operated satisfactorily. No serious interference was encountered.

The following Royal Navy facilities were available for the delivery of traffic by the Broadcast method:

(1) Naples Area Broadcast.
(2) Senior Officers Broadcast.

Use was made of the Naples Area Broadcast for the delivery of traffic to all ships taking part in the operation.

The Senior Officers Broadcast was utilized for the delivery of traffic to flag officers.

A Force Fox circuit was set up by NCWTF for the delivery of operational and air warning traffic to ships in the assault area. Automatic transmission (15 WPM) was employed on this circuit which proved to be very satisfactory.

An indication of the volume of communications conducted is contained in the daily traffic analysis, figure 16. The analysis shows a total of 3,617,891 groups handled by the flagship of NCWTF over a period of 42 days.

A high speed VHF radio teletype circuit was provided for communication between NCWTF and the four assault force commanders. This circuit greatly reduced the load on the Task Force Commanders circuit and operated efficiently when the assault force commanders and NCWTF were in close proximity, about fifteen miles, with no intervening high ground. The development of this means of communication is recommended.

A high speed automatic circuit was used for the Rear Link channel from the flagship of NCWTF to Radio Naples. The rear link traffic could not have been adequately handled manually.

Fire Support communications were satisfactory. There were 44 Shore Fire Control Parties, each equipped with HF. 31 of these parties were also equipped with FM-VHF channels. The Common Fire Support Calling Frequency was guarded by Assault Force Commanders and Commanders of Fire Support Groups. This circuit was used by ships not assigned a shore fire control party to establish communication with these units. Inclusion of SCR 608 sets, or equivalent equipment, in the allowance of DDs is considered highly desirable to improve fire support communications.

Section 7.12

VISUAL

Visual communications functioned more efficiently during the invasion of Southern France than in previous operations of this command.

The volume of operational and tactical traffic was maintained at a low level. This may be attributed to previous experience in amphibious operations by the units involved, strict adherence to basic plan, and the lack of changes thereto, often necessitated by severe enemy action.

An intense period of training was instituted for ships and craft in the Mediterranean theater prior to the operation. This was emphasized particularly between ships of the French, British, and United States Navies. Tactical maneuvers controlled by visual signals were carried out at every opportunity.

Confusion experienced in past operations caused by landing craft employing many different signal books was overcome in this operation by the use of the "Mediterranean Joint Landing Craft Signal Book."

The Operational Call System as prescribed proved to be very satisfactory.

The excellence of visual communications between ships and craft of allied navies is particularly worthy of mention. Difficulties foreseen during the planning stage were eliminated by the assignment of liaison personnel and the use of NCWTF Operational Call Sign Book. No misunderstanding in transmission occurred. British and French ships did not employ any procedure in their transmissions to United States ships but used plain language to indicate precedence, originator, action, and information addressees. Many messages transmitted from United States ships to British and French ships employed complete headings. This operation proved conclusively that combined forces can conduct visual signaling in complete harmony.

LCI(L)s and other control vessels were particularly efficient in their handling of visual communications. Traffic to other landing craft was relayed through them with excellent results.

Communications with merchant ships were far more satisfactory than in the past. The display of number boards was particularly helpful in calling merchant vessels. The signal personnel on these ships have shown distinct improvement.

British 360° Daylight Signaling lanterns proved very valuable in sending "All Ships Present" signals.

Communications with the Seventh Army, while the headquarters was near the beach, were greatly facilitated by establishment of a signal station at their headquarters operated by US Navy personnel. This resulted in speedier transmission and relieved overburdened radio circuits.

It was found necessary to establish more and larger signal stations in captured ports than was at first anticipated. The equipment and personnel available for these stations was very limited, and it was necessary to employ personnel from the ships present. It is recommended that more emphasis be placed on the establishment of visual communications with both army and navy activities on the beach in future operations.

Enemy aircraft warning signals for yellow and red alert proved very useful. Only in distant anchorages and beaches was it observed that ships were slow in repeating.

Excessive transmissions of messages were caused by ships and craft not knowing the positions of the flagships directing the operation in the various areas.

On the signal bridge of all task force flagships, complete ships movement and ships present lists were posted, as well as call signs and other pertinent data. This was of inestimable value in rapid transmission of traffic.

Section 7.13

RADAR AND IFF

Effective use was made of radar during the operation. Surface search radar was used without restrictions. The type SG was particularly satisfactory both for station keeping and for navigation. Use of air search radar was restricted to designated radar guardships, whose duty it was to alert forces enroute to and in the assault area until the air force was established on shore. This plan and the performance of air search radar in its execution were both satisfactory. Although enemy air effort was on a smaller scale than that encountered in previous operations in this theater, it is considered that adequate radar coverage and dissemination of air warnings would have been provided had air opposition been greater. A special FM voice circuit, plus an additional standby intermediate frequency voice circuit, was provided for radar reporting. Prior to the operation, drills were conducted utilizing these circuits.

An IFF guardship plan was not prescribed. Ships were permitted to use their transpondors without restriction. This procedure is not considered sound, and a guardship arrangement for ships in a convoy should be prescribed.

Comment relative to Beedex units is contained in Section 5.2, Part II.

The Radar Planning Device, developed by the Bureau of Aeronautics, was used during the assault phase. The performance of this equipment has been made the subject of a special report to Chief of Naval Operations (Serial 001221 of 30 October 1944).

Section 7.14

COUNTERMEASURES

The services of RCM personnel attached to the staff of Commander US Eighth Fleet were utilized during the planning stage of this operation for the upkeep and testing of the countermeasures material available. Close liaison was maintained with other services in this area.

The program for RCM involved installation of 571 units of equipment, including 152 transmitters on 66 ships. The RCM plan included both "barrage" and "spot" jamming and provision for use of shell and rocket window. Pre-assault bombing was carried out against selected enemy radar installations beginning D-5 day (see Section 4.2, Part II). A special RCM plan for the diversionary group was formulated and proved satisfactory.

Reports from task force commanders indicate that RCM equipment functioned efficiently. The extent to which the enemy was denied effective use of radar and the deception accomplished by the use of RCM is difficult to estimate. Monitoring ships report enemy radar frequencies were effectively blanketed.

Based on experience gained during the invasion of Southern France, the following is considered worthy of note:

(1) Aerial reconnaissance is the most reliable method for pin-pointing enemy radar locations;
(2) RCM equipment should be installed and operators thoroughly indoctrinated well in advance of the assault;
(3) Pre-assault bombing cannot be assumed to have neutralized enemy radar locations.

GUIDED MISSILE COUNTERMEASURES

Sixty warships participating in the invasion of Southern France were equipped with GMCM jammers. All US cruisers, carriers, and battleships were so fitted. Twenty jammers were high-power (CXGE, XCJ) types operated by trained RCM personnel; the remainder were lower powered (MAS, ARQ-8, British 650), operated by ships' personnel. Prior to the operation, an extensive training program was undertaken by the Eighth Fleet GMCM Unit (Countermeasures Unit Z); transmitters were tested and modulation frequency adjusted to within 1 per cent of selected frequency. Doctrine relative to the use of jammers had been in effect within the Eighth Fleet for some months prior to the invasion. Somewhat modified and expanded, this doctrine provided the basis for GMCM instructions. Approximately 17 radio bomb control signals were logged by "J" (jammer) ships during last light 15, 16, 17, and 18 August; all signals were jammed by at least one and frequently as many as 20 jammers. The operation of GMCM equipment was considered satisfactory.

The detailed employment of RCM and GMCM during this operation was made the subject of a separate report to Chief of Naval Operations (Serial 001205 of 19 October 1944).

Section 7.15

RADIO INSTALLATIONS AND EQUIPMENT

Radio equipment was adequate to meet the circuit demands. Temporary installations were made in a number of instances to supplement standard allowances where special requirements existed. In general, all material functioned satisfactorily.

Portable FM SCR 509 equipment was successfully used on the assault boat control circuits.

Each Beach Battalion was equipped with four jeep mounted SCR 284 or TCS transceivers and one jeep mounted SCR 193. The power and mobility of this equipment provided satisfactory communications.

Mobile radio units provided communications between Advanced Base Groups and the assault forces. These groups were provided SCR 399, SCR 284, SCR 193 and TBW transmitters with appropriate receivers, installed in trucks or jeeps as required. Inter-communication was maintained between captured ports and on the rear links to Ajaccio, Naples, and Caserta with this equipment. The mobile radio units which comprised trucks equipped with cryptographic facilities, proved invaluable in the establishment and maintenance of communication with the advanced base groups.

Small radio and radar repair units were set up in LST Mother Ships by Attack Force Commanders. These units were employed in effecting repairs to radio and radar equipment in small craft. Future employment of such units is recommended.

LCVP DRONE VESSELS

LCVP drone vessels were employed during the invasion of Southern France (see "Apex boats," Section 5.9, Part II). The performance of their control equipment has been made the subject of a special report to the Chief of the Bureau of Ships (Serial 001219 of 30 October 1944).

Section 7.16

CONCLUSION

Although the traffic load during the invasion of Southern France was greater than for previous amphibious operations of this command, the conduct of communications was more satisfactory.

Based on the invasion of Sicily, NCWTF outlined the following necessary factors for satisfactory communication in an amphibious combined army-navy-air operation:

(1) Specifically designed "amphibious flagships" for attack force and higher commanders participating in the assault;
(2) Communication personnel adequate in numbers and training;
(3) Communication material available in the theater adequate to meet reasonable needs arising from frequent changes in the planned operational organization;
(4) Planning in close association with other services;
(5) Common procedures, call sign systems and cryptographic aids;
(6) A common landing craft signal book, designed to meet all essential needs of landing ships and craft enroute, in the assault, and during follow-up operations.

The improvement of communications demonstrated in the invasion of Southern France is considered to have resulted from the realization of the above requirements.

New communication arrangements and technique for ship installation were employed during the operation. The continued development and use of the following equipment is recommended:

(1) High speed automatic equipment for use on rear links and force broadcast circuits;
(2) Radio teletype circuits utilizing VHF equipment, between the naval task force commander and attack force commanders;
(3) Drone boats;
(4) Application of information available from the Radar Planning Device.

In addition to the above, need continues for development of efficient scrambling equipment for use with voice circuit transmitters.

Chapter 8

MEDICAL DEPARTMENT OPERATIONS

Section 8.1

GENERAL

The medical annex to the operation plan for the invasion of Southern France was based upon the recognized navy medical responsibilities in a combined army-navy amphibious operation. These are:

(a) Providing medical care for all personnel of all services while in US Navy ships.

(b) Providing seaward evacuation of all casualties from the assault area until the army becomes sufficiently established to treat, hold and evacuate in a routine manner.

The first responsibility was recognized as existing in all US Navy ships and craft. It was not interpreted as precluding cooperation by embarked medical personnel of other services. Their assistance in caring for personnel of their own service was invited but not required and no attempt was made to impose a uniform routine for all ships. Ships' medical officers were directed to provide ample sick call facilities for all hands in the manner best suited for their individual ships. Small boat crews were trained in First Aid procedures to enable them to meet the responsibility to personnel embarked in their craft.

Plans for seaward evacuation of casualties were influenced by experiences gained in previous operations in this theater. The Mediterranean is peculiar in that the distances between friendly shores and target areas are short enough to provide quick turn around times for hospital ships but at the same time they are too long to make the routine use of LSTs desirable for the evacuation of litter cases. During the planning stage, casualty figures for the assault phases of the Sicilian, Salerno and Anzio operation were carefully reviewed and a daily maximum casualty expectancy rate for the invasion was estimated. This rate was broken down into classes and an overall 15% was added as a safety factor. Evacuation facilities were then provided for this number.

The evacuation organization consisted of:

(a) Force and Area Evacuation officers.

(b) Medical sections of Beach Battalions.

(c) Ambulance boats.

(d) Evacuation ships.

(e) Medical units in the rear echelon.

Section 8.2

FORCE AND AREA EVACUATION OFFICERS

The Force Evacuation Officer was embarked in USS Catoctin. He was responsible for the coordination of all parts of the medical plan.

The Area Evacuation Officers were embarked respectively:

(a) For Task Force 84 in USS Duane in the Alpha area.

(b) For Task Force 85 in USS Biscayne in the Delta area.

(c) For Task Force 87 in USS Bayfield in the Camel area.

Area Evacuation Officers were responsible for the coordination of the medical plan within their respective areas.

Section 8.3

MEDICAL SECTIONS OF BEACH BATTALIONS

The medical plan took cognizance of the Beach Group organization. This provided for a clear cut division of responsibility between the medical sections of the army and the navy. The army was responsible for the care of casualties landward of the high water mark, for their transportation to the navy evacuation stations and for the furnishing of a check-off list of all casualties so transported. The navy was responsible for the care of casualties in the navy evacuation stations, for evacuating casualties seaward and for keeping a record of all casualties so evacuated.

Three Beach Battalions took part in the operation, the 1st in the Alpha area, the 4th in the Delta area and the 8th in the Camel area. The medical sections of the 1st and 4th performed their duties in a smooth and efficient manner. They benefited from past experiences and were properly organized to take advantage of lessons learned. The 8th had had no previous combat experience and the medical department was poorly organized to meet its responsibilities. Considerable inefficiency and confusion was noted during the first three days. The Area Evacuation Officer went ashore on D plus 3 and was able to establish proper coordination between the Beach Battalion, the army medical sections and the ambulance boats following which no further difficulty was experienced. The cause of the difficulty appears to have been a lack of appreciation of the importance of the medical sections. The Senior Medical Officer of a Beach Battalion must be recognized as a department head during the training period and must be given the necessary authority and cooperation to properly organize and train the personnel of the medical sections in their responsibilities under combat conditions.

Section 8.4

AMBULANCE BOATS

As in previous operations in this theater, all boats transporting troops and equipment from ship to shore were available to evacuate casualties from shore to ship. Beachmasters as the naval representatives of NCWTF and responsible for naval operations in the vicinity of the beaches were directed to utilize these craft whenever possible. Except for the temporary confusion and difficulties experienced by the 8th Beach Battalion, seaward evacuation from the beaches was handled in a very satisfactory manner. Fortunately, casualties were only a fraction of those anticipated, but this in no way detracts from the excellent work performed by Beach Battalion and small boat personnel in transporting casualties to the evacuation ships.

Section 8.5

EVACUATION SHIPS

The following ships, listed in the order of their suitability, were available for casualty evacuation:

(a) Hospital Ships.

(b) Transports (APAs and XAPs).

(c) LSTs and AKAs.

(d) Task Force Flagships.

(e) Combatant ships and LCI(L)s.

(f) Merchant Marine Ships.

    (a) Hospital Ships.

Hospital ships head the list not only because they are best fitted for this duty but also because the short turn around periods made them easily available at all times. A hospital ship on this type of duty should be expected to provide every hospital facility needed to treat all types of casualties from an active combat area, because they are the only hospitals available during the crucial assault phase. Unless they have both personnel and equipment necessary to meet this qualification they are little better than ambulance ships. The above remarks are inspired by the request of one hospital ship for air transportation for six head injuries on D plus 2. This was arranged with some difficulty but it should not be necessary to transfer any patients from a hospital ship to a shore based hospital for emergency treatment.

The location of US Army and British hospitals in Naples and French Army hospitals in Oran made it necessary to evacuate their respective casualties to these ports. It was estimated that a minimum of 12 hospital ships would be needed to evacuate the maximum load of casualties from the target area to the hospitals in the rear echelon and that 15 would be the ideal number. When this number was requested by NCWTF it was found that the European and Pacific theaters had top priority on American Ships and that the 8th Army and Middle East had top priority on the British Ships. The first allocation of the War Department was for 7, this later was raised to 12. One navy hospital ship, the USS Refuge was allocated for service with combatant ships prior to D-day and made available for the operation. One of the 12 allocated by the Army failed to arrive because of delay in its overhaul and conversion in the United States.

The 12 hospital ships available were placed in a Hospital Ship Pool under the operational control of the Principal Sea Transport Officer (PSTO) of Allied Force Headquarters. They were sent into the combat area on an automatic schedule, beginning D plus 1 and continuing through D plus 6, in the following order:

Ship		Patient capacity	Speed
D plus 1.	1. USAH Algonquin	455	14.5
	2. USAH Chateau Thierry	511	15.3
	3. USAH Shamrock	543	14.5
D plus 2.	1. USAH John Clem	291	14.5
	2. USAH Acadia	788	18
	3. USAH Thistle	462	15
D plus 3.	1. USAH Emily Weder	737	13
D plus 4.	1. USAH Marigold	799	13
	2. USAH Ernest Hines	287	14
D plus 5.	1. USAH Seminole	456	13
	2. USAH Meany	579	11
D plus 6.	1. USS Refuge	630	10.5

In accordance with the practice followed in previous operations in this theater, hospital ships were not taken into the combat area on D day. Experience has shown D day casualties to be relatively lighter than those of succeeding days and that the evacuation facilities afforded by APAs and XAPs are sufficient to meet the requirements. The hospital ships appeared at the outer screen at sunrise and were directed by NCWTF to proceed to anchorages off the beaches where casualties had been collected. Embarkation proceeded until one hour before sunset when the ships departed from the area. Ships less than 50% loaded were directed to proceed beyond the outer screen and to return the following day. Beginning D plus 7 hospital ships were despatched to the combat area by PSTO upon request of the Seventh Army which by that time had established sufficient Evacuation and Field Hospitals in the target area to give them a satisfactory holding capacity. The automatic schedule functioned very satisfactorily. The ships arrived on time and, with the exception of a few minor difficulties with communications during D plus 1 and D plus 2, proceeded without delay to assigned anchorages. Beachmasters were prompt in providing ambulance boats to transport patients from the evacuation stations. Approximately 1800 casualties were evacuated from the beaches to hospital ships during the operation of the automatic schedule. PSTO, the Beach Battalions, the Operations Officer on the staff of NCWTF, the hospital ships and the medical sections of SOS NATOUSA all cooperated in effecting highly efficient casualty evacuation.

(b) Transports (APAs and XAPs).

APAs and XAPs were depended upon for casualty evacuation on D-day. Twelve of these ships took part in the operation and were equally distributed among the three task forces. Their medical staffs were augmented by personnel in the theater, thus permitting them to use their medical department facilities to capacity. D-day casualties were very light on all beaches and the transports were more than sufficient to meet the requirements.

(c) <u>LSTs and AKAs</u>.

Every US Navy LST entering the assault area carried one Navy medical officer and 5 or more hospital corpsmen and were prepared to accept capacity loads of casualties. Cognizance was taken in the medical plan of the length of their return trips and evacuation officers on the beaches were instructed to use them only in case of necessity and to limit their lifts to walking cases as far as possible. It was not necessary to use them for evacuation because casualties were much lighter than anticipated and hospital ships were able to provide all the facilities needed.

(d) <u>Task Force Flagships</u>.

The evacuation possibilities of these ships were explored in an attempt to eliminate one outstanding weakness in the evacuation plans in past operations in this theater. This was the absence of suitable evacuation ships in the target area at night after transports had departed. Hospital ships are not available because they automatically leave the area at sunset. Two of the four flagships in the invasion, USS Catoctin and USS Bayfield are comparable in size and medical facilities to APAs and XAPs. Advantage was taken of this by augmenting their medical department complements and otherwise preparing them in advance to receive casualties if the need arose. It proved to be a wise move since both were used as evacuation ships for casualties resulting at night from enemy air attacks and from minesweepers striking mines. These casualties were received aboard and treated until they could be evacuated to hospital ships.

(e) and (f) <u>Combatant Ships, LCI(L)s and Merchant Ships</u>.

It was not necessary to use these ships for casualty evacuation. Beachmasters made occasional use of LCI(L)s to transport casualties from the beaches to hospital ships.

Section 8.6

HOSPITAL FACILITIES IN THE REAR ECHELON

No attempt was made during the early phases of the operation to classify casualties by nationality on the beaches. All patients were evacuated to Naples where classification was effected. French casualties were sent on to Oran as transportation became available.

Later the French Army was able to use several civilian hospitals which were found operating in the target area. French casualties finding their way into these hospitals were very reluctant to leave, consequently their number on the beaches awaiting evacuation was materially reduced. Later when it became necessary to maintain a satisfactory availability of beds in the invasion area, hospital ships could be loaded with French patients from local hospitals and sent direct to Oran without interferring with the casualty evacuation plan. A small number of French casualties were evacuated to Naples, thence to Oran. American and British casualties were all evacuated to Naples.

As the need for hospital ships to the target area decreased they were released from the pool for other duty and evacuations to the US from Naples began. The USS Refuge was released on D plus 15 and sailed for Oran and the US on D plus 31.

Section 8.7

US NAVY CASUALTIES

Casualties among US Navy personnel participating in the operation up to and including D plus 41 were:

> Killed in Action............................... 35
> Missing in Action............................. 36
> Wounded in Action............................243

These figures are based upon reports available at this time. The majority of those missing in action will eventually be classified as dead because they are members of crews of ships damaged or lost through enemy action. Personnel listed as wounded are those receiving injuries in actual combat or due to enemy action and do not include those due to non-combat causes.

Section 8.8

CASUALTY REPORTS

Casualty reports were reduced to a minimum. Beach Battalions made no separate reports. The Army furnished a list of casualties sent to the evacuation stations which was used to check off the casualties as they were evacuated seaward, and the names of those evacuated independently of the Army were added. The check off list was then forwarded to the Detachment of Patients, Seventh Army.

Evacuation ships prepared a report in triplicate giving the following information on each casualty aboard:

(a) Full name, rate or rank, service or serial number.

(b) Organization.

(c) Hour and date received aboard.

(d) Date disembarked.

(e) Diagnosis and treatment given aboard.

(f) Condition upon disembarkation.

The original was mailed at the port of disembarkation to Detachment of Patients, Seventh Army, one copy was mailed to Com8thFleet, and one copy retained aboard.

Reporting of US Navy casualties was carried out in accordance with the directions in Navy Regulations and the Manual of the Medical Department.

Burial of the dead was under the direction of the Graves Registration Services. There were no burials at sea.

INVASION OF SOUTHERN FRANCE

PART III

CONCLUSIONS & RECOMMENDATIONS

Chapter 1

CONCLUSIONS

Section 1.1

PLANNING

The conclusions herein stated are based upon collective experience of this command in the planning, preparation and execution of the amphibious invasion of Southern France. Some are based upon the results of experimentation and research conducted during the planning period to solve difficulties anticipated in execution of the plan. Still others have grown out of opinion reaffirmed by experience in successive amphibious operations.

The apparent ease and success with which amphibious assaults have frequently been made should not lessen respect for the invariable military maxim, "It depends upon the situation." Given a suitable objective and resources adequate for the execution of the plan to attain it, our developments in methods and equipment for amphibious assault have vastly increased the power of offense and the courses of action available to us in exploitation of the strategic initiative. The enemy's development, construction, and installation on all possible landing sectors, of effective countermeasures to our amphibious assault have lagged behind our employment of amphibious forces. However, this lag may be expected to decrease. Defense against an amphibious invasion is limited principally by the magnitude of the task inherent in a perimeter defense.

1. The mission assigned in this operation was accomplished. The army was firmly established ashore, and the Western Task Force maintained and supported the army over the beaches until the need for such maintenance had ceased.

   The ready cooperation and outstanding degree of coordination attained between the various services and allies involved were a source of greatest satisfaction and were again demonstrated to be the foundation of success in amphibious invasions. There is no reason for complaint or castigation for differences of opinion based on differing experience, and problems that appear at first impossible of solution must be accepted as routine in the planning and preparation of operations of this size.

   For an invasion of this magnitude the efforts to achieve strategic deception and thereby gain and augment strategic initiative were believed to have been well rewarded. No single force even of the size of the Western Task Force by itself could have achieved the degree of strategic deception gained in this invasion. The success was due to the joint efforts of the many sections under AFHQ working with the US Eighth Fleet.

   Having put the enemy in a position of not knowing where we were going to strike, and then exploiting that advantage with such an overwhelming blow of neutralization by air bombing, naval gunfire and rockets, the Western Task Force was able excellently to prepare the beachhead for the army's assault. It was then that the army, fighting a war of movement with vigorous and rapid thrusts inland, successfully kept the enemy from ever making a concerted stand.

2. It cannot be denied that we met a weakened enemy. Having caught the enemy at a weakened point, it is believed that two features above all permitted the establishment of our deep, firm beachheads. They were:

   (a) Well integrated, overwhelming blows by all neutralizing effort;

CONCLUSIONS

   (b) The aggressiveness of the army and the airforce in keeping the defenders off balance.

   The next two factors, from the naval view point, for accomplishing the assigned mission, were in the realm of logistics and supply. These were first, the problem of maintaining the rapidly moving military forces over the beaches, and second, the problem of opening ports to eliminate the necessity of maintenance over beaches.

   The success with which the maintenance was carried out over the beaches is believed due to the careful planning of the supply problem. The success of opening of ports quickly, thereby relieving the necessity of maintenance over the beaches, is believed due to an analysis and exploitation of existing facilities.

3. The compromise which established H-Hour undoubtedly permitted less time for accurately observed gunfire than some gunfire ships deemed desirable. However, the success of the short period of pre-H-Hour neutralization was due to the integration of air and gunfire effort in which the combined effect of both was considered as a whole. While the number of gunfire ships did not meet the Amphibious Force standards, the employment of available air power so augmented the gunfire power that the neutralization was adequate.

4. As in most other major amphibious operations the final plan of NCWTF could not be promulgated until a date which caused commanders of attack forces to be hard pressed in preparing and distributing their detailed plans. With a dynamic situation during the planning period it is believed that this condition is normal. The following measures overcame the handicaps of this condition to a large extent:

   (a) Issuance by NCWTF of Naval Planning Memoranda commencing in the early stages of planning;

   (b) Establishment of Joint Planning Headquarters;

   (c) Procurement, preparation, and distribution by NCWTF of appropriate information, maps, charts and models which could be used by Attack Force Commanders in their own plans or incorporated by reference.

   (a) and (b) permitted concurrent planning of the echelons concerned while (c) greatly reduced the time, personnel and facilities required by Attack Force Commanders for preparation of detailed plans.

Section 1.2

INTELLIGENCE

SURPRISE

5. The foundation of tactical surprise lies in the effective confusion of the enemy. It is attained not by attempting to deny all information to the enemy but rather by a positive program designed to present multiple threats.

AEROLOGY

6. Aerological equipment functioned satisfactorily with the exception of the radio sonde receiver. Soundings attained with the radio sonde equipment were

CONCLUSIONS

uniformly incorrect or non-available, primarily because of interference of shipboard transmitters, principally the TBS equipment.

ENEMY COAST DEFENSES

7. The success of our efforts to breach the German defense system of the south coast of France, which appeared to have been thoroughly planned and was quite formidable, can be attributed to the following factors:

   (a) The enemy had erroneously estimated the most probable place of attack;

   (b) The thinning out of defense personnel, leaving many defenses manned by low category troops and without readily available mobile reserves;

   (c) The success of the invasion of Northern France, and the rapid expansion of FFI activities had caused a deterioration of the enemy situation as efforts were made to move administrative and non-essential supplies and personnel back to Germany;

   (d) Lack of effective enemy air power imposed great difficulty on his movements and permitted more effective bombing, reconnaissance, air spotting, and direct attack on his ground forces by our air forces;

   (e) Our generally accurate knowledge of the enemy defense preparations throughout the planning period.

UNDERWATER OBSTACLES AND MINES

8. Underwater obstacles effective against landing craft were accurately evaluated by aerial photography. Mining of obstacles greatly increases their defensive value. Shallow water, anti-boat, moored and bottom mines are a serious obstruction to amphibious landings because of the time required to clear them. As yet, we have no adequate means for gaining direct information on enemy coastal minefields. Effective mine spotting from aircraft or blimps can be expected to be available only after the area is secured.

BEACH INTELLIGENCE

9. The close agreement between disseminated information and actual conditions encountered effectively contributed to the well ordered landings of the assault waves, the rapid advance of assault troops inland and the lack of congestion on the beaches and movement inland.

10. The contribution of accurate beach intelligence to the assault was evidenced by the efficiency achieved by both naval personnel and army assault troops in knowing clearly in advance what to expect on the beaches and, aided by this information, being thoroughly prepared to carry out their respective tasks.

PHOTOGRAPHIC INTERPRETATION

11. In an operation involving Joint Army and Navy forces a Joint Photo Interreptation Section is highly desirable to ensure that Army and Navy aspects are given full consideration in photo-interpretation and the resulting intelligence meets the needs of all services concerned.

CONCLUSIONS

12. The additional assignment of photo-interpreters to specialized study of various types of enemy defenses and aspects of beach study has the effect of getting better information with less effort than if every interpreter is charged with all types of work.

13. Graphic presentation of information is more effective than written reports particularly for documents to be used by invasion forces.

PANORAMIC BEACH SKETCHES

14. The graphic presentation of all assault intelligence, with the sketching of terrain encountered and its connection with the respective missions of personnel involved in the assault, all in one composite document, has demonstrated its value in the phases of planning, briefing and actual assault.

COMBAT INTELLIGENCE

15. Combat Intelligence officers of suitable qualifications, in addition to the staff intelligence sections of task force commanders, are required to meet the on-shore intelligence requirements of an amphibious force commander and to exploit the intelligence sources of naval interest in the beachhead.

CAPTURED EQUIPMENT AND DOCUMENTS

16. The organization and procedures for recovering and exploiting intelligence from captured enemy documents and equipment produced valuable results.

PRISONER OF WAR INTERROGATION

17. Plans for a large amphibious operation should include provisions for the assignment and functioning of naval prisoner-of-war interrogators and the prompt dissemination of operational intelligence obtained from preliminary interrogation.

Section 1.3

OPERATIONS

DIVERSIONARY SURFACE OPERATIONS

18. The diversionary surface operations required considerable special equipment and were difficult to plan and execute. Their functions varied, but the picture presented to the enemy had to be consistent, and the tactical diversions had to complement the strategic cover plan. If they are to be used in the future, experience in these diversions confirmed the value of air support, the need for considerable fire power, and the importance of communication deception and radar counter-measures.

SITKA ASSAULT

19. The plan was sound and vigorously executed. Some degree of surprise was achieved, especially on the islands. It is possible that the deception achieved by the air and surface diversion groups helped considerably to offset the disclosure

CONCLUSIONS

of allied intentions resulting from the Sitka attack.

20. It was well demonstrated, especially by the Romeo Force, that withholding fire as long as possible in darkness is the best protection for a small group of boats during an attack by stealth, and increases the chances of surprise and ultimate success.

21. It was found that the British LCA was more maneuverable, less noisy and easier to handle than the US LCP(R) in landing on a rocky coast. Both types of craft executed their towing assignments well, and it proved feasible to tow three LCR to a line with three lines per tow at 4 1/2 knots. PT boats were also used satisfactorily for towing LCR but should have been equipped with mufflers and were visible at twice the distance that the LCA was.

ALPHA ASSAULT

22. New weapons such as rockets and drones revealed weaknesses, but nonetheless, established their worth.

23. Smoke was most effective protecting boat waves from enemy fire.

24. Destroyers were employed to great advantage from 1200 to 1500 yards offshore to provide direct support for minesweepers and boat waves.

25. The value of objective and realistic training was thoroughly proved. The men who made the attack carried out their duties efficiently because during weeks of training they had practiced these same duties, using as nearly as possible the same type of terrain, objectives, procedures, equipment, craft, weapons, and organization as they were to use on D-Day.

26. The division of each assault beach area into three sectors commanded by experienced officers worked out well, especially with respect to controlling smoke and keeping the task force commander fully informed. Use of a "W" formation for the first two landing waves, favored by the army, was very successful.

DELTA ASSAULT

27. The success of pre-D-Day pinpoint bombing was so considerable that the anticipated threat from coastal defenses never materialized and was easily disposed of on D-Day by the closely coordinated naval and air attack.

28. As the value of rocket fire has by now been thoroughly demonstrated, it is evident that the risk involved in the danger of rockets falling into the initial waves must be accepted. The danger can be minimized in the future by limiting the maximum distance permissible between rocket boats and the first wave and by improving performance of rockets and rocket launchers to reduce the number of wild shorts.

29. One of the notable features of the assault was the quantity of unloading accomplished over the small Delta Beaches.

30. The flow of traffic was aided by putting the reorganization plan into effect. The use of such a plan was an innovation that proved its worth.

CONCLUSIONS

CAMEL ASSAULT

31. Although amphibious assault has greater success when detailed plans and preparations can be fitted to the requirements indicated by detailed knowledge of enemy situation and defenses, the value of alternate plans to meet the unexpected was well demonstrated by CTF 87 in shifting the landing beach for the 142nd RCT.

THE REDUCTION OF HYERES, TOULON, AND MARSEILLE

32. Enemy gun positions, strong points, etc., in an amphibious operation are reduced by the cumulative efforts of navy, army, and air power. For that reason the integration of all power rather than emphasis on one type produces speediest results.

SCREENING OPERATIONS

33. Conditions of the waters of the Mediterranean for echo ranging and underwater listening were considered poor. The sector type patrol under these conditions was considered more appropriate than the "endless chain" type.

PT OPERATIONS

34. Due to the increased effort by the enemy of anti-boat minelaying and the use of snag lines as a means for detonating them, the shallow draft of the PT is no longer a safety factor when operating in shallow waters.

MINESWEEPING

In the operation relatively few new devices were used by the enemy as regards his mining practice. They are briefly:

35. Laying of the small GZ type shallow contact mines near shore and close together (50-100 feet apart), apparently as a defense against landing craft.

36. Heavy mining of the waters of harbors, which were likely to fall into our hands, with contact mines and influence mines.

37. Laying fields consisting of alternate snag line and shallow contact mines.

38. Using long chain moorings and solid rubber rings fitted to the moorings wire to choke the mechanical cutters.

39. Minespotting introduced a new factor in mine warfare and proved itself the most useful source of mine information in spite of its defects. It cannot be said, at this time, that water covered by minespotting planes with negative results is safe.

THE SEIZURE AND DEVELOPMENT OF PORT DE BOUC

40. The decision made to open Port de Bouc is considered sound and under the circumstances appreciably contributed to the success of the operations in the Rhone Valley.

CONCLUSIONS

BEACHES AND PORTS

41.   The performance of liaison functions necessitates a supporting organization which tends to expand unduly if not carefully checked. The principal reason for the build up is the demands for services made by our own forces of the liaison organization, which can not be ignored, but which can be met only by expanding the organization from our own resources.

ORGANIZATION

42.   During a large scale operation, which may last a month or more, it is particularly important to have on board the flagship a balanced staff in sufficient numbers to carry out its functions efficiently and without physical exhaustion. As long as the air commander is aboard, or the ship is used for fighter direction, a complete air picture must be maintained, and no reduction of air personnel can be made. Under different conditions, fewer allied personnel might suffice.

43.   In accordance with the principle of unity of command, it is believed sound to centralize tactical control of an amphibious invasion as much as practicable.

STORM PLANS

44.   For the invasion of Southern France, where one of the largest landing craft forces ever assembled was to be sent into an area known for its severe autumnal mistrals, a storm plan was an absolute necessity.

REPORTS

45.   Training and indoctrination should emphasize standardization in making reports.

46.   A report plan as an annex of the operation plan containing clear and detailed instructions concerning all special and routine reports required in connection with the operation, is considered desirable for large amphibious operations.

Section 1.4

AIR

PRE-D-DAY BOMBING

47.   Pre-D-Day bombing in preparation for an amphibious invasion can be highly effective if the bombing plan is carefully integrated by navy-air force planners. Selection of targets should be on the basis of attaining neutralization at the proper time of those enemy batteries critical to the success of the naval approach and amphibious assault. Deception as to the sector of assault can be made effective by bombing targets selected to picture impending amphibious assaults on other plausible areas if the selection takes full account of naval considerations and is carefully integrated with the overall cover plan.

PRE-H-HOUR D-DAY BOMBING

48.   It was brought out in this operation by the results of the execution of the scheduled bombing, how highly desirable it is to insure positive control of the tactical support resulting from the air effort, preferably by carefully pre-selecting alternate targets. In the selection of targets and alternates the first object-

CONCLUSIONS

ive should be support of the approach of gunfire ships. If communications then fail for some reason, execution of the air plan will neutralize the defensive strength of the enemy opposing the timely approach of the gunfire ships. By assignment of alternate targets, tactical support to the navy or the army can be controlled to the degree permitted by available communications.

POST-H-HOUR BOMBING

49. The Naval Commander of an amphibious invasion is vitally concerned in the development of post-H-Hour bombing plans with respect to:

    (a). Coordination with available naval gunfire;

    (b) Destruction or neutralization of enemy installations effecting execution of landings or maintenance operations;

    (c) Routes followed by bombers and recognition procedures.

FIGHTER DIRECTION SHIPS

50. Fighter Direction ships or Fighter Control ships are indispensable in any amphibious assault in which a large number of aircraft play a prominent part. The basic requirements or specifications of a Fighter Direction Ship for this use are:

    (a) Adequate radars, including a height-finging type. Until such time as an airborne search radar is developed to insure complete coverage of an invasion coastline regardless of elevations, radar blind spots must be covered by specially stationed fighter patrols.

    (b) Protection.

    (c) Suitably equipped operations room.

    (d) Trained personnel.

FIGHTER COVER

51. Fighter Cover must be assigned on standing patrols with two definite factors in mind:

    (a) Direction from which and altitude at which enemy attack is most probable;

    (b) To fill in blind spots of radar coverage which are almost certain to be present in an amphibious assault.

CARRIER AIRCRAFT OPERATIONS

52. When the enemy air force is weak and dwindling, severe damage can be inflicted by carrier aircraft upon his ground forces.

SPOTTING PLANES

53. Under the condition of little enemy fighter opposition the SOC proved to be most valuable in spotting naval gunfire.

CONCLUSIONS

Section 1.5

GUNNERY

BOMBARDMENT

54.	The construction and location of enemy coast defense batteries and strong points were such that they would have offered serious opposition to the landing had heavy pre-assault bombardment and well coordinated close supporting fire not been carefully integrated and executed according to plan. All weapons - bombs, naval gunfire, explosive boats, rockets, and smoke were combined into a blow which dazed and weakened the enemy so that the army was placed ashore with extremely light losses.

SHORE FIRE CONTROL PARTIES AND NAVAL GUNFIRE LIAISON OFFICERS

55.	The problem of providing a spotting agency to control naval gunfire during the "touchdown" of the troops, extending to the time when the regular Shore Fire Control Parties were landed and functioning was solved, by placing an army artillery officer off each assault beach in an LCC, PC or LCS.

ANTI-AIRCRAFT GUNNERY AND AIRCRAFT RECOGNITION

56.	Efficient aircraft recognition is the best foundation for good fire discipline.

SMOKE PLAN AND EXECUTION

57.	Twenty minutes were normally required to produce an effective smoke cover of a transport area.

Section 1.6

MATERIAL AND LOGISTICS

PLANNING, PREPARATION AND TRAINING PERIOD

58.	The success of this and other amphibious landings in the Mediterranean has been due in large part to the outstanding support rendered by shore based activities and by repair ships based at friendly ports at some distance from the area of assault.

OPENING OF PORTS

59.	Throughout all port clearance operations the most expeditious development of unloading facilities was insured by closest liaison and coordination exercised between the ship salvage and shoreside clearance units.

BEACH CONTROL GROUP AND BEACH BATTALIONS

60.	Two factors led to the success of beach operations:

   (a) Provision of a responsible naval officer (Naval Liaison Officer) to coordinate the naval activities at and between all beaches.

   (b) Beach Battalions trained and rehearsed with the Army Shore Parties with which they were to be associated in the actual operation.

CONCLUSIONS

Section 1.7

COMMUNICATIONS

GENERAL

61. The high degree of cooperation between communication organizations of the Army, Royal Navy, French Navy, and Air Forces was gratifying. The Army and Air Forces were particularly helpful in supplying to naval forces certain radio material which contributed to the successful conclusion of the operation.

PLANNING

62. Successful effort was made through planning to simplify the Communication Annex of the Operation Plan for the invasion of Southern France in comparison with those of previous operations.

FLAGSHIPS

63. A specially equipped amphibious flagship for the naval commander of an amphibious task force, and adequate flagships for the individual attack force commanders are a necessity. Not only during the assault, but particularly in the follow-up period did USS Catoctin prove her worth in handling communications.

DEFICIENCIES

64. During the invasion of Southern France as in previous amphibious operations of this command, deficiencies in communications were noted, the most noticeable being:

(a) Breaking of radio silence on TBS circuits prior to H-Hour;

(b) Overloading and improper use of TBS circuits;

(c) Misuse of higher precedences;

(d) Overloading of Task Force Commanders circuit;

(e) Lack of security on voice circuits.

CALL SIGNS

65. Common operational call-signs for interservice use should be continued throughout the period that assault communications remain in effect.

AUTHENTICATION

66. Although there was little need for an authentication system during the invasion of Southern France, it is considered sound policy to make provision for such a system in future amphibious operations.

VOICE CODES

67. The advantages of speed gained from voice transmission are lost when encryption is necessary. Until efficient scrambling devices are perfected which will permit rapid voice transmission with the requisite security, it is considered loss of speed must be accepted, and the most satisfactory voice code possible

CONCLUSIONS

must be prescribed for use with emphasis placed on necessity for proper procedure, security, and circuit discipline whenever used.

RADIO CHANNELS

68. Fire Support Communications were satisfactory. Inclusion of SCR 608 sets, or equivalent equipment, in the allowance of DDs is considered highly desirable to improve fire support communications.

COUNTERMEASURES

69. Aerial reconnaissance is the most reliable method for pin-pointing enemy radar locations.

70. RCM equipment should be installed and operators thoroughly indoctrinated well in advance of the assault.

71. Pre-assault bombing cannot be assumed to have neutralized enemy radar locations.

Section 1.8

MEDICAL DEPARTMENT OPERATIONS

EVACUATION SHIPS

72. The automatic schedule functioned very satisfactorily. PSTO, the Beach Battalions, the Operations Officer on the staff of NCWTF, the hospital ships and the medical sections of SOS NATOUSA all cooperated in effecting highly efficient casualty evacuation.

Chapter 2

RECOMMENDATIONS

Section 2.1

PLANNING

NAVAL PLANNING MEMORANDA

1. That formalized procedure of issuing planning memoranda and periodically correcting them be used for an operation of this scope.

GUNFIRE SUPPORT

2. That the method of apportioning gunfire support ships based on a mathematical study similar to that outlined in Section 4.2, Part II, be employed for amphibious invasions.

Section 2.2

INTELLIGENCE

SURPRISE

3. That carefully planned measures to deceive the enemy, in respects which will facilitate execution of our plans, be initiated from the earliest planning stages of our amphibious invasion.

AEROLOGY

The recommendations contained in the report of the Sicilian invasion were affirmed as valid. Additionally, it is recommended:

4. That necessary measures be taken to insure complete, accurate surface and upper air reports from friendly and neutral countries in the vicinity of operations.

5. That a rear-echelon unit, be regularly organized to provide information to task force commanders during periods of radio silence in the attacking forces and to make all forecasts in the event of a casualty to the force commander's flagship of such severity as to prevent the functioning of the flagship unit after H-Hour.

6. That radio-sonde equipment be installed ashore as near as practicable to the vicinity of the assault beaches. This could well be a part of the equipment of the rear-echelon unit recommended in 5.

7. That parachute type droppable automatic weather stations be stocked in Aerological Supply Pools.

RECOMMENDATIONS

UNDERWATER OBSTRUCTIONS AND MINES

8. That experiment and research be directed toward means by submarine detection or otherwise of locating minefields off hostile coasts, particularly shallow water mines close inshore.

COMBAT INTELLIGENCE

9. That the training of Amphibious Scout-Transport Intelligence officers and selected boat crews now carried on at Ft. Pierce, Florida, be continued and that training be kept realistic by return to the school after each major amphibious operation of a number of Amphibious Scout Officers who participated in the operation.

10. That for each theater of probable amphibious operations, a pool of combat intelligence officers of appropriate language qualifications and with suitable training and experience be maintained for temporary duty assignments to amphibious task groups. They should receive amphibious training and plans for the assignment of combat intelligence teams should include definite arrangements for transportation and radio communications.

CAPTURED EQUIPMENT AND DOCUMENTS

11. That the intelligence plan for any large amphibious operation include provision for the assignment of an appropriate number of naval combat intelligence officers with enemy document experience and that they be landed with suitable equipment as soon as practicable when a beachhead is secured in order to exploit intelligence from captured enemy documents.

PRESS RELATIONS

12. That additional officers, trained in censorship and public relations, be ordered to a theater for temporary additional duty for major operations.

Section 2.3

OPERATIONS

REHEARSALS

13. That the same organization and procedures to be used during the actual assault should be used both in the training period and the rehearsal.

14. That sufficient time should be allowed between the rehearsal and the final sailing date for the actual operation to permit unloading of vehicles and cargo during the rehearsal.

MOUNTING, STAGING, AND SAILING OF ASSAULT CONVOYS

15. That, for the loading of a large amphibious expedition:

   (a) Separate loading areas be assigned for each type of craft.

   (b) Standard loading plans be distributed to all concerned.

   (c) A Joint Loading Control coordinate craft and troop movements.

RECOMMENDATIONS

SITKA ASSAULT

16. That a boat similar to the British LCA be used in landings by stealth on rocky shores.

ALPHA ASSAULT

17. That organization of each beach assault area into separate sectors of command for the control of smoke, inshore gunfire, and traffic during the assault phase be established.

DELTA ASSAULT

18. In order to make a smooth and orderly transition from the assault to the maintenance and build-up phase of an amphibious invasion, that a reorganization plan, to be placed in effect upon order from the task force commander, be adopted as a standard part of the operation plan.

CAMEL ASSAULT

19. That a gunfire spotter be positioned in a small craft such as an LCC about 1,000 yards offshore for close gunfire support of the assault.

MINESWEEPING

20. That naval commander's staff and the staffs of each task force commander should have an experienced mine officer attached.

21. That for an operation of this size the sweeper force be organized under one command following the assault phase.

22. That minespotting from aircraft should be developed by technical research and its use extended.

23. That high speed sweepers of the SC type, which in this theater have been equipped with German sweep gear, need development.

24. That more satisfactory shallow water sweep than the LCV(P) be developed.

25. That a very shallow draft sweeper of the skid type probably driven by an air screw is required for making a safe cut through fields of snag line and shallow moored mines.

STORM PLANS

26. That training of landing craft personnel should include thorough indoctrination in the art of handling landing craft in storms.

27. That storm plan should be a standard part of any plan for amphibious operations.

CHARTS AND ANCHORAGES

28. That it is essential to have available adequate chart reproduction facilities for an operation such as the invasion of Southern France.

RECOMMENDATIONS

Section 2.4

AIR

FIGHTER DIRECTION SHIPS

29. That when an amphibious flagship (AGC) with communications similar to the USS Catoctin is available, this ship be utilized for the control of offensive air action and that fighter defense be controlled by the Fighter Direction Ship.

AIR RAID WARNINGS

30. That whenever practicable, the representative of the Naval Commander call the air raid warnings from aboard the Fighter Direction Ship until such time as shore facilities can be installed to assume this function.

AIRCRAFT FOR MINESPOTTING

31. That aircraft for minespotting be employed to the fullest extent in the discovery and survey of unknown minefields. Where employed in connection with amphibious operations planning should include provisions for adequate communications for control and reporting minefields, base facilities as near the area of operations as practicable, and close liaison with minesweeping commands

Section 2.5

GUNNERY

ORDNANCE MATERIAL

32. That more attention be given to the employment of white phosphorous projectiles and that a minimum of 100 projectiles be allowed each destroyer assigned fire support duties.

SHORE FIRE CONTROL PARTIES AND NAVAL GUNFIRE LIAISON OFFICERS

33. To insure positive radio contact at all times between the Senior Naval Gunfire Liaison Officer and the Fire Support Group Commander it is considered that an SCR #393 with two receivers (this is a medium powered transmitter with a wide frequency range) and an SCR 608 both mounted in a 2 1/2 ton truck would be the most suitable combination. The truck should be enclosed by a canopy to permit work at night under blackout conditions. A minimum of two jeeps, each with an SCR 609 or SCR 610 would provide the necessary transportation between the various headquarters. Sufficient radio operators are needed to permit twenty-four hour watch standing for extended periods of time. In addition to the Senior Naval Gunfire Liaison Officer, the party should include an army artillery officer, and two junior naval officers for coding, decoding, and general liaison.

NAVAL COMBAT DEMOLITION UNITS

34. That the size of the unit be increased to ten men. A need was felt for an amphibious vehicle that could be used for the transportation of explosives and equipment up and down the beach.

RECOMMENDATIONS

APEX BOATS AND REDDY FOX (DEMOLITION OUTFIT MARK 119)

35. That these boats have distinctive markings so that other craft and ships can avoid them if they go out of control.

36. Despite the somewhat limited success in this operation, that the Apexes be continued in use. In the meantime, vigorous steps must be taken to increase their reliability and positiveness of control.

ROCKET CRAFT - LCT(R), LCM(R), LCS(S)

37. That targets assigned LCT(R)s should, if possible, be so situated that they will not be required to fire over the landing waves and accompanying craft. The destructive effect of rocket fire is so great that it should not be dispensed with on a defended beach.

STANDARD FORM FOR REPORT OF SHORE BOMBARDMENT FIRE MISSIONS

38. In order to facilitate the collection and analysis of shore bombardment data, that a standard form for reporting pertinent data on each land target engaged be devised and issued to the fleet, just as is now done for anti-aircraft actions.

Section 2.6

MATERIAL AND LOGISTICS

BARRAGE BALLOONS

39. That pre-arranged signals by flag hoist be promulgated in the logistics annex, in the communication annex and in the instructions to merchant ships to insure prompt action in close-hauling balloons at sunset, in case of approaching storms or for other reasons.

SALVAGE AND FIRE-FIGHTING

40. That the alterations to LCI(L)s and LCT(5)s for salvage and fire-fighting be standardized and that such craft be organized as shallow water salvage groups. At least fifty percent of the complements of such craft should be composed of personnel trained in salvage and fire-fighting. Each LCI(L) and LCT(5) assigned should be provided with a small shallow draft power boat to facilitate inspection of stranded ships and craft. LCT(5)s fitted for salvage should carry a small repair party with necessary equipment to accomplish minor repairs to damaged ship-borne landing craft and an adequate stock of spare propellers.

EIGHTH FLEET SHIPS AND CRAFT

41. That the Research and Development Center, Amphibious Training Command, US Atlantic Fleet study the problem of landing troops from APDs. Boats with tows provided should be capable of embarking all troops in one wave. Speed is not important. Silence and reliability are mandatory.

42. That electric air compressors be added to allowance lists of APA, XAP and AKA for use in inflating tires of vehicles prior to unloading.

43. That the adequacy of ventilation in the forward section of the well deck of LSDs be investigated. Reports indicate fumes accumulate in the space below

RECOMMENDATIONS

the superstructure when landing craft engines are being warmed up.

44. That a public address system be installed on LSTs with outlets on the main and tank decks.

45. That propeller guards be installed on the smoke producing unit of LCM(3) Smokers.

LOADING AND UNLOADING OF SHIPS AND CRAFT

46. That the present division of responsibilities of Army and Navy for handling the unloading of ships over beaches and transportation of supplies to inland dumps be continued.

Section 2.7

COMMUNICATIONS

That the development and use of the following equipment be continued:

47. High speed automatic equipment for use on rear links and force broadcast circuits;

48. Radio teletype circuits utilizing VHF equipment, between the naval task force commander and assault force commanders;

49. Drone boats;

50. Application of information available from the Radar Planning Device.

51. That efficient scrambling equipment for use with voice circuit transmitters be developed.

Section 2.8

MEDICAL DEPARTMENT OPERATIONS

MEDICAL SECTIONS OF BEACH BATTALIONS

52. That the Senior Medical Officer of a Beach Battalion be recognized as a department head during the training period and be given the necessary authority and cooperation to properly organize and train the personnel of the medical sections under combat conditions.

EVACUATION SHIPS

53. That a hospital ship in an amphibious invasion be prepared to provide every hospital facility needed to treat all types of casualties from an active combat area.

Copy No. _____

File No.
A 16-3-N31
Serial: 00987

WESTERN NAVAL TASK FORCE
OPERATION PLAN NO. 4-44
SHORT TITLE "ANOR-1"

NOTE:
1. This reproduction of the plan includes all corrections issued to 14 August.
2. The classification of this operation plan was changed from Top Secret to Confidential for this report by substitution of non-classified terms for Top Secret code words.
3. The original plan was issued on pages 8 inches wide by 13 inches long.
4. The form otherwise has been exactly reproduced for purposes of analysis.

ANNEX A

File No.
A16-3/N 31

Serial: 00937

NAPLES, ITALY
24 July, 1944; 0400

OPERATION PLAN
No. 4-44

TASK ORGANIZATION

(a) 80 CONTROL FORCE
    80.1 Force Flagship, Commander Comp, U.S.N.
        CATOCTIN (FF)   1 AGC
        PLUNKETT (Relief FF)   1 DD
        MinDiv Twenty-one
            PHEASANT (F), RAVEN, AUK, BROADBILL, CHICK-
            ADEE, NUTHATCH, STAFF, SWIFT, THREAT   9 AMS

    80.2 U.S.N. Liaison, Beach Control Group, Captain Dodds, U.S.N.R.
        Beach Battalions One, Four, Eight.

    80.3 Petroleum Group, Commander Violett, U.S.N.R.
        U.S. Navy Petroleum Division One.

    80.4 Special Operations Group, Captain Johnson, U.S.N.
        ENDICOTT   1 DD
        APHIS, SCARAB   2 PG
        ANTWERP, STUART PRINCE   2 FDS
        ASRC P-403 (Br)   1 ASRC
        ASRC (US)   12 ASRC
        PTs   8 PT
        24th ML Flotilla (plus ML 576)
            ML 299, 357, 451, 456, 461, 478, 576, 581   8 ML

    80.5 Screening Group, Lieutenant Commander Barnes, U.S.N.
        MTBrons 15, 22, 29 (less 24 assigned other groups)   18 PT

    80.6 Anti-Submarine and Convoy Control Group, Captain Clay, U.S.N.
        DesRon Seven
            DesDiv Thirteen (less PLUNKETT, MAYO, GLEAVES
                plus JOUETT)
                JOUETT (F), BENSON, NIBLACK   3 DD
            DesDiv Fourteen
                MADISON (F), HILARY P. JONES, C. F. HUGHES   3 DD
        DesRon Eighteen
            DesDiv Thirty-five
                FRANKFORD (F), CARMICK, DOYLE, McCOOK   4 DD
            DesDiv Thirty-six
                BALDWIN (F), HARDING, SATTERLEE, THOMPSON   4 DD
        Fifth DesFlot
            ALDENHAM (F), BEAUFORT, BELVOIR, WHADDON,
            BLACKMORE, EGGESFORD, LAUDERDALE, PINDOS 8 DD
        Eighteenth DesFlot
            FARNDALE (F), ATHERSTONE, BRECON, CALPE,
            CATTERICK, CLEVELAND, HAYDON   7 DD

File No.
A16-3/N31

OPERATION PLAN
No. 4-44

  Fifty-ninth DesFlot
    BICESTER (F), LIDDESDALE, OAKLEY, ZETLAND,
    CRETE, THEMISTOCLES   6 DD
  CortDiv Forty-seven (plus F.C.DAVIS and H.C.JONES)
    TATUM (F), HAINES, RUNELS, HOLLIS, MARSH,
    CURRIER, F.C.DAVIS, H.C.JONES   8 DE
  French Destroyers
    Third Division Torpilleurs
      FORTUNE (F), FORBIN   2 DD
    Sixth Division Torpilleurs
      SIMOUN, TEMPETE, L'ALCYON   3 DD
  French Escorts
    Second Division Escorteurs
      MOROCAIN (F), TUNISIEN   2 DE
    Fifth Division Escorteurs
      HOVA (F), ALGERIEN, SOMALI   3 DE
  French Sloops
    Tenth Division Avisos (less COMMANDANT DUBOC)
      COMMANDANT DOMINE (F), LA MOQUEUSE, 2 sloops
    Sixth Division Avisos
      COMMANDANT BORY (F), LA GRACIEUSE,
      COMMANDANT DELAGE, LA BOUDEUSE   4 sloops
  MinRon Eleven
    IMPLICIT, INCESSANT, INCREDIBLE, MAINSTAY,
    PINNACLE, IMPROVE   6 AM
  YMS 17, 164, 179, 250, 359, 373   6 YMS
  British Corvettes
    AUBRETIA, COLUMBINE   2 corvettes

80.7 Train, Captain Pike, U.S.N.
  VULCAN, DELTA   2 AR
  DENEBOLA   1 AD
  PLEIADES   1 AKS
  NITRO, MOUNT BAKER   2 AE
  CHEMUNG, WINOOSKI, COWANESQUE, CHIWAWA, VAR,
    ELISE, ELORN, LE MEKONG   8 AO
  CELEROL, ALEXANDER ANDRE, EMPIRE GAWAIN,
    SPINDLE TOP, COTTON VALLEY   5 YO
  NASPRITE, EMPIRE LASS, EMPIRE FAY, EMPIRE DAMSEL 4 YOG
  EMPIRE HARP, EMPIRE FAWN, MYRIEL, PO   4 YW
  AMSTEL, CARA   2 AC
  ACHELOUS   1 ARL
  2 Br. LSE or 2 US ARL (total 2), if assigned
  EMPIRE SPINNEY, EMPIRE GAT, PROCRIS, FENDRIS,
    QUERCY   5 ASIS
  BARFLEUR (Fr.)   1 AE

80.8 U.S. Naval Liaison French Ports, Commodore Doughty, U.S.N.(Ret)

File No.
A16-3/N31
Serial: 00987

OPERATION PLAN
No. 4-44
- -

	80.9	U.S. Naval Detachments, AJACCIO, CALVI - ILE ROUSSE Captain Erskine, U.S.N.(Ret)	
		YMS 271 (Fr.)	1 YMS
		YTL 160, 161	2 YTL
		YW-120 (non self-propelled)	1 YW
		Chasseurs 90, 95	2 SC
(b)	84	ALPHA Attack Force, Rear Admiral Lowry, U.S.N.	
		DUANE (F)	1 AGC
		ULSTER QUEEN	1 FDS
		Assault Ships and Craft	
		TransDiv One	
		HENRICO (F), SAMUEL CHASE, ANNE ARUNDEL,	2 APA
			2 XAP
		THURSTON, OBERON, ANDROMEDA	2 AKA
		DERBYSHIRE, DUNERA	2 LSI(L)
		PARKER	1 AP
		22 LST (including two two-davit pontoon carriers, one of which, LST 906, is fitted with flight deck)	22 LST
		LST 32 (carrying GCI and pontoon causeway)	1 LST
		47 LCI(L) (including three fitted for salvage and fire fighting)	47 LCI(L)
		17 LCT(3)(4)	17 LCT
		22 LCT(5)(6) (including two fitted for salvage)	22 LCT
		Br. LCT(1)9 (smoke tender)	1 LCT
		Br. LCT(2)(E) 160 (with Br. LCRU embarked)	1 LCT
		Br. LCT(2) 135 (balloon tender)	1 LCT
		Br. Fleet Tender 30 (balloon tender)	
		EMPIRE ELAINE	1 LSC
		HIGHWAY (loaded approximately as indicated in Section XI, Logistic Plan, Annex E)	1 LSD
		LCF 4, 8	2 LCF
		LCG 4, 8	2 LCG
		10 LCT(R)	10 LCT(R)
		Escort Sweeper Group	
		PC 557, 591, 626, 1140, 1168, 1169, 1173, 1174, 1226, 1227	10 PC
		SC 524, 526, 651, 666, 690, 693, 695, 1029	8 SC
		PIONEER, SEER, PREVAIL, DEXTROUS	4 AM
		13 M/S Flotilla: ROTHESAY (SO), BUDE, BRIXHAM, POLRUAN, ARIES, STORNOWAY	6 M/S
		NEBB, BOREALIS (Dan Layers)	
		SC 498, 535, 655, 770, 978, 979 (shallow sweeps)	6 SC
		YMS 13, 18, 20, 21, 27, 34, 82, 199, 251, 355	10 YMS
		BARRICADE	1 ACM
		Auxiliary Group	
		YTL 165	1 YTL
		HOPI	1 ATF
		ATR-1	1 ATR
		ATA-170	1 ATA

File No.
A16-3/N31
Serial: 00987

OPERATION PLAN
No. 4-44

	EVEA	1 VTB
	EMPIRE SPITFIRE, EMPIRE ANNE	2 ATR
	BARHOLM (boom vessel)	
	YF-465	1 YF
	MFV 47, 68	2 MFV
	Gunfire Support Group	
	RAMILLIES	1 BB
	QUINCY (2 VOS)	1 CA
	ORION (F), AURORA, AJAX, BLACK PRINCE, GLOIRE	5 CL
	DesDiv Twenty-one	
	LIVERMORE (F), EBERLE, KEARNEY, ERICSSON	4 DD
	TERPSICHORE, TERMAGANT	2 DD
	3rd UNITED STATES Infantry Division (reinforced)	
(c) 85	DELTA Attack Force, Rear Admiral Rodgers, U.S.N.	
	BISCAYNE (F)	1 AGC
	LSF-13	1 LSF
	Assault Ships and Craft	
	TransDiv Five	
	ELIZABETH C. STANTON (F), BARNETT, JOSEPH T.	2 APA
	DICKMAN, LYON, ARCTURUS, PROCYON	2 AP
		2 AKA
	DILWARA	1 LSI(L)
	ASCANIA	1 LSP
	MARINE ROBIN, SANTA ROSA	2 AP
	22 LST (including seven two-davit pontoon carriers, one of which, LST 526, is fitted with flight deck)	22 LST
	LST 140 (carrying GCI and pontoon causeway)	1 LST
	38 LCI(L) (including three fitted for salvage and fire fighting)	38 LCI(L)
	18 LCT(3)(4)	18 LCT
	21 LCT(5)(6) (including one fitted for salvage)	21 LCT
	Br. LCT(1)17 (smoke tender)	1 LCT
	Br. LCT(2)(E) 170 (with Br. LCRU embarked)	1 LCT
	Br. LCT(2) 164 (balloon tender)	1 LCT
	Br. Fleet Tender 6 (balloon tender)	
	ENNERDALE	1 LSG
	LCF 10, 14	2 LCF
	LCG 12, 14	2 LCG
	6 LCT(R)	6 LCT(R)
	Escort Sweeper Group	
	PC 545, 556, 559, 621, 1235, 1593, 1594, 1595, 1596	9 PC
	SC 503, 515, 525, 530, 534	5 SC
	SWAY, SYMBOL	2 AM
	19th M/S Flotilla	
	RINALDO (SO), ANTARES, ARCTURUS, BRAVE, SPANKER, ROSARIO	6 M/S
	ML 556, 557, 566, 568	4 ML

File No.
A16-3/N31
Serial: 00987

OPERATION PLAN
No. 4-44
- -

SATSA, CALM (Dan Layers)	
YMS 3, 18, 19, 37, 43, 55, 69, 83, 226, 248	10 YMS
PLANTER	1 ACM
Auxiliary Group	
YTL 186, 196	2 YTL
NARRAGANSETT, PINTO	2 ATF
ASPIRANT	1 ATR
ATA 125	1 ATA
ATHLETE, CHARON	2 ATA
BARFORD, BARMOND (boom vessels)	
HEBE II (refrigerator ship)	
MFV 90, 77	2 MFV
Gunfire Support Group	
TEXAS (F), NEVADA	2 BB
PHILADELPHIA (2 VOS)	1 CL
GEORGES LEYGUES (F), MONTCALM	2 CL
Tenth Division Contre Torpilleurs	
LE FANTASQUE (F), LE MALIN, LE TERRIBLE	3 DL
DesRon Ten	
DesDiv Nineteen	
ELLYSON (F), HAMBLETON, RODMAN, EMMONS,	
MACOMB	5 DD
DesDiv Twenty	
FORREST (F), FITCH, HOBSON	3 DD

45th UNITED STATES Infantry (reinforced)

(d) 87 CAMEL Attack Force, Rear Admiral Lewis, U.S.N.

BAYFIELD (F)	1 APA
Assault Ships and Craft	
TransDiv Three	
CHARLES CARROLL (F), THOMAS JEFFERSON,	2 APA
DOROTHEA L. DIX, FLORENCE NIGHTINGALE,	2 AP
CEPHEUS, ACHERNAR, BETELGEUSE	3 AKA
WINCHESTER CASTLE, KEREN	2 LSI(L)
GENERAL G. O. SQUIER	1 AP
27 LST (including twelve two-davit pontoon carriers (one of which is fitted with flight deck) one carries Air Force equipment, and four carry French Armored Combat Command)	27 LST
BRUISER, THRUSTER	2 LST
LST 394 (carrying GCI and pontoon causeway)	1 LST
30 LCI(L) (including three fitted for salvage and fire fighting)	30 LCI(L)
17 LCT (3)(4)	17 LCT
21 LCT (5)(6) (including one fitted for salvage)	21 LCT
Br. LCT(1) 4 (smoke tender)	1 LCT
Br. LCT(2) 169 (balloon tender)	1 LCT
DEWDALE	1 LSG

File No.
A16-3/N31
Serial: 00987

OPERATION PLAN
No. 4-44

EASTWAY (loaded approximately as indicated in Section XI, Logistic Plan, Annex E)	1 LSD
LCF 16, 17	2 LCF
LCG 20	1 LCG
14 LCT(R)	14 LCT(R)
Escort Sweeper Group	
PC 542, 546, 551, 625, 627, 1597	6 PC
SC 506, 522, 532, 533, 638, 676, 691, 692, 1030, 1043	10 SC
SPEED, STRIVE, STEADY, SUSTAIN	4 AM
35th Trawler Group	
CROWLIN, AILSA, CRAIG, MEWSTONE, SKOKHOLM	4 M/S
FOULA (Dan Layer)	
ML 121, 134, 554, 563, 565, 569	6 ML
YMS 15, 24, 63, 78, 200, 303	6 YMS
BYMS 2009, 2022, 2026, 2027, 2171, 2172	6 YMS
PRODUCT	1 ACM
YTL 210	1 YTL
Auxiliary Group	
MORENO, ARIKARA	2 ATF
ATA 172	1 ATA
MINDFUL, VAGRANT	2 ATA
EDENSHAW	1 YTB
BARDOLF (boom vessel)	
YF 447	1 YF
MFV 129, 132	2 MFV
Gunfire Support Group	
ARKANSAS	1 BB
TUSCALOOSA (F)	1 CA
BROOKLYN (2 VOS), MARBLEHEAD (2 VOS)	2 CL
ARGONAUT	1 CL
DUGUAY TROUIN, EMILE BERTIN	2 CL
DesRon Sixteen (less LAUB)	
DesDiv Thirty-one	
PARKER (F), KENDRICK, MACKENZIE, McLANAHAN	4 DD
DesDiv Thirty-two	
BOYLE (F), CHAMPLIN, NIELDS, ORDRONAUX	4 DD
DesDiv Twenty-five	
WOOLSEY (F), LUDLOW, EDISON	3 DD

36th UNITED STATES Infantry (reinforced)
French Army Units, as assigned

(e) 86 SUPPORT FORCE, Rear Admiral Davidson, U.S.N.

Gunfire Support Group	
AUGUSTA (F),	1 CA
LORRAINE	1 BB
DIDO	1 CL
SOMERS, GLEAVES	2 DD

File No.
A16-3/N31
Serial: 00987

OPERATION PLAN
No. 4-44

LOOKOUT	1 DD
Gunfire Support Reserves	
CINCINNATI, OMAHA, JEANNE D'ARC, SIRIUS	4 CL
Gunfire Support Group Units released from other forces	
SITKA Assault Ships and Craft	
PRINCESS BEATRIX, PRINCE HENRY, PRINCE DAVID	3 LSI(M)
PRINCE BAUDOUIN, PRINCE ALBERT	2 LSI(S)
TransDiv Thirteen	
TATNALL (F), ROPER, BARRY, GREENE, OSMOND INGRAM	5 APD
PT	16 PT
ASRC	4 ASRC
Escort Sweeper Group	
5th M/S Flotilla: LARNE (SO), CLINTON, OCTAVIA, STORM-CLOUD, WELFARE	5 M/S
ML 559, 560, 562, 567	4 ML
KINTYRE (Dan Layer)	
HACKBERRY, PEPPERWOOD	2 AN
(Additional sweepers for subsequent operations as assigned by Commander Western Naval Task Force)	

UNITED STATES Army and French Army units as assigned.

(f) 88   AIRCRAFT CARRIER FORCE, Rear Admiral Troubridge, R.N.

Aircraft Carriers	
KHEDIVE, EMPEROR, SEARCHER, PURSUER, ATTACKER, STALKER, HUNTER	7 CVE
TULAGI (F), KASAAN BAY	2 CVE
Anti-Aircraft Support Force and Escorts	
ROYALIST (F), COLOMBO, DELHI, CALEDON	4 AACL
24TH DesFlot (less TERPSICHORE, TERMAGANT plus WHEATLAND and NAVARINON)	
TROUBRIDGE (D24), TUSCAN, TYRIAN, TEAZER, TUMULT, TENACIOUS, WHEATLAND, NAVARINON	8 DD
DesRon Seventeen	
DesDiv Thirty-three (less NELSON, GLENNON)	
MURPHY, JEFFERS	2 DD
DesDiv Thirty-four	
BUTLER (F), GHERARDI, HERNDON, SHUBRICK	4 DD
29TH ML Flot	
ML 273, 336, 458, 463, 469, 471	6 ML

1. Information. (1) Information on hostile forces and on characteristics of the Theater of Operations is contained in Information Annex, Annex "A". Additional information, as available, will be separately distributed.

(2) This invasion of Southern FRANCE is an amphibious operation employing United States assault troops with large French reinforcing formations supported by naval forces of GREAT BRITAIN, FRANCE,

File No.
A16-3/N31
Serial: 00987

OPERATION PLAN
No. 4-44

GREECE, POLAND and the UNITED STATES, and the MEDITERRANEAN Allied Air Force. It is designed to assist the invasion of Northern FRANCE by exploitation of the RHONE Valley while maximum pressure is being exerted on the enemy in Northern FRANCE, ITALY and RUSSIA.

(3) This operation is under the joint command of the following:

    Naval - Commander Western Task Force,
            Vice Admiral H. K. Hewitt, U.S. Navy,
            Commander EIGHTH Fleet.
    Army - Commanding General Western Task Force,
            Major General A.M. Patch, U.S. Army,
            Commanding General Seventh Army.
    Air   - Brigadier General G.P. Saville, U.S.A.A.C.,
            Commanding General XII Tactical
            Air Command.

(4) The area of operations of the Western Naval Task Force is bounded:
    (a) On the East by the meridian of ten degrees East.
    (b) On the South by the parallel of forty-one degrees North.
    (c) On the Southwest by a line joining the Spanish border to position Latitude forty-one degrees North and Longitude four degrees East.

(5) The areas of responsibility of Attack Task Force Commanders are as follows: (Use Admiralty Chart of March 4, 1944, F1267, F1268, F1269, F1270).

    (a) TF 87, CAMEL AREA.
Bounded on the Northeast by a line running 310° - 130° true through S477741.
Bounded on the Southwest by a line from U552298 South along the coast line to U549263, then to seaward along a line bearing 120° true; from U552298 inland through U510310, meeting the 36th - 45th Division boundary at the ARGENS RIVER at U497365, then following the division boundary inland along the ARGENS RIVER.

    (b) TF 85, DELTA AREA.
Bounded on the Northeast by the Southwest limit of CAMEL AREA. Bounded on the Southwest by a line through PTE DE LAY U531173, to seaward bearing 126.5° true, and Westerly therefrom along the coast line to LA FOUX, U448163, then inland along the 3rd - 45th Division boundary which passes South of GRIMAUD through U400160, then through U340195.

    (c) TF 84, ALPHA AREA.
Bounded on the Northeast by the Southwest boundary of DELTA AREA.
Bounded on the Southwest by a line from Z276955, bearing 318° true inland, and to seaward South along a tangent to the West tip of BAGAU ISLAND to Latitude 43° 04' North, Eastward along this Latitude to Longitude 06° 46.7' East, then South along this meridian.

File No.
A16-3/N31
Serial: 00987

OPERATION PLAN
No. 4-44
- -

        (d) TF 86, SITKA AREA.
Bounded on the North and East by Latitude 43° 04' North and
Longitude 06° 46.7' East.
Bounded on the West by a line from Z276955 tangent to the West
   tip of BAGAU ISLAND, then seaward along the bearing 220° true.
(6) (a) Paratroops will be dropped in the target area prior to first
light on D day. (For Time Schedule see Air Beacon Directive, Annex
"R"). Troop carrier aircraft will be routed through a corridor
which is:
     Five miles on either side of a line joining CAP DELLI VETTI
(ELBA), Latitude 42° 52' 20" North, Longitude 10° 25' 30"
East, to VIEILLES D' AGAY, Latitude 43° 26' 00" North, Longitude 06° 53' 50" East, and running through position Latitude
43° 02' 50" North, Longitude 09° 24' 50" East, and position
Latitude 43° 19' 30" North, Longitude 07° 39' 40" East; and
North of a line drawn 3,000 yards off the coast from position
Latitude 43° 23' 10" North, Longitude 06° 51' 30" East, paralleling the route as far as position 43° 19' 30" North 07° 39'
40" East.
   (b) All troop carrier aircraft will turn right from the dropping
zones and reach the sea flying on easterly headings at points North
of the corridor but South of CANNES.
   (c) All troop carrier aircraft will display amber lights down-
ward. IFF will be used. Aircraft are equipped with VH/F, Very
pistol and Aldis lamp.
   (d) Troop carrier aircraft will fly at an altitude of 2,000 feet in
a V formation (9 planes) of V's (3 planes) enroute to the Drop Zones.
On return flights the serials may be scattered or dispersed.
   (e) All naval and merchant ships in this corridor are prohibited
from firing anti-aircraft batteries during troop carrier aircraft operations.
   (f) Barrage balloons flying from shipping in the corridor will
be close hauled to 25 feet during airborne operations.
(7) Friendly aircraft participating in the operation will carry no
special distinctive markings except troop carrier aircraft which
are marked with black and white stripes painted on main-planes
and around the fuselage immediately in front of the fin. Absence
of such markings on other troop carrier aircraft does not mean
they are hostile.
(8) Beginning on D day Piper Cub and Stinson Sentinel aircraft will
operate in the vicinity of the beaches at altitudes below 3,000 feet.
These are slow, high-winged, single engine monoplanes having a
fixed landing gear and large glassed-in canopy. The observation
planes are painted dark olive drab with one or two large letters or
with crossed signal flags in red and white on the sides of the fuselage
forward of the National Insignia. They do not carry IFF.
(9) Fighter coverage of the Western Naval Task Force shipping and
convoys will be provided by the MEDITERRANEAN Allied Coastal

File No.
A16-3/N31
Serial: 00987

OPERATION PLAN
No. 4-44
- -
Air Force to cover all movements to within forty miles of the beaches. Cover within forty miles of the beaches will be provided by the Twelfth Tactical Air Command, augmented by carrier based aircraft of this force. When airfields or strips are developed in the target area (probably D plus three) day and night fighter cover will be provided over beaches and shipping from these airfields.
(10) The MEDITERRANEAN Area Fighter Operation Grid (MAFOG) is the standard grid in use throughout this theater for radar reporting, and is used in conjunction with the Combined Air Warning Code. (See Air Plan, Annex "F").
(11) Shipboard anti-aircraft batteries will be strictly controlled in accordance with the rules laid down in the Gunfire Support Plan, Annex "B".
(12) No friendly submarine forces will be operating in the area of operations of the Western Naval Task Force.
(13) It is planned that the small ports of ST. RAPHAEL, ST. MAXIME and ST. TROPEZ will be captured on D day. After capture these ports must be exploited to the fullest in order to ensure adequate maintenance of our military forces.
(14) The LE LAVANDOU beaches will be opened at the earliest moment in support of the advance of the ground forces. A reassignment of mine sweeping forces will be made at that time to sweep and clear areas for gunfire support ships and maintenance shipping.
(15) The Seventh Army plan envisages a rapid coastal advance of the ground forces toward TOULON. This land advance will be supported by naval gunfire support forces which will be reassigned as required to meet the exigencies of the tactical situation.
(16) This force will open the ports of TOULON and MARSEILLES from seaward. These ports will be cleared for operations by the U.S. Navy and U.S. Army and will thereafter be operated by French Port Authority.
(17) Daily "Cositintreps" will be submitted to NCWTF as outlined in Intelligence Plan, Annex "P".
(18) Night Retirement Areas available for Gunfire Support Groups are enclosed by points as follows: CAMEL: Point A is CAP D'ANTIBES Latitude 43° 32.8' North, Longitude 7° 8.8' East, Point B is Latitude 43° 16.2' North, Longitude 9° East, Point C is Latitude 44° North, Longitude 9° East. If the Troop Carrier Aircraft lane is not in use by aircraft then CAMEL Retirement Area will also include the area bounded by Point B above and Point D Latitude 43° 8.3' North, Longitude 9° East, Point E Latitude 43° 25' North, Longitude 7° 15.9' East, Point F Latitude 43° 31.7' North, Longitude 7° 15.9' East. DELTA: Point G is Latitude 43° 14.5' North, Longitude 7° 18.8' East, Point H is Latitude 43° 13.2' North, Longitude 7° 19.3' East, Point I is Latitude 42° 48.2' North, Longitude 8° 24.2' East, Point J is Latitude 43° 00.5' North, Longitude 8° 50.1' East. If the Troop Carrier Aircraft lane is not in use by aircraft, DELTA Retirement Area will also include the area bounded by Point G above, Point J above, Point L Latitude 43°

File No.
A16-3/N31
Serial: 00987

OPERATION PLAN
No. 4-44
- -
20.2' North, Longitude 7° 16 ' East. Point K Latitude 43° 04.5' North, Longitude 8° 53.8' East. ALPHA: Point M is Latitude 43° 10' North, Longitude 7° 19.2' East, Point N is Latitude 42° 45.8' North, Longitude 8° 20' East, Point O Latitude 42° 39' North Longitude 8° 14.6' East, Point P Latitude 43° 02.1' North, Longitude 7° 10' East. SITKA: Point Q is Latitude 43°00.3' North, Longitude 7° 07.5' East, Point R is Latitude 42° 58' North, Longitude 7° 5' East, Point S is Latitude 42° 26.8' North, Longitude 8° 04.3' East, Point T is Latitude 42° 37.3' North, Longitude 8° 13.4' East. Attention of SITKA and ALPHA Gunfire Support Groups is directed to Convoy Route No. 11 described in Appendix 5, Annex "H". Attention is also directed to position of beacon and air sea rescue ships, shown in Annex "R".

(19) For B-26 Medium Bomber Aircraft attacking beach targets on D day, a special lane has been established. This lane is 5 miles wide centered on line from ORISTANO to center of channel between PORQUEROLLES and PORT CROS. Return to base will be by normal route. After D day this lane may be used by special coordination in advance with Naval Task Force Commander via XII Tactical Air Command Advanced.

Assumptions (1) That the initial landing will take place during daylight, about three hours after first light.

(2) That enemy moored mines will be encountered.

(3) That enemy ground mines will not be encountered outside the ten fathom curve.

(4) That the enemy will employ various types of air weapons including mines, circling torpedoes, radio controlled bombs, and glider bombs.

(5) That enemy submarines based at TOULON will attack this force.

(6) That underwater obstacles will be encountered off assault beaches.

(7) That strong enemy resistance will be encountered at the beaches.

(8) That false beaches will not preclude the landing ships and craft from landing on the true beaches.

(9) That the maintenance and build-up of the military forces can be continued over the beaches until adequate ports become available and are rendered usable to meet logistic requirements.

2. This force will
(1) establish the Seventh UNITED STATES Army firmly ashore in the CAVALAIRE - FREJUS area.
(2) support its advance to the westward for the capture of TOULON and MARSEILLES, and
(3) be responsible for army build up and maintenance over the beaches until no longer required due to the capture and utilization of ports; in order to assist in the establishment of Allied Forces in Southern FRANCE for the purpose of assisting the invasion of Northern FRANCE.

3. (a) (1) CONTROL Force, Force Flagship operate as directed by Naval Commander Western Task Force.

File No.
A16-3/N31
Serial: 00987

OPERATION PLAN
No. 4-44
----

(2) <u>U.S. Naval Liaison, Beach Control Group</u> assign Beach Battalions in accordance with previous dispatch orders. Discharge the naval responsibilities under the Standard Operating Procedure for over-the-beach supply as stated in Part Two, Invasion Naval Planning Memorandum number five. Execute Directive to U.S. Naval Liaison, Beach Control Group, Annex "N".

(3) <u>Petroleum Group</u> establish and operate naval fuel facilities on shore in the assault area. Reconstruct damaged installations and erect increased fuel facilities in the ports of TOULON and MARSEILLES in accordance with the plans developed by Allied Force Headquarters. Provide logistic maintenance in base ports of CORSICA.

(4) <u>Special Operations Group</u> conduct diversionary operations in Special Operations Group Directive, Annex "L". Establish navigational markers in accordance with Air Beacon Directive, Annex "R". On D plus two day provide two ASRC to <u>Anti-Submarine and Convoy Control Group</u>.

(5) <u>Screening Group</u> screen the Attack Forces against hostile surface forces approaching from bases northeast of the assault area. Frustrate enemy E-boat raids. Operate in accordance with Screening Group Directive, Annex "M". Establish navigational marker in accordance with Air Beacon Directive, Annex "R". Maintain daily Blood Bank Shuttle between CALVI and DELTA Attack Force beaches beginning on D plus one day to extend to D plus ten day unless otherwise directed. Make deliveries to beaches in other attack areas if so directed by Beachmaster at DELTA beaches. Maintain boat pool at forward base. On D day make available to CTF 84 sufficient PTs to maintain night screens. Base forward on BAIE DE BRIANDE, PORT CROS, ST. TROPEZ GULF.

(6) <u>Anti-Submarine and Convoy Control Group</u> escort convoys to assault area. Establish and maintain protective screen for the defense of shipping in the beach assault areas against submarine and E-boat or other surface attack. Provide jammer protection to important units. Provide relief Destroyers to Fire Support Groups as required by Attack Force Commanders. Assign destroyers for diversionary and other special tasks, as required. Conduct return Convoy Control, organizing convoys and escorts in general conformity with Convoy Plan, Annex "H". Give particular attention to movements of special-use LSTs, and shuttles. Maintain positive communications with <u>U.S. Naval Liaison, Beach Control Group</u>, to ensure receipt of timely information of required diversion of incoming convoys to newly-opened beaches. Base on BAIE DE BRIANDE, BAIE DE BON-PORTE.

(7) <u>Train</u> render logistic support to all Task Forces as required. Base on MERS EL KEBIR, ORAN, ALGIERS, BIZERTA, CAGLIARI, PALERMO, NAPLES, MADDALENA, PROPRIANO, AJACCIO, or as directed.

(8) <u>U.S. Naval Liaison, French Ports</u> establish Port Parties in major ports in accordance with Directive to U.S. Naval Liaison

File No.
A16-3/N31
Serial: 00987

OPERATION PLAN
No. 4-44
- -

French Ports, Annex "O".

(9) U.S. Naval Detachments, AJACCIO, CALVI-ILE ROUSSE provide logistic support in accordance with Logistic Plan, Annex "E". Assign anchorages and berths to units of the Western Naval Task Force. Ensure proper loading and timely sailing of convoys in accordance with Convoy Plan, Annex "H", executing the required signals to interested commands in the forward area. Make every effort possible to sail CALVI shuttle LSTs in advance of scheduled cycle. Expedite refitting of seven LSTs to accommodate lift of mules. Complete arrangements for expeditious loading of aircraft aboard three flight deck LSTs. In conjunction with French naval authorities conduct anti-submarine patrols off harbors being used by units of the Western Naval Task Force. Ensure maintenance of swept channels to those harbors.

(b) ALPHA Attack Force (1) Establish the Third UNITED STATES Infantry Division (Reinforced) on selected beaches in the CAVALAIRE-PAMPELONNE area. Land at H hour of D day in accordance with plan of attack developed by the Commanding General concerned, which involves the capture of ST. TROPEZ, GRIMAUD, and COGOLIN and a rapid advance to secure by D plus one the beachhead CAP DE LECURE-COLLOBRIERES-LES MAYONS. Clear northern half of beach 261 promptly to permit use by Forty-fifth Division.

(2) Be prepared to land over secure beaches, by D plus one day, the Second French Army, consisting of two preloaded infantry divisions, and one Armored Combat Command; by D plus five day, one-half Infantry Division; by D plus nine day, one-half Infantry Division.

(3) Neutralize or destroy enemy batteries which threaten transports, landing craft, or beaches. Conduct bombardment and support the military operations in accordance with Gunfire Support Plan, Annex "B". Release gunfire support ships to TF 86 as directed by NCWTF.

(4) Be prepared on D day to receive and place five pontoon causeways delivered to beach 261 by DELTA Attack Force, and five pontoon causeways delivered to beach 259 by CAMEL Attack Force. When beach 261 is closed, be prepared to move pontoon causeways to newly-opened beaches to westward of beach 259.

(5) Move transports and other shipping inshore when shore batteries have been silenced. Make maximum use of LCT in unloading shipping.

(6) Station LST 32 initially in position Latitude forty-three degrees one minute North, Longitude six degrees forty-six minutes East. Station ULSTER QUEEN initially in position Latitude forty-three degrees six minutes North, Longitude six degrees fifty-four minutes East.

(7) Beginning on D day maintain night anti-E boat screen on left flank between PORT CROS - LEVANT and the mainland to

File No.
A16-3/N31
Serial: 00987

OPERATION PLAN
No. 4-44
- -

frustrate enemy E-boat attacks, employing PTs made available by Screening Group.

(8) On D day station EMPIRE LASS at BAIE DE BRIANDE for logistic support of Special Operations Group and Screening Group. Be prepared to station YOG at PORT CROS on order of NCWTF.

(9) Land special Air Force signal equipment on Island of PORT CROS from LST 32 at earliest opportunity.

(10) Direct LCT(R)s, upon completion their assigned task, to proceed at best speed and report CAMEL Attack Force. All LCT(R) are to endeavor complete reload prior to employment in CAMEL Attack Force area on afternoon of D day.

(c) DELTA Attack Force (1) Establish the Forty-fifth UNITED STATES Infantry Division (reinforced) on selected beaches in the ST. TROPEZ-BOUGNON area. Land at H hour of D day in accordance with plan of attack developed by the Commanding General concerned, which involves the early capture of ST. MAXIME, VILLEPEY, and occupation of high ground immediately west thereof, and a rapid advance to secure the beach head line LES MAYONS-LE CANNET DES MAURESTRANS EN PROVENCE by D plus one. Exploit ST. MAXIME port facilities and open beaches 262, 262A and 263 with all possible speed. Land battalion beach group of reserve RCT over northern end of beach 261 on order after the beach has been cleared by the Third Infantry Division. Operate the northern sector of beach 261 for the landing of vehicles and maintenance stores.

(2) Be prepared to land on order in the ST. TROPEZ area by D plus one day, the Second French Army, consisting of two preloaded infantry divisions and one Armored Combat Command; by D plus five day, one-half Infantry Division; by D plus nine day, one-half Infantry Division. Exploit port facilities of ST. TROPEZ to ensure adequate maintenance of ground forces.

(3) Neutralize or destroy enemy batteries which threaten transports, landing craft or beaches. Conduct bombardment and support military operations in accordance with Gunfire Support Plan, Annex "B". Release gunfire support ships to TF 86 as directed by NCWTF.

(4) If assault beaches cannot be developed and exploited promptly deliver five pontoon causeways on D day to northern half of beach 261 to ensure maintenance of Forty-fifth Infantry Division. When beach 262 is opened, shift to that beach the three pontoon causeways sited on beaches 263 A-B-C.

(5) Move transports and other shipping inshore when shore batteries have been silenced. Make maximum use of LCT in unloading shipping.

(6) Station LST 140 initially in position Latitude forty-three degrees fourteen minutes North, Longitude six degrees fifty-two minutes East. Station LSF 13 initially in position Latitude forty-three degrees fifteen minutes North, Longitude six degrees fifty-

File No.
A16-3/N31
Serial: 00987

OPERATION PLAN
No. 4-44
- -
six minutes East.
    (7) Direct LCT(R)s, upon completion their assigned task, to proceed at best speed and report CAMEL Attack Force. All LCT(R) are to endeavor complete reload prior to employment in CAMEL Attack Force area on afternoon of D day.
  (d) CAMEL Attack Force (1) Establish the Thirty-sixth UNITED STATES Infantry Division (reinforced) and one Combat Command of the First French Armored Division on selected beaches in the ST. RAPHAEL-ANTHEOR area. Land at H hour on D day in accordance with plan of attack developed by the Commanding General concerned, which involves the early capture of ST. RAPHAEL and FREJUS, the seizure of LE MUY and airfield sites in the ARGENS VALLEY, and the advance at utmost speed to the beach head line TRANS EN PROVENCE-BAGNOLS EN FORET-THEOULE SUR MER by D plus one. Clear AGAY ROADS with all possible speed. Develop beach 264 A.
    (2) Be prepared to land one French Armored Combat Command as soon as beaches are cleared. Exploit port facilities of ST. RAPHAEL to ensure adequate maintenance of ground forces. Expedite unloading and turn-around of Air Force LST shuttle. Lay ship moorings at request of Petroleum Group.
    (3) Neutralize or destroy enemy batteries which threaten transports, landing craft or beaches. Conduct bombardment in accordance with Gunfire Support Plan, Annex "B". Release gunfire support ships to TF 86 as directed by NCWTF. Take special measures to ensure safety of troop carrier aircraft.
    (4) Direct LST carrying Air Force equipment and four LST carrying French Armored Combat Command to deliver pontoon causeways to ALPHA Attack Force at beach 259.
    (5) Move transports and other shipping inshore when shore batteries are silenced. Make maximum use of LCT in unloading shipping.
    (6) Station LST 394 initially in position Latitude Forty-three degrees nineteen minutes thirty seconds North, Longitude six degrees fifty-nine minutes thirty seconds East. Tow pontoon causeway carried by LST 394 to CAMEL beaches after dropping from ship on station. Upon releasing LSTs notify Commander Anti-Submarine and Convoy Control Group (CTG 80.6) of identification number of nine LST(2)s to be employed exclusively in CALVI shuttle. Clear THRUSTER, BRUISER promptly for priority Air Force lift from CALVI.
    (7) Be prepared to receive LCT(R) from ALPHA Attack Force and DELTA Attack Force for employment in assault on beach 264A.
  (e) SUPPORT FORCE (1) Establish during darkness on D minus one/D day the First Special Service Force (SITKA Force) on the islands of LEVANT and PORT CROS. Neutralize all enemy batteries on these islands threatening assault shipping and operational forces.
    (2) During darkness on D minus one/D day establish the French Group de Commandos (ROMEO Force) in the vicinity of CAPE

File No.
A16-3/N31
Serial: 00987

OPERATION PLAN
No. 4-44

NEGRE, for the purpose of destroying enemy defenses at CAPE NEGRE, blocking the coastal highway in the vicinity of CAPE NEGRE, seizing the high ground two miles north of that cape, and protection of the left flank of the main assault forces. Destroy or neutralize enemy batteries at CAPE NEGRE (if uncaptured) and CAPE BENAT which threaten CAVALAIRE assault.

(3) As the opportunity permits, release and sail Transdiv Thirteen to AJACCIO for special fast lift of French follow-up elements. Evacuate casualties to combat loaders of ALPHA Attack Force. During daylight on D day release sixteen PTs to CTG 80.5, and four ASRC to Special Operations Group.

(4) Conduct bombardment and support military operations in SITKA area in accordance with Gunfire Support Plan, Annex "B".

(5) As directed by NCWTF reassign gunfire support ships to meet special situations.

(6) After initial assault phases support the westward advance of the Army as directed by NCWTF. Valuable ships and the limited gunfire available are to be employed only against targets of due importance.

(7) Sweeping forces will be assigned as necessary for the westward advance and the clearance of HYERES ROADS.

(8) Battleships base on NAPLES, MALTA, ALGIERS, ORAN, Cruisers base on NAPLES, PALERMO, MALTA, AJACCIO, ALGIERS, MERS EL KEBIR.

(f) AIRCRAFT CARRIER Force (1) Provide maximum practicable fighter protection and spotting aircraft to assigned attack sectors.

(2) Provide close support missions.

(3) Provide own protection against enemy air and submarine forces.

(4) Be prepared to transfer aircraft to captured airfields.

(5) Operate generally in accordance with detailed Air Plan, Annex "F". Operating area is bounded by following positions:
    (A) Latitude forty-two degrees fifty-four minutes North, Longitude five degrees East,
    (B) Latitude forty-two degrees fifty-four minutes North, Longitude seven degrees four minutes East,
    (C) Latitude forty-two degrees thirty-two minutes North, Longitude seven degrees fifty minutes East,
    (D) Latitude forty-one degrees North, Longitude seven degrees fifty minutes East,
    (E) Latitude forty-one degrees North, Longitude five degrees East.

(6) Carriers base on NAPLES, PALERMO, MALTA, ALGIERS, ORAN. Cruisers, destroyers, base on AJACCIO, CAGLIARI, ALGIERS.

(x) (1) This Operation Plan will be placed in effect by dispatch or sealed orders. "Execute Operation Plan No. 4-44."

(2) D day and H hour will be transmitted separately.

(3) Task Force Commanders sail assault convoys in accordance

File No.
A16-3/N31
Serial: 00987

OPERATION PLAN
No. 4-44
- -

with Convoy Plan, Annex "H". Subsequent movements in accordance with Departure and Rendezvous Plan, Annex "G".

(4) The assault is to be pressed home with relentless force regardless of loss or difficulty.

(5) Take every available measure to ensure earliest warning of submarine contacts and vigorous offensive action against these.

(6) Major combatant ships retire seaward during darkness at discretion of Attack Force Commanders, operating in area northward of convoy lanes to CORSICA.

(7) Employ smoke to fullest extend for defense against aircraft attacks.

(8) Maintain alert mine watch and avoid unswept waters.

(9) Take special precautions to avoid firing on friendly aircraft and to ensure strict compliance with rules governing control of anti-aircraft fire.

(10) Attack Force Commanders modify initial positions of GCI/LSTs and Fighter Direction ships as required by Controllers to achieve best results, subject to limitations imposed to ensure safety of ships.

(11) Be prepared to cope with enemy use of gas. Provide impregnated clothing for crews of small craft beaching and all naval personnel landing on hostile shores.

(12) Unless specifically ordered, poison gas will not be employed by this force.

(13) Site pontoon causeways expeditiously. (See Logistic Plan, Annex "E", for LSTs designated to carry pontoon causeways).

(14) Ensure effective boat salvage operations.

(15) Clear empty shipping, LSTs, and LCI(L)s from assault area promptly and direct to report to Anti-Submarine and Convoy Control Group in BAIE DE BRIANDE-BON PORTE area. Upon completion of assigned tasks on D day, release PCs to Anti-Submarine and Convoy Control Group.

(16) Report to Attack Force Commander, info Naval Commander Western Task Force, immediately in case of damage by mine, or observation of mines or mine laying, giving position of suspected field. See Minesweeping Plan, Annex "J".

(17) Take precautions to employ proper and effective recognition signals.

(18) Take steps to prevent flotsam being thrown overboard in assault area.

(19) Annexes to this Operation Plan are effective upon receipt.

(20) Maintain radio and visual silence, including TBS, except as modified by Communication Plan, Annex "C".

(21) The following documents, in the possession of Commanders of Attack Forces, are in effect:
    (a) MEDITERRANEAN Joint Air Orders.
    (b) MEDITERRANEAN Convoy Instructions.
    (c) MEDITERRANEAN Secret General Orders.
    (d) MEDITERRANEAN Navigational Memoranda.

File No.
A16-3/N31
Serial: 00987

OPERATION PLAN
No. 4-44
----

    (22) Landing ships and craft base on NAPLES, AJACCIO; other ships base on NAPLES, AJACCIO, CAGLIARI, PALERMO, MALTA, ALGIERS, ORAN.

4. Evacuation of wounded in accordance with Medical Plan, Annex "D". Logistic support and evacuation of Prisoners of War in accordance with Logistic Plan, Annex "E".

5. (a) Use Communication Plan, Annex "C".
(b) Use zone BAKER time.
(c) Rendezvous Points are listed in Rendezvous and Departure Plan, Annex "G".
(d) Naval Commander Western Task Force in CATOCTIN with Control Force. Second in Command, Western Naval Task Force, Rear Admiral Davidson, USN, in AUGUSTA with Support Force.
(e) (1) Unless otherwise directed by the Supreme Allied Commander, MEDITERRANEAN Theater, Command of the Army and Navy Forces of the Western Task Force, after embarkation, will rest in the Naval Commander Western Task Force under the principle of unity of command, until such time as the Commanding General, Seventh U.S. Army, lands and assumes command.
(2) The naval Attack Force Commanders are similarly in command of all military and naval forces in their respective Attack Forces until the Division Commanding General concerned has landed and assumed command of his unit.
(3) This command is exercised as prescribed in "Joint Action of the Army and Navy (FTP 155, para 10) - Unity of Command."
(f) The Short Title of this Plan is "ANOR 1".

            H. K. Hewitt

            H. K. HEWITT,
            Vice Admiral, U.S. Navy,
          Naval Commander Western Task Force.

ANNEXES: (to be issued separately)
A. Information Annex.
B. Gunfire Support Plan.
C. Communication Plan.
D. Medical Plan.
E. Logistic Plan.
F. Air Plan.
G. Departure and Rendezvous Plan.
H. Convoy Plan.
J. Minesweeping Plan.
K. Salvage Plan.
L. Special Operations Group Directive.
M. Screening Group Directive.
N. Directive to USN Liaison, Beach Control Group.
O. Directive to USN Liaison, French Ports.

File No.
A16-3/N31
Serial: 00987

OPERATION PLAN
No. 4-44
- -
P. Intelligence Annex.
Q. Instructions to Merchant Vessels.
R. Air Beacon Directive.
S. Postponement Directive.

File No.
A16-3/N31
Serial: 00987

OPERATION PLAN
No. 4-44

- -

DISTRIBUTION:

	No. of Copies	Copy No.
SAC Med	5	1-5
DSAC Med	2	6-7
CinC Med	15	8-22
AirCinC Med	5	23-27
CG SOS NATOUSA	2	28, 29
AFHQ (COT)	2	30, 31
CG Peninsular Base Section	2	32, 33
CG Northern Base Section	2	34, 35
CG Mediterranean Base Section	2	36, 37
CG VII Army	5	38-42
CG VI Corps	3	43-45
CG 3rd Inf. Div.	2	46, 47
CG 45th Inf. Div.	2	48, 49
CG 36th Inf. Div.	2	50, 51
CG French Army "B"	4	52-55
CG II French Corps	3	56-58
CG 1st French Inf. Div. (DMI)	2	59, 60
CG 3rd Algerien Inf. Div. (DIA)	2	61, 62
CG 9th Colonial Inf. Div. (DIC)	2	63, 64
CG 1st French Armored Div. (DB)	2	65, 66
CG MATAF	5	67-71
CG MASAF	5	72-76
AOC MACAF	5	77-81
CG XII TAC	5	82-86
CG 7th Army Air Borne Div. (Provisional)	2	87, 88
CTF 80	1	89
CTG 80.1	1	90
CTG 80.2	1	91
CTG 80.3	1	92
CTG 80.4	7‡	93-99
CTG 80.5	4‡	100-103
CTG 80.6	2	104, 105
CTG 80.7	1	106
CTG 80.8	2	107, 108
CTG 80.9	3	109-111
CTF 82	1	112
CTF 83	1	113
CTF 84	2	114, 115
CTF 85	2	116, 117
CTF 86	2	118, 119
CTF 87	2	120, 121
CTF 88	4	122, 125
CTG 89.2	1	126
CTG 89.4	2	127, 128
CTG 89.6	2	129, 130
ComCarrier Group	2	131, 132
ComBatDiv 5	2	133, 134

File No.
A16-3/N31
Serial: 00987

OPERATION PLAN
No. 4-44

DISTRIBUTION: (Continued)

	No. of Copies	Copy No.
ComCruDiv 7	2	135, 136
Com15th Cruiser Squadron	2	137, 138
Com4th French Light CruDiv	1	139
ComNavNAW (Adm)	2	140, 141
Com8thPhib (Adm) Naples	2	142, 143
Com8thPhib (Adm) Bizerte	2	144, 145
Comdt. NOB Palermo	2	146, 147
CO AATB Salerno	1	148
ComNavDet. CAGLIARI	1	149
FOWIT	1	150
FOTALI	1	151
FOGMA	1	152
FOWM	1	153
FOLEM	1	154
FO Tunisia	1	155
VAM	1	156
SOIS	1	157
NOIC Maddelena	1	158
NOIC Naples	1	159
NOIC Cagliari	1	160
NOIC Taranto	1	161
NOIC Brindisi	1	162
NOIC Civitavecchia	1	163
BNLO Ajaccio	1	164
SNOESY	1	165
PSTO	1	166
Navale France	2	167, 168
COMAR CORSE	1	169
Cominch	2	170, 171
CNO	2	172, 173
AGWAR	2	174, 175
CinClant	2	176, 177
ComServLant	1	178
ComDesLant	1	179
ComNavEu	2	180, 181
Secretary to the Admiralty	6	182-187
Staff NCWTF	35	188-222
All Task Groups and Naval Units assigned and reserved for spares.	978	223-1200

‡ For distribution as deemed advisable to units assigned.

J. M. BOIT
Commander, U.S.N.R.
Flag Secretary

PLAN OF ASSAULT
BASED ON
APPENDIX 2 TO
ANNEX "B" TO OPERATION PLAN NO. 4-44
FIRE SUPPORT AND TRANSPORT AREAS

NOT TO BE USED FOR NAVIGATION

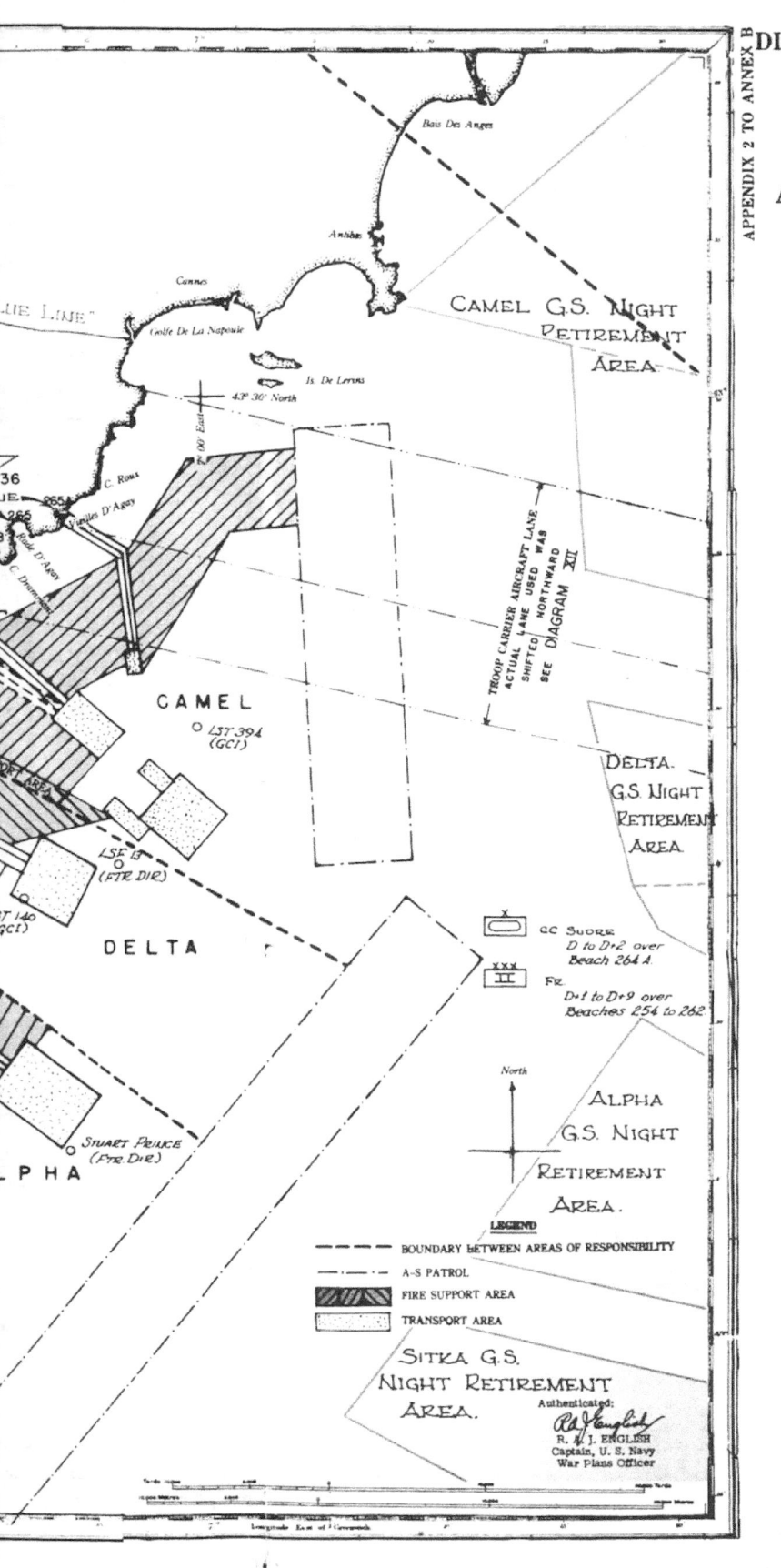

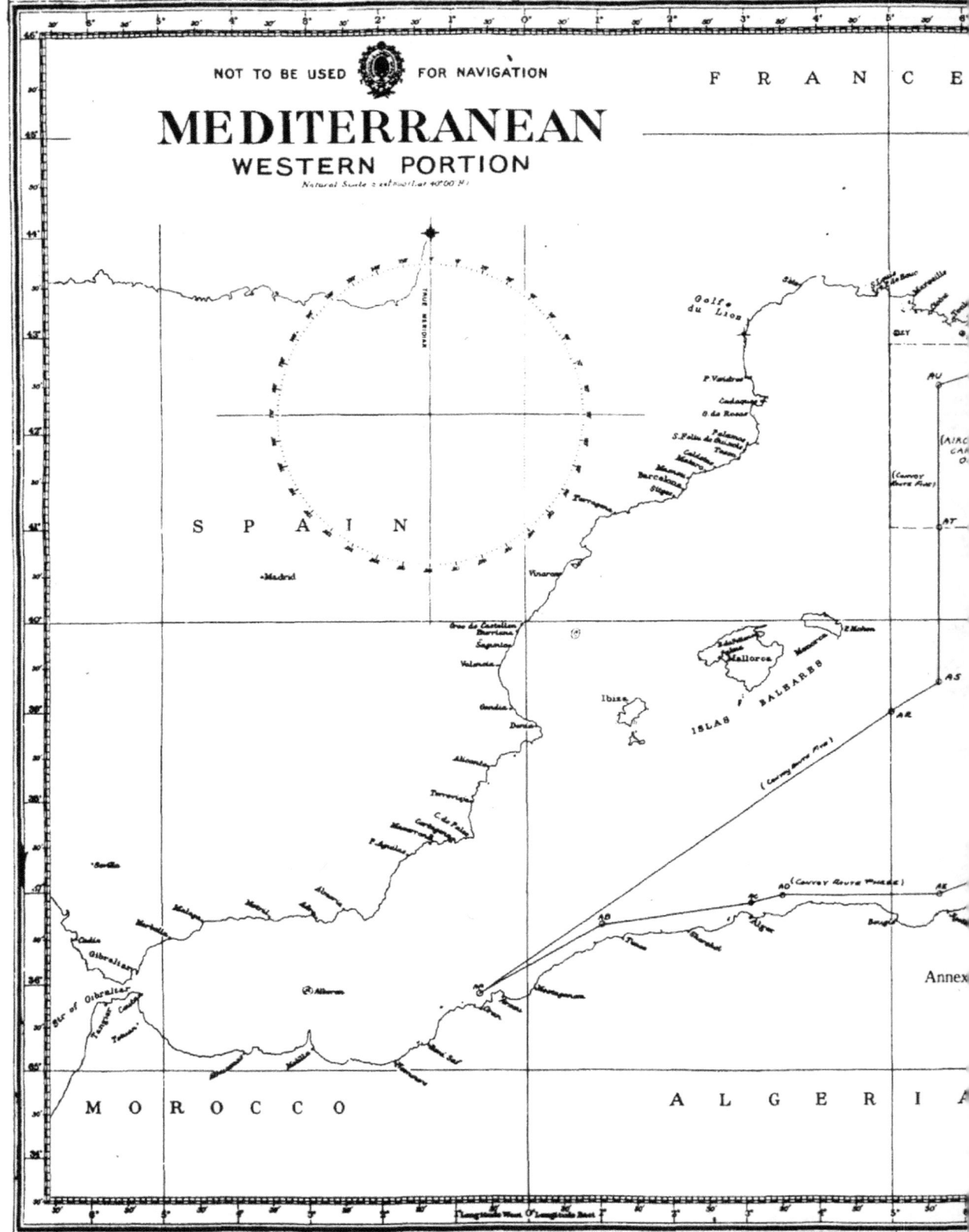

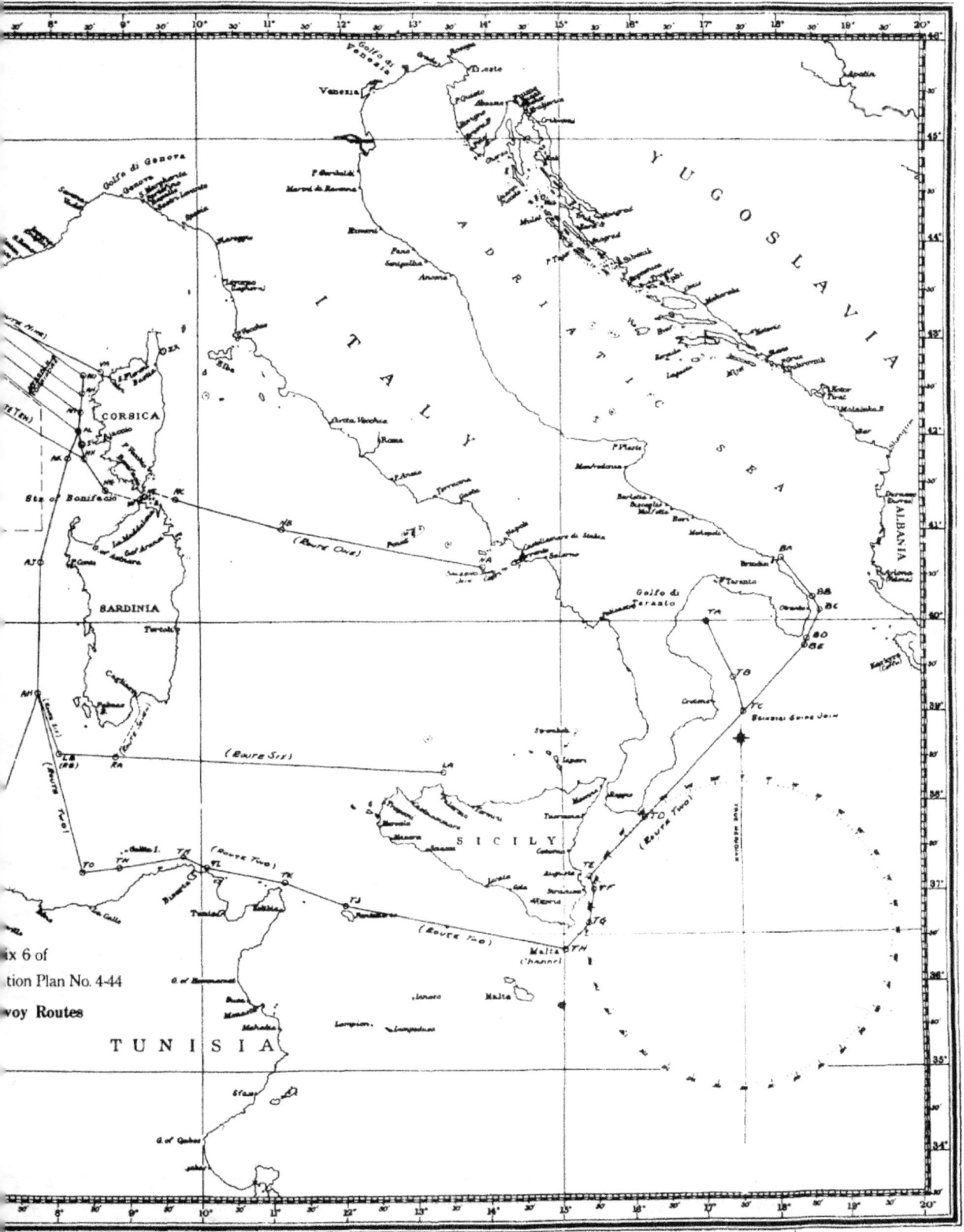

DIAGRAM II

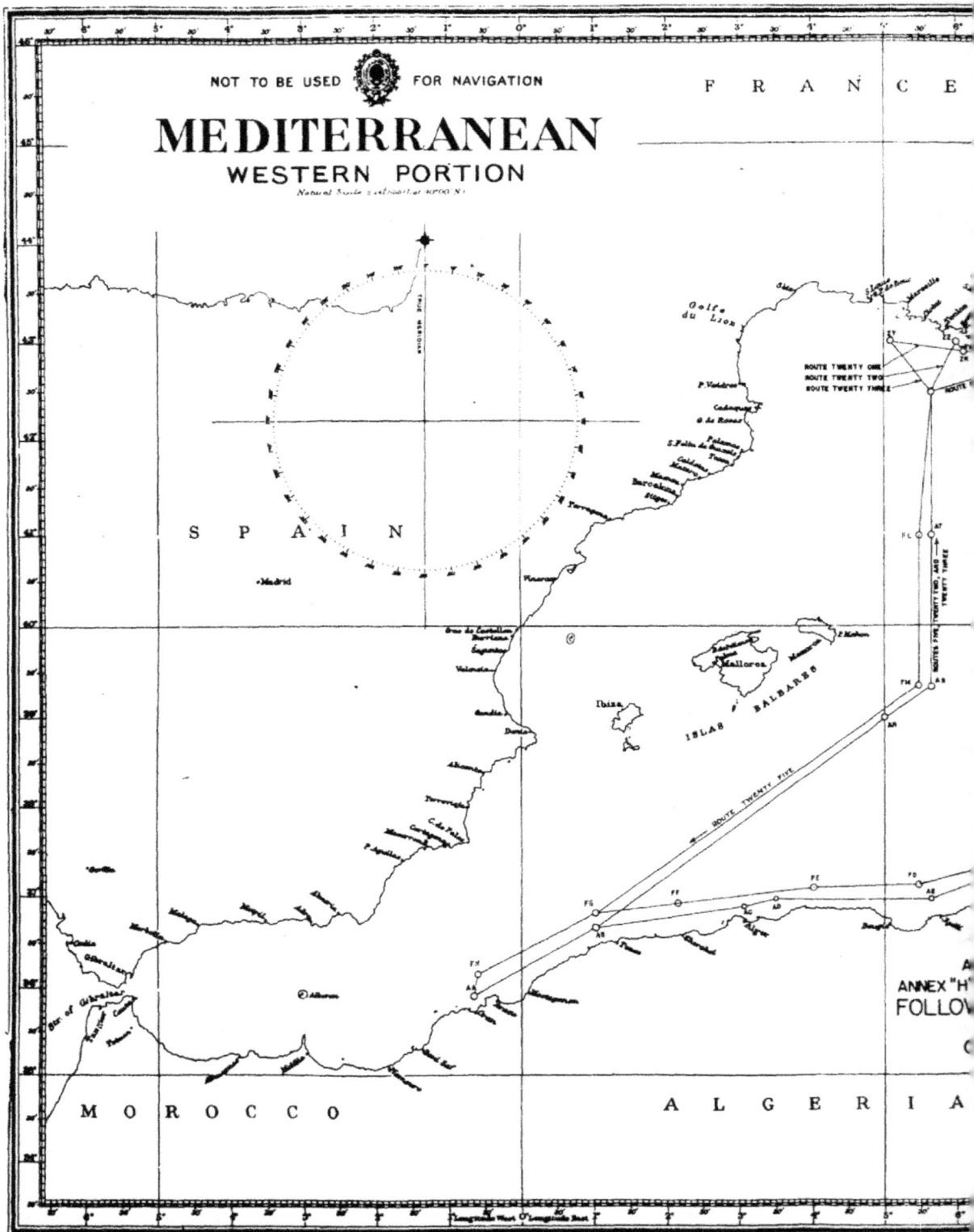

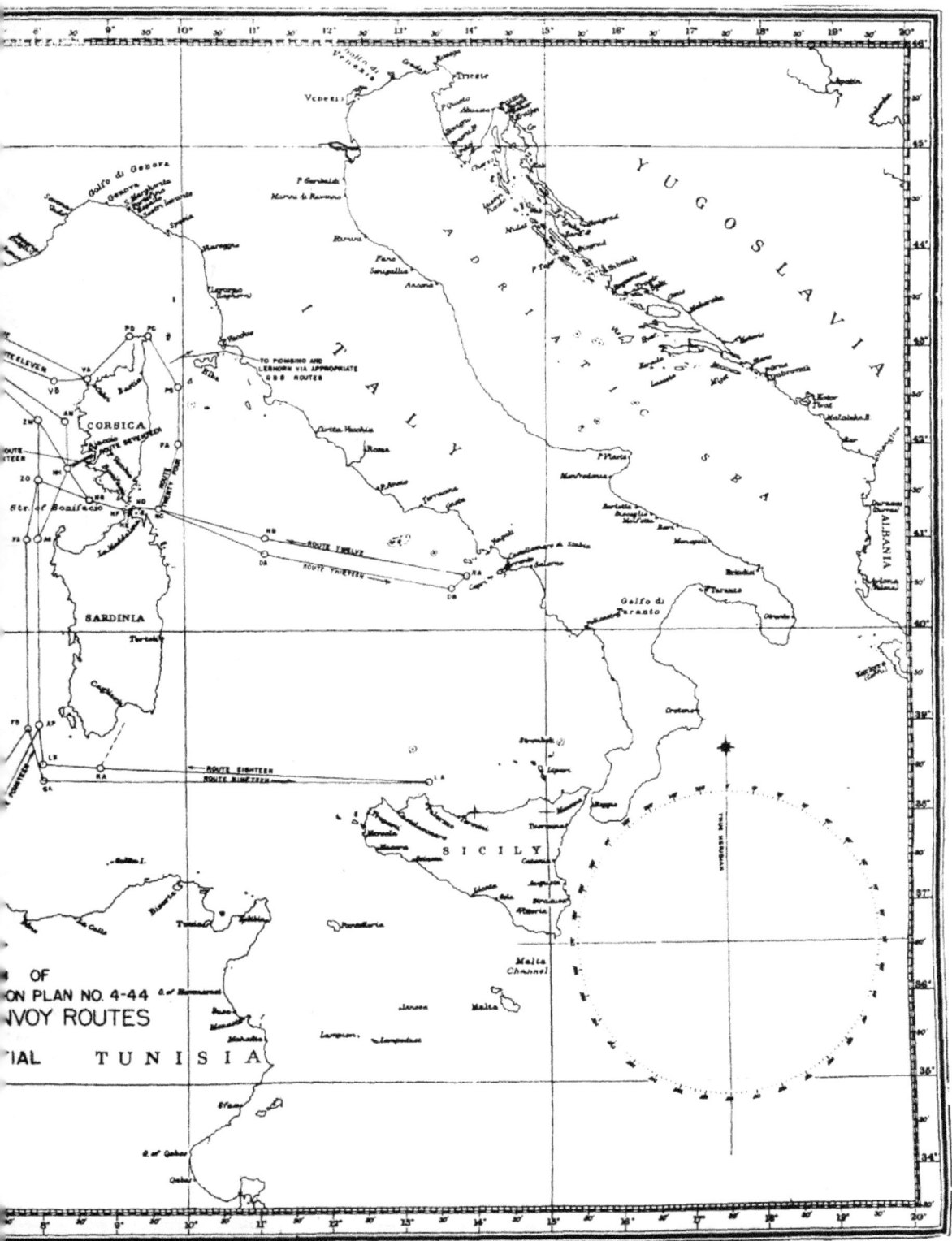

DIAGRAM III

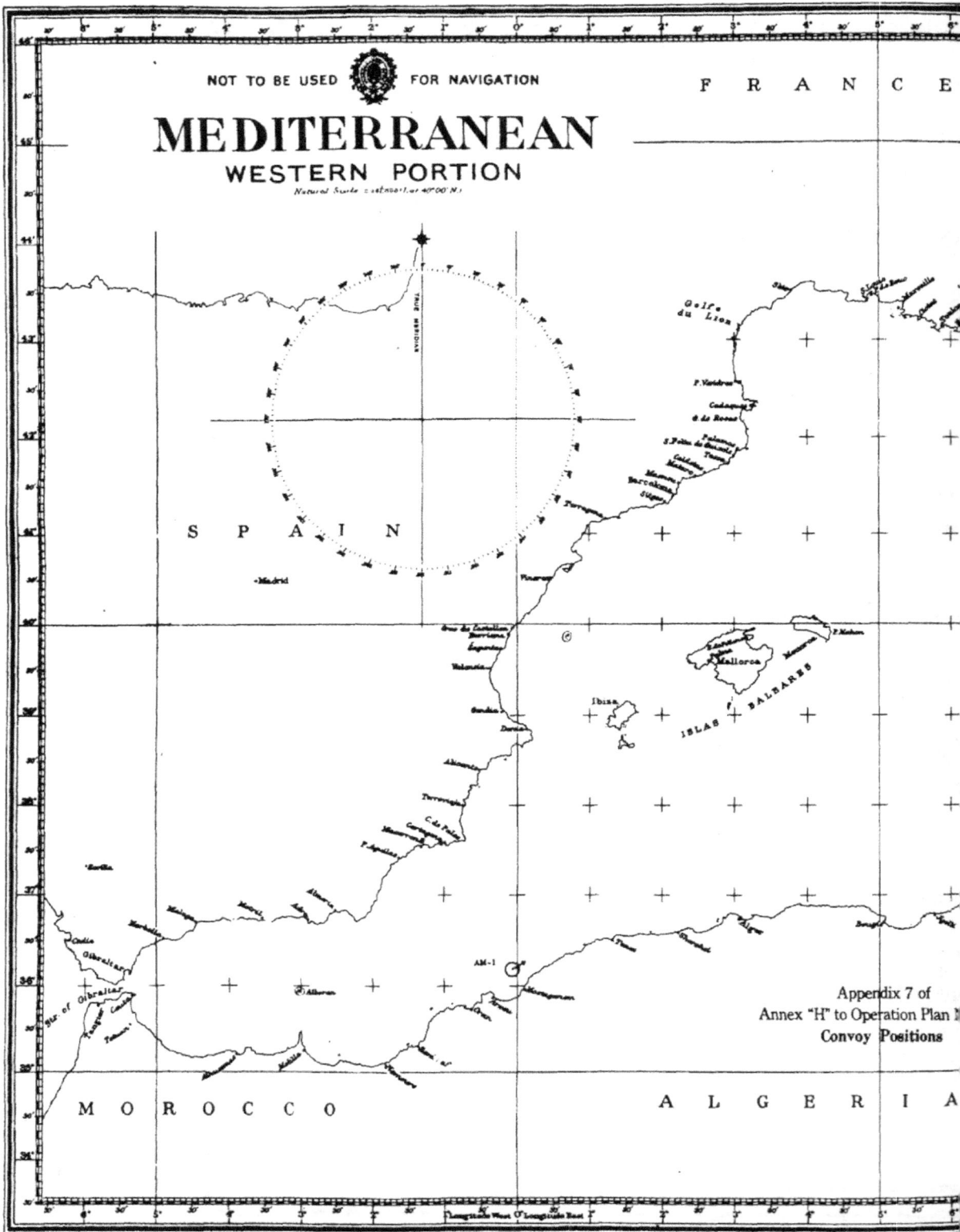

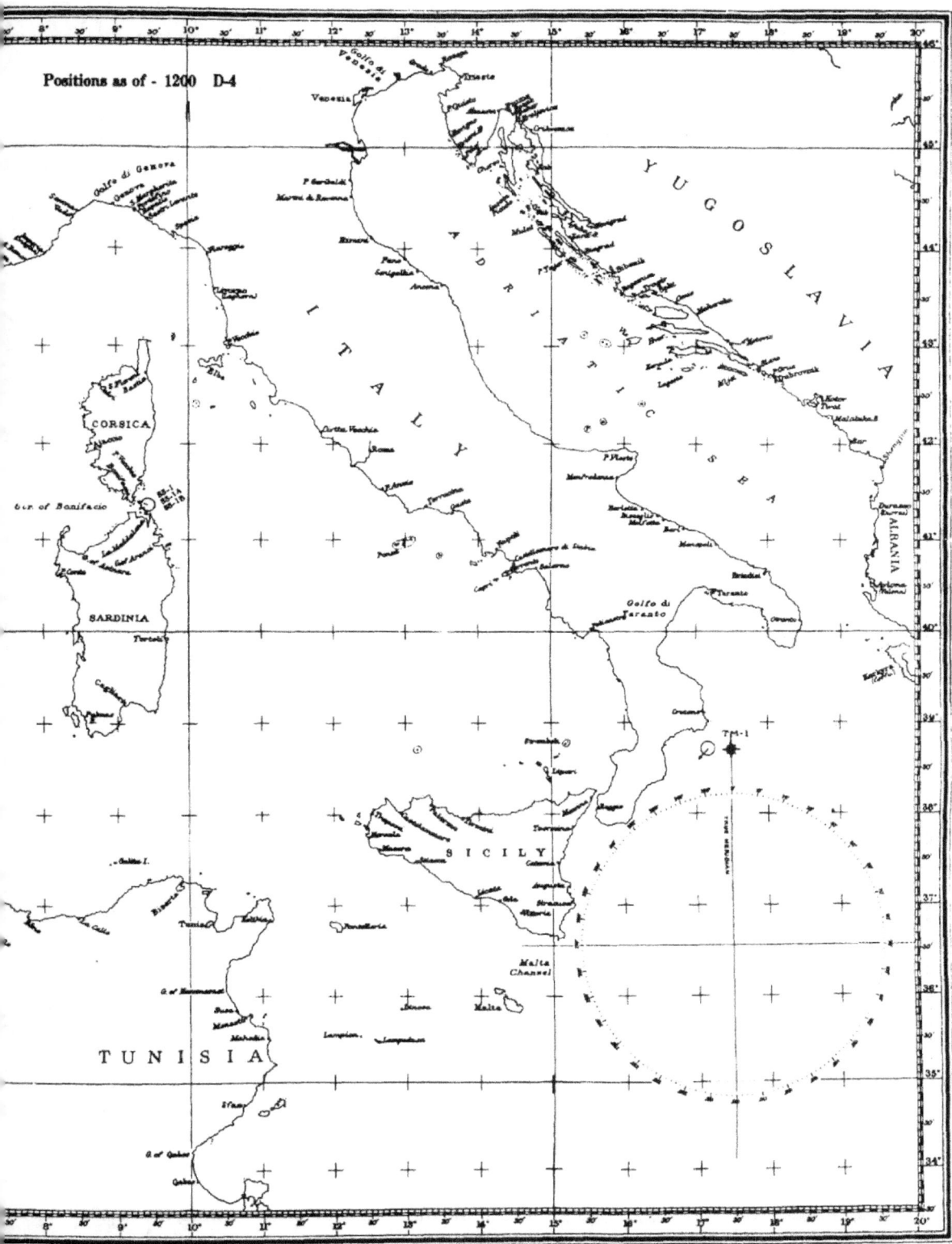

DIAGRAM IV

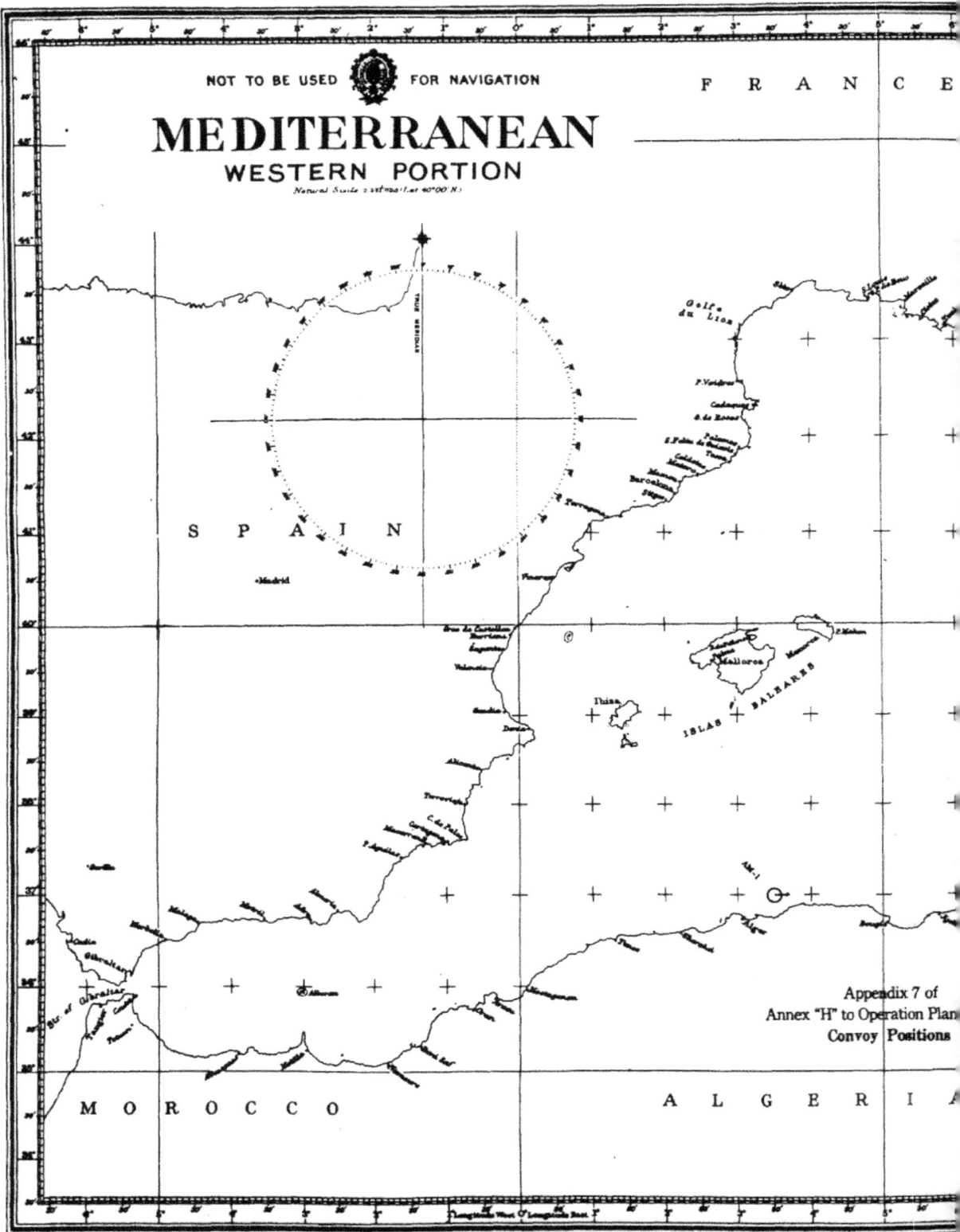

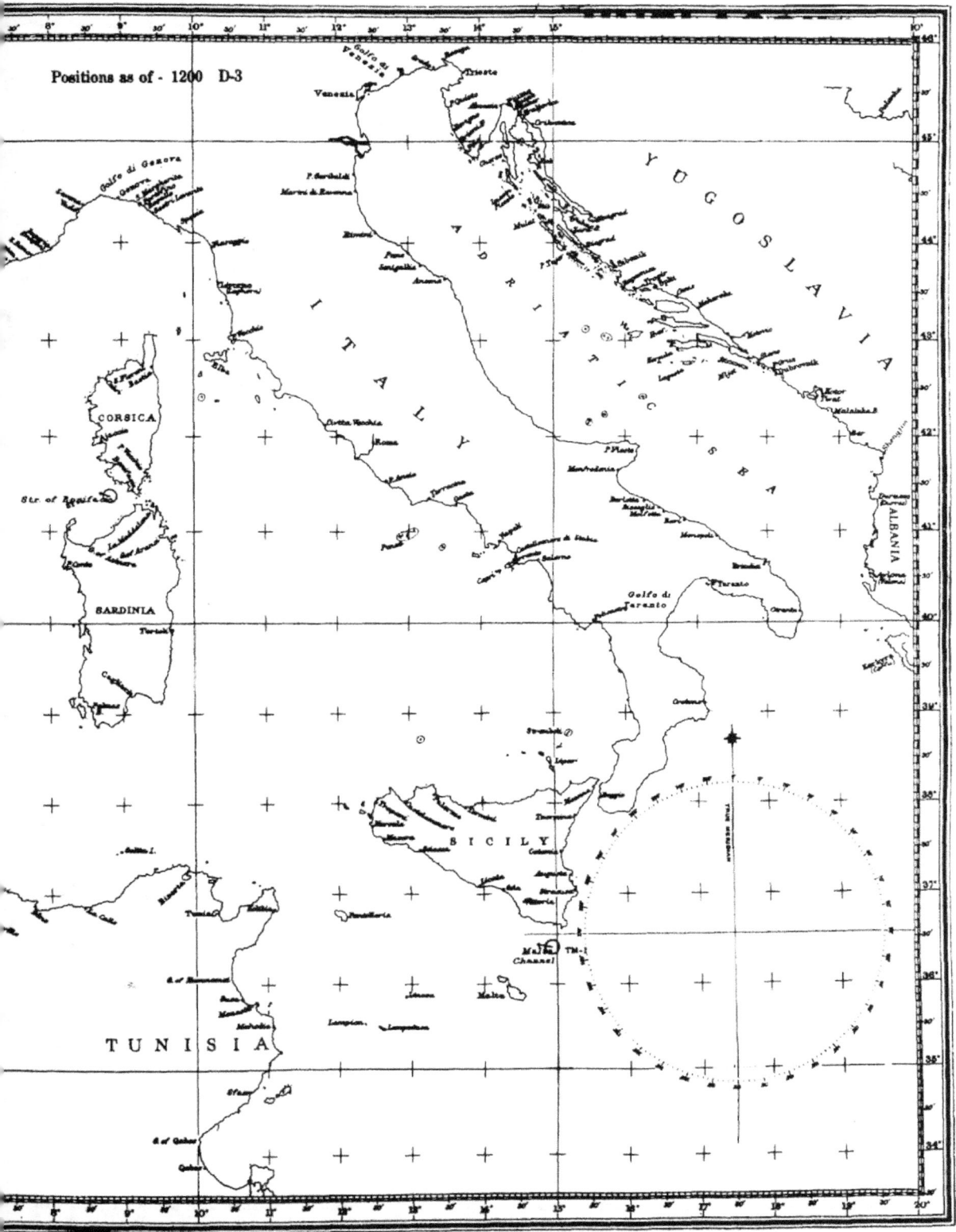

DIAGRAM V

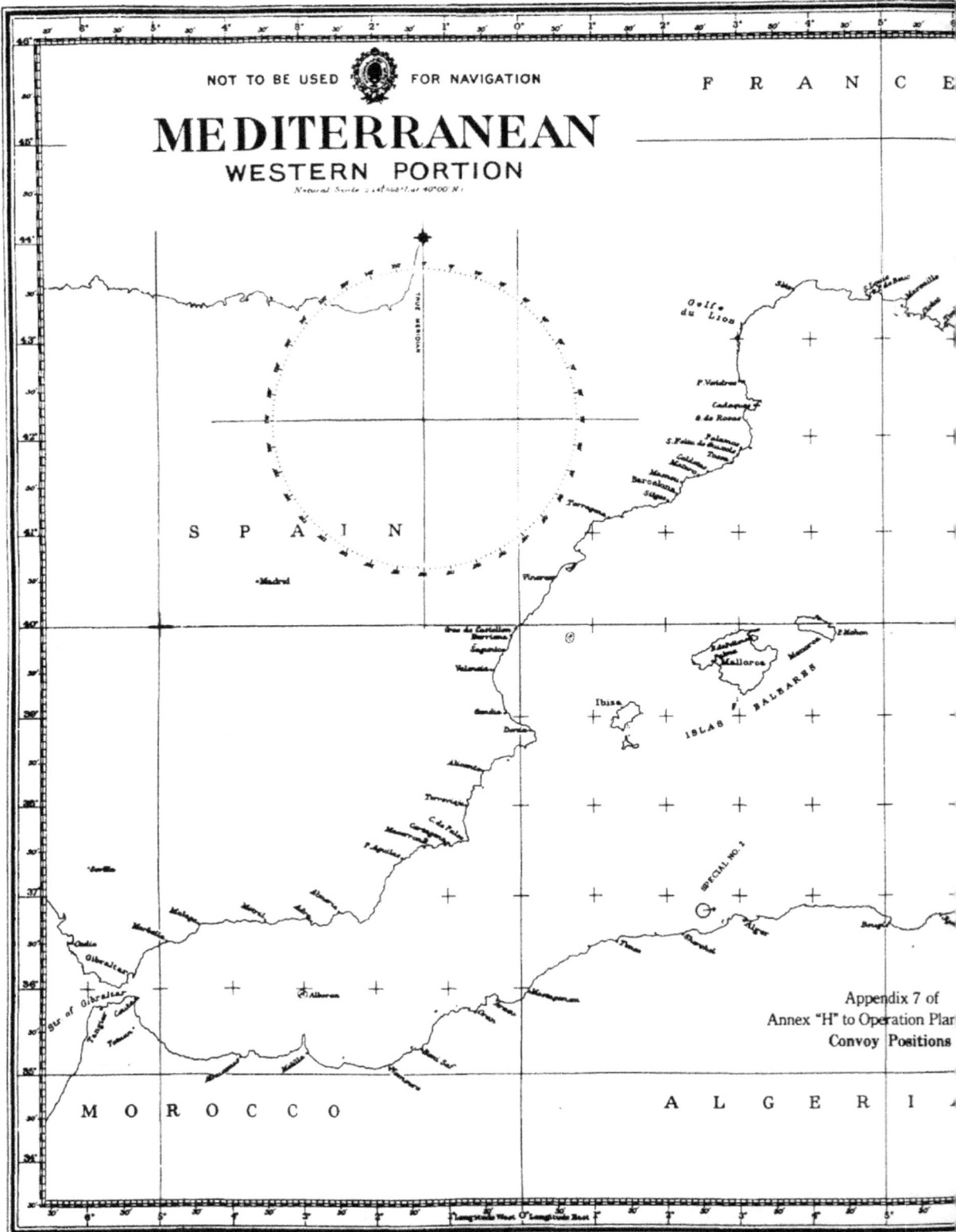

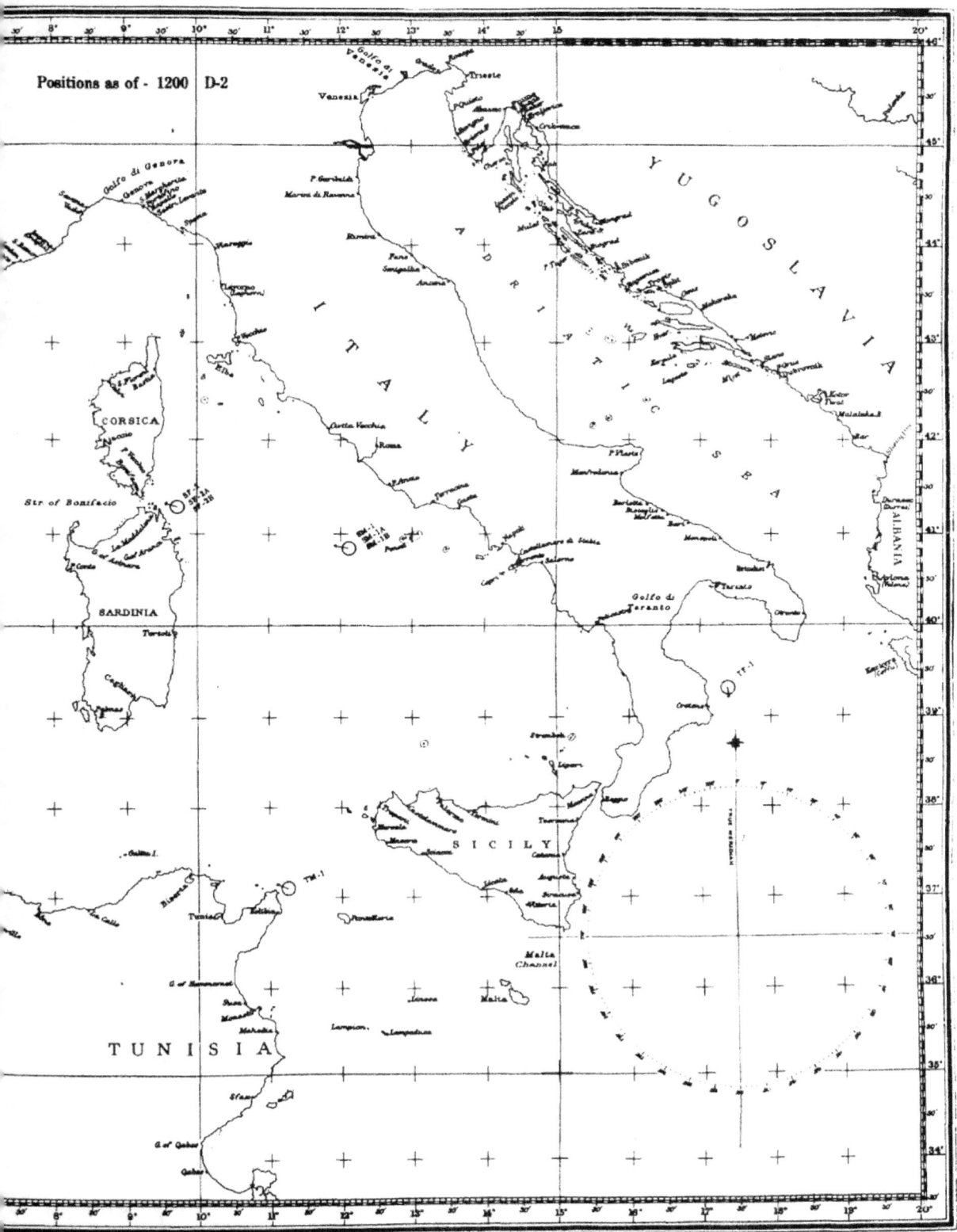

DIAGRAM VI

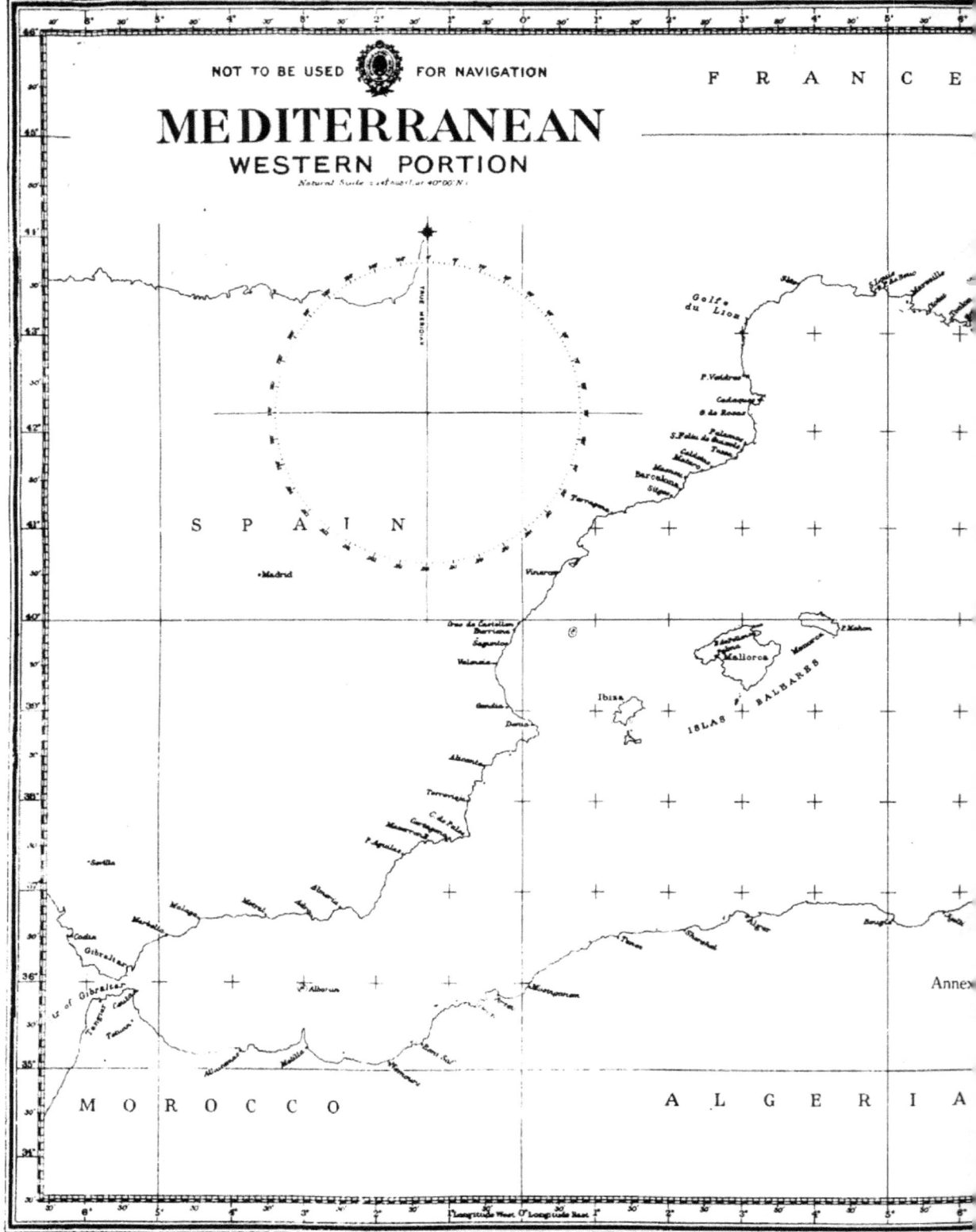

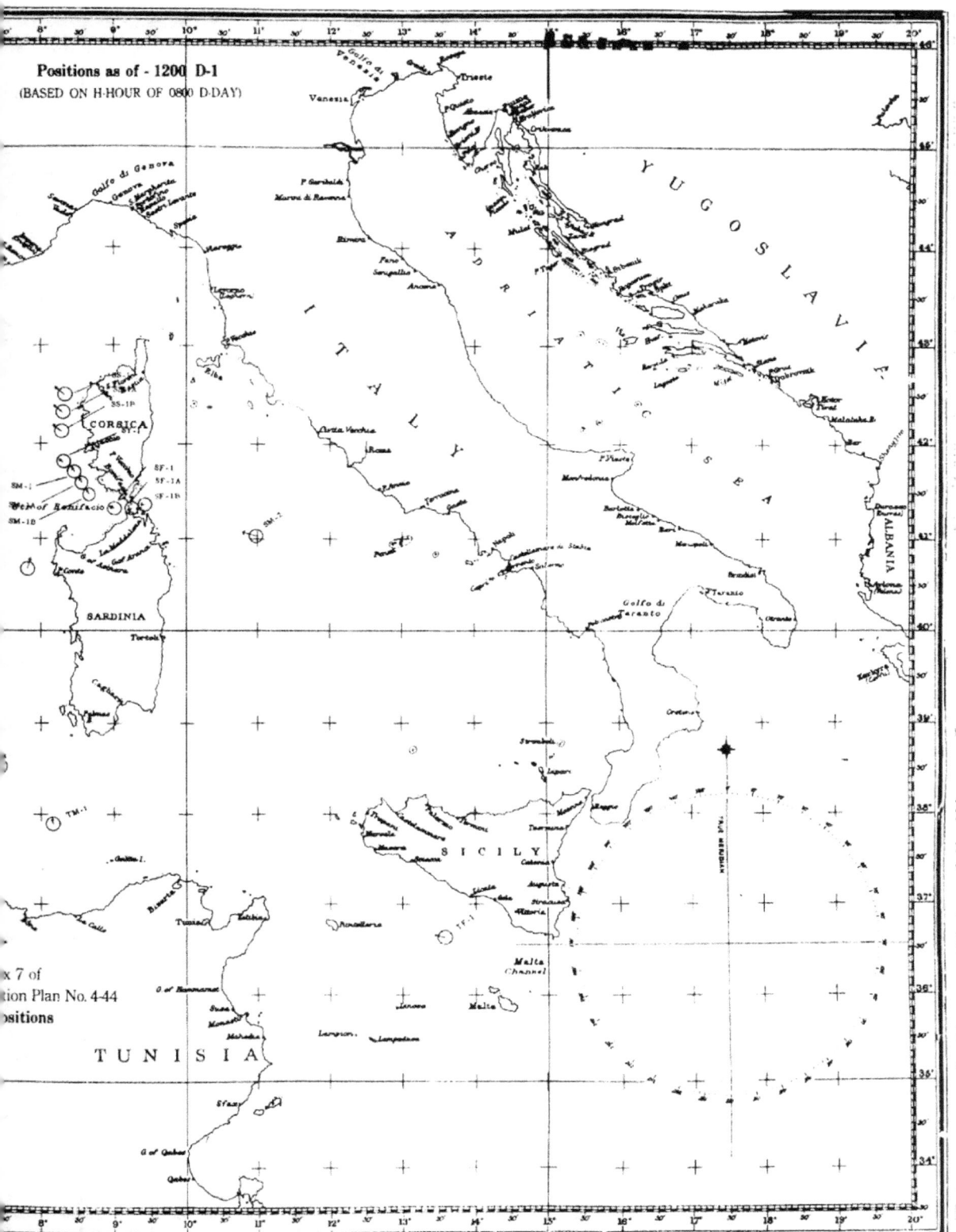

DIAGRAM VII

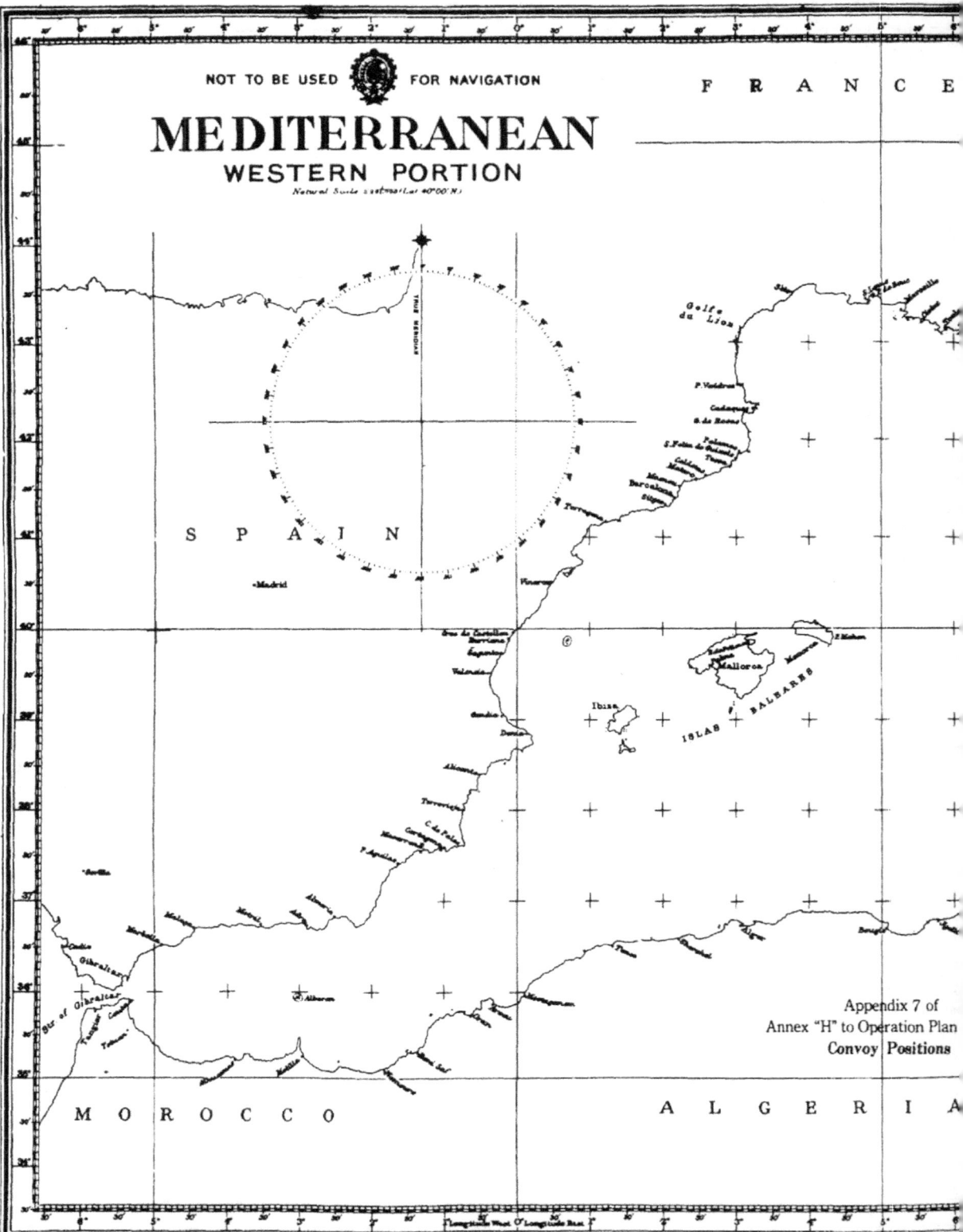

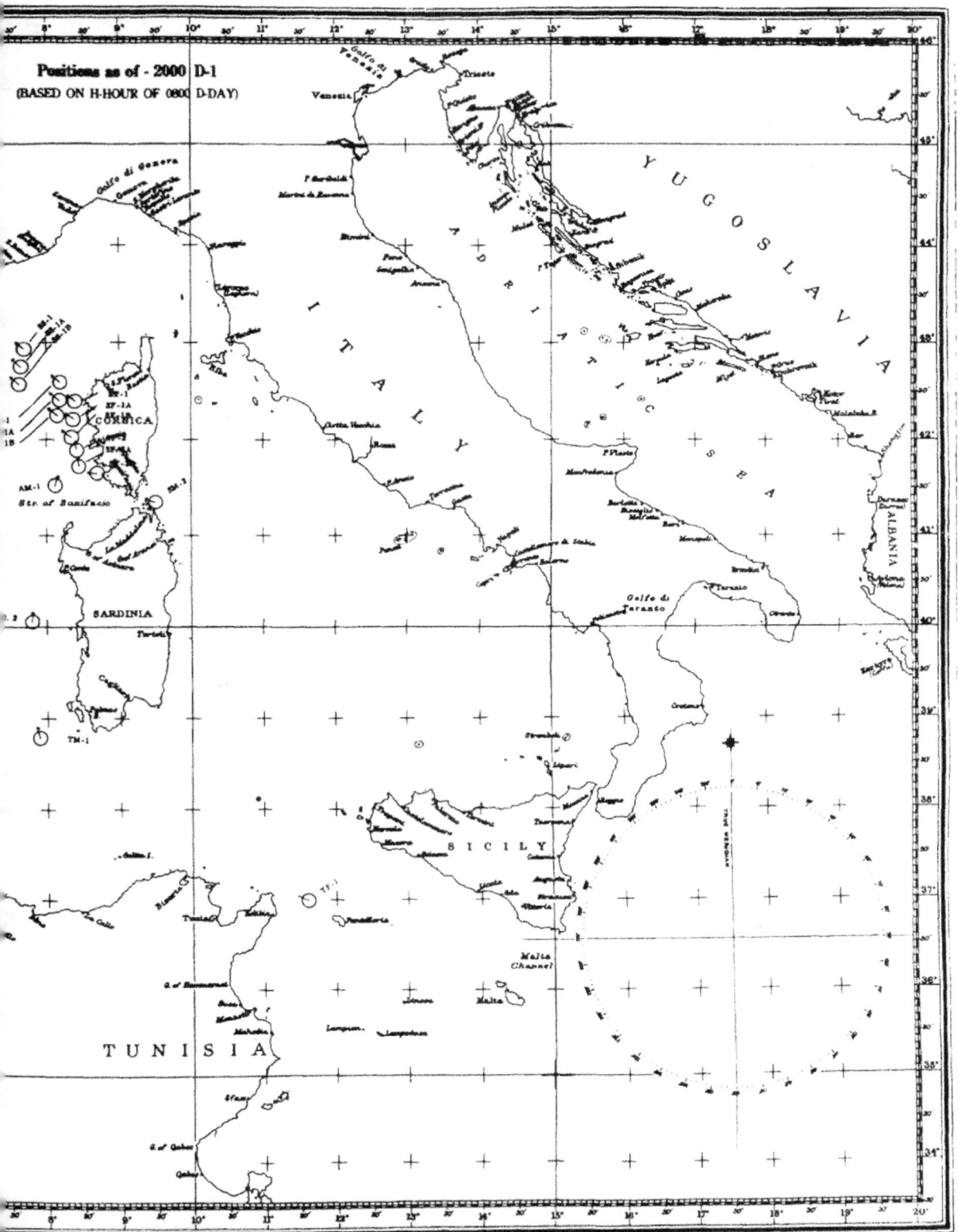

DIAGRAM VIII

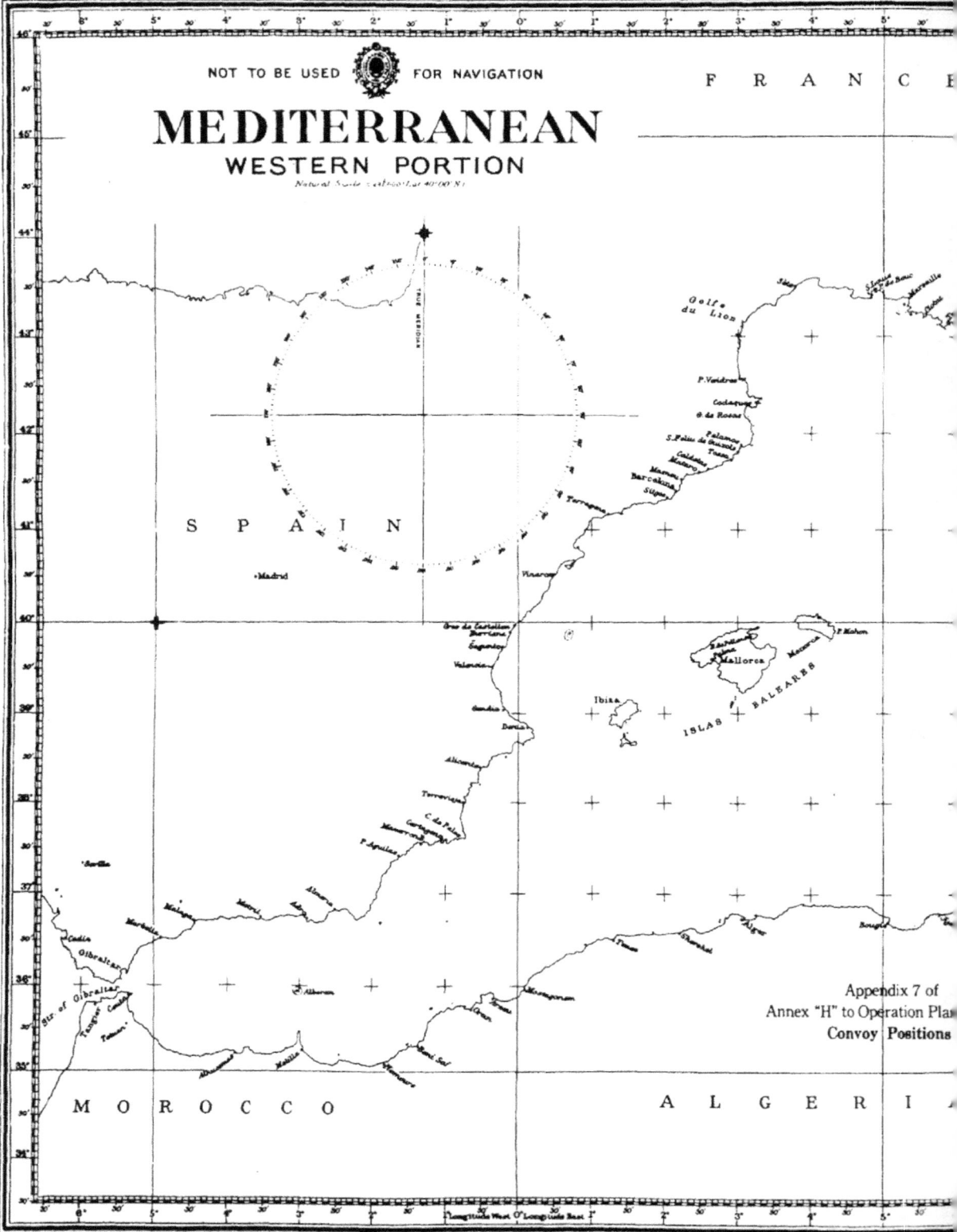

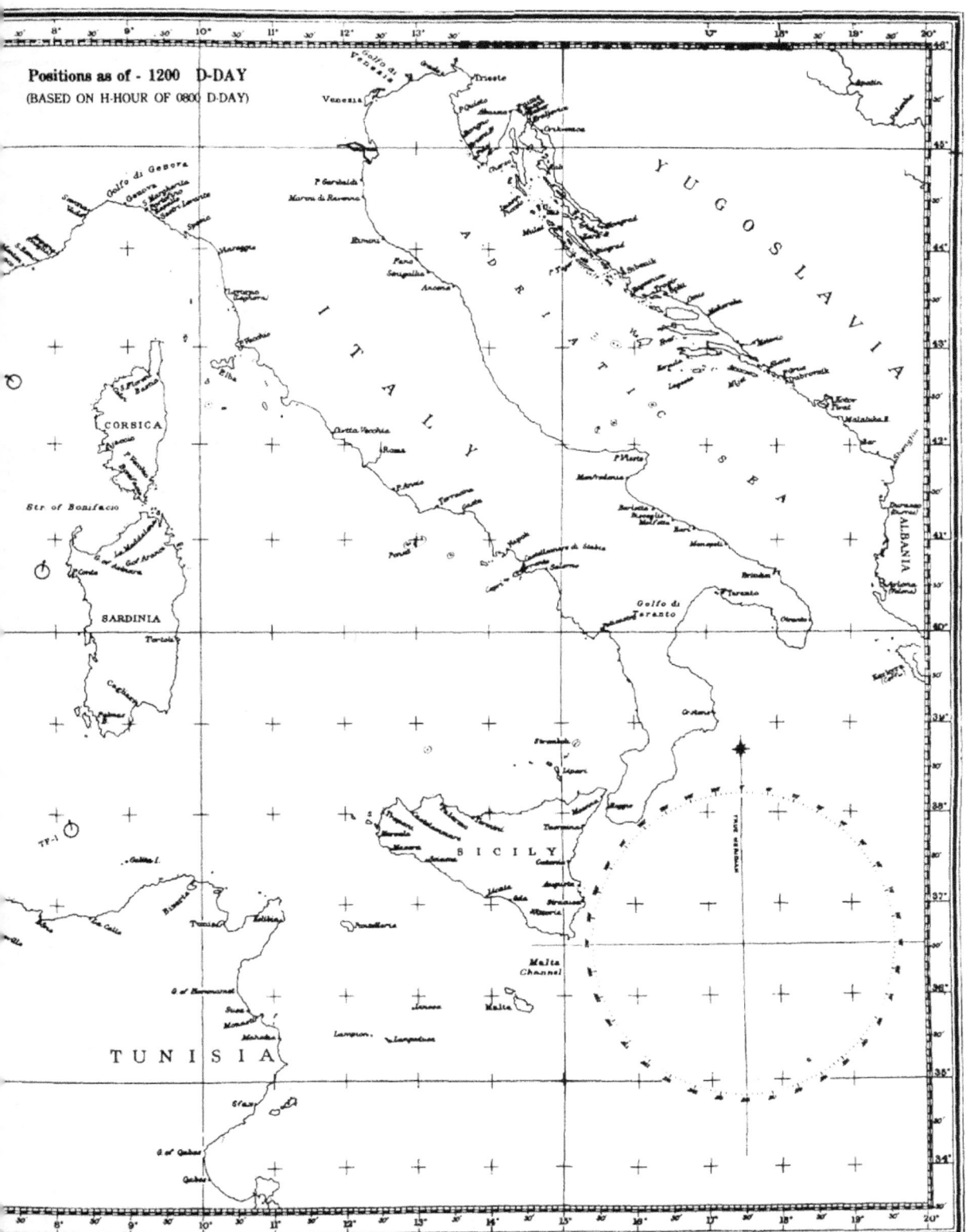

DIAGRAM IX

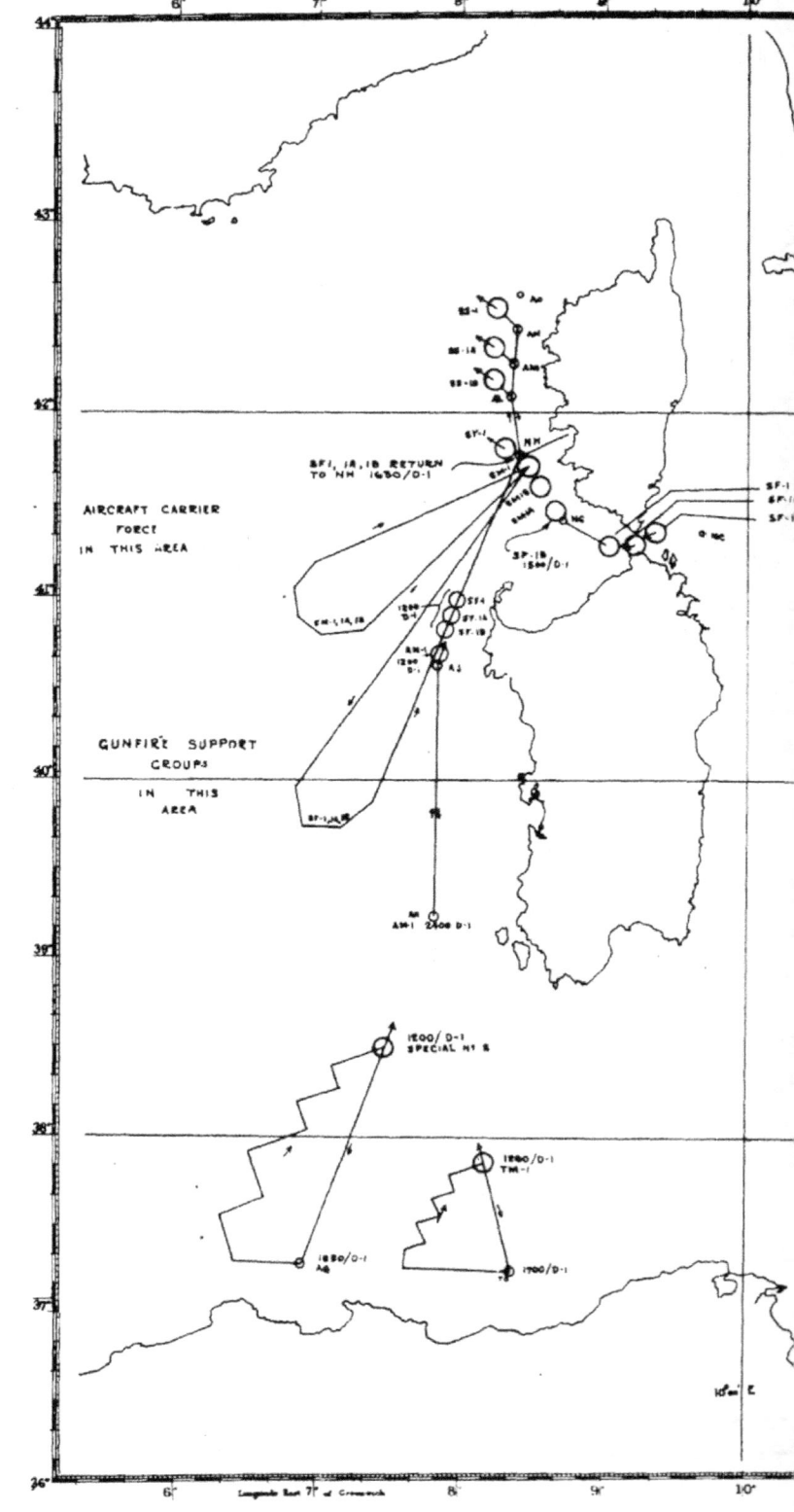

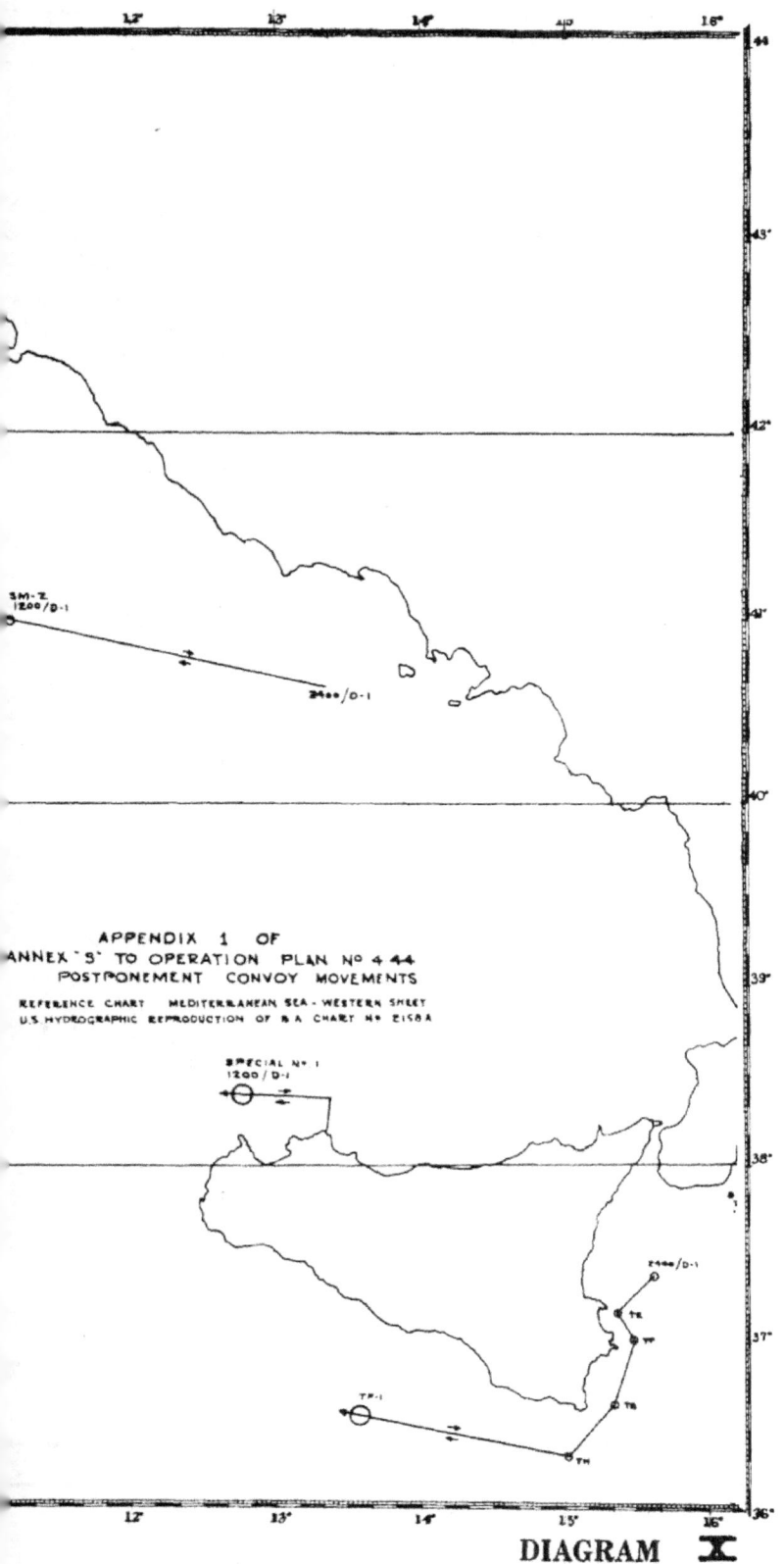

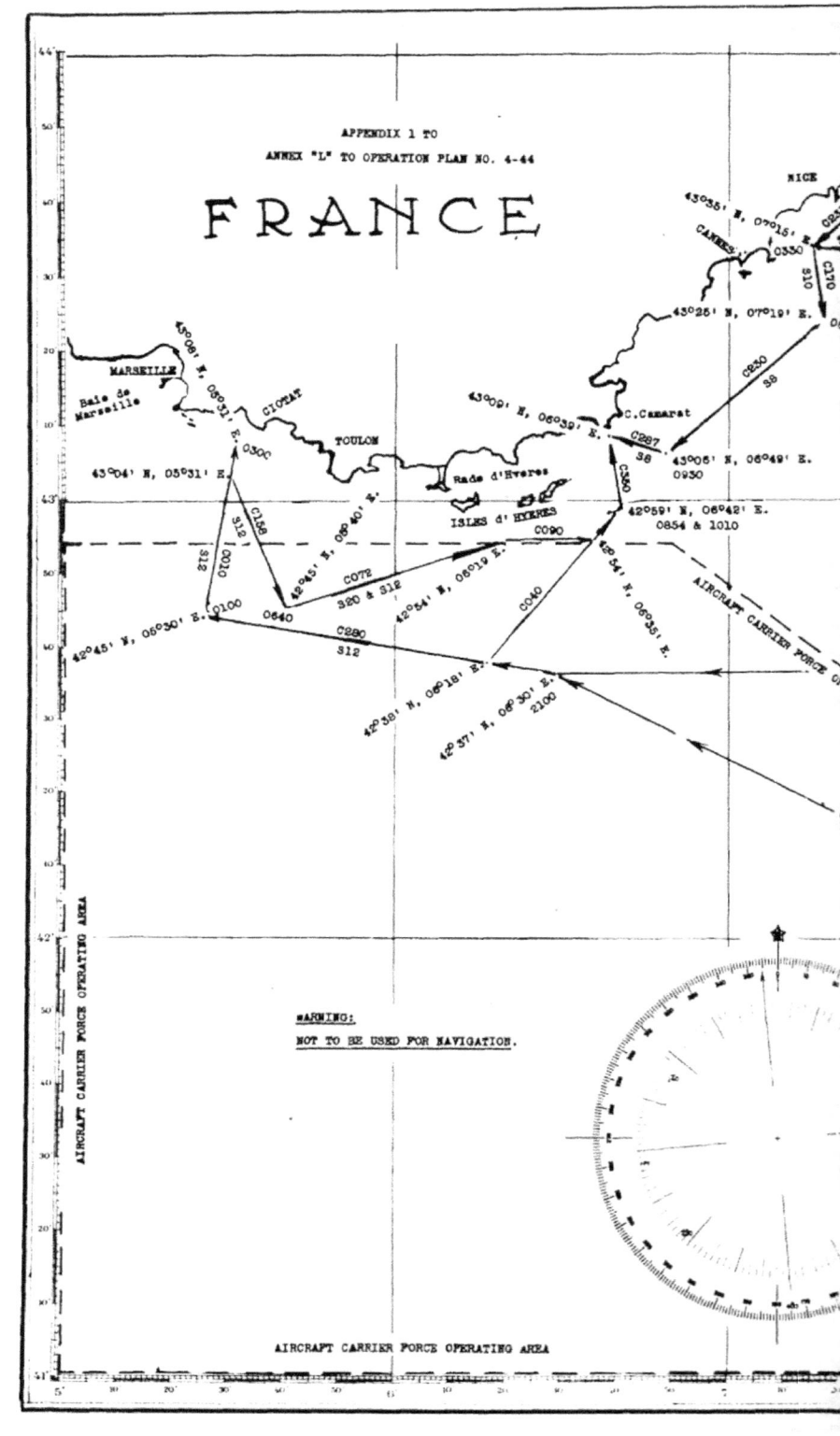

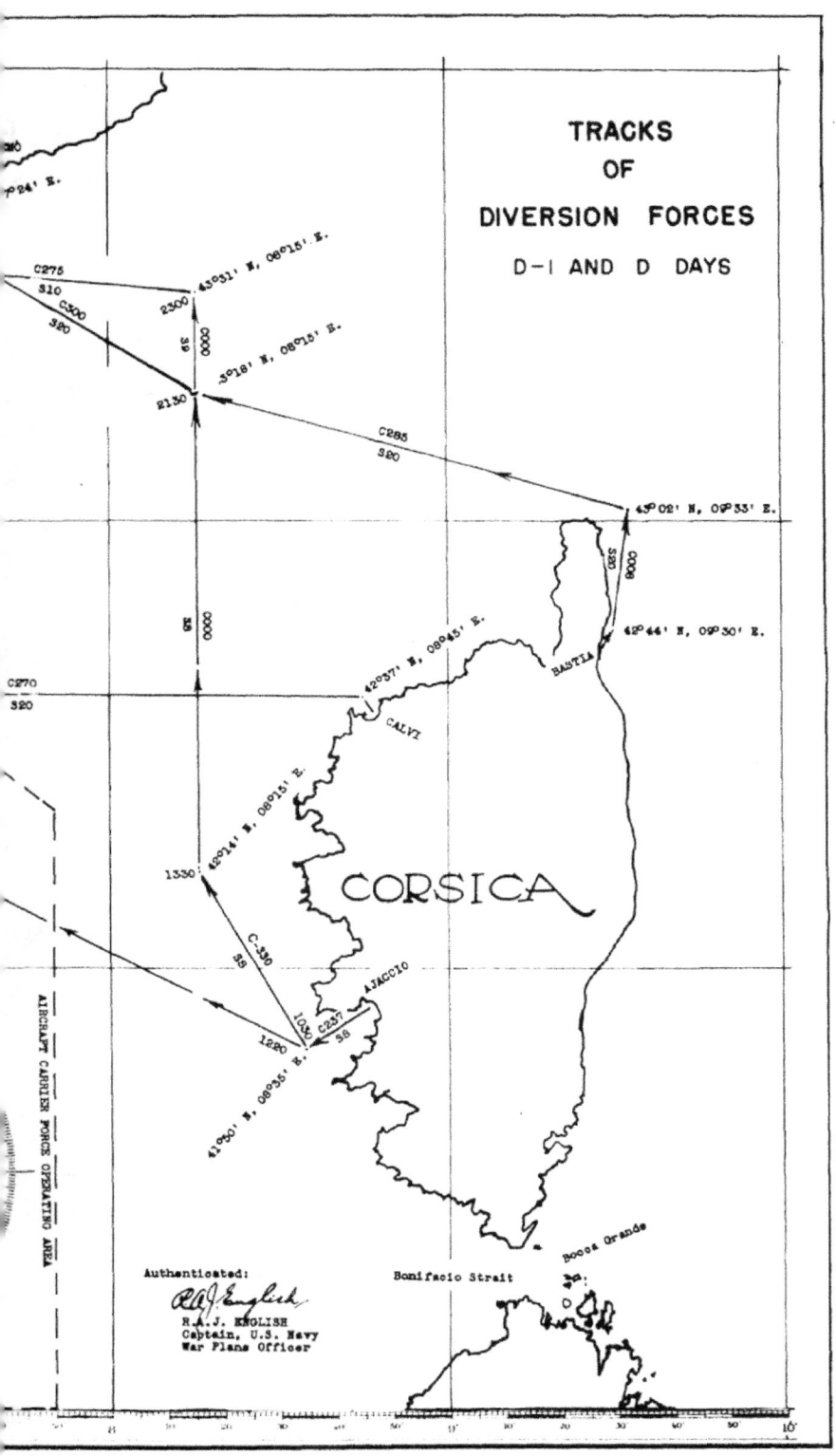

DIAGRAM XI

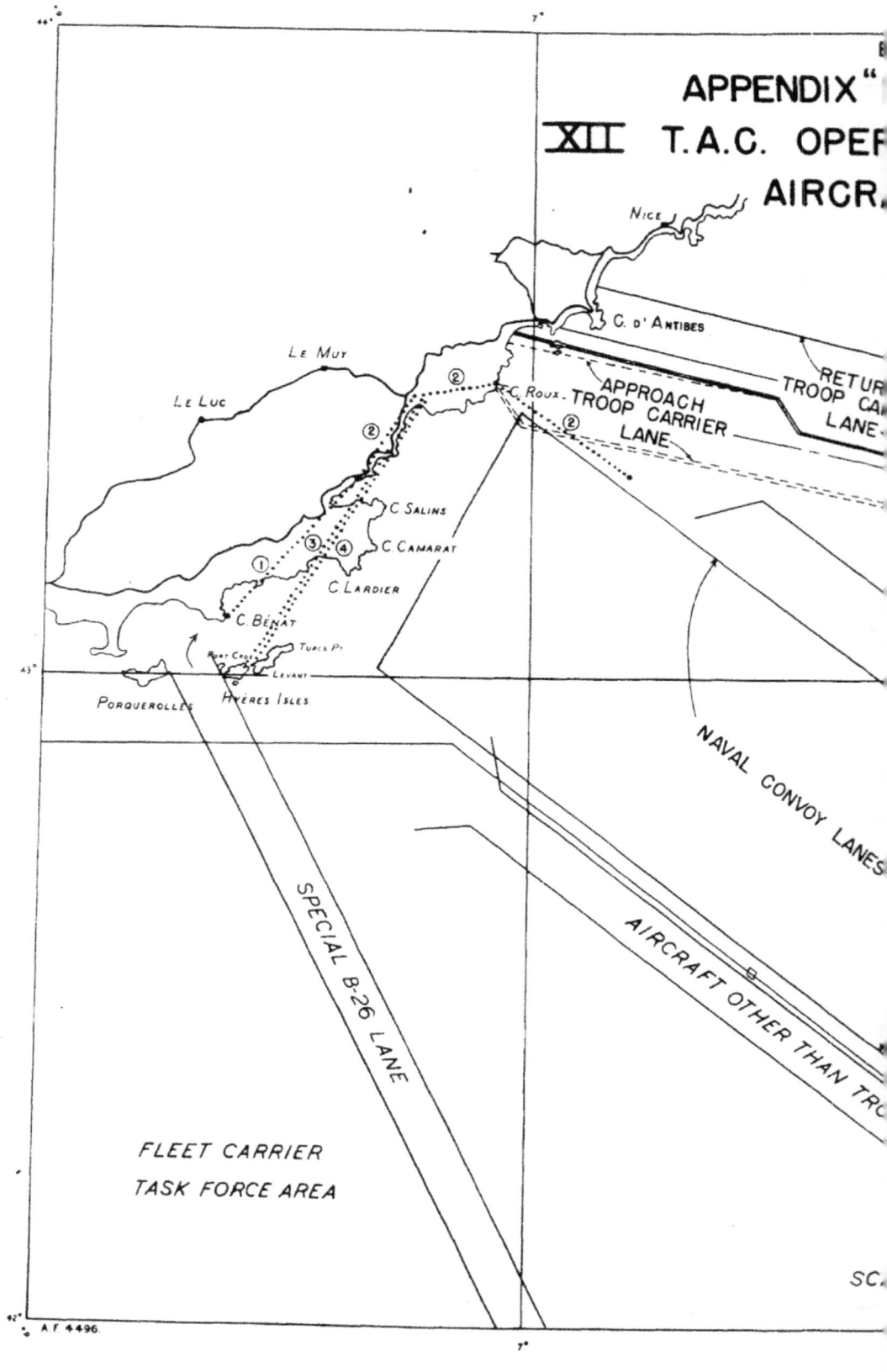

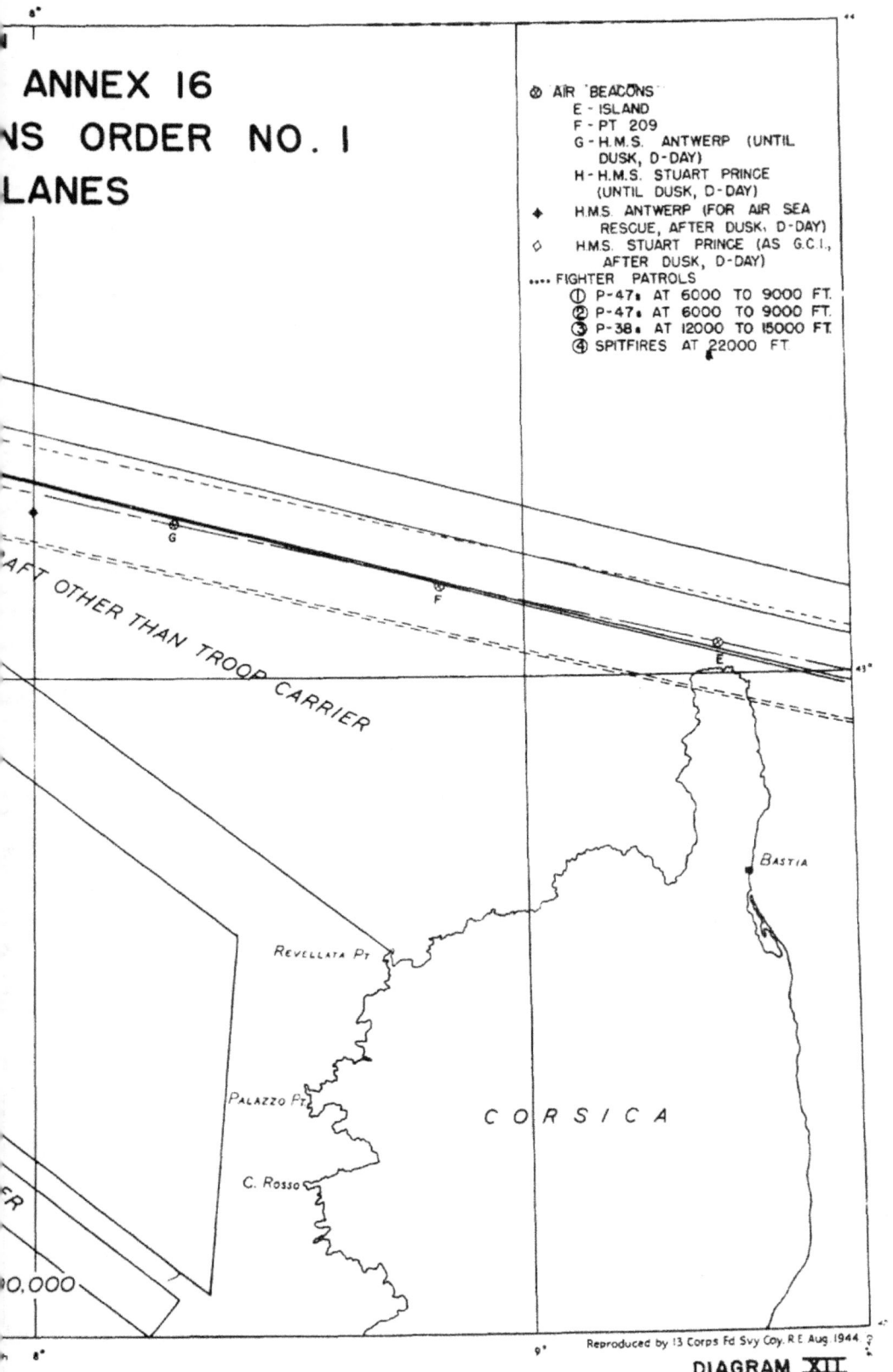

DIAGRAM XII

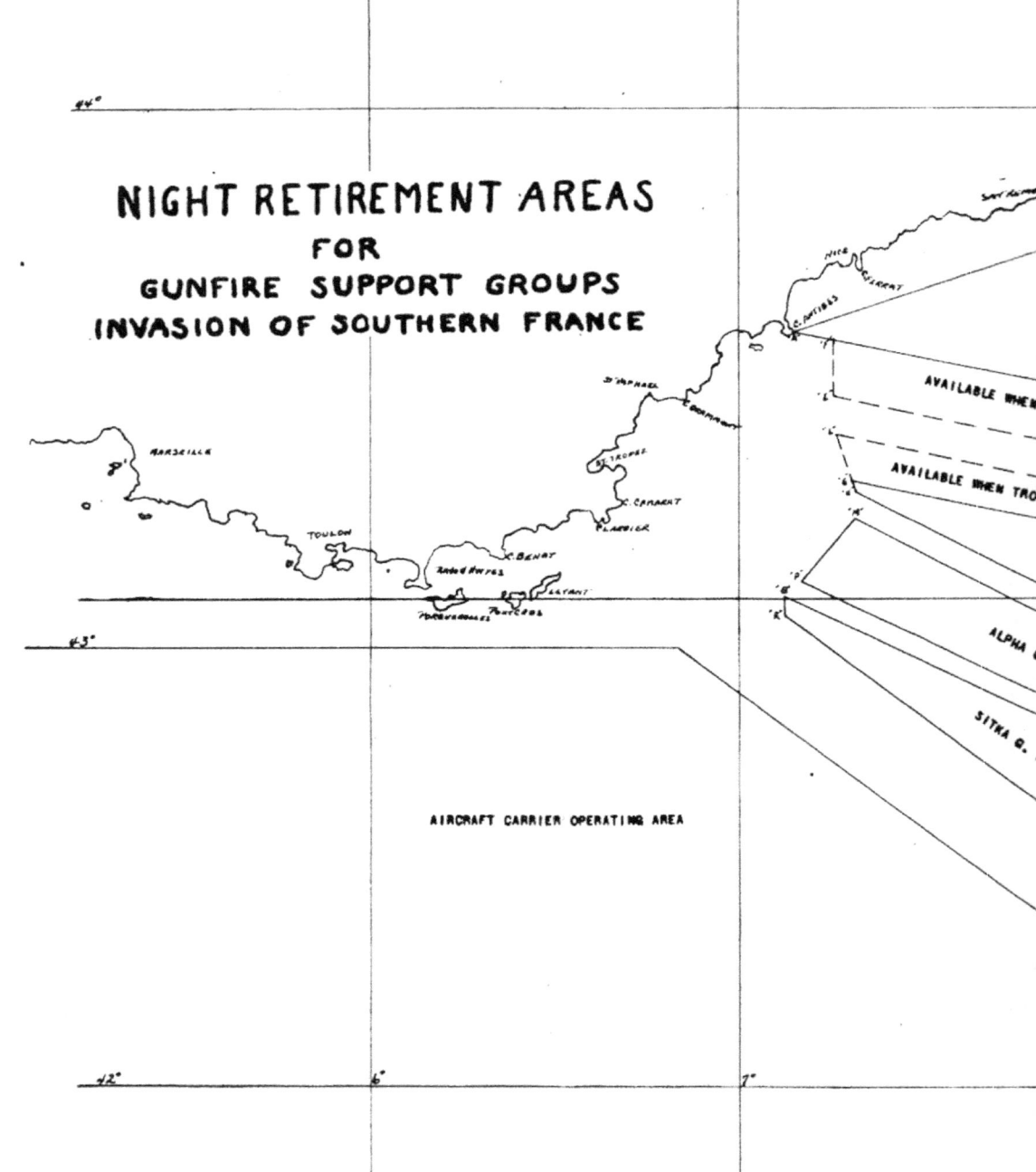

DIAGRAM XIII

INVASION OF SOUTHERN FRANCE

XIITH TACTICAL AIR COMMAND COVER PLAN

SHOWING

THE FOUR AREAS SUBJECTED TO SIMILIAR
BOMBING PLANS PRIOR TO D-DAY

DIAGRAM XIV

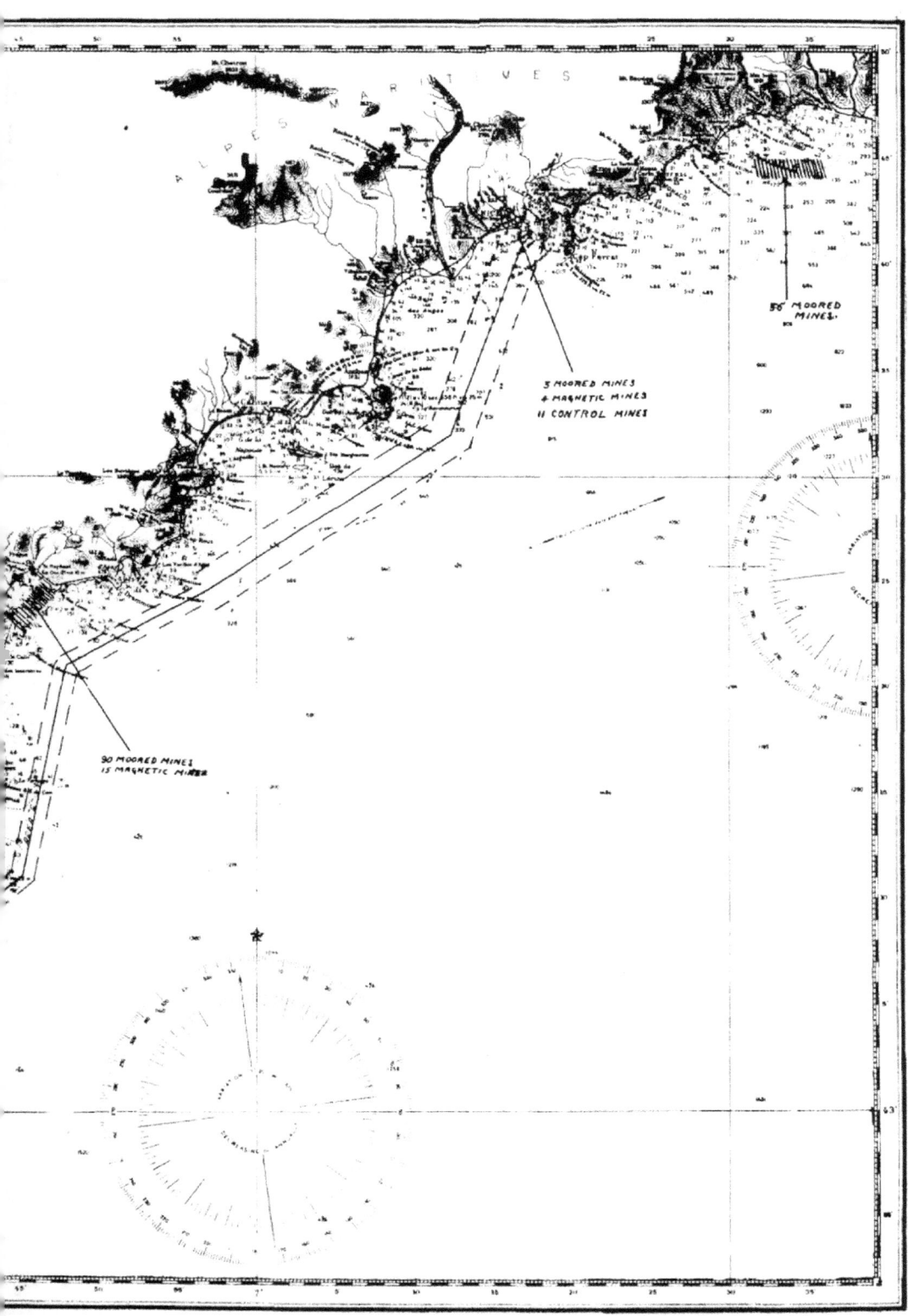

DIAGRAM XV

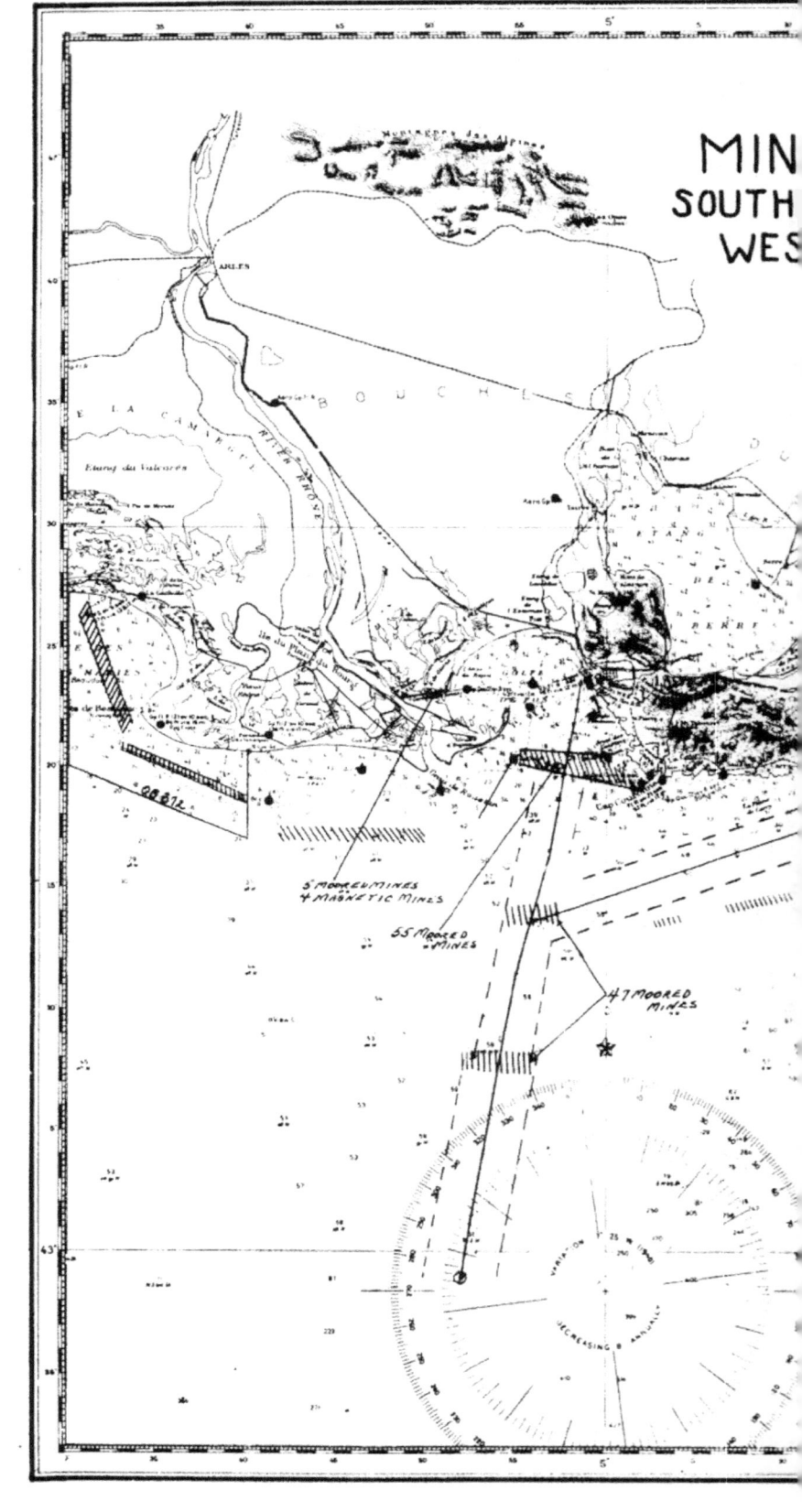

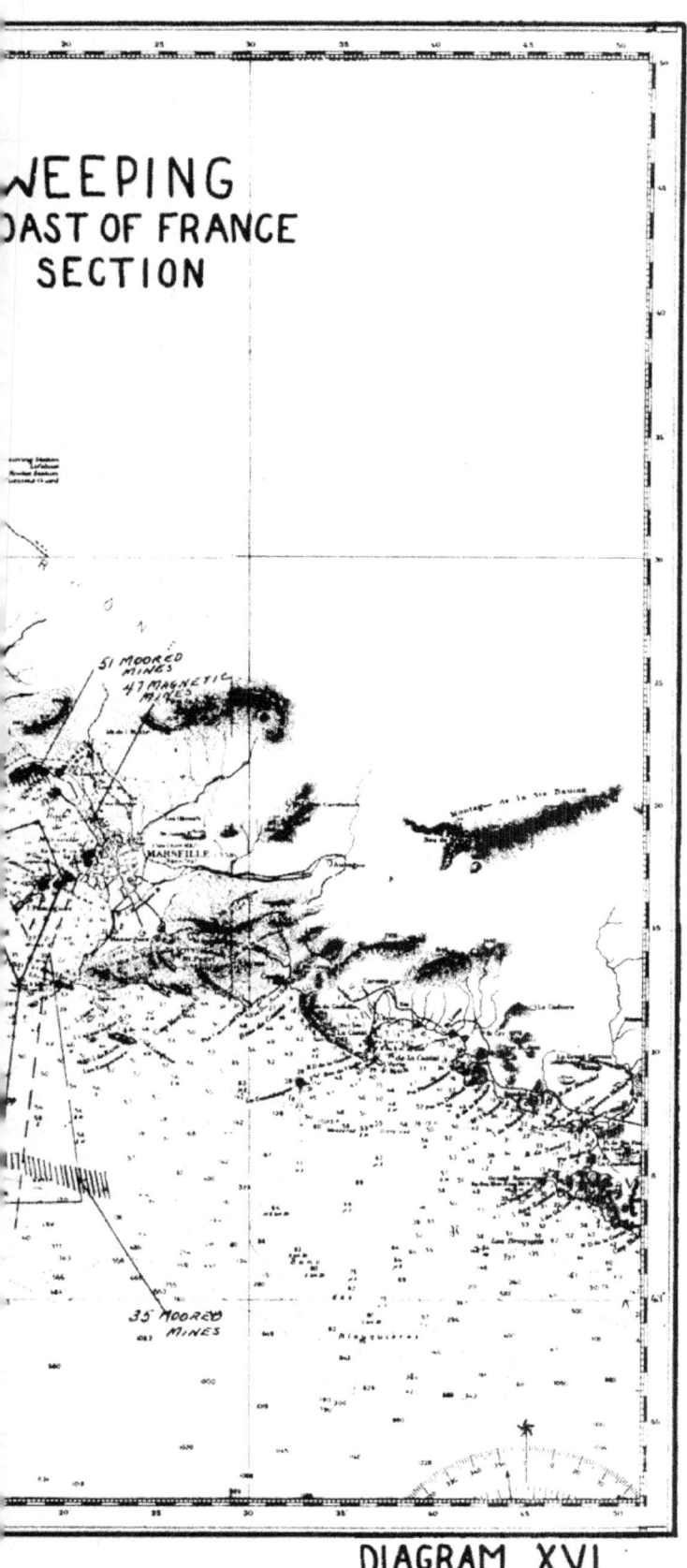

SWEEPING
COAST OF FRANCE
SECTION

DIAGRAM XVI

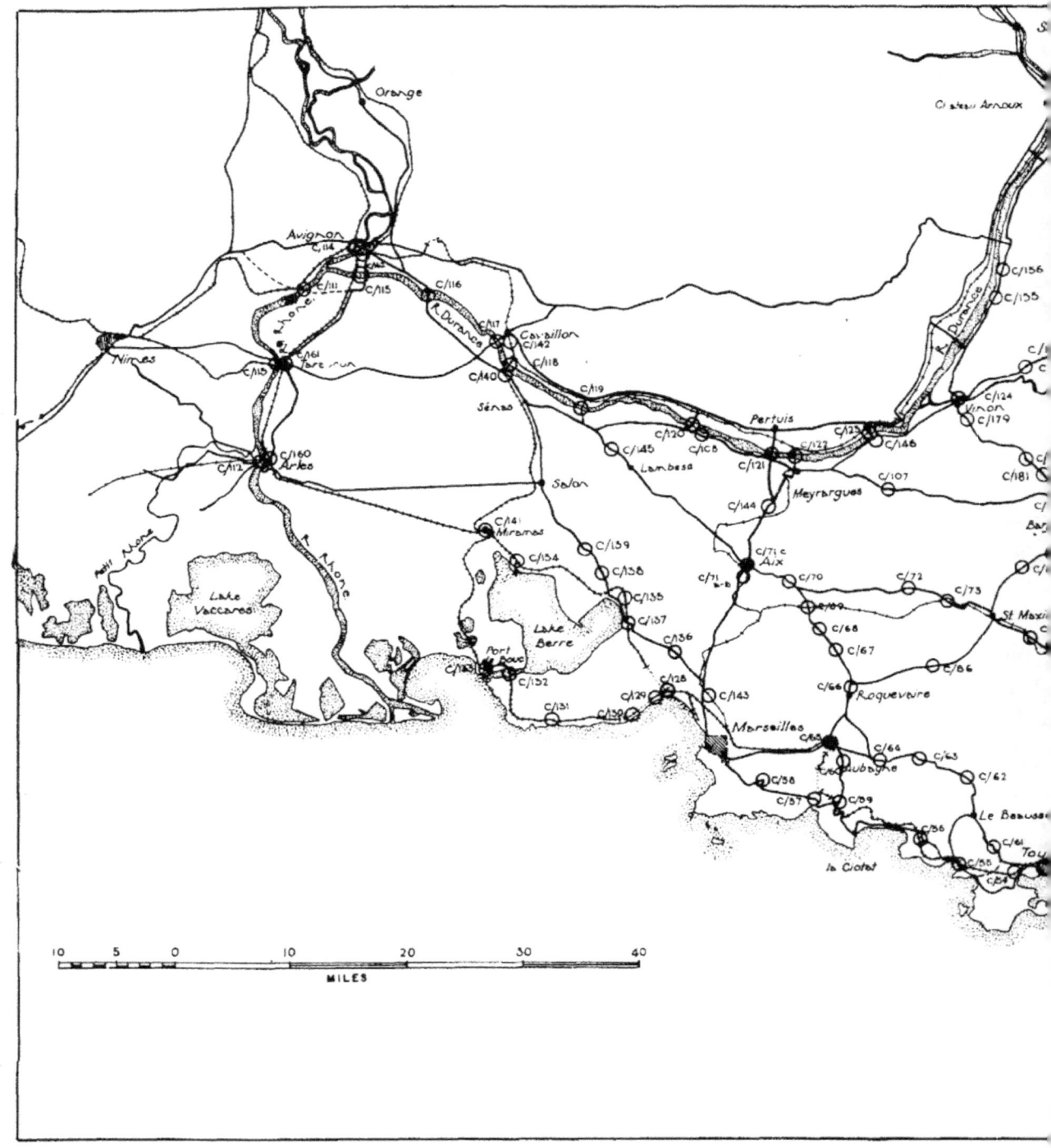

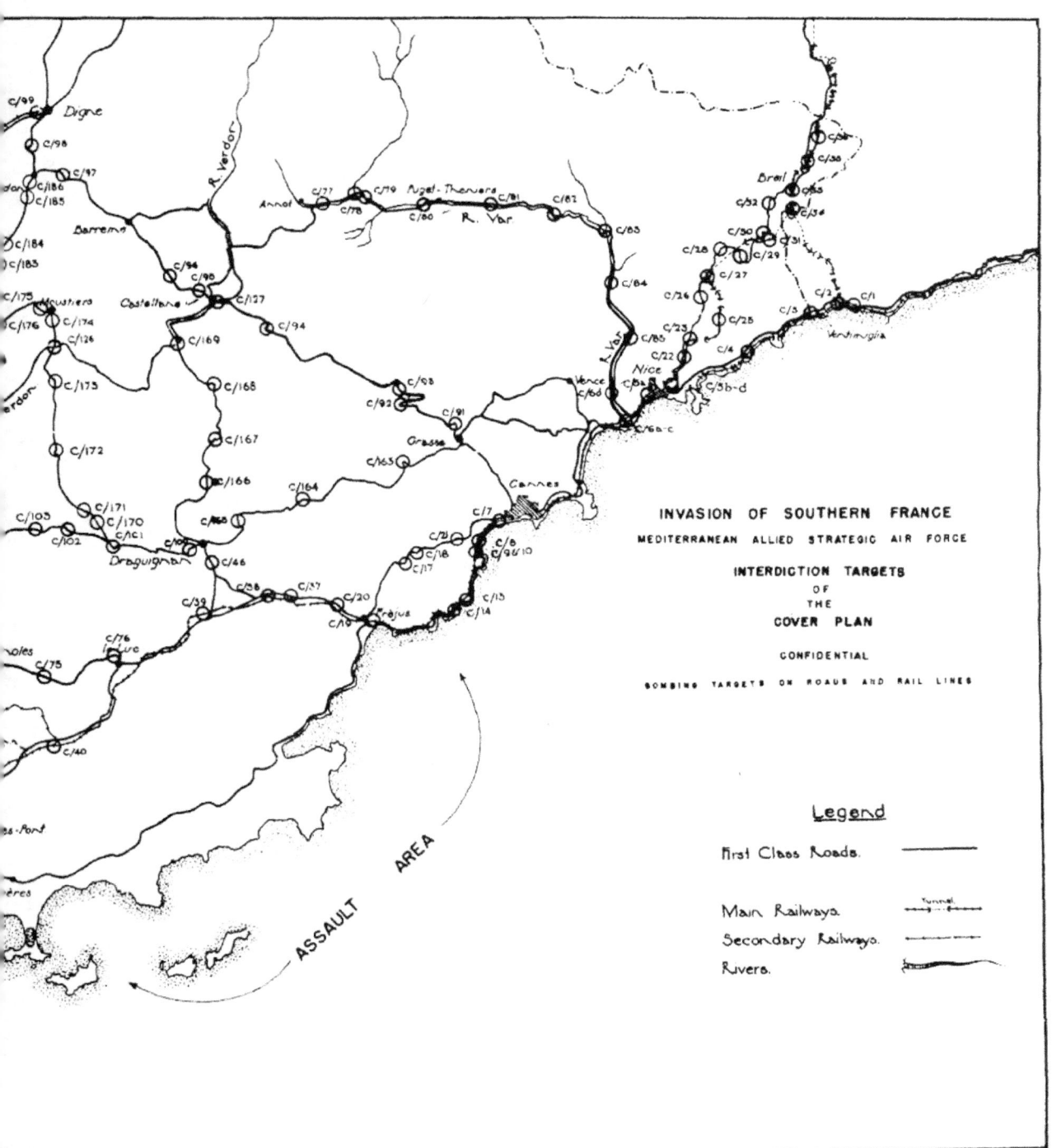

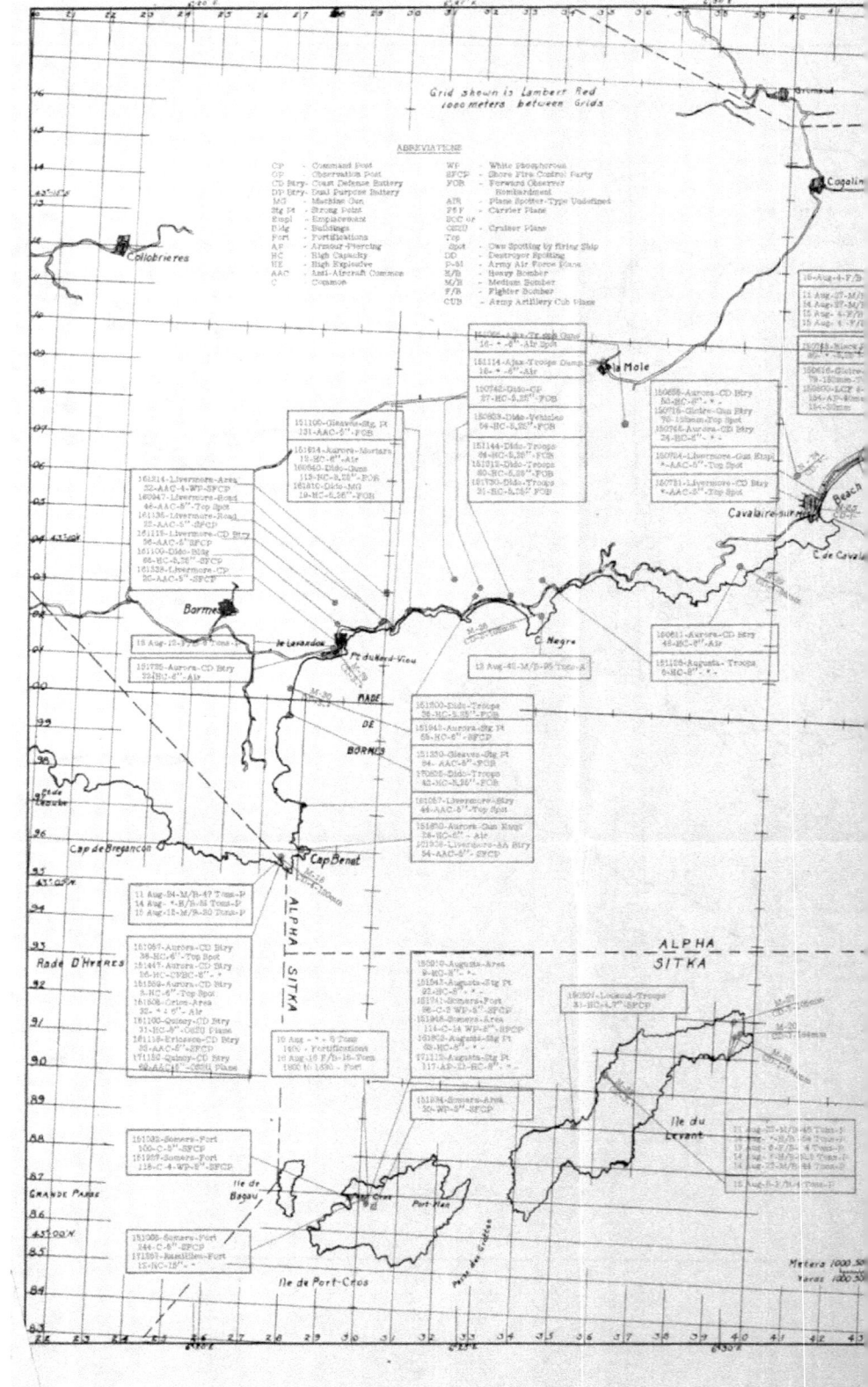

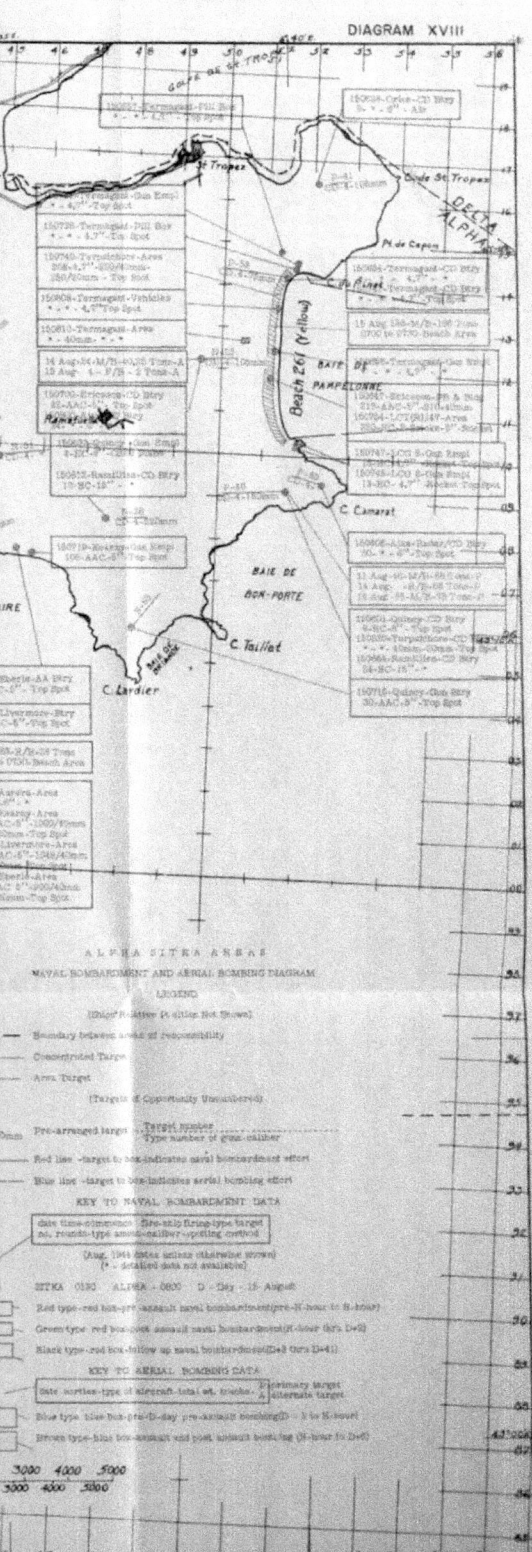

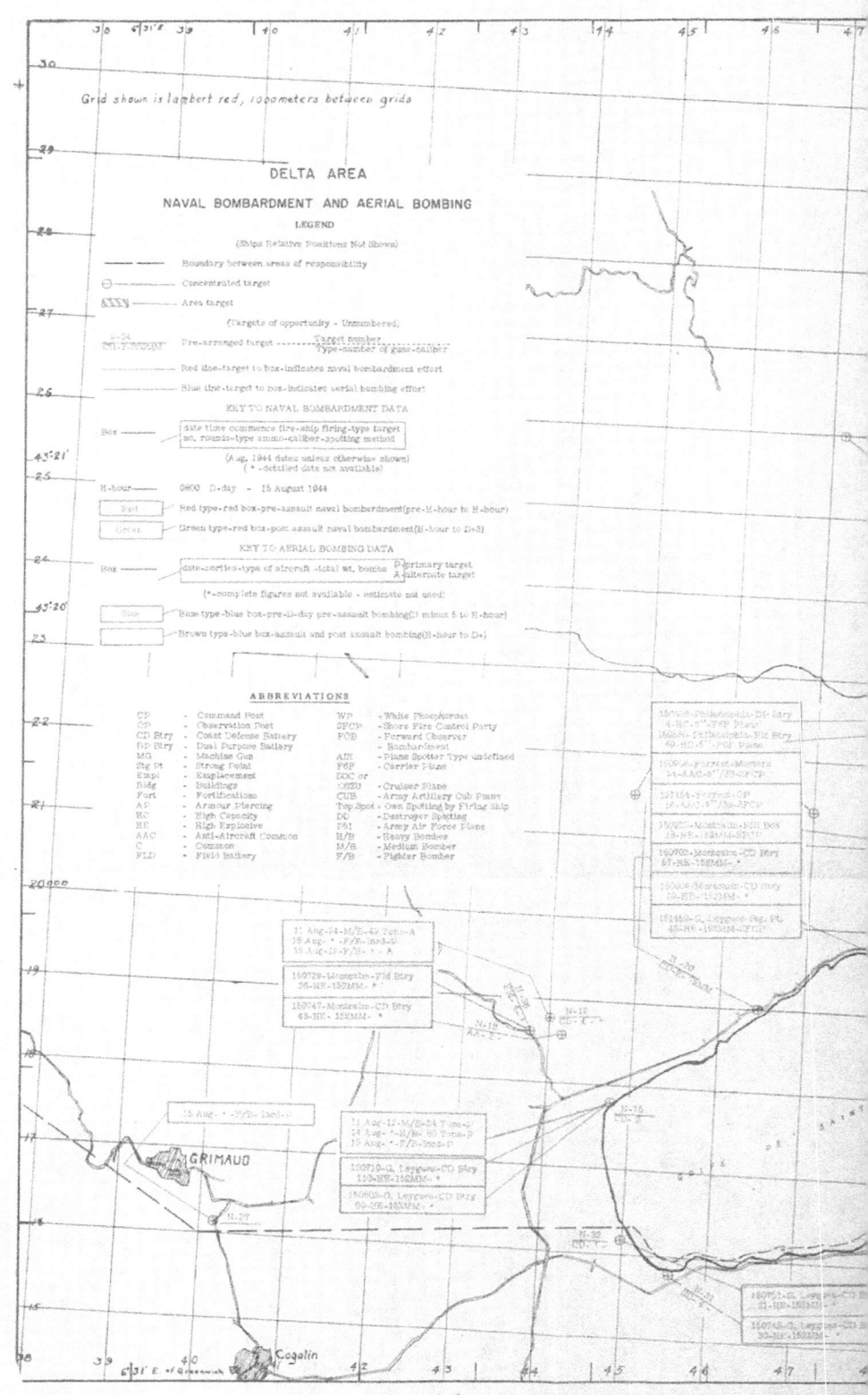

DELTA AREA

NAVAL BOMBARDMENT AND AERIAL BOMBING

LEGEND

(Ships Relative Positions Not Shown)

- ———— Boundary between areas of responsibility
- ⊖———— Concentrated target
- ▨▨▨———— Area target

(Targets of opportunity - Unnumbered)

- Pre-arranged target ······ Target number / Type-number of guns-caliber
- Red line-target to box-indicates naval bombardment effort
- Blue line-target to box-indicates aerial bombing effort

KEY TO NAVAL BOMBARDMENT DATA

Box — date time commence fire-ship firing-type target
no. rounds-type ammo-caliber-spotting method

(Aug. 1944 dates unless otherwise shown)
(* -detailed data not available)

H-hour — 0800 D-day - 15 August 1944

- Red — Red type-red box-pre-assault naval bombardment(pre-H-hour to H-hour)
- Green — Green type-red box-post assault naval bombardment(H-hour to D+3)

KEY TO AERIAL BOMBING DATA

Box — date-sorties-type of aircraft-total wt. bombs P-primary target / A-alternate target

(*-complete figures not available - estimate not used)

- Blue — Blue type-blue box-pre-D-day pre-assault bombing(D minus 5 to H-hour)
- Brown type-blue box-assault and post assault bombing(H-hour to D+)

ABBREVIATIONS

CP	- Command Post	WP	- White Phosphorous
OP	- Observation Post	SFCP	- Shore Fire Control Party
CD Btry	- Coast Defense Battery	FOB	- Forward Observer Bombardment
DP Btry	- Dual Purpose Battery	AIR	- Plane Spotter Type undefined
MG	- Machine Gun	F6F	- Carrier Plane
Stg Pt	- Strong Point	SOC or	
Empl	- Emplacement	OS2U	- Cruiser Plane
Bldg	- Buildings	CUB	- Army Artillery Cub Plane
Fort	- Fortifications	Top Spot	- Own Spotting by Firing Ship
AP	- Armour Piercing	DO	- Destroyer Spotting
HC	- High Capacity	P51	- Army Air Force Plane
HE	- High Explosive	H/B	- Heavy Bomber
AAC	- Anti-Aircraft Common	M/B	- Medium Bomber
C	- Common	F/B	- Fighter Bomber
FLD	- Field Battery		

GRIMAUD

Cogolin

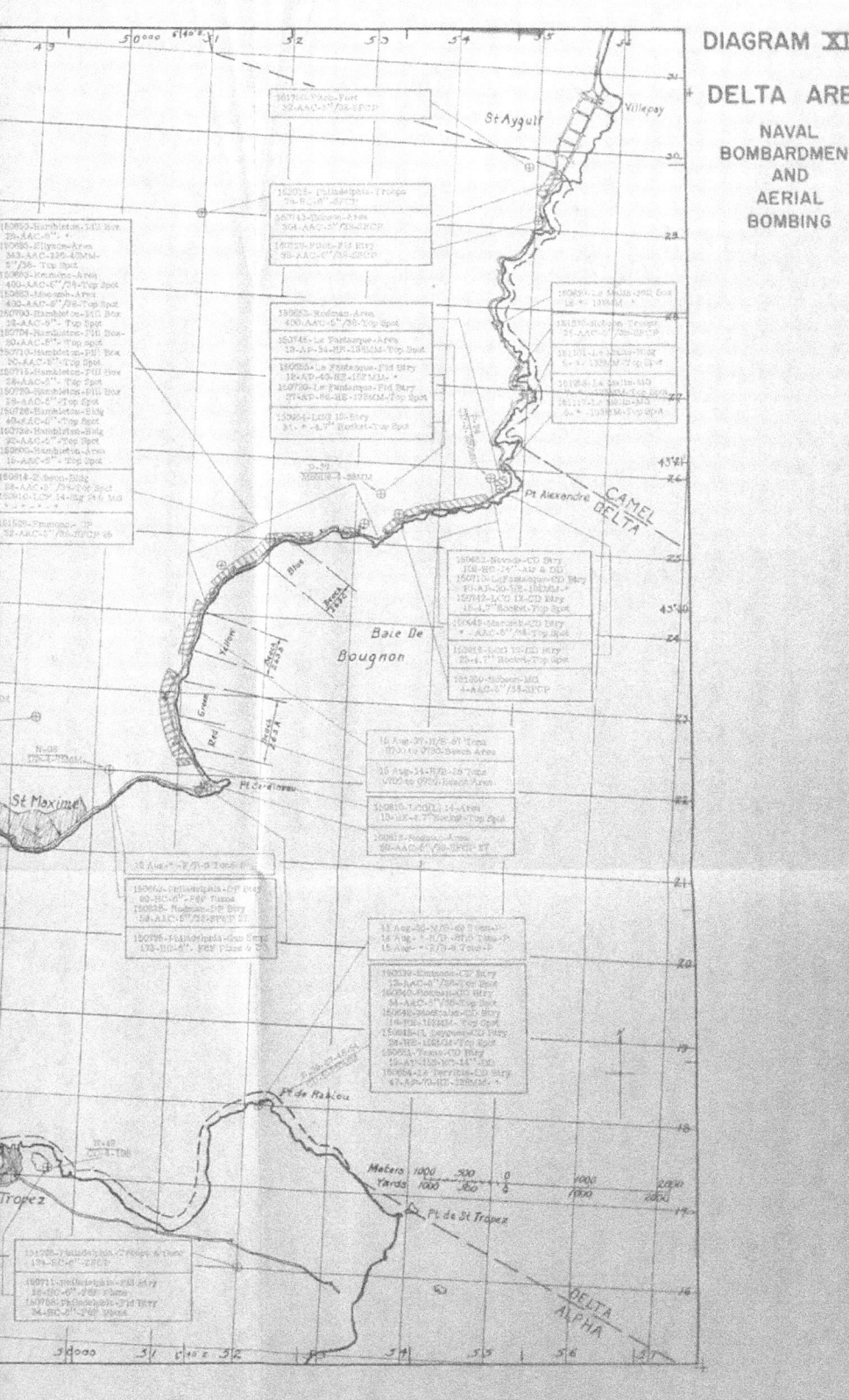

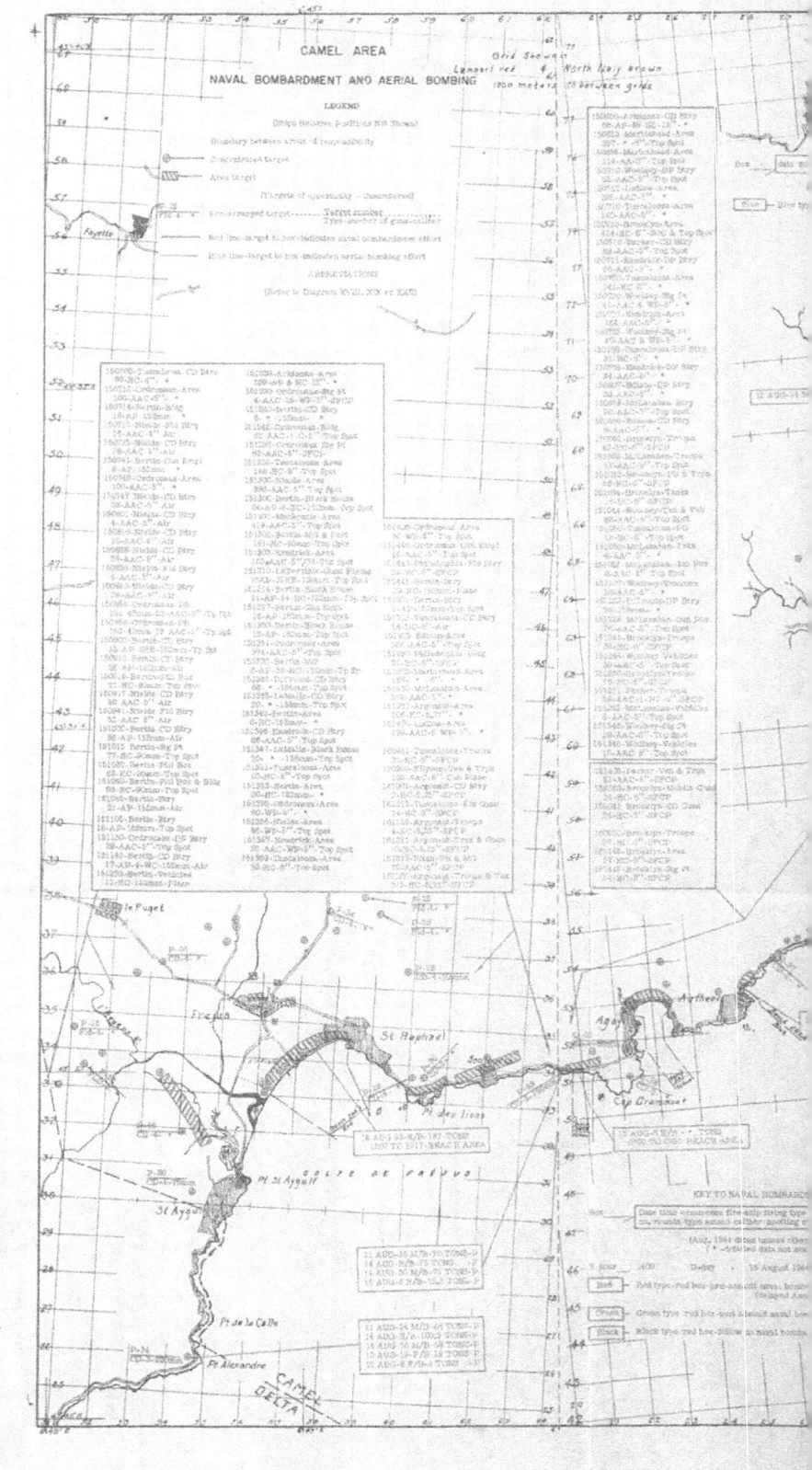

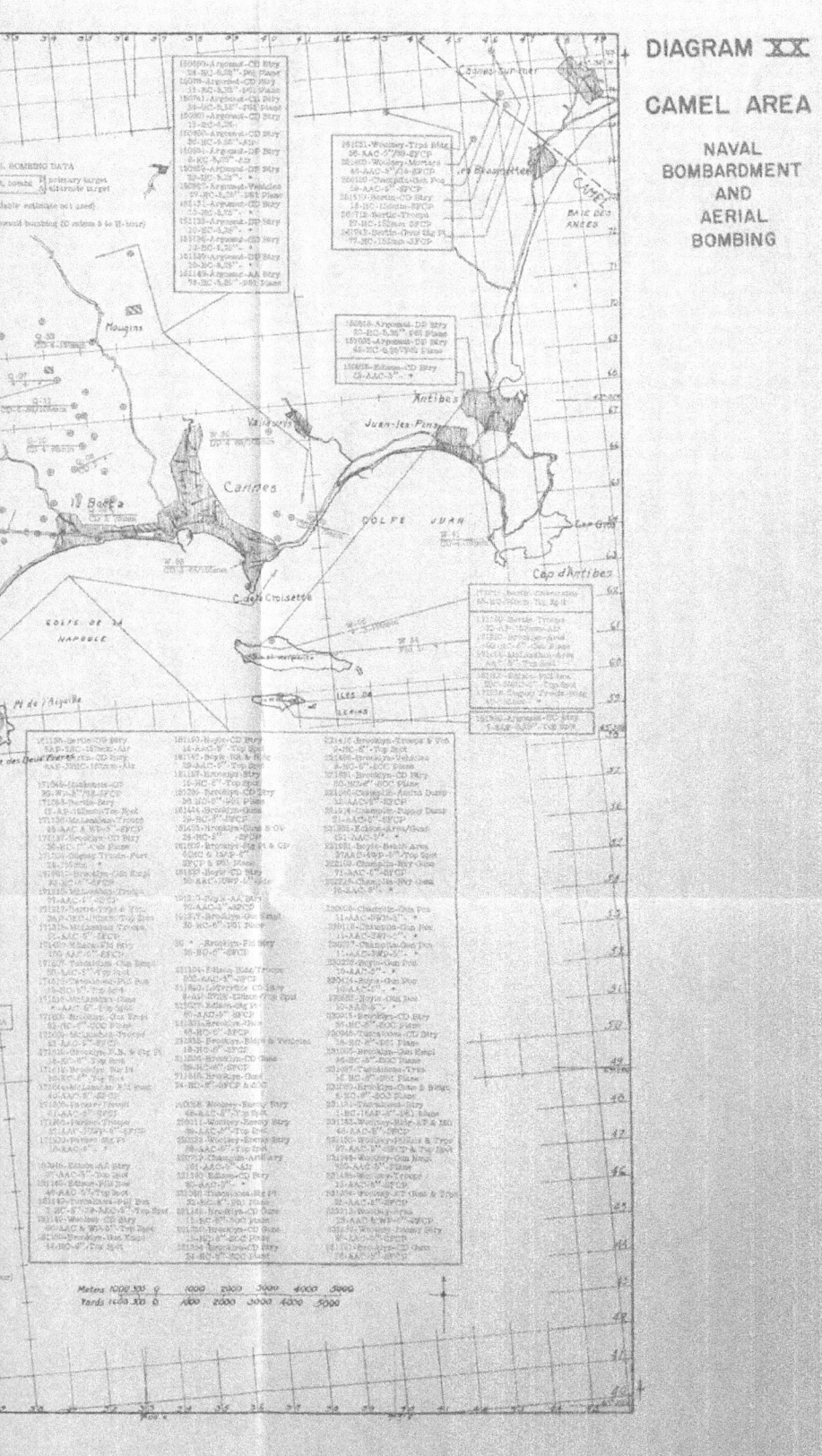

DIAGRAM XX

CAMEL AREA

NAVAL BOMBARDMENT AND AERIAL BOMBING

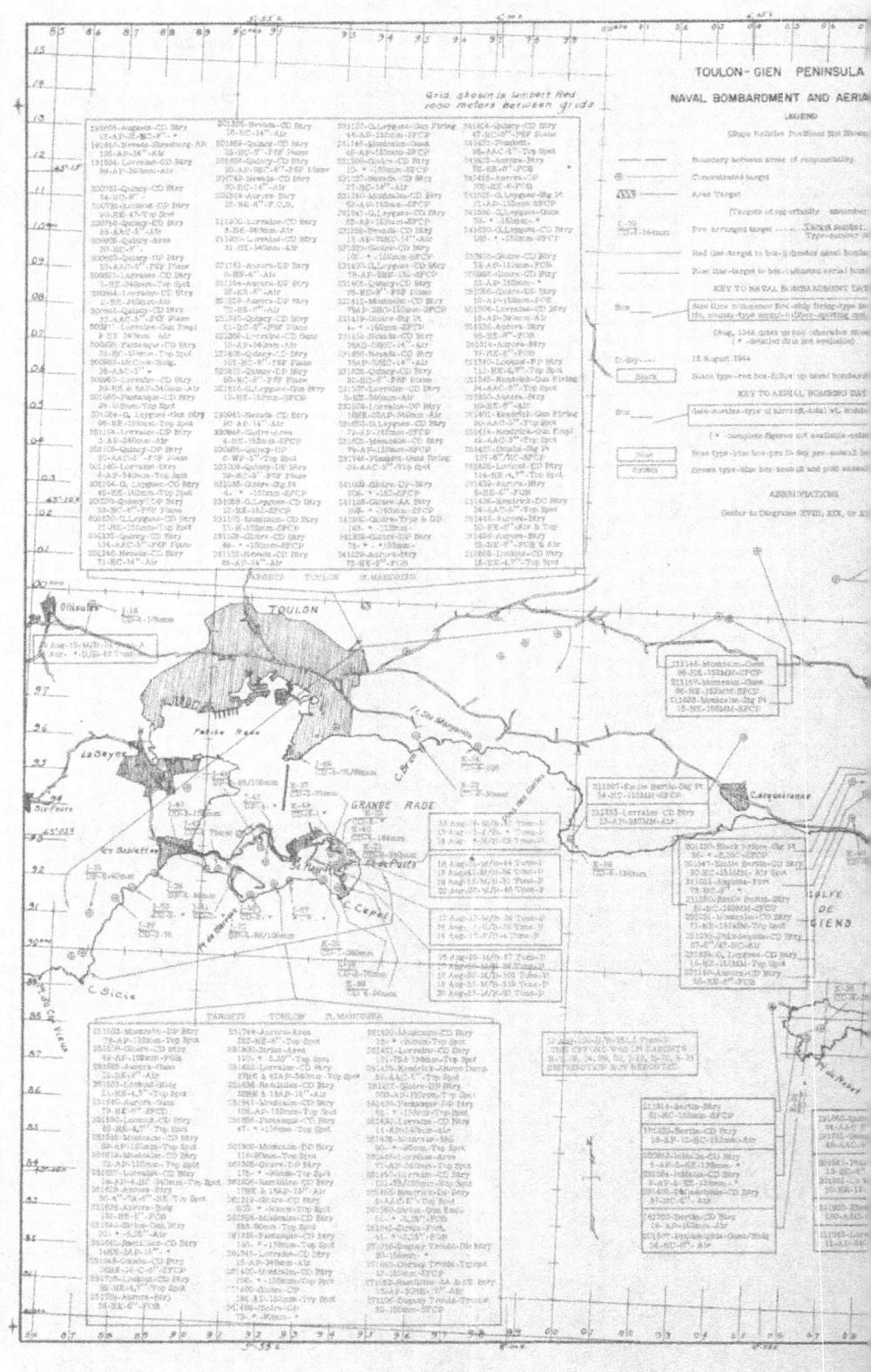

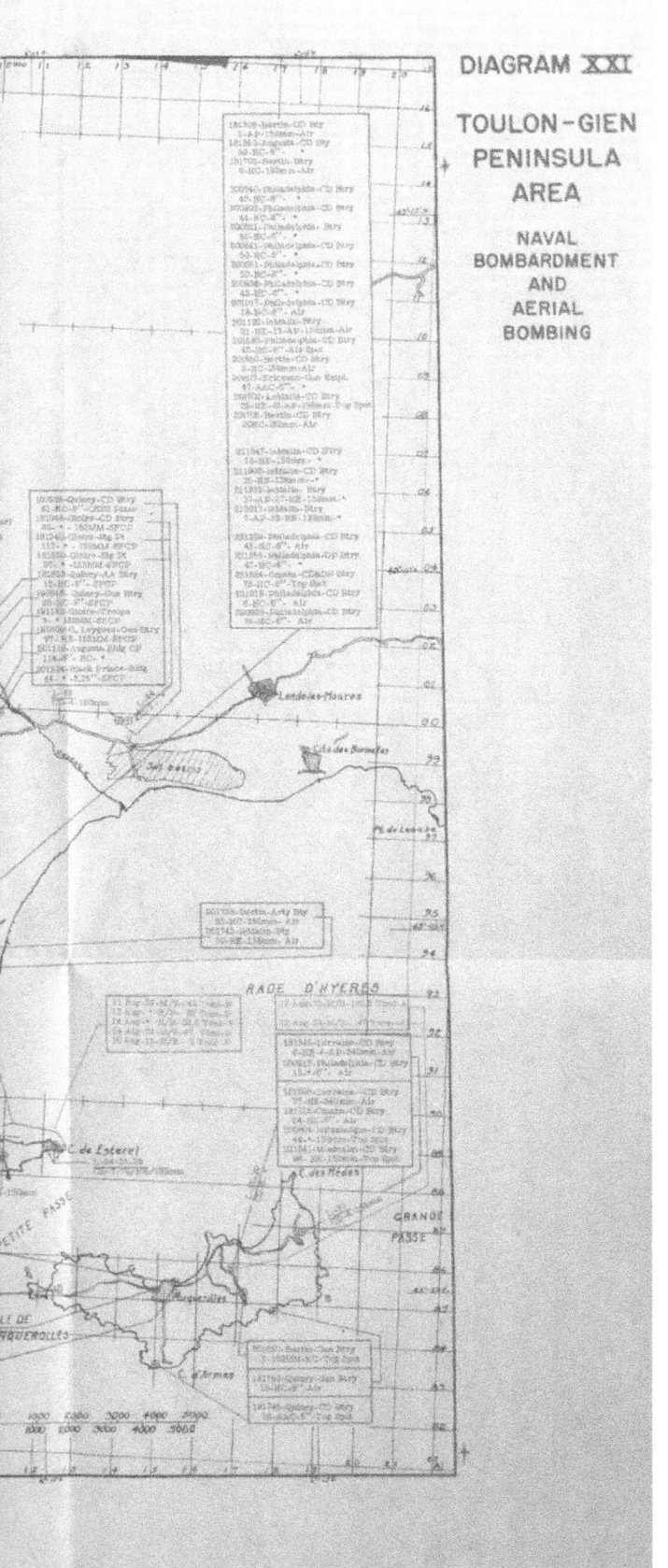

DIAGRAM XXI

TOULON-GIEN PENINSULA AREA

NAVAL BOMBARDMENT AND AERIAL BOMBING

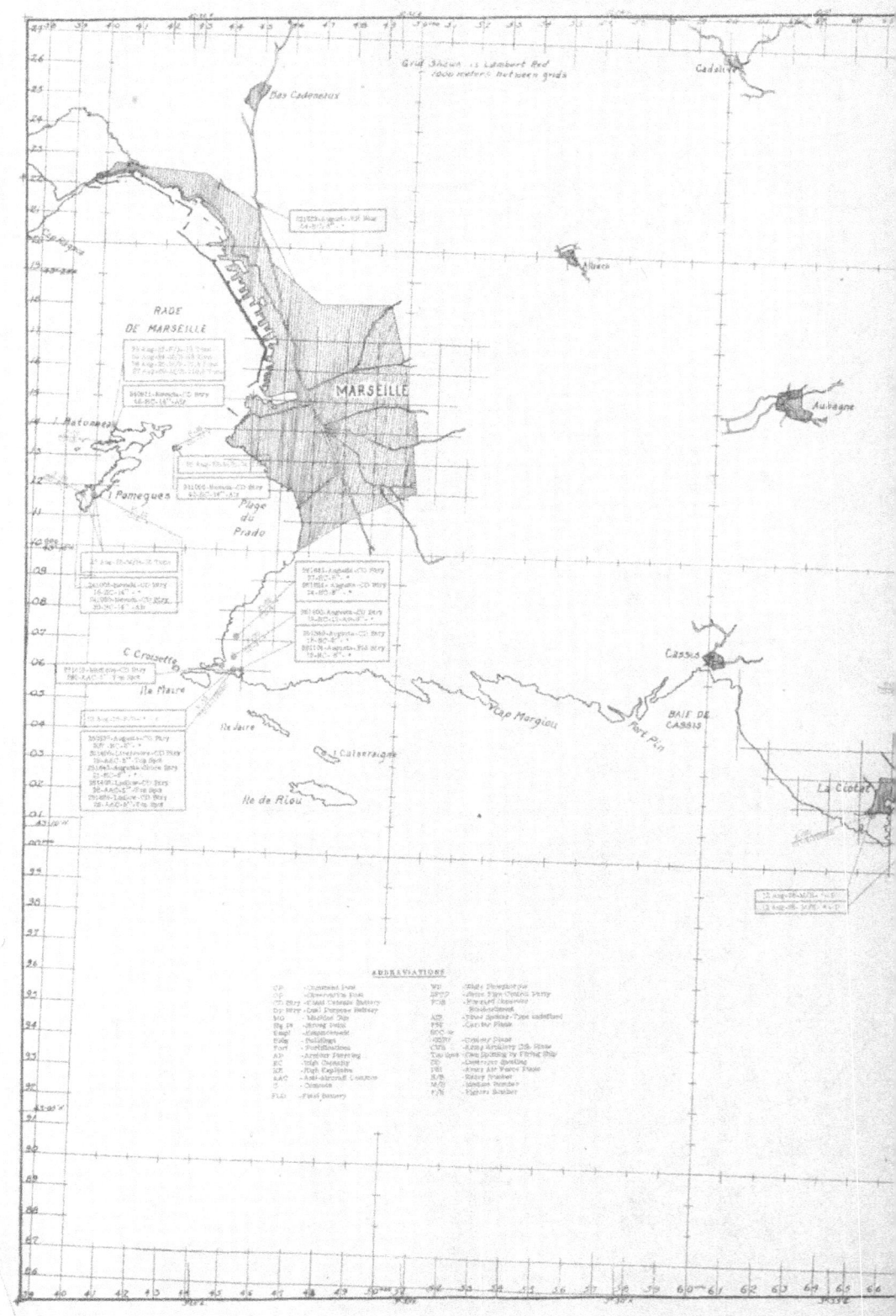

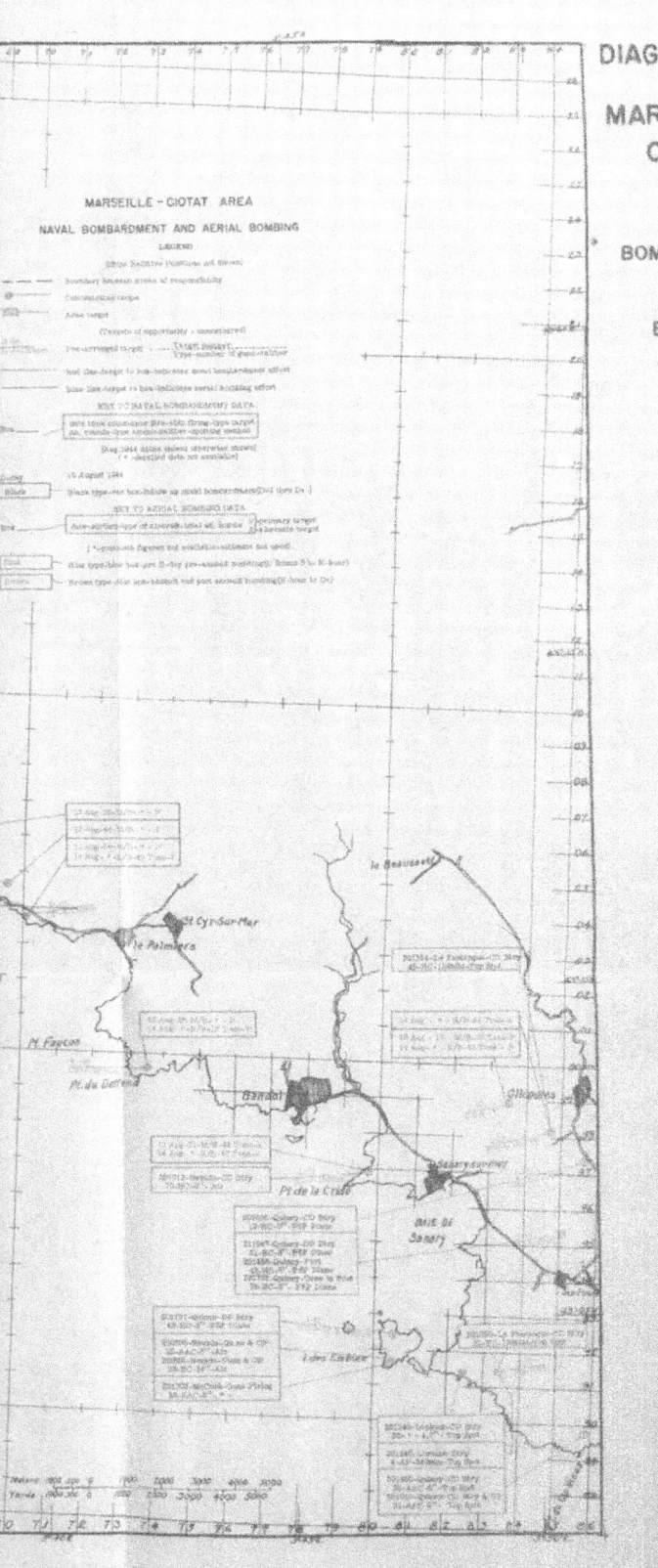

DIAGRAM XXII

MARSEILLE – CIOTAT AREA

NAVAL BOMBARDMENT AND AERIAL BOMBING

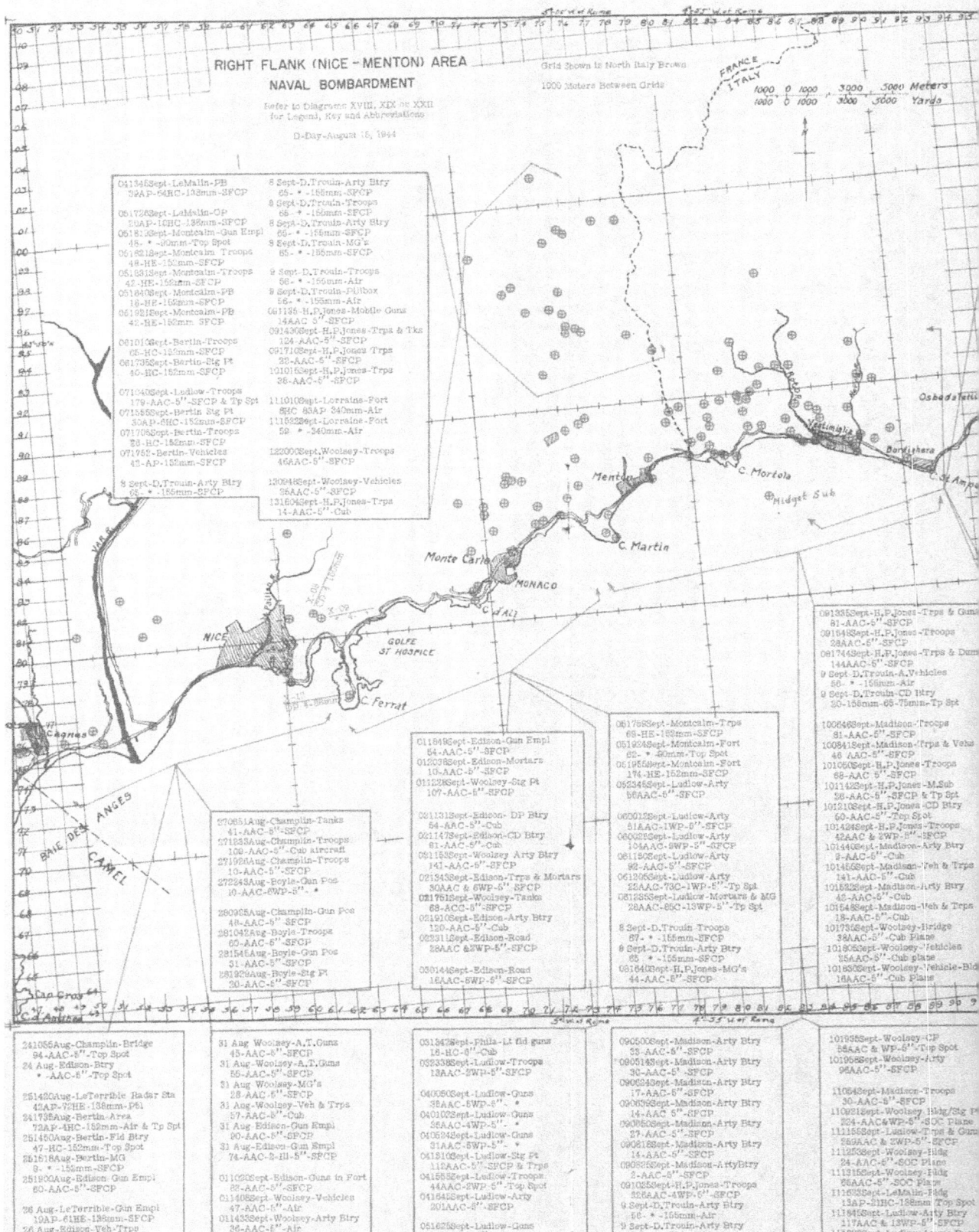

DIAGRAM XXIII

RIGHT FLANK (NICE-MENTON) AREA

NAVAL BOMBARDMENT

Sept-Gloire-Bridge
AC-152mm-Cub Plane
Sept-Gloire-Bridge
P-152mm-Cub
Sept-Woolsey-Arty
AC-5"-Cub
Sept-Ludlow-Troops
AC & 1WP-5"-SFCP
Sept-Ludlow-Troops
AC & 1WP-5"-SFCP

Sept-Woolsey-Trps & Mortars
C-5"-SFCP
Sept-Woolsey-Arty
P-5"-SFCP
Sept-Woolsey-Troops
C-5"-SFCP
Sept-Woolsey-Trps & Mortars
AC & WP-5"-SFCP
Sept-Woolsey-CP-Trps
AC-WP-5"-SFCP
Sept-Ludlow-Troops
C & 6WP-5"-SFCP
Sept-Woolsey-Trps-Vehs
AC-5"-SFCP

Sept-Ludlow-C.A.Trps
AC & 1WP-5"-SFCP
Sept-Ludlow-Trps & Vehs
AAC-5"-SFCP
Sept-Ludlow-Trps & Trks
AC-1WP-5"-Top Spot
Sept-Edison-Vehicles
AC-12WP-5"-Cub

Sept-H P Jones-Troops
AC-5"-CUB
Sept-H.P.Jones-Troops
P-5"-SFCP
Sept-Edison-Bridge
AC-5"-Air & Top Spot
Sept-H.P.Jones-Vehs
AC-6WP-5"-SFCP
Sept-Edison-Trucks
AC-5"-SOC Plane

Sept-H.P.Jones-Road King
AC-5"-Cub
Sept-H.P.Jones-Gun Empl
AC-5"-Cub
Sept-H.P.Jones-CP Bldg
AAC-5"-Cub
Sept-Edison-Guns
AAC-5"-MineSweeper
Sept-H.P.Jones-Guns
AAC-5"-MineSweeper
4Sept-Edison-Trps & Vehs
AC-6WP-5"-SFCP
3Sept-H.P.Jones-Bridge
AAC-5"-Cub
6Sept-Edison-Bldg
AO-14WP-5"-SFCP
7Sept-Edison-Bldg
AC-6WP-5"-Top Spot
8Sept-Edison-Guns-Trps-Vehs
AC-6WP-5"-SFCP

(change 2400-16 Sept from "P"
(c) to "A" (Able) Zone Time

5Sept-H.P.Jones-CD Btry
AAC-5"-Cub
9Sept-Edison-Trps & Vehs
AAC-5"-SFCP
3Sept-Edison-Bridge
AAC-2WP-5"-SFCP
3Sept-Edison-Guns
AAC-5"-SFCP
9Sept-Edison-Gun
AAC-4WP-5"-SFCP
1Sept-Edison-Gun
AAC-6WP-5"-SFCP

5Sept-Ludlow-Arty Btry
AAC-4WP-5"-SFCP
5Sept-Ludlow-Trps & Mortars
AAC-1WP-5"-SFCP

1Sept-Ludlow-Trucks & RR
AAC-1WP-5"-SFCP

4Sept-Ludlow-Dump
AAC-5WP-Cub

06Sept-Edison-Dump Vehs
AAC-5"-Cub Plane
20Sept-Woolsey RR Yard
AAC 5"-SFCP
30Sept-Woolsey-Bridge & RR
AAC-5"-SFCP
17Sept-Edison Vehicles
AAC-5"-SFCP
00-Sept-Woolsey-Btry & Trps
AAC-5"-Cub
30Sept-Woolsey-Arty Btry
AAC-5"-Top Spot

32Sept-Edison-Bridge
AAC-5"-SFCP
33Sept-Woolsey Arty Btry
1-AAC-5"-Top Spot
25Sept-Edison-RR & Trps
AAC-5"-SFCP
45Sept-Woolsey-OP & Fort
5-AAC-5"-Top Spot

05Sept-Edison-Guns
AAC-5"-Cub Plane
47Sept-Edison-Trps & Mortars
4-AAC-5"-SFCP

007Sept-Madison-Supply Train
00-AAC-5"-Cub
263Sept-Madison-OP
1-AAC-5"-SFCP

INVASION OF SOUTHERN FRANCE

AMMUNITION EXPENDITURE BY CALIBER

15 August to 25 September, 1944 Inclusive

CALIBER	HC	AP	AAC	UNSPECIFIED	TOTAL	SEPARATE MISSIONS
15"	135	54	-	-	189	7
14"	745	370	-	-	1115	17
340 mm	190	363	-	59	612	28
12"	48	66	-	269	383	2
8"	2333	246	-	-	2579	64
155 mm	-	-	-	982	982	20
152 mm	2401	2031	-	1620	6052	121
6"	4147	31	-	1393	5571	114
138 mm	818	340[1]	-	503	1661	39
130 mm	-	-	-	34	34	1
5.25"	1326	7[2]	-	383	1716	39
5"/25	-	-	245	-	245	3[3]
5"/38	582[4]	987[5]	23386[6]	-	24955	352
4.7"	575	-	-	305	880[7]	24
4.0"	-	-	-	36	36	0[8]
90 mm	408	-	-	1218	1626	15
75 mm	-	-	-	307	307	2[9]
3"/50	-	-	114	-	114	1
40 mm	900	154	-	2586	3640	1[10]
20 mm	1400	-	-	4311	5711	0
Total	16008	4649	23745	14006	58408	850

NOTES

1 - Includes 47 SAP
2 - All SAP
3 - Plus one mission primarily undertaken by a large caliber battery
4 - White Phosphorus projectiles
5 - 42 illuminating and 945 common projectiles
6 - This figure includes at most 200 rounds of WP
7 - Inadequate data
8 - 4 inch ammunition was fired simultaneously with main battery at the same target
9 - Plus one mission primarily undertaken by main battery
10 - Plus several missions primarily undertaken by main battery
11 - 20 mm ammunition was fired simultaneously with main battery at the same target on five occasions

www.ingramcontent.com/pod-product-compliance
Lightning Source LLC
Chambersburg PA
CBHW060228240426
43671CB00016B/2881